oh my god

P9-EEH-308

156, 137

Nancy is so cool

Nisha wuz here 2000 babe!

Madam
Gr 9 7CA!
Nancy HANIEA!
wuz

Nisha Book

Home

"BLACK LEATHER"

WUZ

WUZ

WUZ up

ADDISON-WESLEY MATHEMATICS 9

Brendan Kelly
Professor of Mathematics
University of Toronto
Toronto, Ontario

Bob Alexander
Assistant Co-ordinator
of Mathematics
Toronto Board of Education
Toronto, Ontario

Paul Atkinson
Principal
Cameron Heights
Collegiate Institute
Kitchener, Ontario

Addison-Wesley Publishers Limited

Don Mills, Ontario
Reading, Massachusetts
Menlo Park, California
New York
Wokingham, England
Amsterdam • Bonn
Sydney • Singapore
Tokyo • Madrid
San Juan

Design
John Zehethofer
Assembly and Technical Art
Frank Zsigo
Illustrative Art
Pronk & Associates
Editorial
Dianne Goffin
Lesley Haynes
Typesetting
Q Composition
Printer
The Bryant Press
Photographic Credits

The publisher wishes to thank the following sources for photographs and other illustrative materials used in this book. We will gladly receive information enabling us to rectify any errors or references in credits.

Cover, Robert Simpson,

Addison-Wesley Photo Library, 24, 79, 101, 166, 195, 200, 237, 292, 306, 360, 390, 425, 466, 478; Air Canada 298; Alberta Wheat Pool, 412; Claus Anderson/Masterfile, 214; Bob Alexander, 306, 331; Bettmann Newsphotos, xvi, 6, 12; Bill Brooks/Masterfile, 480; Jane Burton/Bruce Coleman Incorporated, 466; CBC TV, 10; Canadian Government Travel Bureau, 59; CNE, 375; CN Tower, 177; CP Photos, 1; CP Rail, 490; Christopher Johns Photography, 21; Peter Christopher/Masterfile, 403; Ian Crysler, 84, 93, 119; Lynne Dalkner, 191, 207; De Havilland Aircraft, 204; Department of Fisheries and Ocean-Communications, 49; Fraser Day Photography, 6, 90, 131, 135, 280, 407; Mike Dobel/Masterfile, 324; © M. C. Escher c/o Cordon Art-Baarn Holland 314; Government of the Yukon Territory, 306; James Guthro, 421; Lisa Guthro, 27, 33, 200, 232, 370; Alan Harvey/Masterfile, 26; Hot Shots, 413; Jaguar Canada, 195; Jandec Inc., 11; Jeremy Jones, 74, 93; Michael King, 306; Lee Valley Tools Ltd., 452, 456; MacMillan Bloedel Limited, 183; Metropolitan Toronto Hockey League, 164; Miller Services Ltd., 41, 53, 73, 102, 173, 205, 221, 273, 284, 292, 307, 360, 365, 387, 413, 422, 491; Ministry of Industry and Tourism, 305; Warren Morgan/Masterfile, 338; NASA, 13, 199, 269; National Baseball Library, 206; Joseph Nettis/Masterfile, 110; Steve Powell/Masterfile, 141, 178; Alec Pytlowany/Masterfile, 338; Benjamin Rondel/Masterfile, 360; ROM, Department of Invertebrate Palaeontology, 199; Roy Nicholls Photography, 413; Greg Stott/Masterfile, 187; SSC-Photocentre, 2, 359, 383, 427; Toronto Institute of Medical Technology, 142, 171; John de Visser/Masterfile, 472; Western Airlines, 413.

Credits
We are grateful to the following people, who provided exercises for this text: Bob Borys, Terry Brabazon, Karl Dahlinger, Rosie D'Andrea, Eric Good, Felicia Gudewill, Robert Hamilton, Brian Heimbecker, Father William Moloney, Igor Nowikow, Jim O'Keefe, Mark Templin, and Brian Wright.

Written, printed, and bound in Canada

ISBN   0-201-18640-3

D   E   F   –BP–   92

Features of Mathematics 9

INTRODUCTION

A unique 14-page introductory unit entitled *The Nature of Mathematics* presents six men and women who have worked with mathematics. A quotation from each person is followed by discussion, examples, and exercises which introduce a feature of the text.

This material can be studied at any time as a unit, or the individual sections can be studied separately.

APPLICATIONS OF MATHEMATICS

Students can better understand mathematical principles when they are related to their applications. For this reason, applications are integrated throughout *Mathematics 9*.

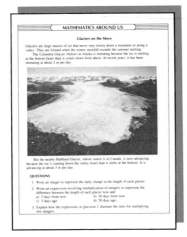

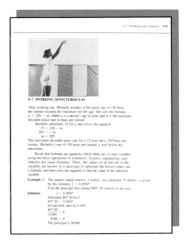

Each chapter begins with an illustrated application of the mathematics in the chapter.

Where appropriate, sections begin with an application which illustrates the necessity for the mathematics that follows. Applications are also included in most of the exercises.

Feature pages entitled *MATHEMATICS AROUND US* outline some applications of mathematics in the sciences, the arts, business, and industry.

CONCEPT DEVELOPMENT

Mathematics 9 is carefully sequenced to develop concepts in mathematics. Concepts are explained with several examples, each of which has a detailed solution.

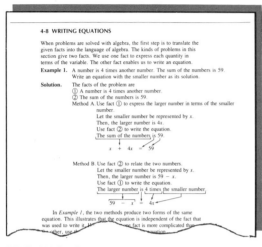

REINFORCEMENT

An abundance of exercises is provided to reinforce skills and concepts. These exercises are graded by difficulty with an appropriate balance of A, B, and C exercises. The A exercises may sometimes be completed mentally and the answers given orally or the questions may be used as additional examples when teaching the lesson. The B exercises are intended for the students to consolidate their learning of the concepts that were taught. The C exercises present a challenge and usually involve extensions of the concepts taught in that section.

Review Exercises and *Cumulative Reviews* provide additional practice. Answers to all questions are included in the text.

TECHNOLOGY

A contemporary mathematics program must reflect the impact of calculators and computers on society.

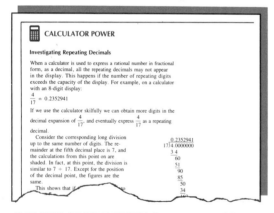

CALCULATOR POWER features provide opportunities for students to explore mathematical problems using a calculator. In addition, keying sequences are given for scientific calculators and 4-function calculators, where appropriate.

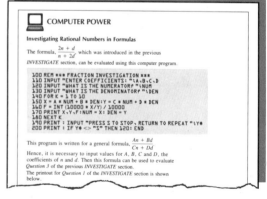

COMPUTER POWER features provide opportunities for students to explore mathematical problems using a computer. It is assumed that students know how to enter a program in BASIC, but it is not necessary for them to understand the program.

PROBLEM SOLVING

Problem solving is integrated throughout the program, with many of the exercises providing challenging problems for the students to solve. In addition, a variety of special features are included which promote the development of problem-solving skills.

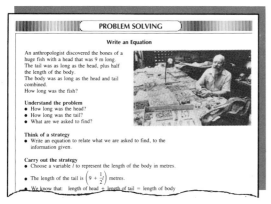

A two-page spread in every chapter focuses on the development of problem-solving strategies.

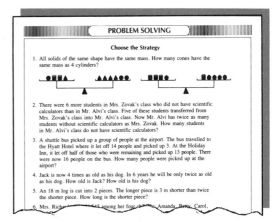

Choose the Strategy pages provide students with the opportunity to select and apply the learned strategies.

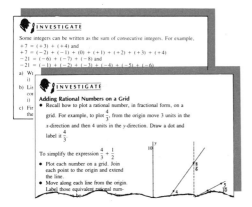

Frequent brief *INVESTIGATE* sections are starting points for mathematical investigations. They always relate to the concepts that are developed in the sections in which they occur.

    Longer *INVESTIGATE* sections lead students to conclusions which they formulate. Students are more likely to retain knowledge that they discover for themselves.

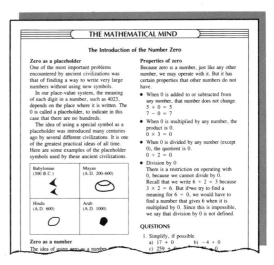

THE MATHEMATICAL MIND highlights historical developments in mathematics, and includes anecdotes of human interest that are part of its history. In this context, interesting problems are presented for the students to solve.

Contents

The Nature of Mathematics

In previous years, your study of mathematics involved learning and practising the fundamental skills of arithmetic, measurement, and geometry. While all of these skills are an important part of this subject, they occupy only a small place in the broad spectrum of mathematics.

Throughout the ages and into the present, people have always appreciated the value of mathematics. Six men and women who have worked with mathematics are presented on the following pages, along with brief quotations which reflect their perceptions of the nature and use of mathematics.

"A mathematician, like a poet or a painter, is a maker of patterns."

Godfrey Harold Hardy
1877-1947

Hardy is famous for his discoveries in the theory of numbers — a branch of mathematics that still contains many unsolved problems.

THE SEARCH FOR PATTERN

Using patterns and relationships, scientists have been able to solve many of life's mysteries and expand their understanding of the world around us. Consider, for example, how remarkable it is that mathematics has enabled us:

- to predict the precise time that a comet, not seen in our lifetime, will reappear
- to estimate with surprising accuracy how long ago dinosaurs roamed the Earth, even though they have been extinct for millions of years
- to prove that the Earth approximates a sphere and to calculate its radius, without leaving the Earth.

These remarkable achievements provide only a glimpse of how far into space and back in time we have reached in our unrelenting search for patterns and relationships. In this book we will explore some patterns and relationships which take us in a natural way from the realm of arithmetic into the realms of algebra and geometry.

Example. In 1682, Sir Edmund Halley saw the comet that now bears his name. He learned that a major comet had also been sighted in the years 1380, 1456, 1531, and 1607. Halley guessed that all these sightings were of the same comet, and he successfully predicted the year when it would return.

a) In what year did Halley's prediction come true?

b) Halley's comet last appeared in 1986. In what year might you next see Halley's comet?

Solution. a) Write down the years when Halley's comet was sighted, and subtract the years which are next to each other.

$$1380 \quad 1456 \quad 1531 \quad 1607 \quad 1682 \ldots$$
$$76 \qquad 75 \qquad 76 \qquad 75$$

If this pattern were to continue, the next sighting would be 76 years after the 1682 sighting. Halley's prediction came true in 1758.

b) Halley's comet should appear again 75 or 76 years after 1986. You might see it in 2061 or 2062.

Looking for a pattern is one of the fundamental problem solving strategies in mathematics. In each chapter of this book you will find a *PROBLEM SOLVING* feature which describes a particular strategy that you may find useful in solving problems.

EXERCISES

1. Check that each line is correct. Then predict the next three lines. Check that your prediction is correct.

   a)
   $$1 = 1 \times 1$$
   $$1 + 3 = 2 \times 2$$
   $$1 + 3 + 5 = 3 \times 3$$

   b)
   $$2 = 1 \times 2$$
   $$2 + 4 = 2 \times 3$$
   $$2 + 4 + 6 = 3 \times 4$$

2. Copy each pattern and predict its next three numbers.

   a) 12, 23, 34, . . .

   b) 1, 5, 10, 14, 19, . . .

   c) 1, 3, 9, 27, . . .

   d) 32, 16, 8, 4, . . .

   e) 392, 400, 405, 413, 418, . . .

   f) 1467, 1562, 1657, 1752, . . .

3. The diagram shows a pattern of whole numbers in three rows. Assume that the pattern continues.

   a) Write the next five numbers in row 2.

   b) In which row will the number 100 appear?

Row 1	1 4 7 10 13 . . .
Row 2	2 5 8 11 14 . . .
Row 3	3 6 9 12 15 . . .

4. These three patterns all start with the numbers 1, 2, 4. Predit the next three numbers in each pattern.

   a) 1, 2, 4, 8, 16, . . .

   b) 1, 2, 4, 7, 11, . . .

   c) 1, 2, 4, 5, 7, 8, 10, . . .

5. Write three different patterns which start with the numbers 1, 2, 3.

6. The first three *triangular numbers* are shown. Write the next three triangular numbers.

7. The first three *square numbers* are shown. Write the next three square numbers.

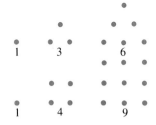

8. This table shows the first six powers of 3.

3^1	3^2	3^3	3^4	3^5	3^6
3	9	27	81	243	729

   Look at the last digit in each power. Extend the pattern and predict the last digit of:

   a) 3^7 b) 3^9 c) 3^{16} d) 3^{21}.

"Many who have never had an opportunity of knowing any more about mathematics confound it with arithmetic and consider it an arid science. In reality, however, it is a science which requires a great deal of imagination."

Sonya Kovalevskaya
1850-1891

Sonya Kovalevskaya was one of the prominent mathematicians of the nineteenth century. She studied the methods of mathematical research and made many brilliant discoveries.

THE VALUE OF MATHEMATICAL INVESTIGATION

Some people view mathematics as a set of rules for solving certain types of problems. They think mathematics is a static subject in which all the important problems have already been solved and only the step-by-step procedures for duplicating the solutions remain. No description of mathematics could be more misleading.

To Sonya Kovalevskaya, mathematics was a dynamic and exciting field. She knew that interesting and challenging problems can be based on simple mathematical concepts. Posing and solving these problems gave her much pleasure and satisfaction.

Example. A regular polyhedron with 12 faces is a *dodecahedron*. A dodecahedron has 20 vertices. How many edges has a dodecahedron?

Solution. The solution can be found by investigating other polyhedrons with fewer vertices, for example, those illustrated below.

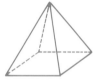   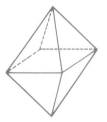

For each polyhedron, count the numbers of its faces, vertices, and edges. Record this information in a table.

	Square-based pyramid	Triangular prism	Cube	Octahedron
Faces	5	5	6	8
Vertices	5	6	8	6
Edges	8	9	12	12

If we study the numbers in each column of the table, we see that the number in the bottom row of each column is 2 less than the sum of the two numbers above it. That is, the number of edges of each polyhedron is 2 less than the total number of faces and vertices. If this relationship is true for the dodecahedron, then the number of edges of a dodecahedron would be: $12 + 20 - 2$, or 30.

That is, we deduce that the dodecahedron has 30 edges.
We can verify that this is the correct answer by counting carefully the edges displayed in the diagram above.

After mathematicians have solved a problem, they usually try to extend the problem or think of related problems. In the above example, we might consider problems such as these.

- Is the number of edges 2 less than the total number of faces and vertices for all polyhedrons?
- Does the same relationship hold for solids with curved surfaces such as the cone or the cylinder?

In this book you will find special questions marked *INVESTIGATE*. Each of these is a mathematical investigation for you to explore. When you do this, you will be doing the kind of mathematics that Sonya Kovalevskaya is referring to in the quotation above.

EXERCISES

1. A truncated octahedron can be formed by cutting off each of the 6 corners of an octahedron. Determine, for a truncated octahedron, the number of:
   a) its faces   b) its vertices
   c) its edges.

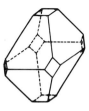

2. A truncated cube can be formed by cutting off each corner.
   a) Draw a diagram of a truncated cube.
   b) Determine, for a truncated cube, the number of:
      i) its faces   ii) its vertices   iii) its edges.

3. Draw a regular pentagon and all its diagonals. How many triangles can you find in the figure?

"How can it be that mathematics, being after all a product of human thought independent of experience, is so admirably adapted to the objects of reality?''

Albert Einstein
1879-1955

This question highlights the power of mathematical reasoning in helping us interpret and understand the world around us.

THE POWER OF MATHEMATICAL REASONING

In Konigsberg, a small town in Prussia, there were two islands in the river which passed through the village. The people wondered if they could walk around the town and cross each bridge exactly once. But whenever they tried it, they ended up either missing a bridge or crossing a bridge twice. They began to think that it was impossible to make the walk, but no one knew why.

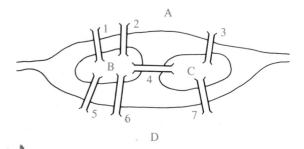

This is one of the most famous problems in mathematics. It was solved about two hundred years ago by the great Swiss mathematician, Leonhard Euler. He drew a simpler diagram by replacing the land by points and the bridges by lines joining them. The problem then is whether it is possible to draw this figure without lifting the pencil from the paper, and without retracing any line. Consider what happens each time a point is approached.

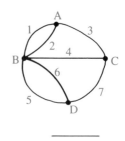

Each time the pencil passes through a point, it draws one line while approaching the point, and another line while leaving it.

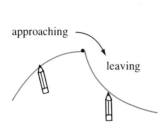

The same thing happens if that point is approached again; there must be one line for approaching and another one for leaving.

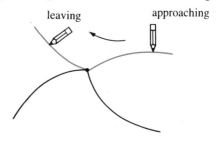

Therefore, the number of lines at each point must be an even number. Since all the points on the figure have an odd number of lines, it is impossible to draw the figure as described. This is the reason why the people in Konigsberg were unable to walk around the town and cross each bridge exactly once.

Example. Is it possible to draw this figure and return to the starting point, without lifting your pencil from the paper or going over any line twice?

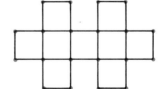

Solution. Count the number of lines at each crossing point. Since they are all even numbers, it is possible to draw the figure as described.

In this book you will see feature pages called *THE MATHEMATICAL MIND*, which describe other famous problems in mathematics. These pages are designed to give you some insights into the history of mathematics and some of the people responsible for it.

EXERCISES

1. Determine if it is possible to draw each diagram without lifting your pencil from the paper, and without going over any line twice.

a)  b)   c) 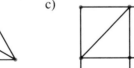 d)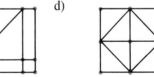

2. Check your answers to *Exercise 1* by drawing those diagrams that can be drawn in the way described.

3. The adjacent diagram shows a floor plan of a house and the location of its doorways. The curve shows a path which passes through each doorway exactly once.

For which of the floor plans below can you sketch a path which passes through each doorway exactly once?

a) 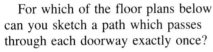 b)  c)

"Thus number may be said to rule the whole world of quantity, and the four rules of arithmetic may be regarded as the complete equipment of the mathematician."

James Clerk Maxwell
1831-1879

Maxwell was a nineteenth-century scientist who made important discoveries in electricity and magnetism.

THE POWER OF THE CALCULATOR

James Clerk Maxwell would have been surprised to learn that his work with electricity would eventually contribute to the invention of inexpensive electronic calculators. Today we take for granted that everyone can use a calculator to do the same kinds of computations that were done in Maxwell's time only by mathematicians.

Some of the ways in which calculators enhance mathematical investigations will be illustrated in the *CALCULATOR POWER* pages in this book. The following example is a problem for which a calculator is essential.

Example. Express as a decimal. $\dfrac{1}{1} + \dfrac{1}{2} + \dfrac{1}{3} + \ldots + \dfrac{1}{10}$

Solution. Using paper and pencil, this problem could be solved by expressing each fraction as a decimal and adding the results. The following strategy is used to solve the problem with a calculator.

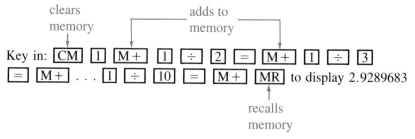

Therefore, $\dfrac{1}{1} + \dfrac{1}{2} + \dfrac{1}{3} + \ldots + \dfrac{1}{10} \doteq 2.928\,968\,3$

The fractions in this example are called *unit fractions*. If you wanted to know the sum of more unit fractions, it would be necessary to continue the additions. But it would be impractical to use a calculator to find the sum of a very large number of unit fractions, say 100. To do this, a computer should be used.

EXERCISES
Use a calculator.

1. Express as a decimal.

   a) $\dfrac{1}{1} + \dfrac{1}{2} + \dfrac{1}{3} + \dfrac{1}{4} + \dfrac{1}{5}$

   b) $\dfrac{1}{1} + \dfrac{1}{2} + \dfrac{1}{3} + \ldots + \dfrac{1}{12}$

   c) $\dfrac{1}{2} + \dfrac{2}{3} + \dfrac{3}{4} + \ldots + \dfrac{9}{10}$

2. Simplify each product. Then predict what the next line should be. Check your prediction with your calculator.

   a) $\qquad 9 \times 7 = $ ▨
   $\qquad 99 \times 67 = $ ▨
   $\qquad 999 \times 667 = $ ▨

   b) $\qquad 6 \times 4 = $ ▨
   $\qquad 66 \times 34 = $ ▨
   $\qquad 666 \times 334 = $ ▨

   c) $\qquad 9 \times 9 = $ ▨
   $\qquad 99 \times 99 = $ ▨
   $\qquad 999 \times 999 = $ ▨

   d) $\qquad 5 \times 5 = $ ▨
   $\qquad 65 \times 65 = $ ▨
   $\qquad 665 \times 665 = $ ▨

   e) $101 \times 101 = $ ▨
   $\quad 202 \times 202 = $ ▨
   $\quad 303 \times 303 = $ ▨

   f) $\quad 1 \times 9 + 2 = $ ▨
   $\quad 12 \times 9 + 3 = $ ▨
   $123 \times 9 + 4 = $ ▨

3. Look for patterns in the numbers given in *Exercise 2* and try similar patterns with other numbers.

4. Choose any three consecutive whole numbers and multiply them together. Then divide the product by 6. Do this for other sets of three consecutive whole numbers. Is the product always divisible by 6? Can you explain why?

5. a) Use the $\boxed{y^x}$ key on your calculator to evaluate 2^{20}.
   b) What is the highest power of 2 which your calculator will display without rounding off?
   c) What is the largest power of 2 which is less than 10^9?

6. The product of the first n natural numbers is $1 \times 2 \times 3 \times 4 \times 5 \times \ldots \times n$. This product is called *factorial n* and is written $n!$.
   a) Calculate $8!$
   b) If $n! = 39\ 916\ 800$, what is the value of n?
   c) For what value of n is $n!$ between 10^{10} and 10^{11}?

7. Use a scientific calculator. Enter as many 9s as your calculator will display then add 1. Assuming a display of 8 digits, it should show 1. 08. Explain this display.

8. For each calculator display, write the number as a decimal.
   a) 2.4   10
   b) 3.7   12
   c) 2.913   09

9. Write each number as it would appear on your calculator.
   a) 983 000 000
   b) 10 300 000 000
   c) 2 345 000 000
   Check by entering each number in your calculator.

"Perhaps the most astonishing achievement of our species has been the invention of a technology, namely the computer, that has the potential to be even more creative and powerful than our own brains."

David Suzuki

David Suzuki has brought science to millions of people through his many articles and television programs.

THE POWER OF THE COMPUTER

The computer has made it possible for us to solve certain problems which were previously considered unsolvable or too complex. For example, the program below can be used to find the sum of any number of consecutive unit fractions.

```
100 REM *** SUM OF UNIT FRACTIONS ***
110 INPUT "HOW MANY UNIT FRACTIONS? ";N
120 S=0
130 FOR K=1 TO N
140    S=S+1/K
150 NEXT K
160 PRINT:PRINT "THE SUM OF THE FIRST ";N
170 PRINT "UNIT FRACTIONS IS ";S
180 END
```

To enter a program such as this one, follow these steps.
- Type NEW and then press RETURN.
- Type each line exactly as it appears.
- After you have entered a line, check that the spacing and punctuation are exactly as shown.
- Make any necessary corrections.
- Press RETURN at the end of each line.
- To begin using the program, type RUN and press RETURN.

Example. Express as a decimal.

a) $\dfrac{1}{1} + \dfrac{1}{2} + \dfrac{1}{3} + \ldots + \dfrac{1}{10}$ b) $\dfrac{1}{1} + \dfrac{1}{2} + \dfrac{1}{3} + \ldots + \dfrac{1}{100}$

Solution. Use the program. Type RUN and then press RETURN. The computer will ask for the number of unit fractions. Enter the number and press RETURN. The computer will then calculate and print the sum in decimal form. Here are the results.

a) HOW MANY UNIT FRACTIONS?
 10
 THE SUM OF THE FIRST 10 UNIT FRACTIONS IS 2.9289683

b) HOW MANY UNIT FRACTIONS?
 100
 THE SUM OF THE FIRST 100 UNIT FRACTIONS IS
 5.18737752

Some of the ways in which the computer enhances mathematical investigations are illustrated in the *COMPUTER POWER* features of this book. These features contain programs in the BASIC computer language, such as the one above. You can use the programs to explore new problems using the power of this technology.

EXERCISES
Use the above program.

1. Express as a decimal.

   a) $\dfrac{1}{1} + \dfrac{1}{2} + \dfrac{1}{3} + \ldots + \dfrac{1}{17} + \dfrac{1}{18} + \dfrac{1}{19} + \dfrac{1}{20}$

   b) $\dfrac{1}{1} + \dfrac{1}{2} + \dfrac{1}{3} + \ldots + \dfrac{1}{47} + \dfrac{1}{48} + \dfrac{1}{49} + \dfrac{1}{50}$

   c) $\dfrac{1}{1} + \dfrac{1}{2} + \dfrac{1}{3} + \ldots + \dfrac{1}{197} + \dfrac{1}{198} + \dfrac{1}{199} + \dfrac{1}{200}$

   d) $\dfrac{1}{1} + \dfrac{1}{2} + \dfrac{1}{3} + \ldots + \dfrac{1}{497} + \dfrac{1}{498} + \dfrac{1}{499} + \dfrac{1}{500}$

   e) $\dfrac{1}{20} + \dfrac{1}{21} + \dfrac{1}{22} + \ldots + \dfrac{1}{27} + \dfrac{1}{28} + \dfrac{1}{29} + \dfrac{1}{30}$

   f) $\dfrac{1}{201} + \dfrac{1}{202} + \dfrac{1}{203} + \ldots + \dfrac{1}{497} + \dfrac{1}{498} + \dfrac{1}{499} + \dfrac{1}{500}$

2. Janet used the program to add some unit fractions, and she obtained the sum 7.380 165 88. Find out how many unit fractions she added.

3. Find how many unit fractions are needed to obtain a sum greater than each number.
   a) 4   b) 5   c) 6   d) 7   e) 8

4. Use a stopwatch to time how long it takes the computer to add different numbers of unit fractions using the program. Graph the results.

". . . tidal friction is gradually slowing down the rotation of the earth.
. . . the spinning of the globe has been so greatly slowed that a rotation now requires, as everyone knows, about 24 hours."

Rachel Carson
1907-1964

Rachel Carson was a biologist and author who was one of the first people to draw attention to environmental issues.

THE UTILITY OF MATHEMATICS

The quotation above is part of Rachel Carson's description of how we know that the Earth's rotation has been gradually slowing down for millions of years. This information has come to us through a knowledge of science and mathematics.

Although we are not aware of it, we are constantly moving in a circle, along with the Earth, making one complete rotation each day. If you were on the equator, you would complete a circle with a radius equal to the Earth's radius. We can use mathematics to find how far you would travel in any given length of time, such as one day or one hour.

Example. The circumference C of a circle is given by the formula $C = 2\pi r$, where $\pi \doteq 3.14$ and r is the radius. The radius of the Earth at the equator is 6378 km. If you were on the equator, find:
a) how far you would travel in one day
b) your speed in kilometres per hour.

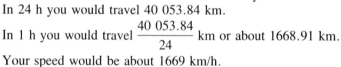

Solution. a) When $r = 6378$, $C \doteq 2(3.14)(6378)$
$= 40\ 053.84$
You would travel about 40 050 km in one day.
b) In 24 h you would travel 40 053.84 km.
In 1 h you would travel $\dfrac{40\ 053.84}{24}$ km or about 1668.91 km.
Your speed would be about 1669 km/h.

EXERCISES

1. How far does someone on the equator travel in:
   a) one minute   b) one second?

2. People who are not on the equator move in smaller circles around the Earth, once every 24 h. The radius of the circle depends on the latitude of the location. Some values for Canadian latitudes are given in the table below.
   a) Consult a map or an atlas to determine the approximate latitude of your location, to the nearest degree.
   b) Use the table to determine the radius of the circle you follow due to the Earth's rotation.
   c) What is the circumference of the circle for your location?
   d) What is your speed in kilometres per hour?

Radii of Circles Due to Earth's Rotation

Latitude (degrees)	Radius (km)	Latitude (degrees)	Radius (km)	Latitude (degrees)	Radius (km)
42	4731	49	4178	56	3562
43	4657	50	4094	57	3470
44	4580	51	4008	58	3376
45	4502	52	3921	59	3281
46	4423	53	3833	60	3186
47	4343	54	3744	61	3089
48	4261	55	3654	62	2991

3. Use the result of *Exercise 2* to determine how far you travel in:
   a) one minute   b) one second.

4. In one year the Earth travels once around the sun. It follows a circle with a radius of approximately 150 000 000 km.
   a) How far does the Earth travel in: i) one year   ii) one day?
   b) What is the Earth's speed in kilometres per hour?

5. In *Exercise 4*, how far does the Earth travel in:
   a) one minute   b) one second?

A FAMOUS UNSOLVED PROBLEM

Despite the best efforts of the world's greatest mathematicians, not all of the important problems in mathematics have been solved. In fact, there are far more unsolved problems than solved ones! One of the most baffling problems in mathematics involves prime numbers.

A *prime number* is one like 13 that has only two factors, the number itself, and 1. The ancient Greek mathematicians noticed that prime numbers frequently occur in pairs differing by 2. Some examples are: 11 and 13; 29 and 31; 347 and 349; 10 006 427 and 10 006 429. These are called *twin primes*, and the question of how many twin primes there are is known as the twin prime problem.

> **The Twin Prime Problem**
> How many pairs of twin primes are there?

Although some of the world's greatest mathematicians have tried to solve this problem, no one knows the answer. There may even be infinitely many twin primes. However, using computer techniques, we have been able to examine all the numbers up to 30 000 000. From this investigation we know that there are 152 892 pairs of twin primes less than 30 000 000. Even as you read this book, computers are finding twin primes far beyond 30 000 000, but it will require a mathematical proof to solve the problem for all possible numbers.

EXERCISES

1. How many pairs of twin primes can you find which are less than 50?

2. a) There are only two pairs of twin primes between 50 and 100. Can you find them?
   b) There are two pairs of twin primes between 100 and 110. Can you find them?

3. Twin primes differ by 2. Find examples of primes which differ by these numbers.
   a) 4   b) 6   c) 8   d) 10   e) 12   f) 14   g) 16

4. If we discovered by computer that there were no twin primes between 30 000 000 and 100 000 000, would that prove that we had found all the twin primes? Why?

5. There is only one pair of primes that differs by 3. Can you find it? Can you explain why there are no other pairs of primes that differ by 3?

6. Explain why the product of two prime numbers is never a multiple of 4.

7. Two prime numbers have a sum which is odd. Explain how you know that the product of those two prime numbers is even.

8. What prime number divides 2159 and 2176?

1 Integers

Ste. Agathe   Altitude 2350 m
Valleville   Altitude   350 m

It is 8°C in Valleville.
The temperature decreases 6.5°C for every 1000 m
increase in altitude. If there is precipitation at the village
of Ste. Agathe, will it be rain or snow? (See Section
1-3, *Example 4*.)

1-1 USING INTEGERS

On a thermometer, $0°$ represents the freezing point of water on the Celsius scale.

Temperatures below freezing are indicated on this thermometer by *negative integers*; temperatures above freezing by *positive integers*.

Newspapers publish charts of the temperatures at different places in the country at a certain time of the day.

From the chart, it can be seen that only Victoria, Vancouver, and Calgary were above freezing.

Which was the coldest place?

Temperatures at 2 p.m. EST yesterday:	
	°C
Whitehorse	−1
Yellowknife	−7
Victoria	7
Vancouver	6
Calgary	4
Edmonton	−6
Prince Albert	−2
Regina	−5
Winnipeg	−10

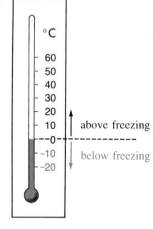

In land elevations, positive integers indicate heights *above* sea level and negative integers indicate heights *below* sea level.

The sectional drawing shows a high point of about $+220$ or 220 m above sea level. The lowest point is about -220 or 220 m below sea level.

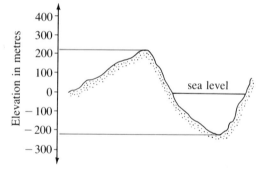

In general, numbers such as 1, 2, 3, . . . (sometimes written +1, +2, +3, . . .) are called positive integers; and numbers such as −1, −2, −3, . . . are called negative integers. The negative integers, zero, and the positive integers make up the set of integers, denoted by *I*.

$$I = \{ \ldots, -3, -2, -1, 0, 1, 2, 3, \ldots \}$$

Integers such as 3 and −3 are called *opposite integers*. We say that 237 is the opposite of −237.

Integers can be represented on a number line.

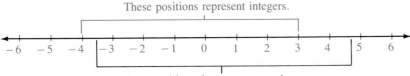

Any integer on the number line is *greater than* all the integers to its *left* and *less than* all the integers to its *right*.
For example, −2 is greater than −5. This is written −2 > −5.
Conversely, −5 is less than −2. This is written −5 < −2.

Example 1. Compare.
      a) −6 and 2   b) −5 and −1 c) 4 and −3   d) 0 and −5

Solution. Draw a number line.

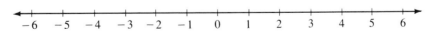

    a) −6 is to the left of 2, so −6 is less than 2, or −6 < 2.
    b) −5 is to the left of −1, so −5 is less than −1, or −5 < −1.
    c) 4 is to the right of −3, so 4 > −3.
    d) 0 is to the right of −5, so 0 > −5.

Example 2. Arrange −5, 6, −3, −1, 0, 4, −2 in order from:
    a) least to greatest   b) greatest to least.

Solution. Draw a number line. Circle the given integers.

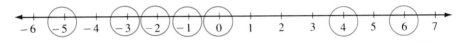

    a) The integers are ordered from least to greatest when written in order
        from left to right. −5, −3, −2, −1, 0, 4, 6

    b) The integers are ordered from greatest to least when written in the
        reverse order. 6, 4, 0, −1, −2, −3, −5

EXERCISES 1-1

(A)

1. State which letters on this number line represent integers.

   Write the integer represented by each letter.

2. Write using integers.
   a) a gain of $9
   b) a loss of $21
   c) 80°C above freezing
   d) 20°C below freezing
   e) a profit of $50
   f) a loss of $75
   g) a debt of $81
   h) a depth of 12 000 m
   i) an altitude of 3000 m

3. If + 100 represents a gain in altitude of 100 m, state what these integers represent.
   a) − 300
   b) + 25
   c) − 100
   d) + 2

4. If − 5 represents a debt of $5, state what these integers represent.
   a) − 12
   b) + 7
   c) + 15
   d) − 53

5. State the opposite.
   a) a gain of $10
   b) an altitude loss of 500 m
   c) a 3 kg loss of mass
   d) a temperature of − 14°C
   e) 18
   f) − 11
   g) the opposite of − 7
   h) the opposite of 5

(B)

6. Compare.
   a) − 3 and 2
   b) 5 and − 6
   c) − 4 and − 1
   d) − 3 and 0
   e) 2 and − 5
   f) − 9 and − 1
   g) − 11 and 10
   h) − 8 and − 9

7. State the least integer.
   a) 1, − 2, 0
   b) − 6, − 3, 1
   c) − 1, 4, − 8
   d) 0, − 2, − 4
   e) 2, − 9, − 3
   f) − 5, 1, − 1
   g) − 4, 7, − 10, 1
   h) 3, − 2, 15, − 18, 7
   i) − 5, 3, 0, − 16, 17

8. Arrange in order from least to greatest.
   a) 3, − 1, 5, − 4
   b) − 2, 8, − 10, 5
   c) − 1, 4, − 8, − 2, 5, 0

9. Arrange in order from greatest to least.
   a) − 2, 7, 1, − 4
   b) − 3, 0, 2, − 1
   c) 5, − 8, − 2, 8, 0, 3

(C)

10. State which integer is
    a) 3 less than 1.
    b) 2 more than − 1.
    c) 6 more than − 4.
    d) 8 less than 5.
    e) 7 more than the opposite of 3.
    f) 5 less than the opposite of − 1.

11. State which integer is
    a) 6 less than 2.
    b) 4 more than − 9.
    c) 3 more than 0.
    d) 5 less than − 2.
    e) 2 more than the opposite of − 3.
    f) 1 less than the opposite of − 1.

THE MATHEMATICAL MIND

Problems and their Solvers of Times Gone By

Some problems involving mathematics have required far more than correct arithmetic and the application of the right formulas. They have required the discovery of new principles, and the invention of special mathematical techniques. Here are three of the world's greatest mathematicians and the kinds of problems they solved.

Why does a small rock sink and a large block of wood float?

What holds up the moon?

Is there a way to send messages around the world instantly?

**Archimedes
287–212 B.C.**

**Sir Isaac Newton
1642–1727**

**Carl Friedrich Gauss
1777–1855**

Archimedes is regarded as the greatest problem solver of the ancient world. Apparently his powers of concentration were so deep that, when working on a problem, he became unaware of his surroundings. The story is told that he was in his bathtub when he discovered the principle of buoyancy. So great was his excitement that he leaped from his tub and ran through the streets naked shouting: ''Eureka! Eureka!'' (I have found it! I have found it!)

Before Isaac Newton, no one understood the idea of gravity. No one knew why the moon travels in an orbit instead of hurtling off into space or crashing to the Earth.

By the time Newton was 25 years old, he had formulated the law of gravitation and cracked the problem — a problem that had baffled scientists from the beginning of time.

Some consider Carl Friedrich Gauss to be the greatest mathematician of all time. In addition to his computer-like skill in performing mental calculations, he had an almost superhuman ability to solve problems. Though his achievements were mainly in pure mathematics, he is also known for his invention of the telegraph. This invention was a giant step forward in communications, and led the way to the development of the telephone and the radio.

1-2 ADDING INTEGERS

An elevator in an apartment block travels from the top floor (the 12th) to the first floor. Then it continues below ground level to the four parking levels beneath the building.

P3	P2	P1	P	1	2	3	4	5	6	7	8	9	10	11	12

Each floor can be considered as an integer on a number line.

- The elevator is on the 8th floor. It goes up 2 floors. Each upward movement can be represented by a positive integer.
$$8 + (+2) = 10$$
  The elevator is then at the 10th floor.
- The elevator moves down 4 floors. Each downward movement can be represented by a negative integer.
$$10 + (-4) = 6$$
  The elevator is then at the 6th floor.

   The addition of integers can be shown by moves on a number line. Start at the first integer. Move to the right for positive integers. Move to the left for negative integers.

Example 1. Simplify.
  a) $(+1) + (+3)$ b) $(-1) + (-3)$
  c) $(+1) + (-3)$ d) $(-1) + (+3)$

Solution. a) $(+1) + (+3)$
  Start at 1. Move 3 to the right.
  $(+1) + (+3) = 4$

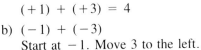

  b) $(-1) + (-3)$
  Start at -1. Move 3 to the left.
  $(-1) + (-3) = -4$

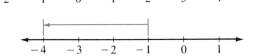

  c) $(+1) + (-3)$
  Start at 1. Move 3 to the left.
  $(+1) + (-3) = -2$

  d) $(-1) + (+3)$
  Start at -1. Move 3 to the right.
  $(-1) + (+3) = 2$

Example 2. Simplify. $(+5) + (-7) + (+3) + (-4)$

Solution. Start at $+5$.
  Move 7 to the left to -2.
  Move 3 to the right to 1.
  Move 4 to the left to -3.

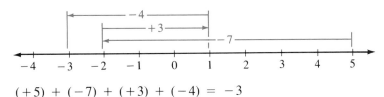

  $(+5) + (-7) + (+3) + (-4) = -3$

  To add several integers, it is easier to add the integers with the same sign first and then use the number line to obtain the final sum.

Example 3. Simplify. $(-25) + (+16) + (-11) + (-28) + (+34)$

Solution. $(-25) + (+16) + (-11) + (-28) + (+34)$
  $= (-25) + (-11) + (-28) + (+16) + (+34)$
  $= (-64) + (+50)$
  $= -14$

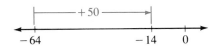

  Positive integers are usually written without the positive sign. For example, the integer sum in *Example 3* could be written as
  $(-25) + 16 + (-11) + (-28) + 34$.
  The number line is a useful device for showing addition of integers. However, after a little practice you should be able to add integers without its help.

EXERCISES 1-2

(A)

1. Simplify.
   a) $(-6) + (+2)$ b) $(+8) + (-5)$ c) $(+5) + (-8)$ d) $(-3) + (+8)$
   e) $(+3) + (+2)$ f) $(-6) + (-4)$ g) $(+5) + (+3)$ h) $(+7) + (-5)$
   i) $(-4) + (+6)$ j) $(+12) + (-3)$ k) $(-5) + (+11)$ l) $(+9) + (-9)$

2. Simplify.
   a) $(+3) + (-6)$ b) $(-9) + (-6)$ c) $(+4) + (-5)$ d) $(+7) + (-3)$
   e) $(+9) + (+5)$ f) $(-3) + (-6)$ g) $(-4) + (-8)$ h) $(-5) + (-7)$
   i) $(-9) + (-7)$ j) $(+3) + (-12)$ k) $(+14) + (-8)$ l) $(-16) + (+7)$

3. Simplify.
   a) $(-3) + (-4) + (+8)$ b) $(+2) + (-5) + (-7)$
   c) $(-2) + (-5) + (-9)$ d) $(+7) + (-8) + (+2)$
   e) $(-9) + (+3) + (+2)$ f) $(+4) + (-6) + (-2)$
   g) $(-8) + (-5) + (+7)$ h) $(-9) + (+7) + (-10)$

(B)

4. Simplify.
   a) $(-8) + (-7) + (+14) + (+1)$ b) $(-13) + (+2) + (+19) + (-7)$
   c) $(-10) + (+7) + (-12) + (+6)$ d) $(+14) + (-3) + (-9) + (-11)$
   e) $(+16) + (+12) + (-11) + (-15)$ f) $(+32) + (+43) + (-29) + (-11)$

5. Simplify.
   a) $5 + (-3) + 7$ b) $(-5) + (-4) + 6$
   c) $2 + (-9) + 4$ d) $(-8) + 1 + (-2)$
   e) $(-13) + 27 + (-11)$ f) $37 + (-21) + (-52)$
   g) $18 + 39 + (-71)$ h) $(-87) + 78 + (-13)$
   i) $(-21) + (-29) + 50$ j) $91 + (-27) + 19 + (-72)$

6. a) Simplify.
      i) $(+4) + (-4)$ ii) $(-7) + (+7)$ iii) $(-36) + (+36)$
      iv) $(+81) + (-81)$ v) $(-23) + (+23)$ vi) $(-57) + (+57)$
   b) What can you conclude about the sum of an integer and its opposite?

7. Copy each chart. Add horizontally and vertically. Find the sum of the integers in each chart in two different ways.

a)

$+4$	-7	$+6$	3
-3	$+10$	-9	-2
$+8$	-3	-11	-6
9	0	-14	

b)

-7	$+3$	-8	
-6	$+5$	$+2$	
$+9$	-4	$+10$	

8. An elevator is at the 14th floor. It goes down 8 floors, then down 5 more floors, then up 4 floors, then down 1 floor. At which floor is the elevator now?

9. The chart shows the normal body temperature and the range of body temperatures that certain animals have survived in.

Animal	Normal Body Temperature	Temperature Range in °C Minimum	Maximum
Catfish	+20°C	+6	+34
Crocodile	+26°C	+23	+29
Garter Snake	+22°C	+4	+39
Horned Lizard	+35°C	+25	+45
Human	+37°C	+16	+44

a) Which animal survived the greatest temperature range?
b) How much did its normal temperature increase before the animal reached the maximum of its range?
c) How much did its normal temperature decrease before the animal reached the minimum of its range?

10. Write an addition statement for each statement.
a) A football team is on the 15-yard line. It gains 15 yards, and on the next play it is penalized 5 yards.
b) Deposit $85 in an account. Write cheques for $29 and $37. Deposit a further $52, and write a cheque for $66.
c) A man's mass was 80 kg. He went on a diet and lost 7 kg. While on vacation he gained 5 kg.

11. Copy and complete the chart. Add $+3$ when moving to the right. Add $+2$ when moving up.

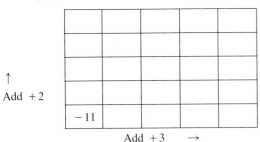

↑
Add $+2$

-11

Add $+3$ →

What pattern do you notice in the diagonals on the chart?

12. Write the integer represented by each square.
a) $7 + ▨ = 3$ b) $2 + ▨ = -5$
c) $(-6) + ▨ = -2$ d) $1 + ▨ = 4$
e) $-7 = (-7) + ▨$ f) $-11 = (-5) + ▨$

13. Copy and complete the chart. Each square should contain an integer such that the rule beneath the chart is obeyed.

			+7				

Add −3 →

14. Find the sum of the integers in the chart in *Exercise 13*.

15. Copy each chart. Insert integers so that their horizontal and vertical sums have the same total.

a)

+8		+5
	−1	
+2		

b)

	−3	−4
+6		
	−2	

c)

	+5	−7
	−3	−9

16. Copy the chart. Find the integer that should be added to each square. Write the rule beneath the chart, then complete the chart.

		−9			6		

Add ? →

17. Copy the chart. Find the integer that should be added in each direction. Complete the chart.

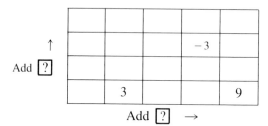

		−3	
	3		9

↑ Add ?

Add ? →

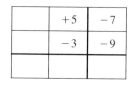

INVESTIGATE

Some integers can be written as the sum of consecutive integers. For example,

$+7 = (+3) + (+4)$ and

$+7 = (−2) + (−1) + (0) + (+1) + (+2) + (+3) + (+4)$

$−21 = (−6) + (−7) + (−8)$ and

$−21 = (−1) + (−2) + (−3) + (−4) + (−5) + (−6)$

a) Write each integer as the sum of consecutive integers.
   i) −11   ii) 18   iii) −14   iv) −17   v) 21   vi) 20

b) List the different ways that these integers can be written as the sum of consecutive integers.
   i) 15   ii) −25   iii) 30   iv) −35

c) Find the five negative integers greater than −40 that *cannot* be written as the sum of consecutive integers.

1-3 SUBTRACTING INTEGERS

Consider these examples of changes in height.

● A hawk at 20 m rises to a height of 25 m.
Change in height = final height − initial height
$$= 25 - 20$$
$$= 5$$
The hawk rose 5 m.

● A dolphin at a depth of 2 m leaps to a height of 1 m above the water surface.
Change in height = final height − initial height
$$= 1 - (-2)$$
$$= 3$$
The dolphin rose 3 m.

● A diver 5 m above a pool dives to a depth of 2 m.
Change in height = final height − initial height
$$= (-2) - (+5)$$
$$= -7$$
The diver dropped 7 m.

● A trout at a depth of 1 m swims to a depth of 3 m.
Change in height = final height − initial height
$$= (-3) - (-1)$$
$$= -2$$
The trout dropped 2 m.

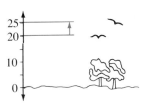

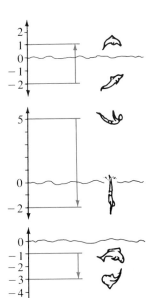

Each example on the previous page illustrates the subtraction of one integer from another. The same results could have been obtained if each expression were written as the sum of integers.

We saw that $25 - 20 = 5$; we know that $25 + (-20) = 5$
Therefore, $25 - 20 = 25 + (-20)$

Similarly,

$1 - (-2) = 3$ but $1 + (+2) = 3$ so $1 - (-2) = 1 + (+2)$
$(-2) - (+5) = -7$ but $(-2) + (-5) = -7$ so
$(-2) - (+5) = (-2) + (-5)$
$(-3) - (-1) = -2$ but $(-3) + (+1) = -2$ so
$(-3) - (-1) = (-3) + (+1)$

This pattern suggests that adding the opposite of an integer gives the same result as subtracting the integer.

> To subtract an integer, add its opposite.

Example 1. Simplify.

    a) $(+6) - (-2)$ b) $(-7) - (+3)$ c) $7 - 9$

Solution.   a) $(+6) - (-2) = (+6) + (+2)$
                       $= 8$
    b) $(-7) - (+3) = (-7) + (-3)$
                       $= -10$
    c) $7 - 9 = -2$

Frequently, expressions involving integers are written without the brackets.

Example 2. Simplify.

    a) $3 - 5 + 6 - 7$ b) $5 - 9 + 2 - 8 - 3 + 6$

Solution.   a) $3 - 5 + 6 - 7$ can be written as $(+3) + (-5) + (+6) + (-7)$.
      Rearranging, $(+3) + (+6) + (-5) + (-7) = (+9) + (-12)$
                                             $= -3$

    b) $5 - 9 + 2 - 8 - 3 + 6$ can be written as
        $(+5) + (-9) + (+2) + (-8) + (-3) + (+6)$
    $= (+5) + (+2) + (+6) + (-9) + (-8) + (-3)$
    $= (+13) + (-20)$
    $= (-7)$

With practice, integer expressions can be simplified directly.

Example 3. Simplify. $-3 + 6 - 5 + 4 - 3 - 7$

Solution. $-3 + 6 - 5 + 4 - 3 - 7 = -3 - 5 - 3 - 7 + 6 + 4$
                                    $= -18 + 10$
                                    $= -8$

The problem posed at the beginning of the chapter can now be solved.

Example 4. It is 8°C in Valleville (altitude 350 m). The temperature decreases 6.5°C for every 1000 m increase in altitude. If there is precipitation in Ste. Agathe (altitude 2350 m), will it be rain or snow?

Solution. The difference in altitude is 2000 m.

Therefore, the temperature in Ste. Agathe is 2(6.5°C) or 13°C lower than the temperature in Valleville.

The temperature in Ste. Agathe is 8°C − 13°C = −5°C.
Any precipitation in Ste. Agathe will probably be snow.

EXERCISES 1-3

Ⓐ

1. The temperature was −6°C. It is now 4°C. How much did the temperature change?

2. A balloon was 600 m above the ground. It is now 250 m above the ground. What is its change in altitude?

3. State the temperature change.
   a) from −12°C to 8°C   b) from −17°C to −5°C   c) from 27°C to −27°C
   d) from −6°C to 18°C   e) from 7°C to −1°C   f) from −1°C to −11°C

4. State the altitude change.
   a) from 3170 m to 525 m   b) from −265 m to 425 m
   c) from −350 m to −580 m   d) from −900 m to −250 m

5. Simplify.
   a) $(+4) - (+6)$ b) $(+7) - (+2)$ c) $(-8) - (+4)$
   d) $(+3) - (+1)$ e) $(+6) - (-1)$ f) $(-4) - (-3)$
   g) $(-6) - (+3)$ h) $(-2) - (+5)$ i) $(+2) - (+1)$
   j) $(+1) - (-5)$ k) $(-4) - (-2)$ l) $(+2) - (-4)$
   m) $(-8) - (-9)$ n) $0 - (-2)$ o) $0 - (+3)$

Ⓑ

6. Simplify.
   a) $(+45) - (-15)$ b) $(-23) - (-13)$ c) $(-14) - (+66)$
   d) $(-145) - (-35)$ e) $(+68) - (+98)$ f) $(-72) - (-42)$
   g) $(+75) - (-15)$ h) $(-187) - (-42)$ i) $(-27) - (+43)$
   j) $(+26) - (+31)$ k) $(-18) - (+42)$ l) $(+37) - (+34)$
   m) $(-29) - (-18)$ n) $(+54) - (-17)$ o) $(-99) - (+91)$

7. Simplify.
   a) $(-9) - (+2) + (-3) - (+5)$ b) $(+8) + (+4) - (+6) - (-3)$
   c) $(+8) - (+3) - (-4) - (-7)$ d) $(-6) - (-3) - (-7) + (-8)$
   e) $(-10) + (+6) - (+5) - (+7)$ f) $(+1) - (-6) - (+3) - (-4)$
   g) $(-7) + (-3) - (-5) - (+8)$ h) $(-2) - (+6) - (-4) - (+7)$

8. Simplify.
   a) $(-3) + (-8) - (+9) - (-7)$
   b) $(+8) - (+13) + (-6) + (+3)$
   c) $(-7) - (-11) + (+3) - (+6)$
   d) $(+15) - (-3) - (+11) + (-8)$
   e) $(+5) - (+10) - (+2) - (-12)$
   f) $(+4) + (-5) + (-11) - (-1)$
   g) $(-9) + (+11) + (-14) - (+5)$
   h) $(-16) - (+8) + (-4) - (-7)$

9. Simplify.
   a) $5 - 2 - 8 + 3 - 1$
   b) $-4 + 6 + 2 - 7 - 3$
   c) $-1 - 5 + 9 - 2 + 3$
   d) $7 - 2 - 6 + 4 - 8 + 2$
   e) $-3 - 9 + 1 - 5 + 7 - 4$
   f) $17 - 14 - 2 + 13 - 9 - 10$
   g) $-7 - 2 + 3 - 6 + 8 - 4$
   h) $14 - 11 - 8 + 12 - 2 - 14$
   i) $36 - 27 + 41 - 81 + 16$
   j) $-40 - 22 + 31 + 17 - 54$

10. Simplify.
    a) $(-4 + 6) - (3 - 7)$
    b) $(8 - 5) - (-4 + 6)$
    c) $(-8 + 3) + (-2 - 5)$
    d) $(-9 + 4) + (-3 - 7)$
    e) $(7 - 4) + (8 - 3)$
    f) $(-6 + 2) - (7 - 9)$
    g) $(8 - 6) + (9 - 4)$
    h) $(-10 + 4) - (8 - 12)$
    i) $(10 - 9) + (8 - 10)$
    j) $(-3 - 6) - (-1 - 8)$

11. Simplify.
    a) $(-3 + 7) + (6 - 4 + 10)$
    b) $(9 - 6 + 13) - (-4 + 5 - 11)$
    c) $(13 - 10 + 1) - (-2 - 8 + 1)$
    d) $(-15 + 18 + 4) + (12 - 3 - 13)$
    e) $(-2 - 16 + 10) + (17 + 9 - 27)$
    f) $(14 + 15 - 17) - (21 - 11 + 3)$
    g) $(18 + 21 - 32) + (-12 - 13 - 15)$

12. The lowest temperature ever recorded in Canada was $-63°C$ in the Yukon in 1947. The highest temperature was $45°C$ in Saskatchewan in 1937. What is the difference between these temperatures?

13. The greatest temperature change in North America in a single day was from $+7°C$ to $-49°C$ in Montana. What is the difference between these temperatures?

14. Write the integer represented by each square.
    a) $17 - (+19) = ▨$
    b) $▨ - (+6) = -4$
    c) $7 - (+3) = ▨$
    d) $-8 - (-5) = ▨$
    e) $11 - ▨ = 3$
    f) $▨ - (+3) = -6$
    g) $-23 - ▨ = 23$
    h) $▨ - (+5) = 3$
    i) $-21 - ▨ = -12$

15. Write the integer represented by each square.
    a) $▨ - (+5) = 13$
    b) $▨ - (+6) = 4$
    c) $7 - ▨ = 45$
    d) $-8 - ▨ = -3$
    e) $-11 - ▨ = 3$
    f) $▨ - (+3) = 6$

Ⓒ

16. The time difference between Toronto and Vancouver is 3 h.
    a) An airplane leaves Vancouver for Toronto at 08:00 and the flying time is 4 h 10 min. What time does it arrive in Toronto?
    b) On the return flight the airplane leaves Toronto at 07:30 and the flying time to Vancouver is 4 h 50 min. What time does it arrive in Vancouver?

17. In August 1978, three Americans made the first crossing of the Atlantic Ocean by balloon. The graph shows the altitude of the balloon along the flight path.

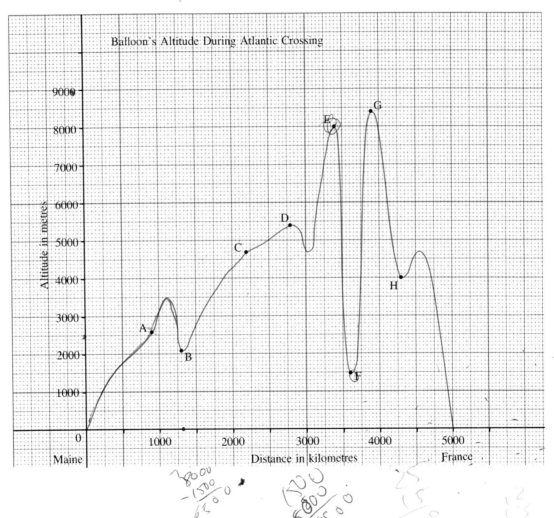

State the approximate change in altitude between each pair of points.
a) from *A* to *B*   b) from *B* to *C*   c) from *A* to *C*   d) from *E* to *F*
e) from *F* to *G*   f) from *E* to *G*   g) from *D* to *H*   h) from *B* to *F*

MATHEMATICS AROUND US

Times of the Day around the World

The time of day changes 1 h for every 15° difference in longitude. This means that when it is midday in London, England (0° longitude), it is midnight at the date line (180° longitude); a new day is just starting there. A place on the date line is 12 h ahead of London.

Find the date line and London, England on a globe.

Times are usually compared with the time in London.

London
England

Standard time difference in hours between London (England) and other cities					
Athens	+2	Halifax	−4	Peking	+8
Bangkok	+7	Jakarta	+7	Rome	+1
Bogota	−5	Jerusalem	+2	Santiago	−4
Brasilia	−3	Mexico City	−6	Washington	−5
Canberra	+10	Moscow	+3	Wellington	+12
Dublin	0	Ottawa	−5	Vancouver	−8

Halifax
Nova Scotia

Halifax −4 means that Halifax is 4 h behind London.

Moscow +3 means that Moscow is 3 h ahead of London.

Therefore, Moscow is 3 h − (−4 h) or 7 h ahead of Halifax.

Moscow
U.S.S.R.

QUESTIONS

1. It is 08:00 in London. State the time in each city.
   a) Ottawa   b) Mexico City   c) Jerusalem   d) Canberra

2. It is 22:00 in Jakarta. State the time in each city.
   a) Bangkok   b) Bogota   c) Wellington   d) Halifax

3. It is 21:00 in Ottawa. State the time in each city.
   a) Vancouver   b) Dublin   c) Washington   d) Peking

4. Team Canada is playing Moscow Selects and the game is being televised live via satellite.
   a) The game is in Moscow at 8 P.M. State the time that a viewer would be watching the game in each city.
      i) Halifax   ii) Vancouver   iii) Ottawa
   b) The game is in Toronto (the same time zone as Ottawa) at 8 P.M. State the time that a viewer in Moscow would be watching it.

5. The scenes of an earthquake in Chile are sent via television satellite from Santiago at 16:00. State the time that the transmission is received in these places.
   a) London   b) Ottawa   c) Bogota   d) Mexico City
   e) Moscow   f) Vancouver   g) Brasilia   h) Wellington

CALCULATOR POWER

If your calculator has a ⎡+/−⎤ key, it can be used to simplify expressions involving integers.

Example 1.   Simplify. $(-5) - (-20)$

Solution.   Key in: ⎡5⎤ ⎡+/−⎤ ⎡−⎤ ⎡2⎤ ⎡0⎤ ⎡+/−⎤ ⎡=⎤ to display 15
$(-5) - (-20) = 15$

If your calculator also has a memory, it can be used to simplify similar expressions.

Example 2.   Simplify. $(-58) - (-39)$

Solution.   Key in: ⎡CM⎤ ⎡3⎤ ⎡9⎤ ⎡+/−⎤ ⎡M+⎤ ⎡5⎤ ⎡8⎤ ⎡+/−⎤ ⎡−⎤ ⎡RM⎤ ⎡=⎤
                         ↑   ↑   ↑
                       clears   adds −39   recalls −39
                       memory   to memory   from memory

                 to display -19
              $(-58) - (-39) = -19$

1. Use the methods of these examples to check the answers to *Exercises 5* and *6* on page 13.

2. Modify the strategy of each example to check the answers to *Exercises 7* and *8* on pages 13 and 14.

1-4   MULTIPLYING INTEGERS

To multiply integers, we must define what we mean by the following products.
    $(+4)(+5)$ $(+4)(-5)$ $(-4)(+5)$ $(-4)(-5)$

To help us define these products, we recall certain facts about multiplication of whole numbers.

Multiplication of whole numbers is defined as repeated addition. For example, 4×5 means $5 + 5 + 5 + 5$.

The multiplication table contains patterns such as this.

The first numbers $4 \times 5 = 20$
decrease by 1; $3 \times 5 = 15$
                     $2 \times 5 = 10$
                     $1 \times 5 = 5$ the products
                     $0 \times 5 = 0$ decrease by 5.

We would like integers to behave as much as possible like whole numbers. Therefore, we will extend these facts to apply to the multiplication of integers. For example, we can use repeated addition to define what we mean by $(+4)(+5)$ and $(+4)(-5)$.

$$(+4)(+5) \text{ means } 4(+5) = (+5) + (+5) + (+5) + (+5)$$
$$= +20$$

$$(+4)(-5) \text{ means } 4(-5) = (-5) + (-5) + (-5) + (-5)$$
$$= -20$$

To define what we mean by $(-4)(+5)$, we write the above number pattern using integers, and extend it to negative integers.

The first numbers decrease by 1;	
$(+4) \times (+5) = +20$	
$(+3) \times (+5) = +15$	
$(+2) \times (+5) = +10$	
$(+1) \times (+5) = +5$	
$0 \times (+5) = 0$	
$(-1) \times (+5) = -5$	
$(-2) \times (+5) = -10$	
$(-3) \times (+5) = -15$	the products
$(-4) \times (+5) = -20$	decrease by 5.

We see that we should define $(-4)(+5)$ to be equal to -20.
To define what we mean by $(-4)(-5)$, we use another number pattern.

The first numbers decrease by 1;	
$(+4) \times (-5) = -20$	
$(+3) \times (-5) = -15$	
$(+2) \times (-5) = -10$	
$(+1) \times (-5) = -5$	
$0 \times (-5) = 0$	
$(-1) \times (-5) = +5$	
$(-2) \times (-5) = +10$	
$(-3) \times (-5) = +15$	the products
$(-4) \times (-5) = +20$	increase by 5.

We see that we should define $(-4)(-5)$ to be equal to $+20$.

Summarizing the above results, we define the multiplication of two integers

> The product of two integers with the same signs is positive.
> The product of two integers with different signs is negative.

These results can be illustrated in a multiplication table.

x	Positive	Negative
Positive	Positive	Negative
Negative	Negative	Positive

Example 1. Simplify.

   a) $(-2)(+6)$ b) $(-7)(-8)$ c) $(+16)(-14)$

Solution.   a) $(-2)(+6) = -12$
   b) $(-7)(-8) = 56$
   c) $(+16)(-14) = -224$

Example 2. Simplify. $(-3)(+2) - (-6)(-2)$

Solution. $(-3)(+2) - (-6)(-2) = (-6) - (+12)$
                $= (-6) + (-12)$
                $= -18$

EXERCISES 1-4

Ⓐ

1. Simplify.
   a) $(-5)(+6)$ b) $(+7)(-8)$ c) $(-7)(-9)$ d) $(+6)(+9)$
   e) $(-12)(+5)$ f) $(-3)(-13)$ g) $(+8)(+9)$ h) $(-5)(+5)$
   i) $(-5)(-5)$ j) $(+7)(-6)$ k) $(+3)(+4)$ l) $(-4)(-8)$
   m) $(+6)(-7)$ n) $(+4)(-7)$ o) $(+9)(+3)$ p) $(0)(-7)$

2. Simplify.
   a) $(+16)(-5)$ b) $(-18)(+3)$ c) $(-14)(-4)$ d) $(-17)(+9)$
   e) $(-11)(+28)$ f) $(+19)(+11)$ g) $(+36)(+72)$ h) $(+47)(-16)$
   i) $(-69)(-89)$ j) $(-74)(-18)$ k) $(+37)(-31)$ l) $(-44)(-22)$

3. Simplify.
   a) $(-2)(+5)(-7)$ b) $(-3)(-4)(-2)$ c) $(+6)(-5)(+4)$
   d) $(-1)(+3)(-3)$ e) $(+2)(-3)(-3)$ f) $(-2)(-2)(-3)$
   g) $(+5)(-1)(-1)(-1)$ h) $(-1)(-2)(-3)(-4)$ i) $(-5)(+4)(+3)(-2)$

Ⓑ

4. Simplify
   a) $(-2)(+3) + (-6)(-2)$ b) $(-4)(-3) + (-1)(-2)$
   c) $(-2)(-6) - (+5)(-2)$ d) $(-3)(+7) - (+1)(+5)$
   e) $(-2)(+8) - (-3)(-3)$ f) $(+4)(-7) + (-8)(+6)$
   g) $(-3)(+9) + (-2)(+7)$ h) $(-7)(-9) - (-6)(-7)$
   i) $(-2)(-2)(+1) + (-3)(-3)(-2)$ j) $(-5)(-2)(-2) - (+2)(-1)(-1)$

5. What must be true of two integers if their product is:
   a) positive   b) negative   c) zero?

6. By comparing the answers in *Exercise 3*, what appears to be true for:
   a) the product of an even number of negative numbers;
   b) the product of an odd number of negative numbers?

Ⓒ

7. Find the integer represented by each square.
   a) $(+5) \times \blacksquare = -20$ b) $(-2) \times \blacksquare = 16$ c) $\blacksquare \times (+7) = -56$
   d) $\blacksquare \times (-6) = 54$ e) $(-8) \times \blacksquare = -72$ f) $\blacksquare \times (-12) = -96$
   g) $-32 = (+8) \times \blacksquare$ h) $48 = (-16) \times \blacksquare$ i) $-39 = \blacksquare \times (-13)$
   j) $-15 \times \blacksquare = -75$ k) $\blacksquare \times 18 = -72$ l) $98 = (-7) \times \blacksquare$

8. Find the integer represented by each square.
   a) $(-2)(+3) \times \blacksquare = -24$
   b) $(+4) \times \blacksquare \times (+2) = -32$
   c) $\blacksquare \times (-1)(-6) = 42$
   d) $(-3) \times \blacksquare \times (+5) = -45$
   e) $96 = (-2)(+6) \times \blacksquare$
   f) $-36 = (-6)(-6) \times \blacksquare$
   g) $56 = \blacksquare \times (-2)(-2)$
   h) $-81 = (-9) \times \blacksquare \times (+3)$

 INVESTIGATE

Models for Multiplying Integers

When mathematicians began working with integers, they had difficulties seeing how the product of two negative numbers can be positive. For example, if you have a negative number, such as -3, and then do something "negative" to it, such as multiplying it by -2, where does the "positive" answer $+6$ come from?

We can gain some insight into this situation by considering models for multiplying integers.

Gains and Losses
Suppose Mr. Ziegler spends \$3 each week on lotteries. We represent this using the integer -3. Suppose also that he never wins anything.

2 weeks from now, he will have \$6 less than he has now.

$(+2)(-3) = -6$

2 weeks ago, he had \$6 more than he has now.

$(-2)(-3) = +6$

Travelling on a Number Line
Suppose the integers on a number line are 1 cm apart. A toy car travels to the left along the number line at 3 cm/s. We represent this using the integer -3.

2 seconds from now, the car will be 6 cm to the left of its present position.

$(+2)(-3) = -6$

2 seconds ago, the car was 6 cm to the right of its present position.

$(-2)(-3) = +6$

Good People and Bad People
In a certain town, all people are identified as being good ($+$) or bad ($-$).

1. For each of the following moves, determine whether it would be good for the town, or bad for the town.
   a) A good person moves to the town. b) A bad person moves to the town.
   c) A good person leaves the town.   d) A bad person leaves the town.

2. Write an expression involving integers for each move in *Question 1*.

3. Suppose there are two families each containing three bad people. Write an expression involving multiplication of integers to represent the effect on the town if these two families leave the town.

MATHEMATICS AROUND US

Glaciers on the Move

Glaciers are large masses of ice that move very slowly down a mountain or along a valley. They are formed when the winter snowfall exceeds the summer melting.

The Columbia Glacier (below) in Alaska is retreating because the ice is melting at the bottom faster than it comes down from above. In recent years, it has been retreating at about 2 m per day.

But the nearby Hubbard Glacier, whose source is in Canada, is now advancing, because the ice is coming down the valley faster than it melts at the bottom. It is advancing at about 3 m per day.

QUESTIONS

1. Write an integer to represent the daily change in the length of each glacier.

2. Write an expression involving multiplication of integers to represent the difference between the length of each glacier now and:
   a) 5 days from now
   b) 50 days from now
   c) 5 days ago
   d) 50 days ago.

3. Explain how the expressions in *Question 2* illustrate the rules for multiplying two integers.

1-5 DIVIDING INTEGERS

Division is the inverse of multiplication.
Since $7 \times 4 = 28$, then $28 \div 4 = 7$ and $28 \div 7 = 4$.
The same is true for integers.
Since $(+5)(-4) = -20$, then $(-20) \div (+5) = -4$ and
$(-20) \div (-4) = +5$

Example 1. Simplify.
   a) $(+6) \div (-3)$ b) $(-24) \div (-6)$

Solution.   a) $(+6) \div (-3)$
            Since $(-3)(-2) = 6$, then $(+6) \div (-3) = -2$
         b) $(-24) \div (-6)$
            Since $(-6)(+4) = -24$, then $(-24) \div (-6) = 4$

Example 2. Simplify.
   a) $(+15) \div (+3)$ b) $(-20) \div (-2)$
   c) $(+24) \div (-8)$ d) $(-33) \div (+3)$

Solution.   a) $(+15) \div (+3) = 5$ b) $(-20) \div (-2) = 10$
         c) $(+24) \div (-8) = -3$ d) $(-33) \div (+3) = -11$

The above examples suggest the following rules.

> The quotient of two integers with *like* signs is *positive*.
> The quotient of two integers with *unlike* signs is *negative*.

Example 3. Simplify.
   a) $\dfrac{63}{-9}$ b) $\dfrac{-42}{-7}$ c) $\dfrac{(-8)(-9)}{3(-4)}$

Solution.   a) $\dfrac{63}{-9} = -7$ b) $\dfrac{-42}{-7} = 6$ c) $\dfrac{(-8)(-9)}{3(-4)} = \dfrac{+72}{-12}$
$$= -6$$

Example 4. Simplify. $\dfrac{(-24)}{4} - \dfrac{10}{(-2)}$

Solution.   Perform the divisions before subtracting.
$$\frac{(-24)}{4} - \frac{10}{(-2)} = (-6) - (-5)$$
$$= -6 + 5$$
$$= -1$$

EXERCISES 1-5

(A)

1. Simplify.
   a) $(-48) \div (+4)$
   b) $(-36) \div (-4)$
   c) $(+32) \div (-8)$
   d) $(-18) \div (+3)$
   e) $(-60) \div (-12)$
   f) $(-40) \div (-5)$

2. Simplify.
   a) $\dfrac{-36}{4}$
   b) $\dfrac{46}{-2}$
   c) $\dfrac{-18}{-9}$
   d) $\dfrac{-85}{5}$
   e) $\dfrac{-49}{-7}$
   f) $\dfrac{81}{-9}$
   g) $\dfrac{-76}{-19}$
   h) $\dfrac{-121}{11}$
   i) $\dfrac{132}{-12}$
   j) $\dfrac{91}{13}$

3. Simplify.
   a) $\dfrac{(-4)(10)}{-8}$
   b) $\dfrac{(6)(-15)}{-5}$
   c) $\dfrac{(-10)(12)}{(5)(-3)}$
   d) $\dfrac{(-15)(-20)}{(-10)(3)}$
   e) $\dfrac{(-50)(9)}{(15)(6)}$
   f) $\dfrac{(14)(-16)}{(-8)(-7)}$
   g) $\dfrac{(-5)(9)(-24)}{(-3)(4)}$
   h) $\dfrac{(-6)(-8)}{(-2)(-1)(-3)}$

(B)

4. Simplify.
   a) $\dfrac{(-30)}{5} + \dfrac{15}{(-3)}$
   b) $\dfrac{(-20)}{10} + \dfrac{8}{(-2)}$
   c) $\dfrac{(-9)}{(-3)} - \dfrac{12}{4}$
   d) $\dfrac{14}{(-2)} - \dfrac{(-16)}{8}$
   e) $\dfrac{(-36)}{4} + \dfrac{(-56)}{(-8)}$
   f) $\dfrac{(-42)}{7} - \dfrac{54}{(-6)}$
   g) $\dfrac{(-63)}{(-7)} - \dfrac{(-56)}{(-8)}$
   h) $\dfrac{(-81)}{(-9)} + \dfrac{(-72)}{(-8)}$
   i) $\dfrac{35}{7} + \dfrac{48}{(-6)}$

5. Canada sells products and services to other countries and buys products and services from them. The Canadian balance of payments is a measure of all yearly business transactions between Canada and the rest of the world.
   a) What does a negative balance of payments indicate?
   b) What was the average monthly balance of payments for each year?

Year	Balance of Payments $ Millions
1979	4 319
1980	− 174
1981	10 468
1982	1 106
1983	5 366
1984	5 307
1985	1 901

6. The temperature is falling at the rate of 3°C/h. Find how long it takes to fall through each temperature range.
   a) $-4°C$ to $-10°C$
   b) $-2°C$ to $-11°C$
   c) $4°C$ to $-11°C$

7. Find the integer represented by each square.
   a) $40 \div \text{▨} = -10$
   b) $\text{▨} \div (-5) = -7$
   c) $\dfrac{\text{▨}}{(-3)} = 6$
   d) $\dfrac{(-20)}{\text{▨}} = -4$
   e) $-3 = \dfrac{\text{▨}}{(-2)}$
   f) $(-65) \div \text{▨} = -13$

8. Find the integer represented by each square.
   a) $3132 \div \blacksquare = -87$ b) $1972 \div \blacksquare = -29$ c) $\blacksquare \div (-47) = 63$
   d) $(-4676) \div \blacksquare = -167$ e) $-33 = \blacksquare \div (-44)$ f) $48 = (-1008) \div \blacksquare$

9. If $x > 0$, $y > 0$, and $z < 0$, decide which expressions are always positive or always negative.

   a) $\dfrac{x}{y}$ b) $\dfrac{x + y}{z}$ c) $\dfrac{xy}{z}$ d) $\dfrac{y - z}{x}$

   e) $\dfrac{z - x}{y}$ f) $\dfrac{z}{x + y}$ g) $\dfrac{z - x}{z}$ h) $\dfrac{y - z}{x + y}$

CALCULATOR POWER

Finding Quotient and Remainder

277 players join a football league.
16 players are needed for each team.
How many teams can be formed?
How many players are left over?

Key in: ☐2☐ ☐7☐ ☐7☐ ☐÷☐ ☐1☐ ☐6☐ ☐=☐ to display 17.3125
Hence, 17 teams can be formed. The remainder is 0.3125.
To display this remainder, subtract 17 from the number in the display.
Then, to display the remainder as a whole number, multiply by 16.
Key in: ☐−☐ ☐1☐ ☐7☐ ☐=☐ ☐x☐ ☐1☐ ☐6☐ ☐=☐ to display 5
Hence, 5 players are left over.

COMPUTER POWER

Finding Quotient and Remainder

The program below can be used to find the quotient and the remainder for any given division problem.

```
100 REM *** QUOTIENTS AND REMAINDERS ***
110 INPUT "WHAT IS THE DIVIDEND? ";A
120 INPUT "WHAT IS THE DIVISOR? ";B
130 Q=INT(A/B)
140 PRINT:PRINT "THE QUOTIENT IS ";Q
150 R=INT((A/B-Q)*B+0.1)
160 PRINT "THE REMAINDER IS ";R
170 END
```

To solve the problem on the facing page, enter the program in a computer. Type RUN and press RETURN. The computer will ask for the dividend. Enter the number 277 and press RETURN. Then the computer will ask for the divisor. Enter 16 and press RETURN. Then the computer will display this result.

```
THE QUOTIENT IS 17
THE REMAINDER IS 5
```

This indicates that 17 teams can be formed, and there will be 5 players left over.

QUESTIONS

1. Use a calculator or a computer to find each quotient and remainder.

   a) $\dfrac{2079}{76}$ b) $\dfrac{68\,075}{82}$ c) $\dfrac{93\,726}{158}$ d) $\dfrac{27\,938}{356}$ e) $\dfrac{80\,079}{283}$

2. Marilyn works in a factory where she makes fruit tarts. On an 8 h shift, her team produced 136 240 tarts. These tarts are packaged in boxes of 12 tarts. The boxes are packed in cases of 24 boxes.
   a) How many cases of tarts were produced?
   b) How many boxes were left over?
   c) How many tarts were left over?

3. Use the computer program to investigate the results of using negative integers.
   a) Use a dividend of −31 and a divisor of 5.
   b) Use a dividend of 38 and a divisor of −6.
   c) Use a dividend of −33 and a divisor of −7.
   Explain the results.

PROBLEM SOLVING

Guess and Check

A theatre charges for admission, as illustrated. A family of 10 paid a total of $58.00. How many children and senior citizens are in the family?

AJAX THEATRE
TICKET PRICES
CHILDREN $4.00 ADULTS $10.00 SENIORS $6.00

Understand the problem
- What is the cost of a ticket for a child? an adult? a senior citizen?
- How many people are in the family?
- What was the total cost of admission?
- What are we asked to find?

Think of a strategy
- Try a guess and check strategy.

Carry out the strategy
- List a possible family of 10, for example, 4 children, 2 adults, 4 seniors.
- Calculate the admission for that family. The admission is $60, which is too high by $2.
- To decrease the admission price by $2, exchange 1 senior citizen for a child. There are 5 children, 3 senior citizens, and 2 adults in the family.

Children	Adults	Seniors	Total
4	2	4	$60

$$4(4) \ + \ 2(10) \ + \ 4(6) \ = \ 60$$

Children	Adults	Seniors	Total
5	2	3	$58

Look back
- Is there a total number of 10 people in the family?
- Is the total cost of admission $58.00?
- Is this the only possible solution?

Solve each problem

1. Ms. McCall cashed a cheque for $63.00. She received 6 bills, none of which was a $1 bill. What were the denominations of the bills she received?

2. An edition of the Daily Planet newspaper has its pages numbered starting at 1. The page numbers have a total of 121 digits. How many pages are in the newspaper?

3. Pietro had 20 problems for homework. His mother paid him 25¢ for each one he solved and deducted 35¢ for each one he couldn't solve. Pietro earned 80¢. How many problems was he able to solve?

4. Six darts were thrown into the dart board shown in the diagram. The total score was 211. Inside which rings did the six darts land? Is there more than one correct answer?

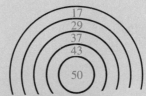

5. A gas station sells an average of 4000 L of gas per day when the price is 60¢ per litre. For each 1¢ increase in the price, the number of litres sold per day is reduced by 50 L. What price gives the greatest possible weekly revenue?

6. Erin collected $6.05 in nickels and dimes. She has 8 more dimes than nickels. How many coins does she have?

7. Minibuses seating 10, 12 or 15 passengers are used to transport hotel guests from the airport to the hotel. A hotel has 5 minibuses of each size available when a party of 120 people arrives. In how many different ways can these guests be transported using some of these minibuses if each bus used must be filled?

1-6 ORDER OF OPERATIONS WITH INTEGERS

Now that we have reviewed the four basic operations with integers, let us review the order in which they must be performed.

- Operations within grouping symbols are performed first, starting with the innermost and working outward.
- Multiplication and division are performed in order from left to right.
- Lastly, addition and subtraction are performed in order from left to right.

Example 1.   Simplify.

a) $(-6) + (-3)(5)$ b) $(-16) \div (-4) + (-8)$

Solution.   a) Perform the multiplication first.

$$(-6) + (-3)(5) = (-6) + (-15)$$
$$= -21$$

b) Perform the division first.

$$(-16) \div (-4) + (-8) = (+4) + (-8)$$
$$= -4$$

Example 2.   Simplify.

a) $[(-7) + (-3)] \div (-5) + (-6)$

b) $-3[2 - 5(2 - 8)(-1 + 3)]$

Solution.   a) Perform the addition within the brackets first.

$$[(-7) + (-3)] \div (-5) + (-6) = (-10) \div (-5) + (-6)$$
$$= (+2) + (-6)$$
$$= -4$$

b) Perform the operations within the innermost brackets first.

$$-3[2 - 5(2 - 8)(-1 + 3)] = -3[2 - 5(-6)(2)]$$
$$= -3[2 - 5(-12)]$$
$$= -3[2 + 60]$$
$$= -3(62)$$
$$= -186$$

A fraction bar is a grouping symbol, like brackets. It indicates that the numerator and the denominator must be simplified before the other operations are performed.

Example 3.   Simplify. $\dfrac{4(-3) + 7(-9 + 5)}{(2 - 3)(2 + 3)}$

Solution.   Perform the operations in the numerator and in the denominator first.

$$\frac{4(-3) + 7(-9 + 5)}{(2 - 3)(2 + 3)} = \frac{(-12) + 7(-4)}{(-1)(5)}$$
$$= \frac{-12 - 28}{-5}$$
$$= \frac{-40}{-5}$$
$$= 8$$

EXERCISES 1-6

(A)

1. Simplify.
   a) $(+4) + (-3)(-2)$
   b) $(-5)(-4) \div (-2)$
   c) $(-18) \div (+3) + (-11)$
   d) $(-6) + (-12) \div (+4)$
   e) $(-6)(0) \div (-4)$
   f) $(+11) - (+9) \div (-3)$
   g) $(-21) \div (+7)(-5)$
   h) $(-1)(-8) \div (+2)$
   i) $(-7) - (-5)(-3)$
   j) $(-3) \times (-4) \div (-6)$

(B)

2. Simplify.
   a) $[(-10) + (-2)] \div (+6) - (+4)$
   b) $(-8) + (+10)[(-12) - (-7)]$
   c) $[(-20) + (+4)] \times [(-10) - (-6)]$
   d) $(-16) \div (-2) + (-8)(+3)$

3. Use brackets with the expression $3 + 5 \times 4 - 2$ so that it simplifies to each value.
   a) 16
   b) 21
   c) 30
   d) 13

4. Simplify.
   a) $3(-2 + 6) - 5(4 - 1)$
   b) $(-5)(-4) + (-6)(3)$
   c) $-2(-4 + 3) + 3(-1 - 5)$
   d) $(-3)(-1)(5) - (-2)(-4)(-1)$
   e) $5(2 - 6)(2 - 6)$
   f) $7(7 - 2) - 5(-3 - 8) + 19$

5. Simplify.
   a) $\dfrac{(-15)}{3} - \dfrac{(-10)}{5}$
   b) $\dfrac{(-7) + 3(-1 + 4)}{-2}$
   c) $\dfrac{4(-5 + 3) - 2(-1 + 5)}{-6 + 2}$
   d) $\dfrac{35 - 81}{27 - 4} - \dfrac{(-4)(3 - 10)}{8 - 15}$

6. Use brackets with each expression so that it simplifies to the answer given.
   a) $1 + 3 \times 5 + 7$; answer 27
   b) $4 + 4 + 4 \times 4$; answer 48
   c) $2 \times 4 + 6 + 8$; answer 28
   d) $5 + 5 \times 5 + 5$; answer 100
   e) $48 \div 8 - 2 \times 3$; answer 24

7. Simplify.
   a) $(12 + 8) \div (2 - 6)$
   b) $(-3 + 4)(8 - 10) - (7 - 9)(4 - 1)$
   c) $(6 - 2 + 3)(-7 + 5 - 1)$
   d) $(4 - 9)(2 + 3) + (8 - 2)(-3 + 2)$
   e) $\dfrac{(-5 + 2)(-4 - 6)}{3 - 9}$
   f) $\dfrac{5(-3 - 4) - (-6)(13 - 6)}{(-1)(11 - 4)}$

8. Simplify.
   a) $5(-4) - [3(-6) + (-3) - 4(2(-4) - 7)] + 3(-8)$
   b) $-2[-7 - 3(4) + 5 - 2(-1)] + 3(-6 + 8)$
   c) $4[-6(-2 - 7) - 5(7 + 2)]$
   d) $-7(-4) - 2[-3(-4 + 6) + 6(7 - 3(-4))] - 8(-4)$

Ⓒ

9. a) Using all the digits in the year 1986, the operations $+$, $-$, $\times$, $\div$, and brackets, if required, form expressions for all the integers from 1 to 10.

   b) Repeat the process for the current year. Are there any integers which cannot be expressed in this way?

INVESTIGATE

- List 4 different integers, for example, -1, -5, $+8$, -3.

- From each integer in turn, subtract all the integers that precede it. That is,
  $(-5) - (-1) = -4$
  $(+8) - (-1) = +9; (+8) - (-5) = +13$
  $(-3) - (-1) = -2; (-3) - (-5) = +2; (-3) - (+8) = -11$

- Use a calculator to find the product of these differences.
  $(-4)(+9)(+13)(-2)(+2)(-11) = -20\,592$

  a) Is this result divisible by 12?

  b) Rewrite the 4 integers in a different order and repeat the procedure of subtraction and multiplication.

  c) Is the resulting integer divisible by 12?

  d) Repeat the procedures for each list of integers.
     i) -7, $+3$, $+2$, -1 ii) $+1$, -4, -2, -1 iii) $+5$, -3, $+4$, -5

  e) Which of these lists result in numbers that are divisible by 12?

  f) Choose 4 different integers and repeat the above procedures. What do you notice?

1. Arrange in order from least to greatest.
   a) $-5, 3, -4, -7, -9, 6$ b) $-6, 6, -5, -9, 9, -7$

2. Simplify.
   a) $(-5) + (+6)$ b) $(-5) + (-3)$ c) $(-6) + (+9)$ d) $(-1) + (+9)$
   e) $(-7) + (+11)$ f) $(+12) + (-13)$ g) $(-19) + (+11)$ h) $(-17) + (-14)$

3. Simplify.
   a) $(-4) + (+3) + (-5)$ b) $(+2) + (-7) + (-4)$
   c) $(-43) + (-17) + (+5)$ d) $(-39) + (+10) + (+31)$
   e) $(-91) + (+13) + (-26)$ f) $(-7) + (+104) + (-110)$

4. The greatest temperature variation in a single day in Alberta's chinook belt was
   from 17°C to -28°C. What was the change in temperature?

5. Simplify.
   a) $(+7) - (+4)$ b) $(-8) - (+2)$ c) $(-9) - (-2)$ d) $(+5) - (-2)$
   e) $(-7) - (-2)$ f) $(+8) - (-5)$ g) $(+6) - (-3)$ h) $(-5) - (+5)$

6. Write the integer represented by each square.
   a) $(+5) + ▩ = 0$ b) $(-13) + ▩ = 0$ c) $(+7) + ▩ = -1$
   d) $▩ + (-5) = -2$ e) $(+4) + ▩ = 3$ f) $▩ + (-3) = 2$
   g) $▩ + (-6) = -4$ h) $▩ + (+5) = -4$ i) $▩ - (+4) = 2$
   j) $▩ - (+3) = -5$ k) $(-5) - ▩ = 2$ l) $▩ - (-9) = 1$

7. Simplify.
   a) $(-8) - (+3) + (-5) - (+7)$
   b) $(-14) - (+12) - (+3)$
   c) $(-103) - (+27) - (-100)$
   d) $(+283) - (-20) + (-60)$
   e) $(+70) - (+90) - (-100)$
   f) $(-100) + (-70) - (+20)$
   g) $(-30) - (-72) + (-43)$
   h) $(+981) - (-19) - (+891)$
   i) $(+45) + (-100) - (-10) - (-40)$
   j) $(-230) - (-300) - (-50) - (-40) + (+230)$

8. Simplify.
   a) $(-8 + 5) - (17 - 9)$
   b) $(-30 - 20) - (-20 - 30)$
   c) $(93 - 84) - (-67 + 89)$
   d) $(-9 - 17) - (11 - 27)$
   e) $(3 - 7) + (5 - 9) - (2 - 7)$
   f) $(284 - 180) - (-3 + 99) + (109 - 47)$
   g) $(33 - 21 + 24) - (47 + 12 - 29)$
   h) $(-74 - 18 - 21) + (-47 + 81 + 10)$

9. Simplify.
   a) $(-7)(+8)$ b) $(-6)(-9)$ c) $(+5)(-7)$ d) $(+3)(-9)$
   e) $(-12)(-6)$ f) $(+10)(+8)$ g) $(-14)(+3)$ h) $(-4)(+15)$
   i) $(-11)(-10)$ j) $(+12)(+12)$ k) $(-16)(-12)$ l) $(-150)(+3)$
   m) $(+13)(+13)$ n) $(-22)(+5)$ o) $(+15)(-15)$ p) $(+16)(-20)$

10. Simplify.
    a) $(-6)(+3)(-4)$ b) $(-8)(-2)(+7)$ c) $(+6)(+5)(+3)$ d) $(-8)(-2)(-3)$
    e) $(+5)(-3)(-4)$ f) $(-7)(-2)(-5)$ g) $(-9)(+9)(-9)$ h) $(+2)(-3)(+4)$

11. Simplify.
    a) $(-2)(-3)(-4)(-5)$ b) $(+8)(-2)(+6)(-3)$ c) $(-5)(+8)(-2)(-10)$
    d) $(+6)(+7)(-2)(0)$ e) $(-1)(+1)(+2)(+9)$ f) $(+5)(+5)(+4)(+4)$

12. Simplify.
    a) $(-16) \div (+4)$ -4 b) $(-18) \div (-9)$ 2 c) $(-48) \div (-16)$ 3
    d) $(+81) \div (-3)$ -27 e) $(-64) \div (-8)$ 8 f) $(-54) \div (+18)$ -1
    g) $(-108) \div (+36)$ -3 h) $(+121) \div (-11)$ -11 i) $(-144) \div (-9)$ -16

13. Simplify.
    a) $\dfrac{(-8)(-12)}{(-24)(-4)}$ 1 b) $\dfrac{(-5)(+39)}{(-13)(-3)}$ -5 c) $\dfrac{(+121)(-7)}{(+77)(-11)}$ 1 d) $\dfrac{(-42)(+6)}{(+14)(-9)}$ 2

    e) $\dfrac{(+65)(-15)}{(+25)(+3)}$ -13 f) $\dfrac{(+85)(+70)}{(-50)(-17)}$ 7 g) $\dfrac{(-51)(-91)}{(-13)(-17)}$ 21 h) $\dfrac{(+92)(+42)}{(+28)(-69)}$ -2

14. Simplify.
    a) $\dfrac{(-40)}{5} + \dfrac{18}{(-6)}$ -11 b) $\dfrac{(-42)}{6} - \dfrac{(-63)}{7}$ 2 c) $\dfrac{42}{(-3)} + \dfrac{(-42)}{7}$ -20

    d) $\dfrac{(-49)}{7} - \dfrac{26}{(-13)}$ -5 e) $\dfrac{(-96)}{(-16)} - \dfrac{132}{12}$ -5 f) $\dfrac{85}{17} + \dfrac{(-95)}{19}$ 0

15. Simplify.
    a) $(-9)(+4) \div (-6)$ b) $(+8) \div (-4) + (-2)(-11)$
    c) $(+25) \div (-5)(-4) - (-3)$ 23 d) $(-3) + (-15) \div (+5)(-6)$ 15

16. Find the integer represented by each square.
    a) $(-4)(+5) \times \blacksquare = -220$ 11 b) $(-2) \times \blacksquare \times (11) = 154$ -7
    c) $189 = (-3)(7) \times \blacksquare$ -9 d) $\blacksquare \times (-3)(-13) = -429$ -11

17. A pilot is flying at an altitude of 5000 m where the temperature is $-21°C$. The nearby airport where he intends to land is at an altitude of 1000 m and the control tower reports precipitation. If the temperature increases 6.5°C for every 1000 m decrease in altitude, will the precipitation be rain or snow? rain

18. Simplify.
    a) $(-36) \div (-4) - (+6)(-5) \div (+3)$
    b) $-2[(-7)(-3) - (+5)(0) + (+2)(-1)]$
    c) $(+8)(-6) \div (+12) - (-3) \div (+1) + (-7)(+1)$
    d) $4[(-11)(-2) + (-6)(+3) - (+4)(+4)]$

2 Rational Numbers

A car's fuel consumption depends on whether it is driven in the city or on the highway. How can the fuel consumption be calculated when it is driven under both conditions? (See Section 2-6, *Example 1*.)

2-1 WHAT ARE RATIONAL NUMBERS?

Just as integers are used to indicate change, so are positive and negative fractions.

Some newspapers publish the prices of stocks.

TORONTO VALUE LEADERS				
INDUSTRIALS	Volume	Value	Last	Change
Noranda	669,465	15,648,294	$23\frac{1}{2}$	$+\frac{1}{2}$
Alcan	312,146	13,334,646	43	$+\frac{7}{8}$
Shell Canada	431,543	12,074,983	$28\frac{1}{4}$	$+\frac{3}{4}$
Alberta Energy	641,158	10,830,158	$16\frac{3}{4}$	$+\frac{1}{4}$
BCE	254,686	10,039,940	$39\frac{3}{8}$	$+\frac{1}{4}$
Laidlaw B	488,262	9,733,485	20	
Cdn Pac Ltd	474,181	9,370,041	$19\frac{1}{2}$	$-\frac{3}{8}$
Bk of Montreal	226,259	8,089,602	$35\frac{5}{8}$	$-\frac{1}{4}$

On the stock market a change of $+\frac{3}{4}$ means that the price of the stock has *risen* by $\frac{3}{4}$ of a dollar, or $0.75, from the day before. A change of $-\frac{1}{4}$ means that the stock has *dropped* by $0.25 from the day before.

The stock market changes are examples of rational numbers. Rational numbers can be represented on a number line.

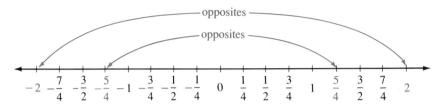

Each positive fraction has an opposite negative fraction, for example, $-\frac{1}{2}$ is the opposite of $\frac{1}{2}$. Similarly, each negative fraction has an opposite positive fraction, for example, $\frac{7}{8}$ is the opposite of $-\frac{7}{8}$.

A positive rational number like $\frac{1}{2}$ is usually written without the positive sign, but it could be written as $+\frac{1}{2}$ or as $\frac{+1}{+2}$. The rules for dividing integers suggest that it can also be written as $\dfrac{-1}{-2}$.

The rules for dividing integers also suggest that a negative rational number like $-\dfrac{1}{2}$ can be written as $\dfrac{-1}{+2}$ or as $\dfrac{+1}{-2}$. We can see why this is true by considering the product $(+2)\left(-\dfrac{1}{2}\right)$.

$$(+2)\left(-\dfrac{1}{2}\right) \text{ means } 2\left(-\dfrac{1}{2}\right) = \left(-\dfrac{1}{2}\right) + \left(-\dfrac{1}{2}\right)$$

$$= -1$$

With whole numbers, we can write, for example,

Since $(3)(4) = 12$, then $\dfrac{12}{3} = 4$

Similarly, with rational numbers,

Since $(+2)\left(-\dfrac{1}{2}\right) = -1$, then $\dfrac{-1}{+2} = -\dfrac{1}{2}$

In a similar manner, it can be shown that

$$\dfrac{+1}{-2} = -\dfrac{1}{2} \text{ and } \dfrac{-1}{-2} = +\dfrac{1}{2}.$$

> Any number which can be written in the form $\dfrac{m}{n}$, where m and n are integers and $n \neq 0$, is called a *rational number*.

Example 1. State which of the following numbers are rational.
$$\dfrac{3}{2}, \dfrac{-8}{20}, 3\tfrac{1}{4}, 5, \dfrac{-6}{-7}, 0, 2.5, -11.27, \dfrac{-60}{-12}$$

Solution. Since $\dfrac{3}{2}, \dfrac{-8}{20}, \dfrac{-6}{-7}, \dfrac{-60}{-12}$ are in quotient form, we know that they are rational numbers.

Check to see if the other numbers can be written in quotient form.

$$3\tfrac{1}{4} = \dfrac{13}{4}; \quad 5 \text{ can be written } \dfrac{5}{1}; \quad 0 \text{ can be written } \dfrac{0}{1}.$$

Recall that 2.5 means 25 tenths or $\dfrac{25}{10}$.

-11.27 means -1127 hundredths or $-\dfrac{1127}{100}$.

All the given numbers are rational numbers.

A rational number can be reduced to lower terms by dividing the numerator and the denominator by a common factor. For example,

$$\frac{-8}{20} = -\frac{8}{20} \qquad\qquad \frac{-60}{-12} = \frac{60}{12}$$

$$= -\frac{8 \div 4}{20 \div 4} \qquad\qquad = \frac{60 \div 12}{12 \div 12}$$

$$= -\frac{2}{5} \qquad\qquad = 5$$

When a rational number cannot be further simplified, it is said to be in *lowest terms* (or in *simplest form*).

The rational numbers $\dfrac{-8}{20}$ and $-\dfrac{2}{5}$ are said to be *equivalent* because

they represent the same quantity. Similarly, $\dfrac{-60}{-12}$ and 5 are equivalent

rational numbers.

Example 2. Find which of these rational numbers are equivalent.

$$\frac{18}{24}, \frac{-6}{8}, \frac{16}{-12}, \frac{-9}{-12}$$

Solution. Reduce each rational number to lowest terms.

$$\frac{18}{24} = \frac{3}{4}, \quad \frac{-6}{8} = -\frac{3}{4}, \quad \frac{16}{-12} = -\frac{4}{3}, \quad \frac{-9}{-12} = \frac{3}{4}$$

Since $\dfrac{18}{24}$ and $\dfrac{-9}{-12}$ both reduce to $\dfrac{3}{4}$, they are equivalent.

A rational number can be raised to higher terms by multiplying the numerator and the denominator by the same number.

Example 3. Arrange these numbers in order from least to greatest.

$$\frac{3}{4}, \frac{-2}{5}, \frac{-7}{-10}, -\frac{-9}{-20}$$

Solution. Express the rational numbers as fractions with a common denominator of 20.

$$\frac{3}{4} = \frac{3 \times 5}{4 \times 5}, \quad \frac{-2}{5} = \frac{-2 \times 4}{5 \times 4}, \quad \frac{-7}{-10} = \frac{-7 \times 2}{-10 \times 2}, \quad -\frac{-9}{-20} = \frac{-9}{20}$$

$$= \frac{15}{20} \qquad = \frac{-8}{20} \qquad = \frac{14}{20}$$

From least to greatest: $\dfrac{-9}{20}, \dfrac{-8}{20}, \dfrac{14}{20}, \dfrac{15}{20}$ or $-\dfrac{-9}{-20}, \dfrac{-2}{5}, \dfrac{-7}{-10}, \dfrac{3}{4}$

EXERCISES 2-1

1. Write the rational numbers for the points indicated.

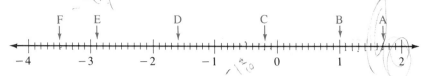

2. Compare each pair of rational numbers. Replace the comma with $>$ or $<$.

a) $\dfrac{1}{2}, \dfrac{3}{2}$

b) $-2.8, 3.1$

c) $\dfrac{7}{4}, \dfrac{-5}{4}$

d) $-1.25, 0.75$

e) $\dfrac{-13}{7}, \dfrac{5}{7}$

f) $0.01, -1.00$

g) $\dfrac{-10}{17}, \dfrac{-5}{17}$

h) $108.6, -116.8$

3. Reduce to lowest terms.

a) $\dfrac{5}{-10}$

b) $\dfrac{10}{-15}$

c) $\dfrac{-12}{-30}$

d) $-\dfrac{6}{15}$

e) $-\dfrac{-6}{11}$

f) $-\dfrac{-6}{18}$

g) $-\dfrac{4}{-14}$

h) $-\dfrac{-14}{-25}$

i) $-\dfrac{-15}{-35}$

j) $-\dfrac{-24}{-72}$

k) $-\dfrac{-42}{-28}$

l) $-\dfrac{54}{-81}$

4. Compare each pair of rational numbers. Replace the comma with $>$ or $<$.

a) $\dfrac{8}{6}, \dfrac{2}{3}$

b) $\dfrac{-7}{10}, \dfrac{-16}{20}$

c) $\dfrac{7}{5}, \dfrac{12}{5}$

d) $\dfrac{-8}{28}, \dfrac{-3}{7}$

e) $\dfrac{-110}{121}, \dfrac{9}{11}$

f) $\dfrac{-27}{24}, \dfrac{-10}{8}$

g) $\dfrac{52}{16}, \dfrac{-11}{4}$

h) $\dfrac{19}{6}, \dfrac{110}{30}$

5. Round each rational number to the nearest integer.

a) -3.7 b) -5.2 c) -6.7 d) -0.4 e) 0.2 f) -0.6

g) -0.97 h) -0.35 i) -7.52 j) $-\dfrac{22}{5}$ k) $-\dfrac{67}{4}$ l) $-\dfrac{37}{5}$

6. The depths reached by divers wearing scuba gear are shown. Arrange the depths in order from greatest to least.

Diver	Depth in metres
Damont	-64.0
Giesler	-99.1
Hilton	-104.9
Trouth	-97.5

7. Write the rational number which is

a) 1 more than -3.

b) 1 less than -4.

c) 5 more than -6.

d) 7 more than -7.8.

e) 6 less than 3.5.

f) 10 less than 6.2.

g) $\dfrac{1}{2}$ more than $-\dfrac{17}{2}$.

h) $\dfrac{1}{2}$ less than $-\dfrac{3}{2}$.

i) $\dfrac{1}{2}$ less than $\dfrac{1}{4}$.

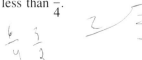

8. Compare each pair of rational numbers. Replace the comma with $>$ or $<$.

   a) $\dfrac{15}{6}, \dfrac{56}{16}$ b) $\dfrac{-35}{15}, \dfrac{-30}{9}$ c) $\dfrac{-72}{40}, \dfrac{72}{45}$ d) $\dfrac{24}{44}, \dfrac{45}{55}$

   e) $\dfrac{-119}{70}, \dfrac{-57}{30}$ f) $\dfrac{77}{28}, \dfrac{78}{32}$ g) $\dfrac{126}{54}, \dfrac{-115}{45}$ h) $\dfrac{-75}{35}, \dfrac{-64}{28}$

9. Reduce each set of rational numbers to lowest terms. Then list them from greatest to least.

   a) $\dfrac{28}{16}, \dfrac{30}{8}, \dfrac{33}{12}, \dfrac{15}{20}$

   b) $\dfrac{-65}{25}, \dfrac{36}{10}, \dfrac{-27}{15}, \dfrac{28}{20}$

   c) $\dfrac{34}{18}, \dfrac{-120}{54}, \dfrac{-91}{63}, \dfrac{-40}{36}$

   d) $\dfrac{-154}{49}, \dfrac{-100}{28}, \dfrac{-45}{21}, \dfrac{-22}{14}$

10. In each set, express the rational numbers with a common denominator. Then list them from least to greatest.

    a) $\dfrac{3}{2}, \dfrac{6}{5}, \dfrac{5}{4}, \dfrac{4}{3}$

    b) $\dfrac{-11}{4}, \dfrac{-8}{3}, \dfrac{-5}{2}, \dfrac{-23}{8}$

    c) $\dfrac{11}{8}, \dfrac{-3}{2}, \dfrac{-16}{10}, \dfrac{-7}{4}$

    d) $\dfrac{-29}{6}, \dfrac{21}{4}, \dfrac{-88}{18}, \dfrac{55}{12}$

11. List these rational numbers from least to greatest.

    $$\dfrac{5}{-10}, \dfrac{-3}{2}, \dfrac{-7}{-28}, \dfrac{-5}{20}, \dfrac{12}{16}, \dfrac{9}{-6}, \dfrac{10}{-8}, \dfrac{-18}{-9}$$

12. List these rational numbers from greatest to least.

    $$-\dfrac{3}{8}, \dfrac{-1}{3}, \dfrac{1}{-4}, -\dfrac{-2}{9}, \dfrac{-7}{-18}, \dfrac{-13}{-36}$$

13. List these rational numbers from least to greatest.

    $$\dfrac{4}{-8}, \dfrac{-3}{-15}, \dfrac{-16}{40}, -\dfrac{19}{-60}, \dfrac{14}{30}, -\dfrac{13}{20}$$

14. Find which five of these rational numbers are equivalent.

    $$\dfrac{-2}{-3}, \dfrac{4}{-6}, \dfrac{-3}{4}, \dfrac{-12}{-20}, \dfrac{15}{-20}, \dfrac{12}{-16}, \dfrac{6}{-10}, -\dfrac{-6}{-8}, \dfrac{-8}{-12}, \dfrac{9}{-12}$$

15. If two numbers have a common factor, it is also a factor of their difference. Use this fact to determine which of these fractions are in lowest terms.

    $$\dfrac{169}{182}, \dfrac{171}{188}, \dfrac{200}{201}, \dfrac{209}{247}$$

16. a) Write a sentence to explain why the sum of two or more rational numbers is a rational number.

    b) Use the result in part a) to explain why any number that can be expressed as a decimal with a finite number of decimal digits is a rational number.

Rational Numbers on a Grid

- Draw a grid, as illustrated, and label each axis from -6 to 6.

- Plot the rational number, $\frac{1}{2}$, on the grid as follows. From the origin, move 2 units in the x-direction and then 1 unit in the y-direction. Draw a dot and label it $\frac{1}{2}$.

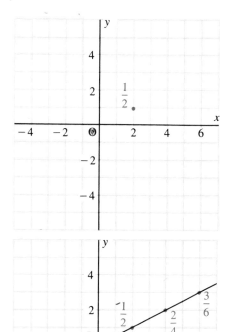

- In a similar way, plot other rational numbers equivalent to $\frac{1}{2}$, for example, $\frac{2}{4}, \frac{3}{6}, \frac{-1}{-2}, \frac{-2}{-4}$, and so on.

- Join the dots representing $\frac{1}{2}$ with a straight line. All points on this line can be considered as rational numbers equivalent to $\frac{1}{2}$.

1. Draw a grid and label each axis from -10 to 10. Plot each rational number listed below. Join its dot to the origin and extend the line in each direction. Use this line to list 4 rational numbers equivalent to the number plotted.
$$\frac{-2}{3}, \quad \frac{3}{4}, \quad \frac{4}{1}, \quad \frac{5}{-2}, \quad -3$$
Remember that the denominator of each rational number indicates how far to move in the x-direction. The numerator indicates how far to move in the y-direction.

2. Choose a rational number. Plot in on a grid. List 6 rational numbers equivalent to the number plotted.

THE MATHEMATICAL MIND

The Introduction of the Number Zero

Zero as a placeholder

One of the most important problems encountered by ancient civilizations was that of finding a way to write very large numbers without using new symbols.

In our place-value system, the meaning of each digit in a number, such as 4023, depends on the place where it is written. The 0 is called a placeholder, to indicate in this case that there are no hundreds.

The idea of using a special symbol as a placeholder was introduced many centuries ago by several different civilizations. It is one of the greatest practical ideas of all time. Here are some examples of the placeholder symbols used by these ancient civilizations.

Babylonian (300 B.C.)	Mayan (A.D. 200–600)
Hindu (A.D. 600)	Arab (A.D. 1000)

Zero as a number

The idea of using zero as a number probably originated about A.D. 800 when the Hindus used positive and negative integers to represent credits and debits. They needed a special number to represent no credit and no debit. This number was gradually picked up by the Arabs, and eventually reached Spain. But mathematicians regarded this number with suspicion, and zero was not completely accepted and used as a number in the western world until after 1500.

Properties of zero

Because zero is a number, just like any other number, we may operate with it. But it has certain properties that other numbers do not have.

- When 0 is added to or subtracted from any number, that number does not change.
  $5 + 0 = 5$
  $7 - 0 = 7$

- When 0 is multiplied by any number, the product is 0.
  $0 \times 3 = 0$

- When 0 is divided by any number (except 0), the quotient is 0.
  $0 \div 2 = 0$

- Division by 0
  There is a restriction on operating with 0, because we cannot divide by 0. Recall that we write $6 \div 2 = 3$ because $3 \times 2 = 6$. But if we try to find a meaning for $6 \div 0$, we would have to find a number that gives 6 when it is multiplied by 0. Since this is impossible, we say that division by 0 is not defined.

QUESTIONS

1. Simplify, if possible.
   a) $17 + 0$ b) $-4 + 0$
   c) $259 + 0$ d) $23 - 0$
   e) $-9 - 0$ f) $319 - 0$

2. Simplify, if possible.
   a) 0×9 b) -6×0
   c) 107×0 d) 0×0
   e) $0 \div 3$ f) $0 \div (-12)$
   g) $5 \div 0$ h) $-8 \div 0$
   i) $0 \div 0$ j) $0 \div (-3)$

3. Give an example to illustrate why 0 is considered to be a number.

2-2 RATIONAL NUMBERS IN DECIMAL FORM

On the stock market, a change of $+\frac{1}{2}$ means an increase in price of $\frac{1}{2}$ a dollar or $0.50.

Consider a change of $-\frac{3}{8}$. To express this as a drop in price, $\frac{3}{8}$ of a dollar is expressed as a decimal. Divide 3 by 8.

$$\begin{array}{r} 0.375 \\ 8\overline{)3.000} \\ \underline{2\,4} \\ 60 \\ \underline{56} \\ 40 \\ \underline{40} \\ 0 \end{array}$$

$\frac{3}{8} = 0.375$

The drop in price is $0.375.

The value $0.375 represents $37\frac{1}{2}$ cents. It is not possible to have $37\frac{1}{2}$ cents. However, shares are usually bought and sold in lots of 100, where a change of $37\frac{1}{2}$ cents per share would become $37.50 per 100 shares.

The decimal, 0.375, is a *terminating* decimal. After the third decimal place, the rest of the digits are zeros.
That is, $0.375 = 0.375\,000\,000\ldots$

This is not always the case. Consider the rational number $\frac{26}{11}$. To express this as a decimal, divide 26 by 11.

$$\begin{array}{r} 2.3636 \\ 11\overline{)26.0000} \\ 22 \\ \hline 40 \\ 33 \\ \hline 70 \\ 66 \\ \hline 40 \\ 33 \\ \hline 70 \end{array}$$

The remainders, after subtracting, alternate between 4 and 7. This produces a sequence of digits which repeats.

$$\frac{26}{11} = 2.3636 \ldots$$

The decimal, 2.3636 . . . , is a *repeating* decimal. It does not terminate. This decimal is written more simply as $2.\overline{36}$ or $2.\dot{3}\dot{6}$ with a line drawn over the repeating digits or periods placed over the first and last digits which repeat.

Example 1.   Express $\frac{100}{7}$ as a decimal

　　　　　　　a) by dividing.　　　　　　　　　b) with a calculator.

Solution.　　a)

$$\begin{array}{r} 14.285\ 714 \\ 7\overline{)100.000\ 000} \\ 7 \\ \hline 30 \\ 28 \\ \hline 20 \\ 14 \\ \hline 60 \\ 56 \\ \hline 40 \\ 35 \\ \hline 50 \\ 49 \\ \hline 10 \\ 7 \\ \hline 30 \end{array}$$

When dividing, bring down zeros until the remainders repeat. This means that the digits in the decimal will repeat. Since there are only 7 possible remainders when dividing by 7 (namely 0, 1, 2, 3, 4, 5, 6) this decimal must repeat on or before the seventh digit.

$$\frac{100}{7} = 14.\overline{285\ 714}$$

　　b) $\frac{100}{7}$, with a calculator

　　　Key in: $\boxed{1}\ \boxed{0}\ \boxed{0}\ \boxed{\div}\ \boxed{7}\ \boxed{=}$ to display 14.285714

Since the calculator displays only 8 digits, it is not always possible to tell what the sequence of repeating digits is. See *CALCULATOR POWER*, page 46.

We can express a terminating decimal as a common fraction.

Example 2. Express these decimals as common fractions in lowest terms.

  a) 3.5   b) 0.65   c) -7.4 d) -0.375

Solution. a) 3.5 means 35 tenths.   b) 0.65 means 65 hundredths.

$$3.5 = \frac{35}{10}$$
$$= \frac{7}{2}$$

$$0.65 = \frac{65}{100}$$
$$= \frac{13}{20}$$

  c) -7.4 means -74 tenths.   d) -0.375 means -375 thousandths.

$$-7.4 = \frac{-74}{10}$$
$$= -\frac{37}{5}$$

$$-0.375 = \frac{-375}{1000}$$
$$= -\frac{15}{40}$$
$$= -\frac{3}{8}$$

Example 3. In football, the pass-completion average of a quarterback is found by dividing the number of passes completed by the number attempted.
  a) Calculate the lifetime pass-completion average, to 3 decimal places, for the following quarterbacks.
  b) List the averages in order from greatest to least.

	Name	Attempted Passes	Completed Passes
i)	Sam Etcheverry	2829	1630
ii)	Russ Jackson	2530	1356
iii)	Joe Paopao	2136	1230
iv)	Jackie Parker	2061	1089

Solution. a)   i) Etcheverry's average $= \dfrac{1630}{2829}$

$$\doteq 0.576\ 175\ 327$$
$$= 0.576 \text{ to 3 decimal places}$$

  ii) Jackson's average is $\dfrac{1356}{2530}$ or 0.536 to 3 decimal places.

  iii) Paopao's average is $\dfrac{1230}{2136}$ or 0.576 to 3 decimal places.

  iv) Parker's average is $\dfrac{1089}{2061}$ or 0.528 to 3 decimal places.

b) From greatest to least: 0.576, 0.576, 0.536, 0.528

EXERCISES 2-2

A

1. Write these numbers to 8 decimal places, rounding where necessary.
   a) $3.\overline{23}$ 　　　b) $42.\overline{307}$ 　　　c) $-81.4\dot{6}$ 　　　d) $690.0\overline{45}$
   e) $-2.6\dot{5}1\dot{3}$ 　　f) $2.\dot{6}51\dot{3}$ 　　g) $0.0\overline{69}$ 　　　h) $-0.007\dot{4}$

2. Write these repeating decimals, using a dot or a bar over the repeating digits.
   a) $6.3333\ldots$ 　　　　　b) $0.17171717\ldots$ 　　　c) $42.135135\ldots$
   d) $0.0363636\ldots$ 　　　e) $-38.348348\ldots$ 　　f) $-46.23333\ldots$
   g) $-0.717171\ldots$ 　　　h) $813.813813\ldots$ 　　i) $-0.0213232\ldots$

3. State which of these numbers are: a) integers 　　b) rational numbers.
   $$\frac{1}{12}, \quad -1.8, \quad -0.611611611\ldots, \quad 0, \quad 2\tfrac{3}{4}, \quad 0.\overline{3}, \quad 7, \quad -13.85\overline{762},$$
   $$-17, \quad 6.432432\ldots, \quad 0.625$$

4. Write in decimal form.
   a) $\dfrac{3}{5}$ 　　b) $\dfrac{2}{-3}$ 　　c) $\dfrac{4}{9}$ 　　d) $-\dfrac{3}{8}$ 　　e) $\dfrac{7}{21}$ 　　f) $\dfrac{-3}{22}$
   g) $\dfrac{15}{7}$ 　　h) $-\dfrac{1}{6}$ 　　i) $\dfrac{5}{16}$ 　　j) $\dfrac{-17}{27}$ 　　k) $\dfrac{11}{12}$ 　　l) $\dfrac{13}{11}$

5. Express in fractional form.
   a) 0.75 　　　　b) 3.25 　　　　c) -0.625 　　　d) 0.0625
   e) -2.75 　　　f) -5.875 　　　g) 16.4 　　　h) -40.0625

B

6. Compare each pair of rational numbers. Replace the comma with $>$ or $<$.
   a) $6.4, \ -\dfrac{25}{4}$ 　　b) $-\dfrac{23}{7}, \ -3.5$ 　　c) $\dfrac{3}{8}, \ -\dfrac{5}{11}$ 　　d) $\dfrac{-57}{100}, \ -0.5$
   e) $-8.6, \ -\dfrac{75}{9}$ 　　f) $-15.8, \ -\dfrac{76}{5}$ 　　g) $\dfrac{51}{16}, \ 3.175$ 　　h) $\dfrac{7}{11}, \dfrac{16}{25}$

7. In the hockey play-offs, a goalkeeper allowed 11 goals in 7 games. The goalkeeper for the opposing team allowed only 8 goals in the same number of games. Calculate "the goals-against" average, to 2 decimal places, for each goalkeeper.

8. A baseball player's batting average is found by dividing the number of hits by the number of times at bat, and rounding to 3 decimal places.
   a) Calculate the batting averages of these players.

	Batter	Year	Times at Bat	Number of Hits
i)	Hugh Duffy	1884	539	236
ii)	Ty Cobb	1911	591	248
iii)	Babe Ruth	1924	529	200
iv)	Lou Gehrig	1927	584	218
v)	Ted Williams	1941	456	185

   b) List the players in the order of their batting averages from greatest to least.

9. Arrange these fractions from greatest to least.

$$\frac{6}{7}, \frac{5}{8}, \frac{9}{11}, \frac{10}{13}, \frac{13}{15}$$

Ⓒ

10. a) Simplify $\frac{2}{3} + \frac{5}{6}$, and write the result in decimal form.

b) Write $\frac{2}{3}$ and $\frac{5}{6}$ in decimal form and find their sum. How does the result compare with that for part a)?

c) Repeat the procedure of parts a) and b) for these expressions.

i) $\frac{3}{4} + \frac{2}{5}$

ii) $\frac{5}{8} - \frac{1}{4}$

iii) $\frac{1}{6} - \frac{5}{9}$

iv) $\frac{2}{9} - \frac{5}{11}$

v) $\frac{7}{16} + \frac{5}{12}$

vi) $\frac{29}{37} - \frac{11}{37}$

11. Use a calculator to express these fractions in decimal form. What do you notice?

a) $\frac{5}{173}$

b) $\frac{50}{173}$

c) $\frac{500}{173}$

d) $\frac{5000}{173}$

12. Use the result of *Exercise 11* to express each fraction to as many decimal places as possible, with your calculator.

a) $\frac{1}{810}$

b) $\frac{6}{5293}$

c) $\frac{6.9}{9572.6}$

d) $\frac{2.3 \times 6.4}{168.7 \times 24.9}$

 INVESTIGATE

a) Use a calculator to express $\frac{1}{7}$ and $\frac{2}{7}$ as repeating decimals. The repeating decimals are the same for both fractions. They can be arranged in a circle.

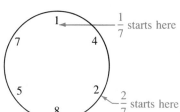

$\frac{1}{7}$ starts here

$\frac{2}{7}$ starts here

b) Find the decimal representations of $\frac{3}{7}, \frac{4}{7}, \frac{5}{7},$ and $\frac{6}{7}$. If they also fit the circle of digits, then the digits of the decimal representation of this set of fractions are said to form a *cyclic pattern*.

c) Investigate the cyclic pattern for each set of fractions.

i) $\frac{1}{13}, \frac{2}{13}, \frac{3}{13}, \ldots$

ii) $\frac{1}{14}, \frac{2}{14}, \frac{3}{14}, \ldots$

iii) $\frac{1}{21}, \frac{2}{21}, \frac{3}{21}, \ldots$

CALCULATOR POWER

Investigating Repeating Decimals

When a calculator is used to express a rational number in fractional form, as a decimal, all the repeating decimals may not appear in the display. This happens if the number of repeating digits exceeds the capacity of the display. For example, on a calculator with an 8-digit display:

$$\frac{4}{17} \doteq 0.2352941$$

If we use the calculator skilfully we can obtain more digits in the decimal expansion of $\frac{4}{17}$, and eventually express $\frac{4}{17}$ as a repeating decimal.

Consider the corresponding long division up to the same number of digits. The remainder at the fifth decimal place is 7, and the calculations from this point on are shaded. In fact, at this point, the division is similar to $7 \div 17$. Except for the position of the decimal point, the figures are the same.

This shows that if we use a calculator to express $\frac{7}{17}$ as a decimal, the first two decimals will be 0.41, and the rest will be the additional decimals for $\frac{4}{17}$.

```
        0.2352941
17) 4.0000000
    3 4
    ___
      60
      51
      __
      90
      85
      __
      50
      34
      ___
      160
      153
      ___
       70
       68
       __
       20
       17
       __
        3
```

```
      0.41
17) 7.00
    6 8
    ___
     20
     17
     __
      3
```

$$\frac{7}{17} \doteq 0.4117647$$

Therefore, $\frac{4}{17} \doteq 0.235294117647$

We can obtain still more decimals if we can find a fraction having a denominator of 17 and a decimal expansion that starts with 0.47. Using a calculator, this can be found by systematic trial.

Key in: ☐1 ☐7 ☐× ☐· ☐4 ☐7 ☐= to display 7.99

This suggests that the fraction required is $\dfrac{8}{17}$.

Key in: ☐8 ☐÷ ☐1 ☐7 ☐= to display 0.4705882

Therefore, $\dfrac{4}{17} \doteq 0.235\ 294\ 117\ 647\ 058\ 82$

Now we want a fraction with a denominator of 17 and a decimal expansion that starts with 0.82.

Key in: ☐1 ☐7 ☐× ☐· ☐8 ☐2 ☐= to display 13.94

This suggests that the fraction required is $\dfrac{14}{17}$.

Key in: ☐1 ☐4 ☐÷ ☐1 ☐7 ☐= to display 0.82 352 94

Therefore, $\dfrac{4}{17} \doteq 0.235\ 294\ 117\ 647\ 058\ 823\ 529\ 4$

The final six digits are a repeat of the first six digits.
The repeating decimal is now evident.

$$\frac{4}{17} = 0.\overline{235\ 294\ 117\ 647\ 058\ 8}$$

1. Express each fraction as a repeating decimal.

   a) $\dfrac{4}{21}$
   b) $\dfrac{87}{137}$
   c) $\dfrac{23}{79}$

   d) $\dfrac{217}{82}$
   e) $\dfrac{19}{84}$
   f) $\dfrac{15}{23}$

2. Express each fraction as a repeating decimal.

   a) $\dfrac{100}{239}$
   b) $\dfrac{328}{271}$
   c) $\dfrac{55}{202}$

   d) $\dfrac{4762}{859}$
   e) $\dfrac{424}{757}$
   f) $\dfrac{155}{353}$

3. Investigate the patterns in the repeating decimals for each set of fractions.

   a) $\dfrac{1}{17}, \dfrac{2}{17}, \dfrac{3}{17}, \ldots$
   b) $\dfrac{1}{41}, \dfrac{2}{41}, \dfrac{3}{41}, \ldots$

4. Investigate other repeating decimals using this method. Write a report of your findings.

COMPUTER POWER

Investigating Repeating Decimals

Since a computer is capable of repeating a sequence of steps very
rapidly and accurately, it can be programmed to perform a division
to any desired number of decimal places. Therefore, a computer
is an ideal tool for investigating the patterns which occur when
rational numbers are expressed as repeating decimals. The following
program will cause the computer to print as many decimal digits as desired.

```
100 REM *** REPEATING DECIMALS ***
110 INPUT "WHAT IS THE NUMERATOR? ";N
120 INPUT "WHAT IS THE DENOMINATOR? ";D
130 INPUT "HOW MANY DECIMAL DIGITS? ";T
140 I=INT(N/D):PRINT
150 PRINT "THE DECIMAL EXPANSION TO ";T;" PLACES IS: "
160 PRINT:PRINT I;".";
170 R=N-I*D
180 FOR J=1 TO T
190    A=INT(R*10/D)
200    PRINT A;
210    R=R*10-D*A
220 NEXT J
230 END
```

To express $\dfrac{39}{17}$ as a repeating decimal, input the program. Type RUN
and press [RETURN]. Answer each question that the computer
asks and then press [RETURN]. Here is a sample of the output.

```
WHAT IS THE NUMERATOR? 39
WHAT IS THE DENOMINATOR? 17
HOW MANY DECIMAL DIGITS? 50
THE DECIMAL EXPANSION TO 50 PLACES IS:
2.29411764705882352941176470588235294117
647058823529
```

The result shows that $\dfrac{39}{17} = 2.2\overline{941176470588235}$

1. Express each fraction as a repeating decimal.

   a) $\dfrac{38}{23}$　　　　b) $\dfrac{27}{31}$　　　　c) $\dfrac{187}{84}$　　　　d) $\dfrac{355}{113}$

2. Investigate the patterns in the repeating decimals for these fractions.

   a) $\dfrac{1}{19}, \dfrac{2}{19}, \dfrac{3}{19}, \ldots$　　　　　　b) $\dfrac{1}{43}, \dfrac{2}{43}, \dfrac{3}{43}, \ldots$

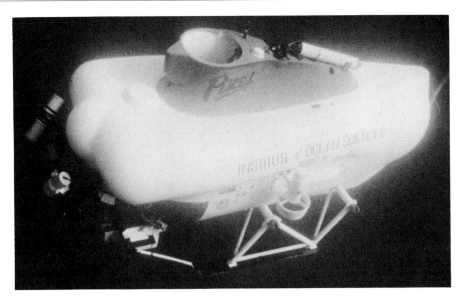

2-3 MULTIPLYING AND DIVIDING RATIONAL NUMBERS

Submersibles like the Pisces III and the Aluminaut can perform numerous deep-water duties, such as search and rescue, repairing oil rigs, under-sea exploration, and scientific research. The maximum operational depth of Pisces III is -1.10 km while the Aluminaut can operate at a depth 4.5 times as great.

What is the maximum depth the Aluminaut can operate in?

Multiply to find the depth. $4.5 \times (-1.10)$

The rules for multiplying decimals and integers also apply when multiplying rational numbers.
$4.5 \times (-1.10) = -4.95$

The Aluminaut can operate to a maximum depth of -4.95 km.

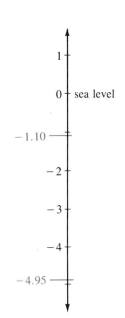

In 1 min, a diver with scuba gear can descend to a depth of -15.2 m. To secure the legs of an oil-drilling rig the diver must descend to a depth of -76 m. How long will it take to reach this depth?

Divide to find the length of time. $(-76) \div (-15.2)$

The rules for dividing decimals and integers apply when dividing rational numbers.
$(-76) \div (-15.2) = +5$

The diver will take 5 min to descend.

The rules for multiplying rational numbers in fractional form are the same as those for multiplying common fractions. The signs obey the same rules as those for multiplying integers.

Example 1. Simplify. $\left(-\dfrac{2}{3}\right)\left(-\dfrac{9}{11}\right)$

Solution. The product of an even number of negative numbers is a positive number.

$$\left(-\frac{2}{3}\right)\left(-\frac{9}{11}\right) = \frac{2}{3} \times \frac{9}{11}$$

$$= \frac{2}{\cancel{3}_{1}} \times \frac{\cancel{9}^{3}}{11}$$

$$= \frac{6}{11}$$

Two rational numbers with a product of 1 are called reciprocals. The reciprocal of a rational number is sometimes called its multiplicative inverse.

> The *reciprocal* of any rational number $\dfrac{m}{n}$ (where m, $n \ne 0$) is
>
> defined to be the rational number $\dfrac{n}{m}$.

Example 2. a) What is the reciprocal of $-\dfrac{2}{5}$?

b) What is the multiplicative inverse of 4?

Solution. a) Since $\left(-\dfrac{2}{5}\right)\left(-\dfrac{5}{2}\right) = +1$, the reciprocal of $-\dfrac{2}{5}$ is $-\dfrac{5}{2}$.

b) The multiplicative inverse of 4 is $\dfrac{1}{4}$.

The rule for dividing rational numbers in fractional form is the same as the rule for dividing common fractions — multiply by the reciprocal.

Example 3. Simplify. $\dfrac{25}{4} \div \left(-\dfrac{5}{8}\right)$

Solution. The reciprocal of $-\dfrac{5}{8}$ is $-\dfrac{8}{5}$.

$$\frac{25}{4} \div \left(-\frac{5}{8}\right) = \frac{25}{4} \times \left(-\frac{8}{5}\right)$$

$$= -10$$

Example 4. Simplify. a) $2.54 \times (-3.86)$ b) $(-9.0272) \div 0.52$

Solution. a) $2.54 \times (-3.86)$

The product is negative. Use a calculator to multiply 2.54 by 3.86.

Key in: $\boxed{2}\ \boxed{\cdot}\ \boxed{5}\ \boxed{4}\ \boxed{\times}\ \boxed{3}\ \boxed{\cdot}\ \boxed{8}\ \boxed{6}\ \boxed{=}$ to display 9.8044

Therefore, $2.54 \times (-3.86) = -9.8044$

b) $(-9.0272) \div 0.52$

The quotient is negative. Use a calculator to divide 9.0272 by 0.52.

Key in: $\boxed{9}\ \boxed{\cdot}\ \boxed{0}\ \boxed{2}\ \boxed{7}\ \boxed{2}\ \boxed{\div}\ \boxed{\cdot}\ \boxed{5}\ \boxed{2}\ \boxed{=}$ to display 17.36

Therefore, $(-9.0272) \div 0.52 = -17.36$

EXERCISES 2-3

Ⓐ

1. Simplify.

a) $\dfrac{1}{2} \times \dfrac{8}{5}$ b) $\left(\dfrac{-2}{3}\right)\left(\dfrac{6}{-7}\right)$ c) $\left(\dfrac{-1}{4}\right)\left(\dfrac{+2}{+3}\right)$ d) $\left(\dfrac{-3}{-8}\right)\left(\dfrac{1}{-21}\right)$

e) $\left(\dfrac{15}{-2}\right)\left(\dfrac{-2}{45}\right)$ f) $-\left(\dfrac{-5}{12}\right)\left(\dfrac{36}{-5}\right)$ g) $\left(-\dfrac{7}{3}\right)\left(\dfrac{-6}{5}\right)$ h) $\dfrac{8}{3}\left(-\dfrac{9}{4}\right)$

2. Simplify.

a) $(7.2) \times 5$ b) $(-3) \times 6.4$ c) $(-4) \times (-0.8)$ d) $(-0.2) \times 0.6$

e) $1.3 \times (-0.5)$ f) 2.8×0.2 g) $(-1.5) \times 1.1$ h) $(-0.9) \times (-1.4)$

3. Write the multiplicative inverse for each rational number.

a) 9 b) -23 c) $\dfrac{16}{19}$ d) $-\dfrac{7}{13}$ e) -1.5 f) 0.8

g) 0.75 h) -2.5 i) $-\dfrac{1}{16}$ j) -0.6 k) -10 l) 0.01

4. Write the rational number represented by each square.

a) $\dfrac{3}{8} \times \blacksquare = 1$ b) $\dfrac{5}{9} \times \blacksquare = 1$ c) $\left(-\dfrac{4}{7}\right) \times \blacksquare = 1$

d) $2.5 \times \blacksquare = 1$ e) $\left(-\dfrac{2}{3}\right) \times \blacksquare = 1$ f) $\left(-\dfrac{7}{15}\right) \times \blacksquare = 1$

g) $\dfrac{3}{5} \times \blacksquare = -1$ h) $\left(-\dfrac{7}{8}\right) \times \blacksquare = -1$ i) $0.6 \times \blacksquare = -1$

5. Simplify.

a) $\dfrac{1}{8} \div \dfrac{1}{2}$ b) $\left(-\dfrac{7}{10}\right) \div \left(\dfrac{4}{-9}\right)$ c) $\left(\dfrac{5}{-8}\right) \div \left(\dfrac{-3}{-4}\right)$

d) $\left(\dfrac{-1}{5}\right) \div \left(\dfrac{8}{-15}\right)$ e) $\left(\dfrac{-8}{2}\right) \div \left(\dfrac{-4}{3}\right)$ f) $\left(-\dfrac{10}{3}\right) \div \dfrac{5}{4}$

g) $\dfrac{5}{4} \div \left(-\dfrac{5}{2}\right)$ h) $\left(-\dfrac{2}{3}\right) \div \dfrac{5}{7}$ i) $\dfrac{11}{6} \div \left(\dfrac{-7}{-12}\right)$

6. Simplify.
   a) $(-8.4) \div 2$
   b) $(-3.6) \div (-4)$
   c) $9.9 \div 0.3$
   d) $(-1.21) \div 1.1$
   e) $16.8 \div (-0.8)$
   f) $1.69 \div 0.13$
   g) $(-10.8) \div (-0.9)$
   h) $0.288 \div (-0.12)$
   i) $(-2.4) \div (-0.16)$

(B)

7. In 1932 the record diving depth in a submersible was about 9 times as deep as the record depth of 1865. The record depth of 1865 was -74.7 m. What was the depth achieved in 1932?

8. The sperm whale is normally found at a depth of -252 m. The greatest depth that a sperm whale has reached is about 4.5 times as great as its normal depth. What depth did the whale reach?

9. Simplify.
   a) $\left(\dfrac{-18}{7}\right) \times \left(\dfrac{-21}{9}\right)$
   b) $\left(\dfrac{-3}{28}\right) \div \dfrac{9}{7}$
   c) $\left(\dfrac{36}{-5}\right) \times \left(\dfrac{-18}{-35}\right)$
   d) $\dfrac{4}{39} \div \left(\dfrac{-64}{13}\right)$
   e) $\dfrac{9}{48} \times \left(\dfrac{-6}{16}\right)$
   f) $\left(\dfrac{-15}{55}\right) \times \left(\dfrac{-2}{-11}\right)$
   g) $\left(-\dfrac{72}{7}\right) \div \left(-\dfrac{12}{49}\right)$
   h) $\left(\dfrac{-75}{3}\right) \div \left(\dfrac{-15}{4}\right)$
   i) $\left(-\dfrac{33}{4}\right) \times \left(\dfrac{7}{22}\right)$

10. Simplify.
    a) $(-2.38) \times 4.47$
    b) $(-3.4336) \div (-9.28)$
    c) $0.046 \times (-10.08)$
    d) $0.164\,15 \div (-24.5)$
    e) $(-313.7) \times (-0.18)$
    f) $(-106.2) \div 236$
    g) $0.000\,161\,2 \div 0.031$
    h) $57.28 \times (-6.04)$
    i) $6.4061 \div (-0.047)$

(C)

11. Without using a calculator or simplifying the expression, replace each comma with $>$ or $<$.
    a) $\dfrac{13}{-14}, \dfrac{-14}{13}$
    b) $\dfrac{-6}{7}, \dfrac{7}{-8}$
    c) $\dfrac{-2387}{3592}, \dfrac{-2388}{3593}$

12. Give an example of a rational number that can be expressed as a terminating decimal, and whose reciprocal can be expressed as a repeating decimal.

13. Write all the single digit numbers whose reciprocal is:
    a) a terminating decimal
    b) a repeating decimal
    c) neither a terminating decimal nor a repeating decimal.

14. Write these expressions in order from least to greatest.
$$\left[(-25) \div \dfrac{2}{3}\right] \div \left(-\dfrac{1}{6}\right); \quad -\left[(-5)^2 \div \dfrac{1}{9} \div \left(\dfrac{4}{-5}\right)\right]; \quad (-3)^2 \div \left[\dfrac{16}{5} \div \left(\dfrac{5}{-4}\right)^2\right]$$

2-4 ADDING AND SUBTRACTING RATIONAL NUMBERS

To swim underwater from the surface of a pool 6 m deep to the bottom and back can be quite a challenge.

To an expert diver like Jacques Mayol, the challenge is to dive deeper than anyone else. In 1973 he held the world's record for breath-held diving at -85.95 m. In 1986 he still held the record but he had reached a depth of -104.85 m.

What is the total depth descended on both dives?

Add to find the total depth. $(-85.95) + (-104.85)$

The rules for adding decimals and integers also apply when adding rational numbers.

$(-85.95) + (-104.85) = -190.80$

Mayol descended 190.8 m on both dives.

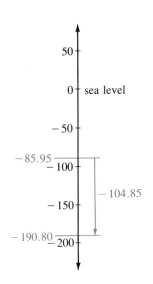

How much deeper is the 1986 record than the 1973 record?

Subtract to find the difference in depth. $(-104.85) - (-85.95)$

The rules for subtracting decimals and integers also apply when subtracting rational numbers.

The opposite of -85.95 is $+85.95$.

Therefore, $(-104.85) - (-85.95)$ becomes

$(-104.85) + (+85.95) = -18.90$

The 1986 record is 18.9 m deeper than the 1973 record.

The rules for adding and subtracting rational numbers in fractional form are the same as those for adding and subtracting common fractions.

The operations are easier if rational numbers with negative denominators are first changed to their equivalents with positive denominators.

The signs obey the same rules as those for operating with integers.

Example 1. Simplify.

a) $\dfrac{3}{4} + \left(\dfrac{2}{-3}\right)$

b) $\left(\dfrac{-5}{6}\right) - \left(\dfrac{12}{-7}\right)$

Solution. a) $\dfrac{3}{4} + \left(\dfrac{2}{-3}\right) = \dfrac{3}{4} + \left(-\dfrac{2}{3}\right)$

$= \dfrac{3}{4} - \dfrac{2}{3}$

$= \dfrac{9}{12} - \dfrac{8}{12}$

$= \dfrac{1}{12}$

b) $\left(\dfrac{-5}{6}\right) - \left(\dfrac{12}{-7}\right) = -\dfrac{5}{6} - \left(-\dfrac{12}{7}\right)$

$= -\dfrac{5}{6} + \dfrac{12}{7}$

$= -\dfrac{35}{42} + \dfrac{72}{42}$

$= \dfrac{37}{42}$

Example 2. Simplify.

a) $(-0.928) + 37.089$ b) $1.37 - (-18.40)$

Solution.   a) $(-0.928) + 37.089$

Rewrite the expression as $37.089 - 0.928$.

Use a calculator to subtract 0.928 from 37.089.

Key in:

$\boxed{3}\ \boxed{7}\ \boxed{\cdot}\ \boxed{0}\ \boxed{8}\ \boxed{9}\ \boxed{-}\ \boxed{\cdot}\ \boxed{9}\ \boxed{2}\ \boxed{8}\ \boxed{=}$ to display 36.161

Therefore, $(-0.928) + 37.089 = 36.161$

b) $1.37 - (-18.40)$

Rewrite the expression as $1.37 + 18.40$.

Use a calculator to add 18.40 to 1.37.

Key in: $\boxed{1}\ \boxed{\cdot}\ \boxed{3}\ \boxed{7}\ \boxed{+}\ \boxed{1}\ \boxed{8}\ \boxed{\cdot}\ \boxed{4}\ \boxed{=}$ to display 19.77

Therefore, $1.37 - (-18.40) = 19.77$

EXERCISES 2-4

(A)

1. Simplify.

   a) $\dfrac{3}{4} + \dfrac{2}{3}$ b) $\dfrac{5}{7} - \dfrac{2}{5}$ c) $\dfrac{3}{8} - \dfrac{5}{6}$ d) $\dfrac{-5}{12} + \left(\dfrac{-3}{8}\right)$

   e) $\dfrac{2}{-9} + \dfrac{5}{6}$ f) $-\dfrac{4}{5} - \dfrac{2}{3}$ g) $\dfrac{3}{-4} - \left(\dfrac{-2}{5}\right)$ h) $-\left(\dfrac{-3}{8}\right) - \left(\dfrac{5}{-4}\right)$

2. Simplify.

   a) $(-1.7) + (-3.1)$ b) $2.8 - 5.9$ c) $(-3.6) - (-2.1)$

   d) $1.7 + (-8.9)$ e) $7.6 + 9.3$ f) $(-6.4) + 11.8$

   g) $(-8.7) - (-9.8)$ h) $(-15.6) + 23.9$ i) $36.3 - (+41.7)$

(B)

3. Simplify.

   a) $-\dfrac{2}{3} + \left(\dfrac{1}{-4}\right)$ b) $-\left(\dfrac{-5}{6}\right) + \dfrac{3}{2}$ c) $\left(\dfrac{3}{-8}\right) - \dfrac{3}{4}$ d) $\dfrac{-5}{8} + \left(\dfrac{-1}{-6}\right)$

   e) $-\left(\dfrac{2}{-3}\right) - \dfrac{3}{10}$ f) $\dfrac{3}{4} - \left(\dfrac{-5}{8}\right)$ g) $\dfrac{9}{4} + \left(\dfrac{-7}{3}\right)$ h) $\dfrac{-20}{6} - \left(-\dfrac{13}{3}\right)$

4. Simplify.

   a) $\dfrac{7}{3} + \dfrac{21}{4}$ b) $\dfrac{47}{8} - \dfrac{8}{3}$ c) $\dfrac{13}{2} - \dfrac{49}{5}$ d) $\dfrac{17}{5} - \dfrac{35}{4}$

   e) $-\dfrac{14}{3} + \dfrac{12}{5}$ f) $\dfrac{9}{7} - \dfrac{9}{5}$ g) $-\dfrac{13}{5} + \dfrac{11}{6}$ h) $\dfrac{43}{3} - \dfrac{47}{7}$

5. Simplify.

   a) $-2.387 + 4.923$ b) $33.78 - (-64.35)$ c) $204.9 - 256.1$

   d) $-0.405 - 18.924$ e) $-12.37 + 8.88$ f) $-45.8 - (-327.6)$

   g) $4.29 + 563.08$ h) $84.91 - 37.08$ i) $-0.046 + (-0.104)$

6. Simplify.

   a) $\dfrac{-7}{10} - \left(\dfrac{-7}{3}\right)$ b) $\dfrac{-15}{4} - \dfrac{13}{6}$ c) $\dfrac{13}{8} + \left(\dfrac{-3}{7}\right)$

   d) $\dfrac{25}{2} - \left(-\dfrac{13}{4}\right)$ e) $\dfrac{-11}{4} + \left(\dfrac{-4}{3}\right)$ f) $\dfrac{20}{9} - \left(\dfrac{-22}{3}\right)$

   g) $-\left(-\dfrac{11}{6}\right) - \left(\dfrac{11}{-18}\right)$ h) $\dfrac{14}{-5} + \left(\dfrac{-3}{7}\right)$ i) $\dfrac{-3}{11} + \dfrac{16}{3}$

7. In 1985 the United States had a federal budget deficit of $-\$179.0$ billion. In 1986 the deficit decreased by $+\$7.1$ billion over 1985.

   a) What was the total deficit at the end of 1986?

   b) In 1987 the deficit is projected to increase by a further $-\$18.2$ billion. What is the total deficit expected at the end of 1987?

8. The table shows the record depths
   achieved by a specially constructed
   submersible called a bathyscaphe.
   a) Calculate the difference in depth
      between consecutive records.
   b) Between which two dives was the
      difference in depth the largest?

Year	Record Depth in metres
1953	− 3150.1
1954	− 4049.9
1959	− 5666.3
1960	− 7315.2

9. Find the integer represented by each square.

   a) $\dfrac{2}{5} + \dfrac{\blacksquare}{5} = \dfrac{6}{5}$

   b) $\dfrac{2}{5} + \dfrac{\blacksquare}{5} = \dfrac{-6}{5}$

   c) $\dfrac{3}{-7} - \dfrac{\blacksquare}{7} = \dfrac{5}{7}$

   d) $\dfrac{3}{-7} - \dfrac{\blacksquare}{7} = \dfrac{5}{7}$

   e) $\dfrac{7}{8} - \dfrac{4}{\blacksquare} = \dfrac{11}{8}$

   f) $\dfrac{5}{9} - \dfrac{8}{\blacksquare} = \dfrac{1}{9}$

10. An editor assigns a value for each letter and space when laying out a book.

Symbols	Value
I, i, letter l, digit 1, punctuation	$\dfrac{1}{2}$
Other digits and lower case letters	1
m, w, and mathematical signs	$1\frac{1}{2}$
Spaces and capitals (except M, W)	2
M, W	$2\frac{1}{2}$

Find the total value of each line.
a) The answer given was $109\frac{1}{2}$.
b) Mass is measured in kilograms. Weight is in newtons.
c) Simplify 3.14 ÷ 4 × 7.2. Give the answer to 2 decimal places.

11. The shares of publicly owned companies are bought and sold on the stock exchange.
    Newspapers list each day's transactions.

COMPANY	Sales	High	Low	Close	Change
Scot Paper	413	$9\frac{3}{4}$	$9\frac{3}{4}$	$9\frac{3}{4}$	$-\frac{3}{4}$
Scot York	14 850	$7\frac{1}{2}$	7	$7\frac{1}{2}$	$+\frac{1}{8}$
Scotts A	1 000	$8\frac{1}{2}$	$8\frac{1}{2}$	$8\frac{1}{2}$	
Seagram	3 815	$35\frac{1}{2}$	$35\frac{1}{4}$	$35\frac{1}{4}$	$-\frac{3}{4}$
Seco Cem	100	$9\frac{1}{2}$	$9\frac{1}{2}$	$9\frac{1}{2}$	$-\frac{1}{4}$
Selkirk A	1 200	$18	17	18	$+2\frac{1}{4}$
Shaw Pipe	10 900	$12\frac{1}{2}$	$12\frac{1}{4}$	$12\frac{3}{8}$	$-\frac{1}{8}$

The clipping shows that on one day 10 900 shares of Shaw Pipe were traded. The highest price paid for a share was $12\frac{1}{2}$ and the lowest price was $12\frac{1}{4}$. This was down $\frac{1}{8}$ on the previous day's closing price.

a) What happened to Scot York shares that day?
b) How much would 500 shares of Seagram's cost at the low price for the day?
c) How many shares of Seco Cem could have been bought for $1900?
d) Calculate the previous day's closing price for each share.

Ⓒ

12. If $x > 0$, $y < 0$, and $z < 0$, which expressions are always positive?

a) $\dfrac{x}{y}$ b) $\dfrac{xy}{z}$ c) $\dfrac{x}{yz}$ d) $\dfrac{y}{xz}$ e) $\dfrac{x}{y+z}$

f) $\dfrac{x-y}{z}$ g) $\dfrac{x}{x-y}$ h) $\dfrac{x-y}{x-z}$ i) $\dfrac{x}{y}+\dfrac{x}{z}$ j) $\dfrac{y}{z}-\dfrac{x}{y}$

▦ CALCULATOR POWER

Adding and Subtracting Rational Numbers in Fractional Form

Many scientific calculators will add and subtract fractions if the numbers are keyed in, in the order in which they appear.

For example, to simplify $\dfrac{2}{5} + \dfrac{3}{4}$,

key in: [2] [÷] [5] [+] [3] [÷] [4] [=] to display 1.15
However, this is usually not the case when using a 4-function calculator. When the above sequence is keyed in, the result, 0.85, is incorrect. This is because the calculator adds 3 to the result of $2 \div 5$ before dividing by 4. However, by altering the sequence of operations, the correct result can be obtained.

Consider the sum $\dfrac{a}{b} + \dfrac{c}{d}$.

This can be written as $\dfrac{ad + bc}{bd} = \left(\dfrac{ad + bc}{b}\right)\dfrac{1}{d}$

$$= \left(\dfrac{ad}{b} + c\right)\dfrac{1}{d}$$

To simplify $\dfrac{2}{5} + \dfrac{3}{4}$,

key in: [2] [×] [4] [÷] [5] [+] [3] [÷] [4] [=]
to display the correct result of 1.15

1. Use your calculator to simplify *Exercises 1* and *3* on page 55.

**INVESTIGATE**

Adding Rational Numbers on a Grid

- Recall how to plot a rational number, in fractional form, on a grid. For example, to plot $\frac{4}{3}$, from the origin move 3 units in the *x*-direction and then 4 units in the *y*-direction. Draw a dot and label it $\frac{4}{3}$.

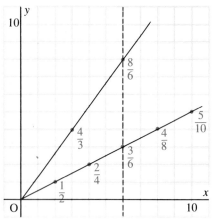

To simplify the expression $\frac{4}{3} + \frac{1}{2}$

- Plot each number on a grid. Join each point to the origin and extend the line.
- Move along each line from the origin. Label those equivalent rational numbers that can be written in the form $\frac{m}{n}$, where *m* and *n* are integers.
- On the two lines drawn, look for two points in the same vertical line, that is, $\frac{8}{6}$ and $\frac{3}{6}$.

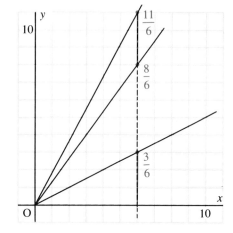

- Add the vertical segments. Slide the line segment, with its upper end on $\frac{3}{6}$, vertically so that its lower end coincides with $\frac{8}{6}$. Then the upper end coincides with the point $\frac{11}{6}$.

- This point, $\frac{11}{6}$, is the sum of $\frac{4}{3}$ and $\frac{1}{2}$.

1. Use a grid to find each sum.

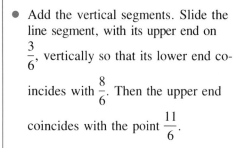
a) $\frac{3}{4} + \frac{5}{3}$ b) $\frac{2}{5} + \frac{3}{2}$ c) $\frac{7}{9} + \frac{5}{6}$ d) $\frac{3}{5} + \frac{5}{3}$

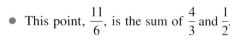
2. Can you think of a method of subtracting rational numbers using a grid?

MATHEMATICS AROUND US

Niagara Falls is Moving!

The flow of water in the Niagara River is about 5700 m³/s. This great volume of water causes erosion at Niagara Falls and they moved upstream about 264 m, between the years 1700 and 1900.

Hydro-electric power plants, requiring the diversion of some of the water around the Falls, were opened in 1905, 1922, 1954, and 1960. Nowadays, as much as 75% of the water may go around, instead of over, the Falls. This has halved the rate of erosion.

QUESTIONS

1. About how far did Niagara Falls move upstream in 1800?

2. About how far does Niagara Falls move upstream each year now?

3. a) How far has Niagara Falls moved since you were born?
   b) How far will it move in your lifetime?

4. How long would it take Niagara Falls to move the length of your classroom?

5. Use the map to answer these questions.
   a) When will Niagara Falls reach the Three Sisters Islands?
   b) When was Niagara Falls at the location of the Rainbow Bridge?

6. What assumptions did you make when answering *Questions 1* to *5*?

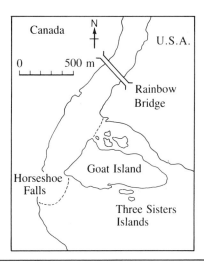

PROBLEM SOLVING

Work Backwards

How much change did Karl have?

Understand the problem
- What operations did Karl perform on the number he started with?
- What are we asked to find?

Think of a strategy
- Try working backwards from the final number to the starting number by reversing the operations.

Carry out the strategy
- Complete a flow chart for the operations that Karl performed.

| Starting Number | → | ×2 | → | +3 | → | ×10 | → | +13 | → | ×5 | → | Final Number |

- Reverse the flow chart by changing multiplication into division and addition into subtraction.
- Start with the final number 6115 and follow the flow chart in reverse to determine the starting number.

| Starting Number | ← | ÷2 | ← | −3 | ← | ÷10 | ← | −13 | ← | ÷5 | ← | Final Number |

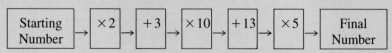

From the reverse flow chart, Karl had 59¢ change.

Look back
- Start with 59 and follow the instructions given to Karl. Do you obtain the final number 6115?

Solve each problem

1. Laura cashed a cheque for $28.65 and put the cash in her purse. Then she purchased 2 magazines for $1.95 each, a book for $6.95, and a record for $5.89. She had $21.60 left in her purse. How much money did she have before cashing her cheque?

2. Todd had more milk than his younger brother Alan so he poured into Alan's glass as much milk as Alan's glass already contained. Then he poured from Alan's glass into his own, as much as his own glass contained. Finally he poured back into Alan's glass as much milk as Alan presently had. Then, both glasses contained 256 mL of milk. How much did each boy start with?

3. Stacey has a 3 L bucket and an 8 L bucket. How can she use these two unmarked buckets to obtain exactly 4 L of water?

4. Mr. Barter didn't have enough money to purchase a book he wanted. He said to the clerk, "If you will give me as much money as I have in my hand, I will spend $6.00." The clerk agreed and after Mr. Barter spent the $6.00 he repeated the offer. The clerk matched the amount Mr. Barter had left, and he spent another $6.00. After Mr. Barter repeated the offer a third time, spending another $6.00, he had no more money. How much money did he start with?

5. Ahmed's plane is to arrive in St. John's at 11:10 Newfoundland time. The flight time is 2 h and 55 min. What time should Ahmed leave his house if it takes about 1 h to drive to Lester B. Pearson airport in Toronto and he wants to arrive 45 min before departure? (Newfoundland is 1.5 h ahead of Toronto.)

6. Each year a car depreciates to $\frac{4}{5}$ of its value one year before. What was the original value of a car that is worth $8000 after 4 years?

7. Lesley boarded a school bus at Oak Street along with 5 other students. The bus drove to Elm Street where it picked up 7 more students. The next stop was Beech Crescent where the bus picked up 6 students. There were now 1.5 times as many students on the bus as there were when it arrived at Oak Street. How many students were on the bus when it left Beech Crescent?

8. The total value of any sum of money that earns interest at 9% per annum doubles every 8 years. What amount of money invested now at 9% per annum will accumulate to $30 000 in 32 years?

2-5 ORDER OF OPERATIONS WITH RATIONAL NUMBERS

CONTEST WINNERS
will be asked to answer correctly
the following skill-testing question.
What is the value of
$$\frac{3}{4} - \left(-\frac{1}{2}\right)\left(\frac{5}{8}\right) \div \left[\left(-\frac{1}{4}\right)\left(-\frac{1}{4}\right)\right]?$$

Merlin wrote:

$$\frac{3}{4} - \left(-\frac{1}{2}\right)\left(\frac{5}{8}\right) \div \left[\left(-\frac{1}{4}\right)\left(-\frac{1}{4}\right)\right]$$

$$= \frac{3}{4} - \left(\frac{-5}{16}\right) \div \frac{1}{16}$$

$$= \frac{3}{4} + \frac{5}{16} \div \frac{1}{16}$$

$$= \frac{17}{16} \div \frac{1}{16}$$

$$= 17$$

Jasmine wrote:

$$\frac{3}{4} - \left(-\frac{1}{2}\right)\left(\frac{5}{8}\right) \div \left[\left(-\frac{1}{4}\right)\left(-\frac{1}{4}\right)\right]$$

$$= \frac{3}{4} - \left(\frac{-5}{16}\right) \div \frac{1}{16}$$

$$= \frac{3}{4} - \left(\frac{-5}{16}\right) \times \frac{16}{1}$$

$$= \frac{3}{4} - (-5)$$

$$= \frac{3}{4} + 5$$

$$= \frac{23}{4}$$

Who is correct?

The order of operations with rational numbers is the same as it is for integers.

- Operations within brackets are performed first.
- Multiplication and division are performed in order from left to right.
- Lastly, addition and subtraction are performed in order from left to right.

In the example above, Jasmine's solution is correct. Merlin made an error when he subtracted $\left(\frac{-5}{16}\right)$ from $\frac{3}{4}$ before he divided by $\frac{1}{16}$.

Example 1. Simplify. $\left(\dfrac{-9}{4}\right) \times \left(\dfrac{-10}{21}\right) \div \left(\dfrac{-45}{7}\right)$

Solution. Multiply and divide in order from left to right.

$$\left(\dfrac{-9}{4}\right) \times \left(\dfrac{-10}{21}\right) \div \left(\dfrac{-45}{7}\right) = \left(\dfrac{-\cancel{9}}{\cancel{4}_2}\right) \times \left(\dfrac{-\cancel{10}}{\cancel{21}_3}\right) \times \left(\dfrac{\cancel{7}}{\cancel{45}_1}\right)$$

$$= -\dfrac{1}{6}$$

Example 2. Simplify. $3\left(\dfrac{-5}{6}\right) + 5\left(\dfrac{-9}{8}\right) - 2\left(\dfrac{-3}{4}\right)$

Solution. Brackets imply multiplication, so perform these operations first.

$$3\left(\dfrac{-5}{6}\right) + 5\left(\dfrac{-9}{8}\right) - 2\left(\dfrac{-3}{4}\right) = 3\left(\dfrac{-5}{6}\right) + 5\left(\dfrac{-9}{8}\right) - 2\left(\dfrac{-3}{4}\right)$$

$$= \dfrac{-5}{2} - \dfrac{45}{8} + \dfrac{3}{2}$$

$$= -\dfrac{20}{8} - \dfrac{45}{8} + \dfrac{12}{8}$$

$$= -\dfrac{53}{8}$$

Example 3. Simplify. $3.78 - \dfrac{14.91}{4.26}(3.8 - 5.9)$

Solution. Use a calculator to do the arithmetic.
Evaluate the expression in the brackets first. Multiply and divide next.

$$3.78 - \dfrac{14.91}{4.26}(3.8 - 5.9) = 3.78 - \dfrac{14.91}{4.26}(-2.1)$$

$$= 3.78 - (-7.35)$$
$$= 3.78 + 7.35$$
$$= 11.13$$

Example 4. Simplify. $\left(-\dfrac{3}{5} + \dfrac{1}{2}\right) \times \left(-\dfrac{2}{3}\right)$

Solution. Simplify the expression in brackets first.

$$\left(-\dfrac{3}{5} + \dfrac{1}{2}\right) \times \left(-\dfrac{2}{3}\right) = \left(-\dfrac{6}{10} + \dfrac{5}{10}\right) \times \left(-\dfrac{2}{3}\right)$$

$$= \left(-\dfrac{1}{10}\right) \times \left(-\dfrac{2}{3}\right)$$

$$= \dfrac{1}{15}$$

EXERCISES 2-5

(B)

1. Simplify.

a) $\dfrac{-2}{3} + \left(\dfrac{1}{-4}\right) - \left(\dfrac{-5}{6}\right)$

b) $\dfrac{3}{2} - \left(\dfrac{3}{-8}\right) - \dfrac{3}{4}$

c) $\dfrac{5}{-8} + \left(\dfrac{-1}{-6}\right) - \left(\dfrac{2}{-3}\right)$

d) $\dfrac{3}{-10} - \dfrac{3}{4} - \left(\dfrac{-5}{8}\right)$

e) $\dfrac{9}{4} + \dfrac{17}{3} - \dfrac{29}{6}$

f) $\dfrac{-3}{5} + \left(\dfrac{-7}{10}\right) - \dfrac{1}{2}$

g) $-\dfrac{7}{2} + \dfrac{4}{3} - \left(-\dfrac{5}{6}\right)$

h) $-\dfrac{5}{9} - \left(-\dfrac{2}{3}\right) + \left(-\dfrac{7}{6}\right)$

i) $\dfrac{13}{2} + \left(\dfrac{-2}{3}\right) - \dfrac{7}{4} + \left(\dfrac{4}{-3}\right)$

j) $\dfrac{4}{7} - \left(\dfrac{3}{-5}\right) + \left(\dfrac{-1}{2}\right) - \dfrac{3}{35}$

2. Simplify.

a) $\left(\dfrac{4}{-9}\right) \times \left(\dfrac{-21}{-32}\right) \times \left(\dfrac{-3}{14}\right)$

b) $\left(\dfrac{-10}{27}\right) \times \left(\dfrac{-8}{20}\right) \times \left(\dfrac{-45}{-28}\right)$

c) $\left(\dfrac{-6}{-25}\right) \div \left(\dfrac{-2}{-21}\right) \div \left(\dfrac{14}{-25}\right)$

d) $\left(\dfrac{12}{-39}\right) \div \left(\dfrac{-10}{-9}\right) \div \left(\dfrac{18}{-5}\right)$

e) $\left(\dfrac{15}{-32}\right) \times \left(\dfrac{-4}{5}\right) \div \left(-\dfrac{9}{16}\right)$

f) $\left(\dfrac{-12}{28}\right) \div \left(\dfrac{-8}{-15}\right) \times \left(\dfrac{-14}{-25}\right)$

g) $\dfrac{5}{2} \div \left(-\dfrac{10}{3}\right) \times \dfrac{8}{3}$

h) $\left(-\dfrac{15}{4}\right) \times \dfrac{8}{5} \div \left(-\dfrac{6}{5}\right)$

i) $\left(\dfrac{20}{-3}\right) \div \left(\dfrac{-35}{9}\right) \times \left(\dfrac{-14}{-6}\right) \div \dfrac{4}{3}$

j) $\dfrac{22}{3} \times \left(\dfrac{-6}{77}\right) \times \left(\dfrac{-3}{-2}\right) \div \left(\dfrac{2}{-7}\right)$

3. Simplify.

a) $3.7 + 0.4 - 17.6$

b) $-0.38 + 2.09 - 8.11$

c) $54.68 + (-18.07) - (+38.46)$

d) $-25.3 - (-27.9) + 60.0$

4. Simplify.

a) $(-14.6) \times (-23.7) \times 10.4$

b) $(-12.958) \div (-2.2) \div 1.9$

c) $(145.0) \times (-14.6) \div (-12.5)$

d) $(966.52) \div (-29.2) \times 0.9$

e) $(0.017\ 67) \div (-0.95) \div (-0.31)$

f) $0.08 \times (-1.03) \times 0.5$

5. Simplify.

a) $\dfrac{4}{5} \times \left[\dfrac{3}{8} + \left(\dfrac{-7}{4}\right)\right]$

b) $\left[\dfrac{-3}{7} - \left(\dfrac{-7}{2}\right)\right] \div \left(\dfrac{-7}{3}\right)$

c) $\left(\dfrac{-6}{7}\right) + \left[\dfrac{3}{4} \times \left(\dfrac{-16}{7}\right)\right]$

d) $\left[\left(\dfrac{-18}{5}\right) \div \dfrac{27}{5}\right] - \left(\dfrac{-6}{11}\right)$

e) $\left[\left(\dfrac{-5}{9}\right) - \dfrac{7}{6}\right] \times \dfrac{9}{5}$

f) $\left(\dfrac{-4}{9}\right) \div \left[\left(\dfrac{-3}{8}\right) + \left(\dfrac{-4}{3}\right)\right]$

6. Simplify.

a) $\left(-\dfrac{5}{6}+\dfrac{2}{3}\right)\times\left(-\dfrac{3}{4}\right)\div\dfrac{5}{6}$

b) $\left(-\dfrac{3}{5}\times\dfrac{2}{3}\right)+\dfrac{5}{6}\div\left(-\dfrac{5}{3}\right)$

c) $\left(-\dfrac{3}{4}\right)\div\dfrac{1}{5}+\left[-\dfrac{1}{3}\times\left(-\dfrac{5}{2}\right)\right]$

d) $\left[\dfrac{3}{16}+\left(-\dfrac{3}{4}\right)\right]\times\left(-\dfrac{3}{8}\right)\div\dfrac{1}{4}$

e) $\dfrac{3}{5}+\left(-\dfrac{2}{3}\right)\times\left[-\dfrac{3}{4}\div\left(-\dfrac{1}{2}\right)\right]$

f) $\left[\dfrac{7}{12}\div(-14)\right]-\dfrac{3}{8}\times\dfrac{5}{3}$

7. Simplify.

a) $[(-3.8)+(-0.9)]\times[7.2-4.7]$

b) $\dfrac{79.12}{9.2}(-2.18+5.27)$

c) $(-4.91)\times(-3.78)+\left(\dfrac{50.827}{-6.85}\right)$

d) $(-74.52)\div(9.2)+(-23.9)\times16.7$

e) $(-0.65)-(-11.82)\times(21.65)\div(-17.32)$

f) $[88.48\div(-15.8)]-[(-34.9)+47.0]$

2-6 RATIONAL NUMBERS AND FORMULAS

A survey was conducted on the heights and the masses of grade 9 students. It was discovered that there is a relationship between the height and the average mass of the students. This relationship can be expressed in a *formula*.

$$M = \dfrac{3}{4}H - 72$$

M represents the average mass of a grade 9 student who is H centimetres tall.

The formula can be used to find the average mass of students of any given height.

Suppose a student, who is 1.5 m tall, wants to know if her mass is above or below the average. She *substitutes* for H in the formula. First she converts her height to centimetres.

$H = 1.5$ m or 150 cm

Then, her mass is given by $M = \dfrac{3}{4}(150) - 72$

$$= 40.5$$

The student knows that students of her age and height have an average mass of 40.5 kg.

Many formulas used in science, business, and industry involve rational numbers. Consider the problem that was posed at the beginning of this chapter.

Example 1. The rate of fuel consumption of a certain model of car is given by this formula.

$$R = -\frac{36}{5}F + \frac{29}{2}$$

F is the fraction of driving on the highway. R is the rate of fuel consumption in litres per 100 km. What will be the rate of fuel consumption, to 1 decimal place, when:
a) three-quarters of the driving is on the highway
b) two-thirds of the driving is in the city?

Solution. a) To find the value of the rate, R, substitute $F = \frac{3}{4}$ into the formula.

$$R = -\frac{36}{5}F + \frac{29}{2}$$
$$= -\frac{36}{5}\left(\frac{3}{4}\right) + \frac{29}{2}$$
$$= -\frac{27}{5} + \frac{29}{2}$$
$$= -5.4 + 14.5$$
$$= 9.1$$

When three-quarters of the driving is on the highway, the rate of fuel consumption is 9.1 L/100 km.

b) If two-thirds of the driving is in the city, then one-third is on the highway. Substitute $F = \frac{1}{3}$ in the formula to find the rate, R.

$$R = -\frac{36}{5}F + \frac{29}{2}$$
$$= -\frac{36}{5}\left(\frac{1}{3}\right) + \frac{29}{2}$$
$$= -\frac{12}{5} + \frac{29}{2}$$
$$= -2.4 + 14.5$$
$$= 12.1$$

When two-thirds of the driving is in the city, the rate of fuel consumption is 12.1 L/100 km.

Why is there such a difference between the fuel consumption rates for city and highway driving?

Example 2. An old reference book gives temperatures in Fahrenheit degrees. The formula relating Celsius degrees, C, and Fahrenheit degrees, F, is

$$C = \frac{5}{9}(F - 32).$$

Find the Celsius temperature which corresponds to $-30°F$.

Solution. Substitute $F = -30$ into the formula.

$$C = \frac{5}{9}(-30 - 32)$$

$$= \frac{5}{9}(-62)$$

$$\doteq -34$$

A temperature of $-30°F$ is equivalent to approximately $-34°C$.

EXERCISES 2-6

Ⓐ

1. Use the formula in *Example 2* to find the Celsius temperature equivalent of each temperature.
   a) 59°F   b) $-4°F$ c) 86°F

2. Find the rate of fuel consumption, R litres per 100 km, when the fraction of the distance the car in *Example 1* is driven:
   a) on the highway is two-thirds of the total
   b) on the highway is five-sixths of the total
   c) in the city is seven-twelfths of the total.

Ⓑ

3. The cost of operating a certain type of aircraft is given by this formula.

$$C = 900 + \frac{m}{200} + \frac{20\ 000\ 000}{m}$$

   m is the cruising altitude in metres. C is the cost in dollars per hour. Find the hourly cost of operating the aircraft at each altitude.
   a) 8000 m   b) 10 000 m
   Why is it cheaper to operate the aircraft at higher altitudes?

4. The power delivered by a high-voltage power line is given by this formula.

$$P = I(132 - \frac{1}{10}I)$$

   I is the current in amperes and P is the power in kilowatts. Find the power, to the nearest kilowatt, that is available when the current is 6.6 A.

5. The efficiency of a jack is given by this formula. E is the efficiency and h is determined by the pitch of the thread. Find the efficiency of a jack with each value of h.

$$E = \frac{h(1 - \frac{1}{2}h)}{h + \frac{1}{2}}$$

   a) $\frac{3}{5}$ b) $\frac{2}{3}$

6. The focal length of a concave spherical mirror is related to the distances of the object and the image from the mirror by this formula.

$$f = \frac{uv}{u + v}$$

f is the focal length of the mirror. u is the distance of the object from the mirror. v is the distance of the image from the mirror. All lengths are measured in the same units. Find the focal length of each spherical mirror.
a) When the object is 3 cm from the mirror, the image is 2 cm from the mirror.

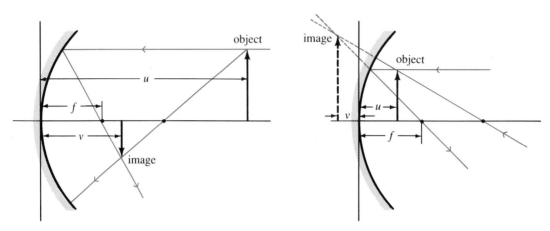

b) When the object is 1.6 m from the mirror, the image is −2.4 m from the mirror.

7. A car-rental firm uses this formula, $C = 28.5D + 0.095(d − 75)$, to calculate the cost, C dollars, of using one of their cars for D days to travel d kilometres ($d > 75$). Find how much the firm will charge a customer who uses the car for 5 days and travels 955 km.

8. A daily-interest savings account pays 9% per annum. The interest is calculated daily and added to the account at the end of each month. The formula,

$$A = P\left(1 + \frac{0.09d}{365}\right),$$ gives the value, A dollars, of the money in the account

d days after depositing P dollars. Calculate the value of the account for each deposit.
a) a deposit of $90 after 30 days   b) a deposit of $10 000 after 5 days

9. A car brakes and decelerates uniformly. The distance, d metres, that it travels in t seconds is given by this formula. $d = ut − 3.5t^2$
u is its speed, in metres per second, before the brakes are applied. Find how far the car travels under these conditions.
a) It is travelling 25 m/s before the brakes are applied. It travels for 5 s after the brakes are applied.
b) It is travelling 35 m/s before the brakes are applied. It travels for 5.5 s after the brakes are applied.

Ⓒ

10. A car-rental firm uses the formula $C = 28.5D + 0.095(d - 75)$ to compute the cost, C dollars, to customers who use one of their cars for D days to travel d kilometres $(d > 75)$. If a customer's bill was \$125.88 for three days of use, how far did the customer drive?

11. Use the formula in *Exercise 8* to find how long a deposit of \$1000 remains in such an account before it has a value of:
    a) \$1001   b) \$1003   c) \$1005.

12. Use the formula in *Example 2* to find the Fahrenheit equivalent of each temperature.
    a) 100°C   b) 215°C   c) 5°C   d) −20°C

13. At what temperature will a Fahrenheit thermometer and a Celsius thermometer show the same reading?

INVESTIGATE

1. Start with any rational number in fractional form, for example, $\frac{3}{5}$. Let n represent its numerator and d its denominator. Form a new fraction by substituting for n and d into this formula.

$$\frac{2n + d}{n + 2d}$$

The result is $\dfrac{2(3) + 5}{3 + 2(5)} = \dfrac{11}{13}$ which is 0.8461 . . . as a decimal.

Repeat the process with the new fraction. That is, substitute $n = 11$ and $d = 13$.

The result is $\dfrac{2(11) + 13}{11 + 2(13)} = \dfrac{35}{37}$ or 0.9459 . . .

Continue this process. What does the result appear to be?

2. Repeat the process several times, each time beginning with a different fraction. What do you notice?

3. Repeat the process with a different formula. For example:
   $$\frac{3n + d}{n + 3d}, \quad \frac{n + d}{4n + d}, \quad \frac{n + 2d}{n + d}, \quad \frac{2n + d}{n + d}.$$

4. Write a report of your findings.

COMPUTER POWER

Investigating Rational Numbers in Formulas

The formula, $\dfrac{2n + d}{n + 2d}$, which was introduced in the previous *INVESTIGATE* section, can be evaluated using this computer program.

```
100 REM *** FRACTION INVESTIGATION ***
110 INPUT "ENTER COEFFICIENTS: ";A,B,C,D
120 INPUT "WHAT IS THE NUMERATOR? ";NUM
130 INPUT "WHAT IS THE DENOMINATOR? ";DEN
140 FOR K = 1 TO 10
150 X = A * NUM + B * DEN:Y = C * NUM + D * DEN
160 F = INT (10000 * X/Y) / 10000
170 PRINT X,Y,F:NUM = X: DEN = Y
180 NEXT K
190 PRINT : INPUT "PRESS S TO STOP, RETURN TO REPEAT ";Y$
200 PRINT : IF Y$ <> "S" THEN 120: END
```

This program is written for a general formula, $\dfrac{An + Bd}{Cn + Dd}$.

Hence, it is necessary to input values for A, B, C and D, the coefficients of n and d. Then this formula can be used to evaluate *Question 3* of the previous *INVESTIGATE* section.

The printout for *Question 1* of the *INVESTIGATE* section is shown below.

```
ENTER COEFFICIENTS: 2,1,1,2
WHAT IS THE NUMERATOR? 3
WHAT IS THE DENOMINATOR? 5
11          13          .8461
35          37          .9459
107         109         .9816
323         325         .9938
971         973         .9979
2915        2917        .9993
8747        8749        .9997
26243       26245       .9999
78731       78733       .9999
236195      236197      .9999

PRESS S TO STOP, RETURN TO REPEAT S
```

1. Input the program. Run the program. Choose values for A, B, C, and D for the formula. Select a fraction to be substituted in the formula.

2. Write a report of your findings.

1. Express as fractions in lowest terms.
   a) -2.5 b) 0.125 c) -1.8 d) -1.11 e) 8.475

2. State which of these rational numbers are equivalent.
   $$\frac{-6}{9}, \quad \frac{16}{-25}, \quad \frac{21}{28}, \quad -\frac{14}{21}, \quad \frac{-30}{-45}, \quad \frac{10}{-15}, \quad \frac{-9}{12}$$

3. Arrange these rational numbers from least to greatest.
   $$-\frac{15}{16}, \quad \frac{-43}{48}, \quad \frac{11}{12}, \quad \frac{5}{6}, \quad \frac{-31}{-32}, \quad \frac{2}{3}$$

4. a) List four rational numbers between 0 and 1.
   b) List four rational numbers between -1 and -2.

5. Express each rational number as a decimal.
   a) $\dfrac{3}{8}$ b) $\dfrac{-4}{7}$ c) $\dfrac{7}{-12}$ d) $\dfrac{20}{9}$ e) $-\dfrac{35}{16}$ f) $\dfrac{2}{3}$

6. Express each decimal as a fraction in lowest terms.
   a) -1.5 b) 20.25 c) 2.007 d) -41.6 e) 10.75 f) -3.875

7. Simplify.
   a) $-\dfrac{2}{3} \times \dfrac{7}{8}$ b) $\left(\dfrac{5}{-8}\right)\left(\dfrac{-9}{12}\right)$ c) $\left(\dfrac{3}{-5}\right)\left(\dfrac{-7}{-8}\right)$

   d) $\left(\dfrac{13}{15}\right)\left(\dfrac{30}{-39}\right)$ e) $\left(-\dfrac{6}{5}\right)\left(\dfrac{12}{-15}\right)\left(\dfrac{-25}{36}\right)$ f) $\left(\dfrac{8}{13}\right)\left(-\dfrac{6}{5}\right)\left(\dfrac{-4}{7}\right)$

8. Simplify.
   a) $\dfrac{3}{7} \div \left(\dfrac{-9}{14}\right)$ b) $-\dfrac{13}{4} \div \left(\dfrac{2}{-3}\right)$

   c) $\dfrac{7}{-8} \div \left(-\dfrac{9}{4}\right)$ d) $\dfrac{-24}{-35} \div \left(\dfrac{16}{-21}\right) \div \dfrac{9}{10}$

   e) $\dfrac{-3}{5} \div \left(\dfrac{-5}{-12}\right) \div \left(\dfrac{-9}{10}\right)$ f) $\dfrac{18}{5} \div (-3) \div \dfrac{3}{2}$

9. Simplify.
   a) $(-56.28) \times (0.09)$ b) $(14.46) \div (-24.1)$
   c) $(143.7) \times (-206.8)$ d) $(-1433.36) \div (43.7)$
   e) $(-7.9808) \div (-92.8)$ f) $(-0.029) \times (-33.370)$

10. Simplify.
   a) $\dfrac{3}{5} + \dfrac{4}{7}$ b) $\dfrac{5}{12} + \dfrac{3}{8}$ c) $\dfrac{2}{9} + \dfrac{7}{12}$ d) $\dfrac{3}{11} + \left(\dfrac{-5}{11}\right)$

   e) $\dfrac{13}{-24} + \left(\dfrac{-7}{24}\right)$ f) $\dfrac{-2}{3} + \left(\dfrac{-4}{9}\right)$ g) $\dfrac{4}{-5} + \dfrac{14}{15}$ h) $\dfrac{-3}{-7} + \left(\dfrac{-2}{5}\right)$

   i) $\dfrac{-4}{9} + \left(\dfrac{17}{-21}\right)$ j) $-\dfrac{5}{12} + \left(\dfrac{7}{-9}\right)$ k) $-\dfrac{32}{15} + \dfrac{19}{6}$ l) $\dfrac{14}{3} + \left(-\dfrac{31}{4}\right)$

11. Simplify.

a) $\dfrac{7}{9} - \dfrac{1}{6}$ b) $\dfrac{5}{6} - \dfrac{3}{10}$ c) $\dfrac{7}{8} - \dfrac{5}{12}$ d) $\dfrac{-5}{8} - \dfrac{3}{8}$

e) $\dfrac{17}{-20} - \left(\dfrac{-12}{20}\right)$ f) $\dfrac{-7}{8} - \left(\dfrac{-1}{4}\right)$ g) $\dfrac{9}{11} - \left(\dfrac{-3}{5}\right)$ h) $-\dfrac{16}{5} - \left(-\dfrac{7}{4}\right)$

12. Simplify.

a) $98.37 - (+102.89)$
b) $(-39.10) + (-9.22)$
c) $(-254.6) - (-748.9)$
d) $58.73 - (-102.99)$
e) $301.7 + (-76.8)$
f) $(-401.01) + (-0.96)$

13. Simplify.

a) $\dfrac{2}{3} \div \dfrac{5}{6} + \left(-\dfrac{1}{4}\right)$

b) $-\dfrac{5}{4} \times \dfrac{-2}{5} + \dfrac{2}{3}$

c) $-\dfrac{7}{6} - \dfrac{3}{5} \div \left(-\dfrac{6}{7}\right)$

d) $\dfrac{3}{8} \times \left(-\dfrac{4}{3}\right) + \dfrac{5}{8} \div \left(-\dfrac{3}{2}\right)$

14. Simplify.

a) $\dfrac{5}{2} - \dfrac{11}{3} + \dfrac{5}{4}$

b) $\dfrac{5}{2} - \dfrac{5}{4} \div \dfrac{5}{4}$

c) $\dfrac{-6}{5} + \left(\dfrac{10}{-2}\right)\left(\dfrac{-3}{5}\right)$

d) $\left[\dfrac{3}{-4} - \left(\dfrac{-3}{4}\right)\right] \div 2$ e) $-6\left(\dfrac{4}{5} - \dfrac{1}{2}\right)$ f) $\left(\dfrac{3}{5}\right)\left(-\dfrac{1}{2}\right)\left(\dfrac{-6}{3}\right) + \dfrac{1}{5}$

15. a) $-9.6 + (-3.2) \times 6.4 \div 1.6$

b) $\dfrac{-27.36}{-5.7} + (37.42)(-0.81)$

c) $(-88.7 + 43.9) \times (-65.96) \div 9.7$

d) $[(-15.5) + (6.2)(-3.4)] - (-7.7) \times (-8.2)$

16. Simplify.

a) $\left(\dfrac{3}{4}\right)\left(\dfrac{1}{-2}\right) + \left(\dfrac{5}{6}\right)\left(\dfrac{-1}{3}\right)$ $-\dfrac{47}{72}$

b) $\dfrac{3}{8} \times \dfrac{2}{3} - \left(\dfrac{1}{2}\right)\left(\dfrac{-5}{6}\right) + \left(\dfrac{3}{5}\right)\left(\dfrac{3}{-4}\right)$ $\dfrac{13}{60}$

c) $\left[\dfrac{5}{2} \div \left(\dfrac{-4}{5}\right)\right] - \left(\dfrac{3}{-4}\right)\left(\dfrac{-8}{9}\right)$ $-\dfrac{91}{24}$

17. For the years 1975 to 2000, the approximate population, P in thousands, of a city is given by this formula.
$P = (y - 1981)(1995 - y) + 500$
y is the year. Find the population in each year.
a) 1977   b) 1984   c) 1990   d) 1999

18. A car-rental firm uses the formula $C = 20.5D + 0.125(d - 80)$ to compute the cost, C dollars, to a customer who uses one of their cars for D days to travel d kilometres ($d > 80$). How much will a customer pay for using a car for 4 days and driving 800 km?

3 From Arithmetic to Algebra

A 4 m log is cut into 2 pieces. Suppose you knew the length of one piece. How could you find the length of the other piece? (See Section 3-5, *Example 1*.)

3-1 WHAT IS ALGEBRA?

A group of grade 9 students decided to participate in Junior Achievement. This involves setting up and running a business. The students decided to make trivets. After a few weeks, the students had a meeting to look at their sales figures. Here is a chart showing the sales for the first 3 weeks.

Trivets Sold	50	70	40
Profit	$300	$420	$240

How could the students calculate their profit if they knew how many trivets they sold?

We need to find a general rule relating the number of trivets sold and the profit. Notice that the profit in dollars is six times the number of trivets sold.

If we let t represent the number of trivets sold, then the profit is $6t$ dollars. This profit of $6t$ dollars represents many different amounts of money. Each amount depends on a value of t, which can vary. For this reason, t is called a *variable*.

The use of a letter to represent a number is the basis of *algebra*. Algebra is used to express patterns in arithmetic, in a general way.

Example 1. Suppose this pattern were continued.

a) How many toothpicks would be needed to make 10 triangles?
b) How could the number of toothpicks be found if the number of triangles were known?

Solution.
a) Identify the pattern. The number of triangles in a figure coincides with its position in the pattern. For example, the third figure has 3 triangles. Every triangle has 3 sides but adjacent triangles have a common side. In any figure, there is 1 toothpick to begin the pattern and each triangle adds 2 toothpicks. Therefore, to make 10 triangles, we would need 1 + 2(10) or 21 toothpicks.

b) For any number of triangles, we need to *generalize* the pattern found in part a). That is, the number of toothpicks is 1 more than twice the number of triangles.

If the pattern were to continue, how many toothpicks would there be on the 150th figure?

Example 2. A rectangle has a length of 16 cm.
a) Calculate the perimeter of the rectangle if its width is:
   i) 10 cm   ii) 8 cm   iii) 5 cm.
b) How could the perimeter of the rectangle be found if its width were known?
c) Write an expression for the perimeter of the rectangle in terms of a variable.

Solution. Draw a diagram.

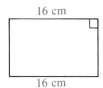

16 cm

16 cm

a) The perimeter is the distance around a rectangle.
   i) The width is 10 cm so the perimeter is [2(10) + 2(16)] cm or 52 cm.
   ii) The width is 8 cm so the perimeter is [2(8) + 32] cm or 48 cm.
   iii) The width is 5 cm so the perimeter is [2(5) + 32] cm or 42 cm.

b) To find the perimeter for any width, look for a pattern in part a) of the solution.
   The perimeter is the sum of twice the width, and 32.

c) Let w represent the width of the rectangle. Then, the perimeter is $(2w + 32)$ centimetres.

EXERCISES 3-1

(A)

1. Suppose this pattern were continued.

a) How many regions would there be in the 14th circle?
b) If the position of the circle in the pattern were known, how could the number of regions be found?

2. Suppose this pattern were continued.

a) On the 8th figure, how many squares are: i) shaded   ii) unshaded?
b) How could the number of unshaded squares be found if the number of shaded squares were known?

3. Suppose this pattern were continued.

```
X       OX      OOX      OOOX
        XO      OXO      OOXO
                XOO      OXOO
                         XOOO
```

a) On the 20th diagram, how many:
   i) Xs are there   ii) Os are there?
b) On any diagram, how could the number of Os be found if the number of Xs were known?
c) Let *a* represent the number of Xs. Write an expression for the corresponding number of Os.

(B)

4. A series of cubes are placed together as shown. The total number of faces that show are counted.

  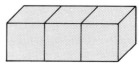

 5 faces   8 faces   11 faces

Suppose this pattern were to continue.
a) How many faces would show on the 12th diagram?
b) How many faces would show on the 30th diagram?
c) If the number of cubes were known, how could the number of faces be found?
d) Write an expression for the number of faces in terms of the number of cubes.

5. Suppose this pattern were continued.

a) How many shaded squares would there be on the 12th diagram?
b) How many unshaded squares would there be on the 12th diagram?
c) If the position of the diagram in the pattern were known, how could:
   i) the number of shaded squares be found
   ii) the number of unshaded squares be found?
d) i) Write an expression for the number of shaded squares in terms of the position of the diagram.
   ii) Write an expression for the number of unshaded squares in terms of the position of the diagram.

6. A cow is milked twice a day. Each time, she gives 11 kg of milk.
a) Calculate the total milk production after:
   i) 16 days   ii) 49 days   iii) 35 weeks.
b) If the number of days that the cow is milked is known, how can the amount of milk be found?
c) Write an expression for the amount of milk produced in terms of the number of days that the cow is milked.
d) If the total amount of milk is known, how can the number of milking days be found?
e) Write an expression for the number of days that the cow has been milked, in terms of the amount of milk produced.

7. The sum of the interior angles of each polygon is shown. Suppose this pattern were continued.

a) Calculate the sum of the interior angles of:
   i) a decagon   ii) a 15-sided polygon.
b) If the number of sides of a polygon is known, how can the sum of the interior angles be found?
c) Write an expression for the sum of the interior angles of a polygon in terms of the number of sides of the polygon.

8

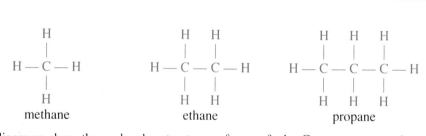

methane   ethane   propane

The diagrams show the molecular structures of some fuels. C represents a carbon atom and H represents a hydrogen atom. How can the number of hydrogen atoms in a molecule of octane be found, if the number of carbon atoms is 8?

9. Suppose this pattern were continued.

a) Which way will:
   i) the 20th arrow point   ii) the 33rd arrow point   iii) the 47th arrow point?

b) If the position of the arrow in the pattern is known, how can the direction of the arrow be found?

Ⓒ ───

10. Suppose this pattern were continued.

```
                           O
              O           OO
O            OO          OOO
XX           XXX         XXXX
```

a) How many Xs would there be on the 10th diagram?
b) How many Os would there be on the 10th diagram?
c) If the number of Xs were known, how could the number of Os be found?
d) Write an expression for the number of Os in terms of the number of Xs.

11. Suppose this pattern were continued.

  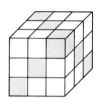 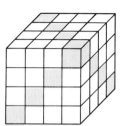

The cubes along one diagonal of each face of a cube are colored, as shown, including the diagonals of the faces that can't be seen.
a) How many cubes are colored on the 5th diagram?
b) How many cubes are plain on the 10th diagram?
c) If the position of the diagram in the pattern were known, how could:
   i) the number of colored cubes be found
   ii) the number of plain cubes be found?

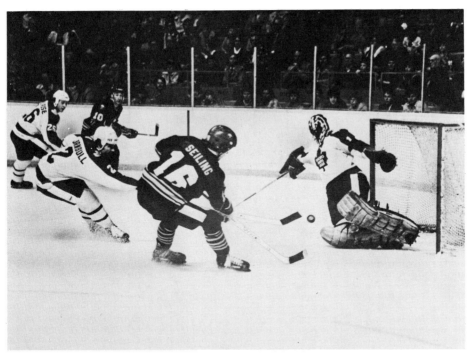

3-2 SUBSTITUTING IN ALGEBRAIC EXPRESSIONS

In hockey standings, 2 points are given for a win and 1 point is given for a tie. Suppose you knew the numbers of wins and ties that a hockey team had in a season. How could you find the total points?

Let w represent the number of wins and t represent the number of ties. The total points scored can be expressed as $2w + t$. This is an example of an *algebraic expression*; $2w$ and t are called the *terms* of this expression.

A term usually has a variable (or variables). The term $2w$ has the variable w. A term always has a *coefficient*. For example, $2w$ has the coefficient 2 and t has the coefficient 1, that is, t represents $1t$. When a term has the coefficient 1, it is not usually written as part of the term.

In the first half of the 1986/87 season, the Maple Leafs had 17 wins and 5 ties. The team's total points can be calculated by *substituting* into the algebraic expression $2w + t$.

Substitute 17 for w and 5 for t.

$$2w + t$$
$$= 2(17) + 5$$
$$= 34 + 5$$
$$= 39$$

The Maple Leafs had a total of 39 points for the first half of the 1986/87 hockey season.

Example 1.   Copy and complete.

Expression	Variables	Terms	Coefficients
$2m - 9n$			
$35x + 17y$			
$5a - 4b + 6c$			

Solution.

Expression	Variables	Terms	Coefficients
$2m - 9n$	m, n	$2m, -9n$	$2, -9$
$-35x + 17y$	x, y	$-35x, 17y$	$-35, 17$
$5a - 4b + 6c$	a, b, c	$5a, -4b, 6c$	$5, -4, 6$

Example 2.   Copy and complete.

a)

+	3	-1	x	w	$3d$
5	8	4	$x + 5$		
1				$w + 1$	
7					

b)

×	3	-1	x	w	$3d$
5	15	-5	$5x$		
1				w	
7					

Solution.

a)

+	3	-1	x	w	$3d$
5	8	4	$x + 5$	$w + 5$	$3d + 5$
1	4	0	$x + 1$	$w + 1$	$3d + 1$
7	10	6	$x + 7$	$w + 7$	$3d + 7$

b)

×	3	-1	x	w	$3d$
5	15	-5	$5x$	$5w$	$15d$
1	3	-1	x	w	$3d$
7	21	-7	$7x$	$7w$	$21d$

Example 3. Evaluate.

       a) $5x + 9$ for $x = 6$

       b) $3a - 7b$ for $a = -9$ and $b = 2$

       c) $2.6m$ for $m = 2.5$

Solution.   a) When $x = 6$, $5x + 9 = 5(6) + 9$

$$= 39$$

       b) When $a = -9$ and $b = 2$, $3a - 7b = 3(-9) - 7(2)$

$$= -41$$

       c) When $m = 2.5$, $2.6m = (2.6)(2.5)$

$$= 6.5$$

EXERCISES 3-2

1. Copy and complete.

	Expression	Variables	Terms	Coefficients
a)	$6p - 2q$			
b)	$a - 2b + 9c$			
c)	$1.8C + 32$			
d)	$2\pi r$			

2. Copy and complete.

a)

+	3	7	a	$2b$	ab
4					
9	v				
x	$x+3$	$7+x$	$x+a$	$2b+x$	$x+ab$
y	$4+3$	$y+7$	$y+a$	$y+2b$	$y+ab$
xy					

b)

×	3	7	a	$2b$	ab
4					
9			$9a$		
x		$7x$	$9a$		
y	$3y$	$7y$	$9x$		$9by$
xy	$3xy$	$7xy$	axy	$2bxy$	

3. The students at the John Cabot Secondary School write their examinations in the gymnasium. How many students can write at one time if:
   a) there are 11 rows and 32 desks in each row
   b) there are 11 rows and d desks in each row
   c) there are r rows and 32 desks in each row
   d) there are r rows and d desks in each row?

4. At a track and field meet, points are awarded as follows:
   first place — 5 points, second place — 3 points, third place — 1 point.
   How many points would be awarded for:
   a) 4 firsts, 2 seconds, and 6 thirds   b) x firsts
   c) y seconds   d) x firsts, y seconds, and z thirds?

5. Evaluate.
   a) $2x + 7$ for $x = 5$
   b) $28 - 5m$ for $m = -3.5$
   c) $9x - 4y$ for $x = -8$ and $y = 7$
   d) $8a + 19b$ for $a = 28$ and $b = -8$
   e) $8a - 4b - c$ for $a = 12$, $b = 18$, and $c = -3$
   f) $-3m + 5n - 6p$ for $m = -3$, $n = 4$, and $p = -5$

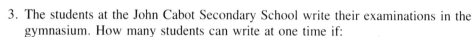

(B)

6. Evaluate.
   a) $2.3x + 0.7y$ for $x = 4$ and $y = -8$
   b) $0.27j - 3k$ for $j = 2.3$ and $k = 0.09$
   c) $3.7a - 2.1b$ for $a = 4.8$ and $b = 3.7$
   d) $5m - 9.2n$ for $m = -2.8$ and $n = 0.6$
   e) $8.3r - 1.27s + 0.6t$ for $r = 0.8$, $s = -5$, and $t = -0.5$
   f) $-4.8d + 2.3f - 2.8g$ for $d = 1.1$, $f = -2.2$, and $g = 0.7$
   g) $-0.6p - 1.3q - 2.5r$ for $p = 2.5$, $q = 1.2$, and $r = 0$

7. Evaluate.
   a) $\frac{3}{4}c + \frac{5}{7}d$ for $c = 12$ and $d = -14$
   b) $\frac{5}{6}m - \frac{2}{9}n$ for $m = \frac{2}{5}$ and $n = \frac{3}{8}$
   c) $\frac{2}{5}x + \frac{1}{3}y$ for $x = \frac{3}{4}$ and $y = -\frac{4}{5}$
   d) $\frac{2}{5}p + \frac{2}{3}q$ for $p = \frac{1}{2}$ and $q = \frac{9}{22}$
   e) $\frac{3}{8}w + \frac{5}{6}y - \frac{3}{4}z$ for $w = \frac{1}{3}$, $y = -\frac{8}{15}$, and $z = \frac{2}{3}$
   f) $-\frac{1}{8}a - \frac{2}{7}b - \frac{3}{4}c$ for $a = \frac{4}{3}$, $b = -14$, and $c = -4$
   g) $-\frac{7}{10}d + \frac{3}{5}e + \frac{2}{15}f$ for $d = -\frac{5}{2}$, $e = -\frac{10}{7}$, and $f = \frac{5}{2}$

8. The cost, C dollars, of installing a steel-panel fence is given by this formula.
   $C = 7l + 15p + 80$
   l is the length of the fence in metres and p is the number of posts required. Find the total cost when:
   a) $l = 120$ and $p = 41$
   b) $l = 32$ and $p = 12$
   c) the fence is 65 m long and requires 25 posts
   d) 85 posts are required for a 250 m fence.

9. The formula for the curved surface area, A, of a cylinder is $A = 2\pi rh$ where r is its radius and h is its height. Find the curved surface area of a cylinder that has a radius 4 cm and a height 15 cm.

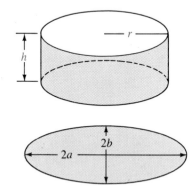

10. The area, A, of an ellipse is given by the formula $A = \pi ab$. Calculate the area when a is 31 cm and b is 19 cm.

11. The intelligence quotient (IQ) is a measure of a student's intellectual ability. The formula is $IQ = \dfrac{100m}{p}$, where m is the mental age and p the physical age. Calculate the IQ of a student who is:
    a) 14 years old with a mental age of 16
    b) 15 years old with a mental age of 13.

Ⓒ

12. A Canadian astronaut, Steve MacLean, predicts that there will be a permanent space station in orbit in the near future. The volume, V, of one proposed station is given by this formula.
    $V = \dfrac{1}{4}\pi^2(a^3 - a^2b - ab^2 + b^3)$
    a and b are the external and internal radii in metres. Find the volume of the space station if $a = 500$ and $b = 400$.

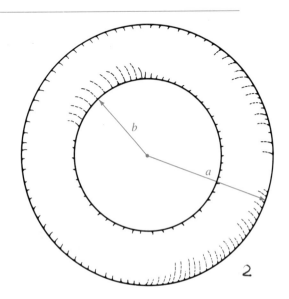

2

3-3 LIKE TERMS

Mrs. Zak wanted to fence her yard. She did not have a measuring tape long enough, so she used a long piece of wood to measure each side. Then, Mrs. Zak drew a plan of the yard. If she knew the length of the wood, how could she find the length of fencing she needed?

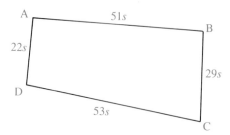

On the plan, the letter s represents the length of the wood.

For side AB, the wood was placed 51 times.
For side BC, the wood was placed 29 times.
For side CD, the wood was placed 53 times.
For side DA, the wood was placed 22 times.

The total number of times the wood was placed is $51 + 29 + 53 + 22$ or 155.

Mrs. Zak measured the piece of wood and it was 83 cm long. She calculated the length of fencing as $155(0.83)$ m or 128.65 m. She ordered 130 m of fencing.

Algebraic terms that have the same variable (or variables) such as $51s$, $29s$, $53s$, and $22s$ are called *like terms*.

The terms $3a$, $4b$, and $10c$ are *unlike terms* because they have different variables. Similarly, $2p$, $7q$, and 9 are unlike terms.

Like terms can be combined into a single term by adding (or subtracting) their coefficients.

Example 1. Simplify.

a) $2x + 3x$ b) $5a - a$ c) $12y + 6 + 3y$

Solution.   a) Since $2x + 3x$ means $x + x + x + x + x$, or $5x$,
then $2x + 3x = 5x$

b) Since $5a - a$ means $a + a + a + a + a - a$, or $4a$,
then $5a - a = 4a$

c) $12y + 6 + 3y = 12y + 3y + 6$
$\qquad\qquad\qquad\quad = 15y + 6$

$15y$ and 6 are unlike terms and cannot be combined.

Example 2. Simplify. $26x - 11y - 12x + 3x - 5y$

Solution. $26x - 11y - 12x + 3x - 5y$ can be written as
$(+26x) + (-11y) + (-12x) + (+3x) + (-5y)$
$= (+26x) + (+3x) + (-12x) + (-11y) + (-5y)$
$= (+29x) + (-12x) + (-16y)$
$= (+17x) + (-16y)$
$= 17x - 16y$

With practice, algebraic expressions can be simplified more directly.

Example 3. Simplify. $-6a + 14b - 13a + 7b + 10a - 11b$

Solution. $\quad -6a + 14b - 13a + 7b + 10a - 11b$
$= -6a - 13a + 10a + 14b + 7b - 11b$
$= -19a + 10a + 21b - 11b$
$= -9a + 10b$

At the beginning of this section, the lengths of the sides of a yard were
represented by like terms.

The perimeter of the yard can be found in two ways.

Method 1.

Perimeter $= 51s + 29s + 53s + 22s$
$\qquad\qquad = 155s$

Substitute 0.83 for s.

Perimeter $= 155(0.83)$
$\qquad\qquad = 128.65$

Method 2.

Perimeter $= 51s + 29s + 53s + 22s$

Substitute 0.83 for s.

Perimeter $= 51(0.83) + 29(0.83) + 53(0.83) + 22(0.83)$
$\qquad\qquad = 42.33 + 24.07 + 43.99 + 18.26$
$\qquad\qquad = 128.65$

These two methods illustrate that when substituting into an algebraic
expression, it is more efficient to simplify by collecting like terms first.

Example 4. Simplify then evaluate.
a) $14p - 5p$ for $p = -5$ b) $16y - 29y - 15$ for $y = 3.7$

Solution.   a) $14p - 5p = 9p$ b) $16y - 29y - 15 = -13y - 15$
When $p = -5$,   When $y = 3.7$,
$9p = 9(-5)$ $-13y - 15 = -13(3.7) - 15$
$ = -45$ $= -48.1 - 15$
          $= -63.1$

EXERCISES 3-3

Ⓐ

1. Simplify.
a) $4a + 7a$ b) $19m - 6m$ c) $-42x + 29x$
d) $14p - 5p$ e) $-21g - 16g$ f) $12b + 37b$
g) $6r + 47r - r$ h) $13w + w - 9w$ i) $36p - 29p - 24p$

2. Simplify.
a) $-7x + 5x + 8y - 3y$ b) $-18m + 7m + 6p - 11p$
c) $9a - 23b - 4a - 11b$ d) $52x + 31y - 31x - 2y$
e) $44u + 17v - 4v + 41u$ f) $-7j + 13k + 5j - k$
g) $4s + 5t - 19t - 37s$ h) $28x + 15y - 19x - 11y$
i) $-6a + 9b - 7c + 5b - 3a - c$ j) $14x - 17y - 5x - 11z - 6y - 2z$

Ⓑ

3. Simplify where possible.
a) $4m + 5 - 3m$ b) $2c + d - 3c - d$ c) $5a + 3b + 5a$
d) $3x + 2y$ e) $8u + 3v - 11v - 7$ f) $5m + 4$
g) $-7x + y - 2x$ h) $15x - 3y - 9x + z$ i) $10p - 5 + 8q - 3p - 2$

4. Simplify.
a) $23a - 42b - 18b + 17a$ b) $12x - 10y - 6x - 6y + x$
c) $45m + 15n - 7 - 5m - 5n$ d) $-32c + 10 - 15c + 4d - 3$
e) $23a + 7a - 13 - 2a$ f) $16x - 17y + x - y$
g) $-2a - 3b - a + 4$ h) $48p - 16q - 3r - 18p - 3r$

5. Simplify.
a) $16a - 3b + 5a + b$ b) $-3 + 2m - 13n - 3n + 2$
c) $-2z + 12 + 10y - 15 + 4z - 15y$ d) $13s - 16r - 4s - 6 + 10 + 3r$
e) $4 + 7x - 3y - 7 - y + 18x$ f) $-4x + 7m - 11x - 10m + 8$
g) $-q + 8q - 11p - 7q + 11p$ h) $-13c - 15d - 18d - 3$

6. Simplify.
a) $14p + 7s - 8r - 2x - 18s + 10r + 2p$
b) $-8z + 13p + 10x - 12z - x - 23p$
c) $5q - 7m + 6q - 11n + m - 8n + 7q$
d) $-10 + a - 13b + 8 - 15a + 2b - 17$
e) $0.3 + 1.5x - 7.0 + 2.4z - 1.0 - 1.3x + 8 - 1.4z$
f) $0.8 + 2.3m - 11.2n - 1.4 - 14.7n + 3.2m$

7. Simplify then evaluate.

a) $4a + 7a$ for $a = 3$

b) $19m - 6m$ for $m = -2.5$

c) $42x - 29x$ for $x = -7$

d) $-14p + 5p$ for $p = \dfrac{2}{3}$

e) $23b + 17b$ for $b = 5$

f) $-64k - 44k$ for $k = -\dfrac{3}{4}$

g) $4x - 7x - 11x$ for $x = 4$

h) $16y - 29y - 15y$ for $y = -\dfrac{1}{2}$

8. Write an expression for the perimeter of each figure.

a)

b)

c)

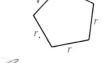

9. Simplify.

a) $3x + 7y - 2z - 6y - 5x - 4z + 12x - 5y$

b) $-10m + 3n - 4p - 7n - 5m - 8p + 17m$

c) $7c - 2a - 5c - 3b + 8a + 6b - 10c$

d) $4x - 6x + 5y - 7y + 3x - 4y - 12y - 7x$

10. Simplify.

a) $3x^2 + 2x - 5x + 4x^2$

b) $6x - x^2 - 4x - 3x^2$

c) $8a - 7b - 6a - 2b + 3ab$

d) $-9p - q^2 + 3r^2 + 4q^2 - 7r$

e) $4y^2 - 3y + 7 - 2y^2$

f) $-6b - 3c + 4c^2 - 6 - 6b$

g) $6x - 3x - 5x + x^2 - 5$

h) $7x^2 - 9b + 5m^2 - 8b - 7x + 1$

i) $-w^2 + 2v - 3w - 9v + 4w^2$

j) $-3a^2 - 3ab + 3b - 4a - 7ab + 3$

11. Simplify.

a) $3xy - 2yz + 5xz - 6yz + 4xy - 10xz$

b) $-4ab - 5bc + 3ac + 8ab - 6bc - 9ac$

c) $-3xyz + 4xyw - 5yzw + 8xyz + 5xyw - 6yzw$

12. Evaluate each expression for $x = 3$, $y = 2$, and $z = -1$.

a) $-3xy + 5yz - 2xz + 6xy + yz - 5xz$

b) $4x^2yz + 5xy^2z - 3xyz + 5xy^2z - 3x^2yz + 6xyz$

13. Write expressions for the perimeter and the area of each figure.

a)

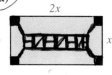

b)

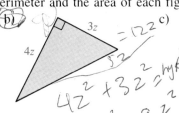

c)

PROBLEM SOLVING

Use a Variable

How old is Janet?

Understand the problem
- How old is Janet's father?
- Is Janet's father more than 3 times Janet's age?
- How many years older than 3 times Janet's age is her father?
- What are we asked to find?

Think of a strategy
- Use a variable to represent Janet's age.
- Express Janet's father's age in terms of the variable.

Carry out the strategy
- Let n represent Janet's age.
- Then, 3 times Janet's age is $3n$.
- To obtain father's age, we add 6 to $3n$.
  $\boxed{3n} \rightarrow \boxed{+6} \rightarrow \boxed{42}$
- To calculate $3n$ we reverse the flow chart.
  $\boxed{36} \leftarrow \boxed{-6} \leftarrow \boxed{42}$
- From a comparison of the flow charts, $3n = 36$ so $n = 12$.
  Janet is 12 years old.

Look back
- What is three times Janet's age plus 6?
- Is that the same as her father's age?
- Is 12 the only solution to the problem?

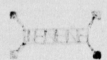

Solve each problem

1. What is the mass of each colored cube?

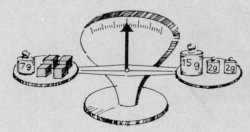

2. One-eighth of a number is 28.5 more than 76. What is the number?

3. The rental cost of a videocassette recorder is $25 plus a fixed daily amount. Ms. Singh was charged $64 for a 4-day rental period. What is the fixed daily rental fee?

4. Sung Choi saved his allowance for eight weeks. When he added to this the $15.50 he received for his birthday, he had a total of $61.50. How much allowance does he receive each week?

5. Margaret handed the cashier a $10 bill for the purchase of 3 tennis balls. After 54¢ tax was added, the clerk gave her $2.71 change. What was the cost of each tennis ball?

6. A rectangular table is twice as long as it is wide. How long is the table if its perimeter is 15.6 m?

7. A gold pen and pencil set cost $69.98. The pen costs $6.50 more than the pencil. What is the cost of the pencil?

8. The sum of two consecutive integers is 25. What are the two integers?

9. In an 18-game hockey tournament between Canada and the U.S.S.R., Canada won 4 more games than they lost. Since there was no tie, how many games did Canada win?

10. Find two integers with a sum of 8 and a difference of 42.

11. When 28 is added to seven times a number, the result is the same as if 16 were subtracted from eleven times that number. What is the number?

12. Find 3 consecutive integers with a sum of 375.

3-4 FROM PRODUCTS TO SUMS AND DIFFERENCES

Mr. Ying grows flowers and vegetables in a rectangular-shaped garden. He needs to buy fertilizer for his garden. Each bag of fertilizer is labelled with the area, in square metres, that the fertilizer should cover. Mr. Ying can calculate the area of his garden in two ways.

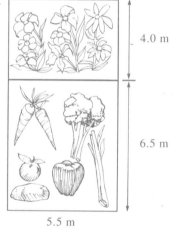

Method 1.
Total area $=$ width $\times$ length
$= 5.5(4.0 + 6.5)$
$= 5.5(10.5)$
$= 57.75$

Method 2.
Total area $=$ area with flowers $+$ area with vegetables
$= 5.5(4.0) + 5.5(6.5)$
$= 22.0 + 35.75$
$= 57.75$

The area of Mr. Ying's garden is about 60 m².
Since both methods gave the same area, it follows that
$5.5(4.0 + 6.5) = 5.5(4.0) + 5.5(6.5)$
This is an example of the *distributive law*. It shows a product expanded into a sum.

It can be shown that this law is true for a product expanded into a difference.
For example, consider $5(9 - 4) = 5(9) - 5(4)$

$$5(9 - 4) = 5(5) \qquad\qquad 5(9) - 5(4) = 45 - 20$$
$$= 25 \qquad\qquad\qquad\qquad\qquad = 25$$

This law can be written algebraically.

Distributive Law
$a(b + c) = ab + ac$
$a(b - c) = ab - ac$

Example 1. Use the distributive law to expand these products.

a) $6(x - 4)$ b) $3(4b + 8)$ c) $4(2x + y - 3)$

Solution. a) $6(x - 4) = 6(x) - 6(4)$
$$= 6x - 24$$

b) $3(4b + 8) = 3(4b) + 3(8)$
$$= 12b + 24$$

c) The distributive law can be extended to the sum or difference of more than two terms.
$$4(2x + y - 3) = 4(2x) + 4(y) - 4(3)$$
$$= 8x + 4y - 12$$

Some expressions must be expanded before they can be simplified.

Example 2. Simplify.

a) $12(3p + q) - 8(q + 2p)$
b) $1.5(2x - y) - 2.5(2y - x)$

Solution. a) Multiply both terms in the second bracket by -8.
$$12(3p + q) - 8(q + 2p) = 36p + 12q - 8q - 16p$$
$$= 20p + 4q$$

b) $1.5(2x - y) - 2.5(2y - x) = 3.0x - 1.5y - 5.0y + 2.5x$
$$= 5.5x - 6.5y$$

EXERCISES 3-4

1. Expand.
   a) $3(m - 8)$ b) $18(x + 5)$ c) $11(p + 7)$ d) $-23(a - 9)$
   e) $7(2p + 6)$ f) $4(a - b + 15)$ g) $-8(7a + b - 1)$ h) $6(2s + 11t - 5)$

2. Simplify.
   a) $5(m + 3) + 63$ b) $18(2x + 4) - 27$
   c) $14 - 3(6x + 7)$ d) $96 + 7(3a - 12)$
   e) $-17(3x + 5) - 2$ f) $7a - 3(2a - 9 - b)$
   g) $15e + 5(12 + e - 4f)$ h) $6t + 9(3t - 4) - 12t$
   i) $-2(5x - 7) - 3x - x$ j) $8w - 6(3w + 5) - 19$
   k) $-3(c + 4) + 2(2c - 3)$ l) $-12t + 3(5 - 2t) - 7$

3. Simplify.
   a) $5m - 2 + 3(4m + 1) - 2m$ b) $-4(2c + 5d) - 2(3c - 7d)$
   c) $5(a + 3) + 2(a - 5) + (a - 1)$ d) $4(2a + 5b + 3) - 3(6b - a - 1)$

4. Simplify.
   a) $3(2x + 5y) + 7(4x - 2y)$ b) $5(7x + 2y) - 3(2y - x)$
   c) $-5(3m + 6n) - 8(9m - 2n)$ d) $5(4a - 16b) + 2(17a - 29b)$
   e) $11(8k + 4l) + 3(13l - 2k)$ f) $3(p + 2q) - 7(2p + q)$
   g) $-11(3r + 2s) + 7(2r + q)$ h) $6(4u + 7v) - 9(u - w)$
   i) $10(3a + 2b + c) - 5(a - b + c)$ j) $-8(12x + 5y + 4) + 3(2x - 4y + 2)$

$(2 \times 7) + 9 \times 9 \div 3$

5. Simplify.
   a) $0.5(4x + 6y) + 1.5(6x + 2y)$
   b) $-1.4(3x + 5y) - 2.8(5x + 2y)$
   c) $2.6(15x + 5y) - 5.2(5x - 3y)$
   d) $-3.8(5y + x) + 7.5(4x + y)$

6. Write the area of each shaded region as a sum or difference of terms.
   a)
   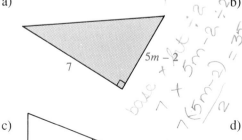
   b)
   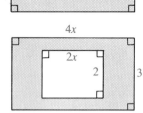

   c)
   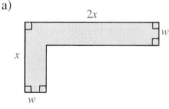
   d)
   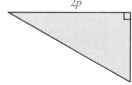

Ⓒ

7. Simplify.
   a) $3a(x - y) - 5a(y - x)$
   b) $8c(b - 3a) - 2c(b - a)$
   c) $4x(x^2 - 2x + 3) - 5x^2(x^2 - x)$
   d) $2x(y - x) + (y - 2x^2)$
   e) $3x - 5y(x - y) + y^2$
   f) $4p(q - p) - (p^2 - q^2)$
   g) $x(x - y) - 3y(y - x)$
   h) $6a(a + b) + 3b(b - a)$

8. Write the area of each shaded region as a sum or difference of terms.
   a)
   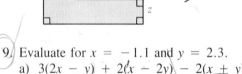
   b)
   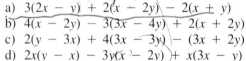

   c)
   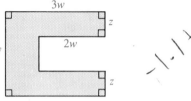
   d)

9. Evaluate for $x = -1.1$ and $y = 2.3$.
   a) $3(2x - y) + 2(x - 2y) - 2(x + y)$
   b) $4(x - 2y) - 3(3x - 4y) + 2(x + 2y)$
   c) $2(y - 3x) + 4(3x - 3y) - (3x + 2y)$
   d) $2x(y - x) - 3y(x - 2y) + x(3x - y)$

3-5 TRANSLATING WORDS INTO SYMBOLS

Five students in Mrs. Iverson's class each invested the same amount in stocks in September. They are now reviewing their gains and losses.
● Ian lost $16.
● Linda gained $7.
● Maria has two-and-a-half times her initial investment.
● Ravi gained $9.
● Susan has half of what she started with.
Suppose you knew how much the students started with. How could you find out whether, collectively, they now have more than or less than that?

This problem is most easily solved with algebra. Let x dollars represent each student's initial investment. Then, an algebraic expression can be written for the amount each student has now.

Student	Verbal Expression	Algebraic Expression
Ian	A loss of $16	$(x - 16)$ dollars
Linda	A gain of $7	$(x + 7)$ dollars
Maria	2.5 times the initial investment	$2.5x$ dollars
Ravi	A gain of $9	$(x + 9)$ dollars
Susan	Half of the initial investment	$0.5x$ dollars

The total amount the students have now is:

$$(x - 16) + (x + 7) + 2.5x + (x + 9) + 0.5x$$
$$= x - 16 + x + 7 + 2.5x + x + 9 + 0.5x$$
$$= x + x + 2.5x + x + 0.5x - 16 + 7 + 9$$
$$= 6x$$

The students started with x dollars each or $5x$ dollars together. Now they have $6x$ dollars. Collectively, the students have more than they started with.

By translating verbal expressions into algebraic expressions, the problem was solved without knowing the initial investment.

Study these verbal expressions and their algebraic equivalents.

Verbal Expression	Algebraic Expression
four more than a number	$n + 4$
a number increased by eight	$p + 8$
nine less than a number	$a - 9$
twice a number	$2d$
one-sixth of a number	$\frac{1}{6}s$ or $\frac{s}{6}$
five more than four times a number	$4f + 5$
the product of one more than a number, and seven	$7(n + 1)$
three less than five times a number	$5l - 3$

Sometimes, two numbers are related. Suppose one of these numbers is known. How can the other number be found? One number can be represented by a variable and the other number expressed in terms of this variable.

Example 1. Choose a variable to represent one quantity. Express the other quantity in terms of this variable.
  a) Two consecutive integers
  b) Two numbers which differ by five
  c) Mary's age now, and in six years
  d) The lengths of the pieces if a 4 m log is cut in two

Solution. a) Two consecutive integers
   Let l represent the lesser integer.
   Then, the greater integer is $(l + 1)$.
   Alternatively, let j represent the greater integer.
   Then, the lesser integer is $(j - 1)$.

  b) Two numbers which differ by five
   Let n represent the greater number.
   Then, the lesser number is $(n - 5)$.
   Can you think of an alternative way to describe the numbers?

  c) Mary's age now, and in six years
   Let a years represent Mary's age now.
   Then in 6 years, Mary will be $(a + 6)$ years old.

  d) The lengths of the pieces of a 4 m log cut into two
   Let l metres represent the length of one piece.
   Then, the length of the other piece is $(4 - l)$ metres.

Example 2. Express each quantity in terms of the variable.
  a) The value in cents of n quarters
  b) The value in dollars of x five-dollar bills
  c) The number of centimetres in k metres
  d) The number of minutes in t hours

Solution. a) The value in cents of n quarters
      1 quarter has a value of 25¢.
      n quarters have a value of $n(25¢)$ or $25n$ cents.

  b) The value in dollars of x five-dollar bills
      1 five-dollar bill has a value of $5.
      x five-dollar bills have a value of $x($5)$ or $5x$ dollars.

  c) The number of centimetres in k metres
      1 metre has a length of 100 cm.
      k metres have a length of $k(100$ cm$)$ or $100k$ centimetres.

  d) The number of minutes in t hours
      1 hour is 60 min.
      t hours are $t(60$ min$)$ or $60t$ minutes.

EXERCISES 3-5

Ⓐ

1. Write an algebraic expression for each verbal expression.
  a) five more than a number
  b) six less than a number
  c) eight times a number
  d) one-fifth of a number
  e) the product of a number and eight
  f) four more than five times a number
  g) two less than eight times a number
  h) the product of two less than a number, and eight
  i) the sum of one-fourth of a number, and three
  j) one-fourth of the sum of a number and three

2. Express each quantity in terms of the variable.
  a) The number of seconds in m minutes
  b) The number of grams in k kilograms
  c) The value in cents of n nickels
  d) The value in dollars of x two-dollar bills
  e) The number of hours in m minutes
  f) The distance in metres of c centimetres

3. Write a verbal expression for each algebraic expression.
  a) $p + 6$ b) $q - 10$ c) $\frac{1}{4}r$ d) $10s$ e) $4 + \frac{3}{10}t$

  f) $3u + 2$ g) $4v - 5$ h) $2(w - 3)$ i) $\frac{1}{3}(x + 5)$ j) $x(x - 3)$

4. Choose a variable to complete the first statement. Using that variable, write an expression that completes the second statement.
   a) Clyde is 12 years older than Bonnie.
      Let Bonnie's age be represented by ▓ years. Then, Clyde's age is ▓ years.
   b) Ian's mass is 1.5 kg less than that of Sean.
      Let Sean's mass be represented by ▓ kilograms. Then, Ian's mass is ▓ kilograms.
   c) A 30 m log is cut into two pieces of unequal lengths.
      Let the length of the longer piece be represented by ▓ metres.
      Then, the length of the shorter piece is ▓ metres.

Ⓑ

5. Write an algebraic expression to complete each statement.
   a) The heights, in centimetres, of Lim and David are consecutive integers. Lim is the taller of the two.
      Let David's height be represented by ▓ centimetres.
      Then, Lim's height is ▓ centimetres.
   b) The ages of Alan, Becky, and Carmen are three consecutive numbers.
      Alan is the oldest and Carmen is the youngest.
      Let Carmen's age be represented by ▓ years.
      Then, Becky's age is ▓ years. Alan's age is ▓ years.
   c) Two numbers have a product of 36.
      Let one number be represented by ▓. Then, the other number is ▓.
   d) Stefa's marks on two tests are consecutive even integers.
      Let one mark be represented by ▓. Then, the other mark is ▓.

6. Express each quantity in terms of the variable.
   a) The area in square centimetres of A square metres
   b) The area in square millimetres of B square centimetres
   c) The volume in cubic centimetres of V cubic metres
   d) The area in square centimetres of M square millimetres

7. Choose a variable to represent one quantity and express the other quantity (or quantities) in terms of the first.
   a) The ages of two brothers if one brother is twelve years older than the other
   b) Two numbers where one number is one-fifth of the other
   c) The ages of Angelo and Mary whose total age is 21 years
   d) The lengths of the jumps if Joan's jump was 15 cm longer than Enid's
   e) The speeds of the two cars if the Jaguar travelled 1.1 times as fast as the Mercedes
   f) Two numbers with a product of 76
   g) Three consecutive integers
   h) Three consecutive odd integers

Ⓒ

8. Choose a variable to represent one quantity and express the other quantity in terms of the first.
   a) Anita's age doubled is 4 years less than Ron's age tripled.
   b) Five times one number is 7 more than eight times a smaller number.
   c) Gloria is now twice as old as Chad was 9 years ago.

Review Exercises

1. Suppose this pattern were continued.

   a) How many matchsticks would be needed to make 12 squares?
   b) How could the number of matchsticks be found if the number of squares were known?
   c) Let s represent the number of squares. Write an expression for the number of matchsticks needed to make s squares.

2. Suzy has a Saturday job where she works 8 h a day and is paid $5/h.
   a) How much money does Suzy make in 1 week?
   b) How much money does Suzy make in 12 weeks?
   c) Suzy wants to buy a stereo system, which will cost $160. How many weeks will she have to work to earn this money?
   d) If the amount of money earned is known, how could:
      i) the number of days worked be found
      ii) the number of hours worked be found?

3. For the expression $6x + 4y - 3z$, list:
   a) the terms   b) the variables   c) the coefficients.

4. Evaluate.
   a) $9 + 3y$ for $y = 16$
   b) $8s - 7$ for $s = 5.4$
   c) $5p + 8q$ for $p = 13$ and $q = -6$
   d) $6s - t$ for $s = -1.7$ and $t = 2.9$
   e) $14u + v - 9w$ for $u = -6$, $v = 29$, and $w = 12$
   f) $21s + 4t$ for $s = 0.4$ and $t = -1.2$

5. Simplify.
   a) $23x - 11x$ b) $4m + 13m$
   c) $15x - 9x + 3x$ d) $12a + 4b - 5a + 3b$
   e) $9x + 4y - x - 2y$ f) $14c + d - 3d + 11c$
   g) $6m - 5m - 5n + 5n$ h) $17w + 8x - 7x - 8w$
   i) $8.5e + 1.5e - 6.2f + 5.7f$ j) $-3.6d + 4.7c - 5.8c - 1.2d$

6. Evaluate.
   a) $\frac{9}{4}x - 3y$ for $x = \frac{2}{3}$ and $y = \frac{3}{8}$

   b) $7y + 9y - 4y$ for $y = \frac{9}{4}$

   c) $3.2x + 4.1y - z$ for $x = 0.3$, $y = -1.1$, and $z = 2.4$

   d) $\frac{3}{8}a - \frac{2}{5}b + \frac{5}{2}c$ for $a = \frac{5}{3}$, $b = \frac{3}{8}$, and $c = -\frac{4}{25}$

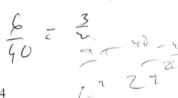

7. Simplify.
   a) $3x - 5x - 3$
   b) $-4a + 3b - 6a$
   c) $5p - 7q - 8p$
   d) $-11m - 9n - 2n + 6m$
   e) $16f - 3e + 10g - 6e$
   f) $-8d - 10b + 2c + 4d$

8. Simplify.
   a) $2(5a + 7) + 17$
   b) $2(3x + 5y) - 4x$
   c) $-7(3x - 2y) - 5(3y - 4x)$
   d) $5(2m + 7n) + 3(m - 4n)$
   e) $-3(2x + 4y) + 3(x - y)$
   f) $7(r + 3s) - 2(2r - 9s)$

9. Simplify.
   a) $4m - 3n - 15 + 14n - 2 + 6n$
   b) $-11 + 3b - 7a + 13 - 8b + 10a$
   c) $10x - 3z + 14 - 11y + 2z - 22$
   d) $14d - 23e + 11d - 16 + 5e$
   e) $4.8x - 3.2y + 2.4z + 1.7y - 3.9x$
   f) $-5.7b + 4.1a - 1.1b + 3.5b - 9.2a$

10. Write an expression for the area of each shaded region.
    a)
    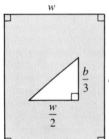
    b)
    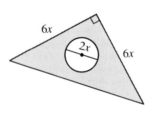
    c)
    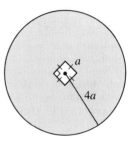

11. Write an algebraic expression for each verbal expression.
    a) one-tenth of a number
    b) eleven times a number
    c) twenty more than a number
    d) thirty-one less than a number
    e) fourteen more than five times a number
    f) the sum of one-seventh of a number, and nineteen

12. Choose a variable to represent one quantity and express the other quantity in terms of the first.
    a) The cost of two cars if one is $1300 more than the other
    b) Two consecutive odd numbers
    c) Three consecutive even numbers
    d) The heights of two trees if one is 2.6 m shorter than the other
    e) Two numbers with a sum of 37.8
    f) The lengths of the pieces of wood if a 15 m log is cut into two
    g) Two numbers which have a difference of 0.4
    h) The ages of two boys if Raj's age is four years less than twice Egino's age

1. Write as an integer.
   a) a gain of $17
   b) a loss of 3 points
   c) a decrease of 12°C
   d) a credit of $425
   e) a drop of 12 m
   f) 210 m below sea level

2. Simplify.
   a) $(-14) + (-23)$
   b) $(+9) - (-26)$
   c) $(+31) + (-48)$
   d) $(-28) - (+17)$
   e) $(-12) + (+35)$
   f) $(-19) - (-11)$

3. Simplify.
   a) $(+7)(-9)$
   b) $(-8)(-5)$
   c) $(-60) \div (-12)$
   d) $(-21)(-7)$
   e) $(-225) \div (+25)$
   f) $(+240) \div (-30) \div (-2)$

4. Simplify.
   a) $\dfrac{(+5)(-8)}{(-4)} + \dfrac{(-4)(-6)}{(+3)}$
   b) $15 - (+8)(-3)$
   c) $(+12)(-5 + 9) - (-3 - 7)$
   d) $14 + (-5) - 3(2 - 9)$
   e) $\dfrac{6 + 15}{-7} - \dfrac{-4 + 19}{3}$
   f) $\dfrac{19 - 28}{-3} - \dfrac{(-11) + 27}{4} + \dfrac{6 - 32}{-2}$

5. Arrange in order from least to greatest.
   a) $-4, \dfrac{5}{2}, \dfrac{22}{3}, -17, 6, -\dfrac{5}{4}, -3$
   b) $12, -4.5, -2.3, \dfrac{17}{5}, -7, -\dfrac{2}{3}, 1.25$

6. Express each rational number as a decimal.
   a) $\dfrac{2}{5}$
   b) $-\dfrac{3}{8}$
   c) $\dfrac{17}{-6}$
   d) $\dfrac{11}{7}$
   e) $\dfrac{-19}{-12}$

7. Express each decimal as a fraction in lowest terms.
   a) 3.25
   b) −7.6
   c) 1.875
   d) −2.145
   e) −11.03

8. Simplify.
   a) $-\dfrac{7}{10} \div \dfrac{2}{-5}$
   b) $\dfrac{-32}{15} \times \dfrac{-25}{-44}$
   c) $-12.25 \div 3.5$
   d) $\dfrac{-21}{16} \div \dfrac{-7}{8} \times \dfrac{3}{-4}$
   e) $(4.2)(-3.5) \div (-2.1)$
   f) $\dfrac{18}{-5} \times \dfrac{10}{-27} \div \dfrac{-9}{2}$

9. Simplify.
   a) $-4.21 + 13.7$
   b) $\dfrac{-9}{4} - \dfrac{-3}{8}$
   c) $\dfrac{-16}{9} + \dfrac{5}{-6}$
   d) $\dfrac{-8}{-15} + \dfrac{3}{-10} - \dfrac{2}{3}$
   e) $3.17 - 5.04 - 1.317$
   f) $\dfrac{11}{6} - \dfrac{4}{3} - \dfrac{-15}{9}$

10. Simplify.
    a) $\dfrac{7}{8} + \left(-\dfrac{3}{4}\right)\left(\dfrac{5}{6}\right)$
    b) $2.17 - \dfrac{9.6}{3.2}(7.6 - 4.3)$
    c) $\left(-\dfrac{5}{8} - \dfrac{1}{2}\right) \times \left(\dfrac{7}{9} - \dfrac{2}{3}\right)$
    d) $\dfrac{17}{5} + \dfrac{-13}{10} - \dfrac{5}{8}\left(\dfrac{-4}{-15}\right)$
    e) $\dfrac{5.6}{-0.14} + \dfrac{7.2}{1.8} - \dfrac{-4.5}{-0.9}$
    f) $\dfrac{11}{18} + \left(\dfrac{-7}{3}\right) - \left(\dfrac{2}{5}\right)\left(\dfrac{-3}{4}\right)$

11. The volume of a cylinder is given by the formula $V = \pi r^2 h$, where r is the radius of the cylinder and h is its height. Find the volume of corn in a full silo, which has a radius of 3.4 m and a height of 8.9 m.

12. A series of tins are stacked as shown. Suppose the pattern were continued.

   a) How many tins would there be on the bottom row of:
      i) the 7th diagram   ii) the 11th diagram?
   b) How many tins would there be in:
      i) the 7th diagram   ii) the 11th diagram?
   c) Write an expression for the number of tins in terms of the position of the diagram.

13. Evaluate.
   a) $\frac{3}{4}x - 5$ for $x = -12$
   b) $3m + 7n - 11m - 5n$ for $m = -4$ and $n = 2$
   c) $1.7x - 4.3y$ for $x = -3$ and $y = 5$
   d) $\frac{-7}{8}a - \frac{5}{3}b + \frac{1}{2}a + \frac{2}{3}b$ for $a = \frac{4}{3}$ and $b = -\frac{2}{5}$
   e) $\frac{5}{4}p + \frac{3}{2}q - \frac{4}{5}r$ for $p = -\frac{2}{3}$, $q = \frac{4}{3}$ and $r = -2$

14. Simplify.
   a) $-7p - 4q - 12p - 5q$
   b) $16x + 7y - 8z - 12x - 15y + 3z$
   c) $3.6a - 2.5b - 1.4a + 3.8b - 7.2a$
   d) $-4x + 11y - 17y + 9x - 3y$
   e) $12m - 4n - 7m - 9n - 8m + 6n$

15. Simplify.
   a) $3a - 2(5a + 4b) - 3b$
   b) $5(4m - 3n) - 8m - 7n$
   c) $-2(7x + 4y) + 6(2x - 5y)$
   d) $8(-3p - 9q) - 3(4p - 12q)$
   e) $2(5c - 3d + e) + 6(c + 2d - 4e) - (3c - d + 2e)$
   f) $-11(3x - 2y + z) - 5(2x + 4y - 9z) + 4(x - 8y - 7z)$

16. Write an algebraic expression for each verbal expression.
   a) the sum of a number and eleven
   b) six times a number, decreased by four
   c) the sum of two consecutive numbers
   d) the difference between a number and twenty-one
   e) eight, plus three times a number
   f) three-quarters of a number, subtracted from ten

4 Solving Equations

If a car's rate of fuel consumption is known, how can the fraction of highway driving be determined? (See Section 4-5.)

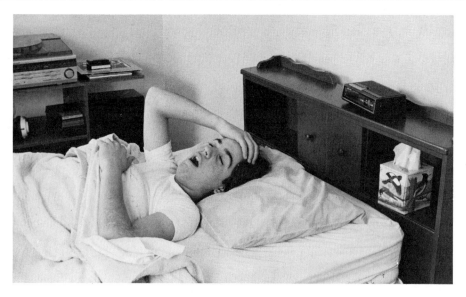

4-1 SOLVING SIMPLE EQUATIONS

The amount of sleep, n hours, that a 15-year-old person needs is given by this equation.

$15 = 34 - 2n$

To find how much sleep is needed at this age, a value must be found for n which *satisfies* this equation. There is exactly one value of n that will make both sides of the equation the same. Finding this value is called *solving* the equation.

The right side of the equation must equal the left side.
So, 34 minus twice a number must equal 15.
We know that 34 minus 19 equals 15.
Hence, twice the number must equal 19.

So, the number must be $\dfrac{19}{2}$ or 9.5.

A 15-year-old person needs 9.5 h sleep.
When an equation is solved in this way, it is called *solving by inspection*.

Example 1. Solve by inspection.

      a) $56 - n = 21$ b) $7d = 28$

Solution.   a) $56 - n = 21$
            This means, ''56 less some number is 21.''
            The number that is subtracted from 56 to give 21 is 35.
            Hence $n = 35$

          b) $7d = 28$
            This means, ''7 times some number is 28.''
            The number that is multiplied by 7 to give 28 is 4.
            Hence $d = 4$

Only very simple equations should be solved by inspection. Another method of solving equations is by *systematic trial*. Systematic trial means substituting values for the variable until the value which satisfies the equation is found.

Example 2. Solve by systematic trial. $54 - 7y = 26$

Solution. A value of y must be found such that $54 - 7y$ equals 26.

Suppose $y = 5$, $54 - 7y = 54 - 7(5)$
$$= 54 - 35$$
$$= 19$$

When $y = 5$, the value of $54 - 7y$ is less than 26.

Try $y = 3$. $\quad 54 - 7y = 54 - 7(3)$
$$= 54 - 21$$
$$= 33$$

When $y = 3$, the value of $54 - 7y$ is greater than 26.

Try $y = 4$. $\quad 54 - 7y = 54 - 7(4)$
$$= 54 - 28$$
$$= 26$$

The solution is $y = 4$.

The method of systematic trial can be a long one. It is the method used by computers to solve more complicated equations.

EXERCISES 4-1

Ⓐ

1. Solve by inspection.
   a) $x + 17 = 32$ b) $29 - x = 12$ c) $x - 7 = 27$ d) $x + 26 = 61$
   e) $43 + x = 79$ f) $11 - x = 11$ g) $15 - x = 0$ h) $20 + x = 15$

2. Solve by inspection.

   a) $4z = 24$ b) $7s = -63$ c) $12q = 132$ d) $\frac{1}{3}y = 12$

   e) $8v = 4$ f) $0.5w = 25$ g) $\frac{1}{4}x = \frac{1}{2}$ h) $0.7t = 3.5$

3. Solve by inspection.
   a) $m - 3.5 = 5$ b) $-8 + x = 12$ c) $t + 2.4 = 5.4$ d) $-9 + q = 7$
   e) $w - 3.6 = 5$ f) $1.3 + z = 3.3$ g) $2.5 - a = 1.5$ h) $1.1 - x = 0.6$

4. Solve by systematic trial.
   a) $3 + 2n = 11$ b) $7 + 3m = 13$ c) $7x - 5 = 30$ d) $4c - 1 = 23$
   e) $24 - 3y = 15$ f) $9k - 27 = 36$ g) $7m - 99 = 6$ h) $7 + 13d = 72$

Ⓑ

5. Solve.
   a) $2x + 7 = 17$ b) $28 - 5m = 18$ c) $6a - 4 = 20$
   d) $9 + 3y = 57$ e) $8s - 7 = 153$ f) $11t + 9 = 130$
   g) $40 - 13v = 1$ h) $110 - 9u = 2$ i) $15 = 3 - 2x$
   j) $-27 = 4a + 1$ k) $31 = -2 - 3y$ l) $-40 = -4 + 4z$

6. The number of hours of sleep that an 18-year-old person needs is given by the value of n in the equation $18 = 34 - 2n$. Solve the equation for n.

7. The rate, in chirps per minute, at which a cricket chirps at 30°C is given by the value of r in the equation $210 = r + 28$. Solve the equation for r.

8. The distance, in kilometres, that a taxi travels for a fare of $9.65 is given by the value of d in the equation $9.65 = 1.40 + 0.75d$. Solve the equation for d.

4-2 ISOLATING THE VARIABLE

An equation is a mathematical sentence that uses an equals sign to relate two expressions.

To solve an equation, it is helpful to think of a level balance. The masses in each pan can be changed but as long as the total masses on both sides are the same, the balance remains level. The same rule applies to equations.

> Whatever change is made to one side of an equation must also be made to the other side.

These changes are made to reduce an equation to its solution in the form $x = a$. In this form, the variable is said to be *isolated*.

Example 1. Solve. $x + 4 = 10$

Solution. $x + 4 = 10$ means $x + 4$ balances 10.
Subtract 4 from both sides to isolate x.
$x + 4 - 4 = 10 - 4$
$\qquad x = 6$

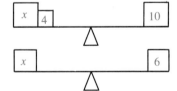

Example 2. Solve. $y - 3 = 18$

Solution. $y - 3 = 18$ means $y - 3$ balances 18.
Add 3 to both sides to isolate y.
$y - 3 + 3 = 18 + 3$
$\qquad y = 21$

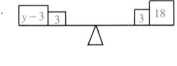

> To solve an equation in the form $x + a = b$, where a and b are numbers, isolate x by subtracting a from both sides.
>
> To solve an equation in the form $x - a = b$, where a and b are numbers, isolate x by adding a to both sides.

Example 3. Solve.

a) $\dfrac{z}{3} = 10$ b) $-2p = 12$

Solution.

a) $\dfrac{z}{3} = 10$

Multiply both sides by 3 to isolate z.

$\dfrac{z}{3}(3) = 10(3)$

$z = 30$

b) $-2p = 12$
Divide both sides by -2 to isolate z.

$\dfrac{-2p}{-2} = \dfrac{12}{-2}$

$p = -6$

To solve an equation in the form $\dfrac{x}{b} = c$, where b and c are
numbers ($b \neq 0$), isolate x by multiplying both sides by b.

To solve an equation in the form $bx = c$, where b and c are
numbers ($b \neq 0$), isolate x by dividing both sides by b.

EXERCISES 4-2

(A)

1. Solve.
   a) $x + 5 = 11$ b) $z - 3 = 10$ c) $y + 7 = 16$ d) $m - 4 = 9$
   e) $a - 11 = 25$ f) $x + 17 = 23$ g) $w - 23 = 61$ h) $p + 19 = 47$

2. Solve.
   a) $\dfrac{x}{5} = 2$ b) $3x = 21$ c) $\dfrac{z}{3} = -4$ d) $5w = 35$ e) $\dfrac{1}{9}m = 5$

   f) $6x = 54$ g) $11a = 88$ h) $\dfrac{y}{4} = -8$ i) $\dfrac{1}{3}p = 18$ j) $7b = 98$

   k) $8a = 128$ l) $-7a = 91$ m) $\dfrac{c}{10} = 80$ n) $\dfrac{x}{12} = 132$ o) $\dfrac{1}{8}x = -9$

3. Solve.
   a) $m + 13 = 9$ b) $x - 4 = -10$ c) $a - 8 = 2$ d) $p + 11 = 5$
   e) $s + 19 = 14$ f) $w - 7 = -18$ g) $y - 3 = 0$ h) $m - 14 = -37$

(B)

4. Solve.

a) $\dfrac{w}{4} = 13$ b) $\dfrac{m}{7} = 4$ c) $5x = -35$ d) $7y = 91$ e) $\dfrac{1}{5}p = 3$

f) $\dfrac{1}{13}x = \dfrac{2}{13}$ g) $\dfrac{x}{7} = -9$ h) $-4s = -28$ i) $-56 = 8p$ j) $\dfrac{x}{-7} = -8$

5. Solve.
   a) $4 + y = -9$ b) $-8 = 2 + x$ c) $3 = y - 5$ d) $20 = 10 + z$
   e) $-11 = n + 21$ f) $-2 = x - 14$ g) $13 + x = 13$ h) $5.2 = 3.7 + p$

6. Solve.

a) $9.3 = a - 2.7$ b) $z - \dfrac{1}{4} = \dfrac{7}{4}$ c) $12 = m - 45$ d) $\dfrac{5}{2} = x + \dfrac{3}{4}$

e) $4.5 = -2.3 + x$ f) $-52 = 27 + y$ g) $q - \dfrac{9}{4} = \dfrac{43}{8}$ h) $\dfrac{2}{5} = a + \dfrac{3}{10}$

7. Solve.

a) $48 = -6y$ b) $-12 = \dfrac{x}{2}$ c) $13x = 169$ d) $5 = \dfrac{n}{15}$

e) $8.5 = 1.7m$ f) $2.5y = -10$ g) $72 = 18m$ h) $\dfrac{9}{4} = \dfrac{x}{12}$

8. A daytime, operator-assisted telephone call from Toronto to Calgary costs $18.40.
   The time, in minutes, for the call is given by the value of t in this equation.
   $18.40 = 0.80 + 1.10t$
   Find how long the call lasted.

9. A car is rented for one day and the charge at the end of the day is $172.95. The
   distance driven, in kilometres, is given by the value of d in this equation.
   $172.95 = 28.50 + 0.15d$
   Find how far the car was driven.

10. A loan company charges a flat rate of $50 to process a loan and charges interest at
    the rate of 27.5% per annum on the principal. After 1 year, the amount a person
    has to pay back is $2600.00. The principal, in dollars, is given by the value of
    p in this equation.
    $2600.00 = 50.00 + 1.275p$
    Find how much the person borrowed.

(C)

11. Solve for x.
    a) $x + a = b$ b) $x - c = d$ c) $3x = m$

    d) $\dfrac{1}{4}x = w$ e) $a - b = x + 2b$ f) $\dfrac{x}{4} = c - d$

    g) $2y + x = z$ h) $b - 2a = c - x$ i) $-ax + b = c$

    j) $n = m - kx$ k) $-b - cx = d$ l) $-p - \dfrac{x}{q} = -r$

4-3 SOLUTIONS REQUIRING SEVERAL STEPS

Many equations require more than one step to isolate the variable. To solve these equations, isolate the term that contains the variable first.

Example 1. Solve.

a) $-5w + 9 = 21$ b) $7.3 = 6.6y - 15.8$

Solution. a) $-5w + 9 = 21$

Subtract 9 from both sides.

$$-5w + 9 - 9 = 21 - 9$$

$$-5w = 12$$

Divide both sides by -5.

$$\frac{-5w}{-5} = \frac{12}{-5}$$

$$w = -\frac{12}{5}$$

b) $7.3 = 6.6y - 15.8$

Add 15.8 to both sides.

$$7.3 + 15.8 = 6.6y - 15.8 + 15.8$$

$$23.1 = 6.6y$$

Divide both sides by 6.6.

$$\frac{23.1}{6.6} = \frac{6.6y}{6.6}$$

$$3.5 = y$$

It may be necessary to expand, using the distributive law, to solve an equation.

Example 2. Solve. $23.98 = 11(1.10w + 2.07)$

Solution. $23.98 = 11(1.10w + 2.07)$

Expand the right side.

$$23.98 = 12.10w + 22.77$$

Subtract 22.77 from both sides.

$$23.98 - 22.77 = 12.10w + 22.77 - 22.77$$

$$1.21 = 12.10w$$

Divide both sides by 12.10.

$$\frac{1.21}{12.10} = \frac{12.10w}{12.10}$$

$$0.1 = w$$

Example 3. The cost, C dollars, of taking n students on a weekend trip to Ottawa is given by this formula.

$$C = 180 + 35n$$

The cost was \$1685. How many students went on the trip?

Solution.

$$C = 180 + 35n$$

Substitute 1685 for C.

$$1685 = 180 + 35n$$

Solve for n. Subtract 180 from both sides.

$$1685 - 180 = 180 + 35n - 180$$
$$1505 = 35n$$

Divide both sides by 35.

$$\frac{1505}{35} = \frac{35n}{35}$$
$$43 = n$$

43 students went on the trip.

EXERCISES 4-3

Ⓐ

1. Solve.
   a) $2w - 5 = 11$
   b) $5n - 8 = 12$
   c) $8 - 2u = 12$
   d) $0 = 7p - 35$
   e) $-9p - 81 = 0$
   f) $10 = -3x - 5$
   g) $-11z - 2 = 20$
   h) $3 - 2y = -7$
   i) $-9 = 8b - 1$
   j) $17 = 5q + 2$
   k) $8 - 3z = -1$
   l) $-13 = 4p - 1$

2. Solve.
   a) $8t + 7 = -10$
   b) $9p - 2 = 6$
   c) $-5r + 6 = 8$
   d) $4x + \frac{3}{4} = \frac{7}{4}$
   e) $3x - \frac{1}{4} = 2$
   f) $-1 = 7x - \frac{5}{12}$
   g) $10t - \frac{2}{5} = \frac{3}{5}$
   h) $7x + \frac{5}{4} = -3$
   i) $11x - \frac{1}{2} = \frac{3}{2}$
   j) $9t - \frac{3}{5} = -\frac{6}{5}$
   k) $1 = 8s - \frac{1}{3}$
   l) $\frac{7}{6} + 8t = \frac{13}{6}$

Ⓑ

3. Solve.
   a) $\frac{1}{3}r - 3 = -6$
   b) $\frac{1}{4}x + 6 = 10$
   c) $\frac{1}{7}x - 1 = \frac{9}{7}$
   d) $1.5x - 3 = -12$
   e) $2.5y + 3 = -8$
   f) $1 = 3.8x - 0.9$
   g) $4.4y + 3 = 5.64$
   h) $1.3w + 65 = 26$
   i) $12.5z - 36 = 64$

4. Solve.
   a) $12 = 9 - 2t$
   b) $23 = 11 - 3r$
   c) $8 - 3z = -19$
   d) $5y + \frac{3}{5} = 3$
   e) $7x - \frac{5}{9} = 3$
   f) $\frac{5}{16} = \frac{11}{16} - \frac{1}{4}x$
   g) $0.2x + 4 = 7$
   h) $-1 = 5 - 0.3t$
   i) $0.25p + 0.25 = 0.5$

5. Solve.

   a) $\dfrac{2}{5}t + 3 = 11$ b) $\dfrac{n}{3} + 4 = -6$ c) $-\dfrac{3}{4}z + 5 = -1$

   d) $1.2(2x - 3) = 7.2$ e) $-3.5(1 + 3r) = 7$ f) $3\left(5.6 + \dfrac{x}{3}\right) = 0$

6. Solve.

   a) $4(x - 2) = 9$ b) $-3 = 5(z + 7)$ c) $-\dfrac{2}{3}(x + 1) = 6$

   d) $-3\left(y - \dfrac{1}{2}\right) = \dfrac{1}{2}$ e) $0.02 = 0.8(y + 0.1)$ f) $1.2(t + 2.3) = 3.96$

   g) $0.6(5s - 6) = 2.4$ h) $1.21 = 11(0.51 + 0.4x)$ i) $2.4(6.7 + 1.2x) = 24.72$

7. If $3w = 6 - 9z$, find:

   a) the value of w for each given value of z
      i) 1   ii) -2 iii) 0.5   iv) -1.4 v) 0

   b) the value of z for each given value of w.
      i) 0   ii) -1 iii) 2.2   iv) -19 v) 110

8. To determine how far away the centre of a storm is, count the number of seconds, t, between a flash of lightning and the sound of thunder. Substitute this value for t in the formula $d = \dfrac{8t}{25}$ to find d, the distance in kilometres.

   a) Find how far away the storm is when the time lapse is:
      i) 5 s   ii) 10 s   iii) 3.5 s.

   b) Find the time lapse when the storm is:
      i) 8 km away   ii) 6 km away.

Ⓒ

9. Typing speed, S, in words per minute, is calculated with the formula $S = \dfrac{w - 10e}{5}$, where w is the number of words typed in 5 min and e is the number of errors made in the same period.

   a) Find how many words must be typed in 5 min if, when 5 errors are made, the typing speed is 40 words/min.

   b) Find how many errors are made for the typing speed to be 30 words/min when 180 words are typed in 5 min.

10. Weekly mathematics tests have 15 questions. Each question has either one, two, or three parts.

   a) If, on one test, 9 questions have one part, 4 questions have two parts, and 2 questions have three parts, how many parts are there altogether?

   b) If a test has a total of 29 parts, 6 questions having one part and 5 questions having three parts, how many questions have two parts?

   c) One test has 8 questions, each with only one part and there is a total of 24 parts. How many questions have two parts and how many have three?

PROBLEM SOLVING

Write an Equation

An anthropologist discovered the bones of a
huge fish with a head that was 9 m long.
The tail was as long as the head, plus half
the length of the body.
The body was as long as the head and tail
combined.
How long was the fish?

Understand the problem
- How long was the head?
- How long was the tail?
- What are we asked to find?

Think of a strategy
- Write an equation to relate what we are asked to find, to the
  information given.

Carry out the strategy
- Choose a variable l to represent the length of the body in metres.

- The length of the tail is $\left(9 + \frac{1}{2}l\right)$ metres.

- We know that: length of head $+$ length of tail $=$ length of body

  that is,
  $$9 + \left(9 + \frac{1}{2}l\right) = l$$

- Solve the equation for l.
  $$18 + \frac{1}{2}l = l$$
  $$18 = \frac{1}{2}l$$
  $$l = 36$$

- The body is 36 m long.
  Length of fish $=$ length of head $+$ length of body $+$ length of tail
  $$= 9 + 36 + 9 + \frac{1}{2}(36)$$
  $$= 72$$
  The fish was 72 m long.

Look back
- Calculate the length of the tail in two ways. Are the answers the
  same?

Solve each problem

1. The lengths of the sides of an isosceles triangle are shown in the diagram (below left). Find the value of x.

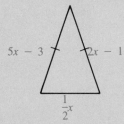

		19
51	50	
		82

2. All rows, columns, and diagonals of a magic square have the same sum. Complete the magic square (above right).

3. Kim lives at the bottom of a mountain. It took her 6 h to ride to the top of the mountain and back. Her average speed up the mountain was 6 km/h and her average speed down the mountain was 24 km/h. How long did it take Kim to ride down the mountain?

4. Peanuts worth $2.80/kg are mixed with pecans worth $4.20/kg. How many grams of each should be mixed to produce a 1 kg mixture worth $3.36?

5. A rectangular walk is a line of 9 identical square cement tiles. The perimeter of the walk is 20 m. What is the area of each cement tile?

6. The total mass of a can and the paint it contains is 5 kg when half full, and 4 kg when one-third full. What is the total mass when the can is:
   a) empty   b) full of paint?

7. A shopkeeper sets retail prices at $p\%$ above cost. On a special sale he reduces these prices by 20%. At these prices he makes no profit. What is the value of p?

8. If a block weighs 7 kg plus half a block, what is the mass of a block and a half?

9. Eric and Lois are trading hockey cards. If Eric gives one card to Lois, they will have the same number. If Lois gives one card to Eric, he will have twice as many as she. How many cards does each person have to start with?

10. The mass of a candy-bar wrapper is $\dfrac{1}{11}$ the mass of the wrapped bar. If the candy bar alone has a mass of 75 g, what is the mass of the wrapper?

11. The sum of the digits of a two-digit number is 9. When the digits are interchanged, the number is decreased by 45. What is the number?

4-4 COMBINING TERMS CONTAINING THE VARIABLE

To solve an equation, it is necessary to isolate the variable on one side of the equation. The numerical terms are combined on the other side of the equation. When several terms contain the variable they must be combined, too.

Example 1. Solve.

    a) $6x - 5 = 2x + 7$ b) $2 - 3y = 7 + y$

Solution.   a) $6x - 5 = 2x + 7$

        Subtract $2x$ from both sides.

$$6x - 5 - 2x = 2x + 7 - 2x$$
$$4x - 5 = 7$$

        Add 5 to both sides.

$$4x - 5 + 5 = 7 + 5$$
$$4x = 12$$

        Divide both sides by 4.

$$\frac{4x}{4} = \frac{12}{4}$$
$$x = 3$$

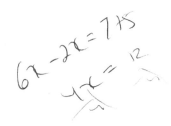

    b) $2 - 3y = 7 + y$

        Add $3y$ to both sides.

$$2 - 3y + 3y = 7 + y + 3y$$
$$2 = 7 + 4y$$

        Subtract 7 from both sides.

$$2 - 7 = 7 + 4y - 7$$
$$-5 = 4y$$

        Divide both sides by 4.

$$\frac{-5}{4} = \frac{4y}{4}$$
$$-\frac{5}{4} = y$$

    These examples illustrate that it doesn't matter on which side of the equation the variable is isolated.

    Sometimes it is necessary to expand before combining the terms and isolating the variable.

Example 2.   Solve.

a) $5(y - 1) = 7(3 + y)$ b) $3(y - 1) - 5y = 2y - (y - 2)$

Solution.   a)

$$5(y - 1) = 7(3 + y)$$
$$5y - 5 = 21 + 7y$$
$$5y - 5 - 5y = 21 + 7y - 5y$$
$$-5 = 21 + 2y$$
$$-5 - 21 = 21 + 2y - 21$$
$$-26 = 2y$$
$$\frac{-26}{2} = \frac{2y}{2}$$
$$-13 = y$$

b)

$$3(y - 1) - 5y = 2y - (y - 2)$$
$$3y - 3 - 5y = 2y - y + 2$$
$$-2y - 3 = y + 2$$

Add 3 to, and subtract y from, both sides.

$$-2y - 3 + 3 - y = y + 2 + 3 - y$$
$$-3y = 5$$
$$\frac{-3y}{-3} = \frac{5}{-3}$$
$$y = -\frac{5}{3}$$

EXERCISES 4-4

Ⓐ

1. Solve.
   a) $7x - 3 = 4x + 3$
   b) $5y + 9 = 2y - 3$
   c) $-4m + 2 = 6m + 12$
   d) $-8t - 5 = -9t - 7$
   e) $3r - 2 = -5r + 14$
   f) $6p - 7 = -6p - 7$
   g) $5 - y = 3 - 2y$
   h) $9 - 2x = 6 - x$
   i) $3 - 2t = 5 - 5t$
   j) $4 - p = 5 - 3p$
   k) $7 - 5p = 6 + p$
   l) $8 - 3r = -6 + r$
   m) $-11 + 6v = -6v + 11$
   n) $-8w = -4 - 6w$

Ⓑ

2. Solve.
   a) $3(x - 1) = 12$
   b) $5(x + 2) = 10$
   c) $-14 = x - 3$
   d) $x - 2 = 2(x - 1)$
   e) $3y - 2 = y + 4$
   f) $4y = -2(9 - y)$
   g) $y + 7 = 3y - 9$
   h) $9y - 3 = 3(y - 4)$

3. Solve.
   a) $2(t - 3) = -3(t - 1)$
   b) $-3(r + 2) = -4(r - 1)$
   c) $7(z + 3) = 5(z - 1)$
   d) $4(2y - 1) = 5(3y + 1)$
   e) $-3(4p + 2) = 4(2p - 2)$
   f) $-2(1 - x) = -3(2 - x)$
   g) $6(-2 - x) = -5(2x + 4)$
   h) $2.5(2 - 3x) = 1.5(3x - 2)$

4. Solve.
   a) $6y - 2 = 5y + 4$ b) $3p + 2 = 5p - 7$
   c) $4 - r = 3 - 2r$ d) $9 - 2p = -8 - p$
   e) $5(x - 1) = 8(1 - x)$ f) $7(y - 2) = 13$
   g) $-2(x - 1) = 3(x + 2)$ h) $-3(y + 1) = -2(y - 1)$
   i) $r - 1 = 5r - 7$ j) $19t - 13 = 2t + 4$
   k) $17y + 3 = 15y - 3$ l) $z - 2 = 2z - 2$
   m) $x + 4 = 11x + 4$ n) $t - 8 = -12t + 18$

5. Solve.
   a) $4(x - 2) + 5 = 3 + 2(x - 3)$ b) $1 + 5(x - 1) = 4(x - 3) + 6$
   c) $-2(m + 4) = 3(5 - m) - 8$ d) $y + 3(y - 6) = 2(3 - y) + 3y$
   e) $3(n - 2) + 12 = 6n - 3(4 - n)$ f) $11 - 2(5 + 3x) = 2(x - 6) + 14$

4-5 EQUATIONS WITH FRACTIONAL COEFFICIENTS

Consider the problem posed at the beginning of the chapter. A car uses gasoline at an average rate of 10.9 L/100 km. The fraction of driving that the car does on the highway is given by the value of f in this equation.

$$10.9 = \frac{-36f}{5} + \frac{29}{2}$$

To find the fraction of highway driving, solve the equation for f.

$$10.9 = \frac{-36f}{5} + \frac{29}{2}$$

Multiply both sides by the common denominator 10.

$$10(10.9) = 10\left(\frac{-36f}{5} + \frac{29}{2}\right)$$

$$109 = 10\left(\frac{-36f}{5}\right) + 10\left(\frac{29}{2}\right)$$

$$109 = -72f + 145$$

$$109 - 145 = -72f + 145 - 145$$

$$-36 = -72f$$

$$\frac{-36}{-72} = \frac{-72f}{-72}$$

$$\frac{1}{2} = f$$

Half the car's driving is done on the highway.

When an equation contains fractions, multiply both sides of the equation by a common denominator of the fractions to obtain an equivalent equation without fractions.

Example 1. Solve. $\dfrac{a}{3} - 3 = \dfrac{3}{4}a + \dfrac{1}{2}$

Solution.
$$\dfrac{a}{3} - 3 = \dfrac{3}{4}a + \dfrac{1}{2}$$

Multiply both sides by the common denominator 12.

$$12\left(\dfrac{a}{3} - 3\right) = 12\left(\dfrac{3a}{4} + \dfrac{1}{2}\right)$$

$$12\left(\dfrac{a}{3}\right) - 12(3) = 12\left(\dfrac{3a}{4}\right) + 12\left(\dfrac{1}{2}\right)$$

$$4a - 36 = 9a + 6$$

$$4a - 36 - 4a - 6 = 9a + 6 - 4a - 6$$

$$-42 = 5a$$

$$-\dfrac{42}{5} = \dfrac{5a}{5}$$

$$-\dfrac{42}{5} = a$$

Example 2. Solve. $\dfrac{3x + 2}{2} - \dfrac{x + 1}{3} = x$

Solution.
$$\dfrac{3x + 2}{2} - \dfrac{x + 1}{3} = x$$

Multiply both sides by 6.

$$6\left(\dfrac{3x + 2}{2} - \dfrac{x + 1}{3}\right) = 6(x)$$

$$\dfrac{6(3x + 2)}{2} - \dfrac{6(x + 1)}{3} = 6x$$

$$9x + 6 - 2x - 2 = 6x$$

$$7x + 4 = 6x$$

$$7x + 4 - 7x = 6x - 7x$$

$$4 = -x$$

$$\dfrac{4}{-1} = \dfrac{-x}{-1}$$

$$-4 = x$$

EXERCISES 4-5

Ⓐ

1. Solve.

a) $\dfrac{a}{4} = \dfrac{1}{2}$

b) $\dfrac{x}{5} = -\dfrac{2}{3}$

c) $\dfrac{1}{3} = \dfrac{-2x}{5}$

d) $\dfrac{1}{2}x + \dfrac{1}{3}x = 10$

e) $\dfrac{1}{4}y - \dfrac{1}{2}y = 4$

f) $\dfrac{y}{3} - \dfrac{2}{3} = 4$

g) $\dfrac{2}{5}a + \dfrac{a}{2} = a - 2$

h) $\dfrac{1}{2}n - \dfrac{2}{3}n + \dfrac{3}{4}n = -7$ i) $\dfrac{x}{3} + \dfrac{1}{2} = -2x$

2. Solve.

a) $-\dfrac{1}{3}x + \dfrac{3}{4}x = 10$ b) $\dfrac{3}{5}x - \dfrac{3}{2}x = 10$ c) $\dfrac{2a}{3} = \dfrac{3a}{5} + 4$

d) $\dfrac{2}{3}x + 9 = \dfrac{3}{4}x - 6$ e) $\dfrac{5x}{2} - 3 = 8 + \dfrac{2x}{3}$ f) $5 - \dfrac{4}{3}x = \dfrac{3}{4}x + \dfrac{5}{2}$

3. Nicole's car uses gasoline at a rate of 11.3 L/100 km. The fraction of driving that Nicole does on the highway is given by the value of f in this formula.

$$11.3 = -\dfrac{25}{4}f + \dfrac{69}{5}$$

Find the fraction of driving that Nicole does on the highway.

B

4. Solve.

a) $\dfrac{a}{5} - a = \dfrac{1}{2}$ b) $\dfrac{2x}{3} = \dfrac{x}{2} - \dfrac{1}{4}$

c) $\dfrac{m}{6} - 5 = \dfrac{1}{2}m$ d) $\dfrac{3k}{4} + \dfrac{1}{2} = \dfrac{k}{3}$

e) $\dfrac{1}{3}(x + 1) = \dfrac{1}{2}(x - 2)$ f) $\dfrac{1}{5}(2n + 1) = \dfrac{2}{3}(n - 1)$

g) $\dfrac{a + 5}{3} = \dfrac{3 - a}{7}$ h) $\dfrac{1}{5}\left(\dfrac{1}{2}x + 4\right) = \dfrac{1}{3}\left(\dfrac{1}{4}x + 3\right)$

i) $\dfrac{1}{4}(2 - x) + \dfrac{1}{2} = \dfrac{1}{2}\left(\dfrac{1}{3}x + 7\right)$ j) $-\dfrac{1}{2}(x - 2) + \dfrac{1}{4} = \dfrac{2}{5}(2 - x)$

5. Solve.

a) $\dfrac{4x}{5} - \dfrac{3}{2} = \dfrac{2}{3} + \dfrac{1}{3}x$ b) $\dfrac{1}{4}(x - 3) + \dfrac{1}{3}(3 + x) = 1$

c) $-\dfrac{x}{3} + \dfrac{x}{4} - \dfrac{x}{6} = \dfrac{1}{10}$ d) $-\dfrac{1}{6}(3 - 5x) = \dfrac{2}{3}(5x + 3)$

e) $-\dfrac{3}{4}x - \dfrac{4x}{5} + \dfrac{7x}{10} = \dfrac{-1}{20}$ f) $-\dfrac{3}{7} = \dfrac{5}{14}(4 - 6x) + \dfrac{2x}{7}$

g) $\dfrac{7}{8}(-x - 6) + \dfrac{3}{4}(2x + 3) = \dfrac{-3}{8}$ h) $\dfrac{3x}{10} - \dfrac{2x}{5} = \dfrac{3x}{2} + \dfrac{1}{2}$

i) $\dfrac{11}{2}(7x - 6) = -\dfrac{1}{4}x + \dfrac{9}{2}(3 - 2x)$ j) $-\dfrac{3}{2}(7 - 4x) = \dfrac{2}{7}x - \dfrac{1}{2}(-3x + 4)$

6. If $y = -\dfrac{3}{5}x - \dfrac{1}{4}$, find:

a) the value of y for each given value of x

   i) 0 ii) $\dfrac{1}{3}$ iii) $-\dfrac{1}{3}$ iv) 2 v) -2

b) the value of x for each given value of y.

   i) 0 ii) $\dfrac{1}{2}$ iii) $-\dfrac{1}{2}$ iv) 1.5 v) -1.5

4-6 CHECKING SOLUTIONS

Solving an equation may require several steps. As the number of steps increases, the greater is the chance of an error. For this reason it is wise to check that the solution is correct. To do this
- Substitute the solution for the variable in each side of the original equation.
- Simplify each side of the equation independently.

The solution is correct if each side of the equation simplifies to the same number.

Example 1. Check that $y = -3$ is the solution of the equation $6y + 5 = 4y - 1$.

Solution. $6y + 5 = 4y - 1$

Substitute -3 for y in each side of the equation and simplify each side independently.

Left side $= 6y + 5$ Right side $= 4y - 1$
$\qquad = 6(-3) + 5$ $\qquad = 4(-3) - 1$
$\qquad = -18 + 5$ $\qquad = -12 - 1$
$\qquad = -13$ $\qquad = -13$

Each side simplifies to the same number.
Hence, $y = -3$ is correct.

Example 2. Solve and check. $3(x - 2) = 5(x + 6)$

Solution. $3(x - 2) = 5(x + 6)$

$3x - 6 = 5x + 30$

$3x - 6 + 6 - 5x = 5x + 30 + 6 - 5x$

$-2x = 36$

$\dfrac{-2x}{-2} = \dfrac{36}{-2}$

$x = -18$

Check. Substitute -18 for x in each side of the equation.

Left side $= 3(x - 2)$ Right side $= 5(x + 6)$
$\qquad = 3(-18 - 2)$ $\qquad = 5(-18 + 6)$
$\qquad = 3(-20)$ $\qquad = 5(-12)$
$\qquad = -60$ $\qquad = -60$

Since the left side equals the right side, $x = -18$ is correct.

EXERCISES 4-6

1. Solve and check.
   a) $2(x + 1) = 3x$
   b) $3(2 - m) = m + 2$
   c) $3 - y = y - 7$
   d) $4a + 6 = 2a - 2$
   e) $2 - x = 5x + 8$
   f) $3m - 5 = 2m + 1$
   g) $3k - 5 = k - 4$
   h) $\dfrac{1}{2}a + 3 = \dfrac{2}{3}a$
   i) $\dfrac{1}{4}(c + 2) = \dfrac{1}{3}(c - 1)$

(B)

2. Solve and check.
   a) $8(y - 5) = 7y$
   b) $-6(3 - x) = -9x - 6$
   c) $9 - v = v - 9$
   d) $8w - 4 = 4 - 8w$
   e) $-5t - 2 = 11t + 16$
   f) $11 - p = 3p - 21$
   g) $6(q + 1) = 3(q - 1)$
   h) $3 - (6s - 15) = 4s + 8$
   i) $-3(2x - 1) - 7 = -41 - 2(x + 0.5)$
   j) $\frac{1}{5}(y + 3) - \frac{5}{4} = \frac{1}{4}(y - 1)$

3. Solve and check.
   a) $3(y - 2) + 6 = 2(y - 3) - 5$
   b) $\frac{1}{2}(m + 3) - 4 = \frac{1}{3}(4 - m) + 7$
   c) $-(a - 7) + 6 = 5(3 - a) - 8$
   d) $3(x - 6) + 2 = 4(x + 2) - 21$
   e) $\frac{1}{4}(8m + 4) - 17 = -\frac{1}{2}(4m - 8)$
   f) $-\frac{1}{3}(6a + 24) = 20 - \frac{1}{4}(12a - 72)$
   g) $0.2t - 0.4 + 0.4t = -0.1t + 0.6$
   h) $0.25(8y + 4) - 17 = -0.5(4y - 8)$
   i) $-1.03 - 0.62m = 0.71 - 0.22m$
   j) $0.125w - 8(3.75 - 0.375w) = -0.875w$

I N V E S T I G A T E

1. Consider the equation $3(x + 2) = x + 2(x + 3)$.
   a) Check that $x = 5$, $x = 8$, and $x = -1$ are all solutions of the equation.
   b) Choose any other number and check that it also is a solution of the equation.
   c) Attempt to solve the equation. Can you suggest why every number is a solution of this equation?
   d) Give another example of an equation like this one, which has infinitely many solutions.

2. Consider the equation $3(x + 2) = x + 2(x + 4)$
   a) Choose any number and show that it is *not* a solution of the equation.
   b) Attempt to solve the equation. Can you explain why it does not have a solution?
   c) Give another example of an equation like this one, which has no solution.

3. *Without solving* these equations, can you tell which have infinitely many solutions, which have no solution, and which have exactly one solution?
   a) $5(n + 2) = n + 6(n - 3)$
   b) $2(p + 1) - 3 = 4(2p + 1) - 11$
   c) $2(y + 1) = y + (1 + y)$
   d) $5(x - 2) = x + 4(x - 3) + 2$
   e) $4(q - 1) = q + 3(q + 3)$
   f) $6(r + 2) = 3r + 3(r - 4)$

4-7 WORKING WITH FORMULAS

After working out, Michelle wonders if her pulse rate of 150 beats per minute exceeds the maximum for her age. She uses the formula $a = 220 - m$, where a is a person's age in years and m is the maximum desirable pulse rate in beats per minute.

Michelle substitutes 15 for a and solves the equation.

$$15 = 220 - m$$
$$-205 = -m$$
$$m = 205$$

The maximum desirable pulse rate for a 15-year-old is 205 beats per minute. Michelle's rate of 150 beats per minute is well below this maximum.

Recall that formulas are equations which relate two or more variables using the basic operations of arithmetic. Science, engineering, and industry use many formulas. Often, the values of all but one of the variables are known. It is necessary to substitute the known values into a formula, and then solve the equation to find the value of the unknown variable.

Example 1. The annual simple interest, I dollars, on a principal, P dollars, is given by this formula. $I = 0.095P$

Find the principal that earned $807.50 interest in one year.

Solution. $I = 0.095P$

Substitute 807.50 for I.

$$807.50 = 0.095P$$

Divide both sides by 0.095.

$$\frac{807.50}{0.095} = P$$

$$8500 = P$$

The principal is $8500.

Example 2. A scientific experiment illustrates that a rubber band stretches according to this formula.

$l = 9.2 + 0.17m$

l is the length of the band in centimetres, and m is the mass in grams, suspended on one end of the band.

a) Calculate the length, to the nearest centimetre, of the rubber band when the mass on the end is 25 g.

b) Calculate the mass, to the nearest gram, that will stretch the band to 86 cm.

Solution.   a) $l = 9.2 + 0.17m$

Substitute 25 for m.

$l = 9.2 + 0.17(25)$

$\quad = 13.45$

The band is about 13 cm long.

b) $\quad l = 9.2 + 0.17m$

Substitute 86 for l.

$\quad 86 = 9.2 + 0.17m$

Solve for m.

$76.8 = 0.17m$

$\dfrac{76.8}{0.17} = m$

$m \doteq 452$

A mass of 452 g will stretch the band to 86 cm.

To find the masses which correspond to several lengths of the rubber band, it is more efficient to solve the equation for m before substituting.

$l = 9.2 + 0.17m$

$l - 9.2 = 0.17m$

$\dfrac{l - 9.2}{0.17} = m$

For other types and thicknesses of rubber, the constant term and the coefficient in this formula would be different. Thus, the general formula for stretching any type of rubber band might be given by this formula.

$l = a + bm$

a and b are constants with values depending on the type of rubber band.

An equation of this type, in which the constants are represented by letters, is called a *literal* equation.

Example 3. a) Solve for F. $C = \frac{5}{9}(F - 32)$

b) Solve for x. $ax + 3c = d$

Solution.   a) $C = \frac{5}{9}(F - 32)$

$$9C = 5(F - 32)$$
$$9C = 5F - 160$$
$$9C + 160 = 5F$$
$$F = \frac{9C + 160}{5}$$

b) $ax + 3c = d$
$$ax = d - 3c$$
$$x = \frac{d - 3c}{a}$$

EXERCISES 4-7

1. The monthly interest, I dollars, on a loan is given by the formula $I = 0.0175P$, where P is the principal. Find the first month's interest on a principal of $1250.

2. The yearly interest, I dollars, is given by the formula $I = 0.11P$, where P is the principal.
   a) Find the interest for one year on each principal.
      i) $100   ii) $1000   iii) $2500   iv) $9000
   b) Find the principal which yields each interest, in one year.
      i) $22   ii) $55   iii) $132   iv) $159.50

3. Solve for x.

   a) $mx + n = p$ b) $\frac{1}{2}x - c = d$ c) $ax - b = d$

   d) $\frac{2}{3}x + 3 = k$ e) $wx + 1 = v$ f) $a - bx = d$

4. Solve for the variable indicated.

   a) $I = Prt$, for t b) $P = 2l + 2w$, for l c) $A = \frac{1}{2}bh$, for b

   d) $C = 2\pi r$, for r e) $l = a + bm$, for m f) $A = 50 + 1.275P$, for P

5. The area, A, of a parallelogram is given by the formula $A = bh$, where b is the length of the base and h is the height.
   a) Find the area of a parallelogram with base 10.3 cm and height 13.6 cm.
   b) Find the height of a parallelogram with area 25.2 cm² and base 5.6 cm.

Ⓑ

6. A person's maximum desirable pulse rate, m beats per minute, can be found from the formula, $m = 220 - a$ if a, the person's age, is known.
   a) Find the maximum desirable pulse rate for a person of each age.
      i) 20 years   ii) 37 years   iii) 63 years
   b) Find the age of a person corresponding to each maximum desirable pulse rate.
      i) 170 beats/min   ii) 192 beats/min   iii) 141 beats/min

7. When an object falls freely from rest, its approximate speed, v metres per second after t seconds, is given by the formula $v = 9.8t$.
   a) Solve the formula for t.
   b) Find the time, to the nearest tenth of a second, it will take the object to reach these speeds.
      i) 54 m/s   ii) 81 m/s   iii) 343 m/s   iv) 1 km/s

8. When the temperature at sea level is $t°C$, the approximate temperature at an altitude h metres is $T°C$, where $T = t - 0.0065h$.
   a) It is 15°C at sea level. Find the temperature, to the nearest degree, at each altitude. i) 1600 m   ii) 4000 m   iii) 12 000 m
   b) The temperature at sea level is 15°C. At what altitude, to the nearest metre, will the temperature be $-8°C$?

9. A company determines the age at which an employee can retire with full pension, from the formula $a + b = 90$, where a is the employee's age and b is the number of years of service.
   a) Find the years of service for retirement with full pension at each age.
      i) 60 years   ii) 65 years   iii) 70 years
   b) Find the minimum age for retirement with full pension after each period.
      i) 30 years of service   ii) 20 years of service   iii) 35 years of service

10. Solve for the variable indicated.
    a) $V = \pi r^2 h$, for h b) $F = \dfrac{Mm}{d}$, for m c) $I = \dfrac{100m}{P}$, for m
    d) $A = \dfrac{1}{2}h(a + b)$, for h e) $n = \dfrac{v}{4l}$, for l f) $\dfrac{1}{3}x + b = c$, for x

11. Solve for the variable indicated.
    a) $S = \dfrac{w - 10e}{5}$, for w b) $n = 17 - \dfrac{1}{2}a$, for a
    c) $L_2 = L_1(1 + at)$, for t d) $C = 3.7 + 0.99(n - 3)$, for n
    e) $S = \dfrac{n}{2}(a + l)$, for l f) $A = \dfrac{1}{2}h(a + b)$, for b

12. The length, l centimetres, of a rubber band suspending a mass of m grams is given by the formula $l = 14.3 + 0.27m$.
    a) Solve the formula for m.
    b) Find the mass, to the nearest gram, that stretches the band to each length.
       i) 98 cm   ii) 103 cm

13. When an object on the moon falls freely from rest, its approximate speed, v metres per second after t seconds, is given by the formula $v = 1.63t$.
   a) Find its speed, to one decimal place, after each time period.
      i) 1 s   ii) 5 s   iii) 8 s   iv) 10 s
   b) Find the time, to the nearest tenth of a second, the object takes to reach each speed.
      i) 5 m/s   ii) 32 m/s   iii) 57 m/s   iv) 0.6 km/s

14. The area, A, of a trapezoid is given by the formula, $A = \frac{1}{2}h(a + b)$, where a and b are the lengths of the parallel sides and h is the distance between them.
   a) Find the distance between the parallel sides if their lengths are 9 cm and 23 cm, and the area is 256 cm².
   b) Find the length of one parallel side if the other parallel side is 3.4 cm, the distance between them is 6.0 cm, and the area is 23.7 cm².

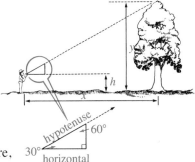

15. The approximate mass, m grams, of a volume of air is given by the formula $m = 1.29V$, where V is the volume in litres. Find the volume, to the nearest litre, of air that has each mass.
   a) 20 g   b) 300 g   c) 22.575 kg

16. To find the height, y, of a tall object
   ● Sight the top of the object along the hypotenuse of a $30° - 60° - 90°$ triangle.
   ● Measure the distance, x, from the object.
   ● Substitute the measured value for x in the formula $y = 0.577x + h$. h is the height of the eye above the ground. (x, y, and h are measured in the same units.)
   Assume h is 1.4 m.
   a) Calculate the height of an object, to the nearest tenth of a metre, for each value of x.
      i) 30 m   ii) 40 m
      iii) 15 m   iv) 17.5 m
   b) Calculate the distance, to the nearest metre, of a viewer from an object which, when correctly sighted, has each of these heights.
      i) 40 m   ii) 55 m
      iii) 100 m   iv) 81 m

 **PROBLEM SOLVING**

Choose the Strategy

1. All solids of the same shape have the same mass. How many cones have the same mass as 4 cylinders?

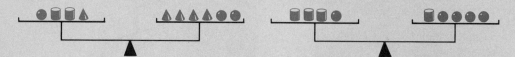

2. There were 6 more students in Mrs. Zovak's class who did not have scientific calculators than in Mr. Alvi's class. Five of these students transferred from Mrs. Zovak's class into Mr. Alvi's class. Now Mr. Alvi has twice as many students without scientific calculators as Mrs. Zovak. How many students in Mr. Alvi's class do not have scientific calculators?

3. A shuttle bus picked up a group of people at the airport. The bus travelled to the Hyatt Hotel where it let off 14 people and picked up 3. At the Holiday Inn, it let off half of those who were remaining and picked up 13 people. There were now 16 people on the bus. How many people were picked up at the airport?

4. Jack is now 4 times as old as his dog. In 6 years he will be only twice as old as his dog. How old is Jack? How old is his dog?

5. An 18 m log is cut into 2 pieces. The longer piece is 3 m shorter than twice the shorter piece. How long is the shorter piece?

6. Mrs. Richards divided $45 among her four children: Amanda, Betty, Carol, and Dan. When the children complained that the shares were not equal, she instructed Betty to give Amanda $2. Then she doubled Carol's share and cut Dan's share in half. Now all of the children have the same amount. How much money do they have in total?

7. a) Explain why every integer can be expressed in exactly one of the forms, $6n$, $6n + 1$, $6n + 2$, $6n + 3$, $6n + 4$, $6n + 5$ for some integer n.
   b) In which of these 5 forms can the prime numbers be expressed?
   c) Show that all prime numbers (except 2 and 3) when divided by 6 leave a remainder of either 1 or 5.

8. Raymond has a box of candy bars. He gave Monique half of what he had plus half a bar. Then he gave Claude half of what he had left plus half a bar. After which he gave Laura half of what he had left plus half a bar. And, finally, he gave Alfred half of what he had left plus half a bar. Then he had no bars left. How many candy bars did Raymond have to start?

4-8 WRITING EQUATIONS

When problems are solved with algebra, the first step is to translate the given facts into the language of algebra. The kinds of problems in this section give two facts. We use one fact to express each quantity in terms of the variable. The other fact enables us to write an equation.

Example 1. A number is 4 times another number. The sum of the numbers is 59. Write an equation with the smaller number as its solution.

Solution. The facts of the problem are
  ① A number is 4 times another number.
  ② The sum of the numbers is 59.
  Method A. Use fact ① to express the larger number in terms of the smaller number.
       Let the smaller number be represented by x.
       Then, the larger number is $4x$.
       Use fact ② to write the equation.
       The sum of the numbers is 59.

$$x \; + \; 4x \; = \; 59$$

  Method B. Use fact ② to relate the two numbers.
       Let the smaller number be represented by x.
       Then, the larger number is $59 - x$.
       Use fact ① to write the equation.
       The larger number is 4 times the smaller number.

$$59 \; - \; x \; = \; 4x$$

In *Example 1*, the two methods produce two forms of the same equation. This illustrates that the equation is independent of the fact that was used to write it. However, when one fact is more complicated than the other, use the complicated fact to write the equation.

Example 2. The sum of two numbers is 117. Five times the smaller number is seven less than three times the larger. Write an equation with the larger number as its solution.

Solution. The simple fact is: The sum of two numbers is 117.
  Let the larger number be represented by x.
  Then, the smaller number is $117 - x$.
  Use the complicated fact to write the equation.

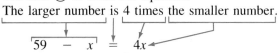

Five times   is   three times   less seven
the smaller   the larger

$$5(117 - x) \; = \; 3x \; - \; 7$$

Example 3. Find two consecutive odd numbers with a sum of 352.
Write an equation with the smaller number as its solution.

Solution. Let the smaller number be represented by x.
Then, the larger number is $x + 2$.
Write the equation.
The sum of
the numbers, is 352

$$x + x + 2 = 352$$

EXERCISES 4-8

Ⓐ

In Exercises 1 to 4, write algebraic expressions to complete parts a) and b). Then write an equation for part c).

1. Ravi is 8 years older than Natasha.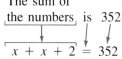
   a) Let Natasha's age be represented by ▨ years.
   b) Then, Ravi's age is ▨ years.
   c) The sum of their ages is 42.

2. Gayle's mass is 2.5 kg less than Maria's.
   a) Let Maria's mass be represented by ▨ kilograms.
   b) Then, Gayle's mass is ▨ kilograms.
   c) The sum of their masses is 97.5 kg.

3. A 12 m tree trunk is cut into two pieces.
   a) Let the length of the shorter piece be represented by ▨ metres.
   b) Then, the length of the longer piece is ▨ metres.
   c) The shorter piece is one-third the length of the longer.

4. The ages of Paul and Judy total 27 years.
   a) Let Paul's age be represented by ▨ years.
   b) Then, Judy's age is ▨ years.
   c) Judy's age plus twice Paul's age is 43.

Ⓑ

Write an equation the solution of which will solve the problem for each of Exercises 5 to 15.

5. Brian ran 2 km less than Tom. They ran a total distance of 12 km. Find how far each boy ran.

6. Marie ran twice as far as Brenda. They ran a total distance of 12 km. Find how far each girl ran.

7. The length of a rectangle is 5 cm longer than the width. The perimeter is 68 cm. Find the dimensions of the rectangle.

8. Find two consecutive numbers with a sum of 263.

9. Find four consecutive numbers with a sum of 234.

10. Find two consecutive even numbers with a sum of 170.

11. One number is one-fifth of another number. The two numbers total 18. Find the numbers.

12. The combined mass of a dog and a cat is 24 kg. The dog is three times as heavy as the cat. Find the mass of each animal.

13. In a class of 33 students, there are 9 fewer boys than girls. Find how many girls there are.

14. Millie is four times as old as Marty. The sum of their ages is 65 years. Find how old the people are.

15. Find two numbers that
    a) are consecutive and have a sum of 83.
    b) differ by 17 and have a sum of 39.

In Exercises 16 to 18, write algebraic expressions to complete parts a) and b). Then write an equation for part c).

16. The sum of two numbers is 54.
    a) Let the smaller number be represented by ▓.
    b) Then, the larger number is ▓.
    c) Twice the smaller is 9 more than the larger.

17. The sum of Millie's and Marty's ages is 65.
    a) Let Millie's age be represented by ▓ years.
    b) Then, Marty's age is ▓ years.
    c) Three times Millie's age is 15 years less than twice Marty's age.

18. Adrienne is twice as old as René.
    a) Let René's age be represented by ▓ years.
    b) Then, Adrienne's age is ▓ years.
    c) The sum of their ages 3 years ago was 48.

Write an equation the solution of which will solve the problem for each of Exercises 19 to 24.

19. The sum of two numbers is 63. Three times the smaller number is 14 more than twice the larger number. Find the numbers.

20. The sum of Julio's and Ramona's ages is 35. Twice Ramona's age is 7 more than Julio's age. Find how old they are.

21. Susan is twice as old as Lana. The sum of their ages 4 years ago was 37. Find how old they are now.

22. The sum of three numbers is 33. The second number is 7 less than the first, and the third number is 2 more than the second. Find the numbers.

23. The sum of three numbers is 75. The second number is 5 more than the first, and the third is three times the second. Find the numbers.

24. James has two-fifths the amount that Lorna has, and Muriel has seven-ninths the amount that James has. Together, they have $770. Find how much each person has.

4-9 SOLVING PROBLEMS USING EQUATIONS – PART ONE

Alexia sees a package deal for skis and boots costing $225. The salesman tells Alexia that the skis cost $60 more than the boots. Alexia wants to know what the skis cost.

She writes an equation, after listing the information in algebraic terms.

Let b dollars represent the cost of the skis.

Since the skis cost $60 more than the boots, the boots cost $(b - 60)$ dollars.

The total cost is $225, so the equation is

$$b + (b - 60) = 225$$
$$2b - 60 = 225$$
$$2b = 285$$
$$b = 142.5$$

The skis cost $142.50.

Solving a problem using an equation involves three steps.

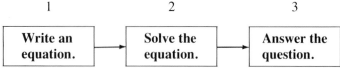

1	2	3
Write an equation.	**Solve the equation.**	**Answer the question.**

The previous sections prepared you for Step 1. Earlier sections in this chapter prepared you for Step 2. Step 3 is merely taking the solution of the equation and answering the question the problem asks.

When you check the solution, do *not* substitute in the equation, substitute in the problem. You could have made a mistake in writing the equation.

Example 1. When four times a number is increased by 25, the result is 77. Find the number.

Solution. Step 1. Let the number be represented by x.
Then, 4 times the number, increased by 25 is $4x + 25$.
The equation is $4x + 25 = 77$.

Step 2. $4x + 25 = 77$
$4x = 52$
$x = 13$

Step 3. The number is 13.

Check. The number is 13.
Four times the number is $4(13)$ or 52.
52 increased by 25 is 77. The solution is correct.

Example 2. In a fishing derby, the mass of fish that Yvonne caught was four times the mass of Michael's catch. Their total catch was 59 kg. How much fish did each person catch?

Solution. Step 1. Let *m* kilograms represent the mass of Michael's fish.
Then, 4*m* kilograms is the mass of Yvonne's fish.
The equation is $m + 4m = 59$.

Step 2. $m + 4m = 59$
$5m = 59$
$m = 11.8$

Step 3. Michael's catch was 11.8 kg.
Yvonne's catch was 4(11.8) kg or 47.2 kg.

Check. The total catch was 11.8 kg + 47.2 kg or 59 kg.
The solution is correct.

In *Step 1* of this solution, the unit of mass was included with the variable
to represent the quantity of fish caught. It is important to state the unit
because a variable represents a number, not a quantity.

In reading the problem, look for the simple fact. Use it to express
each quantity in terms of a variable. Use the more complicated fact
to write the equation. Solve the equation, and answer the question the
problem asks. Check the answer by substituting in the problem.

EXERCISES 4-9

Ⓐ

1. Six times a number increased by 7 is 103. Find the number.

2. When 19 is added to one-quarter of a number the result is 40. Find the number.

3. When 13 is subtracted from three-eighths of a number the result is 11. Find the number.

4. Find two numbers with a difference of 5 and a sum of 27.

5. Find two consecutive numbers with a sum of 45.

6. Mr. Zaluski is 4 years older than Mrs. Zaluski. Their total age is 76 years. How old is each person?

7. A ribbon 22 m long is cut into two pieces. One piece is 10 m longer than the other. How long is each piece?

8. Bruce is 10 years older than Cindy. The sum of their ages is 52. How old is each person?

Ⓑ

9. Ian's mass is 2.5 kg less than that of Sean. The sum of their masses is 121.5 kg. What is the mass of each person?

10. The ages of John and Mary total 27 years. Mary's age plus twice John's age is 40. How old is each person?

11. Joan's jump was longer than Enid's jump by 15 cm. Joan's jump was 1.04 times as long as Enid's jump. How far did each person jump?

12. For two consecutive integers, the sum of the smaller and twice the larger is 38. What are the integers?

13. For two consecutive integers, the sum of twice the larger and three times the smaller is 242. Find the integers.

14. A Jaguar travelled 1.2 times as fast as a Mercedes. The difference in their speeds was 24 km/h. Find the speed of each car.

15. Marie ran twice as far as Brenda. They ran a total distance of 18 km. How far did each person run?

16. One number is five times another number. If the two numbers total 36, find the numbers.

17. The length of a rectangle is 5 cm longer than the width. The perimeter is 54 cm. Find the dimensions of the rectangle.

18. Find two consecutive numbers with a sum of 285.

19. Find three consecutive numbers with a sum of 159.

20. Find four consecutive numbers with a sum of 198.

21. Find two consecutive even numbers with a sum of 226.

22. In a cross-country marathon, Jack and Ted ran a total of 81 km. Ted ran 5 km farther than Jack. How far did each boy run?

23. In a class of 33 students, there are 7 more girls than boys. How many girls are there?

24. Maria is four times as old as Marty. The sum of their ages is 55 years. How old are they?

25. The difference between two numbers is 96. One number is nine times the other. What are the numbers?

26. One number is 0.25 less than another number. The sum of the numbers is 7.25. Find the numbers.

27. The sum of two numbers is 36. Four times the smaller is 1 less than the larger. What are the numbers?

---

28. The sum of three numbers is 33. The second number is 7 less than the first, and the third is three times the second. What are the numbers?

29. The sum of three numbers is 75. The second number is 5 more than the first, and the third is three times the second. What are the numbers?

30. The least of three consecutive integers is divided by 10, the next is divided by 17, the greatest is divided by 26. What are the numbers if the sum of the quotients is 10?

4-10 SOLVING PROBLEMS USING EQUATIONS – PART TWO

In some problems where two facts are given, the statement of the
second fact may seem quite complicated. It may not be immediately
obvious how to write the equation in terms of the chosen variable. In
such cases, it is often helpful to use a table to organize the information.

Example 1.   A parking meter contains \$36.85 in dimes and quarters. If there is a total
of 223 coins, how many quarters does the meter contain?

Solution.   Step 1.   Let x represent the number of quarters.
Then, the number of dimes is $(223 - x)$.
Before writing the equation, write the value of the quarters
and the dimes.

	Number of Coins	**Value in Cents**
Quarters	x	$25x$
Dimes	$223 - x$	$10(223 - x)$

The total value of the coins is \$36.85 or 3685 cents.
The equation is $25x + 10(223 - x) = 3685$.

Step 2. $25x + 10(223 - x) = 3685$
$25x + 2230 - 10x = 3685$
$15x = 1455$
$x = 97$

Step 3.   The parking meter contains 97 quarters.

Check.   Since there are 223 coins, the meter contains 126 dimes.
The value, in cents, of 97 quarters and 126 dimes is
$(25)(97) + (10)(126) = 2425 + 1260$
$= 3685$

This is \$36.85. The solution is correct.

A table can be particularly useful in problems involving ages.

Example 2. A mother is three times as old as her daughter. Six years ago, she was five times as old. How old are the mother and the daughter now?

Solution. Step 1. Let x represent the daughter's age now in years. Then, the mother's age now is $3x$ years.

	Now	**6 years ago**
Daughter's age in years	x	$x - 6$
Mother's age in years	$3x$	$3x - 6$

The equation is $3x - 6 = 5(x - 6)$.

Step 2.
$$3x - 6 = 5(x - 6)$$
$$3x - 6 = 5x - 30$$
$$24 = 2x$$
$$12 = x$$

Step 3. The daughter is 12 years old and the mother is 36.

Check. Six years ago, the daughter's age was $12 - 6$, or 6.
The mother's age was then $36 - 6$, or 30.
Since $5(6) = 30$, the solution is correct.

EXERCISES 4-10

Ⓐ

1. A vending machine contains nickels and dimes only. There is a total of 80 coins. Copy and complete the table to show the value of each kind of coin.

	Number of Coins	**Value in Cents**
Nickels	x	
Dimes	$80 - x$	

Write an algebraic expression for the total value of the coins.

2. A pay telephone contains twice as many dimes as nickels and four times as many quarters as nickels. Copy and complete the table.

	Number of Coins	**Value in Cents**
Nickels	x	$5x$
Dimes		
Quarters		

Write an algebraic expression for the total value of the coins.

3. Debbie is now twice as old as Sandra. Copy and complete the table to show algebraic expressions for their ages at different times.

	Now	Last Year	Next Year	4 Years Ago	3 Years From Now
Debbie's age in years	$2x$				
Sandra's age in years	x				

4. Tracey is 8 years older than Trevor. Copy and complete the table to show algebraic expressions for their ages at different times.

	Now	Last Year	Next Year	5 Years Ago	8 Years From Now
Trevor's age in years	x				
Tracey's age in years	$x + 8$				

5. Jeanne is twice as old as Michel. The sum of their ages three years ago was 45 years. What are their ages now?

6. Yvonne has equal numbers of nickels, dimes, and quarters. Their total value is $2.00. How many of each kind of coin does she have?

7. Tanya is 12 years older than Leah. Three years ago, Tanya was five times as old as Leah. How old is Leah?

8. Find three consecutive odd numbers with a sum of 267.

9. The length of a rectangular pool is 12 m greater than its width. What is the length if the perimeter of the pool is 96 m?

10. Bill is twice as old as his brother Dan. In 7 years, Bill will be only one and one-half times as old as Dan. How old is Bill now?

11. A collection of nickels and dimes has a total value of $8.50. How many coins are there if there are 3 times as many nickels as dimes?

12. Roberta is three years younger than Rebecca. Eight years ago, Roberta was one-half of Rebecca's age. How old is each girl now?

13. A piggy bank contains 91 coins which are nickels, dimes, and quarters. There are twice as many quarters as dimes, and half as many nickels as dimes. How much is in the piggy bank?

14. Sophia's age is four years less than twice Beryl's age. In two years, Beryl's age will be three-quarters of Sophia's age. How old is each girl now?

15. A piece of string, 60 cm long, is cut into three pieces. The middle-sized piece is 2 cm longer than the shortest piece and 2 cm shorter than the longest piece. What is the length of each piece?

16. Girish had $2 more than three times the amount that Joseph had. He gave Joseph $5 who then had one-half as much as Girish. How much did each person have at first?

17. A 500 m track has semicircular ends. If the length of the track is three times its width, what is its width?

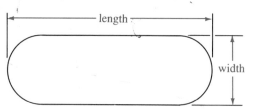

18. At Happy Snack, a milk shake costs twice as much as an order of french fries. If two milk shakes and three orders of french fries cost $4.20, what is the cost of a milk shake?

INVESTIGATE

An inequality is a mathematical sentence that uses the sign $>$ or the sign $<$.
   Investigate whether the rules for solving equations can be used to solve inequalities.

1. Write an inequality that is true, for example, $4 < 8$.

2. Apply each operation listed below. Each time, ask the question, "Is the inequality statement still true?"
    ● Add the same integer to both sides.
    ● Subtract the same integer from both sides.
    ● Multiply both sides by the same positive integer.
    ● Multiply both sides by the same negative integer.
    ● Divide both sides by the same positive integer.
    ● Divide both sides by the same negative integer.

3. What appears to be true?

4. Do the rules for solving equations apply to inequalities?

4-11 SOLVING INEQUALITIES

Boyd sees this sign on a rack of jackets for sale. He calculates that if a jacket has a ticket price of $100, then $\frac{1}{4}$ of $100 is $25. Since the saving is *more than* $\frac{1}{4}$, Boyd realizes that the saving would

be more than $25.

If S represents the saving in dollars, then $S > 25$. Similarly, the sale price would be *less than* $75. If P represents the sale price in dollars, then $P < 75$. $S > 25$ and $P < 75$ are examples of *inequalities*.

Inequalities may also be written using these signs. $\geq$, meaning "is greater than or equal to", and $\leq$, meaning "is less than or equal to".

In the previous investigation, you should have discovered that when both sides of an inequality are multiplied or divided by the same negative number, the statement is no longer true. To keep the statement true, the inequality sign must be reversed, For example,

$$4 < 8$$
$$\text{but } 4(-2) > 8(-2)$$
$$\text{since } -8 > -16$$
$$\text{Also } \frac{4}{-2} > \frac{8}{-2}$$
$$\text{since } -2 > -4$$

> When both sides of an inequality are multiplied or divided by a negative number, the inequality sign must be reversed.

Example 1. Solve. $-3x < 5x + 12$

Solution.

$$3x < 5x + 12$$
$$-12 < 2x$$
$$-6 < x$$
$$x > -6$$

or

$$3x < 5x + 12$$
$$-2x < 12$$
$$x > -6$$

In the alternative solution, the inequality sign was reversed because of the division by -2.

The solution $x > -6$ means that any number greater than -6 satisfies the inequality. This solution can be illustrated on a number line.

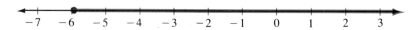

An arrow is drawn in the direction "greater than -6". The open dot at -6 indicates that -6 is not part of the solution.

It is not possible to check the limitless number of solutions to an inequality. However, select one solution and substitute it into the inequality. If the resulting statement is correct, a reasonable conclusion is that the solution is correct.

Example 2. Solve, graph, and check. $3 - 2a \geq a + 9$

Solution.

$$3 - 2a \geq a + 9$$
$$3 \geq 3a + 9$$
$$-6 \geq 3a$$
$$-2 \geq a$$
$$a \leq -2$$

Graph the solution on a number line.

The solid dot at -2 indicates that it is part of the solution.

Check. Since the solution is less than or equal to -2, this includes -5. Substitute $a = -5$ in the inequality.

Left side $= 3 - 2a$ Right side $= a + 9$
$= 3 - 2(-5)$ $= -5 + 9$
$= 3 + 10$ $= 4$
$= 13$

Since $13 > 4$, the left side *is* greater than the right side, and $a = -5$ satisfies the inequality. This suggests that $a \leq -2$ is the correct solution.

EXERCISES 4-11

Ⓐ

1. Solve and graph.
   a) $x + 1 < 4$ b) $x - 1 \leqslant 3$ c) $x + 3 > 2$
   d) $4 > 9 - x$ e) $-13 \geqslant x - 11$ f) $9 \leqslant 15 - x$

2. Write the inequality represented by each graph.

   a)

   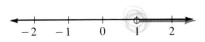

   b)

   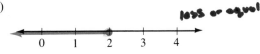

   less or equal

   c)

   d)

Ⓑ

3. Solve and graph.
   a) $7x < 14$ b) $5x \geqslant 10$ c) $9 > -2x$
   d) $3y + 8 > 17$ e) $21 - 5z > 11$ f) $13.5 + 2y \leqslant 18.5$
   g) $13 \leqslant 1 - \dfrac{3}{4}x$ h) $61 < 13w - 4$ i) $18 \geqslant 4.5 - 1.5a$

4. Solve, graph, and check.
   a) $4x - 7 \geqslant 2x + 5$ b) $13 - 2y \leqslant 4y - 14$
   c) $-25 + 11z \leqslant 30 - 11z$ d) $39 + 4w \geqslant 13 - 6w$
   e) $3(x + 2) < 11$ f) $2(x + 8) \leqslant 4(3 + x)$
   g) $5(2 - x) \leqslant 2(x + 7)$ h) $\dfrac{2}{3}(15 - 3x) > \dfrac{1}{2}(2 + 5x)$

5. Solve and check.
   a) $-3y + 8 < 5 - 7y$ b) $18 + 10z \geqslant -12 - 2z$
   c) $14x - 9 \leqslant 17 + x$ d) $-35 - 8a > 6a - 7$
   e) $-4(7 + 2b) \geqslant 3b + 5$ f) $6(-2c - 11) < -5(3c + 8)$
   g) $3(-8 + 2x) > 4 - 2(3x + 5)$ h) $\dfrac{1}{4}(-3y + 7) \leqslant \dfrac{2}{5}(8 - 3y)$

 INVESTIGATE

Which of these statements is false?
- If $\dfrac{a}{b} = \dfrac{c}{d}$ and $a > c$, then $b > d$.
- If $x < y$, then $x < 2y$.

Review Exercises

1. Solve.
   a) $5 + x = -11$
   b) $y - 14 = 83$
   c) $14 - z = -14$
   d) $8 - t = -2$
   e) $w + 21 = -13$
   f) $17 = 19 - t$
   g) $15 = x + 23$
   h) $31 = y - 11$
   i) $-p - 16 = -21$

2. Solve.
   a) $5x = 45$
   b) $-15 = -3n$
   c) $\frac{1}{5}t = -3$
   d) $\frac{n}{14} = -7$
   e) $\frac{s}{5} = \frac{1}{3}$
   f) $8r = 56$
   g) $1.3x = 9.1$
   h) $\frac{x}{17} = \frac{39}{51}$

3. Solve.
   a) $6p - 3 = 15$
   b) $13 = 4 + 3x$
   c) $-6 - 2r = 8$
   d) $5 - 5y = 1$
   e) $8p - 3 = 7$
   f) $3x - \frac{1}{5} = 4$
   g) $3y - 7 = 14$
   h) $\frac{1}{4}x - \frac{2}{3} = 2$
   i) $2.7y - 3.1 = 5$
   j) $\frac{4}{5} - \frac{1}{3}x = \frac{1}{2}x$
   k) $1.69 - 1.3x = 0$
   l) $-64.5 + 2.5x = -2$

4. The cost, C cents, of making copies on a copying machine is given by the formula $C = 90 + 3n$, where n is the number of copies.
   a) What is the cost of making 200 copies?
   b) How many copies can be made for $6.00?

5. The cost, C dollars, of a telephone call from Vancouver, B.C., to St. John's, Newfoundland, is given by the formula $C = 1.20 + 0.95(n - 1)$, where n is the time in minutes, for the call, and $n \geq 1$.
   a) Find the cost of a call that lasts:
      i) 1 min   ii) 3 min   iii) 5 min.
   b) The charge for one call was $24. How long was the call?

6. Solve.
   a) $5y - 2 = 3y + 4$
   b) $-7x + 6 = 2x - 3$
   c) $r - 3 = 2r + 4$
   d) $11 - 1.3x = 4.7x - 7$
   e) $4(x - 3) = -2$
   f) $-5(y + 3) = 14$
   g) $\frac{3}{8}(2 - 4x) = -\frac{5}{4} + \frac{x}{2}$
   h) $0.5(5x - 3) = 1.2$
   i) $3(1 - x) = -2(2 - x)$
   j) $-0.3(0.2a - 0.7) = 0.4(1.1a - 1.2)$
   k) $\frac{3}{4}(2x - 3) = \frac{5}{6}(-2 - 4x)$
   l) $-\frac{2}{3}(7 + 5a) = 1 + \frac{3}{2}(-4 + 5a)$
   m) $-2 + \frac{1}{5}(-4a + 6) = \frac{1}{10}(3 + 2a)$
   n) $\frac{5}{8}(-7c + 3) = -3 - \frac{3}{4}(3 - 7c)$
   o) $3 + \frac{1}{4}(5x + 3) = \frac{3}{8}(x - 4)$
   p) $-\frac{5}{2}(-4 + 3x) = 1 - \frac{3}{4}(3x + 4)$

7. Solve.
   a) $-2z - 3 + 5z = 6 - z - 9$
   b) $-8t + 7 - 5t = 9 - t - 11$
   c) $-13 - q - 9 = 5q - 9 - q$
   d) $-19 - 3r + 6 = 7r - 11 - r$
   e) $4(w - 5) - w = -9 - w + 7$
   f) $-7(p - 3) + 11 = 3p - 12 - p$
   g) $t + 17 - 2t = -3(t - 1) - 3$
   h) $9 - 3(1 - q) = 7 - 4(2 - q)$
   i) $-9(r + 3) - 9r = -3r - (3 - r) + 8$
   j) $3(7v + 8) - 9 = 14 - 2v + 6(3v - 4)$
   k) $5(6w - 3) - 7 = 17 + 3w - 5(2w + 1)$
   l) $-2(5x - 1) - 4 = 22 - 7x + 8(3x - 1)$

8. Solve and check.
   a) $3(x + 1) = 2x$
   b) $4n - 2 = n + 1$
   c) $8 - x = x - 8$
   d) $12 - y = 3y - 14$
   e) $4(t + 1) = 2t + (1 - t)$
   f) $6(w - 2) = 3w + 2(w + 1)$
   g) $7.2x - 7.5 - 1.7x = 4.6 + 4.4x$
   h) $15(0.3 - z) + 14.5z = 2(0.5z - 10)$

9. The speed, s metres per second, of an object is given by the formula $s = \dfrac{d}{t}$, where t seconds is the time taken to travel a distance d metres. Find the distance travelled for each speed and time.
   a) 15 m/s for 3 s
   b) 2 m/s for 12 s
   c) 160 m/s for 15 s
   d) 180 m/s for 6 s
   e) 19 m/s for 13 s
   f) 80 km/h for 1.5 h

10. The sum of the angles of a triangle is 180°. For the triangle shown
    a) Find the value of a when b is:
       i) 30°   ii) 60°.
    b) Find the value of b when a is:
       i) 20°   ii) 50°.

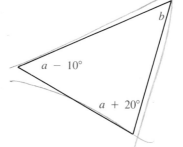

11. A ball, dropped from a height of d centimetres, bounces to a height of b centimetres where $b = \dfrac{3}{4}d$.
    a) Find the height from which the ball was dropped if the height of the bounce is:
       i) 90 cm   ii) 75 cm   iii) 60 cm   iv) 39 cm
    b) The ball is dropped from a height of 160 cm. Find the height of:
       i) its second bounce   ii) its third bounce.

Write an equation the solution of which will solve the problem for each of Exercises 12 to 16.

12. An airplane travels eight times as fast as a car. The difference in their speeds is 420 km/h. Find how fast each vehicle is travelling.

13. Find three consecutive numbers with a sum of 141.

14. In a cross-country marathon, Jack and Jill ran a total of 73 km. Jill ran 5 km farther than Jack. Find how far each person ran.

15. Jeanne is twice as old as Michel. The sum of their ages 3 years ago was 45 years. Find their ages now.

16. Five times a number decreased by 8 is 17. Find the number.

17. Jason is three times as old as Mark. The sum of their ages is 20 years. How old is Mark?

18. Jackie ran 2 km farther than Pat. They ran a total distance of 14 km. How far did each person run?

19. The combined mass of a dog and a cat is 21 kg. The dog is two-and-one-half times as heavy as the cat. What are their masses?

20. Roger has some dimes and quarters with a total value of $2.50. If he has three more quarters than dimes, how many of each kind of coin does he have?

21. Mrs. Jenkins is three times as old as her son, Jerry. In 12 years, Mrs. Jenkins will only be twice as old. How old is Jerry now?

22. One number is seven times one-half of another number. The numbers differ by 35. What are the numbers?

23. Donna's average mark out of three tests was 84 out of 100. Her highest mark was one-and-one-quarter times her lowest mark. The middle mark was 81. What were Donna's marks on the three tests?

24. Write the inequality represented by each graph.

a)

b)

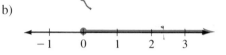

c)

d)

25. Solve and graph.

a) $5x - 17 \leqslant 19 - 4x$

b) $\dfrac{3}{4}y + \dfrac{1}{3} \geqslant \dfrac{1}{2}y + \dfrac{1}{4}$

c) $7(3 - 2z) \leqslant -2(7 + 2z)$

d) $-0.6(3a - 7) > -0.7(-4 + 2a)$

Sunil's copy of this poster is 90 cm by 90 cm. He wants an enlargement that has twice the area. What will be the length of each side of the enlargement? (See Section 5-7, *Example 2*.)

5-1 THE MEANING OF EXPONENTS

Scientists use bacteria in medical research. The bacteria are grown in dishes called petri dishes, named after Julius Petri, a noted bacteriologist. The bacteria 'garden' is called a culture. By counting the bacteria in the culture at regular intervals of time, scientists can study how bacteria grow under controlled conditions.

The table shows a typical bacteria count every hour, starting with a bacteria count of 1000 at midnight.

The number of bacteria doubles every hour.

Time	Number of Bacteria
midnight	1000
01:00	1000×2 or 2000
02:00	$1000 \times 2 \times 2$ or 4000
03:00	$1000 \times 2 \times 2 \times 2$ or 8000

If the pattern in the table is maintained, there would be at 08:00 a total of $1000 \times 2 \times 2 \times 2 \times 2 \times 2 \times 2 \times 2 \times 2$ bacteria. This is a large number which can be written more simply using *exponents*.

The value, $2 \times 2 \times 2 \times 2 \times 2 \times 2 \times 2 \times 2$, is written 2^8.

2^8 is a *power* with an exponent of 8 and a *base* of 2. We say that it is the eighth power of 2.

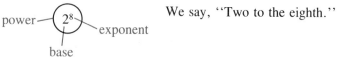

We say, "Two to the eighth."

The base is the number that is repeatedly multiplied. The exponent indicates how many of these numbers are multiplied.

The number of bacteria at 08:00 can be written as 1000×2^8 or 256 000 when expanded.

Example 1. Write each product as a power.
a) $(-9)(-9)(-9)(-9)$

b) $\left(\dfrac{7}{8}\right)\left(\dfrac{7}{8}\right)\left(\dfrac{7}{8}\right)\left(\dfrac{7}{8}\right)\left(\dfrac{7}{8}\right)$

c) $m \times m \times m$

d) $\left(\dfrac{2}{n}\right)\left(\dfrac{2}{n}\right)\left(\dfrac{2}{n}\right)\left(\dfrac{2}{n}\right)$

Solution. a) $(-9)(-9)(-9)(-9) = (-9)^4$

b) $\left(\dfrac{7}{8}\right)\left(\dfrac{7}{8}\right)\left(\dfrac{7}{8}\right)\left(\dfrac{7}{8}\right)\left(\dfrac{7}{8}\right) = \left(\dfrac{7}{8}\right)^5$

c) $m \times m \times m = m^3$

d) $\left(\dfrac{2}{n}\right)\left(\dfrac{2}{n}\right)\left(\dfrac{2}{n}\right)\left(\dfrac{2}{n}\right) = \left(\dfrac{2}{n}\right)^4$

Example 2. If $n = 3$, evaluate: a) n^5 b) 5^n.

Solution.
a) If $n = 3$, $n^5 = 3^5$
$$= (3)(3)(3)(3)(3)$$
$$= 243$$

b) If $n = 3$, $5^n = 5^3$
$$= (5)(5)(5)$$
$$= 125$$

Example 3. Evaluate. a) $(-4)^3$ b) $(-4)^4$

Solution.
a) $(-4)^3 = (-4)(-4)(-4)$
$$= -64$$

b) $(-4)^4 = (-4)(-4)(-4)(-4)$
$$= 256$$

This example illustrates that
- a power with a negative base has a positive value when the exponent is even.
- a power with a negative base has a negative value when the exponent is odd.

The order of operations with exponents is the same as that for rational numbers. When evaluating expressions containing powers, evaluate the powers first unless brackets indicate otherwise.

Example 4. If $x = 5$ and $y = -2$ evaluate:
a) $x^2 - y^2$ b) $(x - y)^2$ c) $-3y^3$ d) $(-3y)^3$.

Solution. If $x = 5$ and $y = -2$

a) $x^2 - y^2 = 5^2 - (-2)^2$
$$= 25 - 4$$
$$= 21$$

b) $(x - y)^2 = [5 - (-2)]^2$
$$= (7)^2$$
$$= 49$$

c) $-3y^3 = -3(-2)^3$
$$= -3(-8)$$
$$= 24$$

d) $(-3y)^3 = [-3(-2)]^3$
$$= (6)^3$$
$$= 216$$

EXERCISES 5-1

Ⓐ

1. Write each product as a power.
   a) $y \times y \times y \times y$
   b) $(-3)(-3)(-3)(-3)(-3)(-3)$
   c) $\dfrac{2}{5} \times \dfrac{2}{5} \times \dfrac{2}{5} \times \dfrac{2}{5} \times \dfrac{2}{5}$
   d) $\left(-\dfrac{3}{8}\right)\left(-\dfrac{3}{8}\right)\left(-\dfrac{3}{8}\right)$
   e) $(4a)(4a)(4a)(4a)(4a)$
   f) $2.9 \times 2.9 \times 2.9 \times 2.9$
   g) $m \times m \times m \times m$
   h) $(-6x)(-6x)(-6x)(-6x)(-6x)$
   i) $\pi \times \pi \times \pi \times \pi \times \pi \times \pi$
   j) $a \times a \times a \times a \times a \times a \times a$

2. Write each phrase as a power.
   a) six cubed
   b) seven to the eighth power
   c) nine to the fourth power
   d) twenty squared
   e) eleven to the fifth power
   f) five to the eleventh power
   g) four to the nth power
   h) $2x$ to the tenth power

3. Evaluate.
   a) 4^3
   b) 3^4
   c) $(-2)^5$
   d) $(-5)^2$
   e) 10^4
   f) $\left(\dfrac{1}{4}\right)^2$

   g) $(0.2)^3$
   h) $(2.1)^2$
   i) $3(2^4)$
   j) $2^3\left(\dfrac{3}{4}\right)^2$
   k) $(3 \times 2)^4$
   l) $2(-3)^4$

4. Express each number as a power of 10.
   a) 1000
   b) 10 000
   c) 100
   d) 1 000 000
   e) 100 000
   f) 10
   g) 100 000 000
   h) 1 000 000 000 000

Ⓑ

5. Using the pattern in the table on page 142, write an expression involving powers of 2 for the number of bacteria in the culture at each time.
   a) 01:00
   b) 02:00
   c) 06:00
   d) 10:00

6. Evaluate.
   a) $2^3 + 3^2$
   b) $3^2 + 4^2$
   c) $(3 + 4)^2$
   d) $5(-4)^3$
   e) $3^2 - 5^2$
   f) $(-4)^2 - 7^2$
   g) $\left(-\dfrac{3}{2}\right)^3 - \left(\dfrac{1}{4}\right)^3$
   h) $(-5)^3 - (-2)^5$

7. Evaluate $2x^2 - 3x + 5$ for each value of x.
   a) 4
   b) -1
   c) -2
   d) 10
   e) -5
   f) $\dfrac{1}{2}$
   g) $-\dfrac{1}{3}$
   h) 1.5
   i) -0.4
   j) 100

8. If $x = -3$ and $y = \dfrac{2}{3}$, evaluate each expression.
   a) x^2
   b) y^3
   c) $-5x^3$
   d) $-x^4$
   e) $(-x)^4$
   f) $x^2 + y^2$
   g) $x^2 - y^2$
   h) $(x + y)^3$
   i) $x^3 + y^3$
   j) $x^3 - y^3$
   k) $(x + y)^9$
   l) $(3x - y)^2$
   m) $5(x^2 - 2y)$
   n) $(3x + y)^3$
   o) $4x^2 - 7y^2$
   p) $4x^2 + y^2$

9. Evaluate each expression for $n = -3$.
   a) n^3
   b) $n^2 - n^3$
   c) $4n^2$
   d) $(4n)^2$
   e) $-(n + 2)^3$
   f) $(-n - 2)^8$
   g) $(2 + n)^{15}$
   h) $-(3n - 7)^4$
   i) $(-4n - 2n^2)^4$
   j) $\left(\dfrac{n}{4}\right)^3$
   k) $\left(\dfrac{2}{n} - 1\right)^5$
   l) $(n - n^2)^3$

10. Arrange from greatest to least.
    a) $2^4, 3^2, 5^2, 2^3, 3^3$
    b) $(-3)^4, 4^3, 7^2, 2^5, 10^2$
    c) $(1.2)^2, (1.1)^3, (1.05)^5, (1.15)^3, (1.3)^1$
    d) $(2.1)^4, (2.9)^3, (2.3)^2, (1.8)^7, (2.4)^5$
    e) $(0.3)^2, (0.2)^3, (0.2)^2, (0.3)^3, (0.4)^2$

$(-4)^2 - 7^2$

$(-4 \times -4) - 7 \times 7$

$(16) - 49$

11. Use the information on page 142.
    a) If you knew how much time had elapsed since midnight, how could you find the number of bacteria in the culture?
    b) Write an expression for the number of bacteria in the culture n hours after midnight.
    c) At 01:30 there are about 2800 bacteria in the culture. Find approximately how many there would be:
       i) 1 h later
       ii) 2 h later
       iii) 1 h earlier.
    d) If a petri dish is half-covered by bacteria at midnight find when it will be completely covered.

12. Identify the greater number in each pair.
    a) $3^{22}, 3^{25}$
    b) $3x^2, (3x)^2$
    c) $(-5n)^3, 5n^3$
    d) $(-2)^{16}, (-2)^{19}$
    e) $(0.9)^{14}, (0.9)^{11}$
    f) $\left(-\dfrac{3}{4}\right)^{10}, (-3.4)^7$

13. a) For what values of y is $y^2 < y$?
    b) For what values of x is $x^3 < x^4$?

14. Solve for n.
    a) $2^n = 8$
    b) $3^n = 81$
    c) $10^n = 1\,000\,000$
    d) $3(2^n) = 48$
    e) $2(5^n) = 50$
    f) $10(3^n) = 810$

15. Identify the greater number in each pair.
    a) $2^5, 5^3$
    b) $3^4, 4^3$
    c) $10^4, 2^{10}$
    d) $6^4, 11^{11}$
    e) $6^3, 3^6$
    f) $9^4, 3^8$

16. Express the first number as a power of the second.
    a) 16, 4
    b) 27, 3
    c) 64, 2
    d) 625, 5
    e) $16, -2$
    f) $-243, -3$
    g) 343, 7
    h) $256, -4$
    i) $81, -3$
    j) 6561, 9
    k) 7776, 6
    l) 1.4641, 1.1

or $(-3)^4$

not -3^4

CALCULATOR POWER

Using a Scientific Calculator to Evaluate Powers

To evaluate $9^2 + (-8)^2$ . . .

. . . Linda pressed these keys on her calculator   . . . Dan pressed these keys

$\boxed{9}\ \boxed{x^2}\ \boxed{+}\ \boxed{8}\ \boxed{+/-}\ \boxed{x^2}\ \boxed{=}$ $\boxed{9}\ \boxed{x^2}\ \boxed{+}\ \boxed{-}\ \boxed{8}\ \boxed{x^2}\ \boxed{=}$

- What answers were obtained by Linda and Dan?
- What is the purpose of the $\boxed{+/-}$ key?
- Whose answer was correct?
- Explain where the error occurred in the incorrect keying sequence.

Evaluate each expression on your scientific calculator.

1. a) $6^2 + 12^2$ b) $5^2 - 9^2$ c) $(0.8^2) + (0.6^2)$ d) $(2.6^2) - (2.4^2)$
   e) $5^2 + (-7)^2$ f) $12^2 + (-5)^2$ g) $1.7(-9)^2$ h) $(2.3 - 12)^2$

   To evaluate, on a scientific calculator, powers with exponents greater than 2 we use the $\boxed{y^x}$ (or $\boxed{a^x}$) key.

To evaluate 3^7, key in: $\boxed{3}\ \boxed{y^x}\ \boxed{7}\ \boxed{=}$ to display 2187

To evaluate $(-2)^9$, key in: $\boxed{2}\ \boxed{+/-}\ \boxed{y^x}\ \boxed{9}\ \boxed{=}$ to display -512

To evaluate $[5(-3)]^4$ . . .

. . . Linda pressed these keys on her calculator   . . . Dan pressed these keys

$\boxed{5}\ \boxed{\times}\ \boxed{3}\ \boxed{+/-}\ \boxed{y^x}\ \boxed{4}\ \boxed{=}$ $\boxed{5}\ \boxed{\times}\ \boxed{3}\ \boxed{+/-}\ \boxed{=}\ \boxed{y^x}\ \boxed{4}\ \boxed{=}$

- What answers did Linda and Dan obtain?
- Explain why their answers differ.
- Whose answer is correct?
- Explain where the error occurred in the incorrect sequence.

Evaluate each expression on your scientific calculator.

2. a) 17^3 b) 29^4 c) $(-3)^3$ d) $(-2)^7$

3. a) $0.3(5)^3$ b) $5.5(-4)^3$ c) $-7(3^4)$ d) $(8^3)(7^4)$
   e) $-6(-3)^7$ f) $(-9.1)^4(-2)^3$ g) $-(-2)^4(-3)^5$ h) $(-2)^3(3^2)(4^3)$

4. a) $2^9 - 3(5.7^4)$ b) $4(-3)^5 - 6(-2.8)^5$

5-2 EXPONENTS IN FORMULAS

In September 1979, an East German family crossed the heavily-guarded frontier into West Germany in a home-made hot air balloon. It was the first escape by this means. The balloon approximated the shape of a sphere with a diameter of about 22 m. What volume of air was in the balloon?

The volume of a sphere is given by the formula $V = \frac{4}{3}\pi r^3$, where r is the radius.

For the balloon, the radius is $\frac{1}{2}(22\text{ m})$ or 11 m.

$$V = \frac{4}{3}\pi r^3$$

$$= \frac{4}{3}\pi(11)^3 \qquad \text{Use a calculator.}$$

Key in: $\boxed{4}$ $\boxed{\div}$ $\boxed{3}$ $\boxed{\times}$ $\boxed{\pi}$ $\boxed{\times}$ $\boxed{1}$ $\boxed{1}$ $\boxed{y^x}$ $\boxed{3}$ $\boxed{=}$ to display 5575.2798

The volume of the balloon was about 5600 m³.

The volume of air is usually expressed in kilolitres (kL).

Since 1 m³ = 1 kL, the volume of air in the balloon was about 5600 kL.

Other formulas which involve exponents are listed below.

$A = s^2$

Area of
a square

$A = \pi r^2$

Area of
a circle

$A = 4\pi r^2$

Surface area
of a sphere

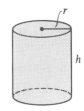

$A = 2\pi r^2 + 2\pi rh$

Surface area of
a cylinder

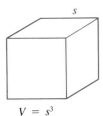

$V = s^3$

Volume of
a cube

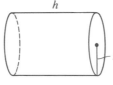

$V = \pi r^2 h$

Volume of
a cylinder

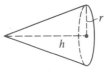

$V = \frac{1}{3}\pi r^2 h$

Volume of
a cone

Example 1. Find the area, to one decimal place, of the shaded region of each figure.

a)

3.6 m

b)

1.6 cm

Solution.   a) Area of square, $A = s^2$

Shaded area of square, $\frac{1}{2}A = \frac{1}{2}s^2$

When $s = 3.6$, $\frac{1}{2}A = \frac{1}{2}(3.6)^2$

$= 6.48$

The shaded region of the square has an area of about 6.5 m².

b) Area of circle, $A = \pi r^2$

Shaded area of circle, $\frac{1}{4}A = \frac{1}{4}\pi r^2$

When $r = 1.6$, $\frac{1}{4}A = \frac{1}{4}\pi(1.6)^2$

$\doteq 2.01$

The shaded region of the circle has an area of about 2.0 cm².

Example 2. Find the volume of each solid, to the nearest unit.

a)

b)

c)

Cube of side
1.9 cm

Sphere of diameter
9.4 cm

Cylinder of height
11.0 cm, diameter 7.4 cm

Solution.   a) Volume of cube, $V = s^3$
When $s = 1.9$, $V = (1.9)^3$
$= 6.859$

The volume of the cube is about 7 cm³.

b) Volume of sphere, $V = \frac{4}{3}\pi r^3$

$r = \frac{1}{2}(9.4)$ or 4.7

$V = \frac{4}{3}\pi(4.7)^3$

$\doteq 434.89$

If your calculator does not have a $\boxed{\pi}$ key,
use $\pi = 3.14$.

The volume of the sphere is about 435 cm³.

c) Volume of cylinder, $V = \pi r^2 h$

$r = \frac{1}{2}(7.4)$ or 3.7 and $h = 11.0$

$V = \pi(3.7)^2(11.0)$

$\doteq 473.09$

The volume of the cylinder is about 473 cm³.

Example 3. The distance d metres that an object falls from rest in t seconds is given by the formula $d \doteq 4.9t^2$. A pebble dropped from the top of a building takes 3.5 s to reach the ground. Find the height of the building.

Solution. Substitute $t = 3.5$ in the formula $d \doteq 4.9t^2$.

$d \doteq 4.9(3.5)^2$

$= 60.025$

The building is about 60 m high.

Example 4. A $500 Canada Savings Bond pays 9% interest annually. This interest compounds (earns more interest) each year. The value V dollars of the bond after n years is given by this formula.

$V = 500(1.09)^n$

Find the value of the bond after: a) 2 years   b) 5 years.

Solution. a) $V = 500(1.09)^n$

Substitute $n = 2$ into the formula.

$V = 500(1.09)^2$

$= 594.05$

After 2 years, the value of the bond is $594.05.

b) $V = 500(1.09)^n$

Substitute $n = 5$ into the formula.

$V = 500(1.09)^5$

$\doteq 769.31$

After 5 years, the value of the bond is $769.31.

EXERCISES 5-2

Ⓐ

1. Express the area of each shaded region using exponents.

a)

2.5

b)

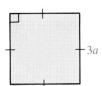

3a

c)

$\frac{2}{3}x$

d)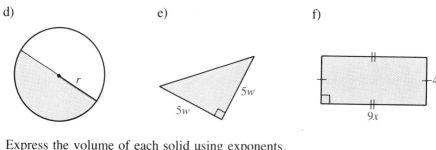

e)

f)

2. Express the volume of each solid using exponents.

a)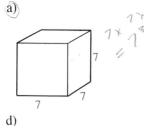

b)

c)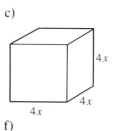

d)

e)

f)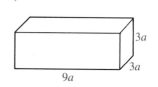

3. Find the area of each square with the given side length.
   a) 5 cm
   b) 9 m
   c) 1.5 cm
   d) 13.7 m
   e) 0.6 cm
   f) 2.6 m
   g) 4a units
   h) 5x units

4. Find the volume of each cube having an edge length the same as that given in *Exercise 3*.

5. Find the area of each shaded region. Give the answers to the nearest square unit.

   a)

   b)

   c)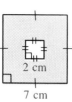

   d)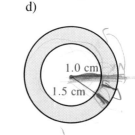

   e)

   f)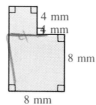

   g)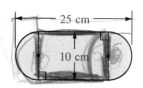

   2 cm
   7 cm
   5 mm
   3 cm
   8 cm
   1.0 cm
   1.5 cm
   12 cm
   4 mm
   4 mm
   8 mm
   8 mm
   25 cm
   10 cm

   dx π

6. A principal of $200 in a savings account that pays 8% interest annually grows to $200(1.08)^n$ in n years. What does the principal grow to in:
   a) 3 years   b) 6 years   c) 10 years?

7. A path 2 m wide is to enclose a circular lawn that has a 25 m radius. What will be the total cost of the material for the path if the cost per square metre is $3.00?

8. A label just covers the curved surface of a soup tin with height 10 cm and diameter 7 cm. What is the area of the label?

9. A punch bowl is hemispherical and 50 cm in diameter. How many litres of punch can it hold? Give the answer to the nearest tenth of a litre.

10. How many bouillon cubes with an edge length of 2 cm can be packed into a cubic box with an edge length of 0.5 m?

11. Find the volume of air contained in a spherical balloon with a radius of 12 cm. Give the answer to the nearest tenth of a litre.

12. A car brakes and decelerates uniformly. The distance d metres that it travels in t seconds is given by this formula.
    $$d = ut - 3.5t^2$$
    u is the speed, in metres per second, just as the brakes are applied.
    Find how far the car travels while braking for 5 s, when it was travelling 25 m/s just as the brakes were applied.

Ⓒ

13. A class found by measuring that the relationship of the area A of the maple leaf on the Canadian flag to the flag's length x is $A \doteq 0.072x^2$.
    a) Find the area of the maple leaf on a flag of each length.
       i)   20 cm   ii)   40 cm
       iii)   80 cm   iv)   1.6 m
    b) Find the length of the flag that has a maple leaf with each area.
       i)   583.2 cm²   ii)   1036.8 cm²
       iii)   0.45 m²   iv)   16.2 mm²

x

14. The balloon that made the first successful crossing of the Atlantic Ocean was filled with helium. It had the shape of a hemisphere on a cone.
    The balloon was 33.0 m high and 19.6 m in diameter.
    Find the volume, to the nearest kilolitre, of helium that the balloon contained.

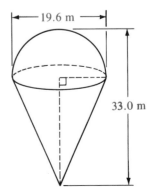

19.6 m

33.0 m

5-3 OPERATIONS WITH POWERS

Three operations involving powers are explained in this section.

- Multiplication of powers with the same base
- Division of powers with the same base
- Exponentiation of a power

All three operations are based on the definition of an exponent.

$$x^n = x \times x \times x \times x \ldots \text{ to } n \text{ factors}$$

Example 1. Simplify.

        a) $5^3 \times 5^4$ b) $y^5 \times y^6$

Solution. a) $5^3 \times 5^4 = 5 \times 5 \times 5 \times 5 \times 5 \times 5 \times 5$

                       $= 5^7$

        b) $y^5 \times y^6 = y \times y \times y \times y \times y \times y \times y \times y \times y \times y \times y$

                     $= y^{11}$

In each part of the example, the exponent of the simplified expression is the sum of the exponents in the original expression. This example illustrates the following rule for multiplying powers.

To multiply powers with the same base, add the exponents.

$$x^m \times x^n = x^{m+n}, \; m > 0, \; n > 0$$

Example 2. Simplify.

        a) $7^8 \div 7^3$ b) $z^9 \div z^2$

Solution.

        a) $7^8 \div 7^3 = \dfrac{7 \times 7 \times 7 \times 7 \times 7 \times 7 \times 7 \times 7}{7 \times 7 \times 7}$

                    $= 7^5$

        b) $z^9 \div z^2 = \dfrac{z \times z \times z \times z \times z \times z \times z \times z \times z}{z \times z}$

                    $= z^7$

In each part of the example, the exponent of the simplified expression is the difference between the exponents in the original expression.

To divide powers with the same base, subtract the exponents.

$$x^m \div x^n = x^{m-n}, \; m > n, \; m > 0, \; n > 0, \; x \neq 0$$

Example 3. Simplify.

    a) $(3^3)^4$ b) $(y^4)^5$

Solution.   a) $(3^3)^4 = 3^3 \times 3^3 \times 3^3 \times 3^3$

                        $= 3^{3+3+3+3}$

                        $= 3^{12}$

        b) $(y^4)^5 = y^4 \times y^4 \times y^4 \times y^4 \times y^4$

                        $= y^{4+4+4+4+4}$

                        $= y^{20}$

In each part of the example, the exponent of the simplified expression is the product of the exponents in the original expression.

> To raise a power to an exponent, multiply the exponents.
> $(x^m)^n = x^{mn}$, $m > 0$, $n > 0$, $x \neq 0$

Example 4. Simplify.

    a) $3a^4 \times 2a^3$ b) $\dfrac{12n^5}{6n^2}$ c) $\dfrac{5(b^2)^3 \times (3b^4)^2}{2b^3}$

Solution.   a) $3a^4 \times 2a^3 = 3 \times 2 \times a^{4+3}$

                        $= 6a^7$

        b) $\dfrac{12n^5}{6n^2} = 2n^{5-2}$

                $= 2n^3$

        c) $\dfrac{5(b^2)^3 \times (3b^4)^2}{2b^3} = \dfrac{5 \times 3^2 \times b^{2\times3} \times b^{4\times2}}{2b^3}$

                          $= \dfrac{45 \times b^6 \times b^8}{2b^3}$

                          $= \dfrac{45b^{6+8-3}}{2}$

                          $= \dfrac{45b^{11}}{2}$

EXERCISES 5-3

Ⓐ

1. Write each product as a power.

    a) $3^4 \times 3^6$ b) $7^4 \times 7^7$ c) $(-5)^{16}(-5)^9$

    d) $(2.1)^5(2.1)^{11}$ e) $(-8)^2(-8)^3(-8)$ f) $(-1.7)^4(-1.7)^2(-1.7)$

    g) $\left(\dfrac{2}{5}\right)^8\left(\dfrac{2}{5}\right)^{14}$ h) $\left(\dfrac{3}{11}\right)^{21}\left(\dfrac{3}{11}\right)^{15}$ i) $\left(-\dfrac{5}{4}\right)\left(-\dfrac{5}{4}\right)^6\left(-\dfrac{5}{4}\right)^7$

2. Simplify.

    a) $x^7x^4 = x^{11}$ b) k^3k^9 c) n^6n^{17} d) $s^4s^5s^2$

    e) $v^{12}v^5v$ f) y^7yy^2 g) $(-a)^4(-a)^6$ h) $(-c)^7(-c)$

3. Simplify.

   a) $3^8 \div 3^3$

   b) $2^{16} \div 2^7$

   c) $m^{20} \div m^5$

   d) $\dfrac{s^{18}}{s^6}$

   e) $\dfrac{14z^{12}}{-2z^4}$

   f) $\dfrac{24r^{24}}{8r^8}$

   g) $\dfrac{6^8}{6^2}$

   h) $\dfrac{(-2)^7}{(-2)^3}$

4. Simplify.

   a) $\dfrac{2^3 \times 2^5}{2^6}$

   b) $\dfrac{3 \times 3^7}{3^2 \times 3^2}$

   c) $\dfrac{m^4 \times m^3}{m^2}$

   d) $\dfrac{b^4 \times b}{b^2}$

   e) $\dfrac{(-a)^5(-a)}{(-a)^2}$

   f) $\dfrac{x^{12} \times x^6}{x^5 \times x^4}$

   g) $\dfrac{c^8 \times c^6}{c^2 \times c^9}$

   h) $\dfrac{(-5)^{41} \times (-5)^{19}}{(-5)^{50}}$

   i) $\dfrac{7^{14}}{7^3 \times 7^4}$

5. Simplify.

   a) $(m^4)^5$

   b) $[(-t)^3]^5$

   c) $(a^7)^7$

   d) $(2^3)^4$

   e) $(12^5)^7$

   f) $(10^2)^6$

   g) $[(-5)^4]^3$

   h) $(z^9)^3$

6. Simplify.

   a) $3a^2 \times 5a^3$

   b) $2m^3 \times 9m^5$

   c) $4x^4 \times 9x^9$

   d) $6y^5(-3y^7)$

   e) $5(3)^8 \times 6(3)^4$

   f) $8(-7)^4 \times 4(-7)^{11}$

   g) $3x \times 19x^{10}$

   h) $2p^5 \times 5p^2 \times 3p^3$

   i) $4s^5 \times 7s^{10} \times 3s$

7. Simplify.

   a) $\dfrac{20d^5}{4d^2}$

   b) $\dfrac{36a^{12}}{-4a^3}$

   c) $\dfrac{-42z^3}{-7z^2}$

   d) $15m^9 \div 5m^3$

   e) $-32x^{12} \div 8x^4$

   f) $50a^{20} \div 20a^5$

   g) $12(2)^7 \div 4(2)^3$

   h) $-24(3)^{18} \div 4(3)^6$

   i) $\dfrac{4n^{12} \times 5n^3}{10n^6}$

   j) $\dfrac{3c^6 \times 2c}{4c^2}$

   k) $\dfrac{18m^{14} \times 5m^7}{10m^3}$

   l) $\dfrac{-9a^7 \times (-8)a^9}{-18a^8}$

8. Simplify.

   a) $(6m^2)^3$

   b) $(4x^5)^2$

   c) $(13a^7)^4$

   d) $(-3p^2)^8$

   e) $(-6c^4)^6$

   f) $(-3x^5)^2$

   g) $\dfrac{(2k^2)^2}{k^3}$

   h) $\dfrac{(3n^4)^3}{(2n)^2}$

   i) $\dfrac{(4a^5)^3(4a^6)^2}{4a^4}$

   j) $\dfrac{-(-2n^4)^2(-n^2)^4}{(3n)^3}$

   k) $\dfrac{(0.5x^2)^3(-2x^3)^2}{(-0.5x)^2}$

   l) $\dfrac{(10m^3)^4(0.1m^2)^4}{(100m^2)(0.01m^2)^2}$

9. Astronomers estimate that there are about 10^{11} galaxies in the universe, and that each galaxy contains about 10^{11} stars. About how many stars are there in the universe?

10. Simplify.

   a) $(a^2b^4)^3$

   b) $(3x^2y^3z)^4$

   c) $(-2mn^3p^4)^3$

   d) $\dfrac{(-36m^2n^3)^2}{(12m^3n^2)^3}$

   e) $\dfrac{(4ab^2c^3)^3}{(-3a^3b^2c)^4}$

11. Evaluate each expression for: i) $a = 2$ ii) $a = 0.5$ iii) $a = -5$.

   a) $a \times a^3$ b) $a^2 \times a^4$ c) $a^9 \div a^7$ d) $\dfrac{a^3 \times a^5}{a^4}$

   e) $\dfrac{15a^3}{5a}$ f) $\dfrac{(-6a^2)(8a^3)}{(4a^2)^2}$ g) $(a^2)^3$    h) $(3a^2)^2$

12. a) Make a table of powers of 2 up to 2^{24}.
   b) Use your table of powers of 2 to evaluate each expression.
     i) 16×64 ii) 32×512 iii) $65\ 536 \div 2048$
     iv) $\dfrac{128 \times 4096}{32}$ v) 64^3 vi) 4^5

13. Fold a piece of paper in half (giving 2
layers of paper). Fold it in half again (giving
4 layers). Fold it in half again (giving 8
layers), and continue folding it in half in
this manner.

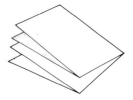

   a) Suppose you could do this 20 times.
     i) How many layers of paper would
       there be?
     ii) About how thick would the resulting
       wad of paper be?

   b) Find out how many times you can
     actually fold a piece of paper in this way.

INVESTIGATE

There are two possible meanings for an expression such as 2^{3^2}, depending on the order in which the exponents are calculated.

2^{3^2} might mean $(2^3)^2$ or it might mean $2^{(3^2)}$.

1. Evaluate the expressions $(2^3)^2$ and $2^{(3^2)}$. Are they the same?

2. Mathematicians have agreed that, in an expression such as 2^{3^2}, the exponents should be evaluated starting at the top. Using this convention, find the value of each expression.
   a) 2^{3^2} b) 3^{2^2} c) 2^{2^3} d) 5^{2^2}

3. Evaluate each expression.
   a) 2^2 b) 2^{2^2} c) $2^{2^{2^2}}$

4. Mathematicians have calculated that $2^{2^{2^{2^2}}}$ is a number with 19 729 digits. Estimate the number of pages of this book that would be needed to print the number $2^{2^{2^{2^2}}}$.

It has been estimated that the number $2^{2^{2^{2^{2^2}}}}$ is so large that it can never be calculated, because the answer would require the age of the universe in computer time, and the space of the universe to hold the printout.

1·2·7

5-4 THE EXPONENT LAWS

Consider the statement, $\dfrac{x^m}{x^n} = x^{m-n}$, $x \neq 0$.

We have shown that this is true if m and n are positive integers and $m > n$. What happens to this equation if the restriction $m > n$ does not hold? That is,

Suppose $m = n$

For example, if $m = 3$ and $n = 3$ and $x \neq 0$,

then $\dfrac{x^3}{x^3} = \dfrac{(x)(x)(x)}{(x)(x)(x)}$ also $\dfrac{x^3}{x^3} = x^{3-3}$

$\qquad\qquad = 1$ $= x^0$

Since x^m is defined only for positive values of m, the expression x^0 has not yet been defined.

However, if we define x^0 to be 1, then $\dfrac{x^3}{x^3} = 1 = x^{3-3}$, for $x \neq 0$.

That is, if we define x^0 to be 1 for $x \neq 0$, then the exponent law $\dfrac{x^m}{x^n} = x^{m-n}$, $x \neq 0$, is true for $m > n$ and $m = n$.

> For any number x, where $x \neq 0$, $x^0 = 1$

Suppose $m < n$

For example, if $m = 3$ and $n = 7$ and $x \neq 0$,

then $\dfrac{x^3}{x^7} = \dfrac{x \times x \times x}{x \times x \times x \times x \times x \times x \times x}$ also $\dfrac{x^3}{x^7} = x^{3-7}$

$\qquad\quad = \dfrac{1}{x^4}$ $= x^{-4}$

Since x^m is defined only for non-negative values of m, the expression x^{-4} has not yet been defined.

However, if we define x^{-4} to mean $\dfrac{1}{x^4}$, then $\dfrac{x^3}{x^7} = x^{-4}$, for $x \neq 0$.

That is, if we define x^{-n} to mean $\dfrac{1}{x^n}$ for $x \neq 0$, then the exponent law, $\dfrac{x^m}{x^n} = x^{m-n}$, $x \neq 0$, is true for all integral values of m and n.

> For any number x and any integer n, x^{-n} is defined to be the reciprocal of x^n.
>
> $$x^{-n} = \dfrac{1}{x^n}, \; x \neq 0$$

These two statements, along with the 3 statements from the previous section, comprise the *exponent laws*.

Exponent Laws
For all integers m and n
- $x^m \times x^n = x^{m+n}$
- $x^m \div x^n = x^{m-n}, x \neq 0$
- $(x^m)^n = x^{mn}$
- $x^0 = 1, x \neq 0$
- $x^{-m} = \dfrac{1}{x^m}, x \neq 0$

The pattern of this table is a further illustration of the relationship between positive and negative exponents.

$$2^4 = 2 \times 2 \times 2 \times 2 = 16$$

Reducing exponents by 1,

$$2^3 = 2 \times 2 \times 2 = 8$$
$$2^2 = 2 \times 2 = 4$$
$$2^1 = 2 = 2$$
$$2^0 = 1 = 1$$
$$2^{-1} = \frac{1}{2} = \frac{1}{2}$$
$$2^{-2} = \frac{1}{2} \times \frac{1}{2} = \frac{1}{4}$$
$$2^{-3} = \frac{1}{2} \times \frac{1}{2} \times \frac{1}{2} = \frac{1}{8}$$ divides answers by 2.
$$2^{-4} = \frac{1}{2} \times \frac{1}{2} \times \frac{1}{2} \times \frac{1}{2} = \frac{1}{16}$$

Example 1. Evaluate.

a) 5^{-2} b) $\left(\dfrac{1}{4}\right)^{-3}$ c) $(3^0 - 3^{-1})^{-2}$

Solution.

a) $5^{-2} = \dfrac{1}{5^2}$

$= \dfrac{1}{25}$

b) $\left(\dfrac{1}{4}\right)^{-3} = \dfrac{1}{\left(\dfrac{1}{4}\right)^3}$

$= \dfrac{1}{\dfrac{1}{64}}$

$= 64$

c) $(3^0 - 3^{-1})^{-2} = \left(1 - \dfrac{1}{3}\right)^{-2}$ or $(3^0 - 3^{-1})^{-2} = \left(1 - \dfrac{1}{3}\right)^{-2}$

$$= \left(\dfrac{2}{3}\right)^{-2} \qquad\qquad = \left(\dfrac{2}{3}\right)^{-2}$$

$$= \dfrac{1}{\left(\dfrac{2}{3}\right)^2} \qquad\qquad = \left(\dfrac{3}{2}\right)^2$$

$$= \dfrac{1}{\dfrac{4}{9}} \qquad\qquad\qquad = \dfrac{9}{4}$$

$$= \dfrac{9}{4}$$

Example 2. Evaluate.

    a) $4^{-3} \times 4^2 \times 4^{-1}$ b) $(-2)^{-4} \div (-2)^{-1}$ c) $(3^{-1})^{-2}$

Solution.   a) $4^{-3} \times 4^2 \times 4^{-1} = 4^{-3+2-1}$

$$= 4^{-2}$$

$$= \dfrac{1}{4^2}$$

$$= \dfrac{1}{16}$$

    b) $(-2)^{-4} \div (-2)^{-1} = (-2)^{-4-(-1)}$

$$= (-2)^{-3}$$

$$= \dfrac{1}{(-2)^3}$$

$$= -\dfrac{1}{8}$$

    c) $(3^{-1})^{-2} = 3^{(-1)(-2)}$

$$= 3^2$$

$$= 9$$

Example 3. Simplify.

    a) $(x^{-2})(x^5)(x^0)$ b) $x^3 \div x^{-5}$ c) $(x^2)^{-3}$

Solution.   a) $(x^{-2})(x^5)(x^0) = x^{-2+5+0}$

$$= x^3$$

    b) $x^3 \div x^{-5} = x^{3-(-5)}$

$$= x^8$$

    c) $(x^2)^{-3} = x^{2(-3)}$

$$= x^{-6}$$

Example 4. Evaluate each expression for $a = -2$ and $b = 3$.

    a) $a^{-2} - b^{-1}$ b) $3a^{-1} + 2b^{-2}$

Solution.   If $a = -2$ and $b = 3$

$$
\begin{aligned}
\text{a) } a^{-2} - b^{-1} &= (-2)^{-2} - (3)^{-1} \\
&= \frac{1}{(-2)^2} - \frac{1}{3} \\
&= \frac{1}{4} - \frac{1}{3} \\
&= \frac{3}{12} - \frac{4}{12} \\
&= -\frac{1}{12}
\end{aligned}
$$

$$
\begin{aligned}
\text{b) } 3a^{-1} + 2b^{-2} &= 3(-2)^{-1} + 2(3)^{-2} \\
&= \frac{3}{-2} + \frac{2}{3^2} \\
&= -\frac{3}{2} + \frac{2}{9} \\
&= -\frac{27}{18} + \frac{4}{18} \\
&= -\frac{23}{18}
\end{aligned}
$$

EXERCISES 5-4

(A)

1. Evaluate.

  a) 2^{-1} b) 5^{-1} c) 3^{-2} d) 2^{-3} e) 5^{-3} f) 10^{-2}

  g) 12^{-3} h) 10^{-4} i) $\left(\frac{1}{2}\right)^0$ j) $\left(\frac{1}{4}\right)^{-2}$ k) 10^{-5} l) $\frac{1}{5^{-1}}$

  m) $\frac{1}{2^{-5}}$ n) $\frac{3}{4^{-2}}$ o) $\left(\frac{3}{4}\right)^{-2}$ p) $\left(\frac{1}{10}\right)^{-1}$ q) $(0.1)^{-3}$ r) $(0.5)^{-2}$

2. Simplify.

  a) $10^3 \times 10^{-5}$ b) $10^{-4} \div 10^{-3}$

  c) $(10^{-4})^2 \times 10^{-1}$ d) $10^0 \times 10^8$

  e) $10^4 \div 10^{-5} \times 10^6$ f) $10^4 \times 10^{-5} \div 10^6$

  g) $(10^{-5})^3(10^5)^3$ h) $(10^4 \times 10^6)^0 \div 10^{-1}$

  i) $(10^{-3})^4(10^{-4})^3 \div (10^{-2})^{-1}$ j) $10^{-5} \div 10^{-3} \times (10^4)^{-2}$

(B)

3. Write each expression as a power.

  a) $5^4 \times 5^7$ b) $2^{-5} \times 2^{11}$ c) $3^4 \div 3^{-11}$

  d) $7^{-8} \div 7^2$ e) $11^{-13} \times 11^{20}$ f) $(-5)^{-11} \div (-5)^{19}$

  g) $6^{-8} \times 6^{-15}$ h) $(-9)^4 \div (-9)^4$ i) $19^{-7} \div 19^{12}$

$-\dfrac{80}{9}$

4. Simplify.
   a) $x^{-9} \times x^{-4}$ x^{-13} b) $p^{-7} \div p^2$ p^{-9} c) $w^{-13} \times w^8$ -5
   d) $y^5 \times y^{-9}$ -4 e) $x^{-5} \div x^{13}$ -18 f) $a^7 \div a^{-4}$ 11
   g) $m^{-14} \div m^{-5}$ -9 h) $s^{-5} \times s^{17}$ 12 i) $t^{-9} \div t^{-17}$ 8

5. Evaluate.
   a) $3^2 + 3^{-2}$ $\dfrac{82}{9}$ b) $3^2 - 3^{-2}$ $\dfrac{80}{9}$ c) $3^{-2} - 3^2$ $-\dfrac{80}{9}$
   d) $3^2 \times 3^{-2}$ 1 e) $3^2 \div 3^{-2}$ 81 f) $3^{-2} \div 3^2$ $\dfrac{1}{81}$

6. Evaluate.
   a) $2^3 - 2^{-1}$ $\dfrac{15}{2}$ b) $5^2 + 5^{-1}$ $\dfrac{126}{5}$ c) $7^{-2} - 7$ $-\dfrac{342}{49}$
   d) $(2 \times 3)^{-2}$ $\dfrac{1}{36}$ e) $4^2 + 4^0$ 17 f) $3^{-1} + 3^{-2}$ $\dfrac{4}{9}$
   g) $6^2 + 6^0 + 6^{-2}$ $\dfrac{1333}{36}$ h) $(2^2 - 1)^{-2}$ $\dfrac{1}{9}$ i) $3^{-2} - 2^{-4}$ $\dfrac{7}{144}$

7. Evaluate.
   a) $(-2)^3$ b) $(-2)^{-3}$ c) $-(-2)^{-3}$
   d) $(-5)^0$ e) $-(5^0)$ f) $(6 - 4)^{-3}$
   g) $(5 - 8)^{-1}$ h) $\left(\dfrac{1}{4} - \dfrac{1}{4^2}\right)^{-2}$ i) $[(-3)^{-2} + (-3)^{-1}]^{-1}$

8. Express as powers of 2, and then arrange in order from greatest to least.
   $\dfrac{1}{32}$, 16, 128, $\dfrac{1}{64}$, 1, $\dfrac{1}{2}$

9. Express as powers of 3, and then arrange in order from least to greatest.
   $\dfrac{1}{9}$, $\dfrac{1}{243}$, $\dfrac{1}{81}$, 27, $\dfrac{1}{729}$, 1

10. Express as powers with positive exponents.
    a) 49   b) $\dfrac{1}{100}$ c) $\dfrac{1}{343}$ d) $\dfrac{1}{-32}$
    e) $\dfrac{1}{1\ 000\ 000}$ f) 0.25   g) 0.001   h) 0.125

11. Express as powers with negative exponents other than -1.
    a) $\dfrac{1}{121}$ b) $\dfrac{1}{169}$ c) 0.01   d) 0.1
    e) 0.000 01   f) 0.008   g) 0.0081   h) $\dfrac{1}{1728}$

12. Simplify.
    a) $a^{-3} \div a^6 \div a^{-8}$ b) $y^{-5} \div y^9 \times y^4$
    c) $(-3)^{-6} \times (-3)^4 \times (-3)^3$ d) $2^3 \times 2^{-7} \div 2^{-5}$
    e) $m^{-6} \div m^{-2} \times m^{-9}$ f) $x^{-4} \times x^{-8} \div x^{-7}$
    g) $p^{11} \div p^{15} \div p^{-9}$ h) $(-7)^{12} \times (-7)^{-8} \div (-7)^{17}$
    i) $11^5 \div 11^{10} \div 11^{-3}$ j) $(0.5)^2 \div (0.5)^{-2} \times (0.5)^{-5}$
    k) $(-0.1)^4 \times 10^6 \times (0.01)^2$ l) $10^{-3} \div 100^{-2} \times (0.1)^{-1}$
    m) $(-2)^{-4} \times (-0.5)^{-5} \times 2^{-2}$ n) $(0.25)^8 \div 4^{-7} \times 2^2$

13. Simplify.
    a) $(x^{-2})^3 \div (x^3)^2$
    b) $(y^4)^2 \times (y^{-2})^3$
    c) $(3^2)^5 \times (3^3)^2$
    d) $(2^{-4})^2 \div (2^2)^6$
    e) $(m^{-3})^4 \div (m^4)^{-3}$
    f) $(8^3)^{-3} \times (8^2)^{-2}$
    g) $(w^2)^{-7} \times (w^{-3})^{-4}$
    h) $(5^{-3})^4 \div (5^2)^3$
    i) $(x^2)^4 \times (x^{-4})^5$

14. Evaluate.

    a) $5^{-1} \div 3^{-2}$
    b) $(3^{-1} - 3^{-2})^{-1}$
    c) $\left(\dfrac{1}{4}\right)^{-1} - \left(\dfrac{1}{3}\right)^{-2}$

    d) $\left(\dfrac{1}{-2}\right)^{-3} + \left(\dfrac{1}{2}\right)^{-2}$
    e) $\left(\dfrac{2}{3^{-1}}\right)^{-3}$
    f) $(0.5)^{-3} + (0.5)^0$

    g) $\dfrac{4}{4^{-1} + 4^0}$
    h) $\dfrac{2^{-1}}{2^{-2} - 2^{-3}}$
    i) $[47(5)^{-2}]^0$

15. Simplify.
    a) $5n^{-4} \times 2n^{17}$
    b) $12t^4 \div 3t^{-3}$
    c) $60x^5 \div 12x^{-5}$
    d) $16w^{-8} \div 4w^{-2}$
    e) $7a^{-4} \times (-4a^{-2})$
    f) $-12y^{-9} \times 6y^{17}$
    g) $15s^{-15} \div 3s^5$
    h) $-4m^{-7} \times (-3m^{-2})$
    i) $18x^5 \div (-3x^8)$

16. Simplify.
    a) $2m^{-3} \times 5m^{-4} \times 3m^{11}$
    b) $6a^2 \div (-2)a^5 \times 4a^{-7}$
    c) $24y^6 \div 3y^2 \div 2y^{-2}$
    d) $45b^{-3} \div 5b^5 \times 3b^{-7}$
    e) $-9m^{-7} \times 8m^{-2} \div (-6m^{-3})$
    f) $-15y^{-4} \div 5y^8 \div 3y^{-12}$

17. Evaluate each expression for $a = -3$, $b = 2$, and $c = -1$.
    a) a^{-1}
    b) $-a^{-1}$
    c) $a^{-1} + b^{-1}$
    d) $(a + b + c)^{-1}$
    e) $a^{-1} + b^{-1} + c^{-1}$
    f) a^b

    g) $\left(\dfrac{a}{b - c}\right)^{-2}$
    h) $\left(\dfrac{2a}{b + 4c}\right)^{-3}$
    i) $\left(\dfrac{-3a}{-2b + c}\right)^{-2}$

18. Evaluate $3a^{-2} + b^c$ for these values of a, b, and c.
    a) $a = 4$, $b = 3$, $c = 0$
    b) $a = 3$, $b = 2$, $c = -1$
    c) $a = -\dfrac{1}{2}$, $b = -2$, $c = 3$
    d) $a = \dfrac{2}{3}$, $b = \dfrac{5}{4}$, $c = -1$

19. Evaluate each expression for: i) $x = 2$ ii) $x = -\dfrac{1}{2}$.

    a) x^3
    b) $(-x)^3$
    c) $-x^3$
    d) $-(-x)^3$
    e) x^{-3}
    f) $(-x)^{-3}$
    g) $-x^{-3}$
    h) $-(-x)^{-3}$

20. Solve.

    a) $5^x = 1$
    b) $2^x = \dfrac{1}{2}$
    c) $(-3)^x = \dfrac{1}{9}$
    d) $x^{-3} = \dfrac{1}{125}$

    e) $2^x = \dfrac{1}{32}$
    f) $x^2 = \dfrac{1}{25}$
    g) $4^{x-1} = \dfrac{1}{64}$
    h) $10^{2-x} = 0.001$

    i) $2^{-x-4} = \dfrac{1}{32}$
    j) $243 = \left(\dfrac{1}{3}\right)^{x+4}$
    k) $64 = (0.5)^{3-x}$
    l) $9^{1+x} = 27$

CALCULATOR POWER

Significant Digits

When measuring the diameter of a circle, we may find that the diameter is 4.3 cm *to the nearest tenth of a centimetre*. This means that the actual diameter is between 4.25 cm and 4.35 cm. We say that the digits 4 and 3 in the measurement 4.3 cm are *significant digits*.

The student in the picture multiplied 4.3 by π to obtain the circumference. When he pressed the $\boxed{\pi}$ key, the calculator used the value 3.141 592 7 for π. Then the student obtained the result 13.508 849. A circumference of 13.508 849 cm represents a measurement that is correct to the nearest millionth of a centimetre. No wonder the teacher was surprised to find that the diameter of a circle known only to the nearest tenth of a centimetre was used to calculate a circumference to the nearest millionth of a centimetre!

When the student multiplied the diameter by π he should have realized that his diameter was known only to be between 4.25 cm and 4.35 cm. If he had used both of these values with his calculator, he would have found the following results for the circumference.

Using a diameter of 4.25 cm, the circumference is:	Using a diameter of 4.35 cm, the circumference is:
$C = \pi d$	$C = \pi d$
$\quad = 3.141\ 592\ 7(4.25)$	$\quad = 3.141\ 592\ 7(4.35)$
$\quad = 13.351\ 769$	$\quad = 13.665\ 928$

Since the student measured the diameter and found it to be 4.3 cm to the nearest tenth of a centimetre, all he knows about the circumference is that it is between 13.351 769 cm and 13.665 928 cm. To overcome this discrepancy, we use the following convention.

> When calculating with measurements, the final answer should be written with the same number of significant digits used in the measurements.

When the student calculated the circumference by multiplying his measured diameter 4.3 cm by π, he should have rounded the circumference to the same number of significant digits as his measurement. That is, his calculated result was 13.508 849, which he should have rounded to two significant digits. He should have written the answer as 14 cm.

There are two important things to realize about the above convention.

- The convention does not always give accurate results. For example, the student's circle could have had a diameter much closer to 4.25 cm than to 4.35 cm. The circumference would then be much closer to 13.351 769 cm than to 13.665 928 cm. To two significant digits, the circumference would be 13 cm and not 14 cm.
- Significant digits are used *only* when the numbers involved in a calculation are actual measurements. For example, we can visualize a circle having a diameter of *exactly* 4.3 cm. The circumference of this circle could be written as 13.508 849 cm, or even as 4.3π cm, without using the convention.

When you consider the significant digits in a number between 0 and 1, the leading zeros, which precede the non-zero digits, are not counted as significant digits. For example, each of the numbers 0.5, 0.006, and 0.000 007 has 1 significant digit.

1. Use your calculator to find the circumferences of the circles with these diameters. Round your answers appropriately.
   a) 1.8 cm   b) 0.09 m   c) 0.6 km   d) 15.7 cm   e) 0.44 m

2. The dimensions of a rectangular solid are measured as 57 cm by 43 cm by 25 cm, to the nearest centimetre.

   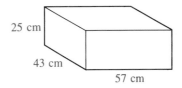

   a) Use these dimensions to calculate the volume of the solid. To how many significant digits should the volume be written?
   b) State the least possible value of each dimension.
   c) Calculate the least possible volume.
   d) State the greatest possible value of each dimension.
   e) Calculate the greatest possible volume.
   f) Express the volumes calculated in parts a), c), and e) to:
      i) 2 significant digits   ii) 1 significant digit.
   g) To how many significant digits should the volume be expressed, to be representative of all possible values?

PROBLEM SOLVING

Solve a Simpler Related Problem

The city of Toronto organized a hockey
league. However, the league organizer discovered that when the players were divided
into teams of 6, teams of 7 or teams of 8,
there was always one player left over. Finally
another player joined the league and now
the players could be divided into teams of 10,
without left overs.
How many teams were in the league?

Understand the problem
- What do we know about the number of players in the league?
- Was the number of players in the league a multiple of 6, 7 or 8
  before the last player joined?
- How is the number of players related to the number of teams?
- What are we asked to find?

Think of a strategy
- Try solving a simpler related problem, for example, what number
  leaves a remainder of 0 when divided by 6, by 7, and by 8?

Carry out the strategy
- Any number which leaves a remainder of 0 when divided by 6, 7 or
  8 is a common multiple of 6, 7, and 8.
- To find the least common multiple of 6, 7, and 8, we write each
  number as a product of its prime factors.
  $6 = 2 \times 3; \quad 7 = 7; \quad 8 = 2^3$
- Then we form the product of all the prime factors to the highest power
  to which they occur. The least common multiple of 6, 7, and 8 is
  therefore $2^3 \times 3 \times 7$, or 168.
- All the common multiples of 6, 7, and 8 are of the form $168n$ where
  n is a integer.
- All numbers which leave a remainder of 1 when divided by 6, 7, or
  8 are of the form $168n + 1$.
- The smallest positive integers which leave a remainder of 1 when
  divided by 6, 7, or 8 are: $168(1) + 1$, or 169;
  $168(2) + 1$, or 337; $\quad 168(3) + 1$, or 505.
- Of these, only 169 is a multiple of 10 when 1 is added. There were
  170 players and hence 17 teams.

Look back
- List the smallest 6 numbers which leave a remainder of 1 when divided by 6, 7, or 8.
- Is 169 the only one of these which is a multiple of 10 when increased by 1?
- If there is another number which leaves a remainder of 1 when divided by 6, 7, or 8 and it is a multiple of 10 when increased by 1, why would it be rejected as an answer to the problem?

Solve each problem

1. What time will it be:
   a) 24 000 h from now   b) 23 999 992 h from now?

2. Let $N = 1 \times 2 \times 3 \times 4 \times 5 \times \ldots \times 19 \times 20$
   a) What is the largest power of 5 of which N is a multiple?
   b) What is the largest power of 2 of which N is a multiple?
   c) How many zeros come at the end of the numeral for N?

3. a) What is the smallest multiple of 300 which has all its prime factors to an even power?
   b) What is the smallest multiple of 300 which is the square of a positive integer?
   c) What is the smallest multiple of 300 which is the cube of a positive integer?

4. What is the area of the shaded kite drawn on 1 cm paper (below left)?

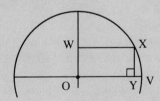

5. In rectangle WXYO, OY = 15 cm and YV = 2 cm. What is the length of WY if O is the centre of the circle (above right)?

6. M and N are the midpoints of the sides of a rectangle. What fraction of the rectangle is shaded?

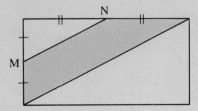

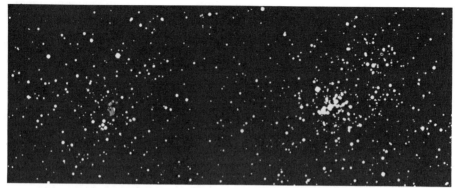

5-5 SCIENTIFIC NOTATION

Scientists tell us that there are about 120 000 000 000 stars in our galaxy, the Milky Way. Only the first two digits in this number are significant, the zeros are place holders to show the position of the decimal point.

Large numbers like this are awkward to write and difficult to read. To express very large numbers (and very small numbers) more simply, we use *scientific notation*.

When a number is expressed in scientific notation, it is written as the product of:
- a number greater than or equal to 1 but less than 10, and
- a power of 10.

To express 120 000 000 000 in scientific notation, write the decimal after the first non-zero digit and drop the trailing zeros, to get 1.2.

Since the true position of the decimal is 11 places to the right, we multiply the number 1.2 by 10^{11}.

That is, $120\ 000\ 000\ 000 = 1.2 \times 10^{11}$

The mass of a hydrogen atom is 0.000 000 000 000 000 000 000 001 67 g. To express this very small number in scientific notation, write the decimal after the first non-zero digit and drop the preceding zeros, to get 1.67.

Since the true position of the decimal is 24 places to the left, we multiply the number 1.67 by 10^{-24}.

That is, $0.000\ 000\ 000\ 000\ 000\ 000\ 000\ 001\ 67 = 1.67 \times 10^{-24}$

Example 1. Simplify. $\dfrac{24\ 000\ 000\ 000 \times 0.000\ 02}{3200}$

Solution. Rewrite the expression using scientific notation.

$$\frac{24\ 000\ 000\ 000 \times 0.000\ 02}{3200} = \frac{2.4 \times 10^{10} \times 2 \times 10^{-5}}{3.2 \times 10^{3}}$$

$$= \frac{2.4 \times 2}{3.2} \times \frac{10^{10} \times 10^{-5}}{10^{3}}$$

$$= 1.5 \times 10^{2}$$

$$= 150$$

Example 2. Write in scientific notation and estimate the answer to one significant digit.

$$\frac{389\ 527 \times 6\ 058\ 732}{4793.82}$$

Solution. Write each number in scientific notation to one significant digit.

$$389\ 527 \doteq 4 \times 10^5; \qquad 6\ 058\ 732 \doteq 6 \times 10^6; \qquad 4793.82 \doteq 5 \times 10^3$$

$$\frac{389\ 527 \times 6\ 058\ 732}{4793.82} \doteq \frac{4 \times 10^5 \times 6 \times 10^6}{5 \times 10^3}$$
$$\doteq 5 \times 10^8$$

Since the factors were rounded to one significant digit, the estimate should not exceed one significant digit.

Example 3. It has been estimated that if the average mass of an automobile were reduced from 1500 kg to 1000 kg, Canada would save about 30 000 000 L of oil each day.
a) Find how much oil Canada would save in one year.
b) Three litres of oil yield 2 L of gasoline. Assume that there are 9 000 000 cars on Canadian roads and gasoline costs 55¢/L. Find the annual saving per car.

Solution.
a) Oil saved per year $= 365 \times 30\ 000\ 000$
$$= 3.65 \times 10^2 \times 3.0 \times 10^7$$
$$= 10.95 \times 10^9$$
$$= 1.095 \times 10^{10}$$

The annual saving of oil would be about 1.1×10^{10} L.

b) 1.095×10^{10} L of oil are saved every year.

Hence, $\frac{2}{3}(1.095 \times 10^{10})$ L of gasoline are saved every year.

There are 9 000 000 cars on the road.

Hence, the gasoline saved per year per car is

$$\frac{1}{9\ 000\ 000} \times \frac{2}{3}(1.095 \times 10^{10})\ \text{L}.$$

Gasoline costs $0.55/L.

Hence, the annual saving per car is

$$\frac{1}{9\ 000\ 000} \times \frac{2}{3}(1.095 \times 10^{10}) \times 0.55\ \text{dollars}$$

$$= \frac{2 \times 1.095 \times 0.55 \times 10^{10}}{9 \times 3 \times 10^6}$$

$$\doteq 0.0446 \times 10^4$$

$$\doteq 446$$

The annual saving per car could be about $450.

What would be the annual saving per car with the price of gasoline today?

EXERCISES 5-5

Ⓐ

1. Write in scientific notation.
   a) 1000
   b) 100 000 000
   c) 100
   d) 750
   e) 1100
   f) 3 700 000
   g) 0.0001
   h) 0.000 000 1
   i) 0.000 001
   j) 0.000 85
   k) 0.000 092
   l) 0.000 000 008 2
   m) 85
   n) 0.038
   o) 9900
   p) 3 210 012

2. Write in scientific notation.
   a) Speed of light, 300 000 km/s
   b) World population in 1985, 4 843 000 000
   c) Mass of the Earth, 5 980 000 000 000 000 000 000 000 kg
   d) Time of fastest camera exposure, 0.000 000 1 s
   e) Mass of the ball in a ball-point pen, 0.004 g

3. What numbers complete this table?

	Physical Quantity	Decimal Notation	Scientific Notation
a)	Temperature of the sun's interior	1 300 000°C	1.3×10^6
b)	Thickness of a plastic film	0.000 01 m	1×10
c)	Mass of an electron		9.2×10^{-28} g
d)	Number of stars in our galaxy	120 000 000 000	1.2×10^{11}
e)	Estimated age of the Earth	4 500 000 000 years	
f)	Diameter of a hydrogen atom	0.000 000 011 3 cm	
g)	Land area of the Earth		1.5×10^8 km²
h)	Ocean area of the Earth		3.6×10^8 km²
i)	Mass of the Earth		5.9×10^{24} kg
j)	Cost of a Concorde aircraft	8 500 000 000 F	

Ⓑ

4. Write in scientific notation.
   a) 32×10^4
   b) 247×10^8
   c) 49.2×10^7
   d) 685×10^{10}
   e) 0.387×10^4
   f) 0.087×10^3
   g) 672×10^{-5}
   h) 43.7×10^{-6}
   i) 0.841×10^{-2}
   j) 0.49×10^{-7}
   k) 125×10^0
   l) $1.85 \div 10^{-2}$

5. Find each value for n.
   a) $1265 = 1.265 \times 10^n$
   b) $76.3 = 7.63 \times 10^n$
   c) $0.0041 = 4.1 \times 10^n$
   d) $0.860 = 8.60 \times 10^n$
   e) $0.005 = 5 \times 10^n$
   f) $0.000 056 3 = 5.63 \times 10^n$
   g) $1150 = 1.150 \times 10^n$
   h) $4 961 000 000 = 4.961 \times 10^n$
   i) $7 430 000 = 7.43 \times 10^n$
   j) $0.000 000 583 1 = 5.831 \times 10^n$

6. Express these distances and measurements in scientific notation.

From Galactic Distances to Atomic Measurements, all in metres

100 000 000 000 000 000 000 000 000	Distance to quasars
14 000 000 000 000 000 000 000	Distance to the nearest galaxy
760 000 000 000 000 000 000	Diameter of our galaxy
41 000 000 000 000 000	Distance to the nearest star
12 000 000 000 000	Diameter of the solar system
150 000 000 000	Distance to the sun
380 000 000	Distance to the moon
13 000 000	Diameter of the Earth
8 800	Height of Mount Everest
2	Height of a person

Size of an insect 0.005
Diameter of a grain of sand 0.000 1
Size of a bacterium 0.000 001
Diameter of an atom 0.000 000 000 1
Diameter of a nucleus 0.000 000 000 000 01
Diameter of a proton 0.000 000 000 000 000 1
Wavelength of cosmic rays 0.000 000 000 000 000 000 01

7. Write in scientific notation and estimate the answer.

a) $\dfrac{582\ 965 \times 7\ 123\ 085}{5034.8}$

b) $\dfrac{9\ 867\ 341 \times 403\ 928}{79\ 386.3}$

c) $\dfrac{1\ 937\ 281 \times 8\ 886\ 432}{2916.5 \times 58\ 034}$

d) $\dfrac{38\ 621 \times 49\ 728 \times 392.6}{79\ 362 \times 193\ 481}$

8. Simplify, and express the answer in scientific notation rounded to two significant digits.

a) $349\ 000 \times 2650 \times 120\ 000$

b) $8600 \times 1\ 500\ 000 \times 0.0003$

c) $\dfrac{480\ 000 \times 62\ 000\ 000}{300\ 000}$

d) $\dfrac{850\ 000 \times 400\ 000}{6\ 200\ 000}$

e) $\dfrac{0.000\ 006 \times 54\ 000}{0.000\ 009}$

f) $\dfrac{2\ 400\ 000 \times 0.000\ 000\ 000\ 8}{0.000\ 000\ 4 \times 12\ 000}$

9. Write in scientific notation and estimate the answer.

a) $\dfrac{392\ 876 \times 48\ 731 \times 0.000\ 186}{0.000\ 007\ 7 \times 3\ 865\ 097}$

b) $\dfrac{0.000\ 000\ 28 \times 78\ 365\ 294}{1873.6 \times 29\ 586 \times 0.0038}$

c) $\dfrac{29\ 307\ 608 \times 30\ 962 \times 567\ 081}{0.000\ 089 \times 5\ 821\ 939}$

d) $\dfrac{23\ 501\ 784 \times 0.000\ 935}{0.000\ 248\ 6 \times 225.69}$

e) $\dfrac{0.000\ 730\ 8 \times 0.017\ 41 \times 642}{52\ 325 \times 0.002\ 79 \times 48}$

f) $\dfrac{3127.98 \times 0.005\ 294 \times 1.4372}{1001 \times 0.9842 \times 0.000\ 55}$

10. Californium 252, one of the world's rarest metals, is used in treating cancer. If one-tenth of a microgram costs $100, what is its cost per gram?

11. The measured daily deposit of the pollutant sulphur dioxide on Metropolitan Toronto is approximately 4.8×10^{-6} g/cm². If Metropolitan Toronto has an area of about 620 km², and the pollutant is distributed evenly, calculate the amount of sulphur dioxide that falls on the city:
    a) in 1 day
    b) in 1 year
    c) in your lifetime.

12. If it takes 1200 silkworm eggs to balance the mass of 1 g, what is the mass of one silkworm egg?

13. The volume of water in the oceans is estimated to be 1.35×10^{18} m³. If the density of sea water is 1025 kg/m³, what is the mass of the oceans?

14. A faucet is leaking at the rate of one drop of water per second. The volume of one drop is 0.1 cm³.
    a) Calculate the volume of water lost in a year.
    b) Calculate how long it would take to fill a rectangular basin 30 cm by 20 cm by 20 cm.

Ⓒ

15. In 1986, astronomers discovered a chain of galaxies, which stretches a billion light-years from one end to the other. It is the largest structure ever found in the universe. A light-year is the distance that light, with a speed of 300 000 km/s, travels in one year.
    a) Calculate the approximate number of kilometres in one light-year.
    b) Calculate the length, in kilometres, of the astronomers' discovery.

16. It has been estimated that the insect population of the world is at least 1 000 000 000 000 000 000. The scientist who made this estimate also reckoned that if the average mass of an insect is 2.5 mg, then the total mass of insects on the Earth is twelve times as great as the total mass of all human beings.
    a) Estimate the total mass of the Earth's insect population.
    b) Estimate the total mass of the Earth's human population.
    c) Use the population estimate in *Exercise 2* and your answer to part b) to calculate the average mass of a person. Is this average reasonable?

17. A drop of oil with a volume of 1 mm³ spreads out on the surface of water until it is a film one molecule thick. If the film has an area of 1 m², what is the thickness of an oil molecule?

18. The number 10^{100} is sometimes called a *googol*. To help you understand how large a number this is, think of the visible universe as a cube with edges of length 2×10^{25} m. Suppose this cube were filled with cubical grains of sand with edges of length 2×10^{-4} m. How many grains of sand would be needed?

19. Write in scientific notation.
    a) The square root of a googol
    b) The fourth root of a googol
    c) The tenth root of a googol

MATHEMATICS AROUND US

How Bacteria Grow and Multiply

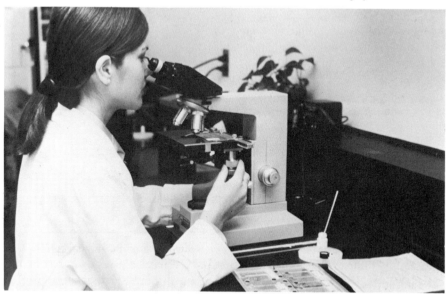

At midnight, there were 1000 bacteria in a culture. The number of bacteria doubles every hour so n hours later there would be $1000(2^n)$. Does this statement make sense if n is negative?

If n were -3, it would be like asking, "How many bacteria were there -3 h after midnight?"; -3 h after midnight is 3 h *before* midnight. To find the number of bacteria 3 h before midnight, multiply 1000 by 2^{-3}.

$$1000(2^{-3}) = 1000\left(\frac{1}{8}\right)$$
$$= 125$$

There were about 125 bacteria in the culture 3 h before midnight.

QUESTIONS

1. About how many bacteria were in the culture:
   a) 1 h before midnight
   b) 2 h before midnight?

2. At 00:30, there were about 1400 bacteria in the culture. About how many were there:
   a) 1 h earlier
   b) 2 h earlier
   c) 3 h earlier?

3. At 03:45, there were about 13 500 bacteria in the culture. About how many were there:
   a) 3 h earlier
   b) 4 h earlier
   c) 5 h earlier?

COMPUTER POWER

Scientific Notation

Most microcomputers can display nine digits in a number. When a computer displays a number in scientific notation, it is likely to use E to indicate that the number is in this form.

Most microcomputers display:
- numbers less than 1 billion in decimal form, for example, the command PRINT 999999999 yields the display 999999999.
- numbers 1 billion or greater in scientific notation, for example, the command PRINT 1000000000 yields the display 1E + 09; the command PRINT 1400000000 yields the display 1.4E + 09.

After each input, press $\boxed{\text{RETURN}}$.

1. Write the display produced by each command.
   a) PRINT 690000000   b) PRINT 7200000000   c) PRINT 42800000000
   Use the computer to check your answers.

2. Determine the largest number of digits your computer will display.

3. Determine the smallest positive number your computer will display in decimal form.

4. Write the display produced by each command.
   a) PRINT 0.052   b) PRINT 0.0035   c) PRINT 0.000096

5. Write, in decimal form, the number expressed in each computer display.
   a) 1.7 E + 09   b) 9.63 E + 10   c) 7.19 E + 12
   d) −6.2 E + 11   e) 9.3 E − 03   f) 3.05 E − 08

6. Input each command on your computer. Record each answer.
   a) PRINT 1E + 09*1E + 10   b) PRINT 1E + 09*1E − 08
   c) PRINT 1E + 10*1E − 13   d) PRINT 1E + 22/1E + 10
   e) PRINT 1E + 08/1E − 03   f) PRINT 1E + 12/1E − 03

7. Study your answers in *Exercise 6*. Can you write a simple rule for:
   a) multiplying powers of 10   b) dividing powers of 10?

8. Use your rules in *Exercise 7* to predict these products and quotients.
   a) 1E + 11*1E + 15   b) 1E + 18*1E − 08
   c) 1E + 29/1E + 16   d) 1E + 31/1E + 14
   Use the computer to check your answers.

9. What happens if:
   a) you enter 2E12 instead of 2E + 12
   b) you enter 1E − 8 instead of 1E − 08
   c) you enter E − 9 instead of 1E − 09

5-6 SQUARE ROOTS

When a skydiver leaves an airplane, the distance fallen during the first few seconds of free fall is related to the time that has elapsed by the formula $t^2 \doteq \frac{1}{5}d$. d is the distance in metres and t is the time in seconds.

How long does it take the skydiver to fall a distance of 80 m?
To find the value of t, substitute $d = 80$ into the equation.

$$t^2 \doteq \frac{1}{5}(80)$$
$$= 16$$

t^2 means $t \times t$. To solve the equation, we need to find the value of t that multiplied by itself gives 16.

We know that $4 \times 4 = 16$ and $(-4) \times (-4) = 16$.
Hence t must equal 4 or -4.

But a negative value for t has no meaning in this context.

Hence, the solution is $t = 4$.

The skydiver takes about 4 s to fall 80 m.

When a number (like 16) can be written as the product of two factors that are the same, each factor is a *square root* of that number.

That is, since $4 \times 4 = 16$ and $(-4) \times (-4) = 16$, then 4 and -4 are the square roots of 16.

Similarly, since $7 \times 7 = 49$ and $(-7) \times (-7) = 49$, then 7 and -7 are the square roots of 49.

Further, since $0.2 \times 0.2 = 0.04$ and $(-0.2) \times (-0.2) = 0.04$, then 0.2 and -0.2 are the square roots of 0.04.

Positive numbers always have two square roots — one positive, the other negative. The symbol, $\sqrt{}$, is the *radical sign* and it always denotes the positive square root.

Thus, $\sqrt{49} = 7$ and $\sqrt{0.04} = 0.2$

Example 1. Evaluate.

    a) $\sqrt{121}$ b) $-\sqrt{1.21}$ c) $-\sqrt{12\ 100}$ d) $\sqrt{0.0121}$

Solution.

    a) Since $11 \times 11 = 121$, then $\sqrt{121} = 11$

    b) Since $1.1 \times 1.1 = 1.21$, then $-\sqrt{1.21} = -1.1$

    c) Since $110 \times 110 = 12\ 100$, then $-\sqrt{12\ 100} = -110$

    d) Since $0.11 \times 0.11 = 0.0121$, then $\sqrt{0.0121} = 0.11$

Example 2. Find the length of the side of each square.

    a)   b)

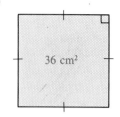
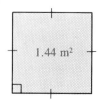

Solution.

The area A of a square is equal to the square of the length of the side s.

That is, $A = s^2$

    a) If $A = 36$, then $s = \sqrt{36}$

                        $= 6$

      The side of the square is 6 cm.

    b) If $A = 1.44$, then $s = \sqrt{1.44}$

      We know that $\sqrt{144} = 12$, so $\sqrt{1.44} = 1.2$.

      The side of the square is 1.2 m.

Radical signs are usually treated like brackets. Operations under radical signs are performed first.

Example 3. Evaluate.

    a) $-3\sqrt{6.25}$ b) $\sqrt{9 + 16}$ c) $5\sqrt{4} - 3(\sqrt{121} - \sqrt{81})$

Solution.

    a) $-3\sqrt{6.25} = -3(2.5)$

                     $= -7.5$

    b) $\sqrt{9 + 16} = \sqrt{25}$

                  $= 5$

    c) $5\sqrt{4} - 3(\sqrt{121} - \sqrt{81}) = 5(2) - 3(11 - 9)$

                                  $= 10 - 3(2)$

                                  $= 10 - 6$

                                  $= 4$

Example 4. Evaluate each expression for $x = -2$ and $y = 3$.

a) $\sqrt{-x + y + 4}$ 　　　　　　　b) $-\sqrt{6x + 5y - xy}$

Solution. 　Substitute the given values for x and y.

a) $\sqrt{-x + y + 4} = \sqrt{-(-2) + 3 + 4}$
$$= \sqrt{2 + 3 + 4}$$
$$= \sqrt{9}$$
$$= 3$$

b) $-\sqrt{6x + 5y - xy} = -\sqrt{6(-2) + 5(3) - (-2)(3)}$
$$= -\sqrt{-12 + 15 + 6}$$
$$= -\sqrt{9}$$
$$= -3$$

EXERCISES 5-6

(A)

1. Find the square roots of each number.
   a) 81　　　　b) 10 000　　　c) 900　　　d) 0.16　　　e) 14 400
   f) 40 000　　g) 0.64　　　h) 0.0001　　i) 4900　　　j) 0.25

2. Evaluate.
   a) $\sqrt{49}$　　　b) $-\sqrt{0.04}$　　c) $\sqrt{1600}$　　d) $\sqrt{169}$　　e) $-\sqrt{3600}$
   f) $\sqrt{1.44}$　　g) $-\sqrt{225}$　　h) $\sqrt{10^{12}}$　　i) $\sqrt{625}$　　j) $-\sqrt{2^4}$

3. Find the side length of each square with the given area.
   a) 16 m²　　　　　　　b) 10 000 mm²　　　　　c) 6.25 cm²
   d) 2^6 m²　　　　　　e) 10^4 m²　　　　　　f) 4900 m²

(B)

4. Simplify.
   a) $\sqrt{64 + 36}$　　　　b) $\sqrt{16} + \sqrt{9}$　　　c) $2\sqrt{16} - 3\sqrt{4}$
   d) $3\sqrt{36} + 2\sqrt{25}$　　e) $5\sqrt{100 - 36}$　　f) $\sqrt{1 + 3 + 5 + 7 + 9}$
   g) $2\sqrt{81} - 7\sqrt{49}$　　h) $4\sqrt{289 - 225}$　　i) $2\sqrt{\sqrt{81}}$

5. Evaluate each expression for $a = 5$ and $b = -3$.

   a) $\sqrt{20a}$　　　　　　b) $\sqrt{9a^2}$　　　　　c) $\sqrt{\dfrac{125}{a}}$

   d) $\sqrt{2a - 13b}$　　　e) $\sqrt{-12b}$　　　f) $-\sqrt{3a - 3b + 1}$
   g) $\sqrt{a^2 + 3b}$　　　h) $\sqrt{7a - 8b + 5}$　　i) $-4\sqrt{11a - 3b}$
   j) $-3\sqrt{2a^2 - 4b^2 + 2}$　k) $0.5\sqrt{a^2 - 2ab + b^2}$　l) $2\sqrt{2a^2 - 3b^2 + 2}$

6. Evaluate each expression for $x = 3$, $y = -4$, and $z = -7$.
   a) $-\sqrt{12x}$　　　　　b) $\sqrt{z^2 + 6y}$　　　　c) $4\sqrt{x^2 + y^2}$
   d) $\sqrt{6x - z}$　　　　e) $5\sqrt{15x - y}$　　　f) $-\sqrt{7x - 4y - 1}$
   g) $2\sqrt{x - 2y - 2z}$　　h) $-\sqrt{2z^2 + 5y + x}$　i) $6\sqrt{3y^2 + x^0}$
   j) $\sqrt{-(-2x + 4y + 2z)}$　k) $\sqrt{x^2 + 2x + z^2}$　l) $-\sqrt{3x^2 + y + 2z^2}$

7. From the area of each square, calculate:
   i)   the length of a side
   ii) the perimeter.

   a)
   289 mm²

   b)
   4.41 cm²

   c) 0.0064 m²

8. The distance d metres that an object falls from rest in t seconds is given by the formula $d \doteq 5t^2$. A pebble is dropped from a cliff 320 m high. Find how long the pebble takes to reach the ground.

Ⓒ

9. For an equilateral triangle of side length x, the area A is given by $A \doteq 0.43x^2$. For each equilateral triangle with the given area, calculate:
   i) the length of a side
   ii) the perimeter.

   a) 10.825 m²   b) 27.712 m²
   c) 0.350 73 m²   d) 389.7 cm²
   e) 0.004 33 km²   f) 97.425 km²

   Give the answers to 2 decimal places.

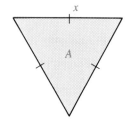

10. In a right triangle with side lengths as shown, the formula $z^2 = x^2 + y^2$ applies. Calculate z for each value of x and y.
    a) 6 mm, 8 mm
    b) 8 mm, 15 mm
    c) 0.5 m, 1.2 m
    d) 24 mm, 7 mm
    e) 0.03 km, 0.04 km
    f) 2.8 km, 9.6 km

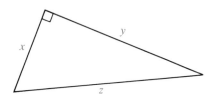

11. In winter, you should have noticed that the stronger the wind the colder it feels. Winter weather forecasts often give ''wind-chill'' temperatures.
    For wind speeds of 10 km/h and higher, the following formula gives an approximate value for the wind-chill temperature.
    $w = 33 - (0.23 \sqrt{v} + 0.45 - 0.01v)(33 - T)$
    w is the wind-chill temperature in degrees Celsius.
    v is the wind speed in kilometres per hour.
    T is the still-air temperature in degrees Celsius.
    For a still-air temperature of $-18°C$, calculate the wind-chill temperatures, to the nearest degree, at these wind speeds.
    a) 100 km/h   b) 80 km/h
    c) 30 km/h   d) 15 km/h

5-7 ESTIMATING AND CALCULATING SQUARE ROOTS

Renata was standing on the observation level of the CN Tower. It was a clear day and she could see to the horizon. She wondered how far away the horizon was.

The formula $d \doteq 3.6\sqrt{h}$ relates the distance d kilometres to the horizon from an observer who is h metres above the ground.

The observation level of the CN Tower is 457 m above the ground.

To find the distance to the horizon, substitute $h = 457$ into the formula $d \doteq 3.6\sqrt{h}$.

Then $d \doteq 3.6\sqrt{457}$

The number 457 has a square root which cannot be written as a terminating decimal. However, an approximation to its value can be found by estimating.

We know that $\sqrt{400} = 20$ so $\sqrt{457}$ will be a little more than 20.

Estimate. $\sqrt{457} = 21$

Check. $21^2 = 441$ so 21 is too small

Try 22. $22^2 = 484$ so 22 is too large

Try 21.5. $21.5^2 = 462.25$ so 21.5 is too large but not by much

Try 21.4. $21.4^2 = 457.96$ so 21.4 is very close

$\sqrt{457}$ is 21.4 to 1 decimal place.

Hence, the distance to the horizon, $d \doteq 3.6(21.4)$
$$= 77.04$$

Renata could see about 77 km to the horizon from the observation level of the CN Tower.

Since a calculator has a ☐√☐ key, the approximate square root of a number can be found easily.

To evaluate $\sqrt{457}$, key in: ▨ ▨ ▨ ▨ to display 21.377558

Example 1. Find, by estimating and checking, the square roots of 8356 to the nearest whole number.

Solution. Start with numbers whose squares are familiar.

$100^2 = 10\ 000$ too high
$90^2 = 8100$ too low but close
$92^2 = 8464$ too high
$91.5^2 = 8372.25$ too high
$91.4^2 = 8353.96$ too low

By inspection, the square root of 8356 is closer to 91.4 than it is to 91.5.

Hence, the square roots of 8356 are 91 and -91 to the nearest whole number.

Consider the problem that was posed at the beginning of the chapter.

Example 2. Find, to the nearest centimetre, the length of each side of the square poster on the right, which is twice the area of the poster on the left.

90 cm

Solution. Area of the smaller poster $= 90^2$
$= 8100$

Area of the larger poster $= 2(8100)$
$= 16\ 200$

The length of each side of a square is equal to the square root of its area.

Side of larger poster $= \sqrt{16\ 200}$
$\doteq 127.28$

Each side of the larger poster is approximately 127 cm long.

Although the area has doubled, the length of the side did not double.

EXERCISES 5-7

(A)

1. State which square roots are between 8 and 9.
   $\sqrt{67}$, $\sqrt{91}$, $\sqrt{78}$, $\sqrt{62}$, $\sqrt{80}$

2. State which of the square roots listed below are between:
   a) 3 and 4   b) 7 and 8   c) 11 and 12
   d) 10 and 11   e) 13 and 14   f) 18 and 19.

   $\sqrt{11}$, $\sqrt{52}$, $\sqrt{61}$, $\sqrt{14}$, $\sqrt{330}$, $\sqrt{360}$, $\sqrt{320}$, $\sqrt{257}$,
   $\sqrt{190}$, $\sqrt{140}$, $\sqrt{171}$, $\sqrt{118}$, $\sqrt{110}$, $\sqrt{130}$, $\sqrt{80}$, $\sqrt{35}$

3. State which of the three estimates is closest to the square root.
   a) $\sqrt{39}$; 6.2, 6.4, 6.6   b) $\sqrt{119}$; 10.3, 10.6, 10.9   c) $\sqrt{172}$; 13.1, 13.3, 13.5

(B)

4. Estimate each square root to one decimal place.
   a) $\sqrt{18}$ b) $\sqrt{7.7}$ c) $\sqrt{111}$ d) $\sqrt{1473}$

5. Estimate each square root to one decimal place.
   a) $\sqrt{29}$ b) $\sqrt{2.9}$ c) $\sqrt{14}$ d) $\sqrt{6.5}$ e) $\sqrt{43.5}$

6. Calculate the length, to one decimal place, of a side of each square with the given area.
   a) 43.67 cm²   b) 2.81 m²   c) 9.48 cm²   d) 37.37 m²

7. Estimate each square root to the nearest unit.
   a) $\sqrt{290}$ b) $\sqrt{1437}$ c) $\sqrt{175}$ d) $\sqrt{640}$ e) $\sqrt{8333}$

8. Use a calculator to find each square root to two decimal places.
   a) $\sqrt{34.72}$ b) $\sqrt{21.38}$ c) $\sqrt{150.46}$ d) $\sqrt{0.62}$ e) $\sqrt{0.05}$

9. What happens when the $\boxed{\sqrt{}}$ key is used in an attempt to evaluate $\sqrt{-3}$? Explain why.

10. a) If you knew the area of a square, how could you find its perimeter?
    b) Write a formula relating the perimeter P and the area A of a square.
    c) Find the perimeters of the squares with these areas.
       i)   25 cm²   ii)   64 cm²   iii) 78 m²   iv) 3.8 m²

11. a) If you knew the diameter of a circle, how could you find its area?
    b) Write a formula for the area A of a circle in terms of its diameter d.
    c) Find the areas of circles with these diameters. Give the answers to the nearest square unit.
       i)   10 cm   ii)   20 cm   iii)   31.8 cm   iv) 4 m
    d) If you knew the area of a circle, how could you find its diameter?
    e) Write a formula for the diameter of a circle in terms of its area.
    f) Find the diameters of the circles with these areas. Give the answers to 1 decimal place.
       i)   22 cm²   ii)   33 cm²   iii)   40 cm²   iv) 5 m²

12. The distance d kilometres of the horizon from an observer at a height h metres is given by the formula $d \doteq 3.6\sqrt{h}$. To the nearest kilometre how far is the horizon from:
   a) the 266 m observation level of the Skylon tower in Niagara Falls
   b) eye level (at a height of 1.5 m) when an observer is standing on the ground?

Ⓒ

13. An object falls a distance d metres when falling from rest for t seconds. The relationship between d and t is given by the formula $d \doteq 4.9t^2$. If it takes 3 s to fall a certain distance, how long, to the nearest tenth of a second, will it take to fall:
   a) twice as far
   c) half as far
   b) five times as far
   d) ten times as far?

14. The length d of the diagonal of a rectangle of length l and width w is given by the formula $d = \sqrt{l^2 + w^2}$.
   a) Calculate the lengths of the diagonals of rectangles with these dimensions.
      i)   8 cm by 3 cm
      iii) 10 m by 7 m
      ii) 2.3 cm by 1.2 cm
      iv) 2 m by 9 m
   b) A rectangle is 9.2 cm long and its diagonal measures 11.5 cm. What is its width?

15. The period of a pendulum is the time taken for one complete swing to and fro. The period T seconds is given by the formula $T \doteq 2\pi\sqrt{\dfrac{l}{9.8}}$, where l is the length of the pendulum in metres.

   a) Find the period, to the nearest tenth of a second, of a pendulum whose length is:
      i)   2.45 m
      ii) 0.5 m.
   b) How long, to the nearest centimetre, is a pendulum whose period is 1 s?

16. The velocity v metres per second with which liquid discharges from a small hole in a container is given by the formula $v \doteq \sqrt{19.6\,h}$, where h is the height in metres of the liquid above the hole.
   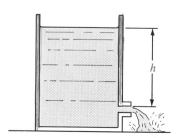
   a) Find the velocity, to the nearest tenth of a unit, of discharge for each height.
      i)   1.0 m
      ii) 0.5 m
      iii) 10 cm
   b) What height, to the nearest centimetre, of liquid gives a discharge velocity of 2 m/s?

Review Exercises

1. Evaluate.
   a) $3^2 + 2^3$
   b) $3^2 \times 2^3$
   c) $(1.6)^2$
   d) $3^2 + 4$
   e) $(-2)^3 + (-3)^2$
   f) $(2 + 3)^3$
   g) $(-4)^2 + (-2)^4$
   h) $\left(-\dfrac{3}{7}\right)^3$

2. If $x = -2$ and $y = 3$, evaluate each expression.
   a) $-5x^2$
   b) $(-5x)^2$
   c) $y^2 - x^2$
   d) $(x + y)^3$
   e) $4x^2 + 3y^2$
   f) $\dfrac{x^2 - y^2}{x - y}$ $x^{-1} - y$
   g) $2(x + y)^2$
   h) $\dfrac{y^2 - x^3}{y - x}$

3. Find the area of the shaded region of each figure. Give the answers to 1 decimal place.
   a)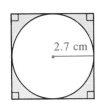
   b)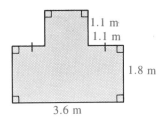
   1.1 m
   1.1 m
   1.8 m
   3.6 m
   c)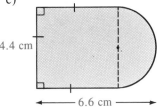
   4.4 cm
   6.6 cm

   2.7 cm

4. Find the volume of each solid. Give the answers to 1 decimal place.
   a)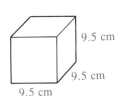
   9.5 cm
   9.5 cm
   9.5 cm
   b)
   2.4 cm
   17.8 cm
   c)
   0.3 m
   25.0 m

5. Simplify.
   a) $x^4 \times x^5$
   b) $x^{36} \div x^{12}$
   c) $x^{12} \times x^6$
   d) $(x)^7$
   e) $3x^2 \times 5x^4$
   f) $2^9 \div 2^4$
   g) $9m^4 \times 3m^2$
   h) $(-3)^{12} \div (-3)^4$
   i) $(5x)^2$
   j) $5(x^2)^3$
   k) $(3x^2)^3$
   l) $-42y^{12} \div 6y^8$

6. Simplify.
   a) $\dfrac{18x^4 \times 5x^2}{15x^3}$
   b) $\dfrac{120x^5}{-15x} \times \dfrac{15x^4}{5x^2}$

7. Evaluate each expression for $x = 4$.
   a) $x^2 \times x^4$
   b) $(2x^2)^2$
   c) $(2x^2)(3x^3)$

8. Evaluate.
   a) 5^{-3}
   b) $\left(\dfrac{1}{2}\right)^{-1}$
   c) $2^{-3} - 4^{-1}$
   d) $7^0 + 2^{-2}$
   e) $3^2 - 3^{-2}$
   f) $\left(\dfrac{2}{3}\right)^{-1} + \left(\dfrac{2}{3}\right)^0$
   g) $\left(\dfrac{1}{2}\right)^{-2} + 2^{-1}$
   h) $\left(\dfrac{1}{2}\right)^{-2} \div 2^{-1}$

9. Simplify.
   a) $w^8 \div w^{-4}$
   b) $w^{-9} \div w^{-12}$
   c) $15x^4 \div (-3x^{-4})$

   d) $-24y^4 \div 3y^{-2}$
   e) $\dfrac{10}{y^4} \div y^2$
   f) $16z^{-2} \div (2z)^2$

10. Evaluate each expression for $a = -2$, $b = 2$, and $c = -1$.
    a) $a^{-1} + b^{-1}$
    b) $(a + b + c)^{-1}$
    c) a^b
    d) $a^{-1} + b^{-1} + c^2$

11. Write in scientific notation.
    a) 10 000
    b) 740 000
    c) 0.000 01
    d) 0.057

12. Express in scientific notation, then simplify.
    a) 49 000 000 × 730 000
    b) 26 500 000 × 7900 × 0.0046
    c) $\dfrac{320\ 000 \times 64\ 000\ 000}{12\ 800\ 000}$

13. Simplify.
    a) $\sqrt{36}$
    b) $-\sqrt{0.25}$
    c) $\sqrt{14\ 400}$
    d) $\sqrt{0.0081}$
    e) $\sqrt{0.36}$
    f) $-\sqrt{640\ 000}$
    g) $\sqrt{0.0121}$
    h) $-\sqrt{0.49}$

14. Simplify.
    a) $-3\sqrt{25} - 5\sqrt{9}$
    b) $\sqrt{225} - \sqrt{49}$
    c) $4\sqrt{169} - \sqrt{25}$

15. Find the side length of each square with the given area.
    a) 64 mm²
    b) 0.81 m²
    c) 49 cm²
    d) 2.25 cm²

16. Calculate each square root to two decimal places.
    a) $\sqrt{28}$
    b) $\sqrt{17.4}$
    c) $\sqrt{250}$
    d) $\sqrt{0.44}$

17. A square, with a side length of 10 cm, is to be reduced in area by one-half. Find the side length, to the nearest centimetre, of the reduced square.

18. Evaluate each expression for $m = 3$ and $n = -2$.
    a) $\sqrt{9m^2}$
    b) $\sqrt{-8n}$
    c) $-\sqrt{m + n}$
    d) $\sqrt{10m + 2n - 1}$
    e) $-\sqrt{m^2 - 3n + 1}$
    f) $\sqrt{m^3 + 2mn + 1}$

19. The approximate velocity v metres per second of an orbiting satellite is given by the formula $v = \sqrt{9.8r}$, where r is the distance in metres of the satellite from the centre of the Earth. Find the velocity of the satellite if:
    a) $r = 2 \times 10^7$ m
    b) $r = 5 \times 10^8$ m.

20. When a ball is dropped from a height of 2 m, the height h metres to which it bounces is given by $h = 2(0.8)^n$, where n is the number of bounces. To what height does the ball bounce after:
    a) the first bounce
    b) the third bounce?

21. The width w of a rectangle with length l and diagonal length d is given by the formula $w = \sqrt{d^2 - l^2}$. Find the width of a rectangle with length 12.2 cm and a diagonal of length 15.8 cm.

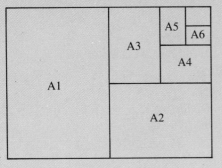

In a move to conserve the Earth's resources, an international standard of paper sizes was created. The largest, A0, has an area of 1 m^2. The ratio of the lengths of its sides are such that cutting it in half results in the next largest size, A1, with side lengths in the same ratio. The next size, A2, is obtained by cutting an A1 sheet in half, and so on. The length-to-width ratio is the same for all sizes.

There is only one length-to-width ratio that yields similar rectangles in this way. Can you find what it is? (See Section 6-3, *Example 3*.)

6-1 RATIOS

The newspaper headline indicates that 80 out of 100 Canadians buy lottery tickets. Therefore, 20 out of 100 do not buy tickets.

80 out of every 100 Canadians buy lottery tickets

The comparison of the numbers of people who do not buy lottery tickets and those who do, can be written as a *ratio*, 20 : 80. This is read, "twenty to eighty".

A ratio is a comparison of quantities measured in the same units. The numbers 20 and 80 are the *terms* of the ratio. The order of the terms is important; they may not be interchanged.

When each term of a ratio is multiplied or divided by the same non-zero number, an equivalent ratio is produced. For example, 20 : 80 = 200 : 800 = 2 : 8 = 1 : 4

The ratio 1 : 4 is in *lowest terms* because the only factor that the terms have in common is 1.

A ratio can be written in fractional form; that is, 20 : 80 can be written as $\frac{20}{80}$.

Although a ratio can be written in fractional form, a ratio is *not* a fraction. A fraction is a comparison of part(s) of an amount (the numerator) to the whole amount (the denominator). A ratio is a comparison of two amounts, the second of which may not be the whole amount.

For example, the ratio described previously, $\frac{20}{80}$, can be written as $\frac{1}{4}$. But this does not mean that $\frac{1}{4}$ of the people do not buy lottery tickets.

In fact, $\frac{1}{4}$ in this context has no meaning as a fraction because the denominator does not represent the whole group of people considered.

Example 1. Write each ratio in lowest terms.

    a) 9 : 6   b) 16 : 12   c) 25 : 20   d) $\frac{60}{15}$

Solution.   a) 9 : 6   b) 16 : 12
                 Divide by 3.   Divide by 4.
                 9 : 6 = 3 : 2   16 : 12 = 4 : 3

           c) 25 : 20   d) $\frac{60}{15}$
                 Divide by 5.   Divide by 15.
                 25 : 20 = 5 : 4 $\frac{60}{15} = \frac{4}{1}$

Example 2. The table shows the knockout records of four boxers in the Winnipeg Boxing Club. Which two boxers have the same ratio of knockouts to fights?

Name	Fights	Knockouts
Doug James	28	7
Mike Seiling	24	8
Gary Burgess	20	5
Dan Stoffer	24	4

Solution The knockouts-to-fights ratios are
James $7 : 28 = 1 : 4$, Seiling $8 : 24 = 1 : 3$, Burgess $5 : 20 = 1 : 4$,
Stoffer $4 : 24 = 1 : 6$
Doug James and Gary Burgess have the same knockouts-to-fights ratio.

Example 3. A parking lot contains domestic and foreign cars in the ratio $7 : 4$. If there are 77 cars in the lot, how many of them are foreign?

Solution. The ratio of domestic cars to foreign cars is $7 : 4$.
Therefore, 7 out of 11 cars are domestic and 4 out of 11 cars are foreign.
The number of foreign cars is $\dfrac{4}{11}(77) = 28$

There are 28 foreign cars in the lot.

Example 4. Fuel X is composed of ingredients A and B in the ratio $3 : 5$. Fuel Y is composed of ingredients A and B in the ratio $4 : 7$. Which fuel is richer in ingredient A?

Solution. Ingredient A is $\dfrac{3}{8}$ of fuel X. Ingredient A is $\dfrac{4}{11}$ of fuel Y.

Raise these fractions to a common denominator.

$\dfrac{3}{8} = \dfrac{33}{88}$ and $\dfrac{4}{11} = \dfrac{32}{88}$

Since $\dfrac{33}{88} > \dfrac{32}{88}$, then $\dfrac{3}{8} > \dfrac{4}{11}$

Fuel X is richer in ingredient A.

EXERCISES 6-1

(A)

1. Explain each statement without using the word "ratio".
   a) Mrs. Adams and Mr. Singh divided the profits in the ratio $3 : 2$.
   b) The ratio of girls to boys in the class is $7 : 5$.
   c) Mrs. Arbor's chain saw runs on a $25 : 1$ mixture of gasoline and oil.
   d) The scale of a map is $1 : 250\ 000$.
   e) Brass is an alloy of copper and zinc in the ratio $3 : 2$.

2. Write each ratio in lowest terms.
   a) 40 : 12
   b) 5 : 65
   c) 28 : 8
   d) 32 : 52
   e) 12 : 72
   f) 50 : 250
   g) $\dfrac{60}{12}$
   h) $\dfrac{144}{9}$

3. State which is the greater ratio.
   a) $\dfrac{5}{8}$ or $\dfrac{3}{5}$
   b) 6 : 7 or 7 : 8
   c) 6 : 5 or 12 : 11
   d) 8 : 3 or 13 : 5

Ⓑ

4. "Gran's" cookies have raisins and chocolate chips in the ratio 3 : 7. "Mum's" cookies have raisins and chocolate chips in the ratio 5 : 11. Which brand has the greater ratio of raisins to chocolate chips?

5. Air consists of oxygen and nitrogen in the approximate ratio 1 : 4, and negligible amounts of other gases.
   a) What fraction of air is oxygen?
   b) What fraction of air is nitrogen?

6. Sterling silver is an alloy of silver and copper in the ratio 37 : 3.
   a) What fraction of a sterling silver fork is silver?
   b) If the mass of a sterling silver ingot is 500 g, how much silver does it contain?

7. Write an equivalent ratio with a second term of 1.
   a) 5 : 2
   b) 2 : 0.5
   c) 3 : 10
   d) 4 : 0.8

8. Write an equivalent ratio with a second term of 24.
   a) 5 : 6
   b) 8 : 48
   c) 27 : 36
   d) 5 : 0.6

9. At a school dance, there are 15 teachers, 275 girls, and 225 boys. Express the following ratios in lowest terms.
   a) girls to boys
   b) teachers to girls
   c) students to teachers

10. A newspaper costs 25¢ each day from Monday to Friday and 75¢ on Saturday. What is the ratio of:
    a) the cost on Saturday to the cost for one week
    b) the cost on Monday to the cost for one week?

11. If the ratio of domestic cars to foreign cars in Metropolitan Toronto is 9 : 5, how many domestic cars might you expect to find in a lot containing 247 cars?

12. The length and the width of a rectangle are in the ratio 9 : 7. If the perimeter is 256 cm, what are the dimensions of the rectangle?

Ⓒ

13. The front gear wheels of a ten-speed bicycle have 40 and 52 teeth. The back gear wheels have 14, 17, 20, 24, and 28 teeth.
    a) Write the ten different gear ratios (front:back).
    b) Arrange the ten gear ratios in order from lowest to highest.

14. The ratio of the mass of a hydrogen atom to the average mass of a person (70 kg) is about the same as the ratio of the average mass of a person to the mass of the sun. The mass of a hydrogen atom is about 1.7×10^{-29} kg. What is the approximate mass of the sun?

6-2 APPLICATIONS OF RATIOS

The amount of gold in jewellery and coins is measured in karats (K) with 24 K representing pure gold.

The mark 14 K on a ring means the ratio of the mass of gold in the ring to the mass of the ring is 14 : 24.

Since the second term of the ratio describing the purity of gold is always 24, it is omitted when describing the gold content.

In many ratios, only the first term is stated. The second term is omitted since it is always the same in each type of application of the ratio. Some further examples of ratios in which only the first terms are stated are Consumer Price Index, Mach numbers, and Intelligence Quotients.

Example 1. A gold bracelet is marked 18 K.
  a) Express the gold content of the bracelet as a fraction in lowest terms.
  b) The mass of the bracelet is 52 g and the value of pure gold is $25.50/g. Find the value of the gold in the bracelet.

Solution. a) Mass of gold : mass of bracelet $= 18 : 24$
$$= 3 : 4$$

  b) Mass of gold in the bracelet $= \dfrac{3}{4}(52 \text{ g})$
$$= 39 \text{ g}$$

Value of gold in the bracelet $= 39(\$25.50)$
$$= \$994.50$$

The gold in the bracelet is worth $994.50.

The *Consumer Price Index (CPI)* is a measure of the change in the cost of living. The ratio compares the price of 300 selected items at any time, to the price of the same items in 1981. The CPI is a ratio with its second term 100.

$$\frac{\text{CPI in year A}}{100} = \frac{\text{Cost of 300 items in year A}}{\text{Cost of 300 items in 1981}}$$

What is the Consumer Price Index today?

Example 2. In 1981 a family spent $14 000. If the CPI in 1990 were 187.4, how much would the family spend, to the nearest $100, in that year for the same items?

Solution.
$$\frac{\text{CPI in 1990}}{100} = \frac{\text{Cost of items in 1990}}{\text{Cost of items in 1981}}$$

Substitute the given information.

$$\frac{187.4}{100} = \frac{\text{Cost of items in 1990}}{\$14\ 000}$$

$$\text{Cost of items in 1990} = \$14\ 000 \left(\frac{187.4}{100}\right)$$

$$= \$26\ 236$$

In 1990, the family would spend about $26 200.

To compare more than two quantities, ratios with more than two terms are used. For example, the gravities of the Earth, Jupiter, and Mars are in the ratio 5 : 13 : 2. This means that a person on Jupiter would weigh $\frac{13}{5}$ of her or his weight on Earth, and $\frac{13}{2}$ of her or his weight on Mars.

Example 3. The profits in a business are to be shared by the three partners in the ratio 2 : 3 : 5. The profit for the year was $176 500. Calculate each partner's share.

Solution. Since the profit is shared in the ratio 2 : 3 : 5, we can think of the profit as consisting of a total of $(2+3+5)$ or 10 shares.

The 1st partner's share is $\frac{2}{10}$($176 500) or $35 300.

The 2nd partner's share is $\frac{3}{10}$ ($176 500) or $52 950.

The 3rd partner's share is $\frac{5}{10}$ ($176 500) or $88 250.

EXERCISES 6-2

1. Express the gold content as a ratio in lowest terms.
   a) a 22 K gold coin
   b) a 16 K gold pin
   c) a charm marked 9 K, the legal minimum for an article to be called gold

2. A 14 K gold ring has a mass of 24.7 g.
   a) Find the mass of the gold in the ring.
   b) At $25.50/g, find the value of the gold in the ring.

(B)

3. In 1986, the Consumer Price Index rose to 131.1. How much did it cost a family in 1986 for goods that cost them $8700 in 1981?

4. Three people contributed to buy a lottery ticket, in the ratio 2 : 5 : 3. If the ticket wins $25 000, how should the prize be divided?

5. Four partners in a business agreed to share the profits in the ratio 4 : 2 : 3 : 6. The first year's profits were $84 000. Calculate each partner's share.

6. a) A 1-cent coin minted before 1860 had a mass of 4.50 g and contained copper, tin, and zinc in the ratio 95 : 4 : 1. What mass of tin did each coin contain?
   b) From 1876 to 1920, the mass of each 1-cent coin minted was 5.67 g, and the ratio of copper to tin to zinc was 95.5 : 3 : 1.5. What mass of copper did each coin contain?
   c) After 1942, each 1-cent coin minted had a mass of 3.24 g and contained copper, tin, and zinc in the ratio 98 : 0.5 : 1.5. What mass of zinc did each coin contain?

7. The *Intelligence Quotient (IQ)* is the first term of a ratio with a second term of 100. The IQ is always stated to the nearest whole number. It is calculated from this formula. The formula applies to physical ages up to 20 years.

   $$\frac{IQ}{100} = \frac{\text{mental age}}{\text{physical age}}$$

   a) Find the IQ of each child.
      i) a twelve-year old with a mental age of 12.5
      ii) a seven-year old with a mental age of 6.8
   b) Find the mental age of each child.
      i) a nine-year old with an IQ of 100
      ii) a six-year old with an IQ of 150 (genius level)

8. A *Mach number* is a ratio with second term 1. The Mach number of an airplane is the ratio of its speed to the speed of sound at the same altitude and temperature. Assume an altitude where the speed of sound is 1085 km/h.
   a) Calculate the Mach number of an airplane flying at each speed. Give the answers to one decimal place.
      i)   3255 km/h   ii)   1302 km/h   iii)   1000 km/h
   b) Find the speed of the North American Aviation X-15A-2 flying at Mach 6.72.

9. The frequencies of the notes in the musical scale of C major are related by an eight-term ratio.

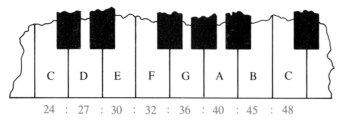

24 : 27 : 30 : 32 : 36 : 40 : 45 : 48

Musical instruments are usually tuned so that A in the scale has a frequency of 440 Hz (cycles per second). Find the frequencies of the other notes in the scale.

10. Chemical fertilizers usually contain nitrogen, phosphorus, and potassium. The amount of each nutrient present is expressed as a percent of the total mass of the fertilizer in the three-term ratio, nitrogen : phosphorus : potassium.

 A, B, and C are 10 kg bags of three kinds of fertilizer.

 a) Which fertilizer contains the most nitrogen?
 b) Which fertilizer has the greatest ratio of nitrogen to phosphorus?
 c) Which fertilizer contains the most nutrients?
 d) Why are the ratios not expressed in lowest terms?

11. The ratio of the approximate distances of the Earth and Uranus from the Sun is 4 : 77, and that of Mars and Uranus from the Sun is 2 : 25.
 a) What is the ratio of the approximate distances of the Earth and Mars from the Sun?
 b) How far is Mars from the Sun if the Earth's distance is 150 Gm?

12. The angles of a triangle are in the ratio 2 : 3 : 4. What are their measures?

13. The angles of a quadrilateral are in the ratio 2 : 3 : 3 : 4. What are their measures?

14. A sphere and a cone are each designed to fit snugly (at separate times) inside a cylinder of radius R and height $2R$.
 a) Write the ratio of the volume of the sphere to the volume of the cone to the volume of the cylinder.
 b) How many times is the volume of the cylinder as great as the volume of the largest sphere it will contain?

6-3 PROPORTIONS

One method of finding the height of a tall tree is to measure its shadow, and then compare that with the length of the shadow of an object whose height is known. If both shadows are measured at the same time of day, the ratio of their lengths will be equal to the ratio of the heights of the object and the tree.

$$\frac{\text{height of tree}}{\text{height of stick}} = \frac{\text{length of tree's shadow}}{\text{length of stick's shadow}}$$

Substitute the known measures.

$$\frac{\text{height of tree}}{1.0} = \frac{12.7}{0.7}$$

$$\text{height of tree} = \frac{12.7}{0.7}$$

$$\doteq 18.1$$

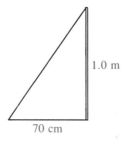

1.0 m

70 cm

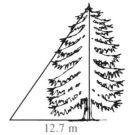

12.7 m

The tree is about 18 m high.

This solution used the fact that two ratios were equal.

A statement that two ratios are equal is called a *proportion*. For example, the statement $a : b = c : d$, is a proportion.

Since ratios can be written in fractional form, the statement $\frac{a}{b} = \frac{c}{d}$ is also a proportion.

To simplify an expression of this type, multiply both sides of the proportion by the lowest common denominator.

$$\frac{a}{b}(bd) = \frac{c}{d}(bd)$$

$$ad = cb$$

This equation can be used to find the unknown term in a proportion when the other three terms are known.

Example 1. Find each value of x.

    a) $\dfrac{7}{30} = \dfrac{14}{x}$ b) $\dfrac{3}{19} = \dfrac{x}{7}$

Solution.   a) $\dfrac{7}{30} = \dfrac{14}{x}$ b) $\dfrac{3}{19} = \dfrac{x}{7}$

                $7x = 14(30)$ Multiply both sides by 7.

                  $x = \dfrac{14(30)}{7}$ $\dfrac{3(7)}{19} = x$

                     $= 60$ $\dfrac{21}{19} = x$

Example 2. The scale, 1 : 300, of the floor plan indicates that 1 mm on the plan corresponds to 300 mm, or 0.3 m, in the actual building.
a) Find the dimensions, in metres, of the living room.
b) Find the total floor area to the nearest square metre.

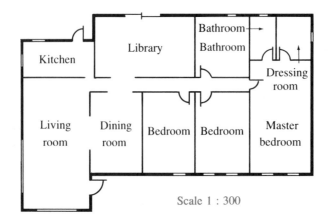

Scale 1 : 300

Solution.   a) By measurement of the floor plan, the living room is 35 mm by 20 mm. This corresponds to 35(0.3 m) by 20(0.3 m), or 10.5 m by 6.0 m.

The living room is 10.5 m by 6.0 m.

      b) The floor plan can be divided into two rectangles. One rectangle comprises the living room and the kitchen. This measures 45 mm by 20 mm, or 45(0.3 m) by 20(0.3 m).

The other rectangle comprises all the other rooms. It measures 60 mm by 42 mm, or 60(0.3 m) by 42(0.3 m).

Total area $= [45(0.3) \times 20(0.3)] + [60(0.3) \times 42(0.3)]$
              $= 307.8$

The floor area is approximately 308 m².

Example 3. A rectangular sheet of paper is 1 m wide. When cut in half, each half has the same length-to-width ratio as the original sheet. How long is the original sheet?

Solution. Draw a diagram.
The width 1 m of the original sheet is the length of the 2 cut sheets.

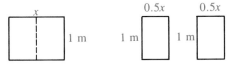

Let x metres represent the length of the original sheet.
Then $0.5x$ metres is the width of the cut sheet.

$$\frac{\text{original length}}{\text{original width}} = \frac{\text{cut length}}{\text{cut width}}$$

$$\frac{x}{1} = \frac{1}{0.5x}$$

$$0.5x^2 = 1$$

$$x^2 = \frac{1}{0.5}$$

$$= 2$$

$$x = \sqrt{2}$$

$$\doteq 1.4$$

When this equation was solved, the negative square root was ignored because a sheet of paper cannot have a negative length.

The original sheet of paper was about 1.4 m long.

This solution relates to the problem posed at the beginning of this chapter. If the paper with size A0 has a length-to-width ratio of $\sqrt{2}$ to 1, when it is cut in half the two sheets produced will have measurements in the same ratio. Subsequent cuts produce smaller sheets with the same ratio of length to width.

EXERCISES 6-3

(A)

1. Find the value of each variable.

a) $\dfrac{3}{8} = \dfrac{m}{24}$ b) $\dfrac{12}{16} = \dfrac{n}{8}$ c) $\dfrac{a}{12} = \dfrac{15}{36}$ d) $\dfrac{x}{18} = \dfrac{9}{54}$

e) $\dfrac{90}{b} = \dfrac{30}{11}$ f) $\dfrac{72}{x} = \dfrac{360}{15}$ g) $\dfrac{9}{8} = \dfrac{144}{d}$ h) $\dfrac{27}{5} = \dfrac{81}{x}$

2. Solve.

a) $\dfrac{11}{16} = \dfrac{n}{8}$ b) $\dfrac{x}{3} = \dfrac{2}{7}$ c) $\dfrac{5}{8} = \dfrac{9}{x}$ d) $\dfrac{7}{11} = \dfrac{9}{x}$

e) $\dfrac{t}{4} = \dfrac{5}{7}$ f) $\dfrac{9}{b} = \dfrac{5}{6}$ g) $\dfrac{3}{5} = \dfrac{w}{7}$ h) $\dfrac{5}{13} = \dfrac{10}{y}$

Ⓑ

3. In a photograph of a mother and her son standing together, the son measures 27 mm and the mother 63 mm. If the mother is actually 180 cm tall, how tall is her son?

4. At a given time of day, the ratio of the height of a tree to the length of its shadow is the same for all trees. A tree 12 m tall casts a shadow 5 m long. How tall is a tree that casts a shadow 3 m long?

5. The ratio of a person's height to her or his arm span is 24 : 32. How tall is a person whose arm span is 184 cm?

6. Assume that the headline statement is correct.
   a) How many out of 30 smokers want to quit?
   b) How many out of 600 smokers want to quit?
   c) How many smokers were polled if 200 want to quit?

5 out of 6 smokers want to quit

7. Find the actual dimensions and the area of the master bedroom shown in the floor plan of *Example 2*.

8. Find each distance from the map.
   a) Halifax to Sable Island
   b) Bathurst to Corner Brook
   c) The width of Cabot Strait
   d) The length of Prince Edward Island
   e) Bridgewater to Grand Bank
   f) Digby to Saint John

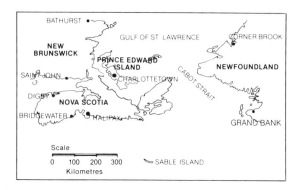

9. The distance between two towns is 180 km. How far apart will they be on a map drawn to a scale of 1 : 1 500 000?

10. Find the approximate length of each part of the mosquito.
    a) the abdomen
    b) the antennae
    c) the wings

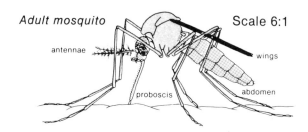

Adult mosquito

Scale 6:1

antennae

wings

proboscis

abdomen

6-4 RATES

When a person buys a car, one of the considerations is usually how much gasoline the car uses. The fuel consumption, in litres, is compared to the distance the car travels, in hundreds of kilometres. Such a comparison is called a *rate* because the two quantities that are compared have different units.

Which of the cars above has the better fuel consumption?

Many familiar measurements are expressed as rates.
- speed in kilometres per hour
- pulse rate in heart beats per minute
- unit pricing on supermarket shelves in cents per 100 g
- wages in dollars per hour
- sports statistics in goals per game

Example 1. A car's fuel consumption is quoted as 5.5 L/100 km.
  a) Find how much fuel is needed to travel 275 km.
  b) Find how far the car will travel on 48 L of gasoline.

Solution. a) A fuel consumption of 5.5 L/100 km means that the fuel for 100 km is 5.5 L.

The fuel for 1 km would be $\left(\dfrac{5.5}{100}\right)$ L.

The fuel for 275 km would be $\left(\dfrac{5.5}{100} \times 275\right)$ L or 15.125 L.

About 15 L of fuel are needed for a trip of 275 km.

b) On 5.5 L of fuel the car travels 100 km.

On 1 L of fuel the car could travel $\left(\dfrac{100}{5.5}\right)$ km.

On 48 L of fuel the car could travel $\left(\dfrac{100}{5.5} \times 48\right)$ km or $872.\overline{72}$ km.

The car travels about 873 km on 48 L of fuel.

Example 2. In one season, Casey batted at the rate of 2 hits for every 5 official times at bat.
   a) At this rate, how many hits should he get in 400 times at bat?
   b) How many times should Casey have at bat to get 180 hits?

Solution. Casey's batting average is $\frac{2}{5}$ or 0.4.

   a) In 400 times at bat, Casey should get 400(0.4) or 160 hits.
      If the rate is constant, Casey should get 160 hits.
   b) Casey bats 5 times to get 2 hits.

      So he will bat $\frac{5}{2}$ times to get 1 hit.

      To get 180 hits, Casey will bat $\frac{5}{2}(180)$ or 450 times.

      If the rate is constant, Casey should bat about 450 times to get 180 hits.

EXERCISES 6-4

Ⓐ

1. Dale drives 45 km on 3 L of gasoline.
   a) Find how far would she drive on:
      i) 2 L of gasoline   ii) 5 L of gasoline.
   b) Find how much gasoline Dale needs to drive:
      i) 60 km   ii) 270 km.

2. Bob can type at the rate of 30 words per minute.
   a) Find how long it would take him to type:
      i) 20 words   ii) 100 words.
   b) Find how many words Bob can type in:
      i) 4 min   ii) 6.5 min.

3. A car uses fuel at the rate of 7.2 L/100 km.
   a) Find how much fuel is needed to travel 360 km.
   b) Find how far the car will travel on a full tank of 85 L.

Ⓑ

4. An electronic typewriter can type 540 words per minute.
   a) Find how long it will take to type:
      i) 1000 words   ii) 1 000 000 words.
   b) How many words can it type in:
      i) 1 h   ii) 1 week.

5. In the first 20 games of the baseball season, Reggie Jackson hit 12 home runs. If he continued at this rate, how many home runs would he hit in 160 games?

6. A 350 g box of cornflakes costs $1.75. A 525 g box of the same cereal costs $2.29.
   a) Find the unit price, in cents per 100 g, for each box of cereal.
   b) Which box is the better buy?

7. Adrian works in a factory making pies. He is paid $9.55 per hour for a 7.5 h shift. He is paid "time and a half" for the first 4 h of overtime in a day. Then he is paid double time for any additional hours worked that day.

   In one week, Adrian worked these hours.

Monday	Tuesday	Wednesday	Thursday	Friday
15	7.5	7.5	11.5	7.5

What are Adrian's gross wages for this week?

8. In the first 6 games of the football season, Dave Cutler scored 83 points. If he continued scoring at this rate, how many points would he score in 14 games?

9. If 18 houses are built in 45 days, find how long at this rate it would take to build:
   a) 63 houses
   b) 144 houses.

10. A brand of liquid detergent is sold in 2 sizes — $2.09 for 500 mL, and $3.55 for 1 L.
    a) Find the unit price for each size of detergent. Which is the better buy?
    b) The smaller size is "on special" for one week at a price of $1.79. For this week, which is the better buy?

11. Marilyn works in a car assembly plant. She is paid $14.50 per hour for an 8 h shift. She receives an additional 72.5¢ per hour for working the night shift.
    In one month, Marilyn works two 40 h day shifts and two 40 h night shifts. Find her gross wages for the month.

12. Milk is sold in 4 L bags and 2 L and 1 L cartons. The milk is priced at $3.49, $2.31, and $1.20, respectively. By how much would the cost of each carton have to be reduced so that its unit price was equal to that of the 4 L bags?

13. Two girls, 60 km apart, start cycling toward each other at the same time. One girl cycles at 18 km/h. How fast must the other girl cycle if they are to meet in 1.5 h?

14. Car A and car B leave Halifax on the same road 1 h apart. Car A leaves first and travels at a steady 80 km/h. How fast must car B travel to overtake car A in 4 h?

15. Machine X makes 200 boxes in 3 min and machine Y makes 200 boxes in 2 min. With both machines working, how long will it take to make 200 boxes?

16. A worker is paid $8.60/h for a 40 h week and time and a half for overtime. How many hours are worked to earn $414.95 in one week?

17. A study shows that an office staff of x people will consume y cups of coffee over a period of z days. At this rate, how long would it take a staff of $3x$ people to consume $\dfrac{y}{12}$ cups of coffee?

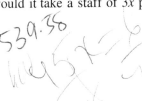

Chapter 6

THE MATHEMATICAL MIND

The Golden Ratio

Twenty-three centuries ago Euclid posed the question, "What are the dimensions of a rectangle that has the property that when it is divided into a square and a rectangle, the smaller rectangle has the same shape as the original?"

The answer to Euclid's question can be found using this proportion.

$$\frac{\text{Length of original rectangle}}{\text{Width of original rectangle}} = \frac{\text{Length of smaller rectangle}}{\text{Width of smaller rectangle}}$$

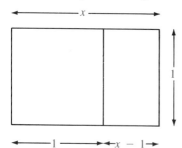

Let the length of the original rectangle be represented by x units and let its width be 1 unit.

The side of the square will then be 1 unit, and the proportion can be written.

$$\frac{x}{1} = \frac{1}{x - 1}$$

Multiply both sides of the proportion by $x - 1$.

$$x^2 - x = 1$$
$$x^2 - x - 1 = 0$$

The positive solution of the equation $x^2 - x - 1 = 0$ is called the *golden ratio*.

QUESTIONS

1. Use your calculator and the method of guess and check to solve the equation $x^2 - x - 1 = 0$.

2. Write down the value of the golden ratio to three decimal places.

3. Simplify this expression.

$$1 + \cfrac{1}{1 + \cfrac{1}{1 + \cfrac{1}{1 + \cfrac{1}{1 + 1}}}}$$

How close is this value to the value of the golden ratio?

A rectangle with a length-to-width ratio of the golden ratio is called a *golden rectangle*. Study the diagram. Then, using a pair of compasses and a straightedge, construct a golden rectangle.

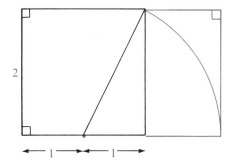

The rectangle obtained by dividing a golden rectangle into a square and a rectangle is itself a golden rectangle. Repeating this process with the small rectangle a number of times gives a set of successively smaller golden rectangles. The result of joining a set of corresponding vertices of these rectangles with a curve is a *spiral*. Such spirals can be found throughout nature, from the spiral galaxy in the heavens to the nautilus shells in the oceans.

Since Euclid's time, the golden ratio has been found in mathematics, architecture, art, and nature. In fact, the golden ratio is probably second only to π in its frequency of occurrence in the mathematical sciences.

6-5 PERCENT

The weather forecast says that there is a 40% chance of rain today.

A store is closing down and offers everything for sale at 50% off.

A car manufacturer offers 6.9% financing to a customer who is buying a car.

A newspaper quotes a cost of living increase of 2.4% last month because of price rises in fuel and fresh produce.

A *percent* is a fraction with a denominator 100. For example,

40% is $\dfrac{40}{100}$ and 6.9% is $\dfrac{6.9}{100}$.

The word ''percent'' means ''per hundred''.

Example 1. Write each ratio as a percent.

a) $\dfrac{27}{100}$ 　　　　 b) 6:100 　　　　 c) 7:25

Solution. 　 a) $\dfrac{27}{100} = 27\%$

b) 6 : 100 written in fractional form is $\dfrac{6}{100}$, which is 6%.

c) 7 : 25 written in fractional form is $\dfrac{7}{25}$.

Multiply numerator and denominator by a factor that produces a denominator of 100.

$$\dfrac{7}{25} = \dfrac{7}{25} \times \dfrac{4}{4}$$
$$= \dfrac{28}{100}$$
$$= 28\%$$

Each solution could have been obtained by writing the ratio in fractional form and then multiplying by 100%.

For example, 7 : 25 can be written as $\left(\dfrac{7}{25}\right)100\%$ which is 28%

Here is a general rule for expressing ratios as percents.

> To change a ratio to a percent, write the ratio in fractional form and multiply by 100%.

Example 2. Write each ratio as a percent.

a) 2 : 5 　　　　 b) 0.1 : 4 　　　　 c) 19 : 6

Solution. 　 Write each ratio in fractional form.

a) $\dfrac{2}{5} = \left(\dfrac{2}{5}\right)100\%$ 　 b) $\dfrac{0.1}{4} = \left(\dfrac{0.1}{4}\right)100\%$ 　 c) $\dfrac{19}{6} = \left(\dfrac{19}{6}\right)100\%$

　　　$= 40\%$ 　　　　　　$= 2.5\%$ 　　　　　$= \dfrac{950}{3}\%$

　　　　　　　　　　　　　　　　　　　　　　　　　　 $\doteq 317\%$

Similarly, decimals can be written as percents by multiplying by 100%.

> To change a decimal to a percent, multiply the decimal by 100%.

Example 3. Express each decimal as a percent.

a) 0.64   b) 0.018   c) 0.0073   d) 2.15

Solution. a) $0.64 = (0.64)100\%$
$= 64\%$

b) $0.018 = (0.018)100\%$
$= 1.8\%$

c) $0.0073 = (0.0073)100\%$
$= 0.73\%$

d) $2.15 = (2.15)100\%$
$= 215\%$

Conversely, to express a percent as a decimal, divide by 100%.

To change a percent to a decimal, divide the percent by 100%.

Example 4. Express each percent as a decimal.

a) 27%   b) 7.5%   c) 156%   d) 0.9%

Solution. a) $27\% = \dfrac{27\%}{100\%}$ b) $7.5\% = \dfrac{7.5\%}{100\%}$
$= 0.27$ $= 0.075$

c) $156\% = \dfrac{156\%}{100\%}$ d) $0.9\% = \dfrac{0.9\%}{100\%}$
$= 1.56$ $= 0.009$

Example 5. Express each percent as a fraction in lowest terms.

a) 18%   b) 175%   c) 12.5%   d) 0.4%

Solution. a) $18\% = \dfrac{18}{100}$ b) $175\% = \dfrac{175}{100}$
$= \dfrac{9}{50}$ $= \dfrac{7}{4}$

c) $12.5\% = \dfrac{12.5}{100}$ d) $0.4\% = \dfrac{0.4}{100}$
$= \dfrac{125}{1000}$ $= \dfrac{4}{1000}$
$= \dfrac{1}{8}$ $= \dfrac{1}{250}$

EXERCISES 6-5

(A)

1. Write each ratio as a percent.
  a) 7 : 100   b) 18.5 : 100   c) 57 : 100   d) 0.8 : 100
  e) 365 : 100   f) 36.5 : 100   g) 540 : 100   h) 1875 : 100

move decimal 2 places to right.

2. Express each decimal as a percent.
  a) 0.38   b) 0.57   c) 0.81   d) 0.06   e) 0.035
  f) 0.072   g) 0.091   h) 0.007   i) 0.0086   j) 0.0051
  k) 0.0007   l) 3.6   m) 3.06   n) 3.006   o) 30.6

3. Express each percent as a decimal.
  a) 24%   b) 39%   c) 57.4%   d) 3%   e) 5.8%
  f) 11.5%   g) 1.6%   h) 0.9%   i) 137%   j) 264%
  k) 375%   l) 375.8%   m) 0.1%   n) 2.03%   o) 0.25%

move decimal 2 places to left.

(B)

4. Write each ratio as a percent.
  a) 1 : 4   b) 5 : 8   c) 7 : 10   d) 11 : 20   e) 5 : 6
  f) 3 : 5   g) 8 : 5   h) 2 : 3   i) 13 : 10   j) 31 : 40
  k) 20 : 3   l) 19 : 50   m) 1 : 25   n) 7 : 40   o) 11 : 200

$\times 100$

5. Estimate what percent of each figure is colored.
  a)   b)   c)   d)

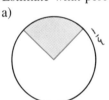

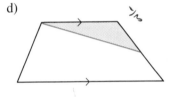

6. Write as a percent.
  a) one-half   b) three-quarters   c) seven-eighths
  d) one-hundredth   e) one-thousandth   f) two-thirds

$\frac{7}{10} \times 100$

$66.6 \rightarrow$

$\frac{244}{3} \times \frac{1}{100} = \frac{244}{300}$

7. Express each percent as a fraction in lowest terms.
  a) 26%   b) 35%   c) 64%   d) 75%

  e) 62.5%   f) 125%   g) $81\frac{1}{3}\%$ h) $16\frac{2}{3}\%$

  i) 185%   j) 360%   k) 0.8%   l) 0.125%

$= \frac{244}{3}$

$\frac{244}{3} \div 100$

8. What percent of the mass of a 16 K gold ring is gold?

9. The weights of a person on Mars and on the Earth are in the ratio 2 : 5. What percent of the weight on Mars is a person's weight on Earth?

(C)

10. A fertilizer contains nitrogen, phosphorus, and potassium in the ratio 1 : 2 : 4 by mass. If 58% of the mass consists of materials other than these nutrients, what percent of the total mass of the fertilizer is phosphorus?

Construct a Table

An aircraft flies from city A to city B against the wind at an average speed of 600 km/h. On the return trip, the average speed is 1000 km/h. What is the average speed for the round trip?

Understand the problem
- What does average speed mean?
- How can it be calculated?
- Is the average speed for the return trip, the average of 600 km/h and 1000 km/h?

Think of a strategy
- Construct a table showing the time, the distance, and the average speed for each journey.

Carry out the strategy
- Write the given information in the table.

	Distance	Time	Speed
A → B			600 km/h
B → A			1000 km/h

- To complete the table, we let d represent the distance between A and B in kilometres.
- Then we use the equation:
  time = distance ÷ speed
  to calculate the times for the trips A to B and B to A. These expressions are entered in the table.

	Distance	Time	Speed
A → B	d km	$\dfrac{d}{600}$ h	600 km/h
B → A	d km	$\dfrac{d}{1000}$ h	1000 km/h

- To calculate the average speed we use the equation:
  Average speed = total distance ÷ total time

$$= \frac{2d}{\dfrac{d}{600} + \dfrac{d}{1000}}$$

  Multiply numerator and denominator by 3000.
  Then divide numerator and denominator by d.

$$= \frac{6000}{5 + 3}$$

$$= 750$$

- The average speed for the round trip is 750 km/h.

Look back

- Is the average speed for the round trip somewhere between 600 km/h and 1000 km/h?
- Should the average speed for the round trip be closer to 600 km/h or to 1000 km/h?
- Does 750 km/h seem to be a reasonable answer?

Solve each problem

1. A boat has an average speed of 50 km/h on the first lap of a two-lap race. On the second lap it averages only 30 km/h. What is its average speed for the whole race?

2. If Mr. Swan drives at an average speed of 100 km/h he arrives at work at 09:00. If he leaves home at the same time but averages 80 km/h, he arrives at 09:06. How far does he live from work?

3. A car's cooling system contains a 25% solution of antifreeze. Half the system is drained and then topped up with pure antifreeze. What is the strength of the antifreeze in the system now?

4. Dianne rode her dirt bike up a hill and down the same distance on the other side. She rode down the hill at 4 times the speed she rode up the hill. If the entire trip took 20 min, how many minutes did it take her to ride down the hill?

5. Marie drove her 18 wheeler 1280 km from Calgary to Winnipeg in 15.2 h. Part of the trip she drove in a snow storm at an average speed of 60 km/h. The rest of the time she drove at 100 km/h. How far did she drive in the storm?

6. Two people, 60 km apart, start cycling towards each other at the same time. One person cycles at 18 km/h. How fast must the other person cycle if the people meet in 1.5 h?

7. Car A and car B leave Halifax on the same road, 1 h apart. Car A leaves first and travels at a steady 80 km/h. How fast must car B travel to overtake car A in 4 h?

MATHEMATICS AROUND US

Election to the Baseball Hall of Fame

To be elected to the Baseball Hall of Fame a player must receive at least 75% of the votes cast by sportswriters who have had 10 or more years of experience. Each sportswriter can vote for up to 10 players.

QUESTIONS

1. In 1982 Henry Aaron was elected to the Hall of Fame with the highest percent of votes since 1936, the year the Hall of Fame started. He received 406 votes out of a total of 415 ballots.
   a) What percent of the votes did Henry Aaron receive?
   b) Frank Robinson, with 370 votes, was also elected in 1982. What percent of the votes did Frank Robinson receive?
   c) What was the minimum number of votes needed for election in 1982?

2. In 1986 there were 425 ballots. Willie McCovey received 81.4% of the votes. Billy Williams just missed being elected, with 74.1% of the votes.
   a) How many votes did each player receive?
   b) How many more votes did Billy Williams need to be elected?

3. Three players were elected to the Hall of Fame in 1936: Ty Cobb with 98.2%; and Babe Ruth and Honus Wagner, each with 95.1%. Ty Cobb received 222 votes.
   a) How many ballots were cast that year?
   b) How many votes did Babe Ruth and Honus Wagner receive?

6-6 APPLICATIONS OF PERCENT

Sita wants to buy a car. On the windshield of a car she sees a price of $8750 with an additional sign, "15% off sticker price". Sita calculates what the car will cost.

The reduction in price is 15%.

The sale price is 100% − 15%, or 85% of the sticker price of $8750.

$$85\% \text{ of } \$8750 = \frac{85}{100}(\$8750)$$
$$= \$7437.50$$

Sita knows that she will have to pay provincial sales tax which is currently 7%. The cost will be $7437.50 plus 7% of $7437.50.

$$\text{Total cost} = 107\% \text{ of } \$7437.50$$
$$= 1.07(\$7437.50)$$
$$= \$7958.13$$

Sita will have to pay $7958.13 for the car.

Example 1. a) Calculate 16% of 85.
  b) 18% of a number is 54. What is the number?
  c) What percent of 65 is 0.13?

Solution. a) $16\% \text{ of } 85 = \frac{16}{100}(85)$
  $= 13.6$

  b) 18% of a number is 54.

  1% of the number is $\frac{54}{18}$.

  100% of the number is $\frac{54}{18}(100)$ or 300.

  c) To find what percent of 65 is 0.13, express 0.13 as a fraction of 65, that is, $\frac{0.13}{65}$.

  Multiply the fraction by 100%.

  $\left(\frac{0.13}{65}\right)100\% = 0.2\%$

  0.13 is 0.2% of 65.

Example 2. Assume that the gas company gets the increase that it wants. A family's natural-gas bill last year was approximately $860. Calculate the gas bill for this year if the same amount of gas is used.

Gas company wants 6% increase in rates

Solution   This year's gas bill will be 106% of last year's bill.

106% of 860 = 1.06(860)
= 911.60

This year's gas bill will be about $910.

Example 3. Which game has the greater percent reduction?

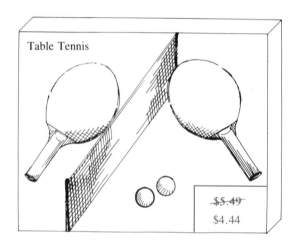

Table Tennis

$~~$5.49$~~$
$4.44

Darts

$~~$4.89$~~$
$3.98

Solution.   To find the percent reduction, express the reduction as a percent of the original price.

Reduction in price of table-tennis set = $5.49 − $4.44
= $1.05

Percent reduction of table-tennis set = $\left(\dfrac{1.05}{5.49}\right)100\%$

$\doteq 19.1\%$

Reduction in price of dart game = $4.89 − $3.98
= $0.91

Percent reduction of dart game = $\left(\dfrac{0.91}{4.89}\right)100\%$

$\doteq 18.6\%$

The table-tennis set has the greater percent reduction.

Example 4. What was the original price of this radio?

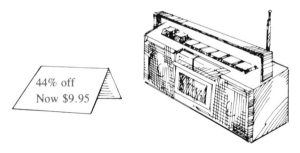

44% off
Now $9.95

Solution. The reduction in price is 44%.
So, $9.95 must represent 100% − 44%, or 56% of the original price.

1% of the original price is $\dfrac{\$9.95}{56}$.

100%, the original price, is $\dfrac{\$9.95}{56}(100)$ or about $17.77.

The radio was originally $17.77.

Interest is the money paid for the use of money. If you have a savings account, the bank pays you interest for the use of your savings. If you borrow money from the bank, it charges you interest for the use of its money. The interest rate is always expressed as a percent.

Tara received $150 from her grandparents as a birthday present. She deposited it into her daily-interest savings account, which pays interest at a rate of 8% per annum.

The interest is calculated daily and is added to the account at the end of each month. How much interest has the money earned in 30 days?

The yearly interest is 8% of $150, or 0.08(150).

The daily interest is $\dfrac{1}{365}$ of this amount, or $\dfrac{1}{365}(0.08)(150)$.

After 30 days, the interest is $\dfrac{30}{365}(0.08)(150)$ or approximately 0.99.

After 30 days, $150 has earned $0.99 interest.

When interest is calculated in this way, it is called *simple interest*. Simple interest can be calculated using this formula.

$I = Prt$

I is the interest in dollars.
P is the principal, the money saved or borrowed.
r is the annual interest rate expressed as a decimal.
t is the time in years for which the money is saved or borrowed.

Example 5. Find the simple interest.

a) On a $324 credit-card bill for 28 days at 21% per annum

b) $6500 in a daily-interest savings account for 25 days at $11\frac{1}{2}$% per annum

Solution.

a) Use the formula.

The rate is 21% or 0.21. The time is 28 days or $\frac{28}{365}$ years.

$I = Prt$

$$= 324(0.21)\left(\frac{28}{365}\right) \qquad \text{Use a calculator.}$$

Key in: $\boxed{3}\ \boxed{2}\ \boxed{4}\ \boxed{\times}\ \boxed{.}\ \boxed{2}\ \boxed{1}\ \boxed{\times}\ \boxed{2}\ \boxed{8}\ \boxed{\div}\ \boxed{3}\ \boxed{6}\ \boxed{5}$

to display 5.2195068

The interest is $5.22.

b) The rate is $11\frac{1}{2}$% or 0.115. The time is 25 days or $\frac{25}{365}$ years.

$I = Prt$

$$= 6500(0.115)\left(\frac{25}{365}\right)$$

$$\doteq 51.20$$

The interest is $51.20.

EXERCISES 6-6

(A)

1. Find.

a) 25% of 40 b) 20% of 40 c) 0.6% of 150 d) 5% of 35

e) 109% of 75 f) 4% of 150 g) 0.7% of 95 h) 65% of 18

2. Determine the number in each statement.

a) 50% of a number is 10. b) 20% of a number is 3.

c) 40% of a number is 10. d) 75% of a number is 30.

e) 60% of a number is 42. f) 15% of a number is 15.

g) $66\frac{2}{3}$% of a number is 18. h) 10% of a number is 8.

i) 104% of a number is 26. j) 130% of a number is 91.

3. a) What percent of 80 is 16? b) What percent of 135 is 15?

c) What percent of 75 is 125? d) What percent of 50 is 45?

e) What percent of 144 is 18? f) What percent of 81 is 270?

g) What percent of 1900 is 1.9? h) What percent of 6000 is 3?

(B)

4. Find the simple interest.

a) On $1200 at 16% per annum for 3 months

b) On $8500 at 18% per annum for 6 months

c) On $3000 at 15% per annum for 30 days

5. A ten-speed bicycle regularly sells for $227.50. What will it cost during a "15% off" sale?

6. Skis are being sold at a discount of 45%. What will be the cost of a pair of skis that regularly sells for $180?

7. Food costs for the coming year are estimated to rise by 11.7%. What will be the coming year's food costs for a family who spent $8400 last year?

8. This year, AKA Ltd. hopes that its sales income will be 160% of last year's sales of $2 500 000. If the company succeeds, what will its sales income be?

9. In April, the unemployment figure was 800 000 people. In May, there was a modest 0.16% decrease. How many people apparently found work in May?

10. In all of William Shakespeare's works, he used 31 534 different words. Of these, 14 356 were used only once. What percent of the words did he use only once?

11. During a "20% off" sale, a clock radio is priced at $29.95. What is its regular price?

12. A calculator is priced at $9.98 during a "25% off" sale. What is its regular price?

13. Express each reduction as a percent, to 1 decimal place, of the original price.
    a) A TV set regularly priced at $540 is selling for $499
    b) An overcoat regularly priced at $195 is selling for $156

14. Sterling silver is an alloy of silver and copper in the ratio 37 : 3.
    a) What percent of a sterling silver bracelet is pure silver?
    b) If the bracelet has a mass of 30 g, how much silver does it contain?

15. Long distance telephone rates are reduced by 35% between 6 P.M. and 11 P.M., and by 60% between 11 P.M. and 8 A.M.
    a) A 5 min call from Ottawa to Charlottetown at 10 A.M. costs $4.30. Calculate the cost of a 5 min call at: i) 8 P.M. ii) 7 A.M.
    b) A 5 min call from Montreal to Vancouver at 9 P.M. costs $3.06. Calculate the cost of a 5 min call at: i) noon ii) 2 A.M.

16. a) In the news item, what percent, to 1 decimal place, of the cars stopped yesterday had defective equipment?
    b) Estimate the number of cars found with defective equipment since the campaign began. What assumption are you making?

Police checks nab 187

Police spot-check crews stopped 860 vehicles yesterday and found 187 with defective equipment, in the holiday safety traffic blitz across the city.

A total of 28 759 cars and trucks have been stopped for safety checks since the campaign began.

17. A pair of skis is priced at $185. Find the cost:
    a) when a 7% sales tax is added b) with a 15% discount and a 7% sales tax.

18. A dress that sells for $80 is placed on sale at "15% off". After two weeks on the rack, the current selling price is reduced another 10%. What is the new selling price?

19. The specifications by mass for the alloy, phosphor bronze, are 85% copper, 7% tin, 0.06% iron, 0.2% lead, 0.3% phosphorus, and the remainder zinc.
    a) What percent of phosphor bronze is the zinc content?
    b) What mass of each element is needed to make 1 t of phosphor bronze?

20. If a worker receives a cut of 20% in salary, what percent increase must he get to regain his original salary?

21. The perimeter of a rectangle doubles such that its length and width remain in the same ratio. By what percent has the area increased?

22. In a recent year, Statistics Canada reported that 8.9 million persons were employed and 810 000 were unemployed.
    a) What was the rate of unemployment, to 1 decimal place?
    b) If the size of the work force does not change, how many of the unemployed need to find jobs to bring the unemployment rate down to 4%?

23. Energy-conservation experts report that there is a 4.5% reduction in home-heating costs for every 1°C reduction in house temperature. A house is kept at a constant 20°C day and night. What percent reduction in heating costs should occur if the house were kept at 18°C from 07:00 to 22:00 and 15°C from 22:00 to 07:00?

24. A company's profit is 5.4% of its sales. It must pay 48% corporate taxes on its profit. It always pays 60% of its after-taxes profit to its stockholders as dividends, and retains the balance as a reserve. How much did the company retain as a reserve in a year when its sales were $10 000 000?

 INVESTIGATE

1. a) Draw a rectangle and measure its dimensions.
   b) Calculate the area of the rectangle.
   c) Calculate the change in area after each change in the dimension(s) listed below.
   d) Express each change in area as a percent of the original area.
      i)   Increase the length by 100%.
      ii) Decrease the width by 50%.
      iii) Increase the length by 50% and increase the width by 50%.
      iv) Decrease the length by 25% and decrease the width by 25%.
      v)   Increase the length by 75% and decrease the width by 75%.
      vi) Increase the length by 75% and decrease the width by 25%.

2. If you knew the percent change(s) in the dimension(s) of a rectangle, how could you find the percent change in its area?

6-7 THE MOST FAMOUS RATIO IN MATHEMATICS

One ratio, above all others, has captured the interest of mathematicians through the ages. This is the ratio of the circumference C of a circle to its diameter d. The value of this ratio is the same for all circles and is denoted by the Greek letter π.

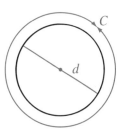

For any circle, $C : d = \pi : 1$ or $\dfrac{C}{d} = \pi$ or $C = \pi d$

In January 1986, a Cray 2 supercomputer calculated π to 29 360 128 decimal places. The calculation took 28 h of computer time. Calculations of π are done to check the calculating ability of a computer. A $\boxed{\pi}$ key on a calculator will give its value to 8 (or 10) decimal places.
Here is the value of π to 50 decimal places.
3.141 592 653 589 793 238 462 643 383 279 502 884 197 169 399 375 10
If your calculator does not have a $\boxed{\pi}$ key, use the approximate value of 3.14.

Example 1. A tree trunk with a circular cross section has a circumference of 172 cm. Find the diameter of the trunk, to the nearest centimetre.

Solution. $C = \pi d$
Divide both sides of the equation by π.
$$\frac{C}{\pi} = d$$
Substitute 172 for C.
$$d = \frac{172}{\pi}$$
$$\doteq 54.7$$
The diameter of the trunk is about 55 cm.

For a circle of radius r and area A, $A : r^2 = \pi : 1$ or $\dfrac{A}{r^2} = \pi$ or $A = \pi r^2$

Example 2. A pipe has a circular cross section of 18 cm². Find the radius of the cross section, to the nearest tenth of a centimetre.

Solution. $A = \pi r^2$
Divide both sides by π.
$$\frac{A}{\pi} = r^2$$
Substitute 18 for A.
$$r^2 = \frac{18}{\pi}$$
$$r \doteq \pm \sqrt{\frac{18}{\pi}}$$
$$\doteq 2.4 \quad r \text{ cannot be negative.}$$
The radius of the pipe is about 2.4 cm.

When throwing a discus, an athlete must stand inside a circle of radius 1.25 m. The region into which the discus is thrown is defined by two lines, at an angle of 40°, diverging from the centre of the circle. That part of the region that lies inside the throwing circle is called a *sector* of the circle. The angle between the lines defining the sector is called the *sector angle*.

The area of a sector is proportional to its sector angle. The area of a circle corresponds to a sector angle of 360°. These statements can be expressed as a proportion.

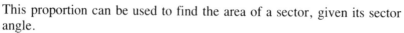

$$\frac{\text{area of sector}}{\text{sector angle}} = \frac{\text{area of circle}}{360°}$$

This proportion can be rearranged.

$$\frac{\text{area of sector}}{\text{area of circle}} = \frac{\text{sector angle}}{360°}$$

This proportion can be used to find the area of a sector, given its sector angle.

Example 3. When throwing the discus, what area of the region into which the discus is thrown lies inside the throwing circle? Give the answer to two decimal places.

Solution. Draw a diagram.
The required area is a sector of a circle with radius 1.25 m.
The sector angle is 40°. Since the areas are proportional to the corresponding sector angles,

$$\frac{\text{sector area}}{\text{circle area}} = \frac{\text{sector angle}}{360°}$$

The circle area is $\pi(1.25)^2$.

$$\frac{\text{sector area}}{\pi(1.25)^2} = \frac{40°}{360°}$$

$$\text{sector area} = \left(\frac{40}{360}\right)(\pi)(1.25)^2$$

$$\doteq 0.545$$

The sector area is about 0.55 m².

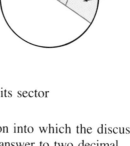

1.25 m

40°

EXERCISES 6-7

(A)

1. For each circumference given below, calculate the corresponding diameter. Express the answers in fractional form, where appropriate.

   a) 5 cm   b) 3π cm   c) π^2 cm   d) $\dfrac{1}{\pi}$ cm

2. Find the radius of each circle with the given area. Give the answer to 1 decimal place, where necessary.

   a) 78.5 cm²   b) 300 mm²   c) 144π mm²   d) $\dfrac{64}{\pi}$ mm²

3. Find the sector angle for each sector.

   a) $\dfrac{1}{6}$ of a circle   b) $\dfrac{2}{3}$ of a circle   c) $\dfrac{5}{8}$ of a circle

(B)

4. Write the area of each shaded sector as a percent of the area of the circle. Give the answer to 1 decimal place, where necessary.

   a)

   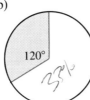

   b)

   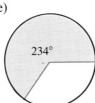

   120°

   c)

   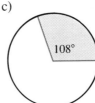

   108°

   d)

   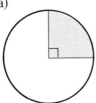

   144°

   e)

   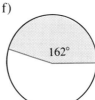

   234°

   f)

   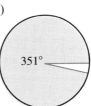

   162°

   g)

   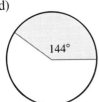

   72°

   h)

   135°

   i)

   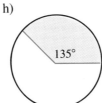

   351°

5. In the shot put event, the shot is thrown from within a circle of diameter 2.14 m.
   a) Find the area of the shot put circle.
   b) The shot must be thrown within a sector having a sector angle of 40°. What area of the region into which the shot is put lies inside the throwing circle?

6. In the sport of pistol shooting, the target consists of ten concentric rings, as shown. The chart shows the outside diameter of each ring.

Ring	Diameter
10	50 mm
9	100 mm
8	150 mm
7	200 mm
6	250 mm
5	300 mm
4	350 mm
3	400 mm
2	450 mm
1	500 mm

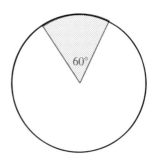

a) Find the area of the 10 ring, to the nearest square millimetre.
b) Find the total target area, to the nearest square centimetre.
c) Express the area of the 10 ring as a percent of the total target area.
d) Find the area of the 1 ring, to the nearest square centimetre.
e) Express the area of the 1 ring as a percent of the total target area.
f) Express the area of the 10 ring as a percent of the area of the 1 ring.

7. A thread of length 36 m is wound around a cylindrical spool of circular cross-section with diameter 2 cm. How many complete revolutions of the spool are needed to unravel all the thread?

8. Through what angle does the hour hand of a clock turn between noon and 05:00?

9. The length of an arc contained in a sector is proportional to the sector angle. The sector angle of the colored sector in the diagram is 60°. Since 60° is $\frac{1}{6}$ of 360°, the colored arc is $\frac{1}{6}$ of the circumference.

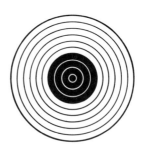

a) Express the arc length corresponding to each sector angle, as a fraction of the circumference.
   i) 90°   ii) 45°   iii) 270°   iv) 120°
b) Calculate each arc length in part a) for a circle with radius 12 cm. Give the answers to the nearest tenth of a centimetre.
c) What sector angle corresponds to an arc length that is $\frac{3}{8}$ of the circumference of the circle?
d) If you knew the sector angle and the circumference, how could you find the length of the arc?

10. The diameter of a spherical weather balloon increases to 1.5 times its initial size by the time it ascends to the cloud base. Find the factors by which these measurements have increased.
    a) the circumference   b) the cross-sectional area

11. Which would drain a tank faster — one drain 4 cm in diameter or two drains each 2 cm in diameter? How many times faster would it drain?

Ⓒ

12. Calculate these ratios concerning the volumes of a cylinder, a sphere, and a cone.
    a) $\dfrac{V \text{ (cylinder)}}{V \text{ (sphere)}}$ when the radius of both the cylinder and the sphere is r and the height of the cylinder is $2r$
    b) $\dfrac{V \text{ (cylinder)}}{V \text{ (cone)}}$ when the cylinder and the cone have the same base and the same height
    c) $\dfrac{V \text{ (sphere)}}{V \text{ (cone)}}$ when the radius of both the sphere and the cone is r and the height of the cone is $2r$

13. Find the angle between the hands of a clock at each time.
    a) 01:00   b) 02:20   c) 03:30   d) 04:45

14. Two circles, with circumferences x and y, are touching. What is the distance between their centres?

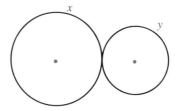

15. A ball just fits into a can, touching the bottom, the sides, and the lid. If it is inserted into the can when the can is full of water, what percent, to 1 decimal place, of the water is displaced?

16. One of Jupiter's moons is three times the diameter of the Earth's moon. How many times greater is the mass of Jupiter's moon than the Earth's? What assumption are you making?

17. Imagine that a steel ring circles the Earth, just touching it at the equator. What length would need to be added to the ring to raise it 1 m from the surface all the way around?

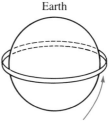

Earth

1 m clearance

1. In a bracelet of 18 K gold, the ratio of gold to copper is 18 : 6.
   a) Write this ratio in lowest terms.
   b) Find the mass of gold in a bracelet with a mass of 72 g.

2. State which is the greater ratio.
   a) $\dfrac{7}{9}$ or $\dfrac{10}{13}$ b) 5 : 6 or 29 : 34   c) 8 : 17 or 11 : 25   d) 21 : 8 or 24 : 9

3. Find the value of each letter.
   a) $\dfrac{7}{10} = \dfrac{m}{15}$ b) $\dfrac{n}{4} = \dfrac{13}{8}$ c) $\dfrac{39}{a} = \dfrac{13}{3}$ d) $\dfrac{17}{21} = \dfrac{51}{b}$

4. Bill contributes $3.50 and Laura $6.50 for the purchase of a $10 lottery ticket. It is drawn for a prize of $125 000. How should the money be divided?

5. The partners in a business agree to share the profits in the ratio 3 : 8 : 4. How much does each partner receive from a total profit of $45 000?

6. The shadow of a tree is 26.5 m long when that of a vertical metre rule is 58 cm long. How high is the tree?

7. On a map, two towns are 85 mm apart. If the scale of the map is 1 : 1 500 000, what is the actual distance between the towns?

8. The ferry crossing of the St. Lawrence River at Baie Comeau is a distance of 61 km. What will this distance be on a map drawn to a scale of 1 : 200 000?

9. A person's heart beats 13 times in 10 s.
   a) How many times does it beat in 1 h?
   b) How long does it take to beat: i) 1000 times   ii) 1 000 000 times?

10. A car's rate of fuel consumption is 8.5 L/100 km.
    a) How much fuel is needed to travel 350 km?
    b) If the car's tank holds a maximum of 58 L of fuel, will one tankful be enough to travel 687 km from Corner Brook to St. John's in Newfoundland?

11. A person's rate of pay increases from $5.00/h to $7.00/h. What is the percent increase?

12. What is the sale price of a $165 bicycle selling at a 15% discount?

13. The price of oil is $150/m^3 and the price is raised 10% every year. What will be its price at the end of three years?

14. Find the simple interest on each amount.
    a) A $215 credit-card bill for 1 month at 18% per annum
    b) $150 in a daily-interest savings account for 20 days at $12\frac{1}{4}$% per annum

15. A tire has a diameter of 58 cm. Find its circumference to the nearest centimetre.

16. A sector of a circle of radius 14.5 cm has a sector angle of 75°. Calculate:
    a) the arc length of the sector
    b) the area of the sector.

Cumulative Review, Chapters 4-6

1. Solve.
   a) $7 + y = -6$
   b) $9 - t = -13$
   c) $-18 = -6p$
   d) $11 = 2.25w$
   e) $\frac{1}{7}x = -2$
   f) $\frac{r}{3} = \frac{1}{5}$
   g) $-2.75x = 16.5$
   h) $5x - 2 = 13$
   i) $3 - 3y = -3$

2. Solve.
   a) $5x - 3 = 2x + 6$
   b) $-3y + 5 = 2y - 10$
   c) $3(r - 1) = -2(r + 8)$
   d) $5(7x - 3) = 17x - (2 - 5x)$
   e) $\frac{4}{3} - \frac{1}{2}x = \frac{2}{3}x$
   f) $1.25 - 0.8x = 0.4x - 0.19$
   g) $2(3a - 5) = 7(2a + 3) - 3$
   h) $\frac{3}{2}p + \frac{1}{4} = \frac{3}{4}p - \frac{7}{8}$

3. Solve and check.
   a) $12 - 4a + 7 = 2a + 31$
   b) $-4(x - 3) = 2(x + 9)$
   c) $7(2s - 3) + 11 = 2(4s + 7)$
   d) $1.4x - 3.6 = 0.4(2x + 1.5)$

4. The cost C dollars of printing a school yearbook is given by this formula.
   $C = 2750 + 9.5n$, where n is the number of books printed
   a) Find the cost of printing:
      i)   600 copies
      ii)   940 copies
      iii)   1050 copies.
   b) How many copies can be printed for $13 010.00?

5. Express each statement as an equation and solve it.
   a) A number multiplied by seven equals fifty-six.
   b) A number divided by fifteen equals seventy-five.
   c) When twenty-nine is subtracted from a number, the result is negative two.

6. A father is three times as old as his daughter. In 12 years time, he will be only twice as old. What are their ages now?

7. Two numbers differ by 3. The sum of the larger and one-fourth the smaller is 13. Find the numbers.

8. Simplify.
   a) $2^3 + 2^4$
   b) $2^3 \times 2^4$
   c) $(-3)^2 + (-3)^3$
   d) $(-2)^7 \div (-2)^4$
   e) $\left(\frac{3}{4}\right)^{-1} + \left(\frac{3}{4}\right)^0$
   f) $2^{-3} \div 2^{-4}$
   g) 3^{-2}
   h) $\left(-\frac{2}{3}\right)^{-2}$

9. If $m = 3$ and $n = -2$, find the value of each expression.
   a) $2m^2$
   b) $-4n^3$
   c) $8m^2 - 5n^2$
   d) $(m + n)^3$
   e) $(m - n)^3$
   f) $\frac{5m^2 - 3n^2}{m - n^3}$
   g) $\frac{3(m - n)^2}{m^2 + n}$
   h) $5n^3 - 2m^2$

10. Simplify.
    a) $x^3 \times x^7$
    b) $x^{14} \div x^8$
    c) $-3p^2 \times 7p^{-9}$
    d) $24m^{-3} \div (-8m^{11})$
    e) $(3x)^2 \times (2x)^3$
    f) $(4y^3)^2$
    g) $35a^3 \div 5a^{-7}$
    h) $3x^5 \times 12x^{-7} \div 4x^{-3}$
    i) $\frac{18s^4 \times 4s^{11}}{12s^7}$

11. Write in scientific notation.
    a) 15 000   b) 2 700 000   c) 21   d) 0.000 016   e) 0.000 37   f) 0.19

12. Simplify.
    a) $\sqrt{2500}$
    b) $-\sqrt{1.96}$
    c) $\sqrt{2\,250\,000}$
    d) $2\sqrt{49} - 3\sqrt{16}$
    e) $9\sqrt{64} + 2\sqrt{9}$
    f) $7\sqrt{81} - 5\sqrt{100}$

13. Evaluate, to 2 decimal places, if $x = -3$ and $y = 2$.
    a) $\sqrt{-14x}$
    b) $\sqrt{2x^2 + 6y^3 - 2}$
    c) $-\sqrt{7x^2 - 4y^2 + 8}$

14. The value of a $3200 investment certificate is given by this formula.
    $V = 3200(1.08)^n$, where n is the number of years after purchase
    Find the value of the certificate after 5 years.

15. Solve each proportion.
    a) $\dfrac{r}{3} = \dfrac{8}{15}$
    b) $\dfrac{16}{25} = \dfrac{48}{x}$
    c) $\dfrac{12}{39} = \dfrac{s}{13}$
    d) $\dfrac{19}{t} = \dfrac{57}{42}$

16. Jacques contributes $4.00 and Jeanne $6.00 for the purchase of a lottery ticket. It is drawn for a prize of $25 000. How should the money be divided?

17. On a map, two cities are 120 mm apart. The scale of the map is 1 : 1 250 000. What is the actual distance between the cities?

18. In an orienteering exercise, Sharon's location is 3.2 cm from town A on the map. If the actual distance is 24 km, what is the scale of the map?

19. a) 24% of a number is 18. What is the number?
    b) What percent of 1210 is 484?

20. A calculator regularly priced at $15.75 is on sale for $12.60. What is the percent of discount?

21. A television that lists for $480 is on sale at a 15% discount. What is the sale price?

22. Find the simple interest on:
    a) a loan of $650 for 3 months at 14% per annum
    b) a deposit of $125 for 90 days at 6.5% per annum.

23. A patio table has a circumference of 353 cm. Find its diameter.

24. A pizza measuring 36 cm in diameter is cut into 6 equal sections.
    a) Find each sector angle.
    b) Find the arc length of each sector.
    c) Find the area of each sector.

25. One sector of a circle graph has a sector angle of 80°. The graph has a radius of 12.5 cm.
    a) Find the arc length of the sector.
    b) Find the area of the sector.

How many tennis rackets must be produced to make a given profit from their sale? (See Section 7-3, *Example 6.*)

7-1 SIMPLIFYING POLYNOMIALS

The simplest algebraic expression is a term. Recall that a term is either a number, called a constant term, or the product of a number (called a coefficient) and one or more variables.

A *polynomial* is the general name for one term or the sum or difference of two or more terms. The variables in the terms have positive integral exponents.

A polynomial with one term is called a *monomial*.

For example, 2, $-3y^2$, $\frac{3}{4}x^2y^3$ are monomials.

A polynomial with two terms is called a *binomial*.

For example, $3x + 7$, $2y^2 - y$, $\frac{1}{2}z^3 - 4zy$ are binomials.

A polynomial with three terms is called a *trinomial*.

For example, $4y^5 - \frac{3}{5}x^2y + y$, $-2 - 6x + 5y$ are trinomials.

These expressions are *not* polynomials.

$$5 + \frac{2}{x}, \sqrt{x} + 3, 3a^{-3} + 2a^2 - 1$$

Can you explain why?

In a polynomial, terms that have the same variable raised to the same exponent are like terms. For example, x, $-x$, and $7x$ are like terms but $7x$ and $7x^2$ are unlike terms. Also, $3x^2y$ and $-9x^2y$ are like terms but the terms xy, x^2y, and xy^2 are unlike terms.

The following example shows how a polynomial can be simplified by combining like terms.

Example 1. Simplify. $5x + 3y - 4x + 9y$

Solution. Combine like terms.
$$5x + 3y - 4x + 9y = 5x - 4x + 3y + 9y$$
$$= x + 12y$$

When the terms of a polynomial are arranged in order from the highest to the lowest powers of the variable, the polynomial is in *descending powers* of the variable. These polynomials are in descending powers.

$$x^3 - 3x^2 + 4x - 5; \quad 4x^2 - 9; \quad 5x^4 - 2x^2 + 11$$

When the terms of a polynomial are arranged from the lowest to the highest powers of the variable, the polynomial is in *ascending powers* of the variable.

Example 2. Simplify and write in descending powers of y.
$$3y - 2y^3 + 5y - 7 + y^2 + y^3$$

Solution.   Combine like terms.
$$3y - 2y^3 + 5y - 7 + y^2 + y^3 = 3y + 5y - 2y^3 + y^3 - 7 + y^2$$
$$= 8y - y^3 - 7 + y^2$$
$$= -y^3 + y^2 + 8y - 7$$

The term with the greatest exponent, or exponent sum, determines the *degree* of the polynomial.

$x + y - 3$ is a first-degree polynomial.

$xy + 4x$ is a second-degree polynomial, since the term xy has the greatest exponent sum, 2.

$x^2 + 3x^3 + 2x - 7$ is a third-degree polynomial.

$x^4 + 2y^3x^2 - 5$ is a fifth-degree polynomial, since the term $2y^3x^2$ has the greatest exponent sum, 5.

The following example shows how we arrange the terms of a polynomial in descending powers before we identify its degree.

Example 3.   Simplify each polynomial and state its degree.
a) $-3x^2 + x^3 - 2x + 7 + 5x^2 + 2x^3 - 8x + 3$
b) $7x^4 + 2y^2 - 5x^4 + 3xy^4 + 5x^3y - 6y^2 + 8$

Solution.   a) $-3x^2 + x^3 - 2x + 7 + 5x^2 + 2x^3 - 8x + 3$
$$= -3x^2 + 5x^2 + x^3 + 2x^3 - 2x - 8x + 7 + 3$$
$$= 2x^2 + 3x^3 - 10x + 10$$
$$= 3x^3 + 2x^2 - 10x + 10$$
It is a third-degree polynomial.

b) $7x^4 + 2y^2 - 5x^4 + 3xy^4 + 5x^3y - 6y^2 + 8$
$$= 7x^4 - 5x^4 + 2y^2 - 6y^2 + 3xy^4 + 5x^3y + 8$$
$$= 2x^4 - 4y^2 + 3xy^4 + 5x^3y + 8$$
$$= 3xy^4 + 5x^3y + 2x^4 - 4y^2 + 8$$
It is a fifth-degree polynomial.

EXERCISES 7-1

Ⓐ

1. State the coefficient in each term.
   a) $14x$ b) $7y^2$ c) a d) $-b^2$ e) $-.4c^3$

2. State the variable in each term.
   a) $5t$ b) $3x^2$ c) $2w^2$ d) $6z^5$ e) 6

3. State whether the terms are like or unlike.
   a) $2a, 3a$ b) $5x, x$ c) $4m, n$ d) $9c, -6c$
   e) $7x^2, 3x^2, -x^2$ f) $8a^2, 8a$ g) $-2a^2, -4b^2$ h) $4t^3, 2t^3, 3t$
   i) $2.3b, 6.9b$ j) $5, \pi, \sqrt{2}$ k) $\frac{3}{4}x, -\frac{2}{3}x, \frac{1}{2}x$ l) $\sqrt{2}n, \frac{3}{2}n$

4. State the like terms.
   a) $5a$, $3b$, $5c$, a^2, $+a$, $3d$, $3e$
   b) $4x$, $3y^2$, $4z$, $2y$, y^2, $4w$
   c) $9g$, $6h$, $9g^2$, $\frac{1}{9}g$, $\frac{1}{6}h^2$, g^2
   d) 16, d^2, d, f, 8, $0.5d$, $7d^3$
   e) $3q^3$, $17q^2$, $-3t^3$, $6q$, $3t^2$, $+15q^2$

5. Simplify.
   a) $3m + 11m$
   b) $-5k + 3k$
   c) $-2x + 7x$
   d) $2n - 6n + n$
   e) $-3a + 4a - 5a$
   f) $-2x^2 + 9x^2 - x^2$
   g) $-y^3 - 5y^3 + 2y^3$
   h) $-3c - 5c$
   i) $2.7m - 6.9m - 5.2m$
   j) $\frac{1}{2}t^2 - t^2 + \frac{1}{2}t^2$
   k) $\frac{3}{4}x + \frac{2}{3}x + \frac{1}{2}x$
   l) $-\frac{1}{3}a + \frac{5}{6}a + \frac{2}{9}a$

6. Simplify.
   a) $3x - 10y + 4y - 7x$
   b) $-2a - 7b + 5a + 11b$
   c) $-4p + 13q - 9q + 8p$
   d) $-5d - 6c - c + 10d$
   e) $m + 11n - 12n - 7m$
   f) $-7h + 12g - 13h + 2g$
   g) $-3e - 7f + 14e - 3f$
   h) $-y - 15x + 13x - 18y$

7. Simplify.
   a) $3t + 5t$
   b) $4a - 3a + 2ab$
   c) $-14m + 5mn - m$
   d) $-5s^2 + s^3 + 9s^2$
   e) $12k^3 - 15k^3 + 2k^3$
   f) $-5c^4 - 3c^2 + 7c^4$
   g) $\frac{1}{2}x + \frac{1}{3}x$
   h) $0.5r + 0.7r$
   i) $\frac{3}{4}a^2 - \frac{2}{5}a^2$
   j) $8.2h - 11.2h$
   k) $\frac{3}{2}c^2 - \frac{11}{3}c^2$
   l) $1.3n - 1.7n + 0.8n$

8. Simplify.
   a) $(+6x) - (+2x)$
   b) $(+3a) - (+7a)$
   c) $(+5p) - (-3p)$
   d) $(-n^2) - (+5n^2)$
   e) $(-7x^3) - (-2x^3)$
   f) $(-y) - (-8y)$
   g) $(+4.5c) - (+5.3c)$
   h) $(+2.9x) - (+9.7x)$
   i) $(+2.5b^2) - (-3.5b^2)$
   j) $\left(+\frac{1}{3}a\right) - \left(-\frac{1}{2}a\right)$
   k) $\left(\frac{1}{4}m\right) - \left(+\frac{3}{4}m\right)$
   l) $\left(+\frac{2}{5}y^2\right) - \left(+\frac{2}{5}y^2\right)$

9. Simplify.
   a) $0.5a + 0.7a - 0.2a$
   b) $-0.6m - 0.9m + m$
   c) $\frac{2}{3}x - \frac{1}{6}x + \frac{1}{4}x$
   d) $\frac{5}{3}y + \frac{1}{4}y - \frac{3}{2}y$
   e) $12c^2 - c^2 - 9c^2$
   f) $24b^2 - 14b^2 + 3b^2$
   g) $-7x^3 - 5x^3 - 4x^3$
   h) $3x^2y - 5x^2y + 7x^2y$
   i) $-3abc + 5bca + bac$
   j) $3mnp - 7mpn + 4npm - 11pmn$
   k) $5xyz + 6yzx - zyx + 2zxy$
   l) $-9fgh + 4gfh - 3fhg - 8hfg$

10. Simplify.
   a) $3x - 5y + 2x - 7x - 6y + 3z$ $-2x \; -11 + 3z$
   b) $-2b - 5a + 3b - 7c + 8a - c$
   c) $8g + 7f + 4g - 3e - 11f - 7e$
   d) $-5m - 6x + 10p + x - 12p + 11m$
   e) $11e - d - 8e + 7f - 4d - 9f$
   f) $4 - 7y + 8 - 3x - 9 + 10y - 11x$
   g) $-1 + 3a - 12b + 8 - 3b + 12a$
   h) $13x + 10 - 2y + 4x + 8y - 15$

11. Simplify.
   a) $8x + 2x - 3x$ b) $-5a - a - 2a$ c) $-3p^2 + p^2 + 5p^2$
   d) $-2y^2 - 3y + y$ e) $5m^2 - 2m - 3m$ f) $7x^3 + 5x^3 - 4x^2$
   g) $-3a^2 + 8a^2 + a^2$ h) $-x^2 - 2x - 3x^2$ i) $2.5c - 3.2c^2 + 1.7c$

12. Simplify.
   a) $32m^2 - 15m - 7m$ b) $-65x^2 + 37x - 27x$
   c) $38c^2 + 45c - 20c$ d) $-18n - 24n + 20n^2$
   e) $6.3x^2 - 9.7x^2 + 2.5x^2$ f) $-4.7x^3 - 3.9x^3 + 11.7x^2$
   g) $-\dfrac{1}{4}c + \dfrac{1}{3}c - \dfrac{1}{2}c$ h) $\dfrac{1}{5}a^2 - \dfrac{1}{2}a - \dfrac{1}{3}a$

13. Simplify. $6n^2 + 7n$
   a) $14n^2 + 7n - 8n^2$ b) $3x^3 - 5x^2 + 8x^2$ c) $5.4y^2 - 1.8y + 1.9y^2$
   d) $-6a^2 + 5a^2 - 3a$ e) $-\dfrac{3}{4}c^2 + \dfrac{2}{3}c + \dfrac{3}{2}c^2$ f) $\dfrac{3}{8}m^3 - \dfrac{3}{4}m^2 + \dfrac{3}{8}m^3$
   g) $0.7x^2 - 0.8x + 0.5x$ h) $-3y + 7y^2 - 2y^2$ i) $5a^3 - 2a - a^3 + 3a$

14. Simplify each expression and write it in descending powers of the variable. State the degree of each expression.
   a) $3a + 2 + 5a + 7$ $8a + 9$ b) $2x - 6 + 8x + 4$
   c) $5n + 1 - 9n + 2$ $-4n + 3$ d) $-6c + 3 - c - 5$ $-7c - 2$
   e) $7x - 2 - 3x - 1$ f) $3x^2 - 5x + x^2 - 2x$ $4x^2 - 7x$
   g) $-4a^2 - 3a - a^2 + 2a$ $-5a^2 - 1a$ h) $-m - 2 + 3m - 1$

15. Simplify where possible.
   a) $3a^2 - 2a - a^2 + a$ b) $5x + 7$
   c) $5x^2 + 3x$ d) $8m^2 - 3 - 2m^2 + 4$
   e) $-c - 3 + 2c - 5$ f) $3a^2 - 3a - 3$
   g) $-2 + 5x - x + 4$ h) $-n^2 - 2n + 4$
   i) $\dfrac{1}{5}m + \dfrac{1}{2}m + m^2$ j) $-\dfrac{1}{2}y^2 + \dfrac{2}{3}y + \dfrac{1}{4}y^2 - \dfrac{1}{6}y$

16. State the like terms.
   a) $2x, x^2, xy, 2y, 3x^2y, 2xy, -5x^2y$
   b) $3a, 4ab, 5ab^2, -7a, 3b, -5ab, 8$
   c) $5ax, 4a, 7x, 3ax, -7a, 6xa, 7ax^2$
   d) $3a^2b, -5ab, 9ab^2, 6ba, -3a^2b$

17. Simplify.
    a) $2xy - 3x^2y + 2xy^2 - 3yx + 5xy^2 - 2yx^2$
    b) $4xy^2 - 3xy + 2yx^2 - 4y^2x^2 + 2yx - 4y^2x + 3$
    c) $9y^2a - 2a^2 + a^2y - 7ay + 3a^2y - 8ay^2$
    d) $9w + 4z - 3wz + 2w^2z - 8zw^2 + 2w - 3z$
    e) $5ab - 6a^2b - 3ab + 8a^2b - 4a + 7ab$
    f) $3xy^2 - 2x^2y + 6x - 2xy^2 + 7x^2y - 4y$
    g) $-m^2n + 3m + 8mn^2 - 5m^2n - 4m + 6mn^2$
    h) $-8 + 6c^2d - 5cd + 8cd^2 + 11cd - 4c^2d$

18. Simplify.
    a) $3x + 4y - 5xy + 3y + 5yx - 4x$
    b) $9xy^2 + 6xy - 8xy^2 - 8x^2y + 6x^2y^2 - 6xy$
    c) $5a^2b + 10ab^2 + 12a^2b^2 + 6ab^2 - 12a^2b - 8a^2b^2 + 7a^2b$
    d) $8x^2y - 6xy^2 - 7yx^2 + 6y^2x - x^2y^2$
    e) $4abc - 5a^2bc + 6abc^2 - 8abc + 7a^2bc + 3abc^2 - 2abc$
    f) $14p^2q + 6pq^2 - 3pq - 4p^2q - 7pq^2 + 5pq - p^2q + 6$
    g) $3xyz - 4x^2yz + 5xy^2z - 7xyz - 8xy^2z + 6x^2yz + 12xy$ $-4xyz$
    h) $1.8s^2t - 7.2st + 0.8st^2 - 0.7s^2t + 4.2st^2 - 4.8st + st^2$

19. a) Complete this multiplication table.
    b) Write the products in your table in descending order.
    c) Write the sum of the products in your table as a polynomial. What is the degree of that polynomial?

×	a	3
a		
4		

20. a) Complete this multiplication table.
    b) Identify the like terms in your table.
    c) Identify and explain any pattern in the positions of the like terms.
    d) Write the products in your table in descending order.
    e) Write the sum of the products in your table as a polynomial. What is the degree of that polynomial?

×	a^2	$2a$	5
a^2			
$4a$			
6			

21. a) Complete this multiplication table.
    b) Write the sum of the products in your table as a polynomial. What is the degree of that polynomial?

×	a	a^2	b
ab			
b			
a			

7-2 EVALUATING POLYNOMIALS

When a particular cannon is fired from a castle wall, the shell's approximate height above the ground at any time can be found from this formula. $h = -4.9t^2 + 25t + 5$

h represents the height, in metres, of the shell.
t represents the time, in seconds, after firing.

To find the height after 3 s, substitute $t = 3$ into the formula.
$$h = -4.9(3)^2 + 25(3) + 5$$
$$= 35.9$$

After 3 s, the shell is about 36 m above the ground.

Many formulas in mathematics, science, and engineering involve polynomials. The application of these formulas usually involves substituting certain values for the variables.

Example 1. The sum S of the first n even numbers is given by this formula.
$$S = n^2 + n$$
a) Show that the formula is true for $n = 5$.
b) Find the sum of the first 30 even numbers.

Solution. a) When $n = 5$, $S = 5^2 + 5$
$$= 30$$
The sum of the first 5 even numbers is $2 + 4 + 6 + 8 + 10$, which does equal 30.
b) Substitute $n = 30$, $S = 30^2 + 30$
$$= 930$$
The sum of the first 30 even numbers is 930.

Example 2. The volume V of air in a tire of inner diameter d and outer diameter D is given by this formula.
$$V = \frac{\pi^2}{32}(D + d)(D - d)^2$$
Find the volume of air, to the nearest 100 cm³, in the tire when $d = 40$ cm and $D = 52$ cm.

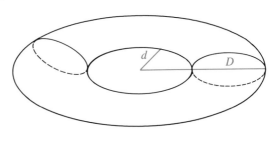

Solution. When $d = 40$ and $D = 52$,
$$V = \frac{\pi^2}{32}(52 + 40)(52 - 40)^2$$
$$= \frac{\pi^2}{32}(92)(12)^2$$

Key in: $\boxed{\pi}$ $\boxed{x^2}$ $\boxed{\div}$ $\boxed{32}$ $\boxed{\times}$ $\boxed{9}$ $\boxed{2}$ $\boxed{\times}$ $\boxed{1}$ $\boxed{2}$ $\boxed{x^2}$ $\boxed{=}$
to display 4086.0162

The volume of air in the tire is about 4100 cm³.

EXERCISES 7-2

(A)

1. Evaluate $n^2 - 3n + 4$ for each value of n.
   a) 1   b) 3   c) 4   d) -1 e) $\dfrac{1}{2}$ f) 1.5

2. Evaluate $2x^2 - 3x^1 - 5$ for each value of x.
   a) 0   b) 1   c) -1 d) 7   e) -4 f) -2.5

3. Find the value of each polynomial when $a = 8$.
   a) $a^2 + 5a + 6$ b) $2a^2 - \dfrac{1}{2}a + 3$ c) $1.5a^2 - 0.4a + 3.6$

4. Find the value of each polynomial when $x = -5$.
   a) $4x^2 - 7x + 3$ b) $-3x^2 + 2x + 5$ c) $2.9 - 0.5x + 3.6x^2$

5. For each polynomial
   i) Write it in descending powers of k.
   ii) State the coefficients and the constant term.
   iii) Evaluate the polynomial when $k = 1$.
   a) $-3 + 7k^2 + 2k$ b) $\dfrac{1}{4}k + \dfrac{1}{2}k^2 + \dfrac{1}{3}$ c) $2.5k - 8.4k^2$

(B)

6. The temperature T degrees Celsius in an oven n minutes after it has been turned on is given by this formula.
   $T = -n^2 + 30n + 20$, for $n < 14$
   Find the temperature:
   a) 7 min after the oven was turned on
   b) 10 min after the oven was turned on.

7. The number of diagonals d in a polygon of n sides is given by this formula.
   $d = \dfrac{1}{2}n^2 - \dfrac{3}{2}n$
   a) Show that the formula is true for $n = 5$ by drawing a pentagon and counting its diagonals.
   b) Find the number of diagonals in:
   i) a hexagon   ii) a decagon (10 sides)   iii) a dodecagon (12 sides)

8. In a traffic study, it was found that the number n of accidents in one month involving drivers x years of age is given by this formula.
   $n = 3x^2 - 200x + 5000$
   Find the number of accidents in one month involving drivers:
   a) 18 years old   b) 25 years old.

9. Find each sum.
   a) the first 50 even numbers   b) the first 100 even numbers

10. Evaluate each polynomial for $a = 3$ and $b = -2$.
    a) $a^2 + 2ab + b^2$ b) $a^3 + 3a^2b + 3ab^2 + b^3$

11. The volume V of the frustum of a cone with top and bottom radii a and b respectively, and height h, is given by this formula.

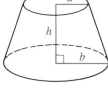

$$V = \frac{1}{3}\pi h(a^2 + ab + b^2)$$

Find the volumes of the frustums with these dimensions.
a) $a = 10$ cm; $b = 15$ cm; $h = 9$ cm
b) $a = 6.7$ m; $b = 9.3$ m; $h = 12.8$ m

12. In an experiment, the stopping distance d metres for a car travelling at v kilometres per hour was found to be given by this formula.
$d = 0.20v + 0.015v^2$
Find the stopping distance for a speed of:
a) 50 km/h   b) 100 km/h.

13. On July 20, 1969, Neil Armstrong became the first man to walk on the moon. The speed v metres per second of his space craft Apollo 11, t seconds before touchdown was given by this formula.
$v = 0.45 + 3.2t$
Its height h metres above the moon's surface was given by this formula.
$h = 0.45t + 1.6t^2$
What was the speed and the height of Apollo 11 1 min before touchdown?

14. In a certain factory, the cost C dollars of producing x bicycles was found to be given by this formula.
$C = -0.04x^2 + 50x + 1000$, for $x \leqslant 600$
Find the cost of producing:
a) 50 bicycles   b) 100 bicycles   c) 250 bicycles   d) 450 bicycles.

Ⓒ

15. a) Use the diagram to find the number of oranges in:
   i)   the top 2 rows
   ii) the top 3 rows
   iii) the top 5 rows.
   b) When there are n oranges in one row of the base of a square pyramid of oranges, the total number of oranges N is given by this formula.

   $$N = \frac{1}{3}n^3 + \frac{1}{2}n^2 + \frac{1}{6}n$$

   i) Verify that this formula is true for $n = 5$. (Use your result from part a) iii) to check.)
   ii) Find the value of the oranges in this display.

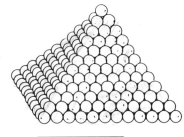

Special
$1.89/dozen

THE MATHEMATICAL MIND

The Search for a Polynomial to Generate Prime Numbers

A prime number is any whole number, greater than 1, which is divisible by only itself and 1. Since the discovery of prime numbers, mathematicians have attempted to find a polynomial for generating them.

Leonhard Euler 1707-1783

In 1772, the great Swiss mathematician, Leonhard Euler, devised the polynomial $n^2 - n + 41$ for the generation of primes.

This polynomial does, in fact, produce primes for $n = 1, 2, 3, 4, \ldots, 40$.

If $n = 1$, $n^2 - n + 41 = 1^2 - 1 + 41$, or 41
If $n = 2$, $n^2 - n + 41 = 2^2 - 2 + 41$, or 43
If $n = 3$, $n^2 - n + 41 = 3^2 - 3 + 41$, or 47
If $n = 4$, $n^2 - n + 41 = 4^2 - 4 + 41$, or 53
However, if $n = 41$, $n^2 - n + 41 = 41^2 - 41 + 41$, or 1681.
This number is divisible by 41 and therefore is not a prime number.

In 1879, E.B. Escott devised the polynomial $n^2 - 79n + 1601$.

1. Test this polynomial for several values of n to see if the results are prime numbers.

2. a) Substitute 80 for n, and show that the result is *not* a prime number.
   b) Find another value of n which gives a result that is not a prime number.

3. Find a value for n for which the following polynomials do *not* produce a prime number.
   a) $n^2 + n - 1$ b) $n^2 - n + 17$ c) $n^2 - n + 41, n \neq 41$

At the present time, there is no known polynomial that produces *only* prime numbers. There is also no known polynomial that will produce all the prime numbers.

COMPUTER POWER

Polynomials to Generate Prime Numbers

Until the arrival of the computer, mathematicians used advanced mathematical techniques together with lengthy computation in the search for a polynomial that would generate only prime numbers. Today, the approach to this problem is made much easier by the use of computers. The following program can be used to determine the values up to any positive integer N for which the polynomial $AN^2 + BN + C$ generates only prime numbers.

```
100 REM *** POLYNOMIALS AND PRIMES ***
110 PRINT  "ENTER THE VALUES OF A, B, AND C"
120 INPUT  "SEPARATED BY COMMAS:   ";A,B,C
130 PRINT  "UP TO WHAT VALUE OF N DO YOU WISH"
140 INPUT  "TO CHECK?  ";M
150 FOR N=1 TO M
160     P=A*N*N+B*N+C
170     PRINT N,P
180     R=INT(SQR(P))
190     FOR D=2 TO R
200         IF P/D=INT(P/D) THEN GO TO 240
210     NEXT D
220 NEXT N
230 PRINT: "EVERY VALUE FOR N=1 TO ";M;" IS PRIME."
240 PRINT "WHEN N = ";N;" THE VALUE IS DIVISIBLE
      BY ";D
260 END
```

1. Use the program to test whether the polynomial $n^2 + n + 17$ generates prime numbers for all positive integers up to 100.

2. Find a value of n for which each of the following polynomials does *not* produce a prime number.
   a) $n^2 + n + 1$ b) $n^2 - n + 17$
   c) $n^2 - n + 41$ d) $n^2 - 79n + 1601$

3. Find the smallest possible integer n for which the polynomial $\dfrac{n^2 + 2n + 653}{16}$ yields a composite integer.

4. Prove that 2 is the greatest integral value of n for which $n^2 - 1$ is a prime number.

7-3 ADDING AND SUBTRACTING POLYNOMIALS

In one factory, the cost of making a model of tennis racket is given by this formula.
$C = 6n + 2000$
C represents the cost in dollars.
n represents the number of rackets made.

The income from the sale of these rackets is given by this formula.
$I = 15n$
The profit from selling these rackets can be found by subtracting the cost from the income.

Profit = Income − Cost

Example 1. Find the profit from the production and sale of 500 rackets.

Solution. The income from the sale of 500 rackets is obtained by substituting $n = 500$ into this formula.
$$I = 15n$$
$$= 15(500)$$
$$= 7500$$
The income is $7500.
The cost of making 500 rackets is obtained by substituting $n = 500$ into this formula.
$$C = 6n + 2000$$
$$= 6(500) + 2000$$
$$= 3000 + 2000$$
$$= 5000$$
The cost is $5000.
Hence, the profit is $7500 − $5000, or $2500.

If we want to know the profit from the sale of different numbers of rackets, it is easier to subtract the polynomials first and then substitute. To do this, we need to learn how to subtract polynomials.

The addition of polynomials resembles the addition of numbers.

Arithmetic		Algebra
7258	$7(10^3) + 2(10^2) + 5(10) + 8$	$7x^3 + 2x^2 + 5x + 8$
$+2431$	$2(10^3) + 4(10^2) + 3(10) + 1$	$+2x^3 + 4x^2 + 3x + 1$
9689	$9(10^3) + 6(10^2) + 8(10) + 9$	$9x^3 + 6x^2 + 8x + 9$

Polynomials, like numbers, can also be added horizontally. We simply combine like terms.

Example 2. Simplify.

a) $(3n + 5) + (2n + 3)$ b) $(-2x^2 + 6x - 7) + (3x^2 - x - 2)$

Solution.   a) $(3n + 5) + (2n + 3) = 3n + 5 + 2n + 3$

$= 3n + 2n + 5 + 3$ grouping like terms

$= 5n + 8$

b) $(-2x^2 + 6x - 7) + (3x^2 - x - 2)$

$= -2x^2 + 6x - 7 + 3x^2 - x - 2$

$= -2x^2 + 3x^2 + 6x - x - 7 - 2$ grouping like terms

$= x^2 + 5x - 9$

Recall that to subtract an integer, we add its opposite (sometimes called its *additive inverse*). The same rule applies to polynomials. To subtract a polynomial, add its *additive inverse*.

To find the additive inverse of a polynomial, multiply it by -1.

Example 3. Find the additive inverse of each polynomial.

a) $7x - 4$ b) $-x^2 + 2x - 6$

Solution.   a) $(-1)(7x - 4) = -7x + 4$

The additive inverse of $7x - 4$ is $-7x + 4$.

b) $(-1)(-x^2 + 2x - 6) = x^2 - 2x + 6$

The additive inverse of $-x^2 + 2x - 6$ is $x^2 - 2x + 6$.

Example 4. Simplify.

a) $(2x + 7) - (6x - 2)$ b) $(8 - n + n^2) - (-2 + 3n - n^2)$

Solution.   Add the additive inverse.

a) $(2x + 7) - (6x - 2) = 2x + 7 + (-1)(6x - 2)$

$= 2x + 7 - 6x + 2$

$= 2x - 6x + 7 + 2$

$= -4x + 9$

b) $(8 - n + n^2) - (-2 + 3n - n^2)$

$= 8 - n + n^2 + (-1)(-2 + 3n - n^2)$

$= 8 - n + n^2 + 2 - 3n + n^2$

$= 8 + 2 - n - 3n + n^2 + n^2$

$= 10 - 4n + 2n^2$

Example 5. Simplify.

a) $(2a - 3) - (a^2 - 5a) + (4 - a)$

b) $3a^2b - (a - b^2) + (a + 8) - (a - 2b^2 + a^2)$

Solution. a) $(2a - 3) - (a^2 - 5a) + (4 - a)$
$= 2a - 3 - a^2 + 5a + 4 - a$
$= -a^2 + 2a + 5a - a - 3 + 4$
$= -a^2 + 6a + 1$

b) $3a^2b - (a - b^2) + (a + 8) - (a - 2b^2 + a^2)$
$= 3a^2b - a + b^2 + a + 8 - a + 2b^2 - a^2$
$= 3a^2b - a + 3b^2 - a^2 + 8$

Consider the problem posed at the beginning of the chapter.

Example 6. a) Find a formula for the profit P dollars on the sale of n tennis rackets. Use the information on page 232.
  b) Use the formula to calculate the profit from the production and sale of:
   i)   500 rackets   ii)   1500 rackets.
  c) If all the rackets that are produced are sold, how many rackets must be sold to earn a profit of $34 000?
  d) How many rackets must be produced and sold for the company to "break even"?

Solution. a) The cost C of making n tennis rackets is given by $C = 6n + 2000$. The income I from the sale of n tennis rackets is given by $I = 15n$. The profit P is the difference between the income I and the cost C. That is, $P = I - C$
$= 15n - (6n + 2000)$
$= 15n - 6n - 2000$
$= 9n - 2000$

The formula $P = 9n - 2000$ gives the profit in dollars on the production and sale of n tennis rackets.

  b) i) If 500 rackets are sold, then the profit $P = 9(500) - 2000$
$= 2500$

The profit is $2500.

   ii) If 1500 rackets are sold, then the profit $P = 9(1500) - 2000$
$= 11\ 500$

The profit is $11 500.

  c) If $P = 34\ 000$, then $34\ 000 = 9n - 2000$
$36\ 000 = 9n$
$4000 = n$

4000 rackets must be sold.

  d) To break even, we must have a zero profit.
$0 = 9n - 2000$
$2000 = 9n$
$n = \dfrac{2000}{9}$
$\doteq 222$

Since n is greater than 222, the company must sell 223 rackets.

Example 6, part b) illustrates that it is easier to find the profit by substituting into the formula, than using the method of *Example 1*.

EXERCISES 7-3

(A)

1. Simplify.
   a) $(6x + 2) + (3x + 4)$ b) $(5a - 3) + (2a + 7)$
   c) $(8 - 4m) + (-3 - 2m)$ d) $(-x + 4) + (7x - 2)$
   e) $(-1 - 3t) + (4 - 5t)$ f) $(9c - 2) + (-5c - 3)$
   g) $(4n^2 - 3n - 1) + (2n^2 - 5n - 3)$ h) $(3x^2 + 6x - 8) + (-5x^2 - x + 4)$
   i) $(2 - 3c + c^2) + (5 - 4c - 4c^2)$ j) $(8 - 2n - n^2) + (-3 - n + 4n^2)$

2. Write the additive inverse of each polynomial.

   a) $2 - 3x$ b) $5a + 4$ c) $\frac{1}{2}x - 5$

   d) $4n^2 - 3n + 1$ e) $-3 - 2t + t^2$ f) $0.2a^2 + 0.4a - 0.6$

3. Simplify.
   a) $(-2x + 3) - (3x + 2)$
   b) $(4 - 5n) - (-6n + 2)$
   c) $(3a - 5) - (6 - 7a)$
   d) $(1 - 3t) - (-2 - 5t)$
   e) $(n + 13) - (7n + 16)$
   f) $(7x - 25) - (17 + 5x)$
   g) $(-2x - 7) - (-14x - 6)$
   h) $(8a^2 + 2a - 3) - (-6a^2 + 4a + 7)$
   i) $(-6x + 5x^2 + 1) - (4x^2 + 5 - 2x)$
   j) $\left(-\frac{1}{2}k - 3 + k^2\right) - \left(-\frac{3}{2}k + 4\right)$

(B)

4. Simplify.
   a) $(3x - 2) - (x - 1) + (4x - 3)$
   b) $(2a + 3) + (6a - 1) - (a - 5)$
   c) $(7c - 5) - (-c + 3) - (2c - 1)$
   d) $(4x^2 - 3x) - (x^2 + 2x) + (3x^2 - x)$
   e) $(2m^2 - 5) + (3m - 2) - (m^2 + 1)$
   f) $(5t - 4) + (3t^2 - t) - (-2t + t^2)$
   g) $(2 - 3n) - (1 - n) + (5 - 2n)$
   h) $(5 - 2s) - (3 - s) + (7s - 2)$
   i) $(3 - 4x + x^2) - (2x - x^2) + (4 - x + 5x^2)$
   j) $(3n^2 - 6n + 5) - (3n^2 - 2n - 1) + (n^2 + 4n - 3)$

5. Simplify.
   a) $(17x - 25) + (34x + 19) - (23x - 11)$
   b) $(45 - 10x) - (-15 - 25x) - (35x + 10)$
   c) $(25n^2 - 6) - (30n^2 - 2n) + (5n^2 + 3n)$
   d) $(37 - 42t) - (61 + 23t) + (21 - 17t)$
   e) $(16n^2 - 10n - 4) + (3n^2 + 25n - 21) - (n^2 - 15n + 19)$
   f) $(2.5x - 3.7) - (1.4x + 4.2) + (-0.8x - 1.3)$

5' UP YALL

6. The cost in dollars of producing n records is $1.9n + 20\ 000$. The income in dollars from selling them is $4.4n$.
   a) Write a formula for the profit earned from producing and selling n records.
   b) Calculate the profit from the production and sale of:
      i)   10 000 records   ii)   20 000 records.
   c) If all the records made are sold, how many must be made and sold:
      i) to earn a profit of $10 000
      ii) to earn a profit of $20 000
      iii) to break even?

7. Simplify.
   a) $(5x^2 - 3y^2) + (x^2 + 4y^2)$
   b) $(3x^2 + 5xy + 7y^2) - (2x^2 - 4xy + 9y^2)$
   c) $(x^2 + 5x^2y - 7) - (3x^2 - 5x^2y + y^2) - (x^2 - 7y^2)$
   d) $(5x^2 - 5x + 7) + (2y^2 - 3x + 7) - (2x^2 - 2x + 7y)$
   e) $(3x^2 - 5x + 7) - [4 - (2x^2 + 3x) - 2]$
   f) $(7y^2 - 3y + 6) - [(2y^2 + 3) - (y^2 + 6y - 8)]$
   g) $(8x^2y^2 + 3xy - 12) - x^2y^2 - (5xy - 6 - 2x^2y^2)$

8. Simplify.
   a) $(4x^2y - 4xy^2 + 2x) - (x^2y - 4y^2x + y)$
   b) $(a^2 - ba) - (b^2 - ab) + (a^2 + b^2 + 2ab)$
   c) $-(3 - x^2y) - (2 - yx^2) - (-3 + x^2y^2)$
   d) $3z - x^2 - [(2x^2y - z) - (3yx^2 + 4z)]$
   e) $b^2a - a^2b - (ab^2 - ba^2) - (2ab^2 + 2a^2b)$
   f) $-3p^2q + 3pq + [p + q^2 - 3qp - (q^2 - 3qp^2)]$

9. The profit P millions of dollars earned from constructing an office building having x storeys is given by this polynomial. $P = 3.5x - (0.5x + 0.1x^2) - 1$
   a) Express P as a polynomial in descending powers of x.
   b) Find the profit earned from constructing an office building with:
      i)   5 storeys   ii)   15 storeys.

ⓒ

10. For $y = (8x - 5) - (x - 4) + (3x + 1)$
   a) Find the value of y for each value of x.
      i)   4   ii) -2 iii) 1   iv) 10
   b) Find the value of x when $y = 30$.

11. Arrange each expression in descending powers of x, then evaluate it for $x = -2$.
   a) $7 - (3x^2 + 2x) - (5x + x^2 - 6) - (3x + 3x^2 - 12)$
   b) $(x^2 + x - 6) - 5x - [(6x - 2x^2 + 3) - (4 - x^2)]$

12. Simplify.
   a) $4a^2b - 5(a - b^2) + a(a + 5)$
   b) $x(x + 4) - 4(x - y^2) + 3x^2y$
   c) $m(n^2 - 3) - 3(n^2 - m) + 6m$
   d) $a(a + b^2) - 2(a^2 - b^2) + ab^2$
   e) $2x^2y^2 - 3(x^2 - 2) + y^2(x^2 - 3) + 7$

7-4 MULTIPLYING POLYNOMIALS BY MONOMIALS

On a farm, in one year, the value of a hectare of wheat is given by this formula.

$V = 0.05x(140 - x)$, for $x \leq 70$

V represents the value of the crop in dollars.
x represents the number of days after planting the wheat.

To express V as a polynomial, we expand the right side of the equation using the distributive law.

$$V = 0.05x(140 - x)$$
$$= 0.05x(140) - 0.05x(x)$$
$$= 7x - 0.05x^2$$

To find the value of the crop, for example, 60 days after planting, substitute $x = 60$ into the polynomial.

$$V = 7(60) - 0.05(60)^2$$
$$= 240$$

The crop is worth $240/ha 60 days after planting.

In earlier work, the product of two monomials was evaluated as follows.

Multiply the coefficients.

$$(3x^5)(4x^2) = 12x^7$$

Add the exponents.

Example 1. Simplify.

a) $(-6b^3)(3b^2)$ b) $(-4x^2)(-5x)(3x^3)$

Solution.   a) $(-6b^3)(3b^2) = (-6)(3)(b^3)(b^2)$
$$= -18b^5$$

b) $(-4x^2)(-5x)(3x^3) = (-4)(-5)(3)(x^2)(x)(x^3)$
$$= 60x^6$$

To multiply monomials in more than one variable, first multiply the coefficients. Then combine like variables using the exponent laws for multiplication.

Example 2. Simplify.

a) $(x^2y^3)(x^3y^4)$ b) $(3p^2q)(2pq^3)$ c) $(5w^2y)(4y^2z)$

Solution. a) $(x^2y^3)(x^3y^4) = (x^2)(x^3)(y^3)(y^4)$
$$= x^5y^7$$

b) $(3p^2q)(2pq^3) = (3)(2)(p^2)(p)(q)(q^3)$
$$= 6p^3q^4$$

c) $(5w^2y)(4y^2z) = (5)(4)(w^2)(y)(y^2)(z)$
$$= 20w^2y^3z$$

When a polynomial is multiplied by a monomial, the distributive law is used.

Example 3. Expand.

a) $3x(5x - 4)$ b) $-6x^2(-3 + x + 2x^2)$

Solution. a) $3x(5x - 4) = 3x(5x) - 3x(4)$
$$= 15x^2 - 12x$$

b) $-6x^2(-3 + x + 2x^2) = -6x^2(-3) + (-6x^2)(x) + (-6x^2)(2x^2)$
$$= 18x^2 - 6x^3 - 12x^4$$

To multiply a polynomial in more than one variable by a monomial, multiply each term in the polynomial by the monomial.

Example 4. Expand.

a) $3m^2(mn - n^2)$ b) $-4xy^3(x^2 + xy - y^2)$

Solution. a) $3m^2(mn - n^2) = (3m^2)(mn) - (3m^2)(n^2)$
$$= 3m^3n - 3m^2n^2$$

b) $-4xy^3(x^2 + xy - y^2) = (-4xy^3)(x^2) + (-4xy^3)(xy) - (-4xy^3)(y^2)$
$$= -4x^3y^3 - 4x^2y^4 + 4xy^5$$

EXERCISES 7-4

(A)

1. Simplify.

a) $(6n)(5n)$ b) $(-2a)(3a)$ c) $(-5x)^2$ d) $(3n)(-6n)$

e) $(-5x^2)(-2x^2)$ f) $(3a)(2a)$ g) $(5x^4)(2x)$ h) $(8y)(-7y)$

i) $(-x)(-5x^3)$ j) $\left(\frac{1}{2}n\right)\left(\frac{1}{4}n\right)$ k) $(2.5m)(1.2m^2)$ l) $(0.5x^3)(3x^2)$

2. Simplify.

a) $(12x)^2$ b) $(-10a)(17a^2)$ c) $(-25n^2)(8n^2)$

d) $(-35c^3)(-4c^2)$ e) $(17x^2)(5x^3)$ f) $(-28n)(5n^3)$

g) $(3x)(5x)(2x)$ h) $(-4n)(-2n)(-3n)$ i) $(3a)^2$

j) $(-2x^2)^2$ k) $(-2x^2)(6x^2)(-3x)$ l) $(-10m)(-8m)(-5m^2)$

3. Simplify.
   a) $(xy^3)(x^2y)$
   b) $(m^2n^3)(mn)$
   c) $(a^2b^2)(ab^2)$
   d) $(c^3d)(c^2d^2)$
   e) $(pq^2)(p^2q^2)$
   f) $(x^4y)(y^4x)$
   g) $(2x^2y)(3xy^2)$
   h) $(-3x^2y)(4y^2x)$
   i) $(-3a^2b^2)(-2ab^3)$
   j) $(2ab^2c)(5a^2bc^2)$
   k) $(4m^2n^2p)(-3mp^2)$
   l) $(-2x^2yz^2)(-5xy^2)$

4. Expand.
   a) $5(x - 3)$
   b) $7(a + 1)$
   c) $-3(2 + n)$
   d) $-4(x - 2)$
   e) $-1(2x - 5)$
   f) $3(6x - 4)$
   g) $-6(5 + 2t)$
   h) $5(x^2 - 6x + 3)$
   i) $-2(-3 + 5n - 3n^2)$
   j) $7(x^2 - 3x + 9)$
   k) $0.4(1.5x - 2.5)$
   l) $\dfrac{1}{2}\left(\dfrac{1}{3} - \dfrac{1}{2}a\right)$

5. Expand.
   a) $x(3x + 2)$
   b) $a(5a - 1)$
   c) $n(3 - 7n)$
   d) $-x(x - 2)$
   e) $-c(3c + 5)$
   f) $x^2(3x - 1)$
   g) $y^3(y - 5)$
   h) $r^2(2 - 7r)$
   i) $n^2(3n^2 - 5n + 1)$
   j) $-x^3(5x^2 - x)$
   k) $a^2(3a^2 - 2a + 1)$
   l) $-s(7 - 2s + s^2)$

6. Expand.
   a) $5x(2x + 3)$
   b) $2a(3a - 4)$
   c) $3c(5 - 2c)$
   d) $-4n(2n - 1)$
   e) $-7y(2y^2 - 5)$
   f) $6k(3 - k + 2k^2)$
   g) $2x^2(3x - 5)$
   h) $-4a^2(3a^2 - 2a)$
   i) $5s(3s^2 - 2s - 7)$
   j) $3p^2(2 - 3p - p^2)$
   k) $-7a^2(3a^2 - 2a - 4)$
   l) $-1.5x^2(4 - 1.5x - 12x^2)$

7. Expand.
   a) $3x^2(xy - y^2)$
   b) $-2a^2(ab^2 - b)$
   c) $4m(mn - n^2)$
   d) $-3p(pq^2 - pq)$
   e) $5a^2(b^2 - a)$
   f) $-4xy(x^2 - y^2)$
   g) $-2m^2n(mn - 3n^2)$
   h) $7ab(2a^2b - 3ab^2)$
   i) $-3pqr(2pq - 4qr)$
   j) $0.25mn^2(5mn - 10m^2)$

8. Expand.
   a) $3x(x^2y + y^2x + xy)$
   b) $-2a(ab^2 - b + a^2b)$
   c) $-3m(mn - m^2n - m)$
   d) $4w(-3zw + w^2z - wz^2)$
   e) $2xy^2(y - 2x^2y + 3xy)$
   f) $-6xyz(-3xz^2 + 2xy^2 - yz^2 + 2xyz)$

9. The number N of baskets of apples that can be produced by x trees in a small orchard $(x \leq 125)$ is given by this formula.
   $N = x(25 - 0.1x)$
   Find how many baskets of apples can be produced by:
   a) 60 trees
   b) 80 trees
   c) 125 trees.

10. A field is x metres wide and $(2x + 3)$ metres long.
    a) Write expressions for the area and the perimeter of the field.
    b) Find the area and the perimeter if $x = 250$.

11. Find the area of each figure in two ways.
    a)
    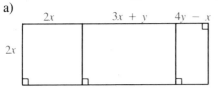
    b)
    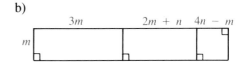

12. A person of mass x kilograms standing on the end of a diving board causes it to dip d centimetres. The relation between d and x is $d = 0.000\ 01x^2(x + 50)$. Find how much the board dips under a person of each mass.
    a) 50 kg   b) 100 kg

Ⓒ

13. The surface area S and the volume V of a right circular cylinder of radius r and height h are given by these formulas.
    $S = 2\pi r^2 + 2\pi rh$ and $V = \pi r^2 h$
    Find the surface area of a can of height 10 cm and volume 160π cm³.
    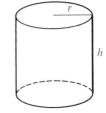

14. The dimensions, in centimetres, of a cereal box are $(5x - 1)$ by $3x$ by x.
    a) Find an expression for:
        i) the volume V of the box
        ii) the surface area S of the box
    b) Find the volume and the surface area when $x = 7$.

15. The dimensions, in metres, of a room are $4x$ by $3x$ by $(x + 2)$.
    a) Find an expression for:
        i) the volume V of the room
        ii) the surface area S of the walls and the ceiling
        iii) the area A of the floor.
    b) If $x = 2$, find the cost of:
        i) carpeting the floor if underlay costs $3.00/m² and carpeting costs $16.99/m²
        ii) painting the walls and the ceiling if 1 L of paint covers 8 m², the walls and the ceiling require 3 coats of paint, and the paint costs $24.99 for a 4 L can.
    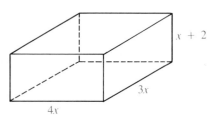

7-5 MULTIPLYING TWO BINOMIALS — PART ONE

A binomial is a polynomial with two terms. The product of two binomials can be illustrated geometrically.

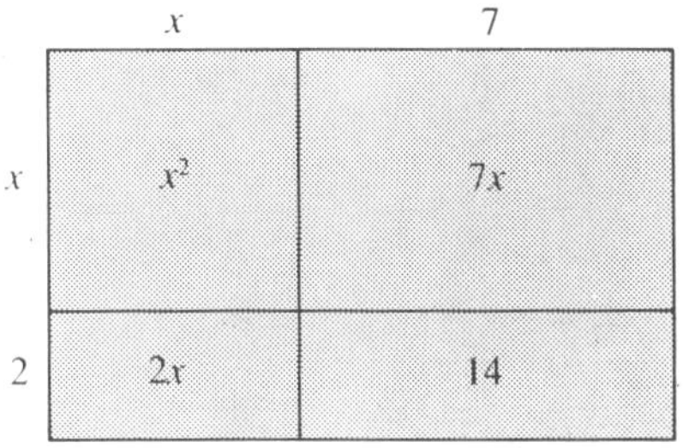

The length of the large rectangle is $(x + 7)$ units and its width is $(x + 2)$ units.

The area of the rectangle is $(x + 7)(x + 2)$.

The area is also the sum of the areas of the four small rectangles, $x^2 + 7x + 2x + 14$.

Therefore, $(x + 7)(x + 2) = x^2 + 7x + 2x + 14$

If we expand the product on the left, using the distributive law, then we obtain the expression on the right.

$$(x + 7)(x + 2) = x(x + 2) + 7(x + 2)$$
$$= x^2 + 2x + 7x + 14$$
$$= x^2 + 9x + 14$$

Example 1. Find the product. $(3a - 2)(a + 4)$

Solution.
$$(3a - 2)(a + 4)$$
$$= 3a(a + 4) - 2(a + 4)$$
$$= 3a^2 + 12a - 2a - 8$$
$$= 3a^2 + 10a - 8$$

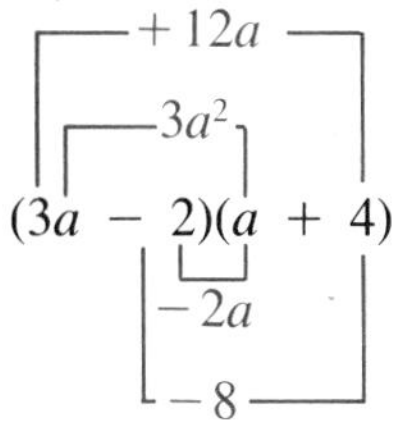

The diagram shows that, to find the product of two binomials, we multiply each term of one binomial by each term of the other binomial.

Example 2. Find each product.

a) $(2x + 1)(7x - 3)$ b) $(n - 3)^2$ c) $5(3 + x)(2 - x^2)$

Solution. a) $(2x + 1)(7x - 3) = (2x + 1)(7x - 3)$

$$= 14x^2 - 6x + 7x - 3$$
$$= 14x^2 + x - 3$$

b) $(n - 3)^2 = (n - 3)(n - 3)$

$$= n^2 - 3n - 3n + 9$$
$$= n^2 - 6n + 9$$

c) First find the product of the two binomials.
$$5(3 + x)(2 - x^2) = 5(6 - 3x^2 + 2x - x^3)$$
$$= 30 - 15x^2 + 10x - 5x^3$$
$$= 30 + 10x - 15x^2 - 5x^3$$

Example 3. Find an expression for the area of the rectangle. Write it as a polynomial in descending powers of x.

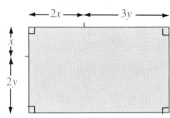

Solution. Area = length × width
The length is $2x + 3y$.
The width is $x + 2y$.
Area $= (2x + 3y)(x + 2y)$
$$= 2x^2 + 4xy + 3xy + 6y^2$$
$$= 2x^2 + 7xy + 6y^2$$
The area of the rectangle can be expressed as $2x^2 + 7xy + 6y^2$.

EXERCISES 7-5

Ⓐ

1. Use the diagram to find the product.
   a) $(x + 3)(x + 5)$ b) $(a + 2)(a + 4)$ c) $(n + 7)(n + 1)$

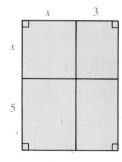
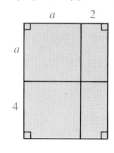
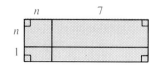

2. Find each product.
   a) $(x + 3)(x + 4)$ b) $(n + 2)(n + 6)$ c) $(a - 5)(a - 3)$
   d) $(t - 1)(t - 4)$ e) $(x - 2)(x + 5)$ f) $(n + 3)(n - 4)$
   g) $(a + 6)(a - 8)$ h) $(x + 9)(x - 7)$ i) $(x + 12)(x - 5)$
   j) $(s - 11)(s - 3)$ k) $\left(n + \dfrac{1}{2}\right)\left(n + \dfrac{1}{2}\right)$ l) $\left(a - \dfrac{2}{3}\right)\left(a + \dfrac{1}{2}\right)$

3. Find each product.
   a) $(a + 1)(a - 2)$ b) $(n - 3)(n - 2)$ c) $(y - 4)(y + 5)$
   d) $(b - 6)(b + 3)$ e) $(a - 10)(a - 6)$ f) $(n + 10)(n + 12)$
   g) $(x - 1)(x + 5)$ h) $(y - 8)(y + 11)$ i) $(z - 5)(z - 6)$
   j) $(a + 2)(a - 3)$ k) $(b + 10)(b + 4)$ l) $(x - 9)(x - 1)$
   $x^2 - 1x - 9x + 9$

Ⓑ

4. Find each product.
   a) $(3x + 2)(x - 1)$ b) $(2a - 5)(a - 3)$ c) $(4n - 7)(n + 5)$
   d) $(x + 3)(6x - 5)$ e) $(12x + 1)(3x - 1)$ f) $(5n - 1)(2n - 2)$
   g) $(7c - 5)(2c + 1)$ h) $(6x - 2)(3x + 1)$ i) $(3x - 1)(x + 2)$
   j) $(3a + 1)(2a - 5)$ k) $(8y - 3)(5y - 1)$ l) $(2x - 3)(4x + 7)$

5. a) $(x - 3)(5x + 2)$ b) $(2a + 1)(2a + 3)$ c) $(8n - 3)(2n - 1)$
   d) $(4a + 3)(4a + 3)$ e) $(3x - 2)(4x - 3)$ f) $(5x + 1)(6x - 4)$
   g) $(6x - 3)(2x - 5)$ h) $(3b + 2)(3b - 2)$ i) $(5a + 1)(4a - 7)$
   j) $(a + 8)(8a + 1)$ k) $(2a - 3)^2$ l) $(3a + 4)^2$
   $(2a - 3)(2a - 3) = (4a^2 + 9)$

6. Find each product.
   a) $(a - 3)(1 - a)$ b) $(x - 1)(1 - x)$ c) $(2y - 1)(5 + y)$

   d) $(2z - 4)(1 + z)$ e) $\left(\frac{1}{2}x + 3\right)\left(3 - \frac{1}{4}x\right)$ f) $(3x - 2)(2 + 5x)$

7. Find each product.
   a) $5(4 - a)(3 + a)$ b) $-(6 - 3n)(2 + n)$ c) $3(x + 3)(4 - x)$
   d) $10(x - 4)(2 + x)$ e) $6(2a - 5)(3 + a)$ f) $-7(c + 3)(5 - 2c)$
   g) $2(5 - a)^2$ h) $4(x - 2)(x - 5)$ i) $3(t - 2)(2 - t)$
   j) $5(4x - 3)(5x + 1)$ k) $-7(3 - x)(2 + 3x)$ l) $-4(x - 0.2)^2$

8. Find each product.
   a) $(x^2 + 3)(x + 5)$ b) $(a^2 + 2)(a - 3)$ c) $(n^2 + 2)(n^2 + 3)$
   d) $(x - 5)(x^2 + 2)$ e) $(x^2 - 1)(x^2 - 4)$ f) $(a^2 - 4)(a^2 - 9)$
   g) $(3x + 2)(x^2 - 5)$ h) $(n - 2)(2n^2 + 1)$ i) $(3a^2 - 1)(2 - a^2)$

9. Find each product.
   a) $(x + 2y)(x + 5y)$ b) $(a - 3b)(a + 2b)$ c) $(3m - n)(2m - n)$
   d) $(5x + 3y)(4x - y)$ e) $(6r + s)(r - 3s)$ f) $(8a + 7b)(7a + 8b)$
   g) $(p - 3q)(2p + 5q)$ h) $(3x - 8y)(2x + 5y)$ i) $(6a + 7b)(7a - 8b)$

10. Find each product.
    a) $(x - y)(y - x)$ b) $(a - 2b)(b - a)$
    c) $(2q - p)(-3p + 4q)$ d) $(x - 2y^2)(y^2 - 3x)$
    e) $(-p^2 + 4q)(-q + 4p^2)$ f) $(-3m - n)(-2n - 6m)$

11. Find the term represented by each square.
    a) $(x + 3)(x - 2) = x^2 + \blacksquare - 6$
    b) $(a + 5)(a + 7) = a^2 + \blacksquare + 35$
    c) $(n - 4)(n - 6) = n^2 + \blacksquare + 24$
    d) $(x - 7)(x + 1) = x^2 + \blacksquare - 7$
    e) $(a - 10)(a - 3) = a^2 + \blacksquare + 30$

12. The revenue R dollars earned from a bus tour carrying x people is given by this formula.

$R = (100 - 0.5x)(x - 10)$, where x is any 2-digit number

a) Write the polynomial for R in descending powers of x.
b) Find the revenue earned when the tour group is:
   i) 60 people   ii) 90 people.

13. a) Find an expression for the area of each rectangle.
    b) Find an expression for the perimeter of each rectangle.
    c) Evaluate each area and perimeter for $x = 10$.
    i)

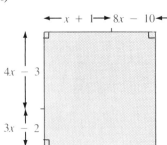

    ii)

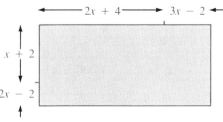

14. The revenue R thousands of dollars from ticket sales and concessions at a football game is given by this formula.

$R = (11 - x)(6 + x) + 1.5(11 - x)$

x represents the increase, in dollars, in the cost of a football ticket.

a) Simplify the expression by writing it as a trinomial in descending powers of x.
b) Find the revenue if ticket prices are increased by:
   i) \$1.00   ii) \$2.00   iii) \$3.00.

15. Find binomials to complete the equalities.
   a) $(n + 2)(n^2 + 5) = n^2 + 7n + 10$
   b) $(x - 3)(x - 4) = x^2 - 7x + 12$
   c) $(x - 2)(x + 6) = x^2 + 4x - 12$
   d) $(a + 2)(a - 5) = a^2 - 3a - 10$
   e) $(x + 2)(x + 3) = x^2 + 5x + 6$
   f) $(t - 4)(t + 5) = t^2 + t - 20$
   g) $(s - 5)(s - 7) = s^2 - 12s + 35$
   h) $(x + 4)(x + 5) = x^2 + 9x + 20$
   i) $(a - 2)(a - 7) = a^2 - 9a + 14$
   j) $(n - 5)(n - 5) = n^2 - 10n + 25$

16. Find each product.
   a) $(x + 5)(x^2 + 2x + 1)$
   b) $(a + 3)(a^2 - 4a + 2)$
   c) $(t - 4)(t^2 + 3t - 5)$
   d) $(2x - 3)(x^2 - 6x + 4)$
   e) $(x + 1)(x + 2)(x + 3)$
   f) $(2x - 1)(3x - 1)(x + 1)$
   g) $3(x - 4)(x^2 - 7x + 5)$
   h) $2x(x + 1)(x - 1)(3x + 2)$

7-6 MULTIPLYING TWO BINOMIALS — PART TWO

Two special cases of the products of two binomials will be considered in this section.

Squaring a Binomial
When we multiply a binomial by itself, we *square* the binomial.

Consider the product $(x + 3)^2$.

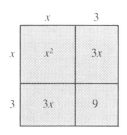

$$(x + 3)^2 = (x + 3)(x + 3)$$
$$= x^2 + 3x + 3x + 9$$
$$= x^2 + 6x + 9$$

The diagram shows how the square of the binomial is represented geometrically.

Because the product involves two equal binomials, there is a pattern in the terms of the expansion. This pattern is illustrated below.

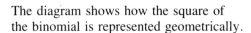

$(x + 3)^2 = x^2 + 6x + 9$
⎡the square of the first term (x) of the binomial
⎡twice the product of the terms (3 and x) of the binomial
⎡the square of the second term (3) of the binomial

$$(x - 4)^2$$
$$x^2 - 8x + 16.$$

This pattern can be used to square a binomial directly.

Example 1. Expand.
    a) $(x - 4)^2$ b) $(3x - 2)^2$ c) $(5 + 6n)^2$

Solution.   a) $(x - 4)^2 = (x)^2 + 2(x)(-4) + (-4)^2$
$$= x^2 - 8x + 16$$
     b) $(3x - 2)^2 = (3x)^2 + 2(3x)(-2) + (-2)^2$
$$= 9x^2 - 12x + 4$$
     c) $(5 + 6n)^2 = 25 + 60n + 36n^2$

$$(5 + 6n)^2$$
$$25 + 60 + 36n^2$$

The pattern resulting from squaring a binomial can be used to square numbers.

Example 2. Calculate.
    a) 41^2 b) 58^2

Solution.   a) $41^2 = (40 + 1)^2$
$$= 40^2 + 2(40)(1) + 1^2$$
$$= 1600 + 80 + 1$$
$$= 1681$$
     b) $58^2 = (60 - 2)^2$
$$= 60^2 + 2(60)(-2) + (-2)^2$$
$$= 3600 - 240 + 4$$
$$= 3364$$

The pattern for squaring a binomial can be expressed in general terms.

$$(a + b)^2 = a^2 + 2ab + b^2$$
$$(a - b)^2 = a^2 - 2ab + b^2$$

Product of a Sum and a Difference

An interesting case of the product of two binomials occurs when one binomial is the sum of two terms and the other binomial is the difference of the *same* two terms.

Consider the product $(x + 6)(x - 6)$.

$$(x + 6)(x - 6) = x^2 - 6x + 6x - 36$$
$$= x^2 - 36$$

The product $x^2 - 36$ is the difference between the squares of the two terms in the binomials. This pattern can be used to find the product of two binomials of this form directly.

Example 3. Expand.

a) $(a - 4)(a + 4)$ b) $(2x - 7)(2x + 7)$ c) $(6 + y)(6 - y)$

Solution. a) $(a - 4)(a + 4) = (a)^2 - (4)^2$
$$= a^2 - 16$$

b) $(2x - 7)(2x + 7) = (2x)^2 - (7)^2$
$$= 4x^2 - 49$$

c) $(6 + y)(6 - y) = 36 - y^2$

The pattern resulting from the product of two binomials of this form can be used to find certain numerical products.

Example 4. Evaluate.

a) 41×39 b) 18×22

Solution. a) $41 \times 39 = (40 + 1)(40 - 1)$
$$= 40^2 - 1^2$$
$$= 1600 - 1$$
$$= 1599$$

b) $18 \times 22 = (20 - 2)(20 + 2)$
$$= 20^2 - 2^2$$
$$= 400 - 4$$
$$= 396$$

How must the two numbers be related to enable us to calculate their product in this way?

The pattern for the product of two binomials, when one binomial is the sum of two terms and the other binomial is the difference of the same terms, can be expressed in general terms.

$$(a - b)(a + b) = a^2 - b^2$$

$x^2 + 14x + 49$

EXERCISES 7-6

A

1. Expand.
   a) $(x + 5)^2$ b) $(x + 1)^2$ c) $(a - 3)^2$ d) $(n - 7)^2$
   e) $(c + 4)^2$ f) $(x - 1)^2$ g) $(a + 2)^2$ h) $(a - 6)^2$
   i) $(2 + a)^2$ j) $(5 - x)^2$ k) $(t + 9)^2$ l) $(10 - m)^2$

2. Expand.
   a) $(x + 2)(x - 2)$ b) $(a - 3)(a + 3)$ c) $(x - 4)(x + 4)$
   d) $(x + 8)(x - 8)$ e) $(y + 1)(y - 1)$ f) $(d + 12)(d - 12)$
   g) $(s + 25)(s - 25)$ h) $(m + 40)(m - 40)$ i) $(x - 11)(x + 11)$
   j) $(8 - x)(8 + x)$ k) $(6 - a)(6 + a)$ l) $(9 - y)(9 + y)$

B

3. Expand.
   a) $(3a - 1)^2$ b) $(2a + 3)^2$ c) $(7x - 5)^2$ d) $(6a + 4)^2$
   e) $(3n - 8)^2$ f) $(5 - 9x)^2$ g) $(10 - 3c)^2$ h) $(12x + 5)^2$

4. Expand.
   a) $(3x + 2)(3x - 2)$ b) $(4x - 3)(4x + 3)$
   c) $(3 - 5x)(3 + 5x)$ d) $(6s - 5)(6s + 5)$
   e) $(12x - 7)(12x + 7)$ f) $(5y + 13)(5y - 13)$
   g) $(10a + 11)(10a - 11)$ h) $(4s - 20)(4s + 20)$

5. Square each binomial.
   a) $x + 7$ b) $a - 2$ c) $n + 4$ d) $2x - 1$
   e) $5c + 3$ f) $2 - 3m$ g) $4 + 5x$ h) $8 - 3x$
   i) $5 + 5s$ j) 4 k) $3 - 7x$ l) $6x - 6$

6. Expand.
   a) $(n + 0.2)^2$ b) $(x + 1.5)(x - 1.5)$

   c) $\left(c + \dfrac{1}{2}\right)\left(c - \dfrac{1}{2}\right)$ d) $\left(x + \dfrac{1}{4}\right)^2$

   e) $\left(k + \dfrac{2}{3}\right)\left(k - \dfrac{2}{3}\right)$ f) $\left(\dfrac{2}{3}a - 1\right)\left(\dfrac{2}{3}a + 1\right)$

   g) $\left(x - \dfrac{1}{3}\right)^2$ h) $\left(2s + \dfrac{1}{5}\right)^2$

   i) $(1.2x - 5)^2$ j) $\left(\dfrac{1}{2}x + \dfrac{1}{3}\right)\left(\dfrac{1}{2}x - \dfrac{1}{3}\right)$

7. Expand.
   a) $(x - 3)^2$ b) $(-x + 3)^2$ c) $(3 - x)^2$ d) $(-3 + x)^2$
   What do you notice?

8. Expand.
   a) $3(x - 2)^2$ b) $4(x + 5)(x - 5)$ c) $5(a + 1)(a - 1)$
   d) $-4(2x - 3)^2$ e) $-3(5 - n)^2$ f) $2(3x - 4)(3x + 4)$

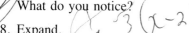

END OF CHAPTER

9. Use the pattern for squaring a binomial to calculate each product.
   a) 31^2 b) 13^2 c) 29^2 d) 103^2 e) 61^2 f) 92^2

10. Calculate each product.
    a) 31×29 b) 32×28 c) 59×61 d) 57×63
    e) 101×99 f) 105×95 g) 302×298 h) 210×190

11. Find the term or coefficient represented by each square.
    a) $(x + \blacksquare)^2 = x^2 + 8x + 16$
    b) $(x + \blacksquare)^2 = x^2 - 12x + 36$
    c) $(a + \blacksquare)^2 = a^2 + \blacksquare a + 49$
    d) $(2a + \blacksquare)^2 = 4a^2 + \blacksquare a + 9$
    e) $(\blacksquare - 2x)^2 = 49 - \blacksquare x + 4x^2$
    f) $(\blacksquare - 5)^2 = 9y^2 - \blacksquare + 25$

©

12. Expand.
    a) $(x - 1)(x + 1)(x - 2)(x + 2)$
    b) $(x + 1)(x - 1)(x^2 + 1)$
    c) $(a - 3)(a + 3)(a - 5)(a + 5)$
    d) $(a + 5)(a - 5)(a^2 + 25)$
    e) $(y - 2)(y + 2)(1 - y)(1 + y)$
    f) $(n - 3)(n + 3)(2 + n)(2 - n)$

13. a) Find each product.
    i) $(x - 1)(x + 1)$
    ii) $(x - 1)(x^2 + x + 1)$
    iii) $(x - 1)(x^3 + x^2 + x + 1)$
    b) Predict the product of $(x - 1)(x^4 + x^3 + x^2 + x + 1)$ and check by multiplying.

14. Calculate mentally.
    a) $(1\ 000\ 000)^2 - (999\ 999)^2$ b) 501×499

INVESTIGATE

1. a) Choose a number, for example, 11.
   b) Square the number. $11^2 = 121$
   c) Subtract 1 from the number and square the result.
      $11 - 1 = 10;\ 10^2 = 100$
   d) Add the original number, the previous number, and its square.
      $11 + 10 + 10^2$
   e) What do you notice?

2. Repeat the procedure for a different number. What do you notice?

3. Repeat the procedure for a negative number. What do you notice?

4. Repeat the procedure for a decimal. What do you notice?

5. Repeat the procedure for any number x.

6. What conclusion can you make from your investigation?

7-7 COMMON FACTORS

To factor a number means to write it as a product, for example,
$15 = 3 \times 5$.

If two or more numbers have the same factor, it is called a *common factor*.

To find the common factors of three numbers, for example, 24, 42, and 60, we express each number as a product.
$24 = 2 \times 2 \times 2 \times 3$
$42 = 2 \times 3 \times 7$
$60 = 2 \times 2 \times 3 \times 5$
2, 3, and 2×3 or 6, are the common factors of 24, 42, and 60.
6 is the *greatest common factor* of 24, 42, and 60.

When the greatest common factor is known, the sum of two or more numbers can be written as a product.
For example, $24 + 42 + 60 = 6(4) + 6(7) + 6(10)$
$$= 6(4 + 7 + 10)$$
$$= 6(21)$$

To factor a polynomial also means to write it as a product. In an earlier section, a product such as $3(2x + 1)$ was written as the sum, $6x + 3$, using the distributive law. Factoring is the reverse process. A sum like $6x + 3$ is written as the product $3(2x + 1)$.

Example 1. a) Find the common factors of $2x^3$, $4x^2$, and $-6x$.
 b) Find the greatest common factor of $2x^3$, $4x^2$, and $-6x$.
 c) Express $2x^3 + 4x^2 - 6x$ as a product.

Solution. a) Express each monomial as a product.
$2x^3 = 2(x)(x)(x)$
$4x^2 = 2(2)(x)(x)$
$-6x = -(2)(3)(x)$
2, x, and $2x$ are the common factors of $2x^3$, $4x^2$, and $-6x$.
 b) The greatest common factor of $2x^3$, $4x^2$, and $-6x$ is $2x$.
 c) Use the greatest common factor found in part b).
$2x^3 + 4x^2 - 6x = 2x(x^2) + 2x(2x) + 2x(-3)$
$$= 2x(x^2 + 2x - 3)$$

Example 2. Factor then check.
 a) $6x - 15$ b) $a^3 - 4a^2 + 2a$

Solution. a) $6x - 15 = 3(2x) - 3(5)$
$$= 3(2x - 5)$$
Check by expanding. $3(2x - 5) = 6x - 15$
 b) $a^3 - 4a^2 + 2a = a(a^2) - a(4a) + a(2)$
$$= a(a^2 - 4a + 2)$$
Check. $a(a^2 - 4a + 2) = a^3 - 4a^2 + 2a$

When factoring, always look for the *greatest* common factor.

Example 3. Factor.

a) $18n^2 - 12n$

b) $36x^3 - 27x^2 + 54x$

c) $-20x^4y + 10x^2y$

d) $24a^3b - 3a^2b^2 + 12ab^2$

Solution. a) $18n^2 - 12n = 6n(3n - 2)$

b) $36x^3 - 27x^2 + 54x = 9x(4x^2 - 3x + 6)$

c) $-20x^4y + 10x^2y = -10x^2y(2x^2 - 1)$

d) $24a^3b - 3a^2b^2 + 12ab^2 = 3ab(8a^2 - ab + 4b)$

In *Example 3* part c), the solution could have been written as $10x^2y(1 - 2x^2)$.

EXERCISES 7-7

(A)

1. Find the greatest common factor.

a) $9, 6, 12$

b) $16, 28, -44$

c) $2x, 4x^2, 6x^3$

d) $-14x, 21x^2, 28x^3$

e) $8y^4, 2y^3, -3y^2$

f) $16z^2, 12z^3, 32z^5$

2. Express as products.

a) $5y - 10$

b) $12a + 18$

c) $-3x^2 + 6x - 12$

d) $2a^2 - 10a + 2$

e) $4w + 3w^2 - 7w^3$

f) $8y^3 - 4y^2 + 2y$

g) $-6s + 2s^2 + 4s^3$

h) $-7k^3 - 35k^4 + 49k^5$

i) $6m^2 - 36m^3 - 54m^4$

3. Factor then check.

a) $14x^2 + 35x - 7$

b) $-10 - 25a + 30a^2$

c) $20n^2 - 30n + 80$

d) $5x + 10x^2 + 15x^3$

e) $9c^3 + 15c$

f) $-x^3 + x^2$

g) $4x - 8x^2 + 12x^3$

h) $-6y^2 - 3y^3 - 12y^4$

i) $12m + 16m^2 - 4m^3$

4. Factor.

a) $16x + 40$

b) $15n - 24$

c) $-2a^2 - 6a$

d) $a^3 - 9a^2 + 3a$

e) $-27x^2 - 9x + 3$

f) $5x^3 + 3x^2 - x$

g) $9a^3 + 7a^2 + 18a$

h) $-8d - 24d^2 - 8d^3$

i) $17k - 85k^2 - 51k^3$

(B)

5. Find the greatest common factor.

a) xy, x^2y

b) $3x^2y^2, 6xy$

c) $ab, -a^2b^2$

d) $-4xy, 16$

e) $-5xy, -10x^2y^2$

f) $6p^2q, -12pq^2$

g) $2m^2n, -4mn^2$

h) $3x^2y, 9x^2y^2$

6. Factor.

a) $xy + x^2y$

b) $-3x^2y^2 + 6xy$

c) $ab - a^2b^2$

d) $-4xy - 16$

e) $5xy + 10x^2y^2$

f) $6p^2q - 12pq^2$

g) $2m^2n - 4mn^2$

h) $3x^2y + 9x^2y^2$

i) $-5x^6y - xy^6$

7. Factor.

a) $b^4 - 3b^3$

b) $3b^4 - 6b^5$

c) $-a^4 + 3a^3 - 2a^2$

d) $21x + 42x^2 + 63x^3$

e) $-d^4 + 5d^5$

f) $24m^3 + 6m^2 - 12m$

g) $-12x - 9x^2 - 3x^3 - 6x^4$

h) $2x^3 + 3x^4 - 4x^5 + 5x^6$

8. The surface area S of a right circular cylinder of radius r and height h is given by this formula.
$$S = 2\pi rh + 2\pi r^2$$
Express S as a product.

9. Factor.
   a) $18a - 6ab^2$
   b) $12x^2y + 16xy$
   c) $-8ab^2c - 12a^2bc^2$
   d) $5m^2 + 15mn + 25n^2$
   e) $4x^2y^2z - 16xy^2z^2$
   f) $3x^2 + 6y^2x - 12x^2y^2$
   g) $-5xy + 6y + 3xy^2$
   h) $9a^3b^2 + 7a^2b^2 + 18a^2b^3$
   i) $-7a^3b^2 + 14a^2b^3 - 21a^2b^2$
   j) $-12p^2q^3 - 20p^3q^3 + 8p^2q^4$

10. Factor.
    a) $3xy^2 + 6x^2y - 9xy$
    b) $-2a^2b + 6ab^2 - 4ab$
    c) $5m^2n^2 - 10m^3n^2 + 25m^2n$
    d) $-28x^2y^2 + 14x^3y^3 - 7x^2y^3$

11. Factor.
    a) $2a^3b - 16a^2b^3 + 4a^3b^2 + 6a^2b^2 - 8a^3b^3 + 12a^2b$
    b) $15x^4y^3 - 25x^3y^4 + 10x^2y^3 - 5x^3y^2 + 30x^4y^4 - 35x^2y^2$

12. Express as products. $an(a+b)$
    a) $a(a + 6) + 7(a + 6)$
    b) $x(x - 9) - 2(x - 9)$
    c) $-8(1 + y) - 3y(1 + y)$
    d) $5(2 - x) + x(2 - x)$
    e) $2x(x + 3) + 4(x + 3)$
    f) $-3a(2a - 1) + 6(2a - 1)$

13. Factor.
    a) $6t(3t - 1) + 9(3t - 1)$
    b) $a^2(a + 2) - a(a + 2)$
    c) $5x^2(x + 7) - 10x(x + 7)$
    d) $-(2n + 3)n - (2n + 3)4$
    e) $(r - 3)2r + (r - 3)8$
    f) $-(x + 4)x^2 + (x + 4)x^3$
    g) $3a^3(a - 1) - 6a^2(a - 1)$
    h) $12a^2(2a - 5) + 16a(2a - 5)$

14. Factor.
    a) $a^2 + 2a + ab + 2b$
    b) $3x - xy + 3y - y^2$
    c) $3a + 3b + ab + b^2$
    d) $4x - 4 + ax - a$
    e) $2p - 2q - p^2 + pq$
    f) $-4x - 4y + xy + y^2$
    g) $-3m + 3n - mn + n^2$
    h) $-5c - 5d - cd - d^2$

 INVESTIGATE

Choose any positive number.
- Add 2.
- Multiply by the original number.
- Add 1.
- Take the positive square root.

How is the result related to the original number?
Show that this pattern applies for any number chosen.

PROBLEM SOLVING

Look For a Pattern

What is the last digit of 7^{134}?

Understand the problem
- What does 7^{134} mean?
- How could this number be calculated?
- What are we asked to find?
- Do we need to know all the digits in the number to answer the question?

Think of a strategy
- Expand 7^2, 7^3, 7^4, 7^5, . . . and look for a pattern in the last digits.

Carry out the strategy
- The table shows the expansions for 7^1, 7^2, 7^3, . . . 7^8, with their last digits in color.
- The last digits of successive powers of 7 appear to run through the sequence 7, 9, 3, 1 and then repeat.
- When the power of 7 is a multiple of 4, the last digit is 1, so 7^{132} has a last digit 1.
- Therefore, 7^{133} has a last digit 7.
- And so 7^{134} has a last digit 9.

Powers of 7	
$7^1 = 7$	$7^5 = 16\ 807$
$7^2 = 49$	$7^6 = 117\ 649$
$7^3 = 343$	$7^7 = 823\ 543$
$7^4 = 2401$	$7^8 = 5\ 764\ 801$

Look back
- There are other ways to consider the pattern, for example,
  $7^{132} = (7^4)^{33}$
  Since 7^4 has a last digit of 1, when this power is raised to a power, the result will always have a last digit of 1.
  Hence 7^{132} has a last digit of 1.
  But $7^{134} = 7^{132} \times 7^2$
  Since 7^{132} has a last digit of 1, and 7^2 has a last digit of 9, the product $7^{132} \times 7^2$ will have a last digit of 9.

Solve each problem

1. Find the next two numbers in each sequence.

   a) $\dfrac{3}{8}, \dfrac{1}{2}, \dfrac{5}{8}, \ldots$ b) $x + y,\ 2x + 3y,\ 3x + 5y,\ \ldots$

   c) 1, 2, 4, 7, . . .   d) 5, 11, 17, 23, . . .

2. What is the missing number? 1, 5, 13, __, 41, 61, . . .

3. Sketch the figures missing from spaces A, B, C, and D (below left).

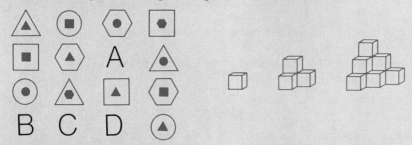

4. How many cubes are in the next figure in this sequence (above right)?

5. Study the pattern in the table. Can you find a formula for the sum of the whole numbers from 1 to *n*?

n	1	2	3	4	5	6	7
Sum to *n*	1	3	6	10	15	21	28
$\dfrac{\text{Sum to } n}{n}$	$\dfrac{1}{1}$	$\dfrac{3}{2}$	$\dfrac{6}{3}$	$\dfrac{10}{4}$	$\dfrac{15}{5}$	$\dfrac{21}{6}$	$\dfrac{28}{7}$

6. Copy and complete the table. Use the table in *Question 5* to complete the last row.

n	1	2	3	4	5	6	7
n^3	1	8					343
Sum of cubes to n^3	1	9					784
$\dfrac{\text{Sum of cubes to } n^3}{\text{Sum to } n}$	1	3					28

Study the pattern in the table. Can you find a formula for the sum of the cubes of the whole numbers from 1 to *n*?

7-8 FACTORING TRINOMIALS

A polynomial with three terms is a trinomial. The product of two binomials is often a trinomial.

For example, $(x + 3)(x + 4) = x^2 + 7x + 12$

Factoring is the reverse process. A sum like $x^2 + 7x + 12$ is written as the product $(x + 3)(x + 4)$.

Consider this expansion.

7 is the sum of 3 and 4

$$x^2 + 7x + 12 = (x + 3)(x + 4)$$

12 is the product of 3 and 4

The coefficient of x in the trinomial is the sum of the constant terms in the binomials.

The constant term in the trinomial is the product of the constant terms in the binomials.

Example 1. Factor then check. $x^2 + 5x + 6$

Solution. $x^2 + 5x + 6$

Find two numbers whose sum is 5 and whose product is 6.
List pairs of factors of 6: 1, 6; -1, -6; 2, 3; -2, -3.
The pair of factors whose sum is 5 is 2, 3.
$x^2 + 5x + 6 = (x + 2)(x + 3)$

Check. $(x + 2)(x + 3) = x^2 + 3x + 2x + 6$
$= x^2 + 5x + 6$

Example 2. Factor then check. $a^2 - 8a + 12$

Solution. $a^2 - 8a + 12$

Find two numbers whose sum is -8 and whose product is 12.
List pairs of factors of 12: 12, 1; -12, -1; 6, 2; -6, -2; 4, 3; -4, -3.
The pair of factors whose sum is -8 is -6, -2.
$a^2 - 8a + 12 = (a - 6)(a - 2)$

Check. $(a - 6)(a - 2) = a^2 - 2a - 6a + 12$
$= a^2 - 8a + 12$

Example 3. Factor then check. $m^2 - 5m - 14$

Solution. $m^2 - 5m - 14$

Find two numbers whose sum is -5 and whose product is -14.
List pairs of factors of -14: -14, 1; 14, -1; -7, 2; 7, -2.
The pair of factors whose sum is -5 is -7, 2.
$m^2 - 5m - 14 = (m - 7)(m + 2)$

Check. $(m - 7)(m + 2) = m^2 + 2m - 7m - 14$
$= m^2 - 5m - 14$

Example 4. Factor.

  a) $n^2 - 14n + 49$ b) $k^2 + 12k + 36$

Solution. a) $n^2 - 14n + 49$

  Find two numbers whose sum is -14 and whose product is 49.
  The numbers are -7, -7.
  $$n^2 - 14n + 49 = (n - 7)(n - 7)$$
  $$= (n - 7)^2$$

  b) $k^2 + 12k + 36$

  Find two numbers whose sum is 12 and whose product is 36.
  The numbers are 6, 6.
  $$k^2 + 12k + 36 = (k + 6)(k + 6)$$
  $$= (k + 6)^2$$

In *Example 4*, the first and last terms of each trinomial are perfect squares; that is, in $n^2 - 14n + 49$, $n^2 = n \times n$ and $49 = (-7) \times (-7)$. Also, the middle term is $2(-7)n$.

If you recognize this pattern in a trinomial, you know that it is a perfect square, with two equal factors.

Not all trinomials can be factored using rational numbers.

Example 5. Factor if possible.

  a) $x^2 + 6x - 7$ b) $x^2 + 9x + 12$

Solution. a) $x^2 + 6x - 7$

  List pairs of factors of -7: -7, 1; 7, -1.
  Select the pair of factors whose sum is 6; that is, 7, -1.
  $$x^2 + 6x - 7 = (x + 7)(x - 1)$$

  b) $x^2 + 9x + 12$

  List pairs of factors of 12: 12, 1; -12, -1; 6, 2; -6, -2; 3, 4;
  -3, -4.
  None of the pairs of factors has a sum of $+9$.
  $x^2 + 9x + 12$ is not factorable.

If the terms of the trinomial have a common factor, it should be removed before the other factors are found.

Example 6. Factor completely.

  a) $3x^2 - 18x + 24$ b) $x^4 + 4x^3 - 5x^2$

Solution. a) $3x^2 - 18x + 24 = 3(x^2 - 6x + 8)$
  $$= 3(x - 4)(x - 2)$$

  b) $x^4 + 4x^3 - 5x^2 = x^2(x^2 + 4x - 5)$
  $$= x^2(x + 5)(x - 1)$$

When factoring, always look for a common factor first.

258

EXERCISES 7-8

A

1. Factor.
   a) $x^2 + 7x + 10$ b) $a^2 + 5a + 6$ c) $m^2 + 10m + 24$
   d) $a^2 + 8a + 7$ e) $x^2 + 6x + 9$ f) $n^2 + 14n + 49$
   g) $t^2 + 13t + 40$ h) $x^2 - 12x + 36$ i) $x^2 + 9x + 20$

2. Factor.
   a) $x^2 - 8x + 15$ b) $c^2 - 12c + 32$ c) $a^2 - 8a + 16$
   d) $x^2 - 6x + 5$ e) $x^2 + 2x + 1$ f) $n^2 - 9n + 14$
   g) $y^2 - 15y + 54$ h) $s^2 - 18s + 81$ i) $k^2 - 11k + 30$

3. Factor.
   a) $x^2 - 8x + 16$ b) $x^2 + 12x + 36$ c) $a^2 + 4a + 4$
   d) $p^2 - 2p + 1$ e) $x^2 - 6x + 9$ f) $t^2 - 10t + 25$
   g) $x^2 + 14x + 49$ h) $b^2 - 16b + 64$ i) $x^2 + 20x + 100$

B

4. Factor.
   a) $x^2 + 6x - 16$ b) $a^2 + 4a - 12$ c) $x^2 + 6x - 27$
   d) $c^2 + 2c - 35$ e) $x^2 + x - 12$ f) $a^2 + a - 30$
   g) $y^2 + y - 56$ h) $t^2 - 2t - 24$ i) $x^2 + 2x - 15$

5. Factor and check.
   a) $x^2 - 6x + 8$ b) $x^2 + 9x + 18$ c) $a^2 - 11a + 18$
   d) $m^2 + 11m + 28$ e) $n^2 - 10n + 25$ f) $30 - 13n + n^2$
   g) $p^2 + 16p + 64$ h) $y^2 - 13y + 42$ i) $x^2 + 15x + 56$

6. Factor.
   a) $r^2 - 5r - 36$ b) $a^2 - 4a - 45$ c) $n^2 - 3n - 54$
   d) $m^2 - 2m - 48$ e) $k^2 - 2k - 63$ f) $x^2 - 7x - 30$
   g) $81 - 18a + a^2$ h) $m^2 + 22m + 121$ i) $n^2 - 4n + 4$

7. Factor and check.
   a) $x^2 - 5x - 24$ b) $x^2 + 5x - 50$ c) $a^2 + a - 72$
   d) $n^2 - 3n - 40$ e) $m^2 + m - 42$ f) $8 - 7x - x^2$
   g) $y^2 + 3y - 4$ h) $s^2 - 7s - 18$ i) $2 + t - t^2$

8. Factor.
   a) $x^2 + 7x - 8$ b) $a^2 + 5a - 14$ c) $t^2 - 2t - 3$
   d) $n^2 + 13n + 42$ e) $x^2 - 17x + 72$ f) $c^2 - 11c + 30$
   g) $m^2 + 6m - 55$ h) $a^2 + 10a + 9$ i) $s^2 + s - 20$
   j) $c^2 + 9c - 36$ k) $12 + 4m - m^2$ l) $15 - 8y + y^2$

9. Consider the trinomial $x^2 - 2x - 15$.
   a) Find its value when $x = 17$.
   b) Factor the trinomial.
   c) Evaluate the factored expression when $x = 17$.

10. Consider the trinomial $x^2 - 13x + 36$.
   a) Find its value when $x = 59$.
   b) Factor the trinomial.
   c) Evaluate the factored expression when $x = 59$.

11. Factor if possible.
   a) $x^2 + 16x + 63$ b) $a^2 + 12a + 30$ c) $x^2 - 4x + 32$
   d) $t^2 + 11t + 24$ e) $n^2 - 12n + 35$ f) $k^2 - 5k - 21$
   g) $x^2 + 7x - 60$ h) $n^2 + 7n - 7$ i) $x^2 - 6x + 24$
   j) $a^2 - a - 45$ k) $56 + t - t^2$ l) $6 - x + x^2$

12. Factor completely.
   a) $2x^2 + 12x + 10$ b) $5a^2 - 10a - 40$ c) $10n^2 + 10n - 20$
   d) $4a^2 - 16a - 20$ e) $3x^2 + 15x + 6$ f) $7a^2 - 35a + 42$
   g) $x^3 - 2x^2 - 3x$ h) $a^3 - 2a^2 - 9a$ i) $2y^3 + 14y^2 + 24y$
   j) $3x^3 + 6x^2 - 24x$ k) $60n + 50n^2 + 10n^3$ l) $14s + 7s^2 - 7s^3$

13. If a hockey arena increases its ticket prices by x dollars, the predicted revenue R thousands of dollars from all ticket sales is given by this formula.
   $R = 35 + 2x - x^2$, where $x < 7$
   a) Factor the trinomial.
   b) Find the predicted revenue if ticket prices are increased by each amount.
      i) $1   ii) $2   iii) $3

14. If a transit company increases its fares by x cents, the total daily revenue R thousands of dollars is given by this formula.
   $R = 55 + 6x - x^2$, where $x < 11$
   a) Factor the trinomial.
   b) Find the total daily revenue for each fare increase.
      i)   1¢   ii)   2¢   iii) 3¢   iv) 5¢   v) 6¢

15. Factor.
   a) $x^2 + 8xy + 15y^2$ b) $x^2 - 9xy + 14y^2$ c) $x^2 - 4xy - 5y^2$
   d) $x^2 + 7xy - 18y^2$ e) $c^2 - 4cd - 21d^2$ f) $m^2 + 14mn + 45n^2$
   g) $6x^2 + xy - y^2$ h) $8a^2 - 2ab - b^2$ i) $28a^2 + 3ab - b^2$
   j) $12x^2 + 8xy + y^2$ k) $25x^2 - 10x + 1$ l) $20a^2 - 9ab + b^2$

16. Find an integer to replace each square so that each trinomial can be factored.
   a) $x^2 + \blacksquare x + 12$ b) $x^2 - \blacksquare x + 20$ c) $x^2 + \blacksquare x - 18$
   d) $x^2 + 5x + \blacksquare$ e) $x^2 + 4x + \blacksquare$ f) $x^2 - 2x + \blacksquare$

17. Consider the equation $y = x^2 + 12x + 11$.
   a) Factor the trinomial.
   b) Evaluate y for $x = 1, 2, 3, \ldots, 10$.
   c) For which values of x is y a perfect square?

18. Find values of x which make these trinomials perfect squares.
   a) $x^2 + 7x + 6$ b) $x^2 + 8x - 9$ c) $x^2 - 11x + 24$

CALCULATOR POWER

Evaluating Polynomials by Factoring

A steep cliff is the boundary of one side of a piece of land which is to be fenced as a rectangular-shaped corral. The rancher has 840 m of fencing. This fencing is to form 3 sides of the corral, so that it has the greatest possible area. What are the dimensions of the corral with the largest area?

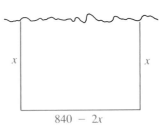

$840 - 2x$

Let x metres represent the length of the two equal sides which are to be fenced. Then, the third side is $(840 - 2x)$ metres.
The area, in square metres, is $x(840 - 2x)$ or $840x - 2x^2$. This can be factored as $2x(420 - x)$.

The total length of the two equal sides, $2x$ metres, must be less than the total length of the fence, 840 m.
Therefore, $2x < 840$
$\qquad\qquad x < 420$

To find the maximum area, the rancher substituted values of x up to 400 into the polynomial. The results are shown below.

x	100	150	200	250	300	350	400
$840x - 2x^2$	64 000	81 000	88 000	85 000	72 000	49 000	16 000

This table suggests that $840x - 2x^2$ is largest when x is between 150 and 250.

The rancher made another table for values of x from 150 to 240.

x	160	170	180	190	200	210	220	230	240
$840x - 2x^2$									

1. Copy the table above.
   a) Use your calculator to evaluate the polynomial $840x - 2x^2$ for $x = 160, 170, 180, 190,$ and 200.
   b) Use your calculator and the product $2x(420 - x)$ to evaluate the polynomial $840x - 2x^2$ for $x = 200, 210, 220, 230,$ and 240.
   c) In which form is it easier to evaluate the polynomial: $840x - 2x^2$ or $2x(420 - x)$? Explain your answer.

2. Use your completed table to estimate the dimensions of the corral of largest area.

3. a) Use your calculator to evaluate the trinomial $x^2 - 24x + 140$ for all integral values of x from 5 to 15. Record your answers in a table.
   b) Use your table to estimate the value of x for which the trinomial $x^2 - 24x + 140$ has its minimum value.

7-9 FACTORING A DIFFERENCE OF SQUARES

Recall the product of two binomials that differ only by one sign.
For example, $(x + 5)(x - 5) = (x)^2 - (5)^2$
$$= x^2 - 25$$
The product is written as a difference of squares.

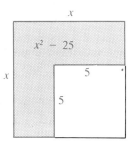

The "difference of squares" can be
illustrated geometrically.

The larger square has area x^2.

The smaller square has area 25.

The area of the shaded region, which is
the difference in areas of the two squares,
is $x^2 - 25$.

Consider the shaded region cut along the dotted line and the two
pieces repositioned.

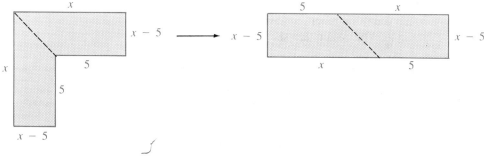

The resulting rectangle has area $(x - 5)(x + 5)$. This is equal to the
area of the original figure, $x^2 - 25$.

If a binomial is expressed as a difference of squares, it can be
factored easily.

Example 1. Factor.
a) $x^2 - 9$ b) $a^2 - 0.16$ c) $49x^2 - 64$

Solution. a) $x^2 - 9$ can be written as $(x)^2 - (3)^2$.
$$x^2 - 9 = (x + 3)(x - 3)$$
b) $a^2 - 0.16$ can be written as $(a)^2 - (0.4)^2$.
$$a^2 - 0.16 = (a + 0.4)(a - 0.4)$$
c) $49x^2 - 64$ can be written as $(7x)^2 - (8)^2$.
$$49x^2 - 64 = (7x + 8)(7x - 8)$$

A difference of squares may occur after a common factor is removed.

Example 2. Factor.

   a) $5x^2 - 45$ b) $8x^3 - 2x$

Solution.   a) $5x^2 - 45$

The terms have a common factor of 5.

$5x^2 - 45 = 5(x^2 - 9)$

Factor the difference of squares.

$= 5(x + 3)(x - 3)$

   b) $8x^3 - 2x = 2x(4x^2 - 1)$

$= 2x(2x + 1)(2x - 1)$

Example 3. Factor.

   a) $x^2 - y^2$ b) $36x^2 - 9y^2$

Solution.   a) $x^2 - y^2 = (x - y)(x + y)$ b) $36x^2 - 9y^2 = 9(4x^2 - y^2)$

$= 9[(2x)^2 - (y)^2]$

$= 9(2x - y)(2x + y)$

EXERCISES 7-9

(A)

1. Factor.

   a) $x^2 - 25$ b) $a^2 - 49$ c) $x^2 - 36$ d) $y^2 - 100$

   e) $x^2 - 1$ f) $x^2 - 4$ g) $m^2 - 64$ h) $n^2 - 144$

(B)

2. Draw two diagrams to illustrate the factoring of each difference of squares.

   a) $x^2 - 1$ b) $x^2 - 16$ c) $x^2 - 36$ d) $x^2 - 4$

3. Factor.

   a) $9a^2 - 4$ b) $25x^2 - 9$ c) $16s^2 - 1$ d) $36 - 100n^2$

   e) $100x^2 - 121$ f) $144p^2 - 49$ g) $\dfrac{1}{4}x^2 - \dfrac{4}{9}$ h) $6.25 - n^2$

4. Factor.

   a) $49a^2 - 1$ b) $4 - 36x^2$ c) $9 - 64m^2$ d) $81y^2 - 49$

   e) $1.44x^2 - 1$ f) $1600a^2 - 81$ g) $0.64x^2 - 1.21$ h) $\dfrac{1}{9} - \dfrac{1}{16}x^2$

5. Factor completely.

   a) $2x^2 - 18$ b) $5x^2 - 5$ c) $3a^2 - 48$ d) $3n^2 + 30$

   e) $7 - 28y^2$ f) $2a^2 + 12$ g) $x^3 - 25x$ h) $a^3 - 49a$

6. Factor.

   a) $a^2 - b^2$ b) $x^2 - 4y^2$ c) $9m^2 - 16n^2$ d) $36x^2 - 49y^2$

   e) $a^2b^2 - c^2$ f) $4a^2b^2 - 9c^2d^2$ g) $4c^4 - 81c^2d^2$ h) $25x^2y^2 - 9y^4$

(C)

7. Factor completely.

   a) $x^4 - 1$ b) $a^4 - 16$ c) $16c^4 - 1$ d) $2 - 2x^4$

7-10 DIVIDING POLYNOMIALS BY MONOMIALS

To divide a monomial by a monomial, recall this exponent law.

$$\frac{x^m}{x^n} = x^{m-n}, \, x \neq 0$$

Example 1. Simplify.

a) $\dfrac{x^5}{x^3}$

b) $\dfrac{21y^6}{3y^2}$

c) $12x^3y^2 \div 8x^2y$

Solution.

a)
$$\frac{x^5}{x^3} = x^{5-3}$$
$$= x^2$$

b)
$$\frac{21y^6}{3y^2} = 7y^{6-2}$$
$$= 7y^4$$

c)
$$12x^3y^2 \div 8x^2y$$
$$= \frac{12x^3y^2}{8x^2y}$$
$$= \frac{3}{2}xy$$

To divide a polynomial by a monomial, perform the division with each term.

Example 2. Simplify.

a) $\dfrac{9a + 15}{3}$

b) $\dfrac{24x^2 - 9x}{-3x}$

c) $\dfrac{20x^4 - 15x^3 + 5x^2}{5x^2}$

Solution.

a)
$$\frac{9a + 15}{3} = \frac{9a}{3} + \frac{15}{3}$$
$$= 3a + 5$$

b)
$$\frac{24x^2 - 9x}{-3x} = \frac{24x^2}{-3x} - \frac{9x}{-3x}$$
$$= -8x + 3$$

c)
$$\frac{20x^4 - 15x^3 + 5x^2}{5x^2} = \frac{20x^4}{5x^2} - \frac{15x^3}{5x^2} + \frac{5x^2}{5x^2}$$
$$= 4x^2 - 3x + 1$$

An alternative method of dividing a polynomial by a monomial is illustrated below.

Example 3. Simplify. $\dfrac{x^3y^2 - 3x^2y^4 + 2x^4y^2}{4x^2y}$

Solution. Factor the polynomial. Then, divide the polynomial and the monomial by their greatest common factor.

$$\frac{x^3y^2 - 3x^2y^4 + 2x^4y^2}{4x^2y} = \frac{x^2y^2(x - 3y^2 + 2x^2)}{4x^2y}$$
$$= \frac{y(x - 3y^2 + 2x^2)}{4}$$

The solution to *Example 3* could be written as the sum of terms.

$$\frac{y(x - 3y^2 + 2x^2)}{4} = \frac{xy}{4} - \frac{3y^3}{4} + \frac{2x^2y}{4}$$
$$= \frac{xy}{4} - \frac{3y^3}{4} + \frac{x^2y}{2} \quad \text{In this solution, all the terms are in lowest form.}$$

EXERCISES 7-10

A

1. Simplify.

a) $\dfrac{12x^3}{3}$ b) $\dfrac{32y^4}{16}$ c) $\dfrac{18y^4}{2y}$ d) $\dfrac{27m^3}{-9m}$

e) $\dfrac{-45y^6}{-5y^4}$ f) $\dfrac{3n^6}{5n^4}$ g) $\dfrac{25x^4}{-5x^4}$ h) $\dfrac{36c^5}{24c^2}$

i) $18x^4 \div 3x$ j) $-52y^6 \div 13y^5$ k) $-45a^5 \div 20a^3$ l) $\dfrac{3}{4}x^3 \div \dfrac{1}{2}x^2$

2. Simplify.

a) $\dfrac{8a + 4}{4}$ b) $\dfrac{12y - 3}{3}$ c) $\dfrac{18x^2 - 6}{6}$ d) $\dfrac{6a + 15}{3}$

e) $\dfrac{24x - 4}{4}$ f) $\dfrac{-10 + 4m}{-2}$ g) $\dfrac{15 - 5n}{-5}$ h) $\dfrac{-21 + 7x}{-7}$

B

3. Simplify.

a) $\dfrac{36x^4y^2}{9xy}$ b) $\dfrac{54a^5b^2}{-9a^3b^2}$ c) $\dfrac{-28m^2n^2}{-4m^2n^2}$

d) $\dfrac{-18a^2b^5}{6a^2b^3}$ e) $\dfrac{42x^5y^5}{-14x^3y^3}$ f) $\dfrac{-25a^2b^3c^4}{-5ab^2c^3}$

4. Simplify.

a) $\dfrac{3x^2 - 6x}{3x}$ b) $\dfrac{5x^2 - 10x}{5x}$ c) $\dfrac{18a - 21a^2}{3a}$

d) $\dfrac{-28n^2 - 7n}{7n}$ e) $\dfrac{36y^3 - 9y^2}{-9y}$ f) $\dfrac{32b^4 + 8b^3}{-4b^2}$

g) $\dfrac{-3m^5 + 18m^2}{-3m^2}$ h) $\dfrac{-4x^5 - 12x^3}{-4x^2}$ i) $\dfrac{-7c^2 + 6c^3}{-6c^2}$

5. Simplify.

a) $\dfrac{18x^2 - 6x + 30}{6}$ b) $\dfrac{-5 - 15c + 10c^2}{-5}$ c) $\dfrac{4x^3 - 12x^2 + 8x}{4x}$

d) $\dfrac{8a + 2a^2 - 2a^3}{2a}$ e) $\dfrac{15x^4 - 30x^3 + 5x^2}{5x^2}$ f) $\dfrac{18a^4 + 6a^3 - 12a^2}{-6a^2}$

g) $\dfrac{-12y^3 + 8y^4 - 4y^5}{-4y^3}$ h) $\dfrac{28x^6 - 35x^4 + 7x^2}{7x^2}$ i) $\dfrac{27w^7 - 54w^5 + 9w^3}{9w^3}$

6. Simplify.

a) $\dfrac{3x^2 - 9x^3 + 27x^5}{3x^2}$ b) $\dfrac{28m^5 - 14m^3 + 7m^2}{-7m^2}$ c) $\dfrac{36a^6 + 18a^4 - 12a^3}{6a^3}$

d) $\dfrac{-10y^6 - 15y^4 + 25y^2}{-5y^2}$ e) $\dfrac{12n^4 - 18n^3 + 24n^2}{9n^2}$ f) $\dfrac{60x^7 - 36x^5 + 12x^3}{-12x^2}$

7. Simplify.

a) $\dfrac{3x^2y^2 - 9x^4y^4 + 18x^3y^5}{3x^2y^2}$

b) $\dfrac{24a^4b^5 - 18a^3b^4 + 12a^2b^3}{6a^2b^2}$

c) $\dfrac{16m^2n^6 - 32m^3n^5 + 48m^4n^4}{-16m^2n^3}$

d) $\dfrac{12x^6y^4 - 8x^5y^3 + 4x^2y^2}{4x^4y^2}$

e) $\dfrac{-27a^5b + 18a^4b^2 - 9a^3b^3}{-9a^3b}$

f) $\dfrac{54x^2y^3z^4 - 36x^3y^4z^5 + 18x^4y^5z^6}{18x^2y^2z^2}$

8. The volume V of a sphere of radius R is given by the formula $V = \dfrac{4}{3}\pi R^3$. The surface area S is given by the formula $S = 4\pi R^2$. Write an expression for the quotient $\dfrac{V}{S}$ for a sphere of radius R.

9. The surface area S of a cylinder of radius R and height h is given by $S = 2\pi Rh + 2\pi R^2$. The volume V is given by $V = \pi R^2 h$. Write an expression for the quotient $\dfrac{V}{S}$ for a cylinder with $h = 2R$.

7-11 RATIONAL EXPRESSIONS

The set of numbers obtained by adding, subtracting, multiplying, or dividing integers is called the set of rational numbers.

Just as integers are the "building blocks" for rational numbers, so polynomials are the building blocks for rational expressions.

> The sum, difference, product or quotient of any two polynomials is called a *rational expression*.

These are rational expressions.

$$3, \quad 4x + 2, \quad 5xy, \quad 3x^2y - 2y, \quad \frac{5x}{7y}, \quad \frac{3x^2 - y}{z}$$

Each expression can be written as the sum, difference, product or quotient of two polynomials. In addition, 3, $4x + 2$, $5xy$, and $3x^2y - 2y$ are polynomials.

These are not rational expressions.

$$\sqrt{x^2 + x + 3}, \quad \frac{1 + \sqrt{x}}{3}, \quad \frac{\sqrt{x} - 1}{3x}$$

These expressions cannot be written as the sums, differences, products, or quotients of polynomials.

Operations with rational expressions are performed in the same way as operations with rational numbers.

It is important to realize that rational expressions are not defined for values of the variables which would make the denominator equal to zero. This is because division by zero is not defined.

Example 1. Simplify.

a) $\dfrac{3m^2n}{4m^2} \times \dfrac{2m^3n}{5n}$ $\dfrac{6m^5n^2}{20m^2n}$

b) $\dfrac{3a^2b}{4} \div \dfrac{2b}{5a}$

c) $\dfrac{x-2}{3} \times \dfrac{2}{x}$

d) $\dfrac{x-1}{2x} \div \dfrac{3}{x}$

Solution.

a) $\dfrac{3m^2n}{4m^2} \times \dfrac{2m^3n}{5n} = \dfrac{6m^5n^2}{20m^2n}$

$= \dfrac{3m^3n}{10}$

$2x-4$

$3x$

b) To divide by a rational expression, multiply by its reciprocal.

$\dfrac{3a^2b}{4} \div \dfrac{2b}{5a} = \dfrac{3a^2b}{4} \times \dfrac{5a}{2b}$

$= \dfrac{15a^3b}{8b}$

$= \dfrac{15a^3}{8}$

c) $\dfrac{x-2}{3} \times \dfrac{2}{x} = \dfrac{2(x-2)}{3x}$

$= \dfrac{2x-4}{3x}$

d) $\dfrac{x-1}{2x} \div \dfrac{3}{x} = \dfrac{x-1}{2x} \times \dfrac{x}{3}$

$= \dfrac{x(x-1)}{6x}$

$= \dfrac{x-1}{6}$

Rational expressions are added and subtracted in the same way as rational numbers.

Example 2. Simplify.

a) $\dfrac{m-4}{3} + \dfrac{m+5}{3}$

b) $\dfrac{x+2}{3x^2} + \dfrac{2(x-3)}{3x^2}$

c) $\dfrac{3}{2y^2} - \dfrac{5-y}{2y^2}$

d) $\dfrac{a-2}{3} - \dfrac{3(a-1)}{4}$

Solution.

a) $\dfrac{m-4}{3} + \dfrac{m+5}{3} = \dfrac{m-4+m+5}{3}$

$= \dfrac{2m+1}{3}$

b) $\dfrac{x+2}{3x^2} + \dfrac{2(x-3)}{3x^2} = \dfrac{x+2+2(x-3)}{3x^2}$

$= \dfrac{x+2+2x-6}{3x^2}$

$= \dfrac{3x-4}{3x^2}$

c) $\dfrac{3}{2y^2} - \dfrac{5 - y}{2y^2} = \dfrac{3 - (5 - y)}{2y^2}$

$= \dfrac{3 - 5 + y}{2y^2}$

$= \dfrac{y - 2}{2y^2}$

d) Write the rational expressions with a common denominator of 12.

$\dfrac{a - 2}{3} - \dfrac{3(a - 1)}{4} = \dfrac{a - 2}{3} \times \dfrac{4}{4} - \dfrac{3(a - 1)}{4} \times \dfrac{3}{3}$

$= \dfrac{4(a - 2) - 9(a - 1)}{12}$

$= \dfrac{4a - 8 - 9a + 9}{12}$

$= \dfrac{-5a + 1}{12}$

EXERCISES 7-11

(A)

1. Which of these expressions are rational expressions?

   a) $\dfrac{3a^2b}{2}$ b) $\dfrac{4m^2n^2}{3mn}$ c) $\dfrac{3}{5}$ ✓   d) $\dfrac{1}{2\sqrt{a}}$ e) $\dfrac{3\sqrt{a}}{4}$ f) $\dfrac{x - 6}{5}$ ✓

   g) $\dfrac{3 - 4y}{2y}$ h) $\dfrac{3x}{1 + \sqrt{x}}$ i) $-\dfrac{4}{3}$ j) $3x^2 + 1$ k) $\dfrac{4 + 3m^2}{2m^3}$ l) $\dfrac{x^2 + \sqrt{x}}{3}$

2. Simplify.

   a) $\dfrac{2x^2}{y} \times \dfrac{3x}{2y^3}$ b) $\dfrac{-4m^2n^2}{m} \times \dfrac{3mn}{n^2}$ c) $\dfrac{8xy^3}{3} \times \dfrac{x^2y}{4x^2y^2}$

   d) $\dfrac{-5n}{3mn} \times \dfrac{-2m^2n^2}{n^2}$ e) $\dfrac{3a}{2b} \times \dfrac{2a^2b}{3ab^2}$ f) $\dfrac{2c^2d^3}{3c^3} \times \dfrac{-4c^2d^2}{d^3}$

   g) $\dfrac{6x^2y^5}{x^2y^2} \times \dfrac{2x^2y}{3xy^2}$ h) $\dfrac{m^2n^3}{3m} \times \dfrac{-4m^2n}{5n}$ i) $\dfrac{2x^5}{3y^2} \times \dfrac{5x^2y^3}{-4x^3}$

3. Simplify.

   a) $\dfrac{x^3y}{2} \div \dfrac{y^2}{4x}$ b) $\dfrac{2x^2y^3}{3} \div \dfrac{6xy^2}{5x^2}$ c) $\dfrac{4m^2n^3}{3mn} \div \dfrac{8mn^2}{m}$

   d) $\dfrac{a^2b^3}{2a} \div \dfrac{ab^2}{3ab}$ e) $\dfrac{-x^4y^3}{2xy} \div \dfrac{xy^2}{4x}$ f) $\dfrac{6c^2d^3}{5cd} \div \dfrac{12cd^2}{25c^2d}$

   g) $\dfrac{3x^2y^4}{2xy^2} \div \dfrac{-4x^2y^2}{3xy}$ h) $\dfrac{-2a^2b^3}{5ab^2} \div \dfrac{-8ab}{15a}$ i) $\dfrac{7x^2y^5}{-3xy} \div \dfrac{-14x^2y^2}{x^2y}$

   j) $\dfrac{3p^2q}{5pq^2} \div \dfrac{-15pq}{20p^3q^4}$ k) $\dfrac{28a^3b^4}{-9ab^7} \div \dfrac{7a^5}{27b^6}$ l) $\dfrac{-6m^3n^4}{55m^4n} \div \dfrac{21mn}{-22mn^4}$

4. Simplify.

a) $\dfrac{a + 3}{2} + \dfrac{2a - 1}{2}$

b) $\dfrac{3x - 1}{5} - \dfrac{x + 1}{5}$

c) $\dfrac{3 + y}{7} + \dfrac{2y - 1}{7}$

d) $\dfrac{3m - 2}{4} + \dfrac{m + 1}{4}$

e) $\dfrac{4 - 3n}{3} - \dfrac{n + 5}{3}$

f) $\dfrac{5x - 2}{6} - \dfrac{3x - 4}{6}$

g) $\dfrac{4y - 5}{5} - \dfrac{2(y + 1)}{5}$

h) $\dfrac{2(x + 4)}{3} + \dfrac{3(x - 2)}{3}$

i) $\dfrac{3(m + 2)}{4} - \dfrac{(4 - m)}{4}$

B

5. Simplify.

a) $\dfrac{3x + 1}{2x^2} + \dfrac{x - 1}{2x^2}$

b) $\dfrac{2a - 5}{3a^2} - \dfrac{6 + a}{3a^2}$

c) $\dfrac{4 - 3m}{2m} - \dfrac{2 + m}{2m}$

d) $\dfrac{2y - 3}{3y^3} + \dfrac{4 + 3y}{3y^3}$

e) $\dfrac{x - 2}{x^4} - \dfrac{5 - 2x}{x^4}$

f) $\dfrac{7 - 2n}{4n^2} + \dfrac{4n - 3}{4n^2}$

g) $\dfrac{2(x - 1)}{3x^2} + \dfrac{4(x + 1)}{3x^2}$

h) $\dfrac{y - 5}{2y^3} - \dfrac{3(y - 1)}{2y^3}$

i) $\dfrac{8a + 3}{5a} - \dfrac{2(3 + a)}{5a}$

6. Simplify.

a) $\dfrac{-3x^2y^2}{2y^3} \times \dfrac{5xy}{3x^2}$

b) $\dfrac{14ab^4}{3ab} \div \dfrac{-7ab^2}{6a^2b}$

c) $\dfrac{3m^2n^4}{2mn} \div \dfrac{6m^4n^2}{m^2n^2}$

d) $\dfrac{2x^2yz^2}{3xy} \times \dfrac{xy^2z}{2yz}$

e) $\dfrac{3a^2bc}{-a^2bc^2} \div \dfrac{6ab^2c}{ab^2c^3}$

f) $\dfrac{-3xyz^2}{2x^2y^2z} \times \dfrac{5x^2y^2z}{-4xyz^3}$

7. Simplify.

a) $\dfrac{3(x + 1)}{2x^2} - \dfrac{2(x - 1)}{2x^2}$

b) $\dfrac{4(1 - y)}{3y^3} + \dfrac{2(y + 3)}{3y^3}$

c) $\dfrac{1 - m}{2m} - \dfrac{3 - 2m}{2m}$

d) $\dfrac{5(2 - a)}{a^3} + \dfrac{3(2a + 1)}{a^3}$

e) $\dfrac{-2(x + 5)}{3x^2} - \dfrac{4(1 - x)}{3x^2}$

f) $\dfrac{3(a + 2)}{4a^3} + \dfrac{5(1 - a)}{4a^3}$

8. Simplify.

a) $\dfrac{x - 1}{3} + \dfrac{2x + 1}{4}$

b) $\dfrac{2a + 3}{3} - \dfrac{a + 4}{2}$

c) $\dfrac{4 - 3m}{2} - \dfrac{5 + m}{5}$

d) $\dfrac{3(y + 1)}{4} + \dfrac{y - 1}{3}$

e) $\dfrac{n - 1}{2} + \dfrac{3(4 - n)}{7}$

f) $\dfrac{2(x + 6)}{5} - \dfrac{x - 3}{4}$

C

9. It takes x hours to fill a swimming pool when only hose #1 is used. It takes y hours to fill the pool if only hose #2 is used. Write a rational expression to show how long it takes to fill the pool if both hoses are used.

10. An aircraft has an air speed of v kilometres per hour. When there is a tail wind of w kilometres per hour, the resultant speed of the aircraft is $(v + w)$ kilometres per hour. When there is a head wind of w kilometres per hour, the resultant speed of the aircraft is $(v - w)$ kilometres per hour.

A and B are two towns D kilometres apart. The aircraft travels from A to B and back to A.

a) Write a rational expression for the total time taken for the round trip.

b) Write a rational expression for the average speed of the round trip.

1. Simplify.
   a) $(-5n) + (+8n)$
   b) $6x - (-2x)$
   c) $3y^2 - (-5y^2)$
   d) $-2y^2 - 3y^2 - 5y^2$
   e) $-5b^2 + 8b^2 - (-2b^2)$
   f) $2.7y^3 - 1.8y^3 + 2y$

2. Simplify each expression. Arrange each polynomial in descending powers, and state its degree.
   a) $5x - 2x + 7 - 4x$
   b) $15y^2 - 3y + 6y^3 - 2y^2 + 7y$
   c) $2a - 5a^4 + 6a^2 - 4a^2 + 7a + 8a^4 - a^3$
   d) $4 - 6a + a^2 - 3 + 4a^2 + 12a - a - 2a^2 + 1$

3. Evaluate $3y^2 - 5y + 2$ for each value of y.
   a) 0
   b) -1
   c) -3
   d) 4.5

4. Simplify.
   a) $(5y - 3) + (2y + 4)$
   b) $(7x - 2) - (5x + 3)$
   c) $(8r - 5) - (-3r + 2)$
   d) $(5y^2 - 3y) + (6y - 2y^2)$
   e) $(4x - 3) - (2x + 1) - (-3x + 4)$
   f) $(1 - 2p + 3p^2) + (-4 + 3p - 7p^2)$
   g) $(3q^2 + 5q - 2) - (8q^2 - 3q + 4)$

5. Simplify.
   a) $(7a)(5a)$
   b) $(-3b)(5b)$
   c) $(-4y)^2$
   d) $(-9x^3)(7x^2)$
   e) $(-2y)^3$
   f) $(4xy^2)(-3x^2y)$

6. Expand.
   a) $4(y - 2)$
   b) $8(a - 3)$
   c) $-4(x + 2)$
   d) $3x(5 - x)$
   e) $2y(y - 6)$
   f) $-5x(3 - x)$
   g) $5y(7 - 2y + 3y^2)$
   h) $-6x(3x^2 + 5x - 12)$
   i) $10a(-4 - 7a + 2a^2)$

7. Factor and check.
   a) $6y + 18y^2$
   b) $-3a + 12a^4$
   c) $5a^2 - 25a^3$
   d) $3a^3 + 4a^2 + 7a$
   e) $6x^2y - 3xy + 9xy^2$
   f) $8ab - 4a^2b^2 + 6ab^2$

8. Find each product.
   a) $(x - 3)(x - 4)$
   b) $(y + 7)(y + 3)$
   c) $(a - 2)(a + 5)$
   d) $(n - 6)(n + 7)$
   e) $(n + 4)(n - 7)$
   f) $(x - 1)(x + 5)$

9. Find each product.
   a) $4(x - 5)(x - 6)$
   b) $y(y - 2)(y + 9)$
   c) $-3y(1 - y)(7 + y)$

10. Expand.
   a) $(x + 3)^2$
   b) $(y - 5)^2$
   c) $(5 - q)^2$
   d) $(6 - 5y)^2$

11. Factor.
   a) $x^2 - 7x + 10$
   b) $x^2 - 6x + 9$
   c) $x^2 + 6x + 5$
   d) $a^2 - 4a - 12$
   e) $x^2 - x + 12$
   f) $15 + 2x - x^2$
   g) $y^2 - y - 72$
   h) $n^2 + 3n - 40$
   i) $8 + 7x - x^2$
   j) $2x^2 - 12x - 72$
   k) $5m^2 + 10m - 40$
   l) $y^3 + 2y^2 - 3y$

12. Find each product.
   a) $(a - 4)(a + 4)$
   b) $(x + 8)(x - 8)$
   c) $(2 - y)(2 + y)$
   d) $\left(\frac{1}{2}n - 1\right)\left(\frac{1}{2}n + 1\right)$
   e) $3(x - 6)(x + 6)$
   f) $-5y(3 - y)(3 + y)$

13. Factor.
   a) $b^2 - 25$
   b) $x^2 - 81$
   c) $y^2 - 121$
   d) $m^2 - \frac{1}{4}$
   e) $9x^2 - 16$
   f) $25 - 4y^2$
   g) $2x^2 - 32$
   h) $64m - 4m^3$

14. A garden plot has the dimensions shown.
   a) Write an expression for the perimeter of the plot.
   b) Write an expression for the area of the plot.
   c) Determine the perimeter and the area when x is 7 m.

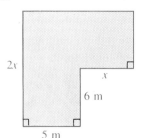

15. The temperature T degrees Celsius in a sauna n minutes after being turned on is given by this formula. $T = -0.04n^2 + 2.5n + 16$, where $n \leqslant 30$
   Find the temperature in the sauna after each time.
   a) 0 min
   b) 15 min
   c) 25 min

16. Simplify.
   a) $\dfrac{15x - 20}{5}$
   b) $\dfrac{-12 + 2x}{-2}$
   c) $\dfrac{12x^2 + 4x}{4x}$
   d) $\dfrac{10a - 6a^2}{2a}$
   e) $\dfrac{3x^3 - 12x^2}{3x^2}$
   f) $\dfrac{10a^3 - 6a^2}{2a^4}$

17. Simplify.
   a) $\dfrac{18c^2 - 6c^3 + 12c^4}{6c^2}$
   b) $\dfrac{5x^5 + 20x^4 - 5x^3}{5x^3}$
   c) $\dfrac{-9m^3 + 12m^4 - 15m^2}{-6m^5}$

18. Simplify.
   a) $\dfrac{a^2b^2}{10bc} \times \dfrac{-25b^2c}{4a^2c}$
   b) $\dfrac{3}{2}x^3 \div \dfrac{1}{4}x^2$
   c) $\dfrac{3m^2n^3}{-5mn^2} \div \dfrac{9m^4n^2}{30mn}$
   d) $\dfrac{13s^2t^2}{-7r^2st} \times \dfrac{49rst^3}{52r^3st}$
   e) $\dfrac{-11u^2v^3w}{100v^2w^2} \div \dfrac{132u^3w^2}{-20uvw}$
   f) $\dfrac{-36abc^4}{-28bc^2d} \times \dfrac{-56b^2cd}{12a^2b^3}$

19. Simplify.
   a) $\dfrac{x + 3}{2} + \dfrac{2x + 5}{2}$
   b) $\dfrac{2m - 7}{3} - \dfrac{3m + 4}{3}$
   c) $\dfrac{5a + b}{2b} + \dfrac{2a - 3b}{2b}$
   d) $\dfrac{4(u + 2v)}{5u} - \dfrac{3(2u - v)}{5u}$
   e) $\dfrac{-7(-2s + 3t)}{2t^2} + \dfrac{6(t - 2s)}{2t^2}$
   f) $\dfrac{4m + 3n}{3} - \dfrac{m + 6n}{2}$

handwritten:
$\dfrac{-9ac^2}{-7d} \times \dfrac{-9cd}{2\,aa^2}$

$\dfrac{-81acd}{14dba^2}$

8 Relations

How can the height of a rocket be determined at any time after it has been fired? (See Section 8-5.)

8-1 THE CARTESIAN COORDINATE SYSTEM

There is a story that the great 17th century French mathematician, René Descartes, in bed because of illness, was watching a spider on the ceiling. As he watched, he thought of how he might describe the position of the spider at any instant. The technique he devised is called the *Cartesian coordinate system*. Although the system is named after Descartes, another French mathematician, Pierre de Fermat, is equally deserving of acclaim. For, quite independently, he developed the same technique at about the same time.

In coordinate geometry, we represent points, lines, circles, and other curves by numbers and equations. Geometric problems can be solved using arithmetic and algebra. Descartes, de Fermat, and others were able to apply these methods to practical problems in astronomy, optics, ballistics, and navigation.

The plane is divided into four regions by the *x*- and *y*-axes, which are perpendicular. These regions are called *quadrants*.

Point A has *coordinates* (3,4). The *x*-coordinate is always written first, hence, (3,4) is an *ordered pair of numbers*. The coordinates of B appear to be $(-4.5, -2.5)$.

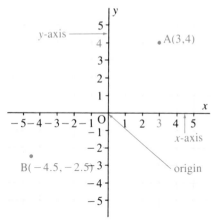

Example 1. a) State the coordinates of the points P, Q, R, and S.
b) Plot these points.
$A(-3, -1)$, $B(4, -4)$, $C(-2,4)$, $D(4,4)$
c) Where are the points with:
i) -3 as their *x*-coordinate
ii) 2 as their *y*-coordinate
iii) 0 as their *y*-coordinate?

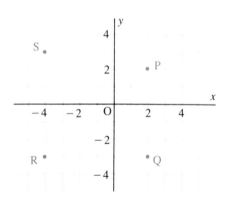

Solution. a) The coordinates are P(2,2), Q(2, − 3), R(− 4, − 3), S(− 4,3).

b)

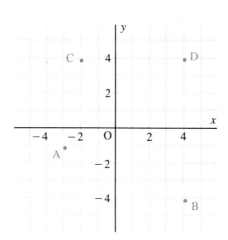

c) i) The points with − 3 as their x-coordinate lie on a line 3 units to the left of the y-axis and parallel to it.

ii) The points with 2 as their y-coordinate lie on a line 2 units above the x-axis and parallel to it.

iii) The points with 0 as their y-coordinate lie on the x-axis.

Example 2. Plot these points. P(− 2.5,2.5), Q(2.5,2.5), R(4, − 1), S(− 1, − 1)
a) Draw PQ, QR, RS, and SP.
b) What polygon have you drawn?

Solution. a)

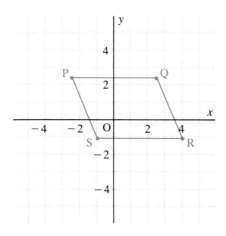

b) The polygon appears to be a parallelogram.

EXERCISES 8-1

1. State the coordinates of the points A to J.

2. Plot these points. M(3,4), N(−2,−6),
   P(−4,5), Q(0,4), R(−4,0), S(−5,−2),
   T(0,−5), U(3,−4)

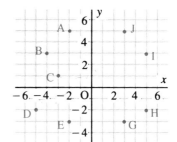

3. Where are the points with:
   a) *x*-coordinate 0
   b) *y*-coordinate −4
   c) *x*-coordinate negative
   d) *x*-coordinate negative, *y*-coordinate positive
   e) *x*-coordinate and *y*-coordinate equal?

4. Plot these points on the same axes and draw the line segments named.
   a) A(−4,3), B(−3,−2), C(−2,1), D(−1,−2), E(0,3); AB, BC, CD, DE
   b) F(2,3), G(2,−2), H(4,3), J(4,−2), K(2,0), L(4,0); FG, HJ, KL
   c) M(6,3), N(8,3), P(7,0), R(7,−2); MP, NP, RP
   d) What word is formed?

5. a) Plot these points. T(−4,1), C(−3,−3), E(5,−1), R(4,3)
   b) Draw these line segments. TC, CE, ER, RT
   c) What polygon have you drawn?

6. Plot each set of points and determine which sets of points do *not* form triangles.
   a) A(−3,1), B(1,−1), C(3,−4)   b) O(0,0), E(6,2), F(9,3)
   c) G(2,−3), H(5,−1), I(8,1)   d) K(4,−6), L(2,−2), M(−4,10)
   e) O(0,0), P(8,3), Q(13,4)   f) R(−1,1), S(2,3), T(5,5)

7. The coordinates of three vertices of a square are given. Find the coordinates of the fourth vertex.
   a) A(3,5), B(−4,5), C(−4,−2)   b) D(1,2), E(5,−2), F(1,−6)
   c) G(−3,−1), H(4,2), J(2,−3)   d) K(−3,−1), L(4,0), M(1,−4)

8. Plot each set of points and join them by line segments to form a quadrilateral. State whether the quadrilateral is a parallelogram, trapezoid, rhombus, rectangle, square, or none of these.
   a) A(1,1), B(−4,1), C(−4,−4), D(1,−4)
   b) E(−2,5), F(−5,−3), G(−5,−5), H(−2,−3)
   c) J(3,0), K(0,3), L(−3,0), M(0,−3)
   d) N(0,4), P(1,0), Q(−1,0), R(0,−4)

9. The coordinates of three vertices of a parallelogram are given. Find the coordinates of a fourth possible vertex.
   a) B(3,0), C(6,3), D(0,3)   b) E(2,1), F(5,3), G(2,7)
   c) H(1,6), J(−5,1), K(3,1)   d) L(0,−3), M(0,3), N(2,0)

10. Which polygon has these vertices? P(*a*,0), Q(*b*,0), R(*a*,*b* − *a*), S(*b*,*b* − *a*)?

8-2 DISPLAYING RELATIONS

Tickets to a theatre cost $6.00 each. The cost of a number of tickets (less than seven for convenience) can be displayed in a table and in a graph.

Number of Tickets	Total Cost ($)
0	0
1	6
2	12
3	18
4	24
5	30
6	36

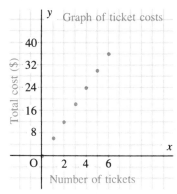

Both the table and the graph relate numbers in pairs. A more concise way of doing this is as a set of ordered pairs.
{(0,0), (1,6), (2,12), (3,18), (4,24), (5,30), (6,36)}
This set of ordered pairs is an example of a *relation*. The first number in each pair is the number of tickets. The second number is the total cost of the tickets. Thus, the ordered pair (3,18) indicates that 3 tickets cost $18.

Example 1. The graph shows the relation between the service charge on a chequing account and the number of cheques written.

    a) From the graph, determine:

        i) the service charge on 4 cheques

        ii) the number of cheques handled for a charge of $1.25.

    b) Write the relation as a set of ordered pairs.

Graph of service charges

Solution.

    a) i) The ordered pair, (4,1.00) indicates that the service charge on 4 cheques is $1.00.

       ii) The ordered pair (5,1.25) indicates that $1.25 is the service charge on 5 cheques.

    b) The relation defined by the graph is:

       {(0,0), (1,0.25), (2,0.50), (3,0.75), (4,1.00), (5,1.25)}

Example 2. When Jessica arrived for the first day of her summer job, she saw this chart on the bulletin board.

    Draw a graph to show the wages earned for working up to 10 h.

Hours worked	Wages earned
3	$20.82
5	$34.70
8	$55.52
10	$69.40

Solution. To draw a graph, follow these steps.

Step 1. *Count the number of squares available in the horizontal direction.*

On the graph paper shown, there are 18 squares in this direction. Some of these will be needed to write the scale along the vertical axis. Therefore, approximately 15 squares are available for the graph.

Step 2. *Compare the number of squares available with the greatest value to be plotted in the horizontal direction. Choose an appropriate value to be represented by each square.*

We plot the number of hours in the horizontal direction. The greatest value to be plotted is 10 h. We can let one square represent 1 h, and the graph will occupy 10 squares horizontally.

Step 3. *Count the number of squares available in the vertical direction.*

There are 20 squares in this direction. Some of these will be needed to write the scale along the horizontal axis. Therefore, approximately 17 squares are available for the graph.

Step 4. *Compare the number of squares available with the greatest value to be plotted in the vertical direction. Choose an appropriate value to be represented by each square.*

We plot wages in the vertical direction. The greatest value to be plotted is $69.40. We can let 2 squares represent $10, and the graph will occupy 14 squares vertically.

Step 5. *Draw a set of axes scaled as in Steps 2 and 4.*

The scale we chose does not enable us to show the cents on the values of the wages earned. Hence, round the values to the nearest dollar before plotting the points. Then draw a straight line through them.

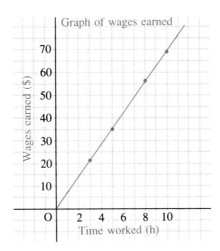

Sometimes there is no simple arithmetical relationship between the numbers in the ordered pairs of a relation.

Example 3. Write the relation as a set of ordered pairs.

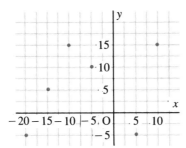

Solution. The relation defined by the graph is this set of ordered pairs.
$\{(-20, -5), (-15, 5), (-10, 15), (-5, 10), (5, -5), (10, 15)\}$
It does not matter in what order the ordered pairs are listed.

EXERCISES 8-2

Ⓐ

1. Write each relation as a set of ordered pairs.

a)

Number	Cost ($)
1	0.50
2	0.95
3	1.35
4	1.70
5	2.00

b)

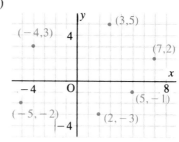

2. Write each relation as a set of ordered pairs.

a)

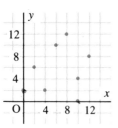

b)

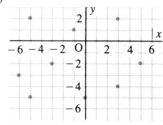

c)

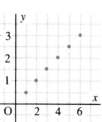

d)

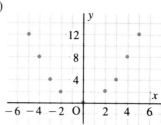

Ⓑ

3. Draw the graph for each relation.

a)

Rectangles with same Perimeter	
Length (cm)	Width (cm)
11	1
10	2
9	3
8	4
7	5
6	6

b)

Average Statistics for Women	
Height (cm)	Mass (kg)
152	47
160	52
167	56
175	63
181	70

c)

Pizza Toppings	
Number of Toppings	Cost ($)
1	5.90
2	6.60
3	7.30
4	8.00
5	8.70
6	9.40

4. The graph represents the sums of the
natural numbers from 1 to 6.
a) From the graph, determine:
i) the sum of the first five numbers
ii) how many numbers are required
for a sum of 10.
b) Write the relation as a set of ordered
pairs.

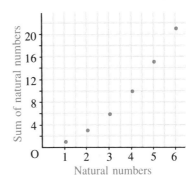

5. For the graph shown
a) State the value(s) of y that corre-
spond(s) to each value of x.
i) 2   ii) 6   iii) 10   iv) 13
b) State the value(s) of x that corre-
spond(s) to each value of y.
i) 15   ii) 25   iii) 30   iv) 40
c) Write the relation as a set of ordered
pairs.

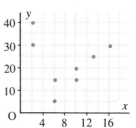

6. A copy shop displays this advertisement.

FOR EACH ORIGINAL		
first 5 copies	second 5 copies	all additional copies
15¢ each	11¢ each	8¢ each

a) Make a table of values for up to 15 copies of one original.
b) Graph the relation between the total cost and the number of copies.

7. A bank allows 3 free cheques per month but makes a service charge of 32¢ for
each cheque after that. Graph the relation between the service charge and the number
of cheques for up to 8 cheques.

8. The local drama group is selling tickets for its latest production. The tickets cost
$5 for adults and $2 for students.
a) Graph the relation between the number of each kind of ticket that can be bought
for each total expenditure.
i)   exactly $20   ii) $20 or less
b) Write the relation for each part of a) as a set of ordered pairs.

9. Some parents decide that their children should receive a weekly allowance from
age 4 to age 16. The amount is 75¢ the first year and increases by 75¢ each year.
a) Make a table of values for the relation.
b) Graph the relation.
c) Find a formula relating the allowance to the child's age.

PROBLEM SOLVING

Use a Graph

What will be the correct time when the slow watch reads 15:00?

Understand the problem
- How many minutes per hour does the slow watch lose?
- What will the slow watch read when the correct time is 15:00?
- What are we asked to find?

Think of a strategy
- Try drawing a graph of the time shown by the slow watch against the correct time. Use the graph to determine the correct time corresponding to the slow watch time of 15:00.

Carry out the strategy
- Since the slow watch loses 10 min every hour, we know the times on the slow watch at 13:00, 14:00, and 15:00. These are shown on the chart below.

Correct time	Time on slow watch
12:00	12:00
13:00	12:50
14:00	13:40
15:00	14:30

- Plot these points and join them with a straight line. From the graph, we see that when the slow watch reads 15:00, the correct time is 15:36.

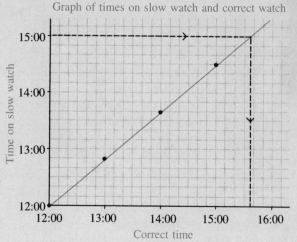

Graph of times on slow watch and correct watch

Look back

- Our answer indicates that it takes 3 h and 36 min for the slow watch to show a time elapse of 3 h. The slow watch moves at $\frac{5}{6}$ of the correct rate. Is $\frac{5}{6}$ of 3 h and 36 min equal to 3 h?

Solve each problem

1. Mr. Jenkins left for work at 9:00 and drove at an average speed of 50 km/h. After he left, Mrs. Jenkins discovered that he had forgotten his briefcase. She set out at 9:15 at an average speed of 70 km/h. Approximately what time did she reach her husband?

2. A graph of temperature in degrees Fahrenheit against temperature in degrees Celsius is a straight line. When the temperature is $-40°C$ it is also $-40°F$. A temperature of 50°F corresponds to 10°C. Use these facts to determine $-13°F$ in degrees Celsius.

3. The table shows the total distance which an object falls during the first few seconds after it is dropped. Estimate the total distance fallen in the first 5.5 s.

Falling time (s)	Distance fallen (m)
1	4.8
2	19.2
3	43.2
4	76.8
5	120.0
6	172.8

4. Anita wired her electrical digital clock so that it would run backwards. If she set the clock to the correct time at 16:00, when will the clock next show the correct time?

5. One side of a field is bounded by a river. A farmer wants to fence a rectangular pasture with the river as one side. She has 192 m of fencing for the three sides. What are the dimensions of the largest pasture that can be enclosed?

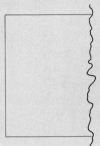

8-3 RELATIONS HAVING MANY ORDERED PAIRS

While Fred was ill, his temperature was taken every 2 h from 8 A.M. to midnight, and then at 4 A.M. This continued for 48 h.

The readings were plotted on a temperature chart and adjacent points connected by a straight line.

From this graph, further information can be determined. The doctor can estimate Fred's temperature at times of the day between those times when it was measured.

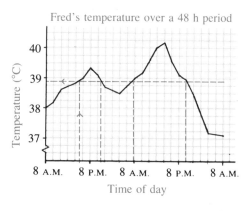

Fred's temperature over a 48 h period

For example, to find Fred's temperature at 5 P.M. on the first day, the doctor would draw a vertical line from 5 P.M. to the graph. Then, she would draw a horizontal line to meet the temperature axis. This indicates a value of about 38.9°C.

Normal body temperature is 36.9°C. The doctor is concerned if Fred's temperature is more than 2°C above normal.

To find the times when Fred's temperature was above 38.9°C, the doctor drew a horizontal line through 38.9°C to meet the graph. Then she drew vertical lines to meet the time axis. This shows that Fred's temperature was above 38.9°C from 5 P.M. to 11 P.M. on the first day and from 8 A.M. to 10 P.M. on the second day.

Using a graph to estimate a *y*-value, which is located between two measured *y*-values is called *interpolation*.

The relation on the previous page has too many ordered pairs for all of them to be listed. A graph is the only way to represent this relation.

Sometimes it is possible to represent a relation with an equation.

Example.   The interest I dollars on a principal P dollars invested for one year at 11% is given by this equation. $I = 0.11P$

a) Draw a graph to show the annual interest earned for principals up to $5000.

b) From the graph
   i) Estimate the annual interest on $2750.
   ii) Estimate the principal that would earn interst of $700.

Solution.   a) Make a table of values. Choose values of P for which I is easily calculated. Substitute each value of P into the equation to get the corresponding value of I.

P ($)	I ($)
1000	110
2000	220
3000	330
4000	440
5000	550

Graph of interest against principal

Plot the points on a grid. They appear to lie on a straight line, so join them.

b) i) Draw a vertical line where P is $2750. Draw a horizontal line from the point where the vertical line intersects the graph. This horizontal line indicates an interest of about $300.

   ii) The graph shows interest up to $550. To find the principal that will earn $700, the line of the graph is extended.
   The interest axis is extended to include $700.
   The principal axis is extended proportionally.
   Then the information can be read from the graph.
   A principal of about $6400 would earn interest of $700.

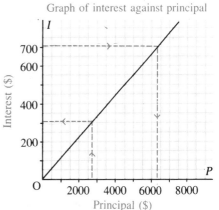

Graph of interest against principal

Using a graph to represent the y-values which are beyond all the measured y-values is called *extrapolation*.

EXERCISES 8-3

Ⓑ

1. The graph shows how the radioactive
   element carbon 14 decays over a long
   period of time
   a) What was the initial mass of the
      carbon?
   b) Find the mass of the carbon after
      each time period.
      i)   3000 years   ii)   6000 years
      iii) 9000 years   iv)   15 000 years
   c) The halflife of a radioactive substance
      is the time required for one-half of
      the atoms in a given mass to dis-
      integrate. What is the halflife of
      carbon 14?

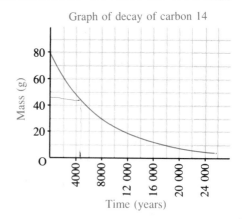

Graph of decay of carbon 14

2. The graph shows how the time of sunset
   in Winnipeg varies with the time of
   year.
   a) Why are there two breaks in the
      curve?
   b) What is the earliest time that the sun
      sets? On what date does it occur?
   c) What is the latest time that the sun
      sets? On what date does it occur?
   d) Find the time of sunset on each date.
      i)   March 1
      ii) August 15
      iii) December 15
   e) Find the approximate date(s) on
      which the sun sets at each time.
      i)   5 P.M.
      ii) 6:30 P.M.
      iii) 8:30 P.M.

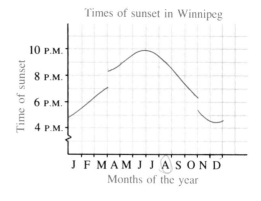

Times of sunset in Winnipeg

3. In a physical fitness program, the maximum pulse rate m beats per minute is related
   to a person's age a years by this formula.
   $m = 220 - a$
   a) Make a table of values for this equation, for people between the ages of 18 and
      50.
   b) Graph the relation defined by the table of values.
   c) From the graph, find the age of a person whose maximum pulse rate is 180.
   d) From the graph, find the maximum pulse rate of a person who is 27 years old.

4. In a science experiment a mass *m* grams is suspended from a beam by a spring. When it is pulled down and released, the mass moves up and down. The graph was drawn from measurements of the heights of the mass above the floor during the first few seconds of motion.
   a) Find the height of the mass after each time.
      i)   1 s   ii)   2 s   iii)   3 s
   b) Find when the mass was at each height.
      i)   6 cm above the floor
      ii)   10 cm above the floor
   c) Find how long it takes the mass to move up and down once.

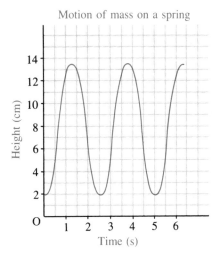

Motion of mass on a spring

5. The temperature of a cup of hot chocolate is taken every 2 min for 10 min.
   a) Graph the relation defined by this table of values.
   b) From the graph
      i) Interpolate to estimate the temperature after 5 min.
      ii) Extrapolate to estimate when the temperature was 30°C.
   c) Find the drop in temperature:
      i)   in the second minute
      ii)   in the fifth minute.

Time (min)	Temperature (°C)
0	100
2	77
4	61
6	49
8	41
10	35

6. The table shows the population of Canada every ten years since Confederation.

Year	1871	1881	1891	1901	1911	1921	1931	1941	1951	1961	1971	1981
Population (millions)	3.7	4.3	4.8	5.4	7.2	8.8	10.4	11.5	14.0	18.2	21.6	24.3

   a) Show this information graphically.
   b) Interpolate to estimate the year when the population was 15 000 000.
   c) Interpolate to estimate the population in 1916.
   d) Extrapolate to estimate the population in 1991. What assumptions are you making?

7. Two numbers are related as follows. Double the first number plus the second number equals 12.
   a) Make a table of values of pairs of numbers that obey this relation.
   b) Graph the relation defined by the table of values.

8-4 LINEAR RELATIONS

The weekly cost of operating a car is $40 for the fixed costs (insurance, maintenance and repairs, depreciation, etc.) and $0.05/km for gasoline and oil. The relation between the weekly cost C dollars and the distance travelled x kilometres is given by this equation.

$C = 40 + 0.05x$

The graph of this relation is a straight line.

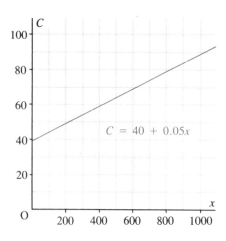

Any relation whose graph is a straight line is called a *linear relation*. Every linear relation is defined by a linear equation; that is, an equation in which each variable term has an exponent sum of 1.

For example, $3x + 5y = 15$
$4x - 7y = -3$
$h = 17 - \dfrac{1}{2}a$

These are linear equations. Each linear equation defines a linear relation.

To graph a linear relation, we require the coordinates of only two points. The coordinates of a third point should be determined, as a check.

Example 1.   Graph the relation defined by $2x - 5y = 10$.

Solution.   Two of the easiest points to find are the ones where the graph intersects the axes.
Substitute $x = 0$ into the equation $2x - 5y = 10$.
$2(0) - 5y = 10$
$\qquad - 5y = 10$
$\qquad\qquad y = -2$
One point on the graph is $(0, -2)$.
Substitute $y = 0$ into the equation $2x - 5y = 10$.
$2x - 5(0) = 10$
$\qquad\quad 2x = 10$
$\qquad\quad x = 5$
Another point on the graph is $(5, 0)$.
For the third point, choose any value of x, for example, $x = 10$.
Substitute $x = 10$ into the equation $2x - 5y = 10$.
$2(10) - 5y = 10$
$\quad 20 - 5y = -10$
$\qquad\qquad y = 2$
A third point on the graph is $(10, 2)$.
For convenience, we record the results in a table of values.

x	y
0	-2
5	0
10	2

Plot these points on a grid. Join them with a straight line. Then label the line with its equation.

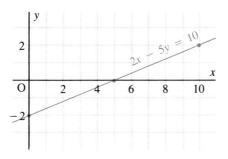

Example 2. The number h of hours of sleep needed by people up to the age of 18 is given by this equation.

$h = 17 - \dfrac{1}{2}a$, where a is the person's age in years

a) Graph the relation defined by this equation.

b) From the graph, find how many hours of sleep a 5-year-old child needs.

Solution. a) The relation is linear because its defining equation is linear.

Select the vertical axis for the values of h and the horizontal axis for the values of a.

Find 3 points which lie on the graph.

Substitute $a = 0$ into $h = 17 - \dfrac{1}{2}a$ to obtain

$h = 17 - \dfrac{1}{2}(0)$

$\quad = 17$

It is not reasonable to substitute $h = 0$ into the equation because everyone needs some sleep. Choose other values for a.

Substitute $a = 10$. Substitute $a = 18$.

$h = 17 - \dfrac{1}{2}(10)$ $\qquad h = 17 - \dfrac{1}{2}(18)$

$\quad = 12$ $\qquad\qquad\qquad = 8$

Record the results in a table of values. Plot the points on a grid. Join the points with a straight line. The graph is restricted to values of a between, and including, 0 and 18 years.

a	h
0	17
10	12
18	8

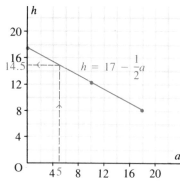

b) From the graph, a 5-year-old child needs 14.5 h sleep.

When graphing relations, care should be taken that only reasonable values of the variable are included.

EXERCISES 8-4

(A)

1. State which graphs represent linear relations.

a)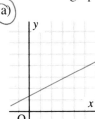

b)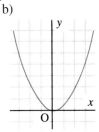

c)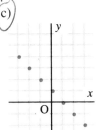

d)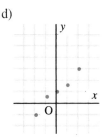

2. State which of these equations define linear relations.

   a) $3x - y = 7$

   b) $7x - 5 = 2y$

   c) $8x + 2xy = 11$

   d) $3x^2 + 16y^2 = 48$

   e) $y = x^2 - 3$

   f) $\dfrac{1}{x} + \dfrac{1}{y} = 1$

3. State the coordinates of the points where each line intersects the axes.

   a)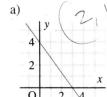

   b)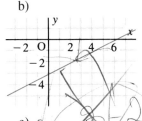

   c)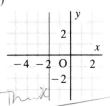

   d)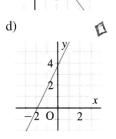

   e)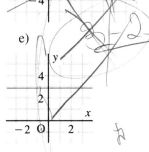

   f)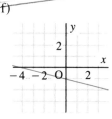

4. Find the coordinates of the points where each line intersects the axes.

   a) $2x + 3y = 18$

   b) $4x - 3y = 12$

   c) $7x - 4y = -28$

   d) $x + 5y = 10$

   e) $y = 2x - 6$

   f) $3x + 6y = 9$

(B)

5. The graph shows the relation between the time required to cook a turkey and the mass of the turkey. Find the cooking time for a turkey of each mass.

   a) 8 kg   b) 5 kg   c) 11 kg

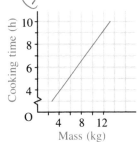

Time required to cook a turkey

6. The graph shows the distance travelled
   by a car over a 6 h period.
   a) How far had the car travelled in 4 h?
   b) How long did it take to travel the
      first 125 km?
   c) How much farther did the car travel
      in the first 3 h than in the last 3 h?
   d) Does the graph represent a linear
      relation?

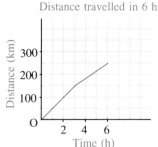
Distance travelled in 6 h

7. Make a table of values then graph the relation defined by each equation.
   a) $4x + 5y = 10$ b) $6x - 8y = 12$ c) $3y = 2x - 8$
   d) $5x - 7y = 0$ e) $y = x - 7$ f) $y = 3$

8. Find which relations are linear.

   a)

x	y
-2	4
-1	1
0	0
1	1
2	4
3	9

   b) $\{(-2,3), (0,2), (2,1), (4,0), (6,-1)\}$
   c) $\{(3,-5), (5,0), (7,5), (9,10)\}$
   d) $\{(-3,-1), (0,1), (3,4), (6,9)\}$

9. A car travels at a constant speed from Edmonton to Calgary. The relation between
   the distance travelled d kilometres and the time taken t hours is given by this
   equation. $d = 280 - 100t$
   a) Graph the relation defined by this equation, after making a table of values.
   b) From the graph, how far is it from Edmonton to Calgary?
   c) What was the total travelling time?
   d) After 2 h
      i) How far was the car from Calgary?
      ii) How far was the car from Edmonton?

10. The thermometer of an old oven is calibrated in Fahrenheit degrees. The relation
    between the Fahrenheit temperature F and the Celsius temperature C is given by
    this equation.
    $$C = \frac{5}{9}(F - 32)$$
    a) Graph the relation defined by this equation.
    b) Find the Fahrenheit setting for each Celsius temperature.
       i)   90°C   ii)   120°C   iii) 200°C
    c) Find the Celsius temperature equivalent to each Fahrenheit temperature.
       i)   90°F   ii)   120°F   iii) 200°F
    d) Extend the graph to find the Celsius temperature equivalent to each Fahrenheit
       temperature.
       i)   20°F   ii) 0°F   iii) -10°F   iv) -20°F

©

11. The relation between Len's height and his age was linear between the ages of 8 and 15 years. He was 132 cm tall when he was 8 and 156 cm tall when he was 12.
   a) Graph the relation between Len's height and age.
   b) Estimate Len's height at each age.
      i)   10 years   ii)   13 years   iii)   14 years
   c) Estimate Len's age for each height.
      i)   140 cm   ii)   145 cm   iii)   150 cm

 INVESTIGATE

Pairs of Linear Equations

1. Graph on the same axes the relations defined by these equations.
   i) $y = 3x + 2$ ii) $y = -2x + 7$
   What do you notice?

2. Graph on the same axes the relations defined by these equations.
   i) $y = 4x - 6$ ii) $y = 4x + 3$
   What do you notice?

3. Graph on the same axes the relations defined by these equations.
   i) $4x - 2y = -10$ ii) $y = 2x + 5$
   What do you notice?

   ● The graphs of two linear relations may intersect at one point.
   ● The graphs of two linear relations may be parallel.
   ● The graphs of two linear relations may coincide.

4. Graph each pair of linear equations. For each pair state whether:
   i) the graphs intersect, if so, state the coordinates of their points of intersection
   ii) the graphs are parallel
   iii) the graphs coincide.
   a) $y = 2x - 2$ b) $y = 5x + 6$ c) $x + 2y = 3$
      $3x + y = 13$ $y = 5x - 3$ $2x + 4y = 6$
   d) $2x + 5y = -3$ e) $5x + 2y = 0$ f) $3x + y = -2$
      $2x + 5y = 4$ $y = x + 7$ $9x + 3y = -6$
   g) $4x + 3y = 1$ h) $y = \dfrac{5}{2}x - \dfrac{7}{2}$ i) $x = -6$
      $-4x - 3y = -1$ $-5x + 2y = -7$ $y = 3x + 17$

5. By inspecting the equations of a pair of linear relations, describe how to tell:
   i) if the graphs will be parallel   ii) if the graphs will coincide.

Choose the Strategy

1. Consider this expression. $1 - 2 + 3 - 4 + \ldots n$
   a) For what values of n is the value of the expression positive?
   b) For what values of n is the value of the expression negative?
   c) Write a formula for the value of the expression:
      i)   when n is even   ii)   when n is odd.

2. The squares ABCD and BEFC (below left) are congruent. Which has the greater perimeter, the colored region or the black region?

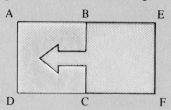

3. a) Use the pattern suggested by the diagram (above right) to evaluate this sum. $1 + 3 + 5 + 7 + \ldots + 15$
   b) Find a formula for this sum.
      $1 + 3 + 5 + 7 + \ldots + (2n - 1)$

4. a) If $x\%$ of x is 16, what is x?   b) If $y\%$ of $y\%$ is 36%, what is y?

5. The pieces of this puzzle fit together to form a square. What is the length of each side of the square that they form?

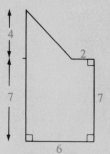
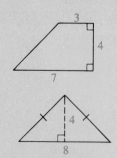
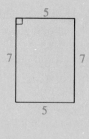

6. At winter ski-camp all the students were required to register for cross-country skiing or alpine skiing or both. If 68% of the students registered for cross-country skiing and 52% signed up for alpine skiing, what percent registered for both?

7. Mrs. McLeod was offered three successive discounts of 10%, 20%, and 25% on a videocassette recorder. The salesperson said that the discounts could be taken in any order she chose. Which would be best for her?

MATHEMATICS AROUND US

The Return of Halley's Comet

In 1705, the English astronomer, Edmund Halley, concluded from observations and calculations that the appearances of a comet in 1531, 1607, and 1682 were the return visits of the same comet. He predicted it would return again in 1758, and it did.

Astronomers now know that this comet travels in a narrow elliptical orbit around the sun once every 75 or 76 years. The time varies slightly owing to the influence of the planets. It reappeared in November, 1985, and was visible in various parts of the world until April, 1986. It is expected again in 2061.

Coordinate geometry can be used to show the relationship between the orbit of Halley's comet and the orbits of the planets.

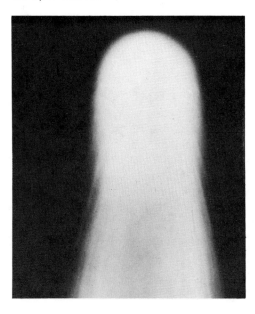

QUESTIONS

1. Draw a pair of axes and on each axis mark a scale from -40 to $+40$. The orgin (0,0) represents the position of the sun.

2. With centre (0,0), draw circles with the following radii to represent the orbits of the planets.

Planet	Earth	Mars	Jupiter	Saturn	Uranus	Neptune
Radius	1	1.5	5	9.5	19	30

3. Each point represents the approximate position of Halley's comet in a certain year. Plot the points on the graph and draw a smooth curve through them.

Year	1918	1933	1948	1963	1978
Position	(17,4.5)	(30,3.0)	(35,0)	(30,-3.0)	(17,-4.5)

Year	1984	1985	1986	1987	1988
Position	(9,-4.0)	(6,-3.5)	(-1,0)	(6,3.5)	(9,4.0)

4. At what points in its orbit is the comet moving fastest and when is it moving slowest?

8-5 NON-LINEAR RELATIONS

When a person stands on the free end of a diving board, it bends under the weight of the person. The relation between the vertical distance d centimetres that the board moves and the mass m kilograms of the person on the board is given by this relation.

$d = 0.000\ 01m^3 + 0.0005m^2$

This equation has a third-degree term, hence the relation it represents is not linear. This non-linear relation is graphed below.

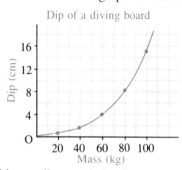

m	d
0	0
25	0.5
50	2.5
75	7.0
100	15.0

Dip of a diving board

The graph of this non-linear relation is a curve. You can use this graph to estimate how far the diving board would move under your weight.

The problem posed at the beginning of the chapter involves another non-linear relation.

Example.   The height h metres of a rocket in the first few seconds after blast-off is given by this formula.

$h = t^2 + 4t$,   where t is the time in seconds since blast-off

a) Graph the relation defined by this equation.
b) From the graph, find how high the rocket is 7.5 s after blast-off.
c) From the graph, find how long the rocket takes to reach a height of 50 m.

Solution.   a) Make a table of values for t and h. Choose values of t which span the value(s) in the question. That is, t must go beyond 7.5 and beyond a value which gives $h = 50$.

Choose values of t from 0 to 10. Find each corresponding value of h by substituting into the equation.

t	h
0	0
1	5
2	12
3	21
4	32
5	45
6	60
7	77
8	96
9	117
10	140

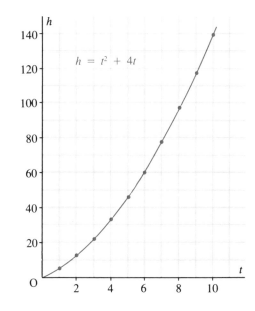

Draw a set of axes, with t horizontal and h vertical. Plot the points and join them with a smooth curve.

b) From the graph, when $t = 7.5$, $h \doteq 85$
The rocket is about 85 m high 7.5 s after blast-off.

c) From the graph, when $h = 50$, $t \doteq 5$
The rocket takes just over 5 s to reach a height of 50 m.

Recall that when graphing a linear relation, only two points are needed. For a non-linear relation, several points are needed to draw its graph.

EXERCISES 8-5

Ⓐ

1. Classify each graph as representing a linear relation or a non-linear relation.

   a)   b)   c)   d)

   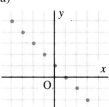   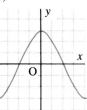   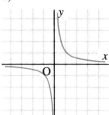   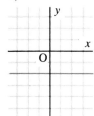

Ⓑ

2. A car, improperly parked, begins to coast down a hill. It rolls d metres in t seconds. The relation between d and t is $d = \frac{1}{2}t^2$.
   a) Make a table of values for t between 0 and 15.
   b) Graph the relation defined by this equation.
   c) Find how far the car rolls in 7.5 s.
   d) Find how long it takes the car to roll 75 m.

3. The height h metres of a pebble t seconds after it is dropped from a height of 335 m is given by this equation. $h = 335 - 4.9t^2$
   a) Make a table of values for t between 0 and 9.
   b) Graph the relation defined by this equation.
   c) How far is the pebble from the ground 4.5 s after it is dropped?
   d) How long after it is dropped is the pebble 90 m from the ground?

4. At 27°C, the pressure P kilopascals and the volume V litres of a sample of oxygen are related by this equation.
   $PV = 300$
   a) Make a table of values for P from 100 to 1000.
   b) Graph the relation defined by this equation.
   c) Find the pressure when the volume is 1.5 L.
   d) Find the volume when the pressure is 250 kPa.

5. The speed v kilometres per hour at which a vehicle was travelling can be estimated from the length l metres of the skid marks it produced when it braked. The equation is $v = -7 + 8.2\sqrt{l}$.
   a) Graph the relation defined by this equation, for values of l between 50 and 300.
   b) From the graph, find the lengths of the skid marks for a car that was travelling at these speeds when it braked.
      i)   80 km/h   ii)   90 km/h   iii) 125 km/h
   c) Find the speeds at which a car was travelling when it braked, if it produced skid marks of these lengths.
      i)   90 m   ii)   150 m   iii) 210 m

6. An aircraft travelling at x kilometres per hour uses fuel at a rate of y litres per hour. The equation relating x and y is $y = 0.01x^2 + 5x + 100$.
   a) Graph the relation defined by this equation, for values of x between 200 and 600.
   b) Find the speed of the aircraft for each rate of fuel consumption.
      i)   2000 L/h   ii)   3000 L/h   iii) 4000 L/h
   c) Find the fuel consumption for each speed of the aircraft.
      i)   325 km/h   ii)   475 km/h   iii) 550 km/h

7. The area A square centimetres of an equilateral triangle of side length x centimetres is given by this formula.
   $$A = \frac{\sqrt{3x^2}}{4}$$
   a) Graph the relation defined by this equation.
   b) If the side length doubles, by what factor does the area increase?

8. A bacterial culture is set up at 12 noon. The number N of bacteria in a culture t hours after it was set up is given by this equation.
   $$N = 1000(2^t)$$
   a) Graph the relation defined by this equation, for values of t between 3 and 9.
   b) Find the number of bacteria at each time.
      i)   4:30 P.M.   ii)   6:45 P.M.   iii) 8:15 P.M.
   c) Find the time at which the culture would contain each number of bacteria.
      i)   5000   ii)   50 000   iii) 100 000

Ⓒ

9. The area A square centimetres of a rectangle of length w centimetres and perimeter 50 cm is given by this formula. $A = 25w - w^2$
   a) Make a table of values using values of w between 0 and 25.
   b) Graph the relation defined by this equation.
   c) From the graph, find the length of the rectangle that has the greatest area.

10. The volume V cubic centimetres of a rectangular prism with a square base of side length s centimetres, and a surface area of 512 cm² is given by this formula.
    $$V = 128s - \frac{1}{2}s^3$$
    a) Make a table of values using values of s between 0 and 15.
    b) Graph the relation defined by this equation.
    c) From the graph, find the length of a side of the base of the prism with the greatest volume.

11. The numbers 3 and 1.5 have the property that their sum equals their product.
    a) Find three more pairs of numbers whose sum equals their product.
    b) Graph the relation between those numbers.
    c) If (x,y) is an ordered pair belonging to this relation, write an equation relating x and y.

12. Write a relation, in terms of x and y, between all numbers whose difference equals their product.

COMPUTER POWER

Creating a Table of Values

To graph a relation, given its defining equation, we must evaluate the expression on the right side of the equation for many values of the variable. This can be tedious if the relation is non-linear, and many points have to be plotted to draw the graph.

The following computer program will generate a table of values for the equation on page 292 which relates the dip of a diving board to the mass of the person on the board. The program can be easily modified to generate a table of values for any other equation.

```
100 REM *** TABLE OF VALUES ***
110 PRINT:INPUT "WHAT IS THE FIRST VALUE OF X? ";X1
120 INPUT "WHAT IS THE CHANGE IN X? ";CX
130 INPUT "WHAT IS THE LAST VALUE OF X? ";X2
140 PRINT:PRINT "VALUEOF X","VALUE OF EXPRESSION"
150 FOR X=X1 TO X2 STEP CX
160    Y=0.00001*X*X*X+0.0005*X*X
170     PRINT X,Y
180 NEXT X
190 END
```

The program assumes that the equation is written in terms of x. For example, the equation given on page 292 is $d = 0.000\,01m^3 + 0.0005m^2$. The program interprets this equation as $y = 0.000\,01x^3 + 0.0005x^2$. This, of course, makes no difference to the numbers in the table of values.

When the program is run, the computer asks for the first value of x in the table, the change in x, and the last value of x. To generate the table on page 292, enter 0 for the first value of x, 25 for the change in x, and 100 for the last value of x. The output appears as follows.

```
WHAT IS THE FIRST VALUE OF X? 0
WHAT IS THE CHANGE IN X? 25
WHAT IS THE LAST VALUE OF X? 100
```

VALUE OF X	VALUE OF EXPRESSION
0	0
25	.46875
50	2.5
75	7.03125
100	15

Notice that the computer calculates the values exactly, and does not round all the results to the same number of decimal places.

To modify the program to print tables of values for other relations, it is necessary to change one line in the program. To see the line which must be changed, type LIST 160 and press RETURN. The computer will print the following line on the screen.

```
160 Y = 0.00001*X*X*X*X + 0.0005*X*X
```

This is the line which instructs the computer to evaluate the expression in the equation on page 292. Suppose we want to use the program to generate a table of values for the equation on page 293 for the height of the rocket. Type the following line exactly as it appears, and then press RETURN.

```
160 Y = X*X+4*X
```

You can now use the program to generate the table of values for this relation.

1. Use the program to generate the tables of values on pages 292 and 293.

2. Use the program to generate the tables of values for some of the exercises in *Exercises 8-5*. For each exercise, the line which must be changed is given.
    a) Exercise 2.   ` 160 Y = 0.5*X*X `
    b) Exercise 3.   ` 160 Y = 335 - 4.9*X*X `
    c) Exercise 4.   ` 160 Y = 300/X `
    d) Exercise 5.   ` 160 Y = -7 + 8.2*SQR(X) `
    e) Exercise 6.   ` 160 Y = 0.01*X*X + 5*X + 100 `
    f) Exercise 7.   ` 160 Y = SQR(3)*X*X/4 `
    g) Exercise 8.   ` 160 Y = 1000*2^X `
    h) Exercise 9.   ` 160 Y = 25*X - X*X `
    i) Exercise 10.   ` 160 Y = 128*X - 0.5*X*X*X `

3. The depth of a well can be estimated by dropping a stone into it and timing the number of seconds it takes before you hear the splash. The depth d metres is given by this formula.
    $$d = 4.9t^2 - 0.015t^3$$
    a) Use the program to obtain a table of values, and then graph the relation. Use the following line in the program.
       ` 160 Y = 4.9*X*X - 0.015*X*X*X `
    b) How deep is the well for the following times?
       i) 2.5 s   ii) 4.5 s   iii) 9.2 s
    c) What is the time interval for wells with these depths?
       i) 200 m   ii) 800 m   iii) 2000 m

8-6 WRITING EQUATIONS

When an airplane reaches its cruising altitude, it flies at a constant speed of 600 km/h. There is a relation between the distance travelled and the time taken. This relation can be illustrated with a table of values.

Time (h)	Distance (km)
1	600
2	1200
3	1800
4	2400
5	3000

After 1 h, the plane has travelled 600 km.
After 2 h, the plane has travelled 1200 km.
After 3 h, the plane has travelled 1800 km.

How could we find the distance travelled if we knew the time taken? We need to find a relation between the time taken and the distance travelled.

From the table of values, we see that the distance travelled is always 600 times the time taken.

If we let t hours represent the time taken, then the distance travelled is $600t$ kilometres.

If we let d kilometres represent the distance travelled, then $d = 600t$.

The equation $d = 600t$ represents the relation between the distance travelled in kilometres and the time taken in hours for an airplane travelling at a constant speed of 600 km/h.

If we want to know how far the airplane has travelled in 3.5 h, we substitute 3.5 for t in the equation.

$$d = 600t$$
$$= 600(3.5)$$
$$= 2100$$

The airplane travelled 2100 km in 3.5 h.

Example 1. Each table of values illustrates a relation between x and y. Write an equation to describe each relation.

a)

x	y
0	0
1	4
2	8
3	12
4	16

$y = 4x$

b)

x	y
0	0
2	-1
4	-2
6	-3
8	-4

$-\frac{1}{2}x = y$

c)

x	y
0	-3
1	-2
2	-1
3	0
4	1

$y = x - 3$

Solution. a) From the table of values, we can see that each y-value is 4 times the corresponding x-value. Expressing this relation as an equation, $y = 4x$.

b) From the table of values, we can see that each y-value is opposite in sign to the corresponding x-value.

Also, each y-value is one-half the corresponding x-value. Expressing these facts in an equation, $y = -\frac{1}{2}x$.

c) From the table of values, we can see that each y-value is 3 less than the corresponding x-value. Expressing this relation as an equation, $y = x - 3$.

Example 2. Suppose this pattern were continued.

   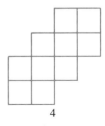

    1   2   3   4

a) Discuss how the pattern is produced.
b) How many squares would there be on the 10th diagram?
c) How many squares would there be on the 100th diagram?
d) Let x represent the number of a diagram. Let y represent the number of squares on the diagram. Write an equation relating x and y.

Solution. a) Each additional diagram has 3 squares added to the top right-hand corner of the previous diagram. Make a table of values showing the number of each diagram and the number of squares it contains. Look for a pattern in the table. As the number of the diagram increases by 1, the number of squares increases by 3. That is, each additional diagram has 3 more squares than the previous diagram.

Number of diagram	Number of squares
1	1
2	4
3	7
4	10

b) The 10th diagram will have 3(9) squares more than the 1st diagram, which has 1 square.
   Hence, the 10th diagram will have [3(9) + 1] squares, or 28 squares.

c) The 100th diagram will have [3(99) + 1] squares, or 298 squares.

d) The xth diagram will have [3(x − 1) + 1] squares.
   But the number of squares is represented by y.
   Hence, $y = 3(x − 1) + 1$
   $$= 3x − 3 + 1$$
   $$= 3x − 2$$
   The equation relating x and y is $y = 3x − 2$.

EXERCISES 8-6

Ⓐ

1. Write an equation to describe each relation.

$y = x(+1)$

a)

x	y
0	0
1	2
2	4
3	6
4	8

$y + 2x$

b)

x	y
0	0
3	−1
6	−2
9	−3
12	−4

$y = -\frac{1}{3}x$

c)

x	y
0	1
1	2
2	3
3	4
4	5

2. Write an equation to describe each relation.

$y = -x$

a)

x	y
0	0
1	1
2	2
3	3
4	4

$y = x$

b)

x	y
0	2
1	3
2	4
3	5
4	6

$y = x + 2$

c)

x	y
0	0
1	−1
2	−2
3	−3
4	−4

3. Suppose this pattern were continued.

1   2   3   4

a) How many triangles would there be on the 10th diagram?
b) How many triangles would there be on the 18th diagram?
c) Let x represent the number of a diagram. Let y represent the number of triangles in the diagram. Write an equation relating x and y.

B)

4. Write an equation to describe each relation.

a)

x	y
0	0
1	1
2	4
3	9
4	16

$y = x^2$

b)

x	y
0	5
1	4
2	3
3	2
4	1

$y = 5 - x$
$x + 5 - y$

c)

x	y
−10	5
−8	4
−6	3
−4	2
−2	1

$y = -\frac{1}{2}x$

5. Suppose this pattern were continued.

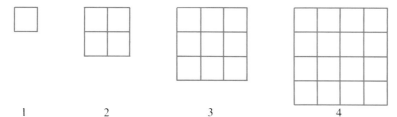

   1   2   3   4

a) How many squares would there be on the 12th diagram?
b) How many squares would there be on the 20th diagram?
c) Let x represent the number of a diagram. Let y represent the number of squares in the diagram. Write an equation relating x and y.

6. Suppose this pattern were continued.

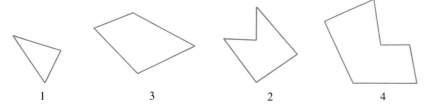

   1   3   2   4

a) How many sides would the 8th diagram have?
b) How many sides would the 30th diagram have?
c) Let x represent the number of a diagram. Let y represent the number of sides in the diagram. Write an equation relating x and y.

7. The base of a triangle is 4 cm.
a) Find the area of the triangle for each height.
   i)   6 cm   ii)   10 cm   iii) 2 cm   iv)   15 cm
b) Let x centimetres represent the height of the triangle. Let y square centimetres represent the area of the triangle. Write an equation relating x and y.

8. Suppose this pattern were continued.

 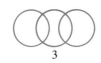 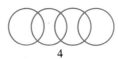

  1   2   3   4

  a) How many regions would there be on the 7th diagram?

  b) How many regions would there be on the 100th diagram?

  c) If *x* represents the number of a diagram and *y* represents the number of its regions, write an equation relating *x* and *y*.

9. Suppose this pattern were continued.

  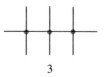 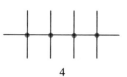

  1   2   3   4

  a) How many dots would there be on the 10th diagram?

  b) How many line segments would there be on the 10th diagram?

  c) How many dots would there be on the 100th diagram?

  d) How many line segments would there be on the 100th diagram?

  e) Let *x* represent the number of dots and *y* represent the number of line segments on a diagram. Write an equation relating *x* and *y*.

Ⓒ

10. Write an equation to describe each relation.

a)

x	*y*
0	1
1	2
2	5
3	10
4	17

b)

x	*y*
0	1
1	3
2	5
3	7
4	9

c)

x	*y*
0	−2
1	1
2	4
3	7
4	10

11. Suppose this pattern were continued.

   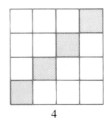

  1   2   3   4

  a) How many shaded squares would there be on the 10th diagram?

  b) How many unshaded squares would there be on the 10th diagram?

  c) Let *x* represent the number of shaded squares and let *y* represent the number of unshaded squares on a diagram. Write an equation relating *x* and *y*.

1. a) Plot these points. K($-4, -1$), L($-1, -4$), M(5,2), N(2,5)
   b) Draw these line segments. KL, LM, MN, NK
   c) What polygon have you drawn?

2. Where are the points with:
   a) x-coordinate -2
   b) y-coordinate 3
   c) x-coordinate positive, y-coordinate negative?

3. Write each relation as a set of ordered pairs.
   a)   b)

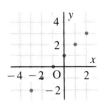   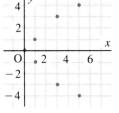

4. The graph shows the relation between the number of sides and the number of diagonals in a polygon.
   a) State how many diagonals each polygon has.
      i) a triangle   ii) a pentagon
      iii) a hexagon   iv) an octagon
   b) State how many sides a polygon has with the following number of diagonals.
      i) 2   ii) 9   iii) 27
   c) A heptagon has 7 sides. How many diagonals does it have?

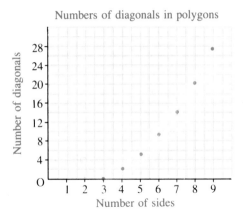

Numbers of diagonals in polygons

5. A ball was dropped from a height of 2 m. The heights to which it bounced were measured for the first 7 bounces. The results are shown in the table.

   a) Graph the relation defined by this table of values.
   b) What height does the ball reach after the sixth bounce?
   c) On what bounce is the height 0.82 m?
   d) For how many bounces did the ball reach a height greater than 75 cm?
   e) How many times did the ball bounce before the height of its bounce was half of its initial height?

Number of bounces	Height (m)
0	2.00
1	1.60
2	1.28
3	1.02
4	0.82
5	0.66
6	0.52
7	0.42

6. Experiments by psychologists have measured how much a person remembers of material that was learned. The number of days that passed since the material was learned and the amount recalled, as a percent, are shown in the chart.

Time (days)	1	5	15	30	60
Amount recalled (%)	84	71	61	56	54

a) Graph this information.
b) After how many days would you expect to recall only 75% of what you had learned for an examination?
c) How much are you likely to *forget* over the March break?

7. Graph the relation defined by each equation.
a) $3x + y = 9$
b) $5x - 3y = 15$
c) $y = 5x$
d) $y = 7 - 2x$

8. The numbers of students, s, and teachers, t, in a school are determined by this relation.

$$t = \frac{1}{23}s + 5$$

a) Graph the relation defined by this equation.
b) How many teachers are required for a school with 460 students?
c) How many students are there in a school having 10 teachers?

9. Write an equation to describe each relation.

a)

x	y
0	0
1	3
2	6
3	9
4	12

b)

x	y
0	-1
1	0
2	1
3	2
4	3

c)

x	y
0	0
4	-1
8	-2
12	-3
16	-4

10. Suppose this pattern were continued.

  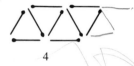

1   2   3   4

a) How many triangles would there be on the 10th diagram?
b) How many matchsticks would there be on the 10th diagram?
c) How many triangles would there be on the 20th diagram?
d) How many matchsticks would there be on the 20th diagram?
e) Let x represent the number of triangles in a diagram. Let y represent the number of matchsticks in the diagram. Write an equation relating x and y.

9 Geometry

Sami and Jane have a measuring tape and a compass.
How can they measure the width of a river they cannot
cross? (See Section 9-5, *Example 2*.)

9-1 WHAT IS GEOMETRY?

Geometry is all around us, as the photographs on these pages show.
Study each photograph and the question that accompanies it. The questions
and your answers involve some of the ideas and the language of
geometry.

Architecture
What shapes do you see?

Sports
Why do runners on an oval track start at
different places?

Nature
What is the shape of the horns?

Navigation
What measurements does a navigator make?

Art
How is the feeling of ''depth'' achieved?

Building and Decorating
What is the purpose of the weighted string?

The answers to these questions required knowledge of the following basic geometric concepts.

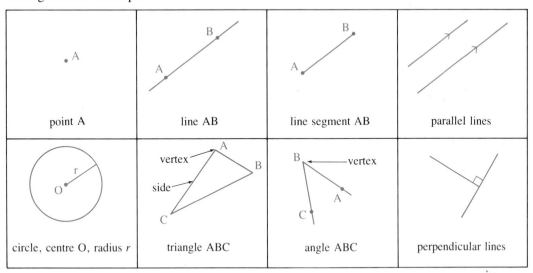

point A	line AB	line segment AB	parallel lines
circle, centre O, radius *r*	triangle ABC	angle ABC	perpendicular lines

The study of these concepts is the basis of geometry. The ancient Egyptians and Babylonians used geometric ideas to determine the areas of fields and the volumes of buildings such as temples and pyramids.

The word *geometry* comes from two Greek words *geos* and *metron* meaning earth measure. It was about 300 B.C. when the Greeks began to study geometry. Their contributions have influenced the study of the subject to the present time.

Example 1. Name all the line segments in this line.

Solution.   The line segments are AB, BC, and AC.

Problems in geometry often involve investigations of relationships among the basic geometric concepts.

Example 2. Find in how many points a line and a circle can intersect.

Solution.   Draw a diagram to show each case.

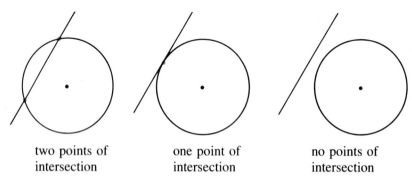

two points of   one point of   no points of
intersection   intersection   intersection

A line and a circle can intersect in 2 points, in 1 point, or not at all.

EXERCISES 9-1

Ⓐ

1. Collect some pictures that show geometry in the world around us.

2. Name all the line segments in this line.

3. Name all the angles in each figure.

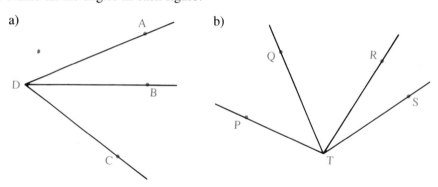

4. Name all the triangles in each figure.

a)

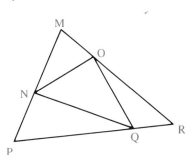

b)

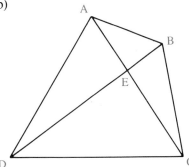

Ⓑ

5. Find in how many points two circles can intersect if:
   a) the circles have equal radii b) the circles have different radii.

6. Find in how many points two lines can intersect.

7. Find in how many points these figures can intersect.
   a) a line segment and a line b) a line and a triangle

8. Find the greatest number of points in which each pair of figures can intersect.
   a) a triangle and a circle b) two triangles c) a square and a circle

---

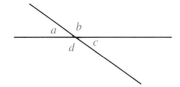 I N V E S T I G A T E

Two intersecting lines form two pairs of angles called *opposite angles*.

a and *c* are opposite angles.
b and *d* are opposite angles.

1. Draw two intersecting lines. Label and measure both pairs of opposite angles.

2. Repeat the procedure for another pair of intersecting lines.

3. Do pairs of opposite angles appear to have a special property?

4. Write a statement to describe a property of a pair of opposite angles formed when two lines intersect.

9-2 ANGLES AND INTERSECTING LINES

Angles are classified according to their measures in degrees.
One degree (1°) is $\frac{1}{360}$ of a complete rotation.

Measure	Angle	Example
Less than 90°	acute	
90°	right	
Between 90° and 180°	obtuse	
180°	straight	
Between 180° and 360°	reflex	

From the previous *INVESTIGATE*, you may have discovered that, in this situation, $a = c$ and $b = d$.

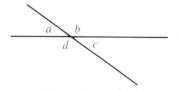

When two lines intersect, the opposite angles are equal.

Two angles with a sum of 180° are
supplementary angles.
ABC is a straight line.
$\angle ABD + \angle DBC = 180°$
$\angle ABD$ and $\angle DBC$ are supplementary.

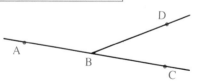

Example 1. ∠BOA and ∠AOC are
supplementary angles.
∠AOC = 65°
Find the measure of ∠BOA.

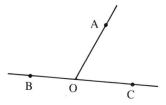

Solution. Since ∠BOA and ∠AOC are supplementary,
∠BOA + ∠AOC = 180°
∠BOA + 65° = 180°
∠BOA = 115°

Example 2. Find the angle measure indicated by each letter.

a) 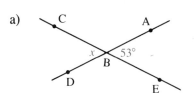   b)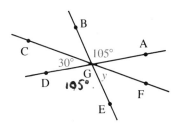

Solution. a) Since ∠CBD and ∠EBA are opposite angles,
∠CBD = ∠EBA
$x = 53°$

b) Since ∠DGE and ∠AGB are opposite angles,
∠DGE = ∠AGB
∠DGE = 105°
Since ∠CGF is a straight angle,
∠CGD + ∠DGE + ∠EGF = 180°
30° + 105° + y = 180°
135° + y = 180°
$y = 45°$

EXERCISES 9-2

1. Identify each angle as acute, right, obtuse, straight, or reflex.

a) 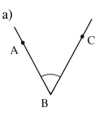   b) 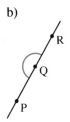   c) 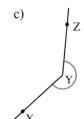   d)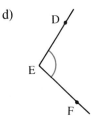

2. Name two pairs of opposite angles in each figure.

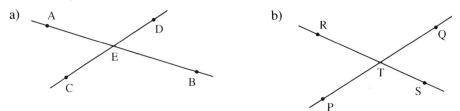

a) A D E C B

b) R Q T P S

3. Find the angle measure indicated by each letter.

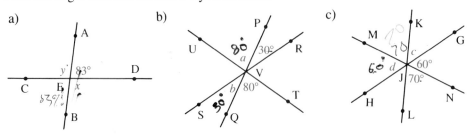

a) A y 83° D C E x B 83°

b) P U 80° 30° R a V b 80° T S Q

c) M K c G 70° 60° d J 70° H L N

(B)

4. Plot these points on a grid: P(8,2), Q(0, −2), R(2,4), and S(6, −4). Draw line segments PQ and RS. Measure the opposite angles formed by PQ and RS.

5. Plot each set of points on a grid. Draw each △ABC. Identify each angle.
   a) A(4,0), B(−3, −2), C(0,5)
   b) A(7, −1), B(2,2), C(−5,0)
   c) A(−4,8), B(−1,2), C(7,6)

6. Two lines intersect to form four equal angles. What can be said about the lines?

7. Find in how many points a line and two parallel lines can intersect. Consider all possible cases.

8. Angle ABC has a measure of 74°. What is the measure of reflex angle ABC?

9. Find the value of each letter.

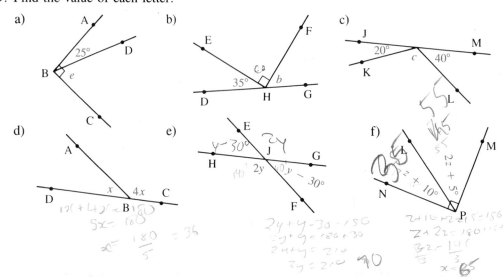

a) A 25° D B e C

b) E F 35° b D H G

c) J 20° M K c 40° L

d) A D x 4x B C

e) E y − 30° J 2y G H y − 30° F

f) L M z + 10° 2z + 5° N P

Ⓒ

10. Find in how many points these figures can intersect. Consider all possible cases.
    a) two parallel lines and a circle
    b) two parallel lines and a line segment

11. The adjacent numbers on the two scales of a double-scale protractor add up to 180°. Explain why.

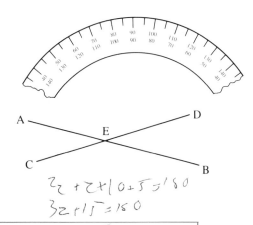

12. a) Two line segments AB and CD intersect at point E. Explain why each statement is true.
       i) $\angle AED + \angle DEB = 180°$
       ii) $\angle AED + \angle AEC = 180°$
    b) Use the equations in part a) to conclude that $\angle DEB = \angle AEC$.

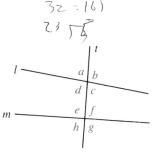

$2z + 2z + 10 + 5 = 180$

$3z + 15 = 180$

$3z = 165$

$z = 55$

INVESTIGATE

A line that intersects two or more lines is called a *transversal*. When a transversal intersects two other lines, the pairs of angles formed are described by their relative positions.

Transversal *t* intersects lines *l* and *m*.

There are two pairs of *alternate angles*: *d* and *f*; *c* and *e*.
There are four pairs of *corresponding angles*: *a* and *e*; *b* and *f*; *d* and *h*; *c* and *g*.
There are two pairs of *interior angles*: *d* and *e*; *c* and *f*.

When a transversal intersects two parallel lines, each pair of angles described above has a special property.

1. Draw two parallel lines and a transversal. Label and measure:
   a) each pair of alternate angles
   b) each pair of corresponding angles
   c) each pair of interior angles.

2. Repeat the procedure for another pair of parallel lines.

3. What property does each pair of angles appear to have?

4. Write a statement to describe for parallel lines a property of:
   a) a pair of alternate angles
   b) a pair of corresponding angles
   c) a pair of interior angles.
Do these properties hold for non-parallel lines?

$3z + 15 = 180$

$z + 10 + 2z + 5 = 90$

$90 - 5 - 10$

$2z + 22$

$3z$

75

$z = 25$

$z = 55$

THE MATHEMATICAL MIND

Misleading Diagrams

Maurits Cornelis Escher was an artist, who was born in the Netherlands in 1898. He travelled extensively through Europe before his death in 1972.

Much of Escher's work is unique; one of his many talents was the ability to design and draw "impossible" pictures. What is impossible in the illustration of the waterfall?

When geometric figures are combined, the resulting diagrams can sometimes deceive the eye. This can happen in different ways.

Reversing Diagrams
Some diagrams can be seen in different ways. What do *you* see?

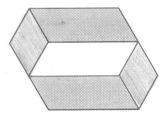

Optical Illusions
An optical illusion can lead to a false conclusion. Are the colored circles the same size?

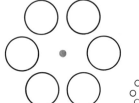

Impossible Objects
A two-dimensional diagram can be drawn of a three-dimensional object that cannot exist. Do you think you could make this object?

Subjective Contours
Sometimes the outline of a figure is visible when it is not really there. Do you see a white triangle? Is it really there?

These examples show how careful we must be when drawing conclusions from a diagram.

QUESTIONS

1. Are the diagonal line segments parallel?

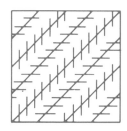

2. Can you make a physical model of this drawing?

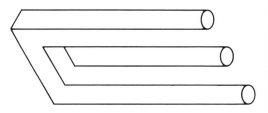

3. Is there really a white square?

4. Do you see a white triangle? Are the line segments equal in length?

5. Can you make a model from this diagram?

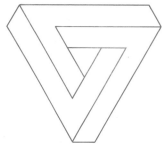

6. Do you see two heads or a birdbath?

7. How many ways does this box open?

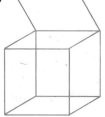

8. Are the horizontal lines "bent"?

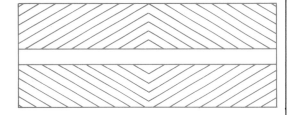

9-3 ANGLES AND PARALLEL LINES

Two lines, in the same plane, that never meet are called *parallel lines.*
From the previous *INVESTIGATE*, you may have discovered the following properties of parallel lines.

When a transversal intersects two parallel lines, the alternate angles are equal.

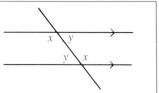

When a transversal intersects two parallel lines, the corresponding angles are equal.

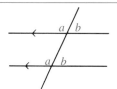 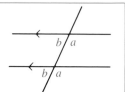

When a transversal intersects two parallel lines, the interior angles are supplementary.

$a + b = 180°$

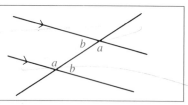

Example 1. Find the angle measure indicated by each letter.

a)

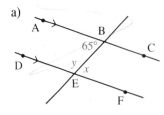

b)

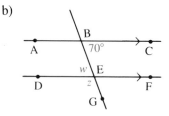

Solution.

a) Since ∠FEB and ∠ABE are alternate angles between parallel lines,
∠FEB = ∠ABE
$x = 65°$
Since ∠DEF is a straight angle,
$y + x = 180°$
$y + 65° = 180°$
$y = 115°$

b) Since ∠DEB and ∠CBE are alternate angles between parallel lines,
∠DEB = ∠CBE
$w = 70°$
Since ∠GEB is a straight angle,
$w + z = 180°$
$70° + z = 180°$
$z = 110°$

Example 2. Find the angle measure indicated by each letter.

a)

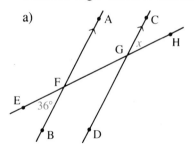

b)

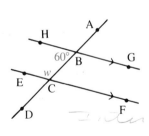

Solution.

a) Since ∠FGD and ∠EFB are corresponding angles between parallel lines,

∠FGD = ∠EFB
   = 36°

Since ∠CGH and ∠FGD are opposite angles,

∠CGH = ∠FGD
   x = 36°

b) Since ∠GFJ and ∠KJB are corresponding angles between parallel lines,

∠GFJ = ∠KJB
   = 55°

∠GFI = ∠GFJ + ∠JFI
   = 55° + 40°
   = 95°

Since ∠GFI and ∠FIJ are interior angles between parallel lines,

∠GFI + ∠FIJ = 180°
   95° + y = 180°
       y = 85°

In this example, can you suggest other ways of finding the values of *x* and *y*?

EXERCISES 9-3

1. In this figure
   a) Name two pairs of alternate angles.
   b) Name four pairs of corresponding angles.
   c) Name two pairs of interior angles.

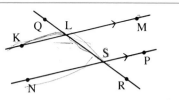

2. Find the angle measure indicated by each letter.

a)

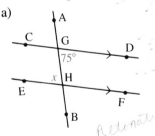

b)

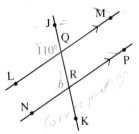

c)

B

3. Find the angle measure indicated by each letter.

a)

b)

c)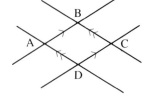
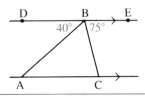

4. Can two intersecting lines both be parallel to a third line? Draw a diagram to support your answer.

5. Can two intersecting lines both be perpendicular to a third line in the same plane? Draw a diagram to support your answer.

6. In how many points can three lines intersect?

C

7. a) Use the diagram to help you explain how you know that in parallelogram ABCD, ∠ABC = ∠ADC.
   b) Use part a) and a property of interior angles to explain why ∠A = ∠C.

8. From the information given in the diagram, find the measures of the angles in △ABC. What is the sum of their measures?

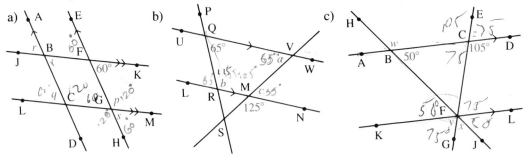

👤 **INVESTIGATE**

1. Draw a triangle with all of its angles less than 90°. Measure the angles. Add these measurements.

2. Draw a triangle with one angle of 90°. Measure the angles. Add these measurements.

3. Draw a triangle with one angle greater than 90°. Measure the angles. Add these measurements.

4. Do the angles of a triangle appear to have a special property?

5. Write a statement to describe a property of the angles of a triangle.

COMPUTER POWER

The Exterior Angles of a Triangle

If the sides of a triangle are extended in one direction, an *exterior angle* is formed at each vertex.

In Turtle Geometry, a small "turtle" which looks like this ▲ can be instructed to construct a triangle by a series of *Logo* commands such as these.

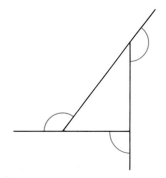

Verbal Command	Logo Command
Start at A.	HOME
Turn right 127°.	RT 127
Move forward 100 units (along AB).	FD 100
Turn right 143°.	RT 143
Move forward 80 units (along BC).	FD 80
Turn right 90°.	RT 90
Move forward 60 units (along CA).	FD 60

Graphics Display

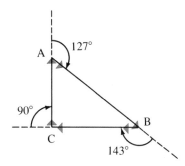

Observe that the turtle turns through the exterior angles as it traces the triangle.

1. What is the total number of degrees through which the turtle turned in drawing the triangle?

2. Write another set of Logo commands that cause the turtle to trace a triangle. (Ensure that the turtle starts and finishes facing upward.) What is the sum of the angles through which your turtle turned?

3. Write a statement about the sum of the three exterior angles of a triangle.

4. What is the sum of the exterior angle and the interior angle at any vertex of a triangle?

5. What is the sum of all three exterior and all three interior angles of a triangle?

6. Use your answers to *Questions 3* and *5* to make a statement about the sum of three interior angles of a triangle.

9-4 ANGLES AND TRIANGLES

Triangles may be classified by the measures of their angles.

Description	Triangle	Example
all angles are acute	acute triangle	
one angle is 90°	right triangle	
one angle is obtuse	obtuse triangle	

From the previous *INVESTIGATE*, you may have discovered that the sum of the measures of the angles of a triangle is 180°.

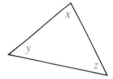

$$x + y + z = 180°$$

For convenience, we delete the phrase ''of the measures'' in the statement above.

> The sum of the angles in any triangle is 180°.

Example. Find the angle measure indicated by each letter.

a)

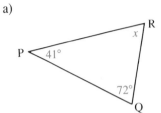

b)

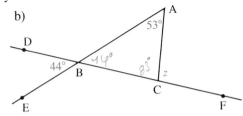

Solution. a) Since the sum of the angles in △PQR is 180°,

$$x + 41° + 72° = 180°$$
$$x + 113° = 180°$$
$$x = 67°$$

b) Since ∠ABC and ∠DBE are opposite angles,

∠ABC = ∠DBE
= 44°

Since the sum of the angles in △ABC is 180°,
$$\angle ABC + \angle BCA + \angle CAB = 180°$$
$$44° + \angle BCA + 53° = 180°$$
$$\angle BCA + 97° = 180°$$
$$\angle BCA = 83°$$
Since ∠BCF is a straight angle,
$$\angle BCA + \angle ACF = 180°$$
$$83° + z = 180°$$
$$z = 97°$$

EXERCISES 9-4

1. Identify each triangle as acute, right, or obtuse.

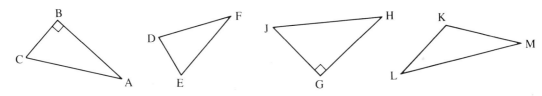

2. Each pair of angles represents the measures of two angles in a triangle. In each case, find the third angle and identify the triangle.
   a) 35°, 65°   b) 70°, 75°   c) 40°, 25°   d) 60°, 30°

3. Find the angle measure indicated by each letter.

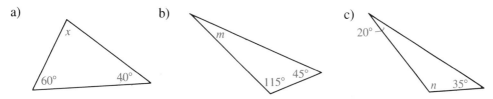

a)   b)   c)

B

4. Plot each set of points on a grid. Draw and identify each triangle.
   a) A(4,4), B(7,0), C(0, −2)
   b) D(5,0), E(−4,6), F(−3,1)
   c) G(−1,6), H(7,4), J(2,1)
   d) K(−4,0), L(1,4), M(2, −2)

5. Cut any triangle from a piece of paper. Label the vertices A, B, and C.
   a) Tear off the corners at A and B and fit them at C, as shown in the diagram. Explain your findings.
   b) Can you fit the angles of a triangle in this way without cutting or tearing?

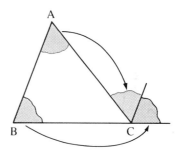

6. Find the angle measure indicated by each letter.

a)

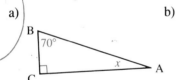

b)

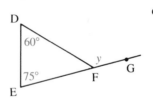

c)

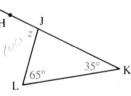

d)

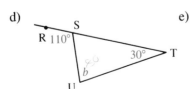

e)

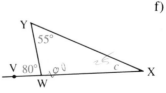

f)

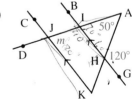

7. State whether a triangle can be drawn having these angles. Give reasons for your answers.
   a) 2 acute angles
   b) 3 acute angles
   c) 2 right angles
   d) 2 obtuse angles
   e) a straight angle
   f) 1 right angle, 1 obtuse angle

8. Explain why every triangle must have at least two acute angles.

9. a) State how many triangles there are in this figure.
   b) Name those that are:
      i)   acute triangles
      ii) right triangles
      iii) obtuse triangles.

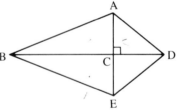

10. In this figure
    a) If the value of x is known, how can the value of y be found?
    b) Find the value of y for each value of x.
       i) x = 30°   ii) x = 50°   iii) x = 87°
    c) If the value of y is known, how can the value of x be found?
    d) Find the value of x for each value of y.
       i) y = 110°   ii) y = 160°   iii) y = 175°
    e) Find an equation relating x and y.

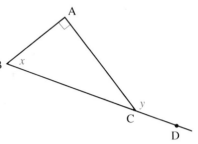

11. Find each value of x.

a)

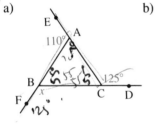

b)

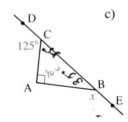

c)

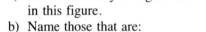

d)

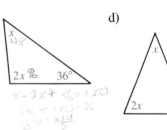

Ⓒ

12. Find the sum of the shaded angles in each figure.

a) b) 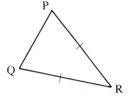 c)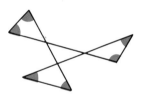

13. What is the sum of the measures of the interior angles of a quadrilateral?

 I N V E S T I G A T E

A triangle with at least two sides equal
is an isosceles triangle.

PR = QR

1. Draw an isosceles △PQR using ruler and compasses.
    ● Draw two equal line segments PR and QR, with the same end point R.
    ● Join PQ.
    ● Measure ∠RPQ and ∠PQR.

2. Repeat the procedure with an isosceles triangle of a different size.

3. Do the angles opposite the equal sides of an isosceles triangle appear to
    have a special property?

4. Write a statement to describe a property of the angles opposite the equal
    sides of an isosceles triangle.

A triangle with three sides equal is an
equilateral triangle.

LM = MN = NL

5. Draw an equilateral △LMN using ruler and compasses.
    ● Draw any line segment LM.
    ● With the distance between compasses point and pencil equal to the length
      of LM, put compasses point on L and draw an arc. Then put compasses
      point on M and draw an arc to intersect the first arc.
    ● Label the intersection of the arcs, N. Join LN and MN.
    ● Measure ∠LMN, ∠MNL, and ∠NLM.

6. Repeat the procedure with an equilateral triangle of a different size.

7. Do the angles of an equilateral triangle appear to have a special property?

8. Write a statement to describe a property of the angles of an equilateral
    triangle.

 **PROBLEM SOLVING**

Draw a Diagram

A 6.5 m ladder is placed against a wall with the foot of the ladder 2.5 m from the wall. If the top of the ladder slips 0.8 m, how far will the bottom of the ladder slip?

Understand the problem
- How long is the ladder?
- How far from the wall is the top of the ladder? the foot of the ladder?
- How far down the wall does the ladder slip?
- What are you asked to find?

Think of a strategy
- Try drawing a diagram to show the lengths and distances.

Carry out the strategy
- Draw a diagram showing the ladder before slipping (AB) and after slipping (A′B′).
- Mark the known lengths and distances on the diagram.
- We need to find the length BB′. We cannot find this directly. So, find AC, then A′C, then B′C.

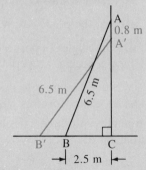

- Use the Pythagorean theorem in △ABC.

  $AB^2 = BC^2 + AC^2$

  $6.5^2 = 2.5^2 + AC^2$

  $AC^2 = 6.5^2 - 2.5^2$

  $AC = \sqrt{6.5^2 - 2.5^2}$

  $ = 6$

  $A'C = AC - AA'$

  $ = 6 - 0.8$

  $ = 5.2$

Use the Pythagorean theorem in △A′B′C.

  $A'B'^2 = B'C^2 + A'C^2$

  $6.5^2 = B'C^2 + 5.2^2$

  $B'C^2 = 6.5^2 - 5.2^2$

  $B'C = \sqrt{6.5^2 - 5.2^2}$

  $ = 3.9$

  $BB' = B'C - BC$

  $ = 3.9 - 2.5$

  $ = 1.4$

The bottom of the ladder slips 1.4 m.

Look back
- Does a 1.4 m slip seem reasonable for a 0.8 m change in the height of the ladder?

Solve each problem

1. The Cougars lead a league of 5 teams and the Dolphins are last. The Bears are halfway between the Cougars and the Dolphins. If the Eagles are ahead of the Dolphins and the Stallions immediately behind the Bears, name the team that is second in the league.

2. During a game of blindfold bluff, Kevin walks 5 m north, 12 m east, 30 m south-west and 8 m north-west. How far is Kevin now from his starting position?

3. The surface area of a cube is 600 cm². The cube is cut into 64 smaller congruent cubes. What is the surface area of one of these cubes?

4. The 40 grade 9 students at Participation H.S. choose to play one or two of the three sports: football, basketball, and hockey. Nineteen play football, 16 play basketball, and 15 play hockey. Included in those numbers are the 6 students who play both football and hockey and 3 who play both football and basketball. How many students play both basketball and hockey?

5. A train leaves at 7:00 A.M. daily from Toronto bound for Vancouver. Simultaneously, another train leaves Vancouver for Toronto. The journey takes exactly 4 days in each direction. If a passenger boards a train in Vancouver, how many Vancouver bound trains will she pass en route to Toronto?

6. How many rectangles can be drawn on a grid of 9 equally spaced dots so that all the vertices are located on dots?

7. A rectangular park is 400 m long and 300 m wide. If it takes 14 min to walk around the perimeter once, how long would it take to walk across a diagonal of the park?

8. How can 10 chairs be arranged along the perimeter of a rectangular room so that there is an equal number of chairs along each wall?

9. The distances between a pine tree, an oak tree, and a maple tree were measured and recorded.

From	To	Distance
Pine	Maple	150 m
Pine	Oak	100 m
Maple	Oak	45 m

Were the measurements correct? Explain your answer.

10. A rectangular field is twice as long as its width. Its perimeter is less than 1.2 km. What does this tell you about the area of the field?

9-5 ISOSCELES AND EQUILATERAL TRIANGLES

In the previous section, triangles were classified according to the measures of their angles. Triangles are also classified according to the lengths of their sides.

Description	Triangle	Example
3 sides equal	equilateral triangle	
at least 2 sides equal	isosceles triangle	
no sides equal	scalene triangle	

From the previous *INVESTIGATE*, you may have discovered these properties of isosceles triangles and equilateral triangles.

In an isosceles triangle, the angles opposite the equal sides are equal.	In an equilateral triangle, the angles are equal and have a measure of 60°.

Example 1. Find the angle measure indicated by each letter.

a)

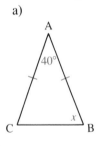

b)

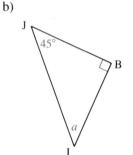

c)

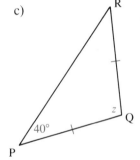

Solution. a) Since AB = AC, then ∠ACB = x
Since the sum of the angles in △ABC is 180°,

$$∠ABC + ∠BCA + ∠CAB = 180°$$
$$x + x + 40° = 180°$$
$$2x + 40° = 180°$$
$$2x = 140°$$
$$x = 70°$$

b) Since the sum of the angles in △BJI is 180°,

$$∠BJI + ∠JIB + ∠IBJ = 180°$$
$$45° + a + 90° = 180°$$
$$a + 135° = 180°$$
$$a = 45°$$

c) Since PQ = QR, ∠PRQ = 40°
Since the sum of the angles in △PQR is 180°,

$$∠PQR + ∠QRP + ∠RPQ = 180°$$
$$z + 40° + 40° = 180°$$
$$z + 80° = 180°$$
$$z = 100°$$

Example 2. Sami and Jane have only a measuring tape and a compass. How can they measure the width of a river that they cannot cross?

Solution. Sami and Jane draw a diagram to help them solve the problem.

On their side of the river, they mark a point S, opposite a large tree T on the far bank. ST represents the width of the river. After taking the compass bearing of T from S, Jane walks in a line perpendicular to ST. She walks until she reaches a point J, where the compass reading indicates that ∠SJT = 45°.

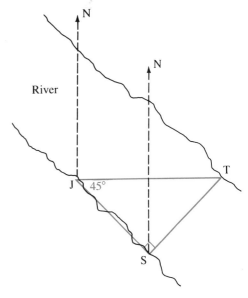

Since the sum of the angles in △SJT is 180°,

$$∠SJT + ∠JTS + ∠TSJ = 180°$$
$$45° + ∠JTS + 90° = 180°$$
$$∠JTS = 45°$$

Since ∠JTS = ∠SJT = 45°, △SJT is isosceles.
Hence, SJ = ST

Sami measures the distance SJ. This is the approximate width of the river.

EXERCISES 9-5

Ⓐ

1. Find the angle measure indicated by each letter.

a)

b)

c)

d)

e)
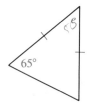

f)

g)

h)
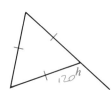

i)
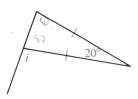

2. a) Are all equilateral triangles isosceles? b) Are all isosceles triangles equilateral?

Ⓑ

3. Find the angle measure indicated by each letter.

a)
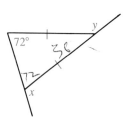

b)
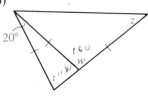

c)
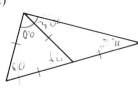

d)
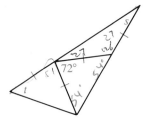

e)
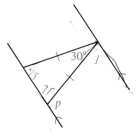

f)
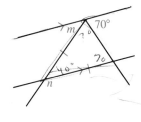

4. Draw an example of each triangle.
   a) an isosceles right triangle
   b) an isosceles obtuse triangle
   c) a scalene right triangle
   d) a scalene obtuse triangle
   e) an isosceles acute triangle
   f) a scalene acute triangle

5. In isosceles $\triangle ABC$
   a) If the value of x is known, how can the value of y be found?
   b) Find the value of y for each value of x.
      i) $x = 70°$ ii) $x = 25°$ iii) $x = 43°$
   c) If the value of y is known, how can the value of x be found?
   d) Find the value of x for each value of y.
      i) $y = 80°$ ii) $y = 110°$ iii) $y = 17°$
   e) Find an equation relating x and y.

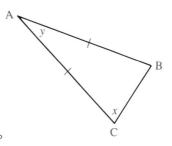

6. In this figure
   a) If the value of x is known, how can the value of y be found?
   b) Find the value of y for each value of x.
      i) $x = 60°$ ii) $x = 40°$ iii) $x = 26°$
   c) If the value of y is known, how can the value of x be found?
   d) Find the value of x for each value of y.
      i) $y = 40°$ ii) $y = 25°$ iii) $y = 81°$
   e) Find an equation relating x and y.

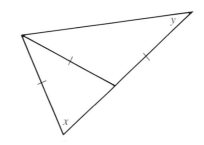

7. Amanda wanted to find the height of a cliff. She drew a diagram in which BC represented this height.

   Amanda had a clinometer for measuring $\angle CAB$. She moved away from the base of the cliff to a point A, where the clinometer showed $\angle CAB$ as 45°. Amanda measured the distance AB as 30 m. How high was the cliff?

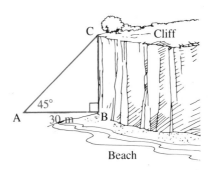

8. Michael and Julie are located at M and J respectively. A large tree is located at T on the opposite bank of the river. The distance MJ cannot be measured with the tape. Determine how Michael and Julie could find the approximate width MT of the river.

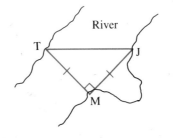

9. The measure of one angle of an isosceles triangle is given. Find the possible measures of the other angles.

a) 30°   b) 40°   c) 80°   d) 90°   e) 110°

 ©

10. A number of equilateral triangles are joined together with whole sides touching. The diagram shows a figure formed with four equilateral triangles. Find how many different figures can be formed for each number of equilateral triangles used.

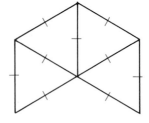

a) 3   b) 4   c) 5

11. Explain how to find the height of a tree with a right, isosceles, plastic triangle and a measuring tape.

 INVESTIGATE

1.   Draw △ABC with AB = 6 cm, BC = 8 cm, and CA = 12 cm.
   - Draw line segment AB 6 cm long.
   - With compasses point on B, and radius 8 cm, drawn an arc.
   - With compasses point on A, and radius 12 cm, draw an arc to intersect the first arc. Label the point of intersection C.
   - Draw BC and CA.

   Can you draw △PQR with PQ = 6 cm, QR = 8 cm, and RP = 12 cm such that its size and shape are different from △ABC?

2.   Draw △ABC with ∠A = 65°, ∠B = 85°, and ∠C = 30°. Can you draw △PQR with ∠P = 65°, ∠Q = 85°, and ∠R = 30° such that its size and shape are different from △ABC?

3.   Draw △ABC with AB = 8 cm, BC = 5 cm, and ∠B = 50°. Can you draw △PQR with PQ = 8 cm, QR = 5 cm, and ∠Q = 50° such that its size and shape are different from △ABC?

4.   Draw △ABC with AB = 7 cm, AC = 4 cm, and ∠B = 30°. Can you draw △PQR with PQ = 7 cm, PR = 4 cm, and ∠Q = 30° such that its size and shape are different from △ABC?

5.   Draw △ABC with ∠A = 62°, ∠B = 80°, and BC = 6 cm. Can you draw △PQR with ∠P = 62°, ∠Q = 80°, and QR = 6 cm such that its size and shape are different from △ABC?

   Which measurements of a triangle would you have to be given so that only one triangle could be drawn?

9-6 CONGRUENT TRIANGLES

If two geometric figures have the same size and shape, they are said to be *congruent*.

Two congruent triangles can be made to coincide because their corresponding sides and corresponding angles are equal.

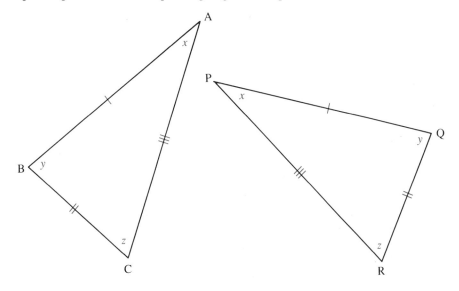

In △ABC and △PQR
  ∠A = ∠P, ∠B = ∠Q, ∠C = ∠R
  AB = PQ, BC = QR, CA = RP
  Therefore, △ABC ≅ △PQR
The sign ≅ is read "is congruent to".

The order in which the vertices are listed when pairs of triangles are congruent indicates which angles and sides correspond.

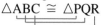

$\triangle ABC \cong \triangle PQR$

If the three sides and the three angles of two triangles are equal, then the triangles are congruent. However, it is not necessary to know this much information to show that two triangles are congruent.

From the previous *INVESTIGATE*, you may have discovered that given certain measurements of a triangle, there is only one possible triangle that can be drawn. This means that if two triangles are each described by this same set of measurements, those triangles must be equal in size and shape, and hence congruent.

The table shows three conditions. Any one of these conditions is sufficient to show that two triangles are congruent.

Conditions for Congruence	**Illustration**	**Abbreviation**
Three sides of one triangle are respectively equal to three sides of another triangle.		SSS (side, side, side)
Two sides and the contained angle of one triangle are respectively equal to two sides and the contained angle of another triangle.		SAS (side, angle, side)
Two angles and one side of one triangle are respectively equal to two corresponding angles and the corresponding side of another triangle.		AAS (angle, angle, side)

Example 1. For each pair of triangles, explain why they are congruent and state the condition for congruence. List the equal sides and the equal angles.

a)

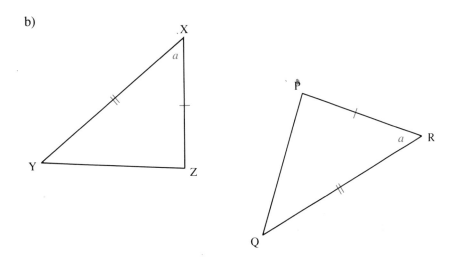

b)

Solution.   a) In △ABC and △DEF
    ∠A and ∠F are equal.
    Side AB and side FE are equal.
    ∠C and ∠D are equal.
    Therefore, △ABC ≅ △FED   AAS

Since △ABC is congruent to △FED,
BC = ED, AC = FD, and ∠B = ∠E

b) In △XYZ and △PQR
    ∠X and ∠R are equal.
    Side XZ and side RP are equal.
    Side XY and side RQ are equal.
    Therefore, △XYZ ≅ △RQP   SAS

Since △XYZ is congruent to △RQP,
YZ = QP, ∠Y = ∠Q, and ∠Z = ∠P

Example 2. △DEF is congruent to △GHK.
a) Find the length of HK.
b) Find the measures of the unmarked angles in the triangles.

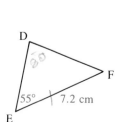

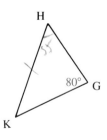

Solution. a) Since △DEF is congruent to △GHK, EF = HK.
But EF = 7.2 cm, so HK = 7.2 cm

b) Since △DEF ≅ △GHK
∠E = ∠H, so ∠H = 55°
∠G = ∠D, so ∠D = 80°
∠F = ∠K
But ∠F = 180° − 80° − 55°
= 45°
So ∠K = 45°

The conclusions from showing that two triangles are congruent
may be used to develop other geometric properties.

Example 3. P is any point on the perpendicular
bisector of line segment AB.
a) Explain why △PNA ≅ △PNB.
b) Explain why PA = PB.
c) State a conclusion about any point on the
perpendicular bisector of a line segment.

Solution. a) Join PA and PB.
In △PAN and △PBN
AN and BN are equal.
∠PNA and ∠PNB are both equal to 90°.
PN is a common side to both triangles.
Therefore, △PNA ≅ △PNB   SAS

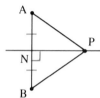

b) Since △PNA ≅ △PNB, corresponding sides are equal.
PA and PB are corresponding sides.
Hence, PA = PB

c) Any point on the perpendicular bisector of a line segment is equidistant
from the ends of the line segment.

EXERCISES 9-6

1. Name the equal angles and the equal sides in each figure.
   a) △MRX ≅ △CLP

   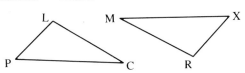

   b) △SQP ≅ △SQR

   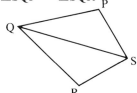

2. Name the equal sides and the equal angles.
   Figure PQRS ≅ figure XWZY

   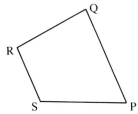

3. State which pairs of triangles are congruent. For those triangles that are congruent, state the condition for congruence.

   a)

   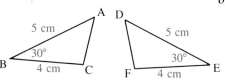

   b)

   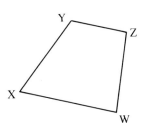

   c)

   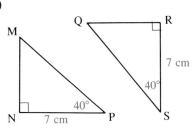

   d)

   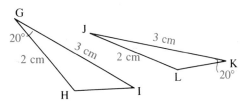

   e)

   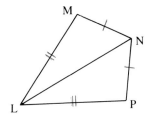

   f)

   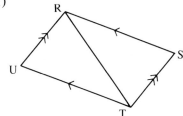

Ⓑ

4. Find pairs of congruent triangles and state the condition for congruence.

a)

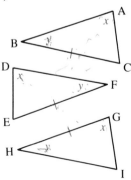

b)

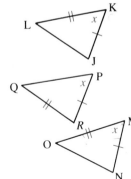

c)

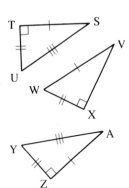

5. Find the value indicated by each letter.

a) △ABC ≅ △DEF

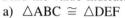
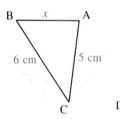

b) △PQR ≅ △STU

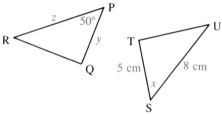

c) △JRC ≅ △MNP

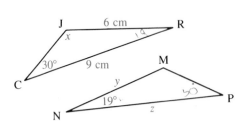

d) △FSN ≅ △TRC

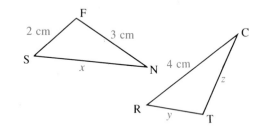

e) △BNA ≅ △AMB

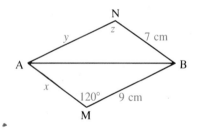

f) △PQB ≅ △RQA

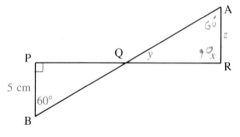

6. N is the midpoint of line segment AB.
   P is any point such that PA = PB.
   a) Explain why △PNA ≅ △PNB.
   b) Explain why
      ∠PNA = ∠PNB = 90°.
   c) State a conclusion about any point
      that is equidistant from the
      endpoints of a line segment.

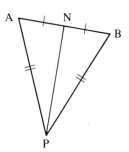

7. Explain why any point on the bisector of an angle is equidistant from the sides of
   the angle.

INVESTIGATE

1. Draw a right triangle on squared
   paper, so that the arms of the
   right angle lie along the lines of
   the paper.

2. Draw a square on each side of
   the triangle.

3. Find the area of each square.
   To find the area of the square on
   the hypotenuse (the longest
   side), you can count the small
   squares and parts of squares.
   Alternatively, you can divide the
   square into right triangles and
   use the formula for the area
   of a triangle.

4. Repeat *Questions 1* to *3* for
   different right triangles. What
   do you notice about the areas
   of the squares?

5. Write a statement to describe a
   property of the areas of the
   squares drawn on the sides of a
   right triangle.

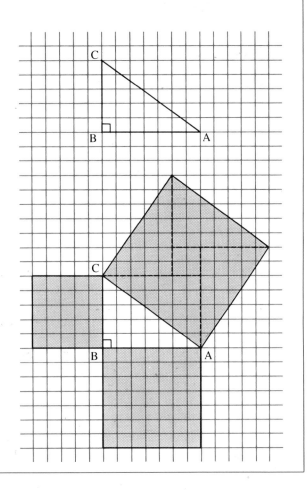

9-7 THE PYTHAGOREAN THEOREM

Anna and Lim are on a hike. They come to a field that is rectangular and measures 3.0 km by 1.6 km. Anna decides to take a short cut and walk diagonally across the field. Lim walks around two sides of the field. Who walks farther and by how much?

To find the distances walked, draw a diagram of the field.

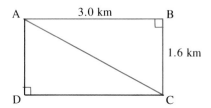

Lim walks (3.0 km + 1.6 km) or 4.6 km.

Anna walks along the path represented by AC. To find the length of the path, use the Pythagorean theorem. Recall that this theorem states that, for a right triangle, the area of the square on the hypotenuse is equal to the sum of the areas of the squares on the other two sides. You may have discovered this result in the previous *INVESTIGATE*.

Since the area of a square is equal to the square of the length of a side, the Pythagorean theorem is usually stated in terms of the lengths of the sides of a right triangle.

Pythagorean Theorem
For any right triangle with sides of lengths a, b, and c, where c is the hypotenuse, $c^2 = a^2 + b^2$

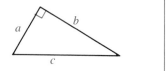

We can apply the Pythagorean Theorem in △ABC, on the facing page.

$$AC^2 = AB^2 + BC^2$$
$$= 3.0^2 + 1.6^2$$
$$= 11.56$$
$$AC = \sqrt{11.56}$$
$$= 3.4$$

Anna walks 3.4 km.

The difference between the distances walked is (4.6 km − 3.4 km) or 1.2 km.

Lim walks 1.2 km farther than Anna.

Example 1. Calculate each value of x.

a)

b)

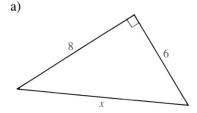

Solution.   a) $x^2 = 6^2 + 8^2$

$$= 36 + 64$$
$$= 100$$
$$x = \sqrt{100}$$
$$= 10$$

b) $17^2 = x^2 + 15^2$

$$289 = x^2 + 225$$
$$289 - 225 = x^2$$
$$64 = x^2$$
$$x = \sqrt{64}$$
$$= 8$$

When taking the square root, ignore the negative root because length cannot be negative.

Example 2. Find the length, to one decimal place, indicated by each letter.

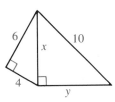

Solution.   Label the diagram.

Use the Pythagorean theorem in each triangle.

In △ABC

$$x^2 = 6^2 + 4^2$$
$$= 52$$
$$x = \sqrt{52}$$
$$\doteq 7.2$$

In △ACD

$$10^2 = x^2 + y^2$$
$$100 = 52 + y^2$$
$$48 = y^2$$
$$y = \sqrt{48}$$
$$\doteq 6.9$$

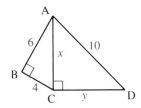

Example 3. The 12th hole at Sandy Dunes golf club is a right-angled "dog leg". What is the distance TG from the tee to the green?

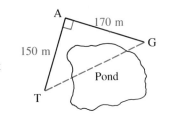

Solution. It follows from the Pythagorean theorem that

$$TG^2 = TA^2 + AG^2$$
$$= 150^2 + 170^2$$
$$= 51\ 400$$
$$TG = \sqrt{51\ 400}$$
$$\doteq 226.7$$

The distance from the tee to the green is approximately 227 m.

EXERCISES 9-7

(A)

1. Find the length indicated by each letter.

a)

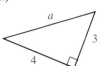

b)

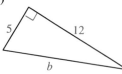

c)

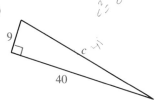

d)

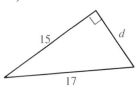

e)

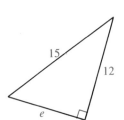

f)

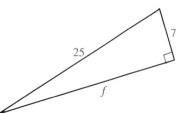

2. Find the length, to one decimal place, indicated by each letter.

a)

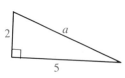

b)

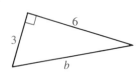

c)

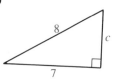

d)

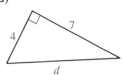

e)

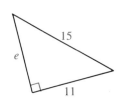

f)

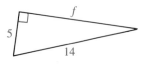

(B)

3. Find the length, to one decimal place, indicated by each letter.

a)

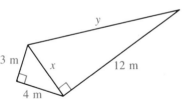

b)

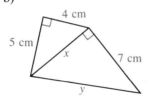

c)

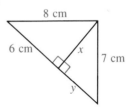

d)

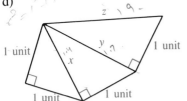

e)

f)

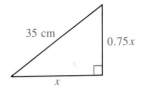

4. A guy wire is attached 50 m up a tower and 12 m from its base. Find the length of the guy wire to the nearest tenth of a metre.

5. A ladder, 8.2 m long, is placed with its foot 1.8 m from a wall. How high up the wall will the ladder reach? Give the answer to the nearest tenth of a metre.

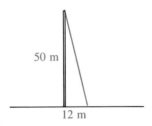

6. Find the length of the rafters for a building, which is 12 000 mm wide and has the peak of the roof 3000 mm above the ceiling. Give the answer to the nearest centimetre.

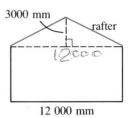

7. Can an umbrella 1.3 m long be packed flat in a box 1.1 m by 0.3 m? Give reasons for your answer.

8. A ramp is to be built from the top level of one parking garage to another. Calculate the length of the ramp to the nearest tenth of a metre.

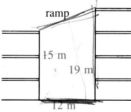

Ⓒ

9. Each colored square has sides 3 cm long.
   a) Find the lengths of the sides of the outer square, to the nearest millimetre.
   b) What percent of the outer square is covered by the five colored squares?

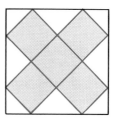

10. A TV set has a screen with a diagonal of length 66 cm. If the screen is 1.2 times as wide as it is high, find its width and height.

11. a) Show that the two isosceles triangles have the same area.
    b) Find another pair of isosceles triangles that have equal areas.

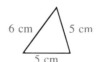

 CALCULATOR POWER

The Pythagorean Theorem

The evaluation of expressions such as $6^2 + 4^2$ (*Example 2*, page 339) is simplified with the use of a calculator.

For a scientific calculator, here is a possible keying sequence.

Key in: ⑥ x^2 ＋ ④ x^2 ＝ √ to display 7.2111026

If the calculator does not have a √ key, this symbol usually occurs above the x^2 key. Here is the keying sequence in this situation.

Key in: ⑥ x^2 ＋ ④ x^2 ＝ INV x^2

A 4-function calculator can be used to evaluate the expression. However, if the numbers are keyed in as they appear,

⑥ × ⑥ ＋ ④ × ④ ＝ √ , the result may be 12.649 111, which is wrong. If this happened, the calculator added the first 4 to the result of 6 times 6 before multiplying by the second 4.

This problem can be solved by rewriting the expression before keying it in.

$$6^2 + 4^2 = \left(\frac{6^2}{4} + 4\right)4$$

Key in: ⑥ × ⑥ ÷ ④ ＋ ④ × ④ ＝ √ , which gives the correct result.

The problem can also be solved by using the memory.

COMPUTER POWER

The Pythagorean Theorem

You can use the following program to find the length of any side
of a right triangle, given the lengths of the other two sides.

```
100 REM *** PYTHAGOREAN THEOREM ***
110 INPUT "DO YOU KNOW THE HYPOTENUSE (Y OR N)? ";Z$
120 IF Z$ = "Y" THEN 170
130 PRINT "ENTER THE LENGTHS OF THE SIDES"
140 INPUT "SEPARATED BY A COMMA: ";X,Y
150 Z = SQR (X * X + Y * Y)
160 PRINT "THE HYPOTENUSE IS: ";Z: GOTO 220
170 INPUT "ENTER THE HYPOTENUSE LENGTH: ";Z
180 INPUT "ENTER THE LENGTH OF THE OTHER SIDE: ";X
190 Y = SQR (Z * Z - X * X)
200 PRINT "THE LENGTH OF THE THIRD SIDE IS:"
210 PRINT Y
220 INPUT "PRESS S TO STOP, RETURN TO CONTINUE: ";Y$
230 IF Y$ <> "S" THEN 110
240 END
```

1. Use the program to find the length of the third side of each triangle.

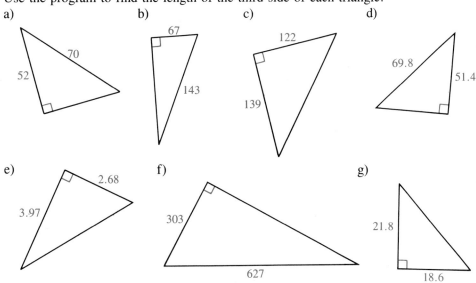

a) 52, 70

b) 67, 143

c) 122, 139

d) 69.8, 51.4

e) 2.68, 3.97

f) 303, 627

g) 21.8, 18.6

2. Find the third side of △ABC, where ∠ABC = 90°.
   a) AB = 2.37 cm, BC = 4.19 cm   b) AB = 7.66 m, BC = 7.66 m
   c) BC = 44.9 cm, AC = 59.3 cm   d) AB = 1.92 m, AC = 3.06 m

INVESTIGATE

Angles in a Circle

1. a) Draw a semicircle with diameter AB.
   b) Mark a point C on the semicircle. Join AC and BC.
   c) Measure ∠C.
   d) Repeat parts b) and c) for other positions of C on the semicircle. What do you notice?
   e) Repeat parts a) to d) for other semicircles.
   f) Write a statement to describe a property of angles in a semicircle.

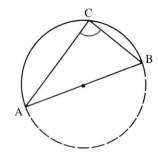

2. a) Mark two points P and Q.
   b) Use a plastic or cardboard right triangle. Position the triangle so that the points P and Q lie on the shorter sides of the triangle. Mark the position of the right angle.
   c) Repeat part b) several times and mark the different positions of the right angles.
   d) What do you notice about the dots marking the positions of the right angle?

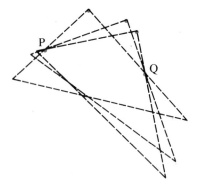

3. a) Draw a circle with any chord AB.
   b) Mark a point C on the circle. Join AC and BC.
   c) Measure ∠C.
   d) Repeat parts b) and c) for other positions of C on the circle. What do you notice?
   e) Repeat parts a) to d) for other circles.
   ● ∠C is called an inscribed angle. An angle is *inscribed* in a circle when its vertex is on the circle and its sides are chords.
   f) Write a statement to describe a property of angles inscribed in a circle.

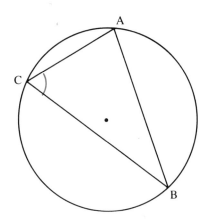

4. a) Mark two points A and B.
   b) Use a plastic or cardboard trian-
      gle.
   c) Choose one angle of the triangle
      and label it R. Position the tri-
      angle so that the points A and B
      lie on the arms of ∠R. Mark
      the position of ∠R.
   d) Repeat part c) several times and
      mark the different positions of ∠R.
   e) What do you notice about the
      dots marking the positions of ∠R?

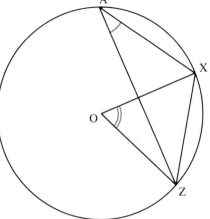

5. a) Draw a circle with any chord XZ.
   b) Mark the centre of the circle O
      and any point A on the
      circumference.
   c) Join OX, OZ, AX, and AZ.
   d) Measure ∠XAZ and ∠XOZ.
      What do you notice?
   e) Repeat parts a) to d) for other
      circles.
   • We say that ∠XAZ and ∠XOZ
     are subtended by the chord
     XZ. A chord *subtends* an angle
     when the angle is formed by
     line segments drawn from the
     ends of the chord.
   f) Write a statement to describe a property of angles in a circle, when
      one angle is at the centre of the circle, one angle is at the circumference,
      and both angles are subtended by the same chord.

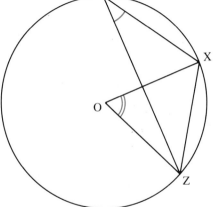

6. a) Draw a circle and mark 4 points
      A, B, C, and D on the
      circumference.
   b) Join AB, BC, CD, and DA.
   c) Measure ∠ABC and ∠ADC.
      What do you notice?
   d) Measure ∠BAD and ∠BCD.
      What do you notice?
   e) Repeat parts a) to d) for other
      circles.
   f) Write a statement to describe a property of opposite angles of a quadri-
      lateral, when the quadrilateral has its vertices on the circumference of
      a circle.

9-8 ANGLES IN A CIRCLE

To learn about angles in a circle, we must be familiar with some terms associated with these angles.

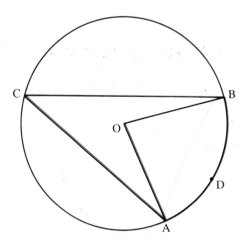

The part of a circle between any two points on the circumference is called an *arc*. An arc is named by its end points and any other point on it. Two points on the circumference denote 2 arcs, the longer one is the *major arc*, and the shorter one is the *minor arc*. The diagram shows major arc AB, or arc ACB, and minor arc AB, or arc ADB.

An angle with its vertex on the circumference and having chords for arms is called an *inscribed angle*. In the diagram, ∠ACB is an inscribed angle.

An angle with its vertex at the centre of the circle and having radii for arms is called a *sector angle*. In the diagram, ∠AOB is a sector angle.

Because ∠ACB and ∠AOB are formed by joining their vertices to the end points of the arc ADB, this arc ADB is said to *subtend* both ∠ACB and ∠AOB.

In a similar way, chord AB subtends both ∠ACB and ∠AOB.

When a quadrilateral is inscribed in a circle; that is, its vertices lie on the circumference of the circle, it is called a *cyclic quadrilateral*.

Quadrilateral EFGH is a cyclic quadrilateral.

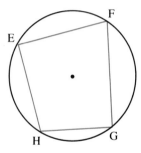

You may have discovered certain properties of the angles in a circle, from the previous *INVESTIGATE*. These properties are listed below.

Inscribed angles subtended by the same arc are equal.
∠PDQ = ∠PCQ;
∠DPC = ∠DQC

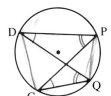

Inscribed angles subtended by a semicircle are 90°.
∠LMN = ∠LPN = 90°

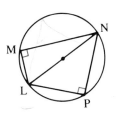

The measure of a sector angle is twice the measure of an inscribed angle subtended by the same arc.
∠EOF = 2∠EGF

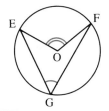

In a cyclic quadrilateral, the opposite angles are supplementary.
∠ABC + ∠ADC = 180°
∠BAD + ∠BCD = 180°

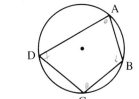

Example 1.   O is the centre of the circle.
Find the measure of each angle.
a) ∠AEB
b) ∠AOB

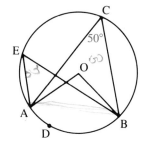

Solution.   a) Since ∠AEB and ∠ACB are subtended by arc ADB,
∠AEB = ∠ACB
= 50°

b) Since ∠AOB is the sector angle subtended by the same arc as the inscribed angle ∠ACB,
∠AOB = 2∠ACB
= 2(50°)
= 100°

Example 2.   BOC is a diameter of the circle.
Find the measure of each angle.
a) ∠ACB   b) ∠OAB

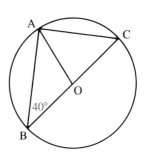

Solution.   a) Since ∠BAC is subtended by a semicircle,
∠BAC = 90°
Since the sum of the angles in △BAC is 180°,
∠BAC + ∠ACB + ∠CBA = 180°
90° + ∠ACB + 40° = 180°
∠ACB + 130° = 180°
∠ACB = 50°

b) Since OA and OB are radii of the circle,
OB = OA
Hence, △OAB is isosceles with ∠OAB = ∠OBA.
Therefore, ∠OAB = 40°

Example 3.   O is the centre of the circle.
Find the measure of each angle.
a) ∠DCO   b) ∠DEC

Solution.   a) Since ∠DCB and ∠DAB are opposite
angles in a cyclic quadrilateral,
∠DCB + ∠DAB = 180°
But ∠DCB = ∠DCO + ∠OCB
∠DCO + ∠OCB + ∠DAB = 180°
∠DCO + 44° + 98° = 180°
∠DCO + 142° = 180°
∠DCO = 38°

b) Since OD and OC are radii, △ODC is isosceles.
∠ODC = ∠DCO = 38°
Since the sum of the angles in △ODC is 180°,
∠DOC + ∠ODC + ∠DCO = 180°
∠DOC + 38° + 38° = 180°
∠DOC + 76° = 180°
∠DOC = 104°
Since inscribed ∠DEC and sector ∠DOC are subtended by the
same arc,

$$\angle DEC = \frac{1}{2}\angle DOC$$

$$= \frac{1}{2}(104°)$$

$$= 52°$$

EXERCISES 9-8

1. For the arc ABC
   i)   Name the inscribed angle(s).   ii)   Name the sector angle.

   a)   b)   c)

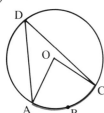   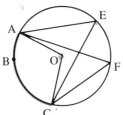   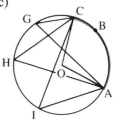

2. Find the angle measure indicated by each letter.

   a)   b)   c)

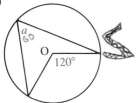   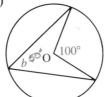   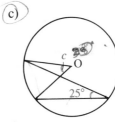

   d)   e)   f)

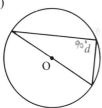      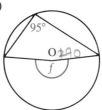

3. Find the angle measure indicated by each letter.

   a)   b)   c)

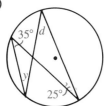   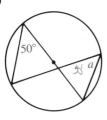   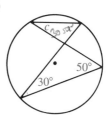

   d)   e)   f)

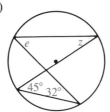   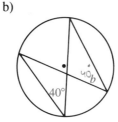   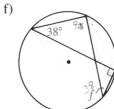

Ⓑ

4. Find the angle measure indicated by each letter.

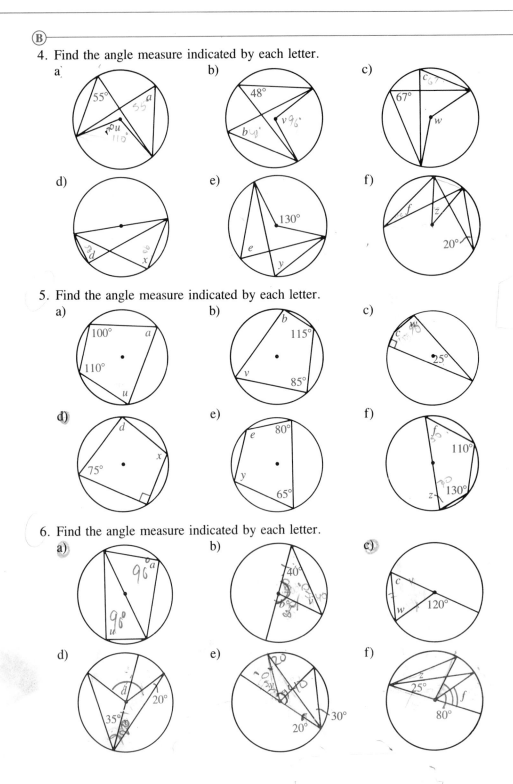

a)

55°
55 a
7°u
110

b)

48°
v 96°
b

c)

67°
c
w

d)

d
x

e)

130°
e
y

f)

f
z
20°

5. Find the angle measure indicated by each letter.

a)

100°
a
110°
u

b)

b
115°
v
85°

c)

25°

d)

d
x
75°

e)

e 80°
y
65°

f)

f
110°
z 130°

6. Find the angle measure indicated by each letter.

a)

96 a
98
u

b)

40°

c)

c
w 120°

d)

d
20°
35°

e)

y
20° 30°

f)

z
25°
f
80°

7. Find the angle measure indicated by each letter.

a)

b)
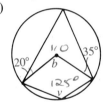

c)
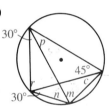

d)
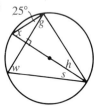
25°

e)
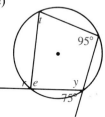
95°
75°

f)
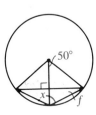
50°

8. For each diagram
   i) If the value of *x* is known, how can the value of *y* be found?
   ii) Write an equation relating *x* and *y*.

a)
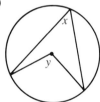

b)
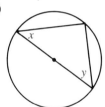

c)
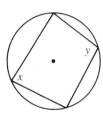

9. Find the area of each shaded region, to 1 decimal place.

a)
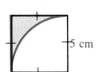
5 cm

b)

5 cm

c)
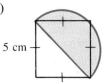
5 cm

10. All the circles have a radius of 10 cm. The dots indicate the centres of the circles. Find the perimeter of each figure, to the nearest millimetre.

a)
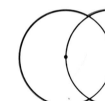

b)
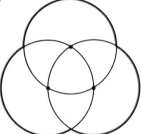

MATHEMATICS AROUND US

Geometry on the Earth's Surface

The geometry in this chapter is called plane geometry because the figures are all drawn on a plane. Geometry on the surface of the Earth is called *spherical geometry* because the figures are drawn on or visualized on a sphere. The shortest distance between two points can be represented by stretching a thread between them. On a plane, this is a straight line.

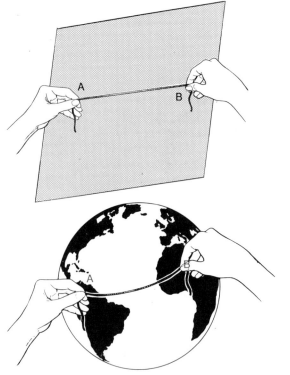

On a globe representing the Earth's surface, the shortest distance between two points is an arc of a *great circle* — the circle that is formed when a plane passes through the two points and the Earth's centre.

The shortest distance between two cities is an arc of a great circle, but it does not look that way on most maps. On the adjacent map the straight line joining Winnipeg and Bombay crosses the Atlantic Provinces and North Africa. This route, however, is actually much longer than the great-circle route which passes near the North Pole. Similarly, the shortest route from Winnipeg to Hong Kong is the great-circle route along the north coast of Alaska.

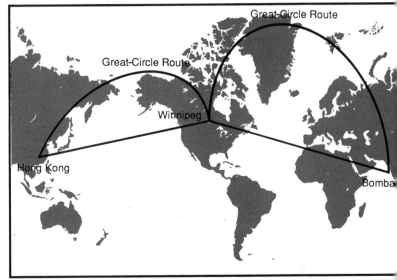

When a triangle is drawn on a plane, its three sides are line segments. The three sides of a *spherical triangle* are arcs of great circles.

On a globe representing the Earth, A is the North Pole, and B and C are points on the Equator. Spherical ∠ABC is 90° because AB is a north/south line and BC is an east/west line. Similarly, spherical ∠ACB is 90°. Spherical ∠BAC is 120° because AC is the 40° E longitude line and AB is the 45° W longitude line. The sum of the angles of spherical △ABC is:
90° + 90° + 120° = 300°

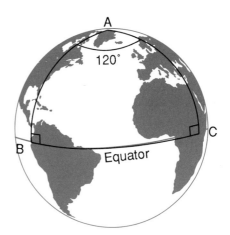

QUESTIONS

1. In the diagram above, if A and C are fixed and B moves along the Equator, how does the sum of the angles in spherical △ABC change?

2. On a globe, using tape and thread, show the great-circle routes from Winnipeg to Hong Kong and Bombay. Compare your routes with those shown on the maps.

3. Which routes do commercial aircraft fly? Why?

4. Which city on the globe is farthest from Winnipeg?

5. On a globe, with tape and thread, show the spherical triangles with vertices at the following cities. Measure their angles with a protractor. What is the sum of the angles in each spherical triangle?
   a) St. John's, Vancouver, Miami (Florida)
   b) Winnipeg, Cairo (Egypt), Rio de Janeiro (Brazil)
   c) Honolulu (Hawaii), Caracas (Venezuela), Nairobi (Kenya)

6. These statements are true for plane geometry. Are they true for spherical geometry? Explain.
   a) When two lines intersect, the opposite angles are equal.
   b) Parallel lines never meet.
   c) Each angle of an equilateral triangle measures 60°.
   d) The angles opposite the equal sides of an isosceles triangle are equal.

Review Exercises

1. Find the angle measure indicated by each letter.

a)

b)

c)

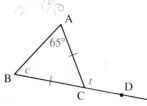

d)

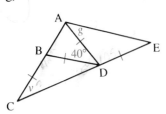

e)

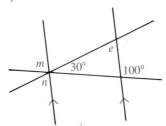

f)

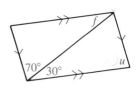

g)

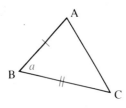

h)

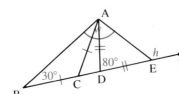

i)

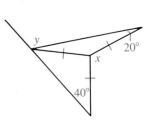

2. Find pairs of congruent triangles and state the condition for congruency.

a)

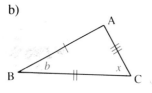

b)

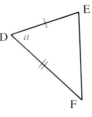

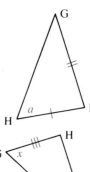

3. Find the length, to one decimal place, indicated by each letter.

a)

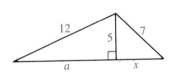

b)

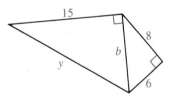

4. The size of a television screen is described by the length of its diagonal. Determine the size of a screen that is 34 cm by 40 cm.

5. Will a sheet of plywood 1200 mm wide fit into the rear of a station wagon if the door opening is 950 mm wide and 700 mm high?

6. The longest side of an isosceles right triangle is 50 cm. Find the length of the other two sides, to the nearest centimetre.

7. Find the angle measure indicated by each letter.

a)

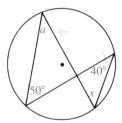

b)

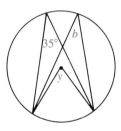

c)

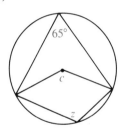

8. Find the angle measure indicated by each letter.

a)

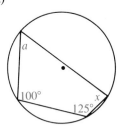

b)

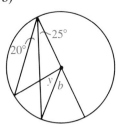

c)

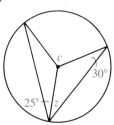

9. Find each sum.
   a) the exterior angles of a triangle
   b) the interior angles of a quadrilateral
   c) the exterior angles of a quadrilateral

10. What is the length of each side of a square with diagonals of length 7 m? Give your answer to 2 decimal places.

11. What is the height of an equilateral triangle with sides 12 cm long? Give your answer to 1 decimal place.

Cumulative Review, Chapters 7-9

1. Simplify.
   a) $14m - 9n - 5m - 3n$
   b) $5a + 7b - 11a - 4b$
   c) $7x - 3 + 2x - 8 - 12x$
   d) $(3y^2 - 7y + 2) - (5y - y^2 + 9)$
   e) $(4x - 7) - (2x + 5) + (9x - 1)$
   f) $(8x - 9y + 4) + (3y - 5 - 6x) - (5x - 4y - 7)$

2. Evaluate, for each value of x.
   a) $5x^2 - 2x + 9$ b) $3(2x + 1) - x(x - 4) + 7$
       i) -2 ii) 5 iii) -1.5

3. Simplify.
   a) $(3m)(-5m)$ b) $\left(-\dfrac{1}{2}x\right)^3$ c) $(-8a^3)(-6a^2)$

   d) $4x(2x^2 - 5x + 3)$ e) $(2xy^2)(-7x^2y^5)$ f) $-2m^2(5m^3 - 2m + 4n)$

4. Find each product.
   a) $(x - 4)(x + 11)$ b) $(2x - 7)(x - 3)$ c) $(4 + 3a)(5 + 9a)$
   d) $(3m - 5)(3m + 5)$ e) $x(2x + 3)(4x - 1)$ f) $-4a(7a + 2)(3a - 8)$

5. Factor.
   a) $6m^2 - 15m$ b) $2y^3 - 6y^2 + 8y$ c) $4x^2 - 49$
   d) $x^2 + 3x - 28$ e) $m^2 - 9m + 18$ f) $20 + a - a^2$

6. Factor.
   a) $y^2 + 16y + 39$ b) $2x^2 - 10x - 12$ c) $4a^3 - 100a$

   d) $-3x^3 + 15x^2 - 6x$ e) $3m^2 - \dfrac{3}{4}$ f) $y^3 - 15y^2 + 56y$

7. The surface area S of a rectangular prism
   with length l, width w, and height h,
   is given by this formula.
   $S = 2(lw + hw + lh)$
   Find the surface areas of prisms with
   these dimensions.
   a) length 20 cm; width 15 cm; height 8 cm
   b) length 17.5 cm; width 6.4 cm; height 3.2 cm

8. The number N of car accidents on a certain street in a week is given by this formula.
   $N = 2c^2 - 6c + 1$, where $c \geq 3$
   c is the number of cars, in thousands, that use the street each week. Find how
   many accidents there are in a week for each number of cars.
   a) 4000   b) 6000   c) 3000   d) 5000

9. Simplify.
   a) $\dfrac{-10x + 35}{-5}$ b) $\dfrac{8x^3 - 12x^2 + 20x}{4x}$ c) $\dfrac{4x^2y}{9xy^2} \times \dfrac{15xy}{16y^3}$

   d) $\dfrac{-17m^2n}{24mn} \times \dfrac{40m^4n^3}{51m^3n}$ e) $\dfrac{9x^5y^2}{16} \div \dfrac{3x^2y}{8}$ f) $\dfrac{-28a^2bc}{33ab^2} \div \dfrac{-21abc^3}{-44b^2c}$

10. Simplify.

a) $\dfrac{3x - 4}{3} + \dfrac{x + 5}{3}$

b) $\dfrac{2m + 7}{5} - \dfrac{3m + 1}{5}$

c) $\dfrac{3(2a - 5)}{4a} + \dfrac{2(a + 3)}{4a}$

d) $\dfrac{2(3x + 2)}{3} - \dfrac{5(2x - 7)}{4}$

11. Plot these points: A(-3,1), B(3,3), C(5,-3), and D(-4,-6). Join the points in order and name the figure drawn.

12. The graph shows the relation between the number of sides of a regular polygon and the size of its interior angles.
    a) What is the size of the interior angle of:
       i) an octagon   ii) a dodecagon?
    b) Name the polygon whose interior angle is:
       i) 120°   ii) 108°.

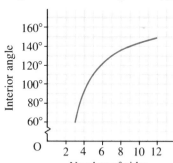

Angles and Sides of Regular Polygons

13. The sum of the first n natural numbers is given by this formula.
    $$S = \dfrac{n(n + 1)}{2}$$
    a) Make a table of values for S if $n = 1, 2, 3, 4, 5,$ and 6.
    b) Graph the relation defined by this table of values.
    c) Why is 12 not a value for S in this relation?

14. Draw a graph of each relation.
    a) $y = 2x + 1$ b) $x + 4y = 12$ c) $3x - 2y = 6$

15. When there is one boxcar on a train, we need 2 links to connect the engine and the caboose. When there are two boxcars, we need 3 links.

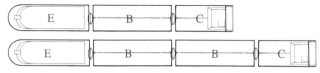

    a) How many links are needed for 10 boxcars?
    b) How many links are needed for 20 boxcars?
    c) Let x represent the number of boxcars and let y represent the number of links in a train. Write an equation relating x and y.

16. The cost C dollars of a long distance telephone call is given by the formula, $C = 1.2m + 1.5$, where m is the time in minutes.
    a) Graph this relation.
    b) How much would each call cost? i) 4 min   ii) 7 min
    c) How long is a call which costs: i) $5.10   ii) $11.70?

17. Find the angle measure indicated by each letter.

a)

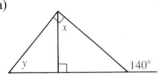

b)

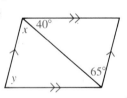

c)

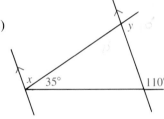

18. For each part, find a pair of congruent triangles and state the condition for their congruence.

a)

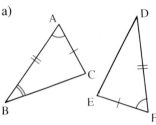

b)

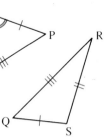

19. Find each value of *x* and *y*, to one decimal place.

a)

b)

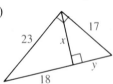

c)

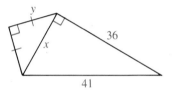

20. A conveyor belt 11.4 m in length is used to raise cartons of produce from one level to another, a distance of 3.7 m. How much floor space, measured in the direction of the conveyor, is required?

21. Find each value of *x* and *y*.

a)

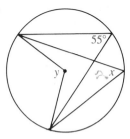

b)

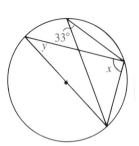

c)

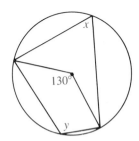

22. Safety procedures require the foot of a ladder to be no more than one-quarter of the length of the ladder away from the base of a building. Will a 10 m ladder safely reach a window 9.5 m high?

23. Draw each triangle.
    a) an isosceles obtuse triangle
    b) an equilateral triangle
    c) an isosceles right triangle
    d) a scalene acute triangle

10 Transformations

Two oil storage tanks, several kilometres apart, are on the same side of a pipeline. Where, along the pipeline, should a pumping station be located to serve both tanks so that the total length of pipe from the pipeline to the tanks is a minimum? (See Section 10-7, *Example 1*.)

10-1 INTRODUCTION TO TRANSFORMATIONS

The photographs above show some familiar transformations.

Whenever the shape, the size, the appearance or the position of an object is changed, it has undergone a *transformation*. Under a transformation, some of the characteristics of an object may be changed while others remain the same. Those characteristics that are unchanged are said to be *invariant*.

For each photograph above, identify some characteristics of the transformation that are invariant as well as some that change.

Transformation geometry is the study of transformations of geometric figures. Three transformations that do not change size or shape are *rotations*, *reflections*, and *translations*. These transformations map a figure onto its image.

A translation, whose direction and length are illustrated by the colored translation arrow, maps the black figure onto its colored image.

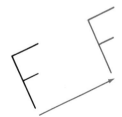

A reflection in the line *l* maps the black figure onto its colored image.

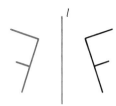

A rotation of 180° about O maps the black figure onto its colored image.

Example 1. State which transformation maps each black letter onto its colored image.

a)   b)   c)

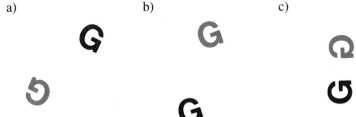

Solution.   a) Since the black G maps onto the colored G by a rotation about a point between the letters, the diagram illustrates a rotation.

b) Since the black G maps onto the colored G by a translation along a line joining the letters, the diagram illustrates a translation.

c) Since the black G maps onto the colored G by a reflection in a line between the letters, the diagram illustrates a reflection.

Example 2. The four parts into which the figure is divided are congruent. Name the transformation that maps:

a) region I onto region IV
b) region II onto region IV
c) region I onto region III
d) region III onto region IV.

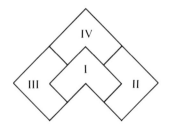

Solution.

a) Region IV is a translation image of region I.

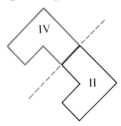

b) Region IV is a reflection image of region II.

Region IV is also a rotation image of region II.

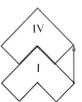

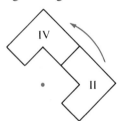

c) Region III is a rotation image of region I.

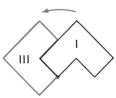

d) Region IV is a reflection image of region III.

Region IV is also a rotation image of region III.

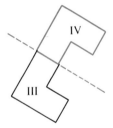

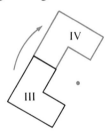

EXERCISES 10-1

1. Name the transformation required to map each letter onto its colored image.

a)   i)   ii)   iii)

J   L   J   ⌐

b)   i)   ii)   iii)

R   R   ᴚ   Я

c)   i)   ii)   iii)

Ш   Ⅎ   Ⴚ   Ⴎ

2. For the figure shown, name a transformation that maps:
   a) region 4 onto region 1
   b) region 3 onto region 4
   c) region 4 onto region 2
   d) region 1 onto region 2
   e) region 3 onto region 1
   f) region 2 onto region 3.

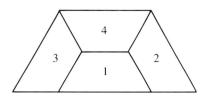

3. For the figure shown, name a transformation that maps:
   a) region C onto region A
   b) region A onto region B
   c) region D onto region C.

4. Copy each diagram. Divide it into two congruent parts. Name the transformation required to map one part onto the other.

a)   b)   c)

d)   e)   f)

INVESTIGATE

1. Plot the points V($-3,6$), W($1,1$), and Z($-1,-8$), and draw △VWZ.

2. Translate △VWZ as follows: move every point 7 units in the negative *x*-direction and 3 units in the positive *y*-direction.

3. Label the image points V′, W′, and Z′. Then, △V′W′Z′ is the translation image of △VWZ.

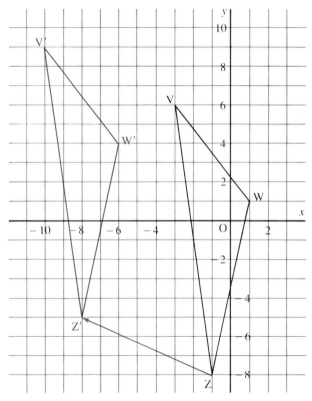

4. Measure VW, WZ, and VZ.

5. Measure V′W′, W′Z′, and V′Z′.
● What appears to be true about the lengths of line segments under a translation?

6. Measure ∠VWZ, ∠WZV, and ∠ZVW.

7. Measure ∠V′W′Z′, ∠W′Z′V′, and ∠Z′V′W′.
● What appears to be true about the measures of angles under a translation?
● What appears to be true about the direction of line segments under a translation?

10-2 TRANSLATIONS

When a hockey puck moves across the ice in a straight line, it is *translated* from one position to another.

When a point or a figure is moved (or translated) in a straight line to another position in the same plane, it is said to have undergone a *translation*.

The translation illustrated here is defined by the length and the direction of the colored arrow.

$\triangle A'B'C'$ is the translation image of $\triangle ABC$.
AB = A'B'; AC = A'C'; BC = B'C'
AB ∥ A'B'; AC ∥ A'C'; BC ∥ B'C'
∠ABC = ∠A'B'C'; ∠BAC = ∠B'A'C';
∠ACB = ∠A'C'B'

Under a translation, any figure and its image are identical in all respects, except location.

You may have discovered the following properties of a translation in the previous *INVESTIGATE*.

- Under a translation, the lengths of line segments are invariant.
- Under a translation, the directions of line segments are invariant; that is, the image line segment is parallel to the original line segment.
- Under a translation, the measures of angles are invariant.

We use these properties to solve problems involving translations.

Example 1. Describe the translation that maps F onto F′.

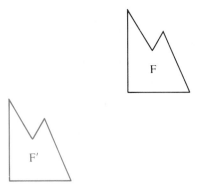

Solution.   Trace the diagram. Join corresponding points Z and Z′ with a straight line segment.
Draw an arrow head at Z′, pointing to Z′.
The length and direction of the arrow ZZ′ represent the translation that maps F onto F′.

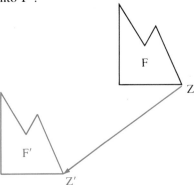

Example 2. A triangle has vertices G(-1,3), H(4,7), and J(3,-3).
  a) Draw the image of △GHJ under this translation: move every point 5 units in the positive *x*-direction and 4 units in the negative *y*-direction.
  b) Write the coordinates of the vertices of the image triangle.

Solution. a) The translation means that every point on △GHJ slides 5 units to the right and 4 units down. Thus, the *x*-coordinate of each point increases by 5 and the *y*-coordinate decreases by 4.
△G′H′J′ is the image of △GHJ under the given translation.

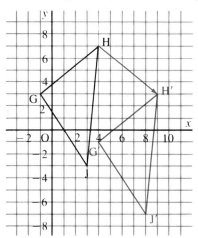

b) G(−1,3) → G′(4,−1)
H(4,7) → H′(9,3)
J(3,−3) → J′(8,−7)

EXERCISES 10-2

Ⓐ

1. Each diagram shows a figure F and its image F′ after a translation. Trace each diagram. Draw the translation arrow.

a)

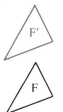

b)

c)

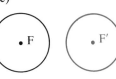

d)

e)

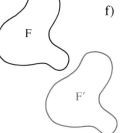

f)

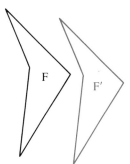

2. A translation maps the point $(1, -2)$ onto $(3,0)$.
   a) Plot the points and draw the translation arrow.
   b) Find the images of these points under this translation.
      i)   A(0,2)   ii)   B(5,6)   iii)   C($-3, -1$)   iv)   D($-4,2$)

Ⓑ

3. The graph shows points A, B, C, D, E, and a translation arrow.

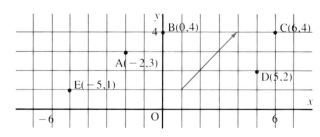

   a) Plot the points and their images under the translation. Label the images A', B', C', D', and E'.
   b) Draw line segments AA' and DD', and compare them with the translation arrow. What do you notice?
   c) Measure and compare the lengths of line segments DE and D'E'. What do you notice?
   d) Measure and compare the sizes of ∠AED and ∠A'E'D'. What do you notice?

4. A translation maps the point $(-2, -3)$ onto $(4,2)$.
   a) Plot the points and draw the translation arrow.
   b) Find the images of A($-1,1$), B(1,4), and C(2, -3) under this translation. Label the image points A', B', and C'.
   c) Describe the effect of this translation on △ABC.

5. A parallelogram has vertices at A($-2,2$), B(2,1), C(4, -4), and D(0, -3). A translation maps points 4 units to the right and 1 unit down. Draw:
   a) the parallelogram
   b) the translation arrow
   c) the image of the parallelogram under this translation.

6. A translation maps the point $(2,5)$ onto $(5, -2)$.
   a) Draw the translation arrow.
   b) If P'($-3, -1$), Q'($-1,3$), and R'($-5,0$) are the images of P, Q, and R under this translation, find the coordinates of P, Q, and R.

7. What properties remain invariant under a translation?

Ⓒ

8. a) Graph this equation. $2x + y = 6$
   b) Draw the image of the graph of the line in part a) under the translation that maps the point $(3,0)$ onto $(0,0)$.

9. a) Graph this equation. $5x - 2y = 10$
   b) Draw the image of the graph of the line in part a) under the translation that maps the point $(-2,1)$ onto $(0,6)$.
   c) Explain the result.

10. Translation T_1 maps the point $(4,1)$ onto $(2,3)$. Translation T_2 maps $(-2,-3)$ onto $(3,0)$.

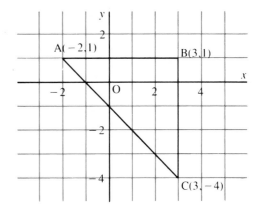

   a) Draw $\triangle ABC$ and its image, $\triangle A'B'C'$, under T_1.
   b) Draw the image of $\triangle A'B'C'$ under T_2. Label it $\triangle A''B''C''$.
   c) Draw a translation arrow for the single translation that maps $\triangle ABC$ onto $\triangle A''B''C''$.
   d) Investigate whether T_1 followed by T_2 gives the same result as T_2 followed by T_1.

 INVESTIGATE

1. Plot the points $S(-3,-5)$, $T(-1,7)$, and $U(-1,-8)$, and draw $\triangle STU$.

2. Reflect $\triangle STU$ in the y-axis. That is, fold the paper along the y-axis. With a sharp pencil or compasses point, mark the positions of S, T, and U so they appear on the other half of the folded paper.

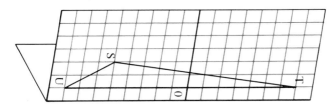

3. Open the paper and label the image points S′, T′, and U′. Then, $\triangle S'T'U'$ is the image of $\triangle STU$ under a reflection in the y-axis.

4. Measure ST, TU, and SU.

5. Measure S′T′, T′U′, and S′U′.
● What appears to be true about the lengths of line segments under a reflection?

6. Measure $\angle STU$, $\angle TUS$, and $\angle UST$.

7. Measure $\angle S'T'U'$, $\angle T'U'S'$, and $\angle U'S'T'$.
● What appears to be true about the measures of angles under a reflection?
● Where is the image of any point on the reflection line?

10-3 REFLECTIONS

When you look in a mirror, you see an image of yourself. The image appears to be as far behind the mirror as you are in front of it. The transformation that relates points and their images in this way is called a *reflection*.

A reflection in line *l* maps each point on a figure, onto its image point on the reflection of the figure.

$\triangle$A′B′C′ is the reflection image of $\triangle$ABC in reflection line *l*.

AB = A′B′; AC = A′C′; BC = B′C′

$\angle$ABC = $\angle$A′B′C′; $\angle$BAC = $\angle$B′A′C′;

$\angle$ACB = $\angle$A′C′B′

The points A and A′ coincide; that is, a point on the reflection line is its own image.

In the diagram, each point on $\triangle$ABC has been joined to its image point on $\triangle$A′B′C′, with a broken line.

BD = DB′; CE = EC′

$\angle$BDA = $\angle$B′DA = 90°; $\angle$CEA = $\angle$C′EA = 90°

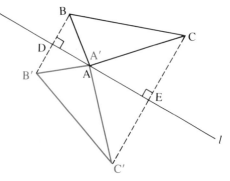

You may have discovered the following properties of a reflection in the previous *INVESTIGATE*.

> - Under a reflection, the lengths of line segments and the measures of angles are invariant.
> - Under a reflection, the points on the reflection line are invariant.
> - The reflection line is the perpendicular bisector of the line segment joining any point to its image point.

We use these properties to solve problems involving reflections.

Example 1. Draw the reflection line that maps F onto F'.

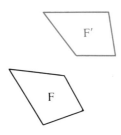

Solution.   Trace the diagram.
Join corresponding points X and X'
with a straight line segment and mark
its midpoint M.
Join another pair of corresponding
points Y and Y' with a straight line
segment and mark its midpoint N.
Join MN. This is the reflection
line that maps F onto F'.

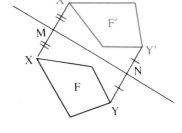

Example 2. A triangle has vertices D(4,7), E(8,3), and F(6, −2). Draw the image of
△DEF after a reflection in the *x*-axis. Write the coordinates of the
vertices of the image triangle.

Solution.   Plot the points on graph paper. Draw △DEF.

Draw a line through D perpendicular to the *x*-axis (that is, parallel
to the *y*-axis). Extend this line to a point D' such that D' is the same
distance from the *x*-axis as D is.

Similarly, draw a line
through E perpendicular to the
x-axis and label E' such that
E' is the same distance from
the *x*-axis as E is.

Also, draw a line through F
perpendicular to the *x*-axis
and label F' such that F' is the
same distance from the *x*-axis
as F is.

△D'E'F' is the image of
△DEF under a reflection in the
x-axis. The coordinates of the
vertices of the image triangle
are D'(4, −7), E'(8, −3), and
F'(6,2).

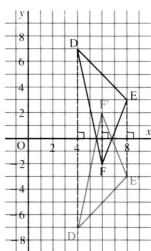

EXERCISES 10-3

(A)

1. Sketch the images of **A**, **3**, **K**, and **5** under reflections in:
   a) a vertical line   b) a horizontal line.

2. State the time shown on the mirror image of each clock face.

   a)   b)   c)   d)

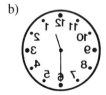 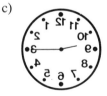 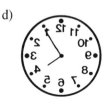

3. Each diagram shows a figure F and its image F′ under a reflection. Trace each diagram and draw the reflection line.

   a)   b)   c)

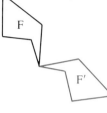

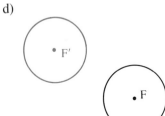

   d)   e)   f)

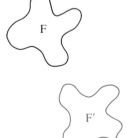
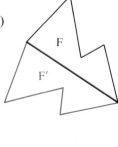

(B)

4. Triangle PQR has vertices P(2,6), Q(6,4), and R(3,2). Draw the image of △PQR under a reflection in:
   a) the *x*-axis   b) the *y*-axis.

5. Quadrilateral ABCD has vertices A(2,5), B(6,5), C(9,1), and D(2,1). Find the coordinates of the image of quadrilateral ABCD under a reflection in:
   a) the *x*-axis   b) the *y*-axis.

6. Triangle ABC has vertices A(4,7), B(7,2), and C(3,3). Its image under a reflection is A′(−2,7), B′(−5,2), and C′(−1,3). Graph both triangles and draw the reflection line.

7. Triangle ABC in *Exercise 6* has another image at A'(4, −11), B'(7, −6), C'(3, −7). Draw the reflection line.

8. For each triangle shown below
   a) Copy the triangle.
   b) Draw its reflection image using the extended side as the reflection line.
   c) Name the figure formed by the triangle and its image.

   i)

   ii)
   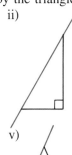

   iii)
   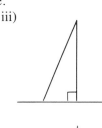

   iv)
   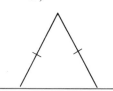

   v)

   vi)
   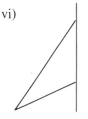

9. Each diagram shows a line OP and its reflection image OP'.
   a) Trace each diagram.
   b) Determine its reflection line.
   c) Verify that the reflection line is the bisector of ∠POP'.

   i)
   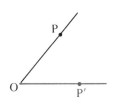

   ii)
   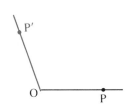

   iii)
   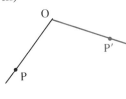

10. Triangle PQR has vertices P(−2,4), Q(4,2), and R(1,−2). Draw the image of △PQR and write the coordinates of the vertices under a reflection in:
    a) the *x*-axis   b) the *y*-axis.

11. Quadrilateral ABCD has vertices A(−2,6), B(4,3), C(3,−3), and D(−5,−2). Write the coordinates of the vertices of its image under a reflection in:
    a) the *x*-axis   b) the *y*-axis.

12. What properties remain invariant under a reflection?

Ⓒ

13. a) Graph this equation. $3x + 2y = 12$
    b) Draw the image of the graph of the line in part a) under a reflection in:
       i) the *x*-axis   ii) the *y*-axis.

INVESTIGATE

Rotations on a Grid

1. Plot the points P(−1,5), Q(−5,4), and R(−2,−4), and draw △PQR.

2. Trace the triangle and the axes on tracing paper. Rotate the tracing paper through 90° counterclockwise about the origin. That is, rotate the paper until the positive y-axis on the tracing paper coincides with the negative x-axis on the base paper.

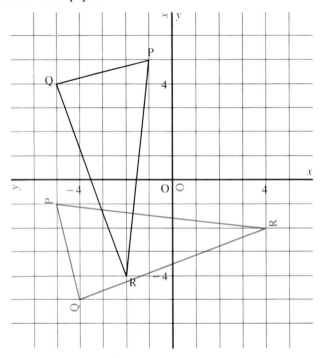

3. Mark the new positions of P, Q, and R and label them P', Q', and R'. △P'Q'R' is the rotation image of △PQR after a counterclockwise rotation of 90° about O.

4. Measure PQ, QR, and PR.

5. Measure P'Q', Q'R', and P'R'.
● What appears to be true about the lengths of line segments under a rotation?

6. Measure ∠PQR, ∠PRQ, and ∠RPQ.

7. Measure ∠P'Q'R', ∠P'R'Q', and ∠R'P'Q'.
● What appears to be true about the measures of angles under a rotation?

10-4 ROTATIONS

A person on a Ferris wheel rotates about the centre of the wheel. When a point or a figure is turned about a fixed point, it is said to have undergone a *rotation*. The fixed point is called the *rotation centre*. A rotation in a counterclockwise direction is a positive rotation. In this chapter, all rotations will be counterclockwise.

A counterclockwise rotation of 90° about O maps each point on a figure, onto its image point on the rotation image.

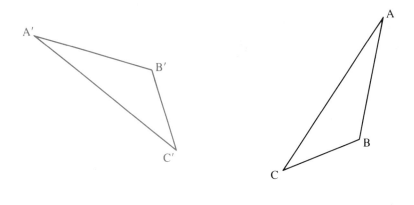

△A′B′C′ is the rotation image of △ABC after a 90° rotation about O.
AB = A′B′; AC = A′C′; BC = B′C′
∠ABC = ∠A′B′C′; ∠BAC = ∠B′A′C′; ∠ACB = ∠A′C′B′

You may have discovered the following properties of a rotation in the previous *INVESTIGATE*.

- Under a rotation, the lengths of line segments are invariant.
- Under a rotation, the measures of angles are invariant.

We can use these properties to solve problems involving rotations.

Example 1. Figure F′ is the image of figure F under a rotation.
  a) Locate the rotation centre.
  b) Measure the rotation angle.

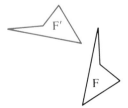

Solution. a) Trace the diagram on tracing paper.
Fold the paper so that a point X on the figure coincides with the corresponding point X′ on the image. Crease the paper.
Unfold the paper and draw a line *l* along the crease.

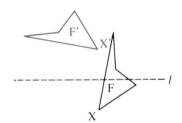

Fold the paper so another point Y on the figure coincides with its corresponding point Y′ on the image. Crease the paper, then unfold it and draw a line *m* along the crease.

The point of intersection O of *l* and *m* is the centre of rotation that maps the figure onto its image.

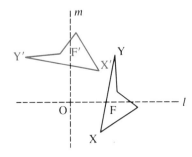

b) Draw lines from O to X and from O to X′.

∠XOX′ is the rotation angle and it is measured to be 90°.

How could you check that the rotation centre and the rotation angle are correct?

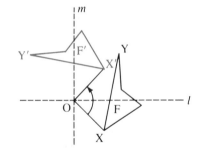

Example 2. A triangle has vertices A(3,5), B(7,1), and C(5, −2).
a) Draw the image of △ABC under a rotation of 90° about the origin.
b) Write the coordinates of the vertices of the image triangle.

Solution. a) Plot the points on graph paper. Draw △ABC.
Draw OA. Place a protractor along OA, centre O and mark
90° counterclockwise. Along this line, label a point A′ such that
OA = OA′.

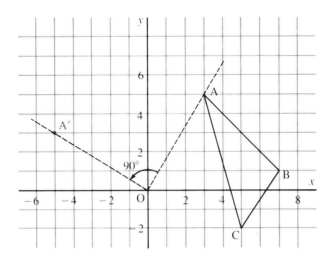

Similarly, mark B′ such that ∠BOB′ is 90° and OB = OB′.
Then mark C′ such that ∠COC′ is 90° and OC = OC′.
△A′B′C′ is the image of △ABC under a rotation of 90° about O.

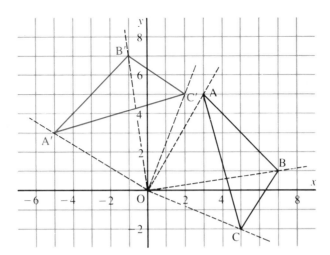

b) The coordinates of the vertices of the image triangle are A′(−5,3),
B′(−1,7), and C′(2,5).

EXERCISES 10-4

Ⓐ

1. Each diagram shows a figure F and its image F' after a rotation. Trace each diagram. Locate the rotation centre and measure the rotation angle.

a)

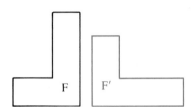

b)

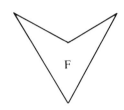

c)

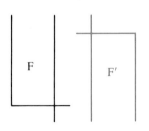

d)

e)

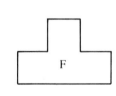

f)

Ⓑ

2. A triangle has vertices A(1,4), B(5,5), and O(0,0). Draw its image and find the coordinates of its vertices under a 180° rotation about O.

3. A quadrilateral has vertices A(1,3), B(4,7), C(6,4), and D(3,1). Draw its image and find the coordinates of its vertices under a 180° rotation about the origin.

4. A triangle has vertices P(−3,5), Q(1,−7), and R(2,1). Draw its image and find the coordinates of its vertices under a 90° rotation about the origin.

5. A quadrilateral has vertices K(−3,4), L(1,6), M(6,−1), and N(−4,−3). Draw its image and find the coordinates of its vertices under a 90° rotation about the origin.

6. a) What can be said about the line segment joining any point P on a figure to its image P', after a 180° rotation?
   b) How do the coordinates of a point and its image under a 180° rotation about (0,0) compare?

7. For each triangle shown below
   a) Copy the triangle.
   b) Draw its image under a 180° rotation about the rotation centre C.
   c) Name the figure formed by the triangle and its image.

   i)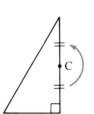
   ii)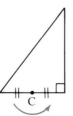
   iii)

   iv)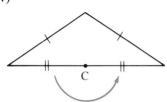
   v)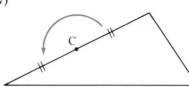

8. Sketch the image of each figure under a 90°, a 180°, a 270°, and a 360° rotation about the rotation centre O. Which image maps onto the original figure when it is rotated through 180°?

   a)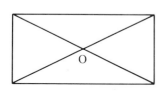
   b)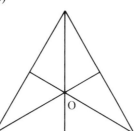
   c)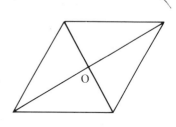

9. What properties remain invariant under a rotation?

10. a) Graph this equation. $y = x + 3$
    b) Draw the image of the graph of the line in part a) under a 180° rotation about the origin.

11. a) Graph this equation. $y = 2x$
    b) Draw the image of the graph of the line in part a) under a 180° rotation about the origin.
    c) Explain the result.

Consider All Possibilities

A box is designed to hold a cube marked with the letters A through F as shown. In how many different ways can the cube be placed in the box?

Understand the problem
- When are two ways of placing the cube in the box to be considered as "different"?
- Is there only one way to place the cube in the box so that face A is on top?
- What are we asked to find?

Think of a strategy
- Consider each letter in turn.
- Think of the number of ways the cube can be placed with that letter on top.

Carry out the strategy
- Count the number of ways of placing the cube in the box so that face A is on top.
- When A is on top, there are four different ways that A can appear, as shown in the diagram.
- Similarly, there are 4 different ways that the cube can be placed in the box when each of B, C, D, E, and F are on top.
- Therefore, the total number of ways of placing the cube in the box is 6 × 4, or 24.

Look back
- Try another method of counting the ways that the cube can be placed in the box. Do you get 24 by this method?

Solve each problem

1. How many lines of symmetry has a regular polygon of 12 sides (below left)?

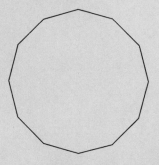

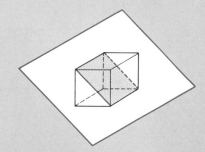

2. A plane which divides a solid into 2 parts such that each part is the reflection of the other in the plane is called a *plane of symmetry* of the solid (above right). How many planes of symmetry has a cube?

3. Place the integers from 1 to 6 inside the circles so that the sums along the sides of the triangle are equal (below left).

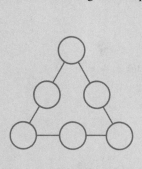

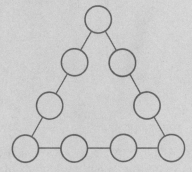

4. Place the integers from 1 to 9 inside the circles so that the sums along the sides of the triangle are equal (above right).

5. a) Choose any two prime numbers greater than 3. Find the difference of their squares. Is the difference a multiple of 24?

   b) Repeat part a) with other pairs of prime numbers.

   c) Make a conjecture about the difference of the squares of two prime numbers greater than 3.

   d) Test your conjecture using other pairs of prime numbers.

   e) Every prime number greater than 3 is either 1 more than a multiple of 4 (such as 17), or 3 more than a multiple of 4 (such as 19). Use this fact to prove your conjecture in part c).

I N V E S T I G A T E

Enlargements and Reductions

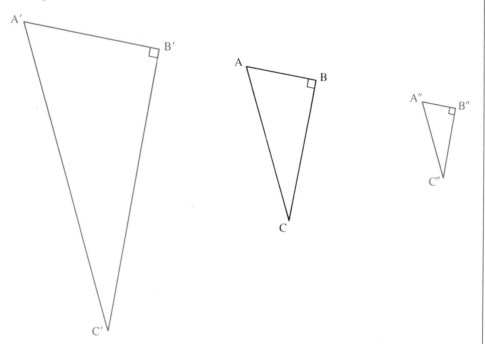

In the diagram, △A′B′C′ is an enlargement of △ABC and △A″B″C″ is a reduction of △ABC.

1. Trace the diagram.

2. Measure AB, BC, and CA.

3. Measure A′B′, B′C′, C′A′, A″B″, B″C″, and C″A″.
   - What appears to be true about the lengths of line segments under an enlargement?
   - What appears to be true about the lengths of line segments under a reduction?

4. Measure ∠ABC, ∠BCA, and ∠CAB.

5. Measure ∠A′B′C′, ∠B′C′A′, ∠C′A′B′, ∠A″B″C″, ∠B″C″A″, and ∠C″A″B″.
   - What appears to be true about the measures of angles under an enlargement?
   - What appears to be true about the measures of angles under a reduction?

6. Find the areas of △ABC, △A′B′C′, and △A″B″C″.
   - What appears to be true about the areas of figures under an enlargement?
   - What appears to be true about the areas of figures under a reduction?

10-5 DILATATIONS

When a photograph has been increased in size, it has been *enlarged*.
When a photograph is decreased in size, it has been *reduced*. In both
cases, the shapes of the objects on the photographs are invariant,
only their dimensions change.

Enlargements and reductions are examples of a transformation called
a dilatation.

A *dilatation* is a transformation that changes all dimensions by
a factor k called the *scale factor*. For enlargements, k is greater
than 1 and for reductions, k is between 0 and 1.

Example 1.   Here are two views of the Canadian flag; F′ is the dilatation image of F.

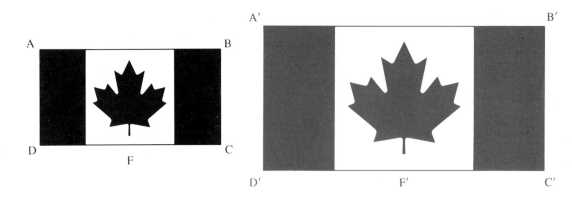

a) Find the scale factor k of the dilatation.

b) Compare the length-to-width ratios of the flags.

c) Find the areas of the flags.

Solution.   a) The scale factor k is the ratio of corresponding lengths.

$$k = \frac{A'B'}{AB} \left(\text{or } \frac{B'C'}{BC} \text{ or } \frac{C'D'}{CD} \text{ or } \frac{A'D'}{AD} \right)$$

By measuring, A′B′ = 7.5 cm and AB = 5.0 cm

$$k = \frac{7.5}{5.0}$$
$$= 1.5$$

The scale factor k of the dilatation is 1.5.

b) For flag F, $\dfrac{\text{length}}{\text{width}} = \dfrac{5.0}{2.5}$

$$= 2.0$$

For flag F′, $\dfrac{\text{length}}{\text{width}} = \dfrac{7.5}{3.8}$

$$\doteq 2.0$$

The length-to-width ratio of the flag is unchanged by the dilatation.

c) For flag F, area = (5.0 × 2.5) cm²

$$= 12.5 \text{ cm}^2$$

For flag F′, area = (7.5 × 3.8) cm²

$$= 28.5 \text{ cm}^2$$

In *Example 1*, the area of F′ is *not* 1.5 times the area of F. Since each dimension of F′ is 1.5 times the corresponding dimension of F, the area of F′ is $(1.5)^2$, or 2.25 times the area of F.

Use your calculator to show that $\dfrac{28.5}{12.5} \doteq 2.25$

In *Example 1*, if we join corresponding points on the flags and extend the lines, we find that they meet at a point called the *dilatation centre*.

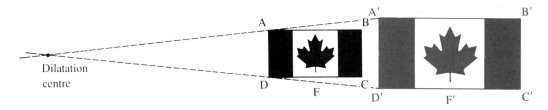

Here are some properties of dilatations. You may have discovered some of these in the *INVESTIGATE* preceding this section.

Under a dilatation with scale factor *k*

- The length of an image line segment is *k* times the length of the original line segment.
- The measures of angles are invariant.
- The area of an image figure is k^2 times the area of the original figure.
- Lines through corresponding points meet at the dilatation centre.

Example 2. The map is a dilatation of the city of Lethbridge with a scale of 1 : 112 000. That is, *x* centimetres on the map corresponds to an actual distance of 112 000*x* centimetres. Use the map to determine the actual distance between 43 Street and 13 Street along 5 Avenue.

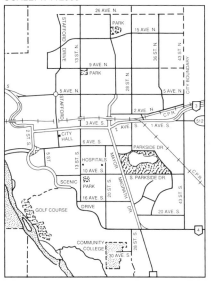

Solution. By measuring, the map distance between 43 Street and 13 Street along 5 Avenue is 2.9 cm.
Actual distance is 112 000 × 2.9 cm
$$= 324\ 800 \text{ cm}$$
$$= 3.248 \text{ km}$$
It is approximately 3.2 km from 43 Street to 13 Street along 5 Avenue.

Example 3. A dilatation maps figure F onto figure F'.
a) Find the scale factor.
b) Locate the dilatation centre.

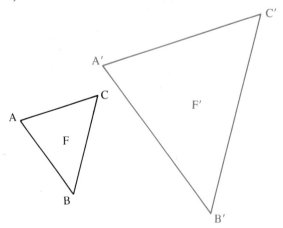

Solution. a) Trace the diagram.
Measure the corresponding lengths AB and A'B'.
The scale factor k of the dilatation is the ratio $\dfrac{A'B'}{AB}$.

$$k = \frac{A'B'}{AB}$$
$$= \frac{5.0}{2.5}$$
$$= 2$$

The scale factor is 2.

b) Join A' to A and extend A'A.
Join B' to B and extend B'B.
The intersection of A'A and B'B is the dilatation centre D.

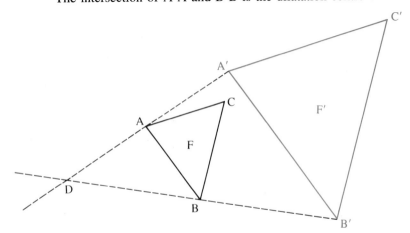

EXERCISES 10-5

1. A figure undergoes a dilatation with the given scale factor. Is the image an enlargement or a reduction?

   a) 3   b) 7   c) $\dfrac{1}{2}$ d) $\dfrac{3}{2}$ e) $\dfrac{1}{4}$ f) $\dfrac{5}{6}$

2. Each diagram shows a figure F and its image F′ under a dilatation. Trace each diagram. Locate the dilatation centre and determine the scale factor.

   a)

   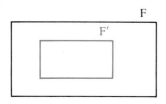

   b)

   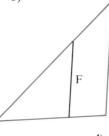

   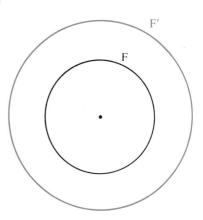

   c)

   d)

3. The larger photograph is a dilatation image of the smaller photograph.

   Measure the photographs.
   a) Find the scale factor of the dilatation.
   b) Find the length-to-width ratios of the photograph and its enlargement.
   c) Find the areas of the photograph and its enlargement.

Ⓑ

4. Trace each figure and its dilatation image.
   i) Find the dilatation centre.
   ii) Determine the scale factor of the dilatation.
   iii) Compare the areas of the figure and its image.
   iv) Compare the angles of the figure and its image.

a)

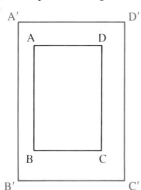

b)

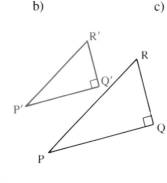

c)

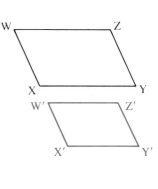

5. A′B′C′D′E′ is a dilatation image of pentagon ABCDE. Trace the diagram onto squared paper.
   a) Find the dilatation centre.
   b) Compare the lengths of corresponding sides.
   c) What is the scale factor of the dilatation?
   d) Compare the measures of corresponding angles.
   e) Compare the areas of the pentagon and its image.

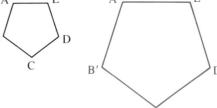

6. Triangle ABC has sides of length 5 cm, 12 cm, and 13 cm. Find the lengths of the sides of its dilatation image for each scale factor.

   a) 2   b) 5   c) $\dfrac{1}{2}$ d) $\dfrac{3}{4}$

7. Using O as the dilatation centre, draw the image of each triangle with each scale factor.
   i) 2.5   ii) 0.75

a)

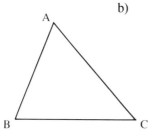

b)

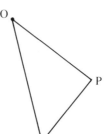

c)

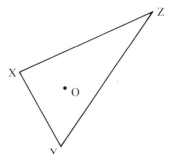

8. On a blueprint, the dimensions of a building are 640 mm by 360 mm. Determine the scale factor of the dilatation if the actual building has these dimensions.
   a) 64 m by 36 m b) 96 m by 54 m
   c) 48 m by 27 m d) 80 m by 45 m

9. From the map in *Example 2*, find the actual distance between each pair of locations.
   a) 9 Ave. N. and 16 Ave. S. along 13 Street
   b) 13 Street and 28 Street along 5 Ave.
   c) the two points where the CPR tracks cross 43 Street

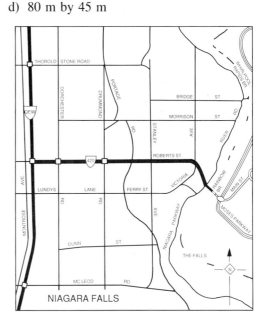

10. The scale for this map of Niagara Falls is 1 : 91 000. How far is it between each pair of locations?
    a) Dorchester Rd. to River Rd. along Morrison St.
    b) Thorold Stone Rd. to McLeod Rd. along Drummond Rd.
    c) the corner of Dorchester Rd. and Dunn St. to the corner of Bridge St. and Stanley Ave.

11. O is the dilatation centre for △ABC and its image △A'B'C'.
    a) Determine the scale factor *k*.
    b) Find these ratios.
       $$\frac{OA'}{OA}, \frac{OB'}{OB}, \frac{OC'}{OC}$$
    c) Copy the diagram and draw △A″B″C″, the dilatation image of △ABC with scale factor 2.

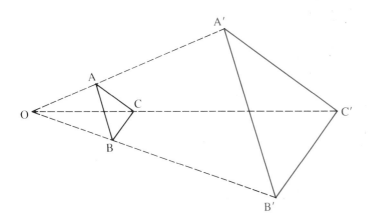

10-6 SIMILAR FIGURES

Two surveyors need to know the distance AB across a pond, which cannot be measured directly.

The surveyors located points D and E such that DE is parallel to AB, and DE can be measured. They completed the triangle at point C.

Triangle CAB can be considered as a dilatation image of △CDE about the dilatation centre C.

Hence, corresponding sides of the triangles are in the same ratio, which is the scale factor of the dilatation.

The surveyors know that $\dfrac{AB}{DE} = \dfrac{AC}{DC}$.

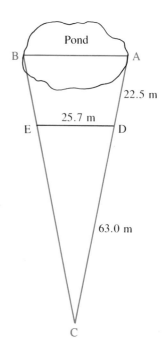

They measured DE, AC, and DC, and these lengths are labelled on the diagram.

Hence, $\dfrac{AB}{25.7} = \dfrac{85.5}{63.0}$

$\qquad AB = \dfrac{85.5}{63.0}(25.7)$

$\qquad\qquad \doteq 34.9$

The distance AB across the pond is about 35 m.

If one geometric figure is the image of another under a dilatation, then the figures are said to be similar.

Two triangles ABC and A′B′C′ are *similar* if the ratios of corresponding sides are equal.

$$\frac{AB}{A'B'} = \frac{AC}{A'C'} = \frac{BC}{B'C'}$$

Two triangles ABC and A′B′C′ are *similar* if pairs of corresponding angles are equal.

$$\angle A = \angle A'; \angle B = \angle B'; \angle C = \angle C'$$

To indicate that △ABC is similar to △A′B′C′, we write △ABC ~ △A′B′C′.

Example 1. Given the figure with the indicated sides parallel

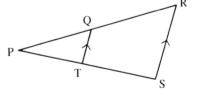

    a) Explain why △PQT is similar to △PRS.

    b) Explain why $\dfrac{QT}{RS} = \dfrac{PT}{PS}$.

Solution.   a) ∠PTQ and ∠PSR are corresponding angles.
        ∠PQT and ∠PRS are corresponding angles.
        Since QT is parallel to RS,
        ∠PTQ = ∠PSR
        ∠PQT = ∠PRS
        ∠P is common to △PQT and △PRS.
        Since pairs of corresponding angles are equal, △PQT ~ △PRS.

    b) The ratios of corresponding sides of △PQT and △PRS are equal.
        Therefore, $\dfrac{QT}{RS} = \dfrac{PT}{PS}$.

Example 2. Find the values of x and y.

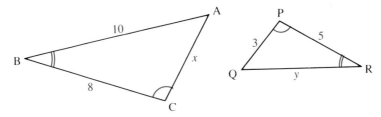

Solution. In $\triangle ABC$ and $\triangle PQR$
$\angle B = \angle R$
$\angle C = \angle P$
Since two pairs of angles in the triangles are equal, the third pair of angles must be equal.
$\angle A = \angle Q$
Since pairs of corresponding angles are equal, $\triangle ABC$ is similar to $\triangle QRP$.
Hence, the ratios of corresponding sides of $\triangle ABC$ and $\triangle QRP$ are equal.
$$\frac{AB}{QR} = \frac{BC}{RP} = \frac{AC}{QP}$$
Substitute the given values.
$$\frac{10}{y} = \frac{8}{5} = \frac{x}{3}$$
Consider these expressions two at a time.

$$\frac{10}{y} = \frac{8}{5}$$
$$5(10) = 8y$$
$$y = \frac{50}{8}$$
$$= 6.25$$

$$\frac{8}{5} = \frac{x}{3}$$
$$\frac{8(3)}{5} = x$$
$$x = \frac{24}{5}$$
$$= 4.8$$

Example 3. The largest international standard paper size is designated by the symbol A0. The A0 size is a rectangle of length 1.19 m and width 0.84 m. The next largest size, A1, is a rectangle similar to A0 but with half the area. What are the dimensions of A1-size paper?

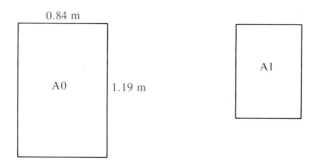

Solution. Since the two rectangles are similar, rectangle A1 is the image of rectangle A0 under a dilatation with scale factor k.

Since the area of rectangle A1 is one-half that of rectangle A0,

$$k^2 = \frac{1}{2}$$

$$k = \frac{1}{\sqrt{2}}$$

Therefore, $\dfrac{\text{length of rectangle A1}}{\text{length of rectangle A0}} = \dfrac{1}{\sqrt{2}}$

$$\text{length of rectangle A1} = \frac{1}{\sqrt{2}}(1.19)$$

$$\doteq 0.84$$

and $\dfrac{\text{width of rectangle A1}}{\text{width of rectangle A0}} = \dfrac{1}{\sqrt{2}}$

$$\text{width of rectangle A1} = \frac{1}{\sqrt{2}}(0.84)$$

$$\doteq 0.59$$

The dimensions of A1-size paper are 0.84 m by 0.59 m.

EXERCISES 10-6

Ⓐ

1. State which figures are similar.

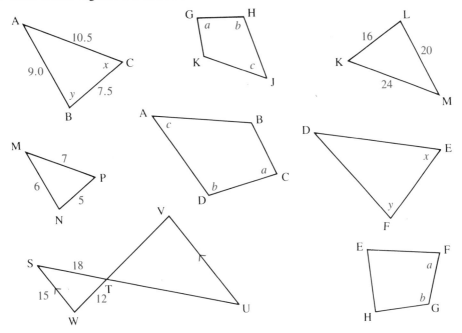

Ⓑ

2. Show that:

a) $\dfrac{AB}{A'B'} = \dfrac{AC}{A'C'}$

b) $\dfrac{AB}{A'B'} = \dfrac{BC}{B'C'}$.

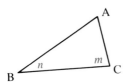

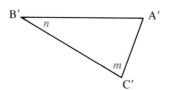

3. Show that:

a) $\dfrac{DE}{DG} = \dfrac{DF}{DH}$

b) $\dfrac{DE}{DG} = \dfrac{EF}{GH}$.

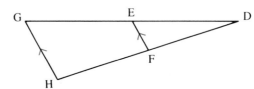

4. Show that:

a) $\dfrac{TR}{TV} = \dfrac{TS}{TU}$

b) $\dfrac{TR}{TV} = \dfrac{RS}{VU}$.

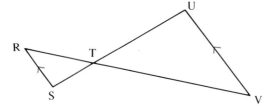

5. Find the values of x and y.

a)

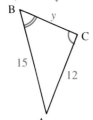

b)

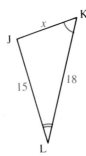

c)

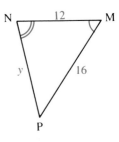

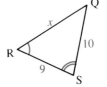

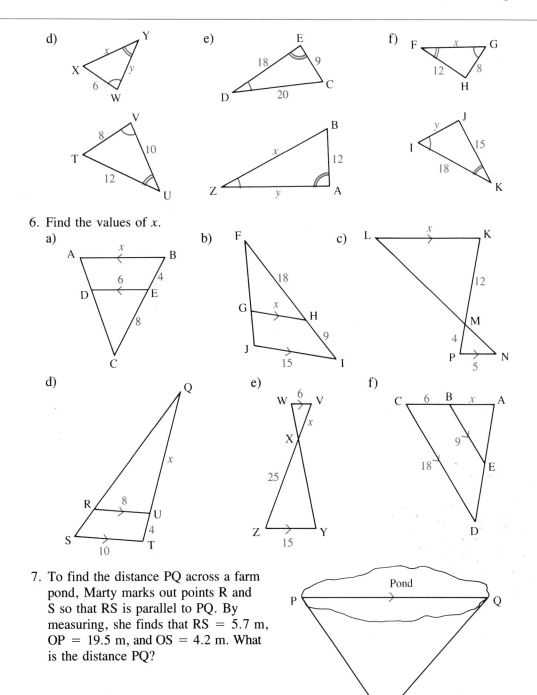

d)

e)

f)

6. Find the values of *x*.

   a)

   b)

   c)

   d)

   e)

   f)

7. To find the distance PQ across a farm
   pond, Marty marks out points R and
   S so that RS is parallel to PQ. By
   measuring, she finds that RS = 5.7 m,
   OP = 19.5 m, and OS = 4.2 m. What
   is the distance PQ?

8. The shadow of a telephone relay tower is 32 m long on level ground. At the same time, a boy 1.8 m tall casts a shadow 1.5 m long. What is the height of the tower?

9. Karen is 37.5 m from a church. She finds that a pencil, 4.8 cm long, which is held with its base 60 mm from her eye, just blocks the church from her sight. How high is the church?

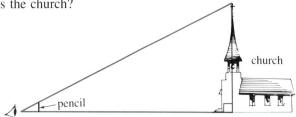

10. The shape of A2-size paper is a rectangle similar to the A1 size but with half its area.
    a) Use the data in *Example 3* to find the dimensions of the A2 size.
    b) What symbol designates paper measuring 30 cm by 21 cm?

11. Sunil has a photograph measuring 20 cm by 25 cm. He wishes to get a copy that is three-quarters the area but with the same length-to-width ratio. What will be the dimensions of the copy?

12. For the photograph in *Exercise 11*, what would be the dimensions of a copy with double the area of the original but with the same shape?

13. Find the values of x and y.
    a) b) c) d)

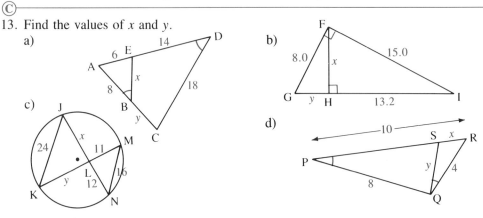

14. To determine the height of a tree, Jerry places a 2 m rod 24 m from the tree. He finds that he can just align the top of the rod with the top of the tree when he stands 1.9 m from the rod. If Jerry's eyes are 1.6 m from the ground, what is the height of the tree?

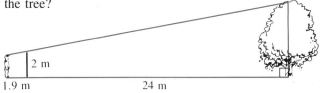

10-7 APPLICATIONS OF TRANSFORMATIONS

We can solve certain apparently difficult problems using transformations.
Consider the problem posed at the beginning of this chapter.

Example 1. A pumping station is to be built somewhere along a pipeline to serve tanks at two points near the pipeline. Where should the pumping station be located so that the total length of the pipe from the pipeline to the tanks is a minimum?

Solution. Draw a diagram. Let A and B represent the tanks, and let *l* represent the pipeline.

Locate B′, the reflection image of B in *l*. The shortest distance between A and B′ is the line segment joining them. Let AB′ intersect *l* at P. Join PB. PB is the reflection image of PB′ in *l*.

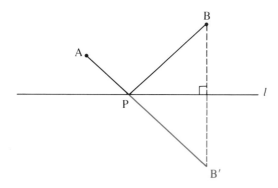

Since AP + PB′ is the shortest distance from A to B′, AP + PB is the shortest distance from A to *l* to B.
The pumping station should be built at P.

When using transformations to solve problems, we make use of the fact that reflections, rotations, and translations preserve lengths, angles, and areas. *Example 1* involved the invariance of length under a reflection.

Although dilatations do not preserve length, they do preserve the ratios of lengths. This property is used in the following example.

Example 2. The image on the screen of a drive-in theatre is projected from a film 35 mm wide. The film is 150 mm in front of the light source and the screen is 14 m high. How far is the screen from the light source?

Solution. Draw a diagram.

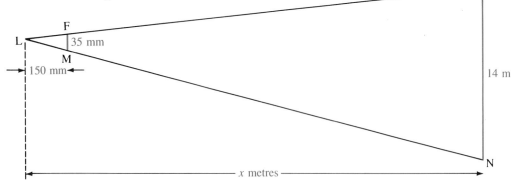

Let the distance from the light source L to the screen SN be x metres. Since the film FM maps onto the screen SN, △LFM maps onto △LSN under a dilatation with centre L.

Hence, △LFM is similar to △LSN.

Therefore, the ratios of corresponding lengths in the two triangles are equal.

$$\frac{150}{FM} = \frac{x}{SN}$$

$$\frac{150}{35} = \frac{x}{14}$$

$$x = \frac{150 \times 14}{35}$$

$$= 60$$

The screen is 60 m from the light source.

EXERCISES 10-7

Ⓐ

1. Show how to locate point R on line l such that PR + QR is a minimum.

_____ l

• P

• Q

2. a) Plot the points A(3,5) and B(7,2) on a grid.
   b) Locate the point M on the x-axis such that AM + MB is a minimum.
   c) Locate the point N on the y-axis such that AN + NB is a minimum.

ⓑ

3. Using points A and B of *Exercise 2*, locate point M on the *y*-axis and point N on the *x*-axis such that AM + MN + NB is a minimum.

4. Copy this diagram.

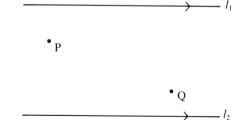

   a) Draw the shortest path from P to l_1 to l_2 to Q.
   b) Draw the shortest path from P to l_2 to l_1 to Q.
   c) In finding the shortest path from P to Q, does it matter which line (l_1 or l_2) you go to first?

5. Two adjacent cushions of a billiard table can be represented by the *x*- and *y*-axes on a grid. Let the points B(3,6) and W(12,6) represent the positions of the brown ball and a white ball respectively.
   a) Find the coordinates of a point on the *x*-axis at which the white ball should be aimed so as to rebound and hit the brown ball.
   b) i) Find the coordinates of the point on the *x*-axis at which the white ball should be aimed so as to rebound from the *x*-axis to the *y*-axis and hit the brown ball.
      ii) What are the coordinates of the point where the ball hits the *y*-axis?

6. A fly lands at the point A(4,6) on a grid. It walks to the *y*-axis, then to the *x*-axis, and finally stops at the point B(8,3). What is the shortest distance the fly could have walked?

7. A film negative, measuring 13 mm by 17 mm, is 32 mm from a camera lens. What are the maximum dimensions of an object that can be photographed from a distance of 12.4 m?

8. To determine the distance AB across a river, a surveyor places a marker at C. She finds a point A′ in alignment with C and a prominent feature A on the far side of the river. Finally, she locates positions B and B′ so that ∠ABC = ∠A′B′C = 90°. If A′B′ = 3.8 m, B′C = 5.2 m, and BC = 14.7 m, how wide is the river at AB?

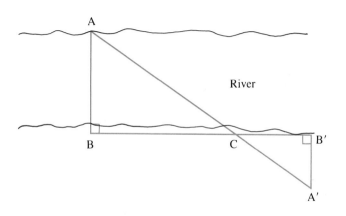

Review Exercises

1. Each triangle is an image of △PQR under a transformation. Identify each transformation.

a)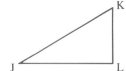

b) D ——— E
   F

c)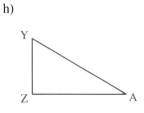

d)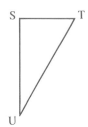

e)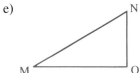

f) S ——— T
   U

g) V ——— W
      X

h) Y
   Z ——— A

2. Each quadrilateral is an image of quadrilateral ABCD under a transformation. Identify each transformation.

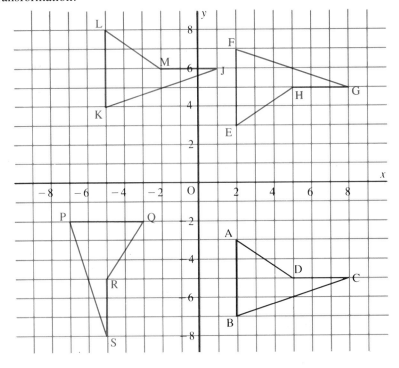

3. State the type of transformation that appears to map each polygon onto its colored image.

a)

b)

c)

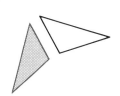  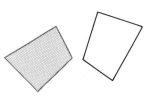

4. Copy each diagram. Divide it along the broken lines into two congruent parts. Name the transformation needed to map one part onto the other.

a)

b)

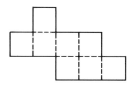 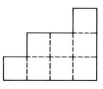

c)

d)

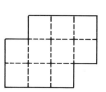 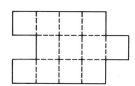

5. A translation maps $(-3, -1)$ onto $(2, -3)$.
   a) Find the images of A$(-2,4)$, B$(1, -5)$, and C$(4,1)$ under this translation.
   b) If P$'(2, -3)$, Q$'(0,4)$, and R$'(-5,1)$ are image points under this translation, find the original points.

6. Graph the points A$(2,5)$, B$(-3,1)$, and C$(1, -4)$. Find the image of each point under a reflection in:
   a) the x-axis
   b) the y-axis.

7. Graph the points L$(-2, -3)$, M$(4, -3)$, and N$(4,5)$. Find the image of each point under a 180° rotation about the origin.

8. The reflection images of A$(1,4)$, B$(3, -2)$, and C$(5,1)$ are A$'(-3,4)$, B$'(-5, -2)$, and C$'(-7,1)$. Graph both triangles and draw the reflection line.

9. Copy $\triangle$XYZ and draw its dilatation image (about a dilatation centre of your choice) using each scale factor.

   a) 2

   b) $\dfrac{3}{4}$

   Compare the area of each image with the area of $\triangle$XYZ.

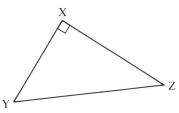

10. Find the values of *x* and *y*.

a)

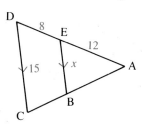

b)

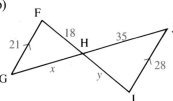

c)

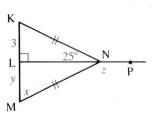

d)

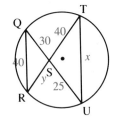

11. A building 18.2 m tall casts a shadow 7.1 m long. At the same time, how long is the shadow of a building that is 15.7 m tall?

12. A poster measures 30 cm by 45 cm. A copy is made, which has three times the area. What are its dimensions?

13. Find the values of *x*, *y*, and *z*.

a)

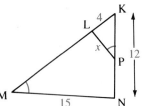

b)

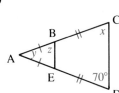

c)

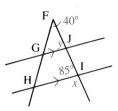

14. Copy the diagram. Draw the shortest path from P to *l* to *m* to Q.

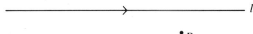

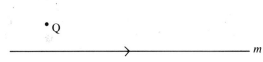

15. Copy this diagram. Translate the exterior angles at vertices B, C, D, and E to vertex A. What is the sum of the exterior angles of the polygon?

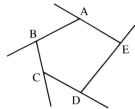

Statistics show that very few accidents occur in the early morning, in fog, at speeds in excess of 150 km/h. Does this mean that these are the safest conditions for driving? (See Section 11-4, *Example 1*.)

11-1 INTERPRETING GRAPHS

In the fast-moving computer age, we encounter vast quantities of data. *Statistics* is the branch of mathematics that deals with the collection, organization, and interpretation of data. These data are usually organized into tables and/or presented as graphs. Some common types of graphs are shown below. Try to answer the question that accompanies each graph.

Pictograph

The graph shown here uses the symbol • to represent 100 million people. A graph that uses a symbol to represent a certain amount is called a *pictograph*.
- What are the populations of North America and Europe?

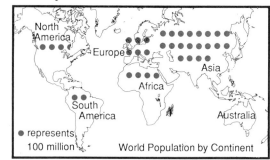

Circle Graph

In a *circle graph*, a complete set of data is presented by the circle. Various parts of the data are represented by the sectors of the circle.
- What percent of Ontario's forest fires are caused by lightning?

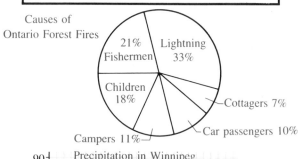

Bar Graph

The graph shown here uses a vertical bar to represent the amount of precipitation each month. Graphs of this type are called *bar graphs*. Bar graphs have horizontal or vertical bars.
- What appears to be the rainy season in Winnipeg?

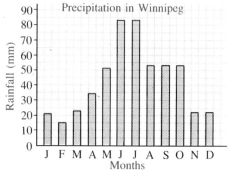

Histogram

A graph that uses bars, where each bar represents a range of values, is called a *histogram*.

The bars on a histogram do not have spaces between them because the data are continuous.

This histogram shows the number of students whose heights fall in each 5 cm interval from 140 cm to 189 cm.
- How many students are at least 170 cm tall?

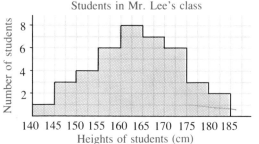

Broken-Line Graph

The graph shown here gives the population of the world at the end of each decade from 1900 to 1980. Since the exact population during each decade is not known, adjacent plotted points are joined by a line segment. Graphs like this are called *broken-line graphs.*

The only points on a broken-line graph that represent data are the endpoints of the segments.

- About how many years did it take the world's population to grow from 3 billion to 4 billion?

Continuous-Line Graph

A graph that shows the value of one variable, such as speed, corresponding to the value of another variable, such as stopping distance, for all values over a given interval is called a *continuous-line graph.*

This graph shows the distance required to bring a car to rest from the moment the brakes are applied, when the car is travelling at speeds up to 100 km/h.

All the points on a continuous-line graph correspond to data.

- What is the car's stopping distance when it is travelling at 60 km/h?

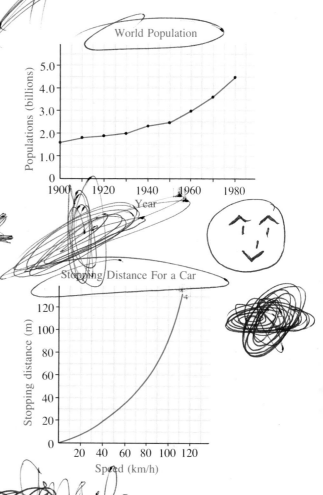

EXERCISES 11-1

Ⓐ

1. Name the type of graph that you think would be most appropriate for displaying each set of data. Explain why you chose that graph.
    a) Kevin's expenditures are divided as follows: 30% for entertainment, 40% for sports equipment, 22% for clothes, and 8% for school supplies.
    b) The approximate populations are given for Canada's 5 most populous provinces.
    c) The average temperature in Vancouver is given for each month of a particular year.
    d) A graph is to be drawn from which temperatures in degrees Celsius can be converted into temperatures in degrees Fahrenheit.
    e) The number of students whose final marks in mathematics were in these intervals: 0-25, 26-50, 51-75, and 76-100.

2. Explain the difference between:
   a) a pictograph and a bar graph
   b) a broken-line graph and a continuous-line graph
   c) a bar graph and a histogram.

3. What is the sum of the percents shown on a circle graph? Explain your answer.

Ⓑ

4. The circle graph shows how an hour of radio time is spent.
   a) What percent of each hour is devoted to news?
   b) How many minutes each hour are devoted to commercials?

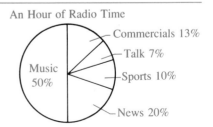

An Hour of Radio Time

5. The bar graph shows the energy in kilojoules per minute used for different activities.
   a) Which activity burns up energy twice as fast as walking?
   b) If you cycled for 30 min, how much energy would you use?
   c) For how long would you have to run to burn up 2200 kJ of energy from a chocolate milkshake?

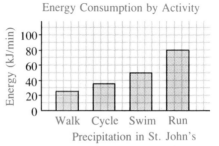

6. The histogram shows the monthly average amount of precipitation in St. John's.
   a) Which month had the most snow?
   b) Which month had the most rain?
   c) During which month did the snowfall equal the rainfall?
   d) What is the average snowfall in a year?

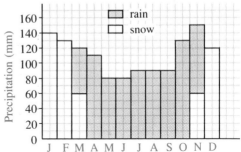

7. The pictograph shows the approximate distances from the sun to the four closest planets.
   a) How far, in kilometres, is each planet from the sun? Write your answers in scientific notation.
   b) About how many times as far from the sun is Mars than Mercury?
   c) Jupiter is about 780 million kilometres from the sun. Write this distance in scientific notation.
   d) What difficulty would you encounter if you tried to show the distances of all the planets from the sun using a pictograph?

Distances of the Four Closest Planets from the Sun

Each ● represents 10^8 km

| Mars | Earth | Venus | Mercury |

11-2 ORGANIZING AND PRESENTING DATA

The heights of the players on a school basketball team were recorded by the coach.

Art	178 cm	Jason	177 cm	Neil	175 cm
Brian	181 cm	Joe	176 cm	Paul	178 cm
Bruce	180 cm	John	175 cm	Scott	177 cm
Dick	177 cm	Kevin	178 cm	Terry	178 cm
Gordon	180 cm	Larry	179 cm		

To get a better idea of the distribution of the heights of his players, the coach made a *tally chart* or *frequency table*. The frequency of a measurement is the number of times it occurs.

Using the frequency table, the coach drew a bar graph. Each height is represented by a bar. The length of a bar corresponds to the frequency of that measurement.

Height (cm)	Number of Players	Frequency
175	ǁ	2
176	ǀ	1
177	ǀǁ	3
178	ǀǁǀ	4
179	ǀ	1
180	ǁ	2
181	ǀ	1

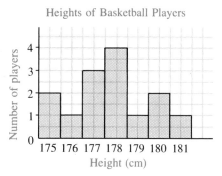

Often, the number of different data is too great for each measurement to be represented by a bar. Then the information is shown on a histogram.

Example 1. Here is a set of marks (out of 100) obtained by a class on a mathematics test.

72	53	73	59	68	83	71	67	77	78	70	67	63
65	56	86	47	78	72	79	67	74	62	84	92	88
71	74	81	70	66	64	75	65	46				

a) Make a tally chart and frequency table for intervals of 10 marks.
b) Draw a histogram.
c) In which interval did most students' marks fall?
d) The pass mark was 50.
   i) How many students passed the test?
   ii) How many students failed the test?

Solution. a) From an inspection of the marks, the lowest mark is 46 and the highest mark is 92.
Choose intervals of 10 marks from 40 to 49, 50 to 59, . . ., 90 to 99. Make a tally chart and frequency table.

Interval	Number of Students	Frequency
40-49	‖	2
50-59	⦀	3
60-69	ҤҤ ҤҤ	10
70-79	ҤҤ ҤҤ ‖‖‖‖	14
80-89	ҤҤ	5
90-99	∣	1

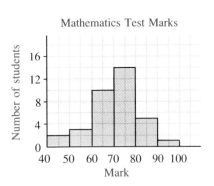

b) Draw a set of axes. Label the horizontal axis with the intervals of marks. Because the intervals begin at 40, the axis between 0 and 40 is interrupted. Label the vertical axis with the numbers of students. Give the graph a title.

c) From the histogram, the interval in which most students' marks fall is the longest bar. That is, most students' marks fall between 70 and 79.

d) i) From the histogram, the number of students who passed the test is the total represented by the lengths of the bars for the interval 50 to 99.
Students who passed: $3 + 10 + 14 + 5 + 1 = 33$
33 students passed the test.

   ii) From the histogram, the students who failed have marks in the interval 40-49. Two students failed the test.

In *Example 1*, suppose the chosen intervals were 45-54, . . ., 85-94. What part of the example could not have been answered from an inspection of the histogram?

Example 2. The chart shows the number of students in each grade of a high school.

Grade	9	10	11	12
Students	266	248	230	142

a) Show this information on a circle graph.
b) What percent, to the nearest whole number, of the students are in:
   i) grade 9   ii) grade 11?

Solution. a) The total student population is 266 + 248 + 230 + 142, or 886.
Each grade will be represented by a sector of the circle.
The sector angle for each grade is proportional to the number of students in that grade.
Express the student population of each grade as a fraction of the total student population, and multiply by 360°.

For grade 9 students, the angle is $\dfrac{266}{886}$ (360°), or 108.1°.

For grade 10 students, the angle is $\dfrac{248}{886}$ (360°), or 100.8°.

For grade 11 students, the angle is $\dfrac{230}{886}$ (360°), or 93.5°.

For grade 12 students, the angle is $\dfrac{142}{886}$ (360°), or 57.7°.

   Write each sector angle to the nearest degree. Check to see if the angles add to 360°.
108° + 101° + 94° + 58° = 361°
   Since several angles were rounded up, the total is 361°. To achieve a total of 360°, round down the angle for grade 11 students to 93°.
   Draw a circle, mark the sector angles, and label each sector. Give the graph a title.

Number of Students
in Each Grade

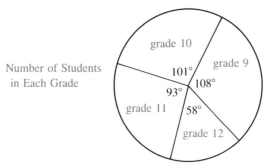

b) i) The grade 9 students represent $\dfrac{266}{886}$ (100%), or about 30%.

   ii) The grade 11 students represent $\dfrac{230}{886}$ (100%), or about 24%.

EXERCISES 11-2

Ⓐ

1. A car dealer hired students to determine the ages of cars owned by the residents of the area. The students listed their findings in this table.

Age of car (years)	0	1	2	3	4	5	6	7
Number of cars	25	40	50	65	45	30	20	15

Display the data on a bar graph.

2. The average daily temperature in Ottawa, for each month, is given in this table.

Month	J	F	M	A	M	J	J	A	S	O	N	D
Temperature (°C)	−11	−10	−3	6	13	18	21	19	14	8	1	−8

a) On a set of axes, plot a point for each temperature from January to December.
b) Join adjacent points with a straight-line segment to form a broken-line graph.

3. The composition of a hot dog is given in this table.

Ingredient	Water	Fat	Protein	Other
Mass (g)	20.4	11.0	4.2	2.3

Draw a circle graph to show this information.

Ⓑ

4. The actual mass of a 2 kg box of chocolates was checked by weighing a selection of 345 boxes. Here are the results.

Mass (kg)	1.91-1.94	1.95-1.98	1.99-2.02	2.03-2.06	2.07-2.10
Frequency	15	85	75	150	20

a) Display this information in a histogram.
b) Quality control dictates that any box under 2 kg must be sold as "seconds".
   i) How many of these checked boxes must be sold as seconds?
   ii) What percent of the boxes are sold as seconds?
c) How could the intervals of mass be organized so that it is possible that fewer boxes would be sold as seconds?

5. A school's grade 9 students obtained these marks (out of 100) in an English examination.

55	66	64	98	56	69	68	62	52	69	65	63	51	90	69
68	32	66	72	44	80	61	84	74	66	79	61	89	78	63
66	59	75	53	69	23	92	78	73	67	38	65	67	41	75
63	71	57	77	66	56	63	73	24	56	76	71	61	51	46
84	55	63	68	86	65	69	66	60	62	68	82	73	65	76
79	88	44												

a) Make a tally chart and frequency table, using intervals of 10 marks.
b) Draw a histogram.
c) The pass mark is 60. How many students passed?
d) What percent of students had marks:
   i) 60 or greater   ii) less than 50?

6. The table shows the amount, as a percent, that a typical family spends in each category.
   a) Draw a circle graph to illustrate this information.
   b) Suppose the family's net annual income is $30 000. How much is spent on:
      i) recreation   ii) transportation
      iii) food   iv) housing?

Item	Amount
Housing	40%
Food	24%
Transportation	15%
Clothing	9%
Savings	5%
Recreation	5%
Miscellaneous	2%

© ——————————————————

7. Use the information in *Example 1*.
   a) Draw a histogram with an interval of 5 marks.
   b) Compare your histogram with that on page 408. What further information could be determined from your histogram?

8. Two groups of students wrote the same mathematics test. Group A was given notice of the test and was able to prepare for it. Group B had the test sprung upon them. The groups obtained the following marks out of 20.

   A 16   17   18   20   11   18   20   19   15   20   15   15   17   12
      19   8   13   16   17   14   19   14   20   12   15
   B 12   11   15   18   12   6   9   11   5   11   11   14   11   16   17
      12   13   9   8   19   10   10   7   11   18

   a) Choose a suitable interval for the marks and draw a histogram for each set of data.
   b) What conclusions can you draw from your histograms?

9. This table shows how Canadians are divided among various age groups.

Age group (years)	1-18	19-34	35-64	65 and over
Canadian population as a percent	32%	25%	32%	11%

   a) Display this information on a circle graph.
   b) Display this information on a histogram.
   c) Which graph do you think is more useful? Explain your answer.
   d) Assume a Canadian population of 26 000 000.
      i) How many Canadians are under 35 years of age?
      ii) How many Canadians are under 65 years of age?

MATHEMATICS AROUND US

Saskatchewan's Wheat Production

Saskatchewan produces more than half of Canada's wheat crop, as illustrated in the table. The wheat production is expressed as a percent of the total Canadian production.

Suppose Canada's wheat production is represented by the area of a 5 cm square. Then, Saskatchewan's wheat production may be represented by the area of a smaller square inside it.

The area of the large square is 25 cm². Therefore, the area of the small square is 0.57(25) cm², or 14.25 cm². The side length of the smaller square is $\sqrt{14.25}$ cm, or about 3.8 cm.

Saskatchewan's wheat production is represented by the area of a square of side length about 3.8 cm. This type of graph is called a *box graph*.

Provincial Wheat Production	
Saskatchewan	57%
Alberta	25%
Manitoba	12%
Other provinces	6%

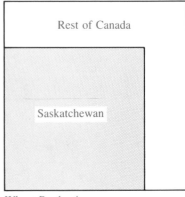

Wheat Production

QUESTIONS

1. a) What would be the side length of the square representing the wheat production of:
      i) Alberta   ii) Manitoba?
   b) Draw the box graphs for part a).

2. Use the data in the table to draw a box graph to represent the population of:
   a) Alberta
   b) Manitoba
   c) Saskatchewan

Population of Canada 1986	
Alberta	2 373 000
Manitoba	1 075 000
Saskatchewan	1 020 000
Other provinces	21 034 000
Total	25 502 000

11-3 MEASURES OF CENTRAL TENDENCY

Police officer	Doctor	Lawyer	Pilot
$35 000	$90 000	$60 000	$55 000

The typical salary of each of four occupations is given above. Who earns more, doctors or lawyers?

It appears from the data given that doctors have greater incomes than lawyers. This can be misleading. Many lawyers earn more than $90 000 per year, and many doctors earn less than $60 000.

We want a single number that best represents the income of all doctors or all lawyers. We are looking for an ''average'' income.

Three of the most commonly used averages are the mean, the median, and the mode.

> The *mean* of a set of numbers is the arithmetical average of the numbers; that is, the sum of all the numbers divided by the number of numbers.

> The *median* of a set of numbers is the middle number when the numbers are arranged in order. If there is an even number of numbers, the median is the mean of the two middle numbers.

> The *mode* of a set of numbers is the most frequently occurring number. There may be more than one mode, or there may be no mode.

The mean, the median, and the mode of a set of numbers are referred to as *measures of central tendency*.

Example 1. The recorded rainfall, in millimetres, for seven consecutive days in Kitimat, British Columbia, is given. 12, 14, 8, 8, 8, 12, 15
Find.
a) the mean rainfall
b) the median rainfall
c) the mode for the rainfall

Solution. a) For the mean, add the numbers and divide by 7.
$$\frac{12 + 14 + 8 + 8 + 8 + 12 + 15}{7} = \frac{77}{7}$$
$$= 11$$
The mean rainfall is 11 mm.
b) For the median, arrange the numbers in order.
8, 8, 8, 12, 12, 14, 15
The middle value is the fourth value, 12.
The median rainfall is 12 mm.
c) The mode is the value which occurs most often. From the list in part b), 8 occurs most often.
The mode for the rainfall is 8 mm.

Example 2. The annual incomes for the people who work at the Beta Metal Works are shown below.
1 Manager: $80 000; 1 Supervisor: $45 000; 3 Mechanics: $35 000;
5 Laborers: $25 000
a) Determine the mean, the median, and the mode for the payroll.
b) Which measure could be used to make the salaries look:
i) high   ii) low?
c) Which measure most fairly represents the average income in the company?

Solution. a) The mean salary, in dollars, is given by:
$$\frac{80\ 000 + 45\ 000 + (3 \times 35\ 000) + (5 \times 25\ 000)}{10}$$
$$= \frac{355\ 000}{10}$$
$$= 35\ 500$$
For the median, arrange the salaries in order.
80 000, 45 000, 35 000, 35 000, 35 000, 25 000, 25 000, 25 000, 25 000, 25 000
Since there is an even number of salaries, the median is the mean of the fifth and sixth values.
$$\frac{35\ 000 + 25\ 000}{2} = \frac{60\ 000}{2}$$
$$= 30\ 000$$
The mode is the salary that occurs most often, $25 000.
The mean is $35 500, the median is $30 000, and the mode is $25 000.

b) i) To make the salaries look high, the mean value of $35 500 would be chosen as being representative.
  ii) To make the salaries look low, the mode value of $25 000 would be chosen as being representative.

c) The mean value of $35 500 is earned by only 2 of the 10 employees. Therefore, it is a high representative value.
  Since every employee earns at least the mode value of $25 000, this is a low representative value.
  The median value of $30 000 probably best represents the average income.

EXERCISES 11-3

Ⓐ

1. Find the mean, the median, and the mode of each set of data. Give the answers to 1 decimal place where necessary.
   a) 10, 12, 8, 9, 12, 14, 11, 15, 9, 12
   b) 1, 2, 2, 3, 3, 3, 4, 4, 4, 4, 4, 4, 5
   c) 2.3, 4.1, 3.7, 3.2, 2.8, 3.6
   d) 15, 18, 16, 21, 18, 14, 12, 19, 11
   e) 9, 12, 7, 5, 18, 15, 5, 11
   f) $\frac{1}{2}, \frac{1}{4}, \frac{2}{3}, \frac{5}{12}, \frac{3}{4}, \frac{2}{3}, \frac{1}{2}, \frac{7}{12}, \frac{1}{6}, \frac{1}{2}$

Ⓑ

2. Over a period of time, some shares were purchased as follows: 10 shares at $8 per share; 20 shares at $9.50 per share; and 15 shares at $8.50 per share. What was the mean price per share?

3. For the numbers 5, 6, 7, 8, 9, find the effect on the mean:
   a) if each number is increased by 2   b) if each number is doubled.

4. If the mean of the numbers 8, 12, 13, 14, x, is 13, what is the value of x?

5. The mean of seven marks on a mathematics test is 68. However, the correction of an error in marking raises one student's mark by 14. Calculate the new mean.

6. The Cabot Manufacturing Company has the following employees at the rates of pay shown.

Position	Weekly Pay ($)	Position	Weekly Pay ($)
1 President	1730	1 Secretary	580
1 Designer	1150	1 Typist	480
1 Supervisor	770	3 Packers	385
3 Assemblers	670	3 Apprentices	290

a) Find the measures of central tendency.
b) Which measure of central tendency most fairly represents the pay structure of the company? Give reasons for your answer.

7. Two groups of students wrote the same mathematics test and obtained the following marks out of 20.

A 16 17 18 20 11 18 20 19 15 20 15 15 17 12
19 8 13 16 17 14 19 14 20 12 15

B 12 11 15 18 12 6 9 11 5 11 11 14 11 16 17
12 13 9 8 19 10 10 7 11 18

   a) Calculate the three measures of central tendency for each group.
   b) Calculate the measures of central tendency for the marks taken together.
   c) How do the results of parts a) and b) compare?

8. The number of accidents at a ski resort for five months is given.
   Which measure of central tendency best describes this data?

	Dec.	Jan.	Feb.	Mar.	Apr.
	25	35	40	35	5

9. Which measure of central tendency is the most suitable to describe each number?
   a) the average number of children in a Canadian family
   b) a person's average weekly salary
   c) a class's average mark in a test
   d) the average rainfall in Quebec City
   e) the average time you spend on homework each night
   f) the average number of hours a ten-year-old child spends watching TV shows each week
   g) the average price of gasoline in a given area
   h) the average size of shoes sold by a store

Ⓒ

10. Find five numbers that have:
    a) a mean of 9 and a median of 8
    b) a mean of 14 and a median of 8.

11. In a set of data, the smallest number is increased by 5 and the largest number is decreased by 5. What changes occur in the measures of central tendency?

12. Mary scored marks of 86, 82, 93, 97, and 78 on term tests in mathematics. What mark must she achieve on the next term test to have a mean score of 90? Explain your answer if the tests are marked out of 100.

13. Akira found that the mean of 100 numbers was exactly 26. Then he subtracted 26 from each of the 100 numbers and added the differences together. What total did he obtain?

14. Use the computer program on page xx to help you find the mean value of the first 100 unit fractions. Is the mean value greater than or less than the median value?

COMPUTER POWER

Calculating Means and Medians

The program below can be used to determine both the mean and the median of three or more numbers. To determine the mean, the computer adds the numbers as they are entered, and then divides the sum by the number of numbers. Then, to determine the median, the computer arranges the numbers in order. If the number of numbers is odd, the computer determines the middle number, and if it is even, the computer determines the mean of the two middle numbers.

```
100 REM *** CALCULATING MEANS AND MEDIANS ***
110 INPUT "HOW MANY NUMBERS ARE THERE? (MINIMUM 3): ";N
120 DIM X(N+1)
130 M=INT((N+1)/2):SUM=0
140 INPUT "ENTER THE FIRST NUMBER: ";X(1):SUM=X(1)
150 FOR I=2 TO N-1
160     INPUT "ENTER THE NEXT NUMBER: ";X(I)
170     SUM=SUM+X(I)
180 NEXT I
190 INPUT "ENTER THE LAST NUMBER: ";X(N):SUM=SUM+X(N)
200 FOR I=1 TO M+1
210     FOR J=I+1 TO N
220         IF X(I)>=X(J) THEN Y=X(I):X(I)=X(J):X(J)=Y
230     NEXT J
240 NEXT I
250 IF N/2<>INT(N/2) THEN X(M+1)=X(M)
260 PRINT:PRINT "THE MEAN IS: ";SUM/N
270 PRINT "THE MEDIAN IS: ";X(M)/2+X(M+1)/2
280 END
```

1. Use the program to find the mean and the median of each set of numbers.

   a) 29 38 26 29 30 41   b) 238 479 506 384 726
       35 33 29 37 25 29   839 448 356 606 928
       32 33 32 28 30 31   335 668 937 46 207
       24 38 28   199 983 663 585 224
                                    669 532 496 355

2. The heights, in centimetres, of 32 students in a grade 9 class at Runnymede Collegiate were recorded as follows.

   153.6 157.9 155.4 156.0 155.8 154.4 149.8 156.5 155.0
   157.1 156.4 153.6 156.8 151.2 166.4 155.3 157.4 152.6
   162.5 158.3 152.4 148.7 153.6 154.2 156.2 150.4 158.1
   159.2 150.1 152.6 153.7 162.8

   a) What are the mean and the median heights of the students in this class?
   b) What is the height of the shortest student in the taller half of the class?

11-4 MISUSING STATISTICS

The table shows the number of cars produced
by one plant of the Standard Automobile
Corporation during a five-year period. These
data were used to construct each broken-
line graph shown below.

Does each graph convey the same
impression?

Year	Cars Produced
1983	20 150
1984	22 300
1985	23 850
1986	25 600
1987	27 100

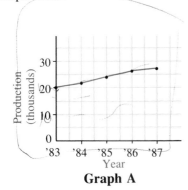

Graph A

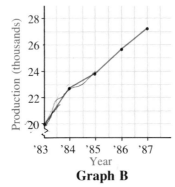

Graph B

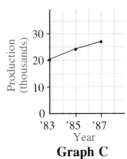

Graph C

Graph A is an honest graph, which shows that the company is
making moderate increases in production.

Graph B is misleading. There appears to be a spectacular increase
in production over the five-year period. This occurs because the vertical
scale does not begin at 0.

Graph C is misleading. This graph also suggests a greater increase
in production than actually took place. This is achieved by making the
vertical axis much longer than the horizontal axis. As a general rule,
the axes should be approximately the same length.

Not all misuses of statistics involve graphs. The following examples
contain statements that are typical of some that can be found in
newspapers and magazines.

Example 1. Comment on the reasoning in this sentence.
"As few accidents happen in the early morning, very few of these as a
result of fog, and fewer still as a result of travelling faster than 150 km/h,
it would be best to travel at high speed on a foggy morning."

Solution. There are few accidents as a result of high speed on a foggy morning
because:
- there is little traffic on the roads in the early morning
- many motorists would wait for the fog to clear, and those who do
  drive would reduce their speeds
- few motorists drive at more than 150 km/h at any time.
Therefore, it would be wrong to conclude from the statistics that it would
be best to travel at high speed on a foggy morning.

Example 2.   Comment on this newspaper report.

Solution.   The headline is inaccurate because
it is based only on the people who
visited Dr. Cole. They very likely
went to see her because they were
not in good health. The 30 patients
were not a representative portion
of the population. Any representative
portion of the population would
include many more people than 30,
most of whom would be healthy.

The Gazette
Two Out of Three Have Heart Trouble

In an interview with a Gazette reporter, Dr.
Cole of Eastern Hospital stated that she was
consulted by 30 patients last week. Of those
30, she found that 20 had had heart trouble.
This is an alarmingly high

EXERCISES 11-4

1. Say whether or not the following statements are correct interpretations of the statistics.
   Give reasons.
   a) A cure for the common cold has been found. In a recent test, 300 cold victims
      took the new wonder drug, Coldgone. After four days, only 7 persons still
      had colds.
   b) Last year, 50 motorists and 8 bicyclists were killed in traffic accidents. This
      proves that it is safer to ride a bicycle than drive a car.
   c) The data in the table show that teen-
      agers are more likely to have a
      skiing accident than persons in other
      age groups. Also, persons over 50
      years of age are the best skiers.
   d) Almost 48% of injuries in downhill
      skiing are to skiers who have never
      had lessons. This means that skiers
      who take lessons are involved in
      more skiing accidents than those who
      do not. It follows that it is better not to take lessons.

Age of Skier (years)	Percent of Skiing Accidents
under 10	10
10-19	61
20-29	19
30-39	5
40-49	3
over 50	2

   e) Last year, there were 45 000 job vacancies in Canada. There were also 500 000
      unemployed workers. This shows that the unemployed are not interested in
      working.

2. You are the Public Relations Manager for an insurance company. A case is being
   made for cheaper insurance rates for persons under 25 years of age based on these
   statistics. What points would you make in reply?

Age Group	Number of Drivers in Fatal Accidents	Percent of Total Fatalities
under 25	98	39.2
over 25	152	60.8

3. Printed on the wrapper of a stick of gum is the statement, "4 out of 5 dentists recommend sugarless gum for their patients who chew gum." Comment on this statement.

4. The table records a company's annual profits for the years 1980 to 1987.
   a) Draw an honest graph to represent the data.
   b) Draw a graph on which the annual profit does not appear to change very much.
   c) Draw a graph that exaggerates the increase in profit.

Year	Profit ($1 000 000s)
1980	5.0
1981	5.2
1982	5.4
1983	5.8
1984	6.5
1985	7.0
1986	7.4
1987	8.5

5. The following table gives a company's monthly sales for a year.

Month	Jan.	Feb.	Mar.	Apr.	May	June	July	Aug.	Sept.	Oct.	Nov.	Dec.
Sales ($1000s)	95	98	98	95	90	85	80	78	75	72	68	64

   a) Draw an honest graph to represent the data.
   b) Draw a graph on which the monthly sales do not appear to change very much.
   c) Draw a graph that exaggerates the decrease in sales.

6. Obtain three examples of statistical data from newspapers and magazines, or from radio and television commercials, and comment on the statements made.

7. The table shows the hitting records of two baseball players, Pops and Rooky, against left-handed and right-handed pitchers.

	Pops	Rooky
Against left-handed pitchers	180 hits out of 540 at bats	20 hits out of 100 at bats
Against right-handed pitchers	230 hits out of 460 at bats	420 hits out of 900 at bats

   Each player was at bat 1000 times.
   a) Calculate the batting averages of Pops and Rooky. Whose average is greater?
   b) Calculate the batting averages of Pops and Rooky against left-handed pitchers. Whose average is greater?
   c) Calculate the batting averages of Pops and Rooky against right-handed pitchers. Whose average is greater?
   d) Compare the answers to parts a), b), and c). What do you notice?

MATHEMATICS AROUND US

Counting Large Populations

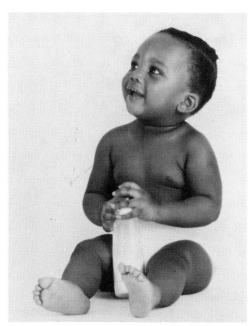

Earth's population estimated to hit 5 billion today

WASHINGTON (AP) — Somewhere on Earth today, the world's five billionth person will be born, say experts at the U.S.-based Population Institute.

If true, the new milestone will come just 10 to 12 years after the four billionth person checked in. But not all experts agree today is the day.

Carl Haub, a demographer at the private Population Reference Bureau, noted United Nations estimates indicate the five billion mark won't be reached until about next March. Other statisticians have said the milestone may have already quietly passed, since many countries simply do not keep very good track of their populations.

In 1986 it was reported that the Earth's population became 5 billion. But, as this newspaper article reveals, a question such as this can never be answered accurately. It takes so long to collect the data that they will be obsolete by the time they are all collected and analysed.

QUESTIONS

1. From an almanac or some other source, obtain the most recent value of the population of the Earth. How accurately is the value given?

2. Do you think there was actually a 5 billionth person? Discuss.

3. Suppose you were counting the people in your community.
   a) Do you think you could do this correct to the nearest person?
   b) Give as many reasons as you can why you might not be able to determine the population correct to the nearest person.
   c) How accurately do you think you could determine the population?

4. Try to determine the population of your school correct to the nearest person. Include both students and staff.

11-5 SAMPLING A POPULATION

What television program is the most popular of those on the air at a particular time?

It is clearly impossible to poll the entire population to find out who is watching what. Instead, a representative portion of the population, called a *sample*, is polled. If the sample is carefully chosen, the viewing preferences of the sample will accurately reflect the preferences of the entire population. For example, the Nielsen ratings which rank the popularity of television shows in North America are determined by a survey which samples less than one home in 10 000, that is, less than 0.01% of the North American population! Gallup polls assess the political preferences of the entire population of Canadians by surveying fewer than 2000 people.

If a sample is truly representative of the population from which it is drawn, then conclusions made about the population are likely to be valid. In statistics, the *population* is the whole of anything of which a sample is being taken.

A sample that is chosen in such a way that it is typical of the population it represents is called a *random sample*. It is very important that a sampling process be purely random in that all members of the population must share an equal chance of being selected.

To obtain information about a population, follow these steps.
- Decide on a sample size.
- Choose a device for selecting a random sample of that size.
- Collect the data from the sample.
- Organize and interpret the data.
- Make inferences about the characteristics of the population.

There are several ways of collecting data.
- Personal interviews — door-to-door, at shopping centres, by telephone
  For example, a roller-skate manufacturer needs to know how many roller skates of each size to make. The manufacturer would arrange to have personal interviews conducted at selected rinks.

- Questionnaires — by mail, with a purchased article, in newspapers
  For example, a politician wants to know how her or his constituents
  feel about an environmental issue. The politician would send questionnaires by mail to the constituents.

- Tests and measurements — recording instruments, quality control,
  time study
  For example, a quality-control engineer for a light bulb manufacturer
  wants to know the life of the light bulbs, and how many are defective. The engineer would conduct tests on a sample of light bulbs
  chosen at random from the production line.

Example. A Vancouver company is hired by a television station to conduct a poll
to predict the outcome of a national election. To gather this information,
the company considers sampling Canadian voters in one of the following
ways.
a) Interview 100 people at random.
b) Poll a random sample of 1000 people in British Columbia.
c) Put an advertisement in all major newspapers asking people to tell
   their political preferences.
d) Send 10 questionnaires to all major businesses to be completed by
   anyone selected at random.
Describe the main weakness(es) of each method.

Solution. a) The sample is probably too small to be reliable.
b) Political preferences are often regional in nature. A sample of voters
   in British Columbia is not likely to be representative of the political
   opinions of all Canadians.
c) Generally, only people with very strong political views will take the
   trouble to respond to an advertisement. The sample will not be
   random.
d) This sample tends to exclude such voting groups as students, farmers,
   homemakers, and senior citizens, and is therefore not a random
   sample.

EXERCISES 11-5

1. A student visited every household within three blocks of her home and recorded
   the number of persons in each household.

Number of persons in household	1	2	3	4	5	6	7
Number of households	3	7	12	21	14	8	5

a) How many households did she visit?
b) How many persons live within three blocks of the student?

2. The make of every third car in a full parking lot is noted and the number of each make is recorded.

Make of car	Ford	General Motors	Chrysler	American Motors	Foreign
Number of each make	47	64	29	25	82

   a) Which is the most popular car?
   b) How many cars were in the lot?
   c) If the parking fee is $3.50 per car, what are the total receipts for these cars?

Ⓑ

3. How would you collect data to find the following information? Give reasons.
   a) The popularity of a TV program
   b) The most popular breakfast cereal
   c) The average number of children in a family
   d) The number of occupants in cars in rush hours
   e) The most popular recording artist
   f) The average family's food budget

4. How would you collect data to find the following information? What kind of people or items would be in your sample?
   a) The player most likely to be voted ''outstanding rookie''
   b) The top 10 movies of the year
   c) The life of flashlight bulbs
   d) The amount spent by car owners on repairs each month
   e) The time required to eat lunch in a cafeteria
   f) The most popular soft drink

5. Explain why data are collected from a sample and not a population, for each situation.
   a) The quality control in the manufacture of flash cubes
   b) The number of pets per family
   c) The purity of processed food
   d) The strength of aluminum extension ladders
   e) The cost of ski equipment
   f) The percent of the population with the various blood types

6. Decide what kind of a sample you need, then work singly, in pairs, or in groups to collect the following data.
   a) The age and the height of the students in your class
   b) The number of persons in cars in the rush hour
   c) The amount spent on lunch in the cafeteria
   d) The most popular musical group
   e) The time spent waiting in line in the cafeteria
   f) The weekly earnings of students
   g) The percent of times a thumbtack lands point up when dropped from a height of 25 cm
   h) The number of letters in English words

11-6 SOURCES OF DATA

What percent of Canadian families have exactly two children?

There are basically two ways to answer this question. We could collect the data directly, or we could seek the data from some other source.

Collecting Data Directly

Since it is impractical to consider every Canadian family, it would be necessary to conduct a survey. We would identify a sample of Canadian families, and determine the number of children in each family. For the sample to be representative of the Canadian population, it would have to be determined randomly. The sample should contain families from all parts of Canada, and families with no children.

Data Accepted From Other Sources

An almanac is likely to contain population data which could be used to answer the question. If the data are based on census figures, they would have been determined by counting all the families in Canada, and not just a sample. Since a census is taken only once every ten years, the data may be somewhat out of date.

Possible sources of data

- almanac
- encyclopedia
- newspaper files
- computer data base
- library
- Statistics Canada publications
- publications of provincial or municipal governments

EXERCISES 11-6

1. Suppose you were estimating the percent of Canadian families with two children. What are the advantages and disadvantages of obtaining the data:
   a) directly
   b) from some other source?

(B)

2. Conduct a survey in your class or your school to determine what percent of the students have at least one brother or sister.
   a) Do you think this would be a reasonable estimate of the percent of Canadian families with two children? Explain.
   b) Is the actual percent of Canadian families with two children likely to be higher or lower than your result in part a)?
   c) Check your prediction in part b) by consulting an almanac.

3. To answer each question, would you seek data from another source? If so, indicate what source you would consult. Or, would you collect the data directly? If so, indicate how you might collect the data.
   a) What fraction of Canadians are under 18 years of age?
   b) What fraction of students in your class have a job during the school year?
   c) What is the world record for the women's high jump?
   d) How much would it cost to buy $100 in U.S. funds?
   e) What percent of the meals eaten by Canadian teenagers are not eaten at home?
   f) What percent of the cars on the road have personalized licence plates?
   g) How many telephone calls does the average person make in one year?
   h) How many television stations can be received in your community?
   i) What percent of the Canadian population was born in Canada?
   j) How many people in your community support the political candidate you are campaigning for?

4. Obtain the following data.
   a) What are the dimensions of a Canadian two-dollar bill?
   b) What is the population of Canada?
   c) What is the current price of gold?
   d) What time does the sun set in your community today?
   e) How many radio stations are there in your city or the city closest to your home?
   f) How many traffic signals are there within 1 km of your school?

 INVESTIGATE

1. Toss a paper cup 20 times.
2. Record the number of times it lands on its top, its bottom, and its side.

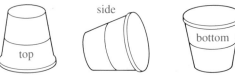

3. Add the results of everyone in the class.
4. Write the number of times each outcome occurs as a fraction of the total number of tosses. This fraction is called the *relative frequency* of each outcome.
5. Discuss the results.

11-7 PREDICTING RESULTS

One of the principal uses of statistics is
in predictions.

By studying samples of voter opinions, we can forecast election outcomes.
These cannot be controlled. We cannot
say for certain what will happen. Never-
theless, sampling enables us to assess
the likelihood that a particular outcome
will occur.

Consider the previous *INVESTIGATE*, where a paper cup was tossed
20 times. Suppose the cup landed on its side 12 times. We say that
the relative frequency of the outcome "landing on its side" is
$\frac{12}{20}$, which simplifies to $\frac{3}{5}$, or 0.6.

> Relative frequency of an outcome $= \dfrac{\text{Number of times the outcome occurs}}{\text{Total number of outcomes}}$

Example. In an experiment, a paper cup is tossed 400 times. Here are the results.

Outcome	top	side	bottom
Frequency	106	246	48

a) Find the relative frequency of each outcome.
b) Predict how many times the cup would land on the bottom in 1000
tosses.

Solution. a) Relative frequency of an outcome $= \dfrac{\text{Number of times the outcome occurs}}{\text{Total number of outcomes}}$

Relative frequency of landing on the top $= \dfrac{106}{400}$
$= 0.265$

Relative frequency of landing on the side $= \dfrac{246}{400}$
$= 0.615$

Relative frequency of landing on the bottom $= \dfrac{48}{400}$
$= 0.12$

b) To predict the number of times a particular outcome will occur, multiply
its relative frequency by the number of tosses.
The number of times a cup will land on the bottom in 1000 tosses is
1000(0.12), or 120.

Jane, the owner of an art shop, decided to make and sell sheets of adhesive letters used for notices and posters. She needed to know how many of each letter to put on a sheet of 500 letters.

To find the frequency with which each letter occurs in the English language, she examined a large sample of poetry. Jane chose the first three verses of *The Tiger* by William Blake.

Tiger, tiger, burning bright
In the forests of the night,
What immortal hand or eye
Could frame thy fearful symmetry?

In what distant deeps or skies
Burnt the fire of thine eyes?
On what wings dare he aspire?
What the hand dare seize the fire?

And what shoulder and what art
Could twist the sinews of thy heart?
And, when thy heart began to beat,
What dread hand and what dread feet?

Jane made a tally chart and frequency table for the letters. She counted the total number of letters in the sample. There are 301 letters. Here is the tally chart for 4 letters.

Letter	a	e	n	s
Tally	⊞⊞ ⊞⊞ ⊞⊞ ⊞⊞ ⊞⊞ ‖‖	⊞⊞ ⊞⊞ ⊞⊞ ⊞⊞ ⊞⊞ ⊞⊞ ⊞⊞ ‖‖|	⊞⊞ ⊞⊞ ⊞⊞ ⊞⊞	⊞⊞ ⊞⊞ ⊞⊞
Frequency	29	39	20	15

Jane found the percent of each letter by multiplying its relative frequency by 100%. For example,

Percent of letter a is $\dfrac{29}{301}$(100%), or about 10%.

Hence, letter a should be 10% of the sheet.
$$10\% \text{ of } 500 = 0.10(500)$$
$$= 50$$

There should be about 50 of letter a on the sheet of letters.

Jane repeated these calculations for each of the letters in the sample poetry.

Would a different poem, or a sample of prose give a different result?

Some letters of the alphabet did not appear in this sample of poetry. Should these letters be included on the sheet?

EXERCISES 11-7

1. A computer simulated the toss of a penny 319 020 times. Heads occured 160 136 times. What was the relative frequency of heads, to 3 decimal places?

2. A die has these faces.

Outcomes on 100 Tosses of a Die

The die was rolled 100 times. The frequency of each outcome is shown on the graph.

a) Find the relative frequency of each face shown below.

   i)   ii)   iii)

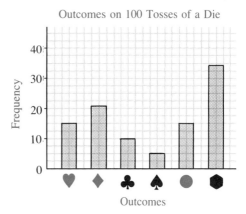

b) Do you think it is a "fair" die? Explain your answer.

3. When a thumbtack is tossed, there are two possible outcomes.

     point up   point down

   a) Toss 10 thumbtacks onto a desk. Record the number that land point up, and calculate the relative frequency.
   b) Combine the results of everyone in the class.
   c) What is the relative frequency for point up after tossing 300 thumbtacks?

4. A thumbtack is tossed 400 times and lands point up 250 times. About how many times should it land point up if it is tossed 5000 times?

5. a) Toss a coin the number of times indicated and record the frequency of heads.
      i) 10 times   ii) 20 times   iii) 30 times
   b) Calculate the relative frequency of heads in each case.
   c) Combine your results with those of other students to obtain the relative frequency of heads for a greater number of tosses.
   d) How does the relative frequency of heads compare with 0.5 for a greater number of tosses?

6. If, in a coin-tossing experiment, you calculated the relative frequency of heads to be 0.47, what should be the relative frequency of tails?

7. Choose 200 lines from a magazine story or newspaper article. Count the number of complete sentences and the number of words in each sentence. What is the relative frequency of sentences containing:
   a) fewer than 9 words
   b) more than 12 words?

8. a) Toss two coins 30 times and record the number of times they show:
      i) two heads   ii) two tails   iii) one head, one tail.
   b) Calculate the relative frequency in each case.
   c) Combine your results with those of other students to find the relative frequencies for a greater number of tosses.
   d) If two coins were tossed 5000 times, about how many times would they show:
      i) two heads   ii) two tails   iii) one head, one tail?

Ⓒ

9. By the end of the second week of the baseball season, a player has had 9 hits out of 20 official times at bat.
   a) Calculate the player's batting average.
   b) In the next game, the player gets 0 hits out of 3 times at bat. Calculate his batting average after this game.
   c) By the final month of the baseball season, the player has had 106 hits out of 425 times at bat. Calculate his batting average now.
   d) The player gets 0 hits out of his next 3 times at bat. What does this make his average?
   e) Why did a game with 0 hits out of 3 times at bat make less difference to the player's batting average at the end of the season than at the beginning?

10. When a cylinder is tossed there are two possible outcomes; it can land on an end or on its side. From a broom handle, cut cylinders 1 cm, 2 cm, 3 cm, and 4 cm long. Record the outcomes of 50 tosses for the four cylinders.

   a) What is the relative frequency of the cylinder landing on an end?
   b) What is the effect of the length to diameter ratio on the way a cylinder lands?

11. You intend to toss a coin 100 times to determine the relative frequency of heads. Investigate whether it makes a significant difference if you toss:
   a) 1 coin, 100 times
   b) 2 coins, 50 times
   c) 4 coins, 25 times
   d) 10 coins, 10 times.

COMPUTER POWER

Counting Characters

Since compiling frequencies and relative frequencies is tedious and time consuming, the computer is now used for this purpose. The following program in BASIC will do this for ten or fewer letters in any passage.

```
100 REM *** COUNTING CHARACTERS ***
110 INPUT "HOW MANY LINES IN YOUR PASSAGE OF TEXT? ";A
120 DIM Q$(10),X$(A),Y$(A,80),R(A),Q(A,10)
130 PRINT "HOW MANY DIFFERENT LETTERS DO YOU WISH"
140 INPUT "TO COUNT? ";N
150 FOR F=1 TO N
160     PRINT "ENTER LETTER NUMBER ";F;" TO BE COUNTED"
170     INPUT Q$(F)
180 NEXT F
190 FOR K=1 TO A
200     PRINT "ENTER LINE #";K
210     INPUT X$(K)
220     FOR J=1 TO LEN(X$(K))
230         Y$(K,J)=MID$(X$(K),J,1)
240         IF Y$(K,J)=" " THEN GOTO 290
250         R(K)=R(K)+1
260         FOR I=1 TO N
270             IF Y$(K,J)=Q$(I) THEN Q(K,I)=Q(K,I)+1
280         NEXT I
290     NEXT J
300     R=R+R(K)
310     FOR L=1 TO N
320         S(L)=S(L)+Q(K,L)
330     NEXT L
340 NEXT K
350 PRINT:PRINT "REL. FREQ.","FREQ.","LETTER"
360 FOR M=1 TO N
370     PRINT S(M)/R,S(M),Q$(M)
380 NEXT M
390 END
```

This program counts all characters, but not spaces. Do not enter punctuation marks or the results may be inaccurate. After entering each line of text, press RETURN and wait for the computer to ask for the next line.

1. Use the program to obtain the frequency and the relative frequency of each letter a, e, i, n, o, s, and t in:
   a) the three verses of ''The Tiger'' on page 428 (do not enter any commas)
   b) the first paragraph of this feature.
   Explain the results.

11-8 PROBABILITY

When spun, the pointer on this wheel may
stop on white, black, or red. Since the three
portions are the same size, we say that each
outcome is *equally likely*.

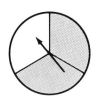

Example 1. For each experiment
    i) List the outcomes.
    ii) State whether the outcomes are equally likely.
      a) A penny is tossed.
      b) A penny and a dime are tossed.
      c) The pointer on the wheel shown is spun.

Solution.   a) i) The outcomes are head (H) and tail (T).
        ii) They are equally likely.
      b) i) The outcomes are: H H, H T, T H, and T T.

        ii) They are equally likely.
      c) i) The outcomes are: red, black, and white.
        ii) Since there are two white portions and only one black and one
           red, the pointer is more likely to stop on white. The outcomes are
           not equally likely.

For the wheel shown, since each outcome
is equally likely, there is one chance in
three that the pointer will stop on black.

We say that the probability that the
pointer will stop on black is $\frac{1}{3}$, and we write:
$P(black) = \frac{1}{3}$.

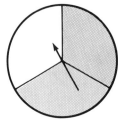

When a die is rolled, the chances that it will show ⊡ are 1 in 6.
We say that the probability that the die will show a 2 is $\frac{1}{6}$, and
we write: $P(2) = \frac{1}{6}$.
Any set of outcomes of an experiment is called an *event*.

    On the roll of a die, there are 6 possible outcomes.

Let A denote the event that we get an even number when we roll a die.
Event A occurs if the outcome of a toss is ⊡ or ⊡⊡ or ⊡⊡⊡ .

We say that the outcomes , and are *favorable* to event A, because if any one of them occurs then event A occurs.

On the toss of two coins, there are 4 possible outcomes.

Let B denote the event that we obtain one head and one tail. Then, the outcomes Ⓗ Ⓣ and Ⓣ Ⓗ are favorable to event B.

The greater the number of equally likely outcomes favorable to an event, the more likely it is that the event will occur.

If the outcomes of an experiment are equally likely, then the probability of an event A is given by:

$$P(A) = \frac{\text{Number of outcomes favorable to A}}{\text{Total number of outcomes}}$$

Example 2. A lottery issued 1000 tickets, which were all sold. What is the probability of your winning if you hold:
a) 1 ticket b) 17 tickets c) 100 tickets?

Solution. Each ticket has an equal chance of being drawn. That is, each outcome is equally likely.

a) $P(\text{win}) = \dfrac{1}{1000}$ b) $P(\text{win}) = \dfrac{17}{1000}$ c) $P(\text{win}) = \dfrac{100}{1000}$, or $\dfrac{1}{10}$

Example 3. A jar contains 3 black balls, 4 white balls, and 5 striped balls. If a ball is picked at random, what is the probability that it is:
a) black b) white c) striped?

Solution. There are 12 balls and each one has an equal chance of being picked. Each outcome is equally likely.

a) $P(\text{black}) = \dfrac{3}{12}$ b) $P(\text{white}) = \dfrac{4}{12}$ c) $P(\text{striped}) = \dfrac{5}{12}$

Example 4. For the wheel shown, determine the probability of each event.
a) Event A: Wheel stops on a number equal to or less than 3.
b) Event B: Wheel stops on a number greater than 6.
c) Event C: Wheel stops on an even number.

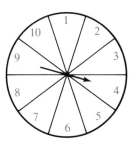

Solution.   There are ten equally likely outcomes.

a) Event A has three favorable outcomes. These are landing on 1, 2, or 3.

$$P(A) = \frac{3}{10}$$

b) Event B has four favorable outcomes. These are landing on 7, 8, 9, or 10.

$$P(B) = \frac{4}{10}$$

c) Event C has five favorable outcomes. These are landing on 2, 4, 6, 8, or 10.

$$P(C) = \frac{5}{10}$$

Example 5.   For the wheel in *Example 4*

a) Event D is that the wheel stops on a number from 1 to 10. What is P(D)?

b) Event E is that the wheel stops on a number greater than 10. What is P(E)?

Solution.   a) Every possible outcome is favorable to event D.

Therefore, $P(D) = \frac{10}{10}$, or 1

b) No outcome is favorable to event E.

Therefore, $P(E) = \frac{0}{10}$, or 0

Probability and relative frequency are closely linked. The probability of an event indicates what the relative frequency should be if the experiment is performed many times.

For the wheel shown, we know that $P(\text{black}) = \frac{1}{3}$. This does not mean that in 30 spins the pointer will stop on black exactly 10 times. It means that it is more probable that it will stop on black 10 times, than any other number of times.

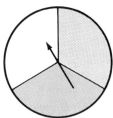

Example 6.   For the wheel above, what is the probable number of times that the pointer should stop on black in 2000 spins?

Solution.   Since $P(\text{black}) = \frac{1}{3}$, the spinner should probably stop on black about $\frac{1}{3}(2000)$ times, or about 667 times.

EXERCISES 11-8

Ⓐ

1. When the pointer is spun, what is the probability that it will stop in the colored sector?

a)

b)

c)

2. In the SCRABBLE™ Brand crossword game, the letters of the alphabet are distributed over the 100 tiles as shown in the table.

From a full bag of tiles, what is the probability of randomly selecting:

a) B   b) E   c) S?

Distribution of Tiles					
A-9	F-2	K-1	P-2	U-4	Z-1
B-2	G-3	L-4	Q-1	V-2	Blank-2
C-2	H-2	M-2	R-6	W-2	
D-4	I-9	N-6	S-4	X-1	
E-12	J-1	O-8	T-6	Y-2	

3. What is the probability that a ball chosen at random from the jar is:

a) black
b) striped
c) colored
d) not black
e) either black or colored
f) neither black nor colored

Ⓑ

4. Cathy and Trevor have birthdays in June. Let A denote the event that Cathy's birthday is a multiple of 5. Let B denote the event that Trevor's birthday is on Wednesday. Let C denote the event that A and B are both true and both birthdays occur on the same day.

JUNE						
Sun	Mon	Tues	Wed	Thurs	Fri	Sat
		1	2	3	4	5
6	7	8	9	10	11	12
13	14	15	16	17	18	19
20	21	22	23	24	25	26
27	28	29	30			

a) If all days are equally likely, what outcomes are favorable to:
i) event A ii) event B iii) event C?
b) Find the probabilities of event A, event B, and event C.

5. For each experiment
i) List the outcomes.
ii) State whether the outcomes are equally likely.
   a) A ball is drawn from a bag containing a red ball, a white ball, and a green ball.
   b) A quarter and a nickel are tossed.
   c) A letter is picked at random from any page of a book printed in English.
   d) A ball is drawn from a bag containing 2 white balls, 3 blue balls, and 5 red balls.
   e) A wheel containing the letters A to H is spun.

6. Five hundred tickets are printed for a lottery. Carla bought 7 tickets. What is the probability of her winning if:
   a) all the tickets were sold
   b) 370 tickets were sold and the rest destroyed?

7. A traffic light is red for 30 s, green for 25 s, and orange for 5 s in every minute. What is the probability that the light is orange when you first see it?

8. A pair of opposite faces of a white die are colored red. If the die is tossed, what is the probability that the top is:
   a) white   b) red?

9. Calculate the probability of tossing a regular tetrahedron so that it lands with the 4 face down. The numbers on the faces are:
   a) 2, 4, 6, 8
   b) 1, 4, 4, 7
   c) 1, 3, 5, 7.

10. What is the probability of receiving a $3 bill in change when groceries are purchased at a store?

11. When the pointer on this wheel is spun, what is the probability that it will stop on :
    a) an odd number   b) an even number
    c) a one-digit number   d) a two-digit number?

12. What is the probability of a regular die, when tossed, showing:
    a) 5   b) an odd number
    c) a prime number   d) a number less than 3
    e) a one-digit number   f) a two-digit number?

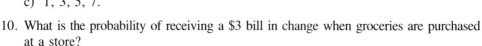

13. What is the probable number of times that a coin should show heads if it is tossed:
    a) 25 times   b) 100 times   c) 1000 times?

14. What is the probable number of times that a die should show 5 if it is tossed:
    a) 25 times   b) 100 times   c) 1000 times?

15. Each wheel is spun 50 times. What is the probable number of times that the wheel should come to rest with the arrow pointing to 2?
    a)   b)   c)   d)

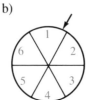

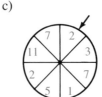
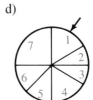

16. What is the probability that all the students in your class are older than 10 years of age?

17. You can pick one marble from any of the three bags. You win a prize if you pick a red marble. Which bag should you choose to have the best chance of winning?

    Bag A contains   Bag B contains   Bag C contains
    3 red and 7 white.   2 red and 3 white.   4 red and 11 white.

18. The words STATISTICS AND PROBABILITY are spelled out with SCRABBLE™ Brand crossword tiles. Then, these tiles are put in a bag. What is the probability that a tile drawn from the bag at random will be:
    a) a vowel
    b) a consonant
    c) one of the first 10 letters of the alphabet?

19. The table lists the number of cars in a parking lot by their ages.

Car's age (years)	0	1	2	3	4	5	6	7
Number	25	40	50	70	45	35	20	15

    Calculate the probability that the age of a car selected at random will be:
    a) 2 years   b) greater than 4 years
    c) less than 3 years   d) 3 to 5 years.

20. What is the probability that a card drawn at random from a deck of 52 cards will be:
    a) red   b) a spade
    c) a black 7   d) a face card (Jack, Queen, or King)?

Ⓒ

21. A die is loaded so that the outcomes have the relative frequencies shown in this table.

Outcome	1	2	3	4	5	6
Relative Frequency	0.12	0.17	0.17	0.08	0.35	0.11

    What is the probability of throwing:
    a) a number less than 3   b) an even number?

22. Life insurance companies use birth and death statistics in calculating the premiums for their policies. The table shows how many of 100 000 people at age 10 are still living at ages 30, 50, 70, and 90.

Age (years)	10	30	50	70	90
Number of People Living	100 000	95 144	83 443	46 774	2220

    a) What is the probability that a 10-year-old child will live:
        i) to age 50   ii) to age 70   iii) to age 50 but not 70?
    b) What is the probability that a 30-year-old person will live to age 90?

PROBLEM SOLVING

Conduct An Experiment

"Each of you", said the judge to the three prisoners before her, "will be given 5 black balls and 5 colored balls. You may distribute these any way you please between two pans. Then you will be blindfolded while the 2 pans are moved around and then you must select a ball from one of the pans. If the ball you select is colored you will be freed. However, if it is black you will be returned to prison."

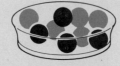

Estimate, for each distribution shown above, the probability that a colored ball will be chosen.

Understand the problem
- Is the probability that a colored ball will be chosen the same for all the distributions?

Think of a strategy
- Try conducting an experiment with the balls placed as illustrated above.

Carry out the strategy
- Get 5 yellow tennis balls and 5 white tennis balls.
- Duplicate the first distribution shown above.
- Conduct the experiment described by the judge. Repeat the selection many times and estimate the probability of selecting a colored ball.
- Repeat the procedure for the other two distributions shown above.
- For which distribution is it most likely that a colored ball will be chosen?

Look back
- Is there a distribution different from those shown above for which it is more likely that a colored ball will be chosen?

Solve each problem

1. Twelve pennies are placed in a row on a table top. Then every second coin is replaced with a nickel. Every third coin is then replaced with a dime. Finally every fourth coin is replaced with a quarter. What is the total value of the 12 coins on the table?

2. Divide a sheet of paper into 3 rectangles of different sizes. Color each rectangle a different color. Toss a penny many times from a distance and record the frequency of landing in each rectangle. Use these frequencies to estimate the area of each rectangle as a fraction of the area of the sheet of paper. Measure the dimensions and calculate the areas to check your answers.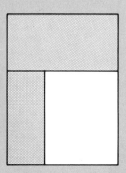

3. Estimate the probability that two cards drawn randomly from a deck of 52 playing cards will both be spades.

4. Estimate the probability that the sum of the numbers obtained on two rolls of a pair of dice exceeds 8.

5. Which of the following figures form a tesselation of the plane; that is, a covering of the plane without gaps or overlapping?

   a) 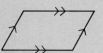   b)   c)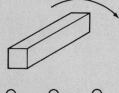

6. A wooden beam with a square cross-section is rolled along the floor. Sketch the path of one corner of the beam.

7. Seven pennies are arranged in 3 lines, with 3 pennies in each line.

   Sketch a diagram to show how 2 of these pennies can be moved so that there are 6 lines with exactly 3 pennies in each line.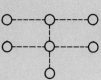

THE MATHEMATICAL MIND

Games of Chance

We know from dice found in the tombs of ancient Greeks and Egyptians that games of chance have been played for thousands of years. However, it was not until the sixteenth and seventeenth centuries that a serious attempt was made to study games of chance using mathematics.

Chevalier de Méré, a professional gambler and amateur mathematician, had many questions about dice probabilities. He turned to the great mathematician Blaise Pascal for the answers. Pascal, with his friend Pierre de Fermat, began a systematic study of games of chance. The theory of probability was founded.

One of de Méré's questions was, "What is the probability of throwing two dice and *not* getting a 1 or 6?"

Pascal answered, "For each die, the probability is $\frac{4}{6}$, or $\frac{2}{3}$. For both, the probability is $\frac{2}{3} \times \frac{2}{3}$, or $\frac{4}{9}$ — about 0.44."

With this information, de Méré offered the equivalent of this gamble.

> Bet $1. Throw 2 dice. If ⚀ or ⚅ do NOT show, you win $2.

He now knew that for every 100 people who played the game, about 44 would win. That meant he would take in $100 and pay out $88. He could expect to win about $12 every time 100 people played. Now that you know this, would you spend $1 to play this game?

QUESTIONS

1. For each of the following games of chance
   a) Determine whether you can expect to win, or lose, money if you play the game a great number of times.
   b) Decide whether you are willing to play the game.
   c) Explain your decision.
      i) Bet $1. Toss a coin. If it shows a head, you win $2.
      ii) Bet $1. Draw a card from a well-shuffled deck. If it shows a spade, you win $5.
      iii) Bet $1. Draw a card from a well-shuffled deck. If it shows an ace, you win $10.
      iv) Bet $1. Toss two coins. If they show two heads, you win $3.

11-9 THE PROBABILITY OF SUCCESSIVE EVENTS

Suppose a coin is tossed and a die is rolled. What is the probability that the coin shows tails *and* the die shows a number less than 3?

To answer this question, we can draw a tree diagram. This illustrates all the possible outcomes of tossing a coin and rolling a die. That is, for each side of the coin, there are 6 faces of the die.

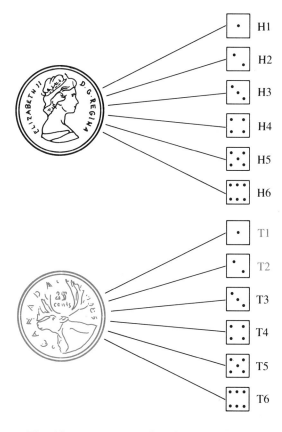

The 12 outcomes are listed at the side of the tree diagram. The outcomes that show tails with a number less than 3 are T1 and T2. These are the favorable outcomes.

The probability of a coin showing tails and a die showing a number less than 3 is

$$P(\text{tails and less than 3}) = \frac{\text{Number of favorable outcomes}}{\text{Total number of outcomes}}$$

$$= \frac{2}{12}$$

$$= \frac{1}{6}$$

Another way of finding P(tails and less than 3) is to notice that the number of outcomes involving tails is $\frac{6}{12}$, or $\frac{1}{2}$ the total number of outcomes. Also, the number of outcomes involving the die showing less than 3 is $\frac{4}{12}$, or $\frac{1}{3}$ the total number of outcomes. Hence, the outcomes for tails *and* the die showing a number less than 3 are $\frac{1}{2}$ of $\frac{1}{3}$ the total outcomes.

$$P(\text{tails and less than 3}) = \frac{1}{2} \times \frac{1}{3}$$
$$= \frac{1}{6}$$

The probability of two (or more) events happening in succession is the product of the probability of each event.
$$P(A \text{ and } B) = P(A) \times P(B)$$

Example 1. A coin is tossed three times. What is the probability that it shows a head each time?

Solution. For each toss, $P(\text{head}) = \frac{1}{2}$

$$P(3 \text{ heads}) = \frac{1}{2} \times \frac{1}{2} \times \frac{1}{2}$$
$$= \frac{1}{8}$$

The rule for successive events must be used carefully, because the probability of the second event may depend on the first event.

Example 2. A bag contains 2 black balls and 2 red balls. Find the probability of drawing 2 red balls in succession if:
a) the first ball is replaced before drawing the second ball
b) the first ball is not replaced.

Solution. a) On the first draw, there are 4 balls of which 2 are red.

$$P(\text{red, on first draw}) = \frac{2}{4}$$
$$= \frac{1}{2}$$

On the second draw, there are 4 balls of which 2 are red.

$$P(\text{red, on second draw}) = \frac{1}{2}$$

$$P(2 \text{ reds in succession}) = \frac{1}{2} \times \frac{1}{2}$$

$$= \frac{1}{4}$$

Since the first ball was replaced before the second ball was drawn, the second event is independent of the first event.

b) $P(\text{red, on first draw}) = \frac{1}{2}$

On the second draw, there are 3 balls of which 1 is red.

$$P(\text{red, on second draw}) = \frac{1}{3}$$

$$P(2 \text{ reds in succession}) = \frac{1}{2} \times \frac{1}{3}$$

$$= \frac{1}{6}$$

Since the first ball was not replaced before the second ball was drawn, the second event is dependent upon the first event.

EXERCISES 11-9

Ⓐ

1. A coin and a regular tetrahedron (with faces marked 1, 2, 3, 4) are tossed. Draw a tree diagram to find the probability of getting:
   a) a head and a 1
   b) a tail and an even number.

2. It is equally likely that a child be born a girl or a boy. Draw a tree diagram to find the probability that:
   a) a family of two children will be both girls
   b) a family of 5 children will be all boys.

3. a) Draw a tree diagram to show the result of tossing a coin five times.
   b) What is the probability of tossing a coin five times and getting tails each time?

4. A True-False test has 6 questions. If all the questions are attempted by guessing, what is the probability of getting all 6 right?

5. What is the probability of rolling three consecutive sixes with one die?

Ⓑ

6. If a thumbtack is tossed, the probability that it lands with the point up is 0.6. What is the probability of tossing a thumbtack four times and having it land with the point up each time?

7. Two people are selected at random. What is the probability that they both have birthdays in September? (Assume a year has 365 days.)

8. A box of 100 flash cubes contains 3 defective ones. If 2 cubes are taken simultaneously from the box, what is the probability that both are defective?

9. Three bags contain black balls and red balls in the numbers shown.

a)   b)   c)

From each bag, find the probability of drawing 2 red balls in succession if:
  i) the first ball is replaced before the second ball is drawn
  ii) the first ball is not replaced.

10. Find the probability of drawing 3 red balls in succession from a bag containing 3 red balls and 3 black balls if:
  a) each ball is replaced before the next ball is drawn
  b) the balls are not replaced after drawing.

11. A card is drawn from each of two well-shuffled decks. Find the probability of drawing two cards that are both:
  a) spades   b) red   c) aces   d) the ace of spades.

12. Find the probability of drawing 4 aces from a deck of cards:
  a) if there is replacement and shuffling after each draw
  b) if there is no replacement of the cards drawn.

13. A die and two coins are tossed. Find the probability of getting:
  a) a 2 and two heads   b) a head, a tail, and an odd number.

Ⓒ

14. Suppose a die is tossed until a 6 appears. Find the probability that the throw on which it appears is:
  a) the second   b) the third   c) the tenth.

15. Two tetrahedrons with faces labelled 1, 2, 3, 4, are tossed. Calculate the probability that they show:
  a) two ones   b) anything but two ones
  c) a sum of 5   d) a sum other than 5.

16. When two dice are tossed, what is the probability that they show:
  a) anything other than two sixes
  b) a sum of 7
  c) a sum of 11
  d) a sum not equal to 7 or 11
  e) at least one 3?

17. On a certain day, the probability of precipitation was 40% in Thunder Bay, 70% in London, and 20% in Ottawa. What was the probability of precipitation in all three cities on that day?

11-10 SIMULATING EXPERIMENTS

Adam, Bradley, Courtney, Dana, Erin, and Franco all volunteered to serve on the school organizing committee for the spring dance. The school charter says that the committee must have exactly 4 members. Mrs. Goreski, the staff supervisor, said she would choose a committee of 4 from the 6 volunteers by random selection. What is the probability that Adam is chosen?

In Section 11-8, we learned that to find the probability that Adam is chosen, we would have to count the number of committees of 4 people of which Adam is a member and divide that number by the total number of possible committees. This would be a long and tedious process.

We can find an approximate value of the probability by *simulating* the random selection as follows.

- First, label 6 identical cards with the first letter of each student's name.

- Then, shuffle the cards and choose any 4 of the 6 cards. These 4 cards name the committee members. For example, the selection of cards **B**, **C**, **E**, and **F** would indicate that the committee was to consist of Bradley, Courtney, Erin, and Franco.

- Do the second step 30 times. The results of one experiment are listed below.

C F E A	**C F E D**	A D B F	**B E F D**	B A E D
B F A C	**D E F B**	B E C A	A C E F	**E C B D**
F A B E	**E F B C**	**F C D B**	F D B A	**B D E C**
F C A E	A D F E	E D A C	A F D C	B A D E
B F D C	C B A D	A B F D	C B F A	A C B D
A B E F	D A C E	F A C B	E A D F	**C D E B**

- From the list of results, the number of times that **A** was chosen is 21.

Then, P(Adam being chosen) $= \dfrac{\text{Number of times } \mathbf{A} \text{ occurred}}{\text{Total number of draws}}$

$$= \frac{21}{30}$$

$$= 0.7$$

The probability that Adam is chosen is 0.7.

The more we repeat step 2 of this simulation, the more likely our estimate will be a close approximation of the true probability.

We use simulations to approximate probabilities when the calculation
of a true probability is difficult or when there are insufficient data.

The following example shows how we can simulate an experiment
by tossing several coins.

Example. Use a simulation to estimate the probability that there will be exactly 3
girls in a family of 5 children.

Solution. We use the fact that the probability that a randomly selected child is a
girl is $\frac{1}{2}$. Therefore, we can simulate the selection of a girl with the outcome of "heads" on the toss of a coin.

Toss 5 coins 40 times and record the results. They are listed below
and those outcomes in which exactly 3 heads appeared are highlighted.

H H T H H   T T H T H   H T H H H   T H T H T   T T H T H
H T T H T   H H H T T   T H H T H   H T T H T   T H T T H
T T H H T   H H T T T   H T T H H   H H H H T   T T T T H
H T T H H   T H H T T   H T T T T   H T T H H   T H H T T
T T T H T   H H T T H   H T H H H   T H T T T   H H H H H
T T H T T   H H T T H   T H H H H   H T T T H   T T H H T
T H T T H   H T H T T   T H T H H   T H H T T   H T H H H
H H H T T   T H T H H   T T H T T   T H H H H   H T H T H

Exactly 3 heads occurred 11 times on 40 tosses so the estimated probability
is $\frac{11}{40}$, or 0.275.

By increasing the number of tosses, we increase the likelihood of
a more accurate estimate.

EXERCISES 11-10

Ⓑ

1. Explain how this spinner could be used
   to estimate the probability of guessing
   at least 3 answers on a 10-question
   multiple-choice test. Each question offers
   4 answers.

2. Describe a simulation you could conduct to estimate each probability.
   a) The probability that in a family of 4 children there are exactly 3 boys.
   b) The probability that you will guess correctly more than 5 answers on an
      8-question true-false test.
   c) The probability that three people born in April are all born on an even-numbered
      day.
   d) The probability that the last two digits in a randomly selected telephone number
      are both even.

3. Conduct a simulation to estimate the probability that a family of 4 children has 2 girls and 2 boys. Use at least 36 trials.

4. Conduct a simulation to estimate the probability of guessing at least 3 correct answers on an 8-question true-false test. Assume the probability of a correct guess is $\frac{1}{2}$.

5. Use dice to conduct a simulation which you can use to estimate the probability of guessing at least 2 correct answers on an 8-question multiple-choice test. Each question offers 6 answers.

6. Use a telephone book to estimate the probability that the last two digits of a telephone number are both even.

7. Use a coin and a die to estimate the probability that at least 2 people in any group of 5 are born in the same month. Assume all months are equally probable. Use at least 15 trials.

INVESTIGATE

Random Numbers

Numbers that are selected at random so that all numbers and all digits are equally likely are called *random numbers*.

Tables of random numbers have been printed, which can be used to estimate the probabilities of certain events.

Here is a list of 200 random numbers.

7813	7191	6347	5646	7021	3575	5608	3257	7225	7593
5149	6646	6674	7952	6267	3078	5721	3502	3224	5082
5166	3831	6934	6965	3025	7346	5883	5451	3482	6223
3256	5295	6413	5325	3557	6079	0148	5742	6781	6540
7707	5662	5186	6524	7383	3965	3718	3287	7075	6541

Use the list the answer these questions.

1. Find the probability that exactly 2 digits out of 4 randomly chosen digits are even. To do this, count how many 4-digit numbers have exactly 2 even digits. Express this number as a fraction of the total, 50.

2. Use the result of *Question 1* to estimate the probability that a family of 4 children has exactly 2 girls and 2 boys.

3. Find the probability that a family of 8 children has exactly 5 boys.

4. Find the probability of guessing at least 4 correct answers on a 10-question true-false test.

5. Find the probability that at least 2 of the 3 digits on a licence plate are the same.

COMPUTER POWER

Simulating Experiments

When a coin is tossed it is just as likely that it will land heads up as tails up. However, when a coin is tossed 1000 times, would we expect it to land heads up exactly 500 times? Is it reasonable to expect the coin to land heads up fewer than 400 times on 1000 tosses?

To obtain answers to such questions we could toss a coin 1000 times and record the results. We might then repeat this experiment many times to verify our results. Tossing a coin a large number of times is a long, tedious process as well as being impractical. It is more appropriate to imitate or *simulate* such experiments.

To simulate a coin toss, we could choose a digit from a table of random numbers. However, the computer has made the use of a random numbers table unnecessary. Microcomputers are equipped with a random number generator. This feature makes the micro-computer an extremely useful device for simulating probability experiments.

The program below selects the numbers 0 and 1 at random and identifies the selection of 0 with a head and the selection of 1 with a tail. The number of heads and tails are tallied and displayed when the program is run.

```
100 REM *** SIMULATING COIN TOSSES ***
110 INPUT "HOW MANY TOSSES DO YOU WISH? ";N
120 H=0
130 FOR K=1 TO N
140    X=INT(2*RND(1))
150    IF X=0 THEN H=H+1:PRINT K, "H"
160    IF X=1 THEN PRINT K, "T"
170 NEXT K
180 PRINT:PRINT "TOSSES","HEADS","TAILS"
190 PRINT N,H,N-H
200 END
```

1. Use the program to determine the number of heads in:
   a) 100 tosses of a coin   b) 500 tosses of a coin   c) 1000 tosses of a coin.

2. What percent of the tosses (simulated in *Question 1*) yielded heads out of:
   a) 100 tosses   b) 500 tosses   c) 1000 tosses?

3. What happens to the percent of tosses which yields heads, as the number of tosses becomes very large?

4. Is it likely that fewer than 400 heads will result on 1000 tosses of a coin? Explain your answer.

1. The diagram shows how heat is lost from a typical two-storey home. Draw a circle graph to show this information.

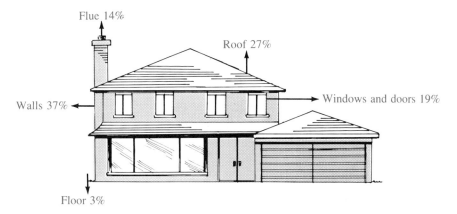

Flue 14%

Roof 27%

Walls 37%

Windows and doors 19%

Floor 3%

2. The workers in a small factory receive these salaries.

$10 000	10 000	10 400	10 800	13 200
10 800	11 200	12 000	12 000	12 400
12 400	12 400	12 400	12 800	10 800
14 000	14 000	14 400	14 800	14 800
15 200	16 000	15 600	15 200	16 000

Display the data on a histogram.

3. The table lists the defence spending of some nations of the North Atlantic Treaty Organization (NATO) as a percent of their gross national product (G.N.P.). Show this information on a suitable graph.

Country	Defence Spending as a Percent of G.N.P.
Britain	4.7
Canada	1.8
Denmark	2.4
France	3.3
Norway	3.2
U.S.A.	5.0
West Germany	3.4

4. Calculate the measures of central tendency for the salaries given in *Exercise 2*.

5. If the mean of the numbers 9, 10, 21, 27, 29, 25, 19, 13, x is 21, what is x?

6. Write nine natural numbers that have a median of 25 and a mean of 21.

7. How would you collect data to determine the following information?
   a) The extent of mercury poisoning in fish in the Great Lakes
   b) The political party most likely to win the next provincial election
   c) The food-purchasing habits of single males
   d) The force required to break a certain gauge of fishing line

8. Shake 5 coins in a paper cup and empty them onto your desk. Record the frequency of heads. Repeat this procedure 24 times. From your results, if you did this a total of 300 times, with what frequency would you expect 5 coins to show:
   a) 3 heads b) 4 heads c) no heads?

9. A manufacturer of widgets has maintained a minimum standard of 95% dependability over the years.
   a) Three widgets in a batch of 75 are found to be defective. Does the batch meet the minimum standard?
   b) How many defective widgets are permissible in a batch of 250?
   c) Workmanship and materials are improved so that only 4 defective widgets are being found in every 250. What is the probability that a widget selected at random is not defective?

10. A ball is selected at random from 15 balls numbered from 1 to 15. What is the probability that the number is:
    a) even   b) prime   c) a multiple of 5   d) a 2-digit number?

11. The bar graph shows the distribution of the heights of students at Montcalm Secondary School. What is the probability that a student selected at random will be:
    a) between 150 cm and 165 cm tall
    b) taller than 175 cm
    c) shorter than 155 cm?

Heights of Students

12. A box of coins contains 36 quarters, 45 dimes, 25 nickels, and 62 pennies. What is the probability that a coin drawn at random will be:
    a) a quarter   b) a nickel or a dime
    c) a quarter or a nickel   d) other than a penny?

13. The faces of two regular tetrahedrons are numbered 1 to 4. If they are tossed, what is the probability of getting:
    a) two numbers the same   b) a total of 5   c) a difference of 1?

14. An aviary has parakeets of four different colors. There are 10 green, 7 blue, 2 yellow, and 1 white. If two birds escape, what is the probability that they will both be:
    a) green   b) blue   c) yellow   d) white?

15. A cafeteria offers a number of choices for lunch.
    3 appetizers: soup, juice, or salad
    4 main courses: beef, chicken, pork, or fish
    2 desserts: pie or ice cream
    If a three-course meal is selected at random, calculate the probability of getting:
    a) soup   b) soup and beef   c) juice, fish, and pie.

16. Conduct a simulation to estimate the probability that a family of 4 children has at least 3 boys. Use at least 36 trials.

12 Geometric Constructions and 3-Dimensional Geometry

Why are silos built with circular bases rather than square ones? (See Section 12-6.)

12-1 GEOMETRIC CONSTRUCTIONS – PART ONE

Any great structure begins as an idea in a person's mind. As an architect translates these ideas into drawings, he or she must construct certain lengths, angles, and geometric figures. Many instruments and techniques are available for this purpose.

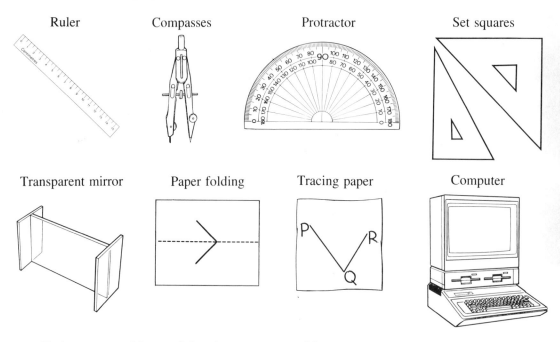

Ruler Compasses Protractor Set squares

Transparent mirror Paper folding Tracing paper Computer

Today, most architectural drawings are prepared by a computer using a process called *computer assisted design*. The person who generates the drawing by computer is using a tool that is much more advanced than ruler and compasses. However, the mathematical principles of these constructions are unchanged.

Constructing the bisector of an angle

We can use geometrical instruments in a variety of ways to construct
the bisector of an angle.

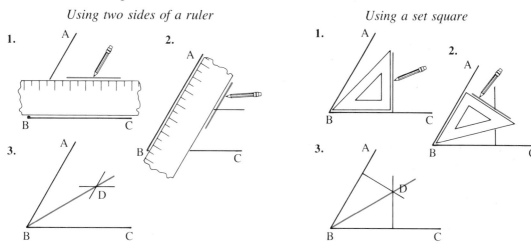

Using two sides of a ruler

Using a set square

BD bisects ∠ABC.

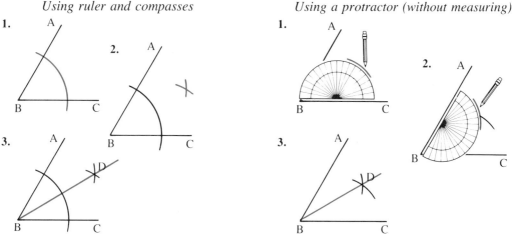

Using ruler and compasses

Using a protractor (without measuring)

BD bisects ∠ABC.

In each construction, we do the same thing on each arm of the angle.
Hence, the constructions work because there is no reason for the line
BD to be closer to one arm than to the other.

 **INVESTIGATE**

Can you construct the bisector of an angle in other ways? How many different
ways can you find?

Example. Using ruler and compasses, construct a 60° angle.

Solution. Draw a line *l* and mark point A on *l*.
Place the compasses point on A and draw part of a circle to cross the line at B.
Without changing the setting of the compasses, place the compasses point on B and draw an arc intersecting the part circle at C.
Join AC. ∠CAB = 60°

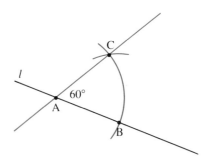

What other 60° angles could be formed by drawing lines on the diagram in this *Example*? Why does the method in this *Example* yield a 60° angle?

EXERCISES 12-1

(A)

1. a) Draw an acute angle and bisect it.
   b) Draw an obtuse angle and bisect it.

2. Construct a 60° angle and bisect it. Check by measuring.

(B)

3. Draw any angle and divide it into four equal parts.

4. Construct each angle.
   a) 60°   b) 30°   c) 15°   d) 120°   e) 150°

5. Copy this diagram.
   a) Construct OD, the bisector of ∠COB.
   b) Construct OE, the bisector of ∠AOC.
   c) Measure ∠DOE.
   d) If the construction were repeated using a different position of line segment OC, would the answer to part c) be the same? Explain.

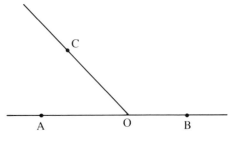

6. a) Construct △ABC in which AB = 7.5 cm, BC = 9.0 cm, and CA = 6.0 cm.
   b) Construct the bisectors of ∠B and ∠C.
   c) Extend the bisectors in part b) to meet at D. Measure ∠BDC.

7. a) Construct △RST in which ∠S = 60°, ST = 6.0 cm, and RS = 10.0 cm.
   b) Measure ∠R, ∠T, and RT.
   c) Construct the bisector of ∠RTS.
   d) Extend the bisector in part b) to meet RS at U. Measure TU and ∠TUR.

8. Triangle ABC has vertices A(3, 8), B(−3, 0), and C(9, 0).
   a) Draw △ABC on a grid.
   b) Construct the bisector of ∠B and extend it to meet AC at D.
   c) Measure ∠ADB and ∠CDB.

9. a) Try to construct a triangle with these side lengths.
      i)   3 cm, 4 cm, 7 cm   ii)   5 cm, 5 cm, 12 cm
   b) What conclusions can you make?

10. a) Construct a regular hexagon with sides of length 4.0 cm.
    b) Measure a diagonal of the hexagon.

11. Copy this diagram. AB is one arm of
    ∠ABC, and BD is the bisector of
    ∠ABC. Construct the other arm of
    ∠ABC.

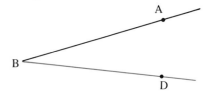

12. Draw an acute angle. Construct an angle with double the measure of the acute angle you drew.

13. Using only a ruler, construct three angles with a sum of 180°.

14. Copy this diagram. Using only a ruler,
    construct a third angle equal to the
    sum of ∠B and ∠C.

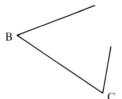

15. a) Construct an isosceles △ABC such that AC = BC.
    b) Extend AC to D.
    c) Construct CE, the bisector of ∠BCD.
    d) What can be said about CE and AB? Explain your answer.

16. Explain the construction for the bisector of an angle which uses a protractor without measuring.

Ⓒ ──

17. The diagram shows the construction for
    the bisector of ∠ABC using two sides
    of a ruler.
    a) Explain why:
       i) FD = FE
       ii) BD = BE
       iii) △FDB ≅ △FEB.
    b) How does part a) explain why FB is
       the bisector of ∠ABC?

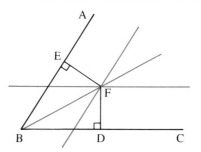

18. Explain the construction for the bisector of an angle which uses a set square.

19. The photograph on page 452 shows an *angle bisector* used by carpenters to bisect angles, and to lay out picture frames.
    a) How is the angle bisector used?
    b) Explain why it works.

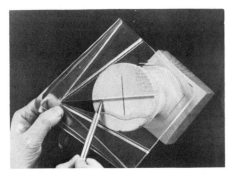

12-2 GEOMETRIC CONSTRUCTIONS – PART TWO

In the preceding section we illustrated four of many ways to construct the bisector of an angle. In this section we present methods of performing other constructions. Each construction can be done in many different ways.

Constructing the perpendicular bisector of a line segment

Infinitely many lines can be drawn perpendicular to a given line segment AB, but only one of them passes through the midpoint of AB. This line is called the *perpendicular bisector* of AB. Here are two methods of constructing the perpendicular bisector of AB.

Using two sides of a ruler

1.

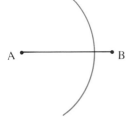

2.

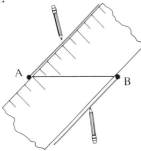

3.

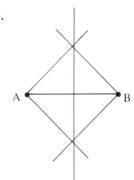

Using ruler and compasses

1.

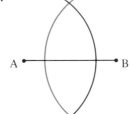

2.

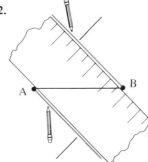

3.

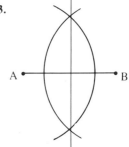

INVESTIGATE

What other ways can you find to construct the perpendicular bisector of a line segment?

Constructing the perpendicular at a point on a line

Using a set square

1.

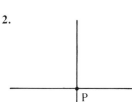

2.

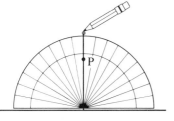

Using ruler and compasses

1.

2.

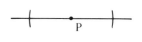

3.

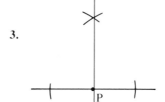

Constructing the perpendicular from a point to a line

Using a protractor

1.

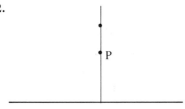

2.

Using ruler and compasses

1.

2.

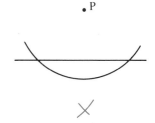

3.

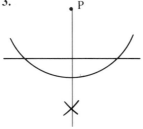

INVESTIGATE

What other ways can you find to construct perpendiculars at a point on a line or from a point to a line?

Example. Using a straightedge and compasses, construct a 45° angle.

Solution. Draw a line *l*.
Construct a perpendicular PB to *l* at any point B on *l*.
Then, ∠PBC = 90°.
Bisect ∠PBC. Line BA is the bisector of ∠PBC.
Hence, ∠PBA = ∠ABC = 45°

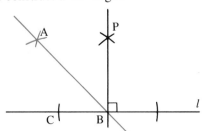

EXERCISES 12-2

Ⓐ

1. Draw a line *l*. Choose any point A on *l*. Construct the perpendicular to *l* at A.

2. Draw a line *l*. Choose any point B not on *l*. Construct the perpendicular from B to *l*.

3. Draw a line segment AB. Construct the perpendicular bisector of AB.

Ⓑ

4. Draw any line segment and divide it into four equal parts.

5. Construct each angle.
   a) 45°   b) 135°   c) 22.5°   d) 75°   e) 67.5°

6. Triangle ABC has vertices at A(7, 9), B(1, 1), and C(11, 3).
   a) Draw △ABC on a grid.
   b) Construct P, the midpoint of AB, and Q, the midpoint of AC.
   c) Compare the lengths of PQ and BC.
   d) Compare the measures of ∠APQ and ∠ABC.

7. Construct △PQR in which ∠Q = 90°, PQ = 5.0 cm, and QR = 5.0 cm. Measure ∠P and ∠R.

8. a) Construct △ABC with BC = 8.0 cm, ∠B = 45°, and ∠C = 30°.
   b) Construct the midpoint M of BC. Draw AM.
   c) Measure.   i) AM   ii) ∠BAC   iii) ∠AMC

9. a) Construct △XYZ such that XY = 4.0 cm, YZ = 5.0 cm, and XZ = 6.0 cm.
   b) Measure each angle of △XYZ.
   c) Construct a line through X perpendicular to YZ.
   d) Construct the bisector of ∠Y.

10. a) Draw △ABC with AB = 7.5 cm, ∠B = 60°, and BC = 10.0 cm.
    b) Construct the perpendicular from A to BC, and measure its length.
    c) Construct the bisector of ∠C, and extend it to meet AB at K. Measure the length of segment CK.
    d) Construct the midpoint M of AC. Draw segment MB and measure its length.

11. Construct a regular octagon with sides of length 4.0 cm.

12. Mark two points A and B on your paper. Construct a circle having AB as a diameter.

13. Draw a line *l*. Choose any point P not on *l*. Construct a line through P parallel to *l*.

14. Which of the constructions described in *Sections 12-1* and *12-2* can be done with ruler and compasses, with the compasses fixed at one setting?

Ⓒ

15. Mark two points A and B on your paper. Construct each square.
    a) A and B are the endpoints of one side.
    b) A and B are the endpoints of a diagonal.
    c) A and B are the midpoints of two opposite sides.
    d) A and B are the midpoints of two adjacent sides.

16. Construct a perpendicular at a point P on a line, using a plastic triangle. Can you do this without placing the right angle of the triangle at P?

17. Explain some of the constructions described on pages 456 and 457.

1. Draw any line segment AB, and construct its perpendicular bisector.

2. Locate any point P on the bisector of AB. Join PA and PB. Measure the lengths of the segments PA and PB.

3. Repeat *Question 2* for other points on the perpendicular bisector of AB.

4. State a probable conclusion about any point on the perpendicular bisector of a line segment.

1. Draw around a circular object such as a jar lid. Locate the centre of the circle. Can you find more than one way to do this?

2. The photograph on page 456 shows a *centre finder* used by carpenters to locate the centre of round stock.
   a) How is the centre finder used?
   b) Explain why it works.

Lines, Triangles, and Circles

The diagrams on these two pages illustrate some particular ways in which lines and triangles intersect.

Investigating Perpendicular Bisectors

A line may be the perpendicular bisector of a side of a triangle.

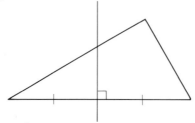

1. Draw a large scalene △ABC.

2. Construct the perpendicular bisector of each side. What do you notice?

3. Let O be the point of intersection of the perpendicular bisectors. Place the compasses point on O and draw a circle which passes through the three vertices of the triangle. We call this circle the *circumcircle* of △ABC. O is called the *circumcentre*.

4. State a probable conclusion about the perpendicular bisectors of the sides of any triangle.

Investigating Angle Bisectors

A line may bisect an angle of a triangle.

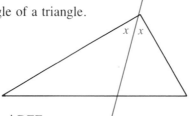

1. Draw a large scalene △DEF.

2. Construct the bisector of each angle. What do you notice?

3. Let I be the point of intersection of the angle bisectors. Place the compasses point on I and draw a circle which touches the three sides of the triangle. We call this circle the *incircle* of △DEF. I is called the *incentre*.

4. State a probable conclusion about the angle bisectors of any triangle.

Investigating Medians

A line may pass through a vertex of a
triangle and the midpoint of the
opposite side. The line segment joining
the vertex to the midpoint is called a
median of the triangle.

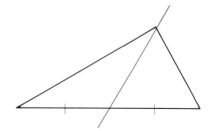

1. Draw a large scalene △PQR on cardboard.

2. Construct the three medians of the triangle. What do you notice?

3. Carefully cut out the triangle.
   a) Try to balance the triangle on the edge of a ruler, with one of the
      medians on the ruler. Do this with each of the three medians.
   b) Let G be the point of intersection of the three medians. Try to balance
      the triangle with a pencil point at G. G is called the *centroid*, or *centre
      of gravity* of the triangle.

4. State a probable conclusion about the medians of any triangle.

Investigating Altitudes

A line may pass through a vertex of a
triangle and be perpendicular to the
opposite side. The line segment joining
the vertex to the opposite side is called an
altitude of the triangle.

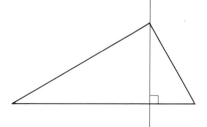

1. Draw a large scalene acute △XYZ.

2. Construct the three altitudes of the triangle. What do you notice?

3. a) Draw examples of triangles to show that an altitude may be:
      i)   a side of the triangle   ii)   outside the triangle.

   b) Repeat the investigation for these triangles.

4. Let H be the point of intersection of the altitudes. H is called the *orthocentre*
   of the triangle. State a probable conclusion about the altitudes of any
   triangle.

12-3 CONSTRUCTING CIRCLES THROUGH SETS OF POINTS

Since ancient times, mathematicians have investigated the circumstances under which circles can be drawn through various numbers of points.

Two Points

Let A and B be any two distinct points. How can we draw a circle through A and B?

In a previous *INVESTIGATE* you may have discovered that any point on the perpendicular bisector of a line segment is equidistant from its endpoints. Hence, any point on the perpendicular bisector of the segment AB can be used as the centre of a circle passing through A and B.

Step 1. Construct the perpendicular bisector of AB.

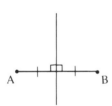

Step 2. Choose any point on the perpendicular bisector as a centre. Draw a circle through A and B.

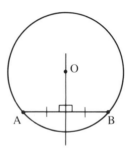

Three Points

Let A, B, and C be three distinct points. How can we draw a circle through A, B, and C?

In a previous *INVESTIGATE* you may have discovered that a circle can be drawn through the three vertices of any triangle. The centre of the circle is the point of intersection of the perpendicular bisectors of the sides of the triangle.

Step 1. Draw △ABC and construct the perpendicular bisectors of any two sides of the triangle (using any method).

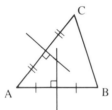

Step 2. Using the point of intersection of the perpendicular bisectors as a centre, draw a circle through A, B, and C.

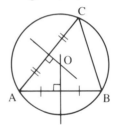

Example Construct the circle which passes through A(1, 0), B(3, 2), and C(7, 0).

Solution. Plot the points on a grid. Construct the perpendicular bisectors of AB and BC. Label their point of intersection D. Place the compasses point on D and draw a circle to pass through A, B, and C.

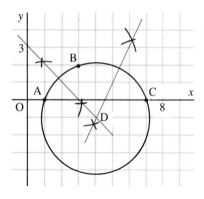

EXERCISES 12-3

(A)

1. Draw *x*- and *y*-axes on a grid.
   a) Construct a circle C_1 with centre (0,0) and diameter 8 units.
   b) Construct a circle C_2 with centre (4,0) and radius 4 units.
   c) Name the coordinates of the two points at which C_1 and C_2 intersect.

2. On a grid, construct a circle with centre (3,2) which passes through the point (5,5). Measure the diameter of the circle.

(B)

3. Construct a circle which passes through each set of points.
   a) A(3,0), B(5,5), C(8,3)
   b) D(2, − 3), O(0,0), E(− 4, − 3)
   c) F(1,3), G(− 5,2), H(1, − 3)

4. a) Can you construct a circle through the points R(1, − 1), P(0, − 4), and S(2,2)? Explain your answer.
   b) Under what conditions can a circle be constructed through three given points?

5. If any three distinct points are given, is it always possible to draw a circle which passes through them? Give examples to illustrate your answer.

6. If more than three distinct points are given, is it always possible to draw a circle which passes through them? Give an explanation, or draw some diagrams to illustrate your answer.

7. Construct △XYZ with base XY = 4 cm and altitude ZM = 3 cm. How many different triangles can be drawn?

8. Construct △XYZ with base XY = 4 cm and median ZN = 3 cm. How many different triangles can be drawn?

9. When would the triangle in *Exercise 7* and the triangle in *Exercise 8* be the same triangle?

Ⓒ

10. a) Draw △ABC with AB = 11.5 cm, BC = 13.0 cm, and AC = 9.0 cm.
    b) Construct the perpendicular bisector of each side and label the circumcentre O.
    c) Construct the three altitudes and label the orthocentre H.
    d) Construct the three medians and label the centroid G.
    e) If you have worked carefully, you should be able to draw a line through O, H, and G. It is called the *Euler line*.
    f) Measure segments OH, HG, and OG. How are the lengths related?
    g) Determine whether the incentre lies on the Euler line.

11. An altitude, a median, and an angle bisector are drawn from the same vertex of a scalene triangle and extended to meet the opposite side. Which of the three line segments divides the triangle into two equal areas?

12. An interesting series of constructions leads to a circle that can be drawn through *nine* seemingly unrelated points.
    a) Draw a large scalene △ABC with sides longer than 20 cm.
    b) Construct the midpoints of AB, BC, and CA, and label them as P_1, P_2, and P_3 respectively.
    c) Construct the orthocentre of △ABC and label it H. Mark P_4, P_5, and P_6, the points where the altitudes meet AB, BC, and CA, respectively.
    d) Label the midpoints of HA, HB, and HC as P_7, P_8, and P_9, respectively.
    e) Construct the circumcentre of △ABC and label it O.
    f) Label the midpoint of OH as F. Using F as the centre, draw the circle which passes through P_1, P_2, P_3, P_4, P_5, P_6, P_7, P_8, and P_9. This is called the *nine-point circle* of △ABC.
    g) Determine whether the centre of the nine-point circle lies on the Euler line (see *Exercise 10*).

INVESTIGATE

Circle Patterns

Draw a circle and a line with point P, as shown. Use a protractor to mark several equally-spaced points on the circle. Using each point as a centre, draw a circle through P. The result should look like the design shown.

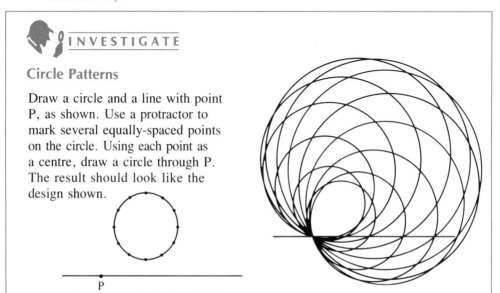

THE MATHEMATICAL MIND

A Problem that took Thousands of Years to Solve

1
The ancient Greeks established rules for constructing geometric figures. Since they considered the line and the circle to be the basic figures, only compasses and an unmarked straightedge could be used.

2
One of the constructions, which the Greek mathematicians attempted, was to *trisect* any given angle using compasses and a straightedge.

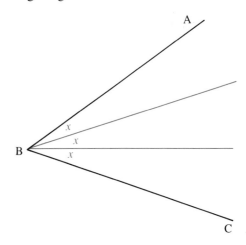

3
Since the 5th century B.C., mathematicians have tried to trisect any given angle using compasses and a straightedge. However, none has succeeded.

4
Finally, in 1837, P.L. Wantzel *proved* that such a construction is impossible! He did this by showing that a 20° angle cannot be constructed using compasses and a straightedge. This means that a 60° angle cannot be trisected.

Certain angles can be trisected using compasses and a straightedge, but there is no general method that works for all angles. If the restriction on compasses and a straightedge is removed, an angle can be trisected using a variety of other instruments.

QUESTIONS

For each of these angles
i) 180°   ii) 90°   iii) 30°   iv) 45°   v) 120°
a) Construct the angle using compasses and a straightedge.
b) Determine if it is possible to trisect it using compasses and a straightedge.
c) Trisect it if you can.

12-4 SURFACE AREAS OF PRISMS AND PYRAMIDS

We see many examples of prisms and pyramids.

When the Earth's minerals are analyzed, they are found to contain crystals of various kinds. The crystals have flat (rather than curved) faces. They are examples of solids called prisms.

The Muttart Conservatory in Edmonton consists of two pyramidal buildings. The faces of a pyramid (other than the base) all meet at the top of the pyramid.

Here are four types of prisms.

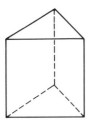
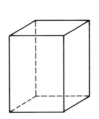
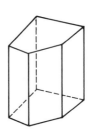
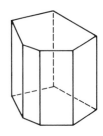

| triangular prism | rectangular prism | pentagonal prism | hexagonal prism |

A *prism* is a solid with two congruent and parallel faces called *bases*. The other faces of the prism are parallelograms.

A plane parallel to the bases of a prism intersects the prism in a figure that is *congruent* to the bases.

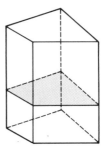

Here are four types of pyramids.

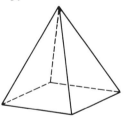

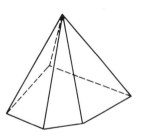

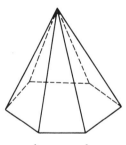

triangular
pyramid

rectangular
pyramid

pentagonal
pyramid

hexagonal
pyramid

A *pyramid* is a solid with a polygonal base. The other faces are triangles with a common vertex.

A plane parallel to the base of a pyramid intersects the pyramid in a figure that is *similar* to the base.

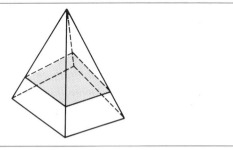

The faces of a prism or a pyramid can be arranged in a pattern called a *net*. Such a pattern could be cut from cardboard, and folded to form the solid. Since the area of a net does not change when it is folded into the solid, we can calculate the area of the net to determine the *surface area* of the solid.

Example 1.　a)　Identify the solid formed by each net.

　　　　　　　b)　Calculate the surface area of each solid.

i)

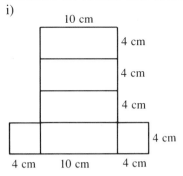

10 cm

4 cm

4 cm

4 cm

4 cm

4 cm　　10 cm　　4 cm

ii)

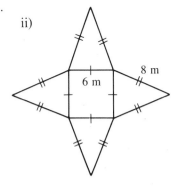

8 m

6 m

Solution.　i) a)　The net will fold to form a rectangular prism.

　　　　　　b)　The net consists of four rectangles each with area 40 cm²
　　　　　　　　and two squares each with area 16 cm².

　　　　　　　　Area of net = 4(40) + 2(16)
　　　　　　　　　　　　　　 = 192

　　　　　　　　The surface area of the prism is 192 cm².

ii) a) The net will fold to form a square-based pyramid.
b) The net consists of a square with area 36 m² and four triangles
with sides 8 m, 8 m, and 6 m.
Before finding the area of each triangle, we use the Pythagorean
Theorem to calculate its height h.

$$h = \sqrt{8^2 - 3^2}$$
$$= \sqrt{55}$$

Area of each triangle $= \dfrac{1}{2}$(base)(height)

$$= \frac{1}{2}(6)(\sqrt{55})$$
$$= 3\sqrt{55}$$

Area of net $= 4(3\sqrt{55}) + 36$
$$\doteq 124.99$$

The surface area of the pyramid is about 125 m².

Example 2. A nation plans to construct, for a World's Fair, a glass pavilion on a
square base measuring 20 m along each side. Plan A calls for a rectangular
prism 25 m high. Plan B calls for a pyramid 50 m high. Which plan
would use less glass?

Solution. Draw a diagram of each pavilion.

Plan A
The surface area, in square metres,
of the rectangular prism (excluding
the base) is
$4(20 \times 25) + (20 \times 20)$, or 2400.

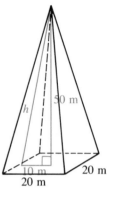

Plan B
To find the area of the triangular
faces of the pyramid, we must
first calculate their height h.
From the diagram, we see that h
is the hypotenuse of a right triangle
with sides 50 m and 10 m.

$$h = \sqrt{50^2 + 10^2}$$
$$= \sqrt{2600}$$

Area of each triangular face $= \dfrac{1}{2}$(base)(height)

$$= \frac{1}{2}(20)(\sqrt{2600})$$
$$= 10\sqrt{2600}$$

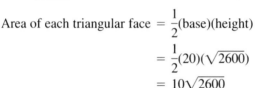

The surface area, in square metres, of the glass pyramid (excluding
the base) is $4(10)\sqrt{2600}$, or about 2040.
The pyramid uses less glass than the prism.

EXERCISES 12-4

Ⓐ

1. Which solids are prisms? Which are pyramids?

   a)

   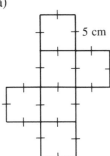

   b)

   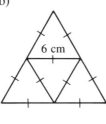

   c)

   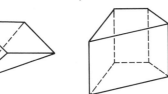

   d)

   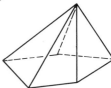

2. Find the area of each net.

   a)

   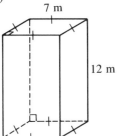

   5 cm

   b)

   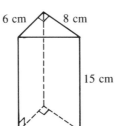

   6 cm

   c)

   7.5 cm

   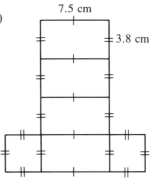

   3.8 cm

3. Find each surface area.

   a)

   7 m

   12 m

   b)

   6 cm   8 cm

   15 cm

   c)

   15 cm

   18 cm

Ⓑ

4. Draw a net and find each surface area.

   a)

   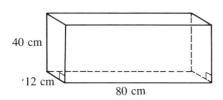

   40 cm

   12 cm

   80 cm

   b)

   12 m

   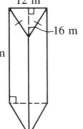

   16 m

   30 m

   c)

   35 cm

   18 cm

   25 cm

5. Find each surface area.

   a)   b)   c)

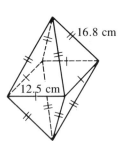
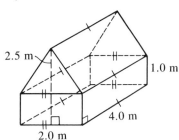

   3.0 m

   1.5 m

   2.5 m

   3.5 m

   16.8 cm

   12.5 cm

   2.5 m

   1.0 m

   4.0 m

   2.0 m

6. A hexagonal prism, with a height of 27 cm, has a base consisting of six equilateral
   triangles with edges 32 mm long.
   a) Draw the net.   b) Find the total surface area.

7. If you know how many sides there are in the base of a prism, how could you
   determine the number of:
   a) faces   b) vertices   c) edges?

8. If you know how many sides there are in the base of a pyramid, how could you
   determine the number of:
   a) faces   b) vertices   c) edges?

Ⓒ ───

9. Susan is going to redecorate her bedroom, which has the floor plan shown.
   The ceiling is 2.4 m high. The paint
   costs $0.70/m², the wallpaper costs
   $9.50/m², and the carpet costs
   $32.50/m². How much will it cost:
   a) to carpet the floor
   b) to paint the walls and the ceiling
   c) to paper the walls and paint the
      ceiling?

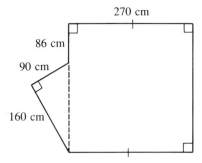

   270 cm

   86 cm

   90 cm

   160 cm

┌───┐
│  **INVESTIGATE**   │
│   │
│ 1. Construct two copies of this net, and   │
│   use tape to make two solids with them.   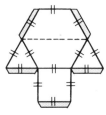 │
│   │
│ 2. Fit these solids together to make a pyramid.   │
│   │
│ 3. Calculate the surface area of the pyramid.   │
└───┘

Constructing a Pyramid

To construct a pyramid and investigate its volume you will need these materials: a rectangular box, some pieces of cardboard, and some tape.

Use the steps below to construct a pyramid which will fit inside the box.

Step 1. Measure the length, the width, and the height of the box. Record the results.

Step 2. Use the Pythagorean Theorem to calculate the slant height s of a face whose base is the length of the box.

Step 3. Construct two triangles with this height and with bases equal to the length of the box.

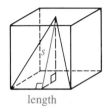

length

length   length

Step 4. Repeat Steps 2 and 3 for a face whose base is the width of the box.

Step 5. Construct a rectangle which is congruent to the base of the box.

Step 6. Tape the four triangles and the rectangle together to form a pyramid.

Estimating the Volume of a Pyramid

Use the pyramid you constructed above, with the base removed. Without the base, the pyramid will not be rigid, and it may be necessary to reinforce it with tape.

1. Suppose the pyramid were filled with sand, and then emptied into the box. Estimate how many times this could be done until the box is full.

2. Check your estimate. Instead of using sand, use some other material such as loose styrofoam pieces which are often used as packing material.

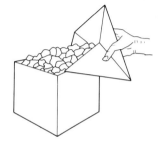

3. What probable conclusion can you make about the volume of a pyramid compared with the volume of a rectangular prism which has the same height and the same base?

12-5 VOLUMES OF PRISMS AND PYRAMIDS

To conserve energy, some houses are heated by solar power that is collected in the daytime in large collectors on the roof. To store the heat for later use, air in the collectors is pumped into a large container of rocks buried under the house. The volume of the container is an important consideration since it must be large enough to heat the house properly.

Volume of a Prism

The rock container shown is a rectangular prism measuring 3 m by 3 m by 2 m. To determine the volume of the container, think of filling it with unit cubes in layers.
The area of the base is the number of cubes which cover it: 3×3, or 9. If this is multiplied by the number of layers, the result is the number of cubes which fill the container. Hence, the volume of the container is the base area multiplied by the height: 9×2, or 18.
The rock container has a volume of 18 m³.

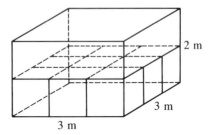

The volume V of a rectangular prism is given by this formula.
V = (base area)(height)

height

base area

Example 1. Find the volume of this triangular prism.

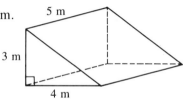

Solution. A rectangular prism, measuring
3 m by 4 m by 5 m, can be
divided into two triangular prisms
congruent to the one given. This
suggests that the volume of the
triangular prism is one-half of the
volume of the rectangular prism.

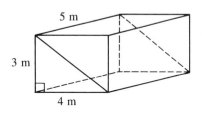

$$V = \frac{1}{2}(3)(4)(5)$$
$$= 30$$

The volume of the triangular prism is 30 m³.

In *Example 1*, the expression $\frac{1}{2}(3)(4)$ represents the area of the
base of the triangular prism. Since the volume was obtained by multiplying this expression by the height, this suggests a general formula for
the volume of any prism.

The volume *V* of any prism
is given by this formula.

$$V = \text{(base area)(height)}$$

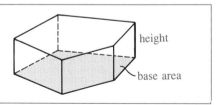

Example 2. Calculate the volume of each solid, to the nearest unit.

a)

b)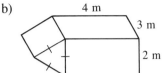

Solution. a) The solid is a triangular prism, with its base an equilateral triangle.
To find the area of the base, we use the Pythagorean Theorem to
calculate the height of the triangle.

$$h = \sqrt{2^2 - 1^2}$$
$$= \sqrt{3}$$

Area of the triangular base $= \frac{1}{2}(2)(\sqrt{3})$
$$= \sqrt{3}$$

Volume of the prism, V = (base area)(height)

$\qquad = (\sqrt{3})(5)$

$\qquad \doteq 8.7$

The volume of the prism is about 9 m³.

b) The solid comprises a rectangular prism and a triangular prism. The rectangular prism has a base measuring 2 m by 3 m.

Volume of the rectangular prism, V = (base area)(height)

$\qquad = (2 \times 3)(4)$

$\qquad = 24$

The triangular prism has a base area equal to that of the prism in part a).

Volume of the triangular prism, V = (base area)(height)

$\qquad = (\sqrt{3})(3)$

$\qquad = 3\sqrt{3}$

Total volume = $24 + 3\sqrt{3}$

$\qquad \doteq 29.2$

The volume of the solid is about 29 m³.

Volume of a Pyramid

In a preceding *INVESTIGATE* you should have found that there is a simple relationship between the volumes of certain pyramids and prisms. If a pyramid and a prism have the same base and the same height, then the volume of the pyramid is one-third of the volume of the prism.

The volume V of a pyramid is given by this formula.

$$V = \frac{1}{3}(\text{base area})(\text{height})$$

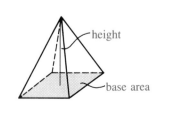

Example 3. Find the volume of the pyramid.

Solution. The base is a rectangle with area 80 cm². Hence, the volume of the pyramid is

$$V = \frac{1}{3}(\text{base area})(\text{height})$$

$$= \frac{1}{3}(80)(12)$$

$$= 320$$

The volume of the pyramid is 320 cm³.

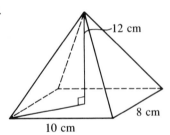

EXERCISES 12-5

Ⓐ

1. Calculate each volume to the nearest unit.

a)
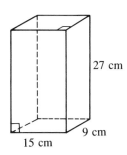
27 cm
9 cm
15 cm

b)
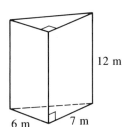
12 m
6 m   7 m

c)
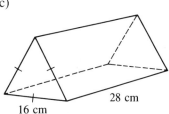
28 cm
16 cm

d)
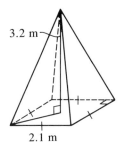
3.2 m
2.1 m

e)
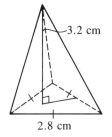
3.2 cm
2.8 cm

f)
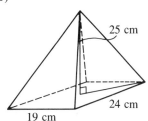
25 cm
24 cm
19 cm

2. Calculate the volume of space enclosed by each tent, to the nearest unit.

a)
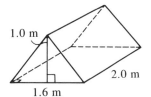
1.0 m
2.0 m
1.6 m

b)
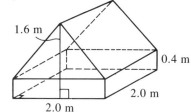
1.6 m
0.4 m
2.0 m
2.0 m

c)
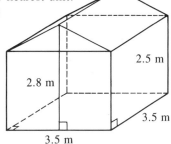
2.5 m
2.8 m
3.5 m
3.5 m

3. Shipping companies often use *CAST* containers to reduce handling costs. One such container measures 3.2 m by 2.6 m by 2.2 m. What volume of goods can be shipped in it?

4. A granary measures 1.8 m by 2.6 m by 2.2 m. What is its capacity?

Ⓑ

5. The bucket on a front-end loader measures 1.2 m by 2.3 m by 1.8 m. The bin of a dump truck measures 4.2 m by 2.5 m by 1.9 m. How many bucket loads will it take to fill the truck?

6. Meridian Frozen Foods sells its products in boxes measuring 38 cm by 28 cm by 7.0 cm. How many of these boxes can be packed into a freezer space measuring 3.50 m by 1.52 m by 0.84 m?

7. Calculate each volume to the nearest unit.

a)

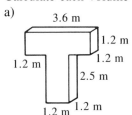

3.6 m
1.2 m
1.2 m
1.2 m
2.5 m
1.2 m
1.2 m

b)

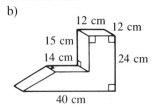

12 cm
12 cm
15 cm
14 cm
24 cm
40 cm

c)

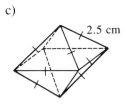

2.5 cm

8. Juice drinks come in 250 mL containers shaped like a rectangular prism.
   a) Measure a container like this one.
   b) Calculate its volume in cubic centimetres.
   c) Does the result confirm that the container holds 250 mL of juice?

9. An aquarium measures 60 cm by 30 cm by 30 cm. If 10 L of water are poured in, how high will the water level rise?

10. A cube is divided into six congruent pyramids. The base of each pyramid is a face of the cube. If the edges of the cube are 30 cm long, what is the volume of each pyramid?

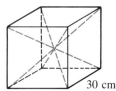

30 cm

Ⓒ

11. In *Exercise 6*, the food boxes filled the freezer space exactly; there was no wasted space. Suppose the freezer space were 1.11 m by 1.40 m by 2.10 m.
    a) How many boxes could be packed into the freezer?
    b) How much wasted space would there be?

12. The surface area of a cube is 100 cm². Calculate its volume to three significant digits.

13. The Great Pyramid in Egypt has a square base of 230 m. Its original height was 147 m; now its height is 146 m.
    a) Find the volume of stone that was used to build the pyramid.
    b) About 2.3×10^6 blocks of stone were used to build the pyramid. Find the volume of one block.
    c) One block of stone has a mass of about 2.5 t. Find the mass of stone in the pyramid today.

14. During a snowstorm, 8 cm of snow fell. When snow melts, the volume of the water is about $\frac{1}{10}$ of the volume of the snow.
    a) What volume of snow fell on a lawn measuring 20 m by 15 m?
    b) If the water from the melted snow were collected, how many aquariums like the one in *Exercise 9* would it fill?

 INVESTIGATE

The Volume of a Cone

To investigate the volume of a cone, follow these steps. You will need an empty tin can such as a soup can, a piece of paper, and some tape.

Step 1.
Roll the piece of paper into the shape of a cone, and adjust it such that it just fits in the tin can.

Step 2.
Secure the cone with tape so that it does not unroll. Mark the rim of the can on the cone, and cut off the excess.

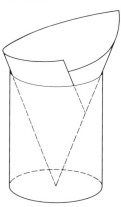

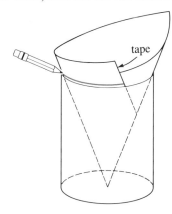

Step 3.
Suppose the cone were filled with water, and then emptied into the can. Estimate how many times this could be done until the can is full.

Step 4.
Check your estimate with water.

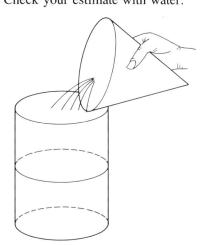

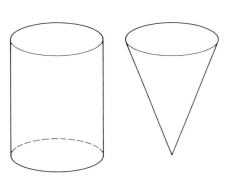

What probable conclusion can you make about the volume of a cone compared with the volume of a cylinder which has the same height and the same base radius?

Use Spatial Visualization

A firecracker is in the shape of a cone. The base radius is 4.0 cm, and the slant height is 6.0 cm. What area of paper is needed to cover the curved surface of the firecracker?

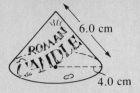

6.0 cm

4.0 cm

Understand the problem

● Can the curved surface be covered with one piece of paper?
● What does *slant height* mean?

Think of a strategy

● Visualize cutting the curved surface and unrolling it.

Carry out the strategy

● When the curved surface is unrolled, it forms part of a circle.
  The radius of the circle is the slant height of the cone.
  The area of the curved surface of the cone is equal to the area
  of the part circle.

● We can find the area of the curved surface from this proportion.

$$\frac{\text{Area of cone}}{\text{Area of circle}} = \frac{\text{Circumference of cone}}{\text{Circumference of circle}}$$

$$\frac{\text{Area of cone}}{\pi(6)^2} = \frac{2\pi(4)}{2\pi(6)}$$

$$\text{Area of cone} = 36\pi\left(\frac{4}{6}\right)$$

$$\doteq 75.3982$$

6.0 cm

ROMAN CANDLE

$2\pi(4)$ cm

The area of the curved surface of the cone is about 75 cm².

Look back

● What is the total surface area of the cone (including the base)?

Solve each problem

1. Find the area of the curved surface of each cone.

a)   b)   c)

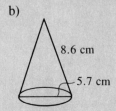

7 m

2 m

8.6 cm

5.7 cm

4.5 cm

9.3 cm

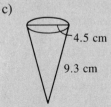

2. Find the total surface area of the cones in *Question 1*.

3. A tepee has the shape of a cone with a slant height of 2.0 m, and a base diameter of 3.0 m. Find the area of the material needed to make the tepee.

4. For Hallowe'en, a witch's hat is made by stapling together the straight edges of a quarter of a circle of radius 30 cm.
   a) How high is the hat?
   b) What is the radius of the base of the hat?

5. There are two balls on a billiard table (below left). Where should the black ball be aimed so that after one bounce it hits the colored ball?

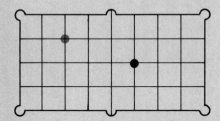

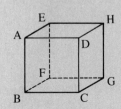

E

H

A

D

F

G

B

C

6. For the cube shown (above right), describe the figure formed by these points.
   a) DCGH   b) ADGF   c) ADCG

7. You have an empty tin can with no markings on it. How can you put the right amount of water in it so that it is exactly half full? No other container may be used.

8. A silver dollar with an inked edge leaves the trace shown when making one complete roll on paper. Find the volume of the coin, to the nearest cubic millimetre.

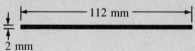

112 mm

2 mm

12-6 CYLINDERS AND CONES

Why are silos built with circular bases rather than square ones?

In the construction of tanks, granaries, silos, and other storage facilities, the shape of the structure is an important consideration. A cylinder, a cone, a prism, and a pyramid constructed from the same amount of material will have different storage capacities, or volumes.

Surface Area of a Cylinder

The net for a cylinder is a rectangle and two circles. The length of the rectangle is the circumference of either circle. The width of the rectangle is the height of the cylinder. The surface area of the cylinder formed from the net is the sum of the areas of the rectangle and the two circles.

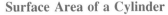

Example 1. Find the surface area of the cylinder.

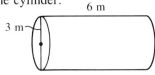

Solution. Draw the net of the cylinder. Since the diameter is 3 m, the radius of each circle is 1.5 m.

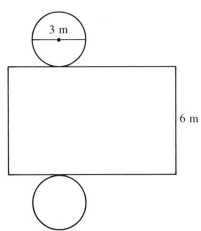

$$\text{Area of each circle} = \pi r^2$$
$$= \pi(1.5)^2$$
$$= 2.25\pi$$

The length of the rectangle is the circumference of either circle.

$$\text{Circumference of each circle} = \pi d$$
$$= \pi(3)$$

$$\text{Area of the rectangle} = \pi(3)(6)$$
$$= 18\pi$$

$$\text{Area of the net} = 2(2.25\pi) + 18\pi$$
$$= 22.5\pi$$
$$\doteq 70.7$$

The surface area of the cylinder is about 71 m².

Volume of a Cylinder

We visualize the volume of a cylinder in the
same way that we visualize the volume of a
prism. Imagine that the cylinder is filled with
layers of unit cubes. The area of the base is the
number of cubes, including part cubes, which
cover it. If this area is multiplied by the number
of layers, the result is the total number of unit
cubes which fill the cylinder. But this is the
volume of the cylinder. Hence, the volume
can be found by multiplying the area of the base
by the height.

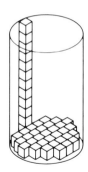

The volume V of a cylinder
is given by this formula.
V = (base area)(height)

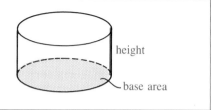

height

base area

Example 2. Find the volume, to the nearest 100 m³, of the storage tank with the
dimensions shown.

Solution. Volume of the tank, V = (base area)(height)
Since base area = πr^2, $V = \pi r^2$(height)
Substitute 10 for r and 15 for height.
$V = \pi(10)^2(15)$
$\doteq 4712$
The volume of the storage tank is about 4700 m³.

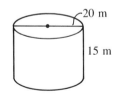

20 m

15 m

Volume of a Cone

In the preceding *INVESTIGATE* you should have found that there is a
simple relationship between the volumes of certain cylinders and cones.
If a cone and a cylinder have the same height and the same base radius,
then the volume of the cone is one-third the volume of the cylinder.

The volume V of a cone
is given by this formula.

$V = \dfrac{1}{3}$(base area)(height)

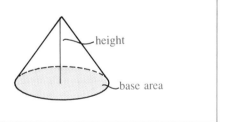

height

base area

Example 3. A firecracker has the shape of a cone with a base radius of 3.0 cm and a height of 5.0 cm. Calculate the volume of the cone, to two significant digits.

Solution. Draw a diagram. The base is a circle with radius 3.0 cm.

Base area $= \pi r^2$

$\qquad = \pi(9)$

The height is 5.0 cm.

Hence, the volume of the cone is

$$V = \frac{1}{3}(\text{base area})(\text{height})$$

$$= \frac{1}{3}\pi(9)(5.0)$$

$$\doteq 47.1$$

To two significant digits, the volume of the cone is 47 cm³.

EXERCISES 12-6

Ⓐ

1. Find the volume of each solid, to the nearest unit.

a)
145 cm
35 cm

b)
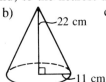
22 cm
11 cm

c)
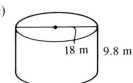
18 m | 9.8 m

d)
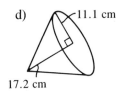
11.1 cm
17.2 cm

2. Find the surface area of each cylinder in *Exercise 1*.

Ⓑ

3. Find the volume of each solid, to the nearest unit.

a)
18 cm
22 cm
25 cm

b)
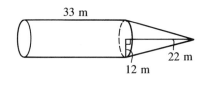
33 m
12 m
22 m

4. A cylinder (below left) just fits inside a cubical box with edges 10 cm long. What is the volume of the cylinder?

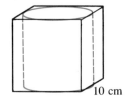
10 cm

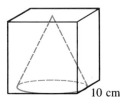
10 cm

5. A cone (above right) just fits inside a cubical box with edges 10 cm long. What is the volume of the cone?

6. A square-based prism with edges 4.4 cm and a cylinder with 5.6 cm diameter have heights of 24 cm. Calculate the areas of their bases, and their volumes, to two significant digits.

7. An ice-cream cone has a diameter of 5 cm and a height of 10 cm. If it were filled with ice cream, and levelled off, how much ice cream would it contain?

8. A refinery has five cylindrical storage tanks each measuring 13.4 m in diameter and 8.7 m high. What is the total storage capacity of the refinery?

9. Tanker trucks have cylindrical tanks 18.4 m long and 2.3 m in diameter. How many truck loads would be needed to empty one of the tanks in *Exercise 8*?

10. A livestock feeder has the dimensions shown. What is the cost of the steel sheet used in its construction if steel costs $6.25/m²?

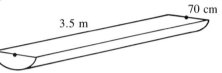

11. A square-based prism with edges 14.0 cm and a cylinder with 15.8 cm diameter have heights of 20.0 cm.
    a) Calculate the areas of their bases.
    b) Find the cost of electroplating the prism and the cylinder at 1.7¢/cm².

12. A cylindrical silo has a height of 12.5 m and a base diameter of 6.4 m. Its top is a cone with the same diameter, and height 1.2 m. Calculate the volume of the silo.

13. A cylindrical can with a base diameter of 6.4 cm is partially filled with water. When a stone is placed in the can, the water level rises 1.5 cm. Calculate the volume of the stone, to the nearest tenth of a cubic centimetre.

14. A can of paint is marked 978 mL. It has a base diameter of 10.4 cm and a height of 12.5 cm. Calculate the volume of the can, in cubic centimetres. Does the result confirm that the can's capacity is 978 mL?

15. A pipeline connects a natural-gas well to a storage depot 3.2 km away. The diameter of the pipe is 0.92 m. What volume of gas, to the nearest 1000 L, will be in the pipe?

16. Pronto gas bar sells unleaded gas at a profit of 1.6¢/L. This gas is stored underground in a cylindrical tank 2.2 m in diameter and 4.5 m long.
    a) If the average fill-up is 40 L, how many cars can be filled up?
    b) How much profit will be made?

ⓒ

17. A farmer plans to build a silo 5.2 m high to hold 72 m³ of corn.
    a) If the silo were cylindrical, what would the diameter of the base be?
    b) If the silo were a square-based prism, how wide would the base be?
    c) What area of metal would be needed to make the sides of the silos in parts a) and b)?
    d) Why are silos normally built with circular bases?

INVESTIGATE

The Styrofoam Cup

Obtain a styrofoam cup, and make the measurements shown in the diagram. Record the results for use in the investigations below.

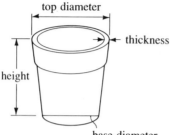

1. Place the cup on its side, and let it roll in a large circle. Do this on a large table or on the floor.
   a) Estimate the diameter of the circle.
   b) Locate the centre of the circle as accurately as you can.
   c) Measure the radius of the circle from the centre to the larger end of the styrofoam cup.

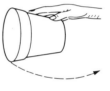

2. In *Question 1*, as the styrofoam cup traces out the circle, it rotates on its axis.
   a) Put a mark on the rim of the styrofoam cup, and let it roll around the circle. How many complete rotations does the styrofoam cup make on its axis?
   b) Confirm the result of part a) by calculation.

3. Styrofoam cups are packed by stacking them together. If you know how many cups there are, how could you determine the height of the stack?

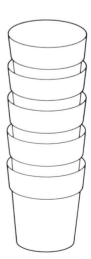

4. The styrofoam cup has the shape of a *truncated cone*. This means that if the curved part of the cup were extended past the smaller end, a cone would result. Determine the height of this cone.

5. Calculate the capacity of the styrofoam cup, in cubic centimetres. Check by filling it with water, and measuring the volume of the water.

6. Find an approximation for the volume of styrofoam used to make the cup. Make any assumptions that seem reasonable.

INVESTIGATE

The Surface Area of a Sphere

To investigate the surface area of a sphere, Lesley used a beach ball which was nearly spherical in shape. She carefully measured its diameter. It was approximately 37 cm.

The beach ball was divided into six congruent sections. Lesley approximated the surface area by dividing each section into two triangles and a rectangle.

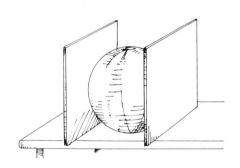

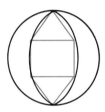

She measured the dimensions of the triangles and the rectangle, and used the results to approximate the surface area of the beach ball.

Area of two triangles: $2 \times \dfrac{1}{2} \times 18$ cm $\times 21$ cm $= 378$ cm^2

Area of rectangle: $\qquad$ 17 cm $\times 21$ cm $= \underline{357 \text{ cm}^2}$
Total area of one section: $\qquad\qquad\qquad\quad 735 \text{ cm}^2$

Approximate surface area of beach ball: 6×735 cm^2, or 4410 cm^2

Then Lesley divided the surface area of the beach ball by the square of its diameter. She discovered a surprising result, and used it to form a probable conclusion about the surface area of a sphere.

1. Complete Lesley's calculation. What did she discover?

2. a) Obtain a beach ball like the one shown and measure its diameter.
   b) Find an approximation of the surface area of the beach ball.
   c) Divide the area by the *square* of the diameter. Record the result.

3. If possible, repeat the investigation with a different beach ball, or with some other ball such as a basketball. Find the *average* value of the results in *Question 2c)*.

4. A beach ball is an example of a sphere. What probable conclusion can you make about the surface area of a sphere?

12-7 SURFACE AREA AND VOLUME OF A SPHERE

The Cinesphere in Ontario Place, Toronto, has the shape of part of a sphere. How can we find the surface area and the volume of a sphere?

A *sphere* is a set of points in space which are the same distance from a fixed point, called the *centre*. A line segment joining the centre to any point on the sphere is called its *radius*. A line segment joining two points on a sphere and passing through the centre is called its *diameter*.

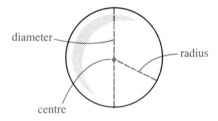

Finding the Surface Area of a Sphere

In the preceding *INVESTIGATE*, you should have found that the surface area of a sphere is slightly more than 3 times the square of the diameter. This suggests that the surface area A of a sphere with diameter d is πd^2. Since $d = 2r$, we may write

$$A = \pi(2r)^2$$
$$= 4\pi r^2$$

The surface area A of a sphere with radius r is given by this formula.
$$A = 4\pi r^2$$

Finding the Volume of a Sphere

We can use the formula for the surface area of a sphere to find a formula for the volume of a sphere.

Imagine that the surface of a sphere with radius r is divided into a very large number of small "polygons" with base areas A_1, A_2, A_3, and so on. Now imagine joining the vertices of these polygons to the centre of the sphere. This forms a large number of "pyramids" with heights equal to the radius of the sphere, and base areas A_1, A_2, A_3, and so on.

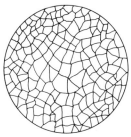

The volume V of the sphere is the sum of the volumes of all the pyramids. Hence,

$$V = \frac{1}{3}A_1r + \frac{1}{3}A_2r + \frac{1}{3}A_3r + \ldots$$

$$= \frac{1}{3}r(A_1 + A_2 + A_3 + \ldots)$$

But the expression in the brackets, $A_1 + A_2 + A_3 + \ldots$, represents the sum of the areas of the bases of all the pyramids. This is equal to the surface area of the sphere, which we know is $4\pi r^2$. Hence, we may substitute $4\pi r^2$ for the expression in the brackets. Therefore,

$$V = \frac{1}{3}r(4\pi r^2)$$

$$= \frac{4}{3}\pi r^3$$

The volume V of a sphere with radius r is given by this formula.

$$V = \frac{4}{3}\pi r^3$$

Example. The sculpture at the Japanese Embassy in Ottawa is in the shape of a sphere with a diameter of 3.2 m.
a) What is the volume of the sculpture, to the nearest cubic metre?
b) What is the surface area of the sculpture, to the nearest square metre?

Solution. The radius of the sphere is $\frac{1}{2}(3.2)$ m, or 1.6 m.

a) Substitute 1.6 for r in the formula for the volume of a sphere.

$$V = \frac{4}{3}\pi r^3$$
$$= \frac{4}{3}\pi(1.6)^3$$
$$\doteq 17.2$$

The volume of the sculpture is approximately 17 m³.

b) Substitute 1.6 for r in the formula for the surface area of a sphere.

$$A = 4\pi r^2$$
$$= 4\pi(1.6)^2$$
$$\doteq 32.2$$

The surface area of the sculpture is approximately 32 m².

EXERCISES 12-7

Ⓐ

1. Calculate the surface area and the volume of each sphere, to the nearest unit.

a)

7.0 cm

b)

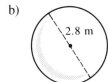

2.8 m

c)

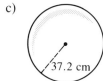

37.2 cm

2. Find the surface area and the volume of each ball.

	Sport	Diameter of ball
a)	Basketball	25 cm
b)	Squash	13 mm
c)	Tennis	6.5 cm

Ⓑ

3. A balloon was blown up to the shape of a sphere, 20 cm in diameter. How much air did it contain?

4. Find a formula for the volume of a sphere in terms of its diameter d.

5. The radii of the Earth, the moon, and the sun are shown. Calculate each surface area and volume.

		Radius
a)	Earth	6370 km
b)	Moon	1740 km
c)	Sun	694 000 km

6. A sphere just fits inside a cube with edges of length 10.0 cm (below left). Calculate, to three significant digits:
   a) the surface area of the sphere   b) the volume of the sphere.

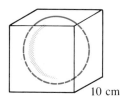

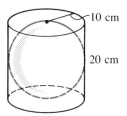

7. A sphere just fits inside a cylinder with base radius 10.0 cm and height 20.0 cm (above right). Calculate, to three significant digits:
   a) the surface area of the sphere   b) the volume of the sphere.

8. A sphere with radius r is contained in a cylinder with radius r and height $2r$, as shown.

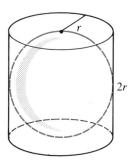

   a) Determine the surface area of the sphere and the total surface area of the cylinder. How do the areas compare?
   b) Determine the total volume of the sphere and the total volume of the cylinder. How do the volumes compare?

9. A sphere has a surface area of 100 cm². Calculate the radius of the sphere, to the nearest tenth of a centimetre.

10. A sphere has a volume of 100 cm³. Calculate the radius of the sphere, to the nearest tenth of a centimetre.

11. If we did not know that the moon's shape was spherical, we might think that it was a circle. How does the surface area of the part of the moon we see when the moon is full compare with the area of the circle that it appears to be?

Ⓒ

12. A balloon was blown up to the shape of a sphere with a circumference of 60 cm. Calculate, to three significant digits:
   a) the surface area of the balloon   b) the volume of air it contained.

13. A spherical soap bubble has a radius of 2.0 cm. It lands on a flat surface and changes into a hemisphere.
   a) Assuming that none of the air inside the bubble escapes, calculate the radius of the hemisphere.
   b) What was the percent change in the surface area of the soap film?

14. The circumference of a sphere is C. Find expressions in terms of C for:
   a) the surface area   b) the volume.

PROBLEM SOLVING

Choose the Strategy

1. A train 1 km long travels at 30 km/h through a tunnel 1 km long. How long does it take the train to clear the tunnel?

2. For which integers, n, do n and n^5 have the same ones digit?

3. a) Given 10 points on a circle, how many chords can be drawn joining them?
   b) How many chords can be drawn joining n points on a circle?

4. A sheet of 50 stamps is printed in 10 rows of 5 stamps. The edges of the stamps forming the sides of the sheet are straight. How many stamps have:
   a) 2 straight edges   b) 1 straight edge   c) no straight edge?

5. A girl is standing in line to buy a ticket. She observes that $\frac{1}{7}$ of all the people in line are in front of her while $\frac{5}{6}$ of all the people are behind her. How many people are in line?

6. a) Use the pattern suggested by the diagram to evaluate this expression.
   $$1 + 2 + 3 + \ldots + 9 + 10 + 9 + \ldots + 3 + 2 + 1$$
   b) Find a formula for this expression.
   $$1 + 2 + 3 + \ldots + (n - 1) + n + (n - 1) + \ldots + 3 + 2 + 1$$

7. Estimate the probability that a hand of 4 cards dealt from a standard deck of 52 cards contains exactly 2 black cards and 2 red cards.

8. The cost of printing greeting cards is a fixed amount, plus a fixed rate per card. The total cost of printing 8 greeting cards is $19.75 and the total cost of printing 20 greeting cards is $34.75. What is the cost of printing 15 cards?

9. What is the least number of pieces into which a circular pie can be divided by n cuts, where a cut corresponds to a chord of the circular pie?

MATHEMATICS AROUND US

Why Polar Bears and Penguins Don't Freeze

Scientists studying different species of fox discovered that foxes living in warmer climates had long ears while those living in the cold climates had very short ears.

Further investigation revealed that animals living in the cold regions of the world have smaller appendages (limbs, ears, and tails) than animals in tropical areas. This principle is called *Allen's rule*.

Furthermore, it was discovered that polar animals tend to be bulkier; that is, less elongated than tropical animals. This principle is called *Bergmann's rule*.

Both Allen's and Bergmann's rules can be understood in mathematical terms. Animals produce heat in proportion to their body size but they lose heat in proportion to their surface area. Therefore, the animal which is shaped so that it has the smallest value of $\frac{\text{surface area}}{\text{volume}}$, is best adapted to a cold climate.

QUESTIONS

1. Consider the snake as a cylinder, with radius 0.5 cm and length 64 cm.

   Calculate the surface area and the volume of the snake, in terms of π. Write down the fraction, $\frac{\text{surface area}}{\text{volume}}$.

2. Consider the bear as a sphere, with radius 1.5 m.

   Calculate the surface area and the volume of the bear, in terms of π. Write down the fraction, $\frac{\text{surface area}}{\text{volume}}$.

3. Which of the two animals, the bear or the snake, has the better shape for surviving cold temperatures? Explain your answer.

4. If you started with a lump of plasticine, what shape would you mould it to have minimum surface area?

Review Exercises

1. a) Construct the bisector of an acute angle.
   b) Construct the perpendicular to a line through a point not on the line.
   c) Construct the perpendicular to a line through a point on the line.
   d) Construct the perpendicular bisector of a line segment.
   e) Construct an angle of 60°.

2. a) Construct △ABC with BC = 8 cm, ∠B = 45°, and ∠C = 30°.
   b) Construct the bisector of ∠C.
   c) Construct the median from B to AC.
   d) Construct the altitude from A to BC.

3. a) Construct △XYZ with YZ = 6.5 cm, ∠Y = 75°, and ∠Z = 60°.
   b) Construct the perpendicular bisector of XY.
   c) Construct the altitude from Y to XZ.

4. The diagram shows the construction for the bisector of ∠ABC using ruler and compasses.
   a) Explain why:
      i) FD = FE
      ii) BD = BE
      iii) △FDB ≅ △FEB.
   b) How does part a) explain why FB is the bisector of ∠ABC?

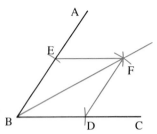

5. Construct a circle which passes through A(−5, −6), B(3, −4), and C(1,4).

6. Draw the net for each solid.
   a) a 2 cm cube
   b) a tetrahedron with 3 cm edges
   c) a 12 cm high prism having a square base with 1.5 cm edges
   d) a 5 cm high cylinder with the radius of the base 2 cm

7. Draw the net for each solid and find its surface area to the nearest square millimetre.

   a)

   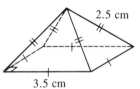

   2.5 cm

   3.5 cm

   b)

   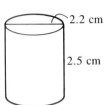

   2.2 cm

   2.5 cm

   c)

   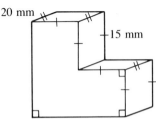

   20 mm

   15 mm

8. The Far North Pavilion at Ontario Place, Toronto, consists of a number of cylindrical silos of various sizes. One silo, with a diameter of 10.2 m, is 8.6 m high. It is to be painted with paint costing $3.75/L. If 1 L of paint covers 5.3 m², what will be the total cost of the paint?

9. A pyramid, 12 m high, has a square base with 15 m edges. How much would it cost to paint the pyramid if 1 L of paint costs $5.50 and covers 7.2 m²?

10. Calculate each volume to the nearest unit.

a)

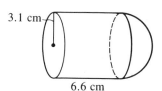

3.1 cm

6.6 cm

b)

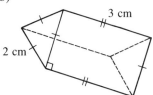

3 cm

2 cm

c)

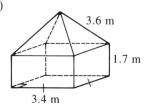

3.6 m

1.7 m

3.4 m

11. Tennis balls are packed in cans 8.4 cm in diameter and 25.5 cm high. Three dozen of these cans are packed in a box 51 cm by 51 cm by 26 cm. What is the total volume of wasted space?

12. An ice-cream manufacturer plans to build a giant ice-cream cone as an advertisement for its product. The cone will be 2 m high and 1 m in diameter. The ice cream in the top of the cone will be hemispherical in shape.

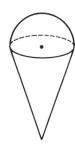

Four litres of paint cover 35 m². How much paint will be needed for 3 coats?

13. A pyramid is supposed to have magical properties. A manufacturer built a pyramid large enough for a person to sit inside and be rejuvenated! The pyramid is 1 m high and its square base has edges of length 1 m. What is the volume of air inside the pyramid, to the nearest tenth of a cubic metre?

14. A smaller pyramid is built, which the manufacturers claim will sharpen a razor blade that is hung inside. The pyramid is 12 cm high and has a square base of edge length 8 cm. The pyramid does not have a base. What is the area of the material necessary to build the pyramid, to the nearest square centimetre?

15. A paper cup has a conical shape, with a base diameter of 5 cm and a height of 7 cm.
    a) Find the volume of water a cup will contain when it's filled to the brim.
    b) How high, to the nearest millimetre, would the level of water be if it were poured into a cylindrical tumbler with the same radius?

16. A cylindrical can of orange concentrate has a diameter of 6 cm and a height of 12 cm. The instructions on the can are to mix the orange with 3 cans of water.
    a) Will the mixture fit into a cylindrical jug with diameter 10 cm and height 20 cm?
    b) How high would a jug with diameter 10 cm have to be, to hold the mixture?
    c) How many paper cups from *Exercise 15* would the mixture fill?

17. An apartment building in Aylmer, Ontario, is heated by solar heating. Water is stored in a buried cylindrical tank 6.7 m deep and 15 m in diameter.
    a) What area of material was needed to make the tank, to the nearest square metre?
    b) What is the volume of the tank, to the nearest cubic metre?

Cumulative Review, Chapters 10-12

1. Triangle ABC has vertices A($-1,4$), B($-1,1$), and C($4,1$). Draw the image of △ABC under:
   a) a translation which maps P($3,5$) onto P'($6,7$)
   b) a reflection in the line $y = -1$
   c) a rotation of 90° about the origin
   d) a dilatation with a scale factor of 2 and rotation centre the origin.

2. A translation maps ($-2,1$) onto ($3,-1$).
   a) Find the images of P($2,4$), Q($-1,0$), and R($4,-2$) under this translation.
   b) If D'($-4,2$), E'($-2,-2$), and F'($1,3$) are image points under this translation, find the coordinates of the original points.

3. The reflection images of A($3,8$), B($1,3$), and C($6,7$) are A'($8,3$), B'($3,1$), and C'($7,6$). Graph these points and draw the reflection line.

4. The dilatation image of a figure has an area of 450 cm². Find the area of the original figure for each dilatation factor.

   a) 3   b) $\dfrac{5}{8}$

5. The cenotaph in the town square casts a shadow of length 12.8 m. At the same time, a 1.5 m post casts a 2.1 m shadow. How tall is the cenotaph?

6. A 2.4 kg sample of nuts is found to contain 384 g of pecans, 864 g of peanuts, 768 g of hazel nuts, and the rest are cashews.
   a) What is the mass of the cashews?
   b) Draw a circle graph to display this information.
   c) What percent of the nuts are:
      i) pecans   ii) peanuts   iii) cashews?

7. The maximum daily temperatures in Vancouver, during July, over a five-year period are shown in this table.

Maximum Temperature (°C)	13-15	16-18	19-21	22-24	25-27	28-30	31-33
Frequency (days)	4	14	22	32	40	30	13

   Draw a histogram for this data.

8. Find the measures of central tendency for the following mathematics marks.

82	78	75	72	68	88	98	67	65	75
43	53	69	86	64	81	72	34	80	71
67	72	41	75	75	73	54	74	73	70

9. If each number in a set of data is increased by 3, how would:
   a) the mean   b) the median and   c) the mode change?

10. The probability of getting 4 heads on the toss of 4 coins is $\dfrac{1}{16}$.

    a) What is the probability of not getting 4 heads?
    b) What is the probability of getting 4 tails?

11. A pair of dice is rolled. Let A denote the event that the total number shown is even. Let B denote the event that the total number shown is less than 7.
   a) What outcomes are favorable to:
       i) event A   ii) event B   iii) both events A and B?
   b) What is the probability of:
       i) event A   ii) event B   iii) events A and B together?

12. In a card game known as "In Between", a player is dealt two cards. To win, the player must be dealt a third card with a value in between the first two. Calculate the probability of winning if the two cards already dealt are:
   a) a three and a seven   b) a nine and a Queen
   c) a four and a ten   d) a six and a seven

13. What is the probability that in any year chosen at random the month of February has:
   a) exactly 28 days   b) 29 days
   c) 30 days   d) more than 27 days?

14. Kara says that the probability that a person can cross a street safely is $\frac{1}{2}$ because there are two possible outcomes, crossing safely or not crossing safely. Do you agree? Why?

15. Construct △PQR with PQ perpendicular to QR, $\angle R = 60°$, and QR = 3.5 cm. Construct the median from P to QR and the bisector of $\angle Q$.

16. Construct a circle which passes through the points A($-2,1$), B($8,4$), and C($5,-3$).

17. Find the surface area of:
   a) a cube of side 5.6 cm
   b) a cylinder 16 cm long and 3 cm in diameter   c) a sphere of radius 7.5 cm.

18. Find the volume of:
   a) a rectangular prism 28 cm long, 12 cm wide, and 8 cm high
   b) a cone of radius 10 cm and height 32 cm
   c) a cylinder of radius 6.4 cm and height 22 cm
   d) a pyramid with a 15 cm square base and a height of 40 cm.

19. How much oil is in a barrel of height 1.2 m and radius 0.65 m?

20. What would it cost to paint the outside of 1200 barrels similar to the one in *Exercise 19* if the paint costs $8.40/L and 1 L covers 9.5 m²?

21. A square pyramid with the length of a side of the base 24 cm and height 52 cm is cut. A pyramid 39 cm high is formed. What is the volume of the remaining portion?

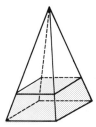

Answers

The Nature of Mathematics

The Search for Pattern

Exercises, page xiii

1. a) $1 + 3 + 5 + 7 = 4 \times 4$
   $1 + 3 + 5 + 7 + 9 = 5 \times 5$
   $1 + 3 + 5 + 7 + 9 + 11 = 6 \times 6$
   b) $2 + 4 + 6 + 8 = 4 \times 5$
   $2 + 4 + 6 + 8 + 10 = 5 \times 6$
   $2 + 4 + 6 + 8 + 10 + 12 = 6 \times 7$
2. a) 45, 56, 67   b) 23, 28, 32   c) 81, 243, 729
   d) 2, 1, 0.5   e) 426, 431, 439
   f) 1847, 1942, 2037
3. a) 17, 20, 23, 26, 29   b) Row 1
4. a) 32, 64, 128   b) 16, 22, 29   c) 11, 13, 14
5. Answers may vary, for example,
   1, 2, 3, 4, 5, 6, ...; 1, 2, 3, 1, 2, 3, 1, 2, 3, ...;
   1, 2, 3, 5, 7, 10, 13, ...
6. 10, 15, 21   7. 16, 25, 36
8. a) 7   b) 3   c) 1   d) 3

The Value of Mathematical Investigation

Exercises, page xv

1. a) 14   b) 24   c) 36
2. b) i) 14   ii) 24   iii) 36   3. 35

The Power of Mathematical Reasoning

Exercises, page xvii

1. a) Yes   b) No   c) No   d) No
3. a), c)

The Power of the Calculator

Exercises, page xix

1. a) 2.283 333 3   b) 3.103 210 7
   c) 7.071 031 7
2. a) 63, 6633, 666 333;
   $9999 \times 6667 = 66\ 663\ 333$
   b) 24, 2244, 222 444;
   $6666 \times 3334 = 22\ 224\ 444$
   c) 81, 9801, 998 001;
   $9999 \times 9999 = 99\ 980\ 001$
   d) 25, 4225, 442 225;
   $6665 \times 6665 = 44\ 422\ 225$
   e) 10 201, 40 804, 91 809;
   $404 \times 404 = 163\ 216$
   f) 11, 111, 1111; $1234 \times 9 + 5 = 11\ 111$
3. Answers may vary.
4. Yes, because 3 consecutive numbers contain the factors 2 and 3.
5. a) 1 048 576   b) Answers may vary, with an 8-digit display, 2^{26} c) 2^{29}

6. a) 40 320   b) 11   c) 14
7. Scientific notation 1×10^8
8. a) 2.4×10^{10} b) 3.7×10^{12} c) 2.913×10^9
9. a) 9.83   08   b) 1.03   10   c) 2.345   09

The Power of the Computer

Exercises, page xxi

1. a) 3.597 739 66   b) 4.499 205 34
   c) 5.878 030 95   d) 6.792 823 42
   e) 0.447 247 47   f) 0.914 792 47   2. 900
3. a) 31   b) 83   c) 227   d) 616   e) 1674

The Utility of Mathematics

Exercises, page xxiii

1. a) About 27.82 km   b) About 464 m
2., 3. Answers may vary.
4. a) i) About 940 000 000 km
   ii) About 2 600 000 km   b) About 110 000 km/h
5. a) About 1800 km   b) About 30 km

A Famous Unsolved Problem

Exercises, page xxiv

1. 6:3,5; 5,7; 11,13; 17,19; 29,31; 41,43
2. a) 59, 61; 71, 73   b) 101,103; 107,109
3. Answers may vary. a) 3,7   b) 5,13   c) 11,19
   d) 13,23   e) 17,29   f) 17,31   g) 3,19
4. No, because there might be some after 100 000 000.
5. 2,5; because one prime would have to be even, and 2 is the only prime that is even.
6. Because there is only one even prime number.
7. One number is odd, one is even, hence their product is even.   8. 17

Chapter 1

Exercises 1-1, page 4

1. B, -7; C, -5; F,0; H,4; I,6; K,9
2. a) $+9$ b) $-\$21$ c) $+80°C$ d) $-20°C$
   e) $+\$50$ f) $-\$75$ g) $-\$81$
   h) $-12\ 000$ m   i) $+3000$ m
3. a) a loss in altitude of 300 m
   b) a gain in altitude of 25 m
   c) a loss in altitude of 100 m
   d) a gain in altitude of 2 m
4. a) a debt of $12   b) a credit of $7
   c) a credit of $15   d) a debt of $53

5. a) a loss of $10   **b)** an altitude gain of 500 m
   c) a 3 kg increase in mass
   d) a temperature of $+14°C$
   e) -18 **f)** $+11$ **g)** -7 **h)** 5
6. a) $-3 < 2$ **b)** $5 > -6$ **c)** $-4 < -1$
   d) $-3 < 0$ **e)** $2 > -5$ **f)** $-9 < -1$
   g) $-11 < 10$ **h)** $-8 > -9$
7. a) -2 **b)** -6 **c)** -8 **d)** -4 **e)** -9
   f) -5 **g)** -10 **h)** -18 **i)** -16
8. a) $-4, -1, 3, 5$ **b)** $-10, -2, 5, 8$
   c) $-8, -2, -1, 0, 4, 5$
9. a) $7, 1, -2, -4$ **b)** $2, 0, -1, -3$ **c)** $8, 5, 3, 0, -2, -8$
10. a) -2 **b)** 1   **c)** 2   **d)** -3 **e)** 4   **f)** -4
11. a) -4 **b)** -5 **c)** 3   **d)** -7 **e)** 5   **f)** 0

Exercises 1-2, page 8

1. a) -4 **b)** 3   **c)** -3 **d)** 5   **e)** 5
   f) -10 **g)** 8 **h)** 2 **i)** 2 **j)** 9 **k)** 6 **l)** 0
2. a) -3 **b)** -15 **c)** -1 **d)** 4   **e)** 14
   f) -9 **g)** -12 **h)** -12 **i)** -16
   j) -9 **k)** 6   **l)** -9
3. a) 1   **b)** -10 **c)** -16 **d)** 1   **e)** -4
   f) -4 **g)** -6 **h)** -12
4. a) 0   **b)** 1   **c)** -9 **d)** -9 **e)** 2   **f)** 35
5. a) 9   **b)** -3 **c)** -3 **d)** -9 **e)** 3
   f) -36 **g)** -14 **h)** -22 **i)** 0   **j)** 11
6. a) i) 0   **ii)** 0   **iii)** 0   **iv)** 0   **v)** 0
   vi) 0   **b)** The sum is zero.

7. a)

$+4$	-7	$+6$	3
-3	$+10$	-9	-2
$+8$	-3	-11	-6
9	0	-14	-5

b)

-7	$+3$	-8	-12
-6	$+5$	$+2$	1
$+9$	-4	$+10$	15
-4	4	4	4

8. 4th floor   **9. a)** garter snake **b)** 17°C **c)** 18°C
10. a) $15 + (+15) + (-5)$
   b) $85 + (-29) + (-37) + (+52) + (-66)$
   c) $80 + (-7) + (+5)$

11.

-3	0	3	6	9
-5	-2	1	4	7
-7	-4	-1	2	5
-9	-6	-3	0	3
-11	-8	-5	-2	1

From bottom left to top right, the numbers
increase by 5. From bottom right to top left,
the numbers decrease by 1.
12. a) -4 **b)** -7 **c)** 4 **d)** 3 **e)** 0 **f)** -6
13. $+16, +13, +10, +7, +4, +1, -2, -5$ **14.** 44

15. a)

$+8$	-3	$+5$
-6	-1	-7
$+2$	-4	-2

b)

-1	-3	-4
$+6$	$+1$	$+7$
$+5$	-2	$+3$

c)

-12	$+5$	-7
-6	-3	-9
-18	$+2$	-16

16. $-19, -14, -9, -4, 1, 6, 11, 16$; Add 5

17.

-14	-12	-10	-8	-6
-9	-7	-5	-3	-1
-4	-2	0	2	4
1	3	5	7	9

Add -5 vertically; add 2 horizontally

Investigate, page 10

Answers may vary.
a) i) $(-5) + (-6)$ **ii)** $(+5) + (+6) + (+7)$
   iii) $(+2) + (+3) + (+4) + (+5)$
   iv) $(-8) + (-9)$ **v)** $(+6) + (+7) + (+8)$
   vi) $(+2) + (+3) + (+4) + (+5) + (+6)$
b) i) $(+7) + (+8); (+4) + (+5) + (+6);$
   $(+1) + (+2) + (+3) + (+4) + (+5)$
   ii) $(-12) + (-13);$
   $(-3) + (-4) + (-5) + (-6) + (-7)$
   $(+2) + (+1) + 0 + (-1) + (-2) + (-3)$
   $+ (-4) + (-5) + (-6) + (-7)$
   iii) $(+9) + (+10) + (+11);$
   $(+4) + (+5) + (+6) + (+7) + (+8)$
   iv) $(-17) + (-18);$
   $(-5) + (-6) + (-7) + (-8) + (-9);$
   $(-2) + (-3) + (-4) + (-5) + (-6) +$
   $(-7) + (-8)$ **c)** $-1, -4, -8, -16, -32$

Exercises 1-3, page 13

1. $+10°C$ **2.** -350 m
3. a) $+20°C$ **b)** $+12°C$ **c)** $-54°C$
   d) $+24°C$ **e)** $-8°C$ **f)** $-10°C$
4. a) -2645 m   **b)** $+690$ m   **c)** -230 m
   d) $+650$ m
5. a) -2 **b)** 5   **c)** -12 **d)** 2   **e)** 7
   f) -1 **g)** -9 **h)** -7 **i)** 1   **j)** 6
   k) -2 **l)** 6   **m)** 1   **n)** 2   **o)** -3

6. a) 60   **b)** −10   **c)** −80   **d)** −110
   e) −30   **f)** −30   **g)** 90
   h) −145   **i)** −70   **j)** −5   **k)** −60
   l) 3   **m)** −11   **n)** 71   **o)** −190

7. a) −19   **b)** 9   **c)** 16   **d)** −4   **e)** −16
   f) 8   **g)** −13   **h)** −11

8. a) −13   **b)** −8   **c)** 1   **d)** −1   **e)** 5
   f) −11   **g)** −17   **h)** −21

9. a) −3   **b)** −6   **c)** 4   **d)** −3   **e)** −13
   f) −5   **g)** −8   **h)** −9   **i)** −15   **j)** −68

10. a) 6   **b)** 1   **c)** −12   **d)** −15   **e)** 8
   f) −2   **g)** 7   **h)** −2   **i)** −1   **j)** 0

11. a) 16   **b)** 26   **c)** 13   **d)** 3   **e)** −9
   f) −1   **g)** −33   **12.** 108°C   **13.** 56°C

14. a) −2   **b)** 2   **c)** 4   **d)** −3   **e)** 8
   f) −3   **g)** −46   **h)** 8   **i)** −9

15. a) 18   **b)** 10   **c)** −38   **d)** −5   **e)** −14
   f) 9   **16. a)** 15:10   **b)** 09:20

17. a) −500 m   **b)** +2600 m   **c)** +2100 m
   d) −6500 m   **e)** +6900 m   **f)** +400 m
   g) −1400 m   **h)** −600 m

Mathematics Around Us, page 16

1. a) 03:00   **b)** 02:00   **c)** 10:00   **d)** 18:00

2. a) 22:00   **b)** 10:00   **c)** 03:00 next day   **d)** 11:00

3. a) 18:00   **b)** 02:00 next day   **c)** 21:00
   d) 10:00 next day   **4. a) i)** 1 P.M.   **ii)** 9 A.M.
iii) 12 noon   **b)** 4 A.M. next day

5. a) 20:00   **b)** 15:00   **c)** 15:00   **d)** 14:00
   e) 23:00   **f)** 12:00   **g)** 17:00   **h)** 08:00
next day

Exercises 1-4, page 19

1. a) −30   **b)** −56   **c)** 63   **d)** 54
   e) −60   **f)** 39   **g)** 72   **h)** −25   **i)** 25
   j) −42   **k)** 12   **l)** 32   **m)** −42
   n) −28   **o)** 27   **p)** 0

2. a) −80   **b)** −54   **c)** 56   **d)** −153
   e) −308   **f)** 209   **g)** 2592   **h)** −752
   i) 6141   **j)** 1332   **k)** −1147   **l)** 968

3. a) 70   **b)** −24   **c)** −120   **d)** 9   **e)** 18
   f) −12   **g)** −5   **h)** 24   **i)** 120

4. a) 6   **b)** 14   **c)** 22   **d)** −26   **e)** −25
   f) −76   **g)** −41   **h)** 21   **i)** −14   **j)** −22

5. a) The integers have the same sign.
   b) The integers have opposite signs.
   c) One of the integers is zero.

6. a) The product is positive.
   b) The product is negative.

7. a) −4   **b)** −8   **c)** −8   **d)** −9   **e)** 9
   f) 8   **g)** −4   **h)** −3   **i)** 3   **j)** 5
   k) −4   **l)** −14   **8. a)** 4   **b)** −4   **c)** 7
   d) 3   **e)** −8   **f)** −1   **g)** 14   **h)** 3

Investigate, page 20

1. a) Good   **b)** Bad   **c)** Bad   **d)** Good
2. a) +(+1)   **b)** +(−1)   **c)** −(+1)
   d) −(−1)   **3.** −(+2)(−3)

Mathematics Around Us, page 21

1. −2 m, +3 m   **2. a)** (−2)(+5); (+3)(+5)
b) (−2)(+50); (+3)(+50)
c) (−2)(−5); (+3)(−5)
d) (−2)(−50); (+3)(−50)   **3.** Answers may vary.

Exercises 1-5, page 23

1. a) −12   **b)** 9   **c)** −4   **d)** −6   **e)** 5   **f)** 8
2. a) −9   **b)** −23   **c)** 2   **d)** −17   **e)** 7
   f) −9   **g)** 4   **h)** −11   **i)** −11   **j)** 7
3. a) 5   **b)** 18   **c)** 8   **d)** −10   **e)** −5
   f) −4   **g)** −90   **h)** −8
4. a) −11   **b)** −6   **c)** 0   **d)** −5   **e)** −2
   f) 3   **g)** 2   **h)** 18   **i)** −3
5. a) We bought more than we sold.
   b) $359.92; −$14.50; $872.33; $92.17; $447.17;
   $442.25; $158.42
6. a) 2 h   **b)** 3 h   **c)** 5 h
7. a) −4   **b)** 35   **c)** −18   **d)** 5   **e)** 6   **f)** 5
8. a) −36   **b)** −68   **c)** −2961   **d)** 28
   e) 1452   **f)** −21
9. a), d), g), h) positive;   **b), c), e), f)** negative

Computer Power, page 25

1. a) 27 R 27   **b)** 830 R 15   **c)** 593 R 32
   d) 78 R 170   **e)** 282 R 273
2. a) 473   **b)** 1   **c)** 4
3. a) −7R4   **b)** −7R−4   **c)** 4R−5
   Dividend = (divisor)(quotient) + remainder

Problem Solving, page 27

1. $50, $5, $2, $2, $2, $2   **2.** 65 pages   **3.** 13
4. 3 in 29, 2 in 37, 1 in 50   **5.** 70¢/L   **6.** 78
7. 2 ways: 3 @ 10, 5 @ 12, 2 @ 15;
   5 @ 12, 4 @ 15

Exercises 1-6, page 29

1. a) 10 **b)** -10 **c)** -17 **d)** -9 **e)** 0
f) 14 **g)** 15 **h)** 4 **i)** -22 **j)** -2

2. a) -6 **b)** -58 **c)** 64 **d)** -16

3. a) $(3 + 5) \times (4 - 2)$ **b)** $3 + (5 \times 4) - 2$
c) $(3 + 5) \times 4 - 2$ **d)** $3 + 5 \times (4 - 2)$

4. a) -3 **b)** 2 **c)** -16 **d)** 23 **e)** 80 **f)** 109

5. a) -3 **b)** -1 **c)** 4 **d)** 2

6. a) $(1 + 3) \times 5 + 7$ **b)** $(4 + 4 + 4) \times 4$
c) $2 \times (4 + 6) + 8$ **d)** $(5 + 5) \times (5 + 5)$
e) $48 \div (8 - 2) \times 3$

7. a) -5 **b)** 4 **c)** -21 **d)** -31 **e)** -5 **f)** -1

8. a) -83 **b)** 30 **c)** 36 **d)** -156

9. a) Answers may vary: $(9 + 8) - 16$; $(1 + 9 + 6) \div 8$; $18 - 9 - 6$; $8 + 6 - 1 - 9$; $19 - 8 - 6$; $8 + 1 - 9 + 6$; $(9 \div 1) - 8 + 6$; $1 + 9 - 8 + 6$; $(8 - 1 - 6) \times 9$; $8 + 9 - 1 - 6$ **b)** Answers may vary.

Review Exercises, page 31

1. a) $-9, -7, -5, -4, 3, 6$
b) $-9, -7, -6, -5, 6, 9$

2. a) 1 **b)** -8 **c)** 3 **d)** 8 **e)** 4
f) -1 **g)** -8 **h)** -31

3. a) -6 **b)** -9 **c)** -55 **d)** 2
e) -104 **f)** -13 **4.** $-45°C$

5. a) 3 **b)** -10 **c)** -7 **d)** 7 **e)** -5
f) 13 **g)** 9 **h)** -10

6. a) -5 **b)** 13 **c)** -8 **d)** 3 **e)** -1 **f)** 5
g) 2 **h)** -9 **i)** 6 **j)** -2 **k)** -7 **l)** -8

7. a) -23 **b)** -29 **c)** -30 **d)** 243 **e)** 80
f) -190 **g)** -1 **h)** 109 **i)** -5 **j)** 390

8. a) -11 **b)** 0 **c)** -13 **d)** -10
e) -3 **f)** 70 **g)** 6 **h)** -69

9. a) -56 **b)** 54 **c)** -35 **d)** -27
e) 72 **f)** 80 **g)** -42 **h)** -60 **i)** 110
j) 144 **k)** 192 **l)** -450 **m)** 169
n) -110 **o)** -225 **p)** -320

10. a) 72 **b)** 112 **c)** 90 **d)** -48 **e)** 60
f) -70 **g)** 729 **h)** -24

11. a) 120 **b)** 288 **c)** -800 **d)** 0
e) -18 **f)** 400

12. a) -4 **b)** 2 **c)** 3 **d)** -27 **e)** 8
f) -3 **g)** -3 **h)** -11 **i)** 16

13. a) 1 **b)** -5 **c)** 1 **d)** 2 **e)** -13
f) 7 **g)** 21 **h)** -2

14. a) -11 **b)** 2 **c)** -20 **d)** -5 **e)** -5 **f)** 0

15. a) 6 **b)** 20 **c)** 23 **d)** 15

16. a) 11 **b)** -7 **c)** -9 **d)** 11

17. Probably rain

18. a) 19 **b)** -38 **c)** -8 **d)** -48

Chapter 2

Exercises 2-1, page 37

1. A, 1.7; B, 1.0; C, -0.2; D, -1.6; E, -2.9; F, -3.5

2. a) $\dfrac{1}{2} < \dfrac{3}{2}$ **b)** $-2.8 < 3.1$ **c)** $\dfrac{7}{4} > -\dfrac{5}{4}$

d) $-1.25 < 0.75$ **e)** $\dfrac{-13}{7} < \dfrac{5}{7}$ **f)** $0.01 > -1.00$

g) $\dfrac{-10}{17} < -\dfrac{5}{17}$ **h)** $108.6 > -116.8$

3. a) $-\dfrac{1}{2}$ **b)** $-\dfrac{2}{3}$ **c)** $\dfrac{2}{5}$ **d)** $-\dfrac{2}{5}$ **e)** $\dfrac{6}{11}$ **f)** $\dfrac{1}{3}$

g) $\dfrac{2}{7}$ **h)** $-\dfrac{14}{25}$ **i)** $-\dfrac{3}{7}$ **j)** $-\dfrac{1}{3}$ **k)** $-\dfrac{3}{2}$ **l)** $\dfrac{2}{3}$

4. a) $\dfrac{8}{6} > \dfrac{2}{3}$ **b)** $\dfrac{-7}{10} > \dfrac{-16}{20}$ **c)** $\dfrac{7}{5} < \dfrac{12}{5}$

d) $\dfrac{-8}{28} > \dfrac{-3}{7}$ **e)** $\dfrac{-110}{121} < \dfrac{9}{11}$ **f)** $\dfrac{-27}{24} > \dfrac{-10}{8}$

g) $\dfrac{52}{16} > \dfrac{-11}{4}$ **h)** $\dfrac{19}{6} < \dfrac{110}{30}$

5. a) -4 **b)** -5 **c)** -7 **d)** 0 **e)** 0 **f)** -1
g) -1 **h)** 0 **i)** -8 **j)** -4 **k)** -17 **l)** -7

6. $-104.9, -99.1, -97.5, -64.0$

7. a) -2 **b)** -5 **c)** -1 **d)** -0.8

e) -2.5 **f)** -3.8 **g)** -8 **h)** -2 **i)** $-\dfrac{1}{4}$

8. a) $\dfrac{15}{6} < \dfrac{56}{16}$ **b)** $\dfrac{-35}{15} > \dfrac{-30}{9}$ **c)** $\dfrac{-72}{40} < \dfrac{72}{45}$

d) $\dfrac{24}{44} < \dfrac{45}{55}$ **e)** $\dfrac{-119}{70} > \dfrac{-57}{30}$ **f)** $\dfrac{77}{28} > \dfrac{78}{32}$

g) $\dfrac{126}{54} > \dfrac{-115}{45}$ **h)** $\dfrac{-75}{35} > \dfrac{-64}{28}$

9. a) $\dfrac{15}{4}, \dfrac{11}{4}, \dfrac{7}{4}, \dfrac{3}{4}$ **b)** $\dfrac{18}{5}, \dfrac{7}{5}, -\dfrac{9}{5}, -\dfrac{13}{5}$

c) $\dfrac{17}{9}, -\dfrac{10}{9}, -\dfrac{13}{9}, -\dfrac{20}{9}$ **d)** $-\dfrac{11}{7}, -\dfrac{15}{7}, -\dfrac{22}{7}, -\dfrac{25}{7}$

10. a) $\dfrac{6}{5}, \dfrac{5}{4}, \dfrac{4}{3}, \dfrac{3}{2}$ **b)** $-\dfrac{23}{8}, -\dfrac{11}{4}, -\dfrac{8}{3}, -\dfrac{5}{2}$

c) $-\dfrac{7}{4}, -\dfrac{16}{10}, -\dfrac{3}{2}, \dfrac{11}{8}$ **d)** $-\dfrac{88}{18}, -\dfrac{29}{6}, \dfrac{55}{12}, \dfrac{21}{4}$

11. $-\dfrac{-18}{-9}, \dfrac{-3}{2}, \dfrac{10}{-8}, \dfrac{-12}{16}, \dfrac{5}{-10}, \dfrac{-5}{20}, \dfrac{-7}{-28}, -\dfrac{9}{-6}$

12. $\dfrac{-7}{-18}, -\dfrac{-2}{9}, \dfrac{1}{-4}, \dfrac{-1}{3}, -\dfrac{-13}{36}, \dfrac{-3}{8}$

13. $\dfrac{-13}{20}, \dfrac{4}{-8}, \dfrac{-16}{40}, \dfrac{-3}{-15}, -\dfrac{19}{-60}, \dfrac{14}{30}$

14. $\dfrac{-3}{4}, \dfrac{15}{-20}, \dfrac{12}{-16}, -\dfrac{-6}{-8}, \dfrac{9}{-12}$

15. $\dfrac{171}{188}, \dfrac{200}{201}$ **16.** Answers may vary.

Investigate, page 39

Answers may vary.

1. $\dfrac{-4}{6}, \dfrac{2}{-3}, \dfrac{4}{-6}, \dfrac{6}{-9}, \dfrac{-3}{-4}, \dfrac{6}{8}, \dfrac{-6}{-8}, \dfrac{9}{12};$
$\dfrac{-4}{-1}, \dfrac{-8}{-2}, \dfrac{8}{2}, \dfrac{12}{3}, \dfrac{-5}{12}, \dfrac{-10}{4}, \dfrac{10}{-4}, \dfrac{-15}{6};$
$\dfrac{-3}{1}, \dfrac{3}{-1}, \dfrac{6}{-2}, \dfrac{-9}{3}$ **2.** Answers may vary.

The Mathematical Mind, page 40

1. a) 17 **b)** -4 **c)** 259 **d)** 23 **e)** -9
f) 319 **2. a)** 0 **b)** 0 **c)** 0 **d)** 0
e) 0 **f)** 0 **g), h), i)** Not possible **j)** 0
3. Answers may vary.

Exercises 2-2, page 44

1. a) 3.232 323 23 **b)** 42.307 307 31
c) $-81.466\ 666\ 67$ **d)** 690.045 454 55
e) $-2.651\ 351\ 35$ **f)** 2.651 365 14
g) 0.069 069 07 **h)** $-0.007\ 474\ 75$
2. a) $6.\overline{3}$ **b)** $0.\overline{17}$ **c)** $42.1\overline{35}$ **d)** $0.0\overline{36}$
e) $-38.\overline{348}$ **f)** $-46.2\overline{3}$ **g)** $-0.7\overline{1}$
h) $813.\overline{813}$ **i)** $-0.021\ \overline{32}$
3. a) $0, 7, -17$ **b)** All are rational
4. a) 0.6 **b)** $-0.\overline{6}$ **c)** $0.\overline{4}$ **d)** -0.375
e) $0.\overline{3}$ **f)** $-0.1\overline{36}$ **g)** $2.\overline{142\ 857}$
h) $-0.1\overline{6}$ **i)** 0.3125 **j)** -0.629
k) $0.91\overline{6}$ **l)** $1.\overline{18}$
5. a) $\dfrac{3}{4}$ **b)** $\dfrac{13}{4}$ **c)** $-\dfrac{5}{8}$ **d)** $\dfrac{1}{16}$ **e)** $-\dfrac{11}{4}$
f) $-\dfrac{47}{8}$ **g)** $\dfrac{82}{5}$ **h)** $-\dfrac{641}{16}$
6. a) $6.4 > -\dfrac{25}{4}$ **b)** $-\dfrac{23}{7} > -3.5$
c) $\dfrac{3}{8} > -\dfrac{5}{11}$ **d)** $-\dfrac{57}{100} < -0.5$
e) $-8.6 < -\dfrac{75}{9}$ **f)** $-15.8 < -\dfrac{76}{5}$
g) $\dfrac{51}{16} > 3.175$ **h)** $\dfrac{7}{11} < \dfrac{16}{25}$ **7.** 1.57, 1.14
8. a) i) 0.438 **ii)** 0.420 **iii)** 0.378
iv) 0.373 **v)** 0.406
b) Duffy, Cobb, Williams, Ruth, Gehrig
9. $\dfrac{13}{15}, \dfrac{6}{7}, \dfrac{9}{11}, \dfrac{10}{13}, \dfrac{5}{8}$
10. a) 1.5 **b)** $1.4\overline{9}$ **c) i)** 1.15 **ii)** 0.375
iii) $-0.3\overline{8}$ **iv)** $-0.2\overline{3}$ **v)** 0.854 16 **vi)** $0.48\overline{6}$

11. a) 0.028 901 7 **b)** 0.289 017 3
c) 2.890 173 4 **d)** 28.901 734
12. a) 0.001 234 567 9 **b)** 0.001 133 572 6
c) 0.000 720 807 30 **d)** 0.003 504 236 3

Investigate, page 45

a) $0.\overline{142\ 857}, 0.\overline{285\ 714}$
b) $0.\overline{428\ 571}, 0.\overline{561\ 428}, 0.\overline{714\ 285}, 0.\overline{857\ 142}$
c) Not every fraction fits the cyclic pattern.

Calculator Power, page 47

1. a) $0.\overline{190\ 476}$ **b)** $0.\overline{635\ 036\ 49}$
c) $0.\overline{291\ 139\ 240\ 506\ 3}$ **d)** $2.\overline{646\ 341\ 4}$
e) $0.\overline{226\ 190\ 47}$
f) $0.\overline{652\ 173\ 913\ 043\ 478\ 260\ 869\ 5}$
2. a) $0.\overline{418\ 410\ 0}$ **b)** $1.\overline{210\ 33}$ **c)** $0.\overline{272\ 277}$
d) $5.\overline{543\ 655\ 413\ 271\ 245\ 634\ 458\ 672\ 87}$
e) $0.\overline{560\ 105\ 680\ 317\ 040\ 951\ 122\ 853\ 368}$
f) $0.\overline{439\ 093\ 484\ 419\ 263\ 456\ 090\ 651\ 558\ 073\ 65}$

3. a) All have the digits that appeared in $\dfrac{4}{17}$, but
beginning at a different digit.
b) $0.\overline{024\ 39}, 0.\overline{048\ 78}, 0.\overline{073\ 17}$

Computer Power, page 48

1. a) $1.\overline{652\ 173\ 913\ 043\ 478\ 260\ 869\ 5}$
b) $0.\overline{870\ 967\ 741\ 935\ 483}$ **c)** $2.22\overline{6\ 190\ 47}$
d) $3.141\ 592\ 920\ 353\ 982\ 300\ 884\ ...$

Exercises 2-3, page 51

1. a) $\dfrac{4}{5}$ **b)** $\dfrac{4}{7}$ **c)** $-\dfrac{1}{6}$ **d)** $-\dfrac{1}{56}$ **e)** $\dfrac{1}{3}$
f) -3 **g)** $\dfrac{14}{5}$ **h)** -6
2. a) 36 **b)** -19.2 **c)** 3.2 **d)** -0.12
e) -0.65 **f)** 0.56 **g)** -1.65 **h)** 1.26
3. a) $\dfrac{1}{9}$ **b)** $-\dfrac{1}{23}$ **c)** $\dfrac{19}{16}$ **d)** $-\dfrac{13}{7}$ **e)** $-\dfrac{2}{3}$
f) 1.25 **g)** $\dfrac{4}{3}$ **h)** -0.4 **i)** -16
j) $-\dfrac{5}{3}$ **k)** $-\dfrac{1}{10}$ **l)** 100
4. a) $\dfrac{8}{3}$ **b)** $\dfrac{9}{5}$ **c)** $-\dfrac{7}{4}$ **d)** 0.4 **e)** $-\dfrac{3}{2}$
f) $-\dfrac{15}{7}$ **g)** $-\dfrac{5}{3}$ **h)** $\dfrac{8}{7}$ **i)** $-\dfrac{5}{3}$

5. a) $\frac{1}{4}$ **b)** $\frac{63}{40}$ **c)** $-\frac{5}{6}$ **d)** $\frac{3}{8}$ **e)** 3

  f) $-\frac{8}{3}$ **g)** $-\frac{1}{2}$ **h)** $-\frac{14}{15}$ **i)** $\frac{22}{7}$

6. a) -4.2 **b)** 0.9 **c)** 33 **d)** -1.1
  e) -21 **f)** 13 **g)** 12 **h)** -2.4 **i)** 15

7. About -672.3 m **8.** About -1134 m

9. a) 6 **b)** $-\frac{1}{12}$ **c)** $-\frac{648}{175}$ **d)** $-\frac{1}{48}$

  e) $-\frac{9}{128}$ **f)** $-\frac{6}{121}$ **g)** 42 **h)** $\frac{20}{3}$ **i)** $-\frac{21}{8}$

10. a) -10.6386 **b)** 0.37 **c)** $-0.463\,68$
  d) -0.0067 **e)** 56.466 **f)** -0.45
  g) 0.0052 **h)** -345.9712 **i)** -136.3

11. a) $\frac{13}{-14} > \frac{-14}{13}$ **b)** $\frac{-6}{7} > \frac{7}{-8}$

  c) $\frac{-2387}{3592} > \frac{-2388}{3593}$

12. Answers may vary, for example, 1.5, $0.\overline{6}$
13. a) 1, 2, 4, 5, 8 **b)** 3, 6, 7, 9 **c)** 0

14. $-\left[(-5)^2 \div \frac{1}{9} \div \left(\frac{4}{-5}\right)\right],$

  $\left[-25 \div \frac{2}{3}\right] \div \left(-\frac{1}{6}\right), [-3]^2 \div \left[\frac{16}{5} \div \left(\frac{5}{-4}\right)^2\right]$

Exercises 2-4, page 55

1. a) $\frac{17}{12}$ **b)** $\frac{11}{35}$ **c)** $-\frac{11}{24}$ **d)** $-\frac{19}{24}$ **e)** $\frac{11}{18}$

  f) $-\frac{22}{15}$ **g)** $-\frac{7}{20}$ **h)** $\frac{13}{8}$

2. a) -4.8 **b)** -3.1 **c)** -1.5 **d)** -7.2
  e) 16.9 **f)** 5.4 **g)** 1.1 **h)** 8.3 **i)** -5.4

3. a) $-\frac{11}{12}$ **b)** $\frac{7}{3}$ **c)** $-\frac{9}{8}$ **d)** $-\frac{11}{24}$ **e)** $\frac{11}{30}$

  f) $\frac{11}{8}$ **g)** $-\frac{1}{12}$ **h)** 1

4. a) $\frac{91}{12}$ **b)** $\frac{77}{24}$ **c)** $-\frac{33}{10}$ **d)** $-\frac{107}{20}$

  e) $-\frac{34}{15}$ **f)** $-\frac{18}{35}$ **g)** $-\frac{23}{30}$ **h)** $\frac{160}{21}$

5. a) 2.536 **b)** 98.13 **c)** -51.2
  d) -19.329 **e)** -3.49 **f)** 281.8
  g) 567.37 **h)** 47.83 **i)** -0.15

6. a) $\frac{49}{30}$ **b)** $-\frac{71}{12}$ **c)** $\frac{67}{56}$ **d)** $\frac{63}{4}$ **e)** $-\frac{49}{12}$

  f) $\frac{86}{9}$ **g)** $\frac{22}{9}$ **h)** $-\frac{113}{35}$ **i)** $\frac{167}{33}$

7. a) $-\$171.9$ billion **b)** $-\$190.1$ billion
8. a) -899.8 m, -1616.4 m, -1648.9 m
  b) 1959 and 1960
9. a) 4 **b)** -8 **c)** 2 **d)** -8 **e)** -8 **f)** 18
10. a) 30.5 **b)** 60 **c)** 71.5
11. a) They were up $\frac{1}{8}$ on the day before.

  b) $\$17\,625.00$ **c)** 200 shares **d)** $\$10\frac{1}{2}$, $\$7\frac{3}{8}$,

  $\$8\frac{1}{2}$, $\$36$, $\$9\frac{3}{4}$, $\$15\frac{3}{4}$, $\$12\frac{1}{2}$

12. b), c), d), g), h), j)

Mathematics Around Us, page 59

Answers may vary.
1. About 1.32 m **2.** About 0.66 m
3. a) Answers may vary, for example, 9.24 m
  b) Answers may vary, for example, 46.2 m
4. a) Answers may vary, for example, about 16 years
5. a) About 900 years from when the map was drawn
  b) About 900 years ago
6. The erosion will continue at 0.66 m per year. The
  erosion was 1.32 m up to 1960 and 0.66 m from
  1960 onward.

Problem Solving, page 61

1. $9.69 **2.** 352 mL; 160 mL
3. Fill 8 L bucket 3 times from 3 L bucket, so have
  1 L left in 3 L bucket. Empty 8 L bucket, pour in
  1 L from 3 L bucket. Fill 3 L bucket and pour into
  8 L bucket.
4. $5.25 **5.** 5:00 A.M. **6.** $19\,531.25
7. 57 **8.** $1875

Exercises 2-5, page 64

1. a) $-\frac{1}{12}$ **b)** $\frac{9}{8}$ **c)** $\frac{5}{24}$ **d)** $-\frac{17}{40}$ **e)** $\frac{37}{12}$

  f) $-\frac{9}{5}$ **g)** $-\frac{4}{3}$ **h)** $-\frac{19}{18}$ **i)** $\frac{11}{4}$ **j)** $\frac{41}{70}$

2. a) $\frac{1}{16}$ **b)** $\frac{5}{21}$ **c)** $-\frac{9}{2}$ **d)** $\frac{1}{13}$ **e)** $-\frac{2}{3}$

  f) $-\frac{9}{20}$ **g)** -2 **h)** 5 **i)** 3 **j)** 3

3. a) -13.5 **b)** -6.4 **c)** -1.85 **d)** 62.6
4. a) 3598.608 **b)** 3.1 **c)** 169.36
  d) -29.79 **e)** 0.06 **f)** -0.0412

5. a) $-\frac{11}{10}$ **b)** $-\frac{129}{98}$ **c)** $-\frac{18}{7}$ **d)** $-\frac{4}{33}$

f) $\dfrac{32}{123}$ **6. a)** $\dfrac{3}{20}$ **b)** $-\dfrac{9}{10}$

d) $\dfrac{27}{32}$ **e)** $-\dfrac{2}{5}$ **f)** $-\dfrac{2}{3}$

11.75   **b)** 26.574   **c)** 11.1398
-407.23   **e)** -15.425 **f)** -17.7

es 2-6, page 67

15°C   **b)** -20°C   **c)** 30°C
) 9.7 L/100 km   **b)** 8.5 L/100 km
c) 11.5 L/100 km
a) \$3440/h   **b)** \$2950/h   **4.** 867 kW

. **a)** $\dfrac{21}{55}$ **b)** $\dfrac{8}{21}$ **6. a)** 1.2 cm   **b)** 4.8 cm

7. \$226.10   **8. a)** \$90.67   **b)** \$10 012.33
9. a) 37.5 m   **b)** 86.6 m   **10.** 500 km
11. a) 4 days   **b)** 12 days   **c)** 20 days
12. a) 212°F   **b)** 419°F   **c)** 41°F   **d)** -4°F
13. -40°

Review Exercises, page 71

1. a) $-\dfrac{5}{2}$ **b)** $\dfrac{1}{8}$ **c)** $-\dfrac{9}{5}$ **d)** $-\dfrac{111}{100}$ **e)** $\dfrac{339}{40}$

2. $-\dfrac{6}{9}, -\dfrac{14}{21}, \dfrac{10}{-15}$ **3.** $-\dfrac{31}{32}, -\dfrac{15}{16}, -\dfrac{43}{48}, \dfrac{2}{3}, \dfrac{5}{6}, \dfrac{11}{12}$

4. Answers may vary.   **a)** 0.1, 0.2, 0.3, 0.4
b) $-1.2, -1.4, -1.6, -1.8$

5. a) 0.375 **b)** $-0.\overline{571\ 428}$ **c)** $-0.58\overline{3}$
d) $2.\overline{2}$ **e)** -2.1875 **f)** $0.\overline{6}$

6. a) $-\dfrac{3}{2}$ **b)** $\dfrac{81}{4}$ **c)** $\dfrac{2007}{1000}$ **d)** $-\dfrac{208}{5}$

e) $\dfrac{43}{4}$ **f)** $-\dfrac{31}{8}$ **7. a)** $-\dfrac{7}{12}$ **b)** $\dfrac{15}{32}$

c) $-\dfrac{21}{40}$ **d)** $-\dfrac{2}{3}$ **e)** $-\dfrac{2}{3}$ **f)** $\dfrac{192}{455}$

8. a) $-\dfrac{2}{3}$ **b)** $\dfrac{39}{8}$ **c)** $\dfrac{7}{18}$ **d)** -1 **e)** $\dfrac{8}{5}$ **f)** $-\dfrac{4}{5}$

9. a) -5.0652 **b)** -0.6 **c)** $-29\ 717.16$
d) -32.8 **e)** 0.086 **f)** $0.967\ 73$

10. a) $\dfrac{41}{35}$ **b)** $\dfrac{19}{24}$ **c)** $\dfrac{29}{36}$ **d)** $-\dfrac{2}{11}$ **e)** $-\dfrac{5}{6}$

f) $-\dfrac{10}{9}$ **g)** $\dfrac{2}{15}$ **h)** $\dfrac{1}{35}$ **i)** $-\dfrac{79}{63}$

j) $-\dfrac{43}{36}$ **k)** $\dfrac{31}{30}$ **l)** $-\dfrac{37}{12}$

11. a) $\dfrac{11}{18}$ **b)** $\dfrac{8}{15}$ **c)** $\dfrac{11}{24}$ **d)** -1 **e)** $-\dfrac{1}{4}$

f) $-\dfrac{5}{8}$ **g)** $\dfrac{78}{55}$ **h)** $-\dfrac{29}{20}$

12. a) -4.52 **b)** -48.32 **c)** 494.3
d) 161.72   **e)** 224.9   **f)** -401.97

13. a) $\dfrac{11}{20}$ **b)** $\dfrac{7}{6}$ **c)** $-\dfrac{7}{15}$ **d)** $-\dfrac{11}{12}$

14. a) $\dfrac{1}{12}$ **b)** $\dfrac{3}{2}$ **c)** $\dfrac{9}{5}$ **d)** 0 **e)** $-\dfrac{9}{5}$ **f)** $\dfrac{4}{5}$

15. a) -22.4 **b)** -25.5102 **c)** 304.64
d) -99.72

16. a) $-\dfrac{47}{72}$ **b)** $\dfrac{13}{60}$ **c)** $-\dfrac{91}{24}$

17. a) 428 000   **b)** 533 000   **c)** 545 000
d) 428 000   **18.** \$172.00

Chapter 3

Exercises 3-1, page 76

1. a) 15   **b)** The number of regions is 1 more than
the position of the circle.

2. a) i) 8   **ii)** 19   **b)** The number of unshaded
squares is 3 more than twice the number of
shaded squares.

3. a) i) 20   **ii)** 380   **b)** The number of 0s is the
number of Xs, multiplied by 1 less than the
number of Xs.   **c)** $a(a - 1)$

4. a) 38 **b)** 92 **c)** The number of faces is 3 times
the number of cubes, plus 2.   **d)** $3c + 2$

5. a) 144   **b)** 25
c) i) The number of shaded squares is the number
of the diagram multiplied by itself.
ii) The number of unshaded squares is twice the
number of the diagram, plus 1.
d) i) $d \times d$ **ii)** $2d + 1$

6. a) i) 352 kg   **ii)** 1078 kg   **iii)** 5390 kg
b) The amount of milk is the number of days
multiplied by 22 kg.
c) $22d$ kilograms   **d)** Divide the amount of milk
by 22 kg.   **e)** $\dfrac{A}{22}$

7. a) i) 1440°   **ii)** 2340°   **b)** The sum of the
interior angles is 180° multiplied by 2 less than
the number of sides.   **c)** $180°(s - 2)$

8. Multiply the number of carbon atoms by 2, then
add 2.

9. a) i) To the right   **ii)** Up   **iii)** Down
b) The pattern repeats every 4th arrow. Divide the
number of the position of the arrow by 4. The
remainder determines the position of the arrow.

Remainder	0	1	2	3
Arrow	$\rightarrow$	$\uparrow$	$\leftarrow$	$\downarrow$

10. a) 11 **b)** 55 **c)** The number of 0s is half the number of Xs, multiplied by 1 less than the number of Xs. **d)** $\frac{1}{2}x(x - 1)$

11. a) 22 **b)** 948
  c) i) Multiply the number of the diagram by 6 and subtract 8.
  ii) Cube the number of the diagram, then subtract the number of colored cubes.

Exercises 3-2, page 81

1. a) $p, q; 6p, -2q; 6, -2$ **b)** $a, b, c; a, -2b, 9c;$
  $1, -2, 9$ **c)** $C; 1.8C, 32; 1.8, 32$ **d)** $r, 2\pi r, 2\pi$
2. a)

7	11	$4 + a$	$4 + 2b$	$4 + ab$
12	16	$9 + a$	$9 + 2b$	$9 + ab$
$x + 3$	$x + 7$	$x + a$	$x + 2b$	$x + ab$
$y + 3$	$y + 7$	$y + a$	$y + 2b$	$y + ab$
$xy + 3$	$xy + 7$	$xy + a$	$xy + 2b$	$xy + ab$

b)

12	28	$4a$	$8b$	$4ab$
27	63	$9a$	$18b$	$9ab$
$3x$	$7x$	ax	$2bx$	abx
$3y$	$7y$	ay	$2by$	aby
$3xy$	$7xy$	axy	$2bxy$	$abxy$

3. a) 352 **b)** $11d$ **c)** $32r$ **d)** dr
4. a) 32 **b)** $5x$ **c)** $3y$ **d)** $5x + 3y + z$
5. a) 17 **b)** 45.5 **c)** -100 **d)** 72 **e)** 27 **f)** 59
6. a) 3.6 **b)** 0.351 **c)** 9.99 **d)** -19.52
  e) 12.69 **f)** -12.3 **g)** -3.06
7. a) -1 **b)** $\frac{1}{4}$ **c)** $\frac{1}{30}$ **d)** $\frac{26}{55}$ **e)** $-\frac{59}{72}$
  f) $\frac{41}{6}$ **g)** $\frac{103}{84}$
8. a) \$1535.00 **b)** \$484.00
  c) \$910.00 **d)** \$3105.00
9. 120π cm² **10.** 589π cm² **11. a)** 114
b) 87 **12.** 2 250 000π^2 m³

Exercises 3-3, page 86

1. a) $11a$ **b)** $13m$ **c)** $-13x$ **d)** $9p$
  e) $-37g$ **f)** $49b$ **g)** $52r$ **h)** $5w$ **i)** $-17p$
2. a) $-2x + 5y$ **b)** $-11m - 5p$
  c) $5a - 34b$ **d)** $21x + 29y$ **e)** $85u + 13v$
  f) $-2j + 12k$ **g)** $-33s - 14t$ **h)** $9x + 4y$
  i) $-9a + 14b - 8c$ **j)** $9x - 23y - 13z$

3. a) $m + 5$ **b)** $-c$ **c)** $10a + 3b$
  d) $3x + 2y$ **e)** $8u - 8v - 7$
  f) $5m + 4$ **g)** $-9x + y$ **h)** $6x - 3y + z$
  i) $7p + 8q - 7$
4. a) $40a - 60b$ **b)** $7x - 16y$
  c) $40m + 10n - 7$ **d)** $-47c + 4d + 7$
  e) $28a - 13$ **f)** $17x - 18y$
  g) $-3a - 3b + 4$ **h)** $30p - 16q - 6r$
5. a) $21a - 2b$ **b)** $-1 + 2m - 16n$
  c) $-5y + 2z - 3$ **d)** $-13r + 9s + 4$
  e) $25x - 4y - 3$ **f)** $-3m - 15x + 8$
  g) 0 **h)** $-13c - 33d - 3$
6. a) $-2p + 2r - 13s$ **b)** $-10p + 9x - 20z$
  c) $-6m - 19n + 18q$ **d)** $-14a - 11b - 19$
  e) $0.2x + z + 0.3$ **f)** $5.5m - 25.9n - 0.6$
7. a) 33 **b)** -32.5 **c)** -91 **d)** -6
  e) 200 **f)** 81 **g)** -56 **h)** 14
8. a) $5r$ **b)** $2y + 4z$ **c)** $2p + 2(q + r) + 2q$
9. a) $10x - 4y - 6z$ **b)** $2m - 4n - 12p$
  c) $6a + 3b - 8c$ **d)** $-6x - 18y$
10. a) $-x^2 - 3x$ **b)** $-4x^2 + 2x$
  c) $2a - 9b + 3ab$ **d)** $3q^2 + 3r^2 - 9p - 7r$
  e) $2y^2 - 3y + 7$ **f)** $4c^2 - 12b - 3c - 6$
  g) $x^2 - 2x - 5$
  h) $5m^2 + 7x^2 - 17b - 7x + 1$
  i) $3w^2 - 7v - 3w$
  j) $-3a^2 - 10ab - 4a + 3b + 3$
11. a) $7xy - 8yz - 5xz$ **b)** $4ab - 11bc - 6ac$
  c) $5xyz + 9wxy - 11wyz$

12. a) 27 **b)** -156 **13. a)** $6x; 2x^2$
  b) $12z; 6z^2$ **c)** $2w + 2z; xy + zw - zy$

Problem Solving, page 89

1. 3 g **2.** 836 **3.** \$9.75 **4.** \$5.75
5. \$2.25 **6.** 5.2 m **7.** \$31.74 **8.** 12, 13
9. 11 **10.** $-17, 25$ **11.** 11 **12.** 124, 125, 126

Exercises 3-4, page 91

1. a) $3m - 24$ **b)** $18x + 90$ **c)** $11p + 77$
  d) $-23a + 207$ **e)** $14p + 42$
  f) $4a - 4b + 60$ **g)** $-56a - 8b + 8$
  h) $12s + 66t - 30$
2. a) $5m + 78$ **b)** $36x + 45$ **c)** $-7 - 18x$
  d) $12 + 21a$ **e)** $-51x - 87$
  f) $a + 3b + 27$ **g)** $20e - 20f + 60$
  h) $21t - 36$ **i)** $-14x + 14$
  j) $-10w - 49$ **k)** $c - 18$ **l)** $-18t + 8$
3. a) $15m + 1$ **b)** $-14c - 6d$ **c)** $8a + 4$
  d) $11a + 2b + 15$

4. a) $34x + y$ **b)** $38x + 4y$ **c)** $-87m - 14n$
d) $54a - 138b$ **e)** $82k + 83l$
f) $-11p - q$ **g)** $7q - 19r - 22s$
h) $15u + 42v + 9w$ **i)** $25a + 25b + 15c$
j) $-90x - 52y - 26$
5. a) $11x + 6y$ **b)** $-18.2x - 12.6y$
c) $13x + 28.6y$ **d)** $26.2x - 11.5y$
6. a) $\dfrac{35}{2}m - 7$ **b)** $12x - 12$ **c)** $2z - 16$

d) $12x - 4x$ **7. a)** $8ax - 8ay$ **b)** $6bc - 22ac$
c) $-5x^4 + 9x^3 - 8x^2 + 12x$ **d)** $2xy - 4x^2 + y$
e) $3x + 6y^2 - 5xy$ **f)** $4pq - 5p^2 + q^2$
g) $x^2 + 2xy - 3y^2$ **h)** $6a^2 + 3ab + 3b^2$
8. a) $3wx - w^2$ **b)** $3p^2 - pq$ **c)** $wy + 4wz$
d) $4\pi x^2 - 7.5x^2$
9. a) -27.3 **b)** 21.7 **c)** -30.9 **d)** 38.01

Exercises 3-5, page 95

Letters may vary.

1. a) $n + 5$ **b)** $m - 6$ **c)** $8x$ **d)** $\dfrac{1}{5}f$

e) $8e$ **f)** $5f + 4$ **g)** $8t - 2$ **h)** $8(b - 2)$

i) $\dfrac{1}{4}c + 3$ **j)** $\dfrac{1}{4}(s + 3)$ **2. a)** $60m$ **b)** $1000k$

c) $5n$ **d)** $2x$ **e)** $\dfrac{m}{60}$ **f)** $\dfrac{c}{100}$

3. a) Six more than a number   **b)** Ten less than a
number   **c)** One-quarter of a number
d) Ten times a number
e) Three-tenths of a number, and four
f) Three times a number, and two
g) Five less than four times a number
h) The product of three less than a number, and two
i) One-third of the sum of a number and five
j) The product of a number, and three less than the
number.
4. a) $x, x + 12$ **b)** $m, m - 1.5$ **c)** $l, 30 - l$
5. a) $h, h + 1$ **b)** $a, a + 1, a + 2$

c) $p, \dfrac{36}{p}$ **d)** $t, t + 2$ **6. a)** $10\,000A$

b) $100B$ **c)** $1\,000\,000V$ **d)** $\dfrac{M}{100}$

7. a) a years, $(a + 12)$ years   **b)** $f, \dfrac{1}{5}f$

c) a years, $(21 - a)$ years   **d)** j centimetres,

$(j + 15)$ centimetres   **e)** $s, 1.1s$ **f)** $p, \dfrac{76}{p}$

g) $i, i + 1, i + 2$ **h)** $p, p + 2, p + 4$
8. Answers may vary.

a) $x, \dfrac{3x - 4}{2}$ **b)** $x, \dfrac{8x + 7}{5}$ **c)** $x, 2(x - 9)$

Review Exercises, page 97

1. a) 37 **b)** The number of matchsticks is one
more than three times the number of squares.
c) $3s + 1$ **2. a)** \$40 **b)** \$480 **c)** 4 weeks
d) i) Divide the amount of money by \$40.
ii) Divide the amount of money by \$5.
3. a) $6x, 4y, 3z$ **b)** x, y, z **c)** 6, 4, 3
4. a) 57 **b)** 36.2 **c)** 17 **d)** -13.1
e) -163 **f)** 3.6 **5. a)** $12x$ **b)** $17m$ **c)** $9x$
d) $7a + 7b$ **e)** $8x + 2y$ **f)** $25c - 2d$ **g)** m
h) $9w + x$ **i)** $10e - 0.5f$ **j)** $-1.1c - 4.8d$

6. a) $\dfrac{3}{8}$ **b)** 27 **c)** -5.95 **d)** $\dfrac{3}{40}$

7. a) $-2x - 3$ **b)** $-10a + 3b$
c) $-3p - 7q$ **d)** $-5m - 11n$
e) $-9e + 16f + 10g$ **f)** $-10b + 2c - 4d$
8. a) $10a + 31$ **b)** $2x + 10y$ **c)** $-x - y$
d) $13m + 23n$ **e)** $-3x - 15y$ **f)** $3r + 39s$
9. a) $4m + 17n - 17$ **b)** $3a - 5b + 2$
c) $10x - 11y - z - 8$ **d)** $25d - 18e - 16$
e) $0.9x - 1.5y + 2.4z$ **f)** $-5.1a - 3.3b$

10. a) $\dfrac{11wb}{12}$ **b)** $18x^2 - \pi x^2$ **c)** $16\pi a^2 - a^2$

11. a) $\dfrac{1}{10}n$ **b)** $11p$ **c)** $q + 20$ **d)** $r - 31$

e) $5s + 14$ **f)** $\dfrac{1}{7}t + 19$

12. Answers may vary.
a) x dollars, $(x + 1300)$ dollars
b) $y, y + 2$ **c)** $n, n + 2, n + 4$
d) x metres, $(x - 2.6)$ metres   **e)** $n, 37.8 - n$
f) x metres, $(15 - x)$ metres   **g)** $d, d + 0.4$
h) a years, $(2a - 4)$ years

Cumulative Review, Chapters 1-3, page 99

1. a) $+\$17$ **b)** -3 **c)** $-12°C$ **d)** $+\$425$
e) -12 m **f)** -210 m **2. a)** -37 **b)** 35
c) -17 **d)** -45 **e)** 23 **f)** -8
3. a) -63 **b)** 40 **c)** 5 **d)** 147 **e)** -9 **f)** 4
4. a) 18 **b)** 39 **c)** 58 **d)** 30 **e)** -8 **f)** 12
5. a) $-17, -4, -3, -\dfrac{5}{4}, \dfrac{5}{2}, 6, \dfrac{22}{3}$

b) $-7, -4.5, -2.3, -\dfrac{2}{3}, 1.25, \dfrac{17}{5}, 12$

6. a) 0.4 **b)** -0.375 **c)** $-2.8\overline{3}$
d) $1.571\,428$ **e)** $1.58\overline{3}$

7. a) $\dfrac{13}{4}$ **b)** $-\dfrac{38}{5}$ **c)** $\dfrac{15}{8}$ **d)** $-\dfrac{429}{200}$

e) $-\dfrac{1103}{100}$ **8. a)** $\dfrac{7}{4}$ **b)** $-\dfrac{40}{33}$ **c)** -3.5

d) $-\dfrac{9}{8}$ **e)** 7   **f)** $-\dfrac{8}{27}$

9. a) 9.49   **b)** $-\dfrac{15}{8}$ **c)** $-\dfrac{47}{18}$ **d)** $-\dfrac{13}{30}$

e) -3.187 **f)** $\dfrac{13}{6}$ **10. a)** $\dfrac{1}{4}$ **b)** -7.73

c) $-\dfrac{1}{8}$ **d)** $\dfrac{29}{15}$ **e)** -41 **f)** $-\dfrac{64}{45}$

11. 323 m³   **12. a) i)** 7   **ii)** 11   **b) i)** 28

ii) 66   **c)** $\dfrac{n(n+1)}{2}$ **13. a)** -14 **b)** 36

c) -26.6 **d)** $-\dfrac{1}{10}$ **e)** $\dfrac{83}{30}$

14. a) $-19p - 9q$ **b)** $4x - 8y - 5z$
c) $-5a + 1.3b$ **d)** $5x - 9y$ **e)** $-3m - 7n$

15. a) $-7a - 11b$ **b)** $12m - 22n$
c) $-2x - 38y$ **d)** $-36p - 36q$
e) $13c + 7d - 24e$ **f)** $-39x - 30y + 6z$

16. a) $a + 11$ **b)** $6b - 4$ **c)** $c + c + 1$

d) $d - 21$ **e)** $8 + 3e$ **f)** $10 - \dfrac{3}{4}f$

Chapter 4

Exercises 4-1, page 103

1. a) 15   **b)** 17   **c)** 34   **d)** 35   **e)** 36
f) 0   **g)** 15   **h)** -5 **2. a)** 6   **b)** -9

c) 11   **d)** 36   **e)** $\dfrac{1}{2}$ **f)** 50   **g)** 2   **h)** 5

3. a) 8.5   **b)** 20   **c)** 3   **d)** 16   **e)** 8.6
f) 2   **g)** 1   **h)** 0.5   **4. a)** 4   **b)** 2   **c)** 5
d) 6   **e)** 3   **f)** 7   **g)** 15   **h)** 5

5. a) 5   **b)** 2   **c)** 4   **d)** 16   **e)** 20
f) 11   **g)** 3   **h)** 12   **i)** -6 **j)** -7
k) -11 **l)** -9

6. 8 h   **7.** 182 chirps/min   **8.** 11 km

Exercises 4-2, page 105

1. a) 6   **b)** 13   **c)** 9   **d)** 13   **e)** 36
f) 6   **g)** 84   **h)** 28

2. a) 10   **b)** 7   **c)** -12 **d)** 7   **e)** 45
f) 9   **g)** 8   **h)** -32 **i)** 54   **j)** 14
k) 16   **l)** -13 **m)** 800   **n)** 1584   **o)** -72

3. a) -4 **b)** -6 **c)** 10   **d)** -6 **e)** -5
f) -11 **g)** 3   **h)** -23 **4. a)** 52   **b)** 28
c) -7 **d)** 13   **e)** 15   **f)** 2   **g)** -63 **h)** 7
i) -7 **j)** 56   **5. a)** -13 **b)** -10 **c)** 8
d) 10   **e)** -32 **f)** 12   **g)** 0   **h)** 1.5

6. a) 12   **b)** 2   **c)** 57   **d)** $\dfrac{7}{4}$ **e)** 6.8

f) -79 **g)** $\dfrac{61}{8}$ **h)** $\dfrac{1}{10}$ **7. a)** -8 **b)** -24

c) 13   **d)** 75   **e)** 5   **f)** -4 **g)** 4   **h)** 27
8. 16 min   **9.** 963 km   **10.** \$2000

11. a) $b - a$ **b)** $d + c$ **c)** $\dfrac{m}{3}$ **d)** $4w$

e) $a - 3b$ **f)** $4c - 4d$ **g)** $z - 2y$

h) $2a - b + c$ **i)** $\dfrac{b-c}{a}$ **j)** $\dfrac{m-n}{k}$

k) $\dfrac{-b-d}{c}$ **l)** $qr - pq$

Exercises 4-3, page 108

1. a) 8   **b)** 4   **c)** -2 **d)** 5   **e)** -9 **f)** -5
g) -2 **h)** 5   **i)** -1 **j)** 3   **k)** 3   **l)** -3

2. a) $-\dfrac{17}{8}$ **b)** $\dfrac{8}{9}$ **c)** $-\dfrac{2}{5}$ **d)** $\dfrac{1}{4}$ **e)** $\dfrac{3}{4}$

f) $-\dfrac{1}{12}$ **g)** $\dfrac{1}{10}$ **h)** $-\dfrac{17}{28}$ **i)** $\dfrac{2}{11}$

j) $-\dfrac{1}{15}$ **k)** $\dfrac{1}{6}$ **l)** $\dfrac{1}{8}$

3. a) -9 **b)** 16   **c)** 16   **d)** -6 **e)** -4.4
f) 0.5   **g)** 0.6   **h)** -30 **i)** 8

4. a) $-\dfrac{3}{2}$ **b)** -4 **c)** 9   **d)** $\dfrac{12}{25}$ **e)** $\dfrac{32}{63}$

f) $\dfrac{3}{2}$ **g)** 15   **h)** 20   **i)** 1

5. a) 20   **b)** -30 **c)** 8   **d)** 4.5   **e)** -1 **f)** -16.8

6. a) $\dfrac{17}{4}$ **b)** $-\dfrac{38}{5}$ **c)** -10 **d)** $\dfrac{1}{3}$

e) -0.075 **f)** 1   **g)** 2   **h)** -1 **i)** 3

7. a) i) -1 **ii)** 8   **iii)** 0.5   **iv)** 6.2   **v)** 2

b) i) $\dfrac{2}{3}$ **ii)** 1   **iii)** $-\dfrac{1}{15}$ **iv)** 7   **v)** -36

8. a) i) 1.6 km   **ii)** 3.2 km   **iii)** 1.12 km
b) i) 25 s   **ii)** 19 s   **9. a)** 250   **b)** 3

10. a) 23   **b)** 4   **c)** 5 questions have 2 parts, 2
questions have 3 parts.

Problem Solving, page 111

1. $\dfrac{2}{3}$ **2.**

18	113	19
51	50	49
81	-13	82

3. 1 h 12 min   **4.** 600 g peanuts, 400 g pecans
5. 1 m²   **6. a)** 2 kg   **b)** 8 kg   **7.** 25%
8. 21 kg   **9.** 7 cards, 5 cards   **10.** 7.5 g   **11.** 72

Exercises 4-4, page 113

1. a) 2 **b)** −4 **c)** −1 **d)** −2 **e)** 2
f) 0 **g)** −2 **h)** 3 **i)** $\frac{2}{3}$ **j)** $\frac{1}{2}$ **k)** $\frac{1}{6}$
l) $\frac{7}{2}$ **m)** $\frac{11}{6}$ **n)** 2 **2. a)** 5 **b)** 0 **c)** −11
d) 0 **e)** 3 **f)** −9 **g)** 8 **h)** $-\frac{3}{2}$

3. a) $\frac{9}{5}$ **b)** 10 **c)** −13 **d)** $-\frac{9}{7}$ **e)** $\frac{1}{10}$
f) 4 **g)** −2 **h)** $\frac{2}{3}$

4. a) 6 **b)** $\frac{9}{2}$ **c)** −1 **d)** 17 **e)** 1
f) $\frac{27}{7}$ **g)** $-\frac{4}{5}$ **h)** −5 **i)** $\frac{3}{2}$ **j)** 1
k) 3 **l)** 0 **m)** 0 **n)** 2

5. a) 0 **b)** −2 **c)** 15 **d)** 8 **e)** 3 **f)** $-\frac{1}{8}$

Exercises 4-5, page 115

1. a) 2 **b)** $-\frac{10}{3}$ **c)** $-\frac{5}{6}$ **d)** 12 **e)** −16
f) 14 **g)** 20 **h)** −12 **i)** $-\frac{3}{14}$

2. a) 24 **b)** $-\frac{100}{9}$ **c)** 60 **d)** 180 **e)** 6
f) $\frac{6}{5}$ **3.** $\frac{2}{5}$

4. a) $-\frac{5}{8}$ **b)** $-\frac{3}{2}$ **c)** −15 **d)** $-\frac{6}{5}$ **e)** 8
f) $\frac{13}{4}$ **g)** $-\frac{13}{5}$ **h)** 12 **i)** −6 **j)** 4.5

5. a) $\frac{65}{14}$ **b)** $\frac{9}{7}$ **c)** $-\frac{2}{5}$ **d)** −1 **e)** $\frac{1}{17}$
f) 1 **g)** $\frac{21}{5}$ **h)** $-\frac{5}{16}$ **i)** $\frac{186}{191}$ **j)** $\frac{119}{59}$

6. a) i) $-\frac{1}{4}$ **ii)** $-\frac{9}{20}$ **iii)** $-\frac{1}{20}$ **iv)** $-\frac{29}{20}$
v) $\frac{19}{20}$ **b) i)** $-\frac{5}{12}$ **ii)** $-\frac{5}{4}$ **iii)** $\frac{5}{12}$
iv) $-\frac{35}{12}$ **v)** $\frac{25}{12}$

Exercises 4-6, page 117

1. a) 2 **b)** 1 **c)** 5 **d)** −4 **e)** −1
f) 6 **g)** $\frac{1}{2}$ **h)** 18 **i)** 10

2. a) 40 **b)** $\frac{4}{5}$ **c)** 9 **d)** $\frac{1}{2}$ **e)** $-\frac{9}{8}$
f) 8 **g)** −3 **h)** 1 **i)** $\frac{19}{2}$ **j)** −8

3. a) −11 **b)** 13 **c)** $-\frac{3}{2}$ **d)** −3 **e)** 5
f) 46 **g)** $\frac{10}{7}$ **h)** 5 **i)** −4.35 **j)** 7.5

Investigate, page 118

3. a) 1 **b)** 1 **c)** none **d)** infinite
e) none **f)** none

Exercises 4-7, page 121

1. $21.88 **2. a) i)** $11.00 **ii)** $110.00
iii) $275.00 **iv)** $990.00 **b) i)** $200.00
ii) $500.00 **iii)** $1200.00 **iv)** $1450.00

3. a) $\frac{p - n}{m}$ **b)** $2c + 2d$ **c)** $\frac{b + d}{a}$
d) $\frac{3(k - 3)}{2}$ **e)** $\frac{v - 1}{w}$ **f)** $\frac{a - d}{b}$

4. a) $\frac{I}{Pr}$ **b)** $\frac{P - 2w}{2}$ **c)** $\frac{2A}{h}$ **d)** $\frac{C}{2\pi}$
e) $\frac{l - a}{b}$ **f)** $\frac{A - 50}{1.275}$ **5. a)** 140.1 cm²
b) 4.5 cm **6. a) i)** 200 beats/min
ii) 183 beats/min **iii)** 157 beats/min
b) i) 50 years **ii)** 28 years **iii)** 79 years

7. a) $t = \frac{v}{9.8}$ **b) i)** 5.5 s **ii)** 8.3 s **iii)** 35 s
iv) 102 s **8. a) i)** 5°C **ii)** −11°C
iii) −63°C **b)** 3538 m
9. a) i) 30 years **ii)** 25 years **iii)** 20 years
b) i) 60 years **ii)** 70 years **iii)** 55 years
10. a) $\frac{V}{\pi r^2}$ **b)** $\frac{Fd}{M}$ **c)** $\frac{IP}{100}$ **d)** $\frac{2A}{a + b}$
e) $\frac{v}{4n}$ **f)** $3c - 3b$

11. a) $5S + 10e$ **b)** $34 - 2n$ **c)** $\frac{L_2 - L_1}{aL_1}$
d) $\frac{C - 0.73}{0.99}$ **e)** $\frac{2S - an}{n}$ **f)** $\frac{2A - ah}{h}$
12. a) $\frac{l - 14.3}{0.27}$ **b) i)** 310 g **ii)** 329 g
13. a) i) 1.6 m/s **ii)** 8.2 m/s **iii)** 13.0 m/s
iv) 16.3 m/s **b) i)** 3.1 s **ii)** 19.6 s

iii) 35.0 s   **iv)** 6 min 8.1 s
14. a) 16 cm   **b)** 4.5 cm
15. a) 16 L   **b)** 233 L   **c)** 17 500 L
16. a) i) 18.7 m   **ii)** 24.5 m   **iii)** 10.1 m
    iv) 11.5 m **b) i)** 67 m **ii)** 93 m **iii)** 171 m
    iv) 138 m

Problem Solving, page 124

1. 9 cones   **2.** 3   **3.** 17   **4.** 12 years, 3 years
5. 7 m   **6.** $40
7. a) Answers may vary, for example, every number
    can be considered as a multiple of 6 plus 1, 2,
    3, 4 or 5.   **b)** $6n + 1$, $6n + 5$ **8.** 15 bars

Exercises 4-8, page 126

1. a) x **b)** $x + 8$ **c)** $x + x + 8 = 42$
2. a) k **b)** $k - 2.5$ **c)** $k + k - 2.5 = 97.5$
3. a) m **b)** $12 - m$ **c)** $m = \frac{1}{3}(12 - m)$
4. a) a **b)** $27 - a$ **c)** $27 - a + 2a = 43$
Equations may vary.   **5.** $d + d - 2 = 12$
6. $f + 2f = 12$ **7.** $2(w + w + 5) = 68$
8. $n + n + 1 = 263$
9. $n + n + 1 + n + 2 + n + 3 = 234$
10. $n + n + 2 = 170$
11. $x + \frac{1}{5}x = 18$ **12.** $c + 3c = 24$
13. $g + g - 9 = 33$ **14.** $m + 4m = 65$
15. a) $x + x + 1 = 83$ **b)** $x + x - 17 = 39$
16. a) x **b)** $54 - x$ **c)** $2x - 9 = 54 - x$
17. a) y **b)** $65 - y$ **c)** $3y + 15 = 2(65 - y)$
18. a) r **b)** $2r$ **c)** $r - 3 + 2r - 3 = 48$
19. $3x = 14 + 2(63 - x)$ **20.** $2r = 7 + 35 - r$
21. $l - 4 + 2l - 4 = 37$
22. $x + x - 7 + x - 5 = 33$
23. $x + x + 5 + 3(x + 5) = 75$
24. $l + \frac{2}{5}l + \frac{7}{9}\left(\frac{2}{5}l\right) = 770$

Exercises 4-9, page 129

1. 16   **2.** 84   **3.** 64   **4.** 11, 16   **5.** 22, 23
6. 40 years, 36 years   **7.** 6 m, 16 m
8. 31 years, 21 years   **9.** 59.5 kg, 62.0 kg
10. 13 years, 14 years   **11.** 3.90 m, 3.75 m
12. 12, 13   **13.** 48, 49   **14.** 144 km/h, 120 km/h
15. 12 km, 6 km   **16.** 30, 6   **17.** 16 cm, 11 cm

18. 142, 143   **19.** 52, 53, 54   **20.** 48, 49, 50, 51
21. 112, 114   **22.** 43 km, 38 km   **23.** 20
24. 44 years, 11 years   **25.** 108, 12   **26.** 3.5, 3.75
27. 7, 29   **28.** $\frac{61}{5}, \frac{26}{5}, \frac{78}{5}$ **29.** 11, 16, 48
30. 50, 51, 52

Exercises 4-10, page 132

1. $[5x + 10(80 - x)]$ cents
2. $[5x + 2x(10) + 4x(25)]$ cents
3. $2x - 1, 2x + 1, 2x - 4, 2x + 3; x - 1, x + 1,$
    $x - 4, x + 3,$ **4.** $x - 1, x + 1, x - 5, x + 8;$
    $x + 7, x + 9, x + 3, x + 16$
5. 34 years, 17 years   **6.** 5   **7.** 6 years
8. 87, 89, 91   **9.** 30 m   **10.** 14 years
11. 136   **12.** 11 years, 14 years   **13.** $16.25
14. 10 years, 7 years   **15.** 18 cm, 20 cm, 22 cm
16. $41, $13   **17.** 70 m   **18.** $1.20

Exercises 4-11, page 137

1. a) $x < 3$ **b)** $x \le 4$ **c)** $x > -1$
    d) $x > 5$ **e)** $x \le -2$ **f)** $x \le 6$
2. a) $x > 1$ **b)** $x \le 2$ **c)** $x < -10$
    d) $x \ge 8$
3. a) $x < 2$ **b)** $x \ge 2$ **c)** $x > -\frac{9}{2}$
    d) $y > 3$ **e)** $z < 2$ **f)** $y \le 2.5$
    g) $x \le -16$ **h)** $w > 5$ **i)** $a \ge -9$
4. a) $x \ge 6$ **b)** $y > \frac{9}{2}$ **c)** $z \le \frac{5}{2}$
    d) $w \ge -2.6$ **e)** $x < \frac{5}{3}$ **f)** $x \ge 2$
    g) $x \ge -\frac{4}{7}$ **h)** $x < 2$
5. a) $y < -\frac{3}{4}$ **b)** $z \ge -\frac{5}{2}$ **c)** $x \le 2$
    d) $a < -2$ **e)** $b \le -3$ **f)** $c < \frac{26}{3}$
    g) $x > \frac{3}{2}$ **h)** $y \le \frac{29}{9}$

Investigate, page 137

The second statement is false.

Review Exercises, page 138

1. a) -16 **b)** 97   **c)** 28   **d)** 10   **e)** -34
    f) 2   **g)** -8 **h)** 42   **i)** 5
2. a) 9   **b)** 5   **c)** -15 **d)** -98 **e)** $\frac{5}{3}$

f) 7   **g)** 7   **h)** 13

3. a) 3   **b)** 3   **c)** -7 **d)** $\dfrac{4}{5}$ **e)** $\dfrac{5}{4}$ **f)** $\dfrac{7}{5}$

g) 7 **h)** $\dfrac{32}{3}$ **i)** 3 **j)** $\dfrac{24}{25}$ **k)** 1.3 **l)** 25

4. a) \$6.90   **b)** 170 copies

5. a) i) \$1.20   **ii)** \$3.10   **iii)** \$5.00   **b)** 25 min

6. a) 3   **b)** 1   **c)** -7 **d)** 3   **e)** $\dfrac{5}{2}$

f) $-\dfrac{29}{5}$ **g)** 1   **h)** 1.08   **i)** 1.4   **j)** 1.38

k) $\dfrac{7}{58}$ **l)** $\dfrac{2}{65}$ **m)** -1.1 **n)** $\dfrac{57}{77}$ **o)** -6 **p)** $\dfrac{16}{7}$

7. a) 0   **b)** 0.75   **c)** -2.6 **d)** $-\dfrac{2}{9}$ **e)** 4.5

f) $\dfrac{44}{9}$ **g)** -8.5 **h)** 7   **i)** -2 **j)** -5

k) $\dfrac{34}{37}$ **l)** $-\dfrac{16}{27}$ **8. a)** -3 **b)** 1 **c)** 8

d) 6.5 **e)** -1 **f)** 14 **g)** 11 **h)** $\dfrac{49}{3}$

9. a) 45 m   **b)** 24 m   **c)** 2.4 km   **d)** 1.08 km
e) 247 m   **f)** 120 km

10. a) i) 70°   **ii)** 55°   **b) i)** 130°   **ii)** 70°

11. a) i) 120 cm   **ii)** 100 cm   **iii)** 80 cm
iv) 52 cm   **b) i)** 90 cm   **ii)** 67.5 cm

12. $8x - x = 420$ **13.** $x + x + 1 + x + 2 = 141$

14. $73 - x - x = 5$ **15.** $x - 3 + 2x - 3 = 45$

16. $5x - 8 = 17$ **17.** 5 years   **18.** 8 km, 6 km

19. 15 kg, 6 kg   **20.** 5 dimes, 8 quarters

21. 12 years   **22.** 49, 14   **23.** 76, 81, 95

24. a) $x < -4$ **b)** $x \geqslant 0$ **c)** $x > -2$ **d)** $x \leqslant 1$

25. a) $x < 4$ **b)** $y \geqslant -\dfrac{1}{3}$ **c)** $z \geqslant 3.5$ **d)** $a < 3.5$

Chapter 5

Exercises 5-1, page 144

1. a) y^4 **b)** $(-3)^6$ **c)** $\left(\dfrac{2}{5}\right)^5$ **d)** $\left(-\dfrac{3}{8}\right)^3$

e) $(4a)^5$ **f)** 2.9^4 **g)** m^4 **h)** $(-6x)^5$
i) π^6 **j)** a^7 **2. a)** 6^3 **b)** 7^8 **c)** 9^4
d) 20^2 **e)** 11^5 **f)** 5^{11} **g)** 4^n **h)** $(2x)^{10}$
3. a) 64   **b)** 81   **c)** -32 **d)** 25

e) 10 000   **f)** $\dfrac{1}{16}$ **g)** 0.008   **h)** 4.41

i) 48   **j)** $\dfrac{9}{2}$ **k)** 1296   **l)** 162

4. a) 10^3 **b)** 10^4 **c)** 10^2 **d)** 10^6 **e)** 10^5
f) 10^1 **g)** 10^8 **h)** 10^{12} **5. a)** $1000(2)^1$
b) $1000(2)^2$ **c)** $1000(2)^6$ **d)** $1000(2)^{10}$

6. a) 17   **b)** 25   **c)** 49   **d)** -320 **e)** -16
f) -33 **g)** $-\dfrac{217}{64}$ **h)** -93

7. a) 25   **b)** 10   **c)** 19   **d)** 175   **e)** 70
f) 4   **g)** $\dfrac{56}{9}$ **h)** 5   **i)** 6.52   **j)** 19 705

8. a) 9   **b)** $\dfrac{8}{27}$ **c)** 135   **d)** -81 **e)** 81
f) $\dfrac{85}{9}$ **g)** $\dfrac{77}{9}$ **h)** $-\dfrac{343}{27}$ **i)** $-\dfrac{721}{27}$
j) $-\dfrac{737}{27}$ **k)** $-\dfrac{40\,353\,607}{19\,683}$ **l)** $\dfrac{841}{9}$
m) $\dfrac{115}{3}$ **n)** $-\dfrac{15\,625}{27}$ **o)** $\dfrac{296}{9}$ **p)** $\dfrac{328}{9}$

9. a) -27 **b)** 36   **c)** 36   **d)** 144   **e)** 1
f) 1   **g)** -1 **h)** $-65\,536$ **i)** 1296
j) $-\dfrac{27}{64}$ **k)** $-\dfrac{3125}{243}$ **l)** -1728

10. a) $3^3,\ 5^2,\ 2^4,\ 3^2,\ 2^3$ **b)** $10^2,\ (-3)^4,\ 4^3,\ 7^2,\ 2^5$
c) $(1.15)^3,\ (1.2)^2,\ (1.1)^3,\ (1.3)^1,\ (1.05)^5$
d) $(2.4)^5,\ (1.8)^7,\ (2.9)^3,\ (2.1)^4,\ (2.3)^2$
e) $(0.4)^2,\ (0.3)^2,\ (0.2)^2,\ (0.3)^3,\ (0.2)^3$

11. a) Multiply 1000 by 2 raised to a power equal to
the time elapsed in hours.   **b)** $1000(2)^n$
c) i) 5600   **ii)** 11 200   **iii)** 1400 **d)** 01:00

12. a) 3^{25} **b)** $(3x)^2$ **c)** $5n^3$ **d)** $(-2)^{16}$

e) $(0.9)^{11}$ **f)** $\left(-\dfrac{3}{4}\right)^{10}$

13. a) $0 < y < 1$ **b)** $x > 1;\ x < 0$

14. a) 3   **b)** 4   **c)** 6   **d)** 4   **e)** 2   **f)** 4

15. a) 5^3 **b)** 3^4 **c)** 10^4 **d)** 11^{11} **e)** 3^6
f) Numbers are equal.   **16. a)** 4^2 **b)** 3^3 **c)** 2^6
d) 5^4 **e)** $(-2)^4$ **f)** $(-3)^5$ **g)** 7^3 **h)** $(-4)^4$
i) $(-3)^4$ **j)** 9^4 **k)** 6^5 **l)** 1.1^4

Calculator Power, page 146

1. a) 180   **b)** -56 **c)** 1   **d)** 1   **e)** 74
f) 169   **g)** 137.7   **h)** 94.09
2. a) 4913   **b)** 707 281   **c)** -27 **d)** -128
3. a) 37.5   **b)** -352 **c)** -567
d) 1 229 312   **e)** 13 122   **f)** $-54\,859.9688$
g) 3888   **h)** -4608
4. a) -2654.8003 **b)** 60.622 08

Exercises 5-2, page 149

1. a) 2.5^2 **b)** $(3a)^2$ **c)** $\left(\dfrac{2}{3}x\right)^2$ **d)** $\dfrac{1}{2}\pi r^2$

e) $\dfrac{1}{2}(5w)^2$ **f)** $36x^2$ **2. a)** 7^3 **b)** $\dfrac{4}{3}\pi(2a)^3$

c) $(4x)^3$ **d)** $\dfrac{1}{3}\pi r^3$ **e)** $\dfrac{4}{3}\pi(4s)^3$ **f)** $81a^3$

3. a) 25 cm² **b)** 81 m² **c)** 2.25 cm²
d) 187.69 m² **e)** 0.36 cm² **f)** 6.76 m²
g) $16a^2$ square units **h)** $25x^2$ square units

4. a) 125 cm³ **b)** 729 m³ **c)** 3.375 cm³
d) 2571.353 m³ **e)** 0.216 cm³ **f)** 17.576 m³
g) $64a^3$ cubic units **h)** $125x^3$ cubic units

5. a) 45 cm² **b)** 59 mm² **c)** 55 cm²
d) 4 cm² **e)** 85 cm² **f)** 80 mm² **g)** 229 cm²

6. a) \$251.94 **b)** \$317.37 **c)** \$431.78

7. \$980.18 **8.** 220 cm² **9.** 32.7 L **10.** 15 625

11. 7.2 L **12.** 37.5 m **13. a) i)** 29 cm²
ii) 115 cm² **iii)** 461 cm² **iv)** 0.2 m²
b) i) 90 cm **ii)** 120 cm **iii)** 2.5 m
iv) 15 mm **14.** 4305 kL

Exercises 5-3, page 153

1. a) 3^{10} **b)** 7^{11} **c)** $(-5)^{25}$ **d)** $(2.1)^{16}$

e) $(-8)^6$ **f)** $(-1.7)^7$ **g)** $\left(\dfrac{2}{5}\right)^{22}$

h) $\left(\dfrac{3}{11}\right)^{36}$ **i)** $\left(-\dfrac{5}{4}\right)^{14}$

2. a) x^{11} **b)** k^{12} **c)** n^{23} **d)** s^{11} **e)** v^{18}
f) y^{10} **g)** $(-a)^{10}$ **h)** $(-c)^8$

3. a) 3^5 **b)** 2^9 **c)** m^{15} **d)** s^{12} **e)** $-7z^8$
f) $3r^{16}$ **g)** 6^6 **h)** $(-2)^4$

4. a) 2^2 **b)** 3^4 **c)** m^5 **d)** b^3 **e)** $(-a)^4$
f) x^9 **g)** c^3 **h)** $(-5)^{10}$ **i)** 7^7

5. a) m^{20} **b)** $(-t)^{15}$ **c)** a^{49} **d)** 2^{12}
e) 12^{35} **f)** 10^{12} **g)** $(-5)^{12}$ **h)** z^{27}

6. a) $15a^5$ **b)** $18m^8$ **c)** $36x^{13}$ **d)** $-18y^{12}$
e) $30(3)^{12}$ **f)** $32(-7)^{15}$ **g)** $57x^{11}$ **h)** $30p^{10}$
i) $84s^{16}$ **7. a)** $5d^3$ **b)** $-9a^9$ **c)** $6z$ **d)** $3m^6$

e) $-4x^8$ **f)** $\dfrac{5a^{15}}{2}$ **g)** $3(2)^4$ **h)** $-6(3)^{12}$

i) $2n^9$ **j)** $\dfrac{3c^5}{2}$ **k)** $9m^{18}$ **l)** $-4a^8$

8. a) $216m^6$ **b)** $16x^{10}$ **c)** $28\,561\,a^{28}$
d) $6561p^{16}$ **e)** $46\,656c^{24}$ **f)** $9x^{10}$ **g)** $4k$

h) $\dfrac{27n^{10}}{4}$ **i)** $256a^{23}$ **j)** $-\dfrac{4n^{13}}{27}$ **k)** $2x^{10}$

l) $100m^{16}$ **9.** 10^{22} **10. a)** a^6b^{12} **b)** $81x^8y^{12}z^4$

c) $-8m^3n^9p^{12}$ **d)** $\dfrac{3}{4m^5}$ **e)** $\dfrac{64c^5}{81a^9b^2}$

11. a) i) 16 **ii)** 0.0625 **iii)** 625 **b) i)** 64
ii) 0.015 625 **iii)** 15 625 **c) i)** 4 **ii)** 0.25
iii) 25 **d) i)** 16 **ii)** 0.0625 **iii)** 625
e) i) 12 **ii)** 0.75 **iii)** 75
f) i) −6 **ii)** −1.5 **iii)** 15
g) i) 64 **ii)** 0.015 625 **iii)** 15 625
h) i) 144 **ii)** 0.5625 **iii)** 5625

12. b) i) $2^{10} = 1024$ **ii)** $2^{14} = 16\,384$
iii) $2^5 = 32$ **iv)** $2^{14} = 16\,384$
v) $2^{18} = 262\,144$ **vi)** $2^{10} = 1024$

13. a) i) 1 048 576 **ii)** Over 100 m

Investigate, page 155

1. 64, 512 **2. a)** 512 **b)** 81 **c)** 256 **d)** 625
3. a) 4 **b)** 16 **c)** 65 536
4. Answers may vary. 6 pages

Exercises 5-4, page 159

1. a) $\dfrac{1}{2}$ **b)** $\dfrac{1}{5}$ **c)** $\dfrac{1}{9}$ **d)** $\dfrac{1}{8}$ **e)** $\dfrac{1}{125}$

f) $\dfrac{1}{100}$ **g)** $\dfrac{1}{1728}$ **h)** $\dfrac{1}{10\,000}$ **i)** 1 **j)** 16

k) $\dfrac{1}{100\,000}$ **l)** 5 **m)** 32 **n)** 48 **o)** $\dfrac{16}{9}$

p) 10 **q)** 1000 **r)** 4

2. a) 10^{-2} **b)** 10^{-1} **c)** 10^{-9} **d)** 10^8
e) 10^{15} **f)** 10^{-7} **g)** 1 **h)** 10 **i)** 10^{-26} **j)** 10^{-10}

3. a) 5^{11} **b)** 2^6 **c)** 3^{15} **d)** 7^{-10} **e)** 11^7
f) $(-5)^{-30}$ **g)** 6^{-23} **h)** $(-9)^0$ **i)** 19^{-19}

4. a) x^{-13} **b)** p^{-9} **c)** w^{-5} **d)** y^{-4} **e)** x^{-18}
f) a^{11} **g)** m^{-9} **h)** s^{12} **i)** t^8

5. a) $\dfrac{82}{9}$ **b)** $\dfrac{80}{9}$ **c)** $-\dfrac{80}{9}$ **d)** 1 **e)** 81 **f)** $\dfrac{1}{81}$

6. a) $\dfrac{15}{2}$ **b)** $\dfrac{126}{5}$ **c)** $-\dfrac{342}{49}$ **d)** $\dfrac{1}{36}$ **e)** 17

f) $\dfrac{4}{9}$ **g)** $\dfrac{1333}{36}$ **h)** $\dfrac{1}{9}$ **i)** $\dfrac{7}{144}$

7. a) −8 **b)** $-\dfrac{1}{8}$ **c)** $\dfrac{1}{8}$ **d)** 1 **e)** −1

f) $\dfrac{1}{8}$ **g)** $-\dfrac{1}{3}$ **h)** $\dfrac{256}{9}$ **i)** $-\dfrac{9}{2}$

8. 2^{-5}, 2^4, 2^7, 2^{-6}, 2^0, 2^{-1}; 128, 16, 1, $\dfrac{1}{2}$, $\dfrac{1}{32}$, $\dfrac{1}{64}$

9. 3^{-2}, 3^{-5}, 3^{-4}, 3^3, 3^{-6}, 3^0; $\dfrac{1}{729}$, $\dfrac{1}{243}$, $\dfrac{1}{81}$, $\dfrac{1}{9}$, 1, 27

10. a) 7^2 **b)** $\left(\dfrac{1}{10}\right)^2$ **c)** $\left(\dfrac{1}{7}\right)^3$ **d)** $\left(-\dfrac{1}{2}\right)^5$

e) $\left(\dfrac{1}{10}\right)^6$ **f)** $(0.5)^2$ **g)** $(0.1)^3$ **h)** $(0.5)^3$

11. a) 11^{-2} **b)** 13^{-2} **c)** 10^{-2} **d)** $10(10^{-2})$
e) 10^{-5} **f)** 5^{-3} **g)** $\left(\dfrac{100}{9}\right)^{-2}$ **h)** 12^{-3}

12. a) a^{-1} **b)** y^{-10} **c)** -3 **d)** 2 **e)** m^{-13}
f) x^{-5} **g)** p^5 **h)** $(-7)^{-13}$ **i)** $\dfrac{1}{121}$ **j)** 2

k) 0.01 **l)** 100 **m)** $-\dfrac{1}{2}$ **n)** 1

13. a) x^{-12} **b)** y^2 **c)** 3^{16} **d)** 2^{-20} **e)** 1
f) 8^{-13} **g)** w^{-2} **h)** 5^{-18} **i)** x^{-12}

14. a) $\dfrac{9}{5}$ **b)** $\dfrac{9}{2}$ **c)** -5 **d)** -4 **e)** $\dfrac{1}{216}$

f) 9 **g)** $\dfrac{16}{5}$ **h)** 4 **i)** 1

15. a) $10n^{13}$ **b)** $4t^7$ **c)** $5x^{10}$ **d)** $4w^{-6}$ **e)** $-28a^{-6}$
f) $-72y^8$ **g)** $5s^{-20}$ **h)** $12m^{-9}$ **i)** $-6x^{-3}$

16. a) $30m^4$ **b)** $-12a^{-10}$ **c)** $4y^6$ **d)** $27b^{-15}$
e) $12m^{-6}$ **f)** -1

17. a) $-\dfrac{1}{3}$ **b)** $\dfrac{1}{3}$ **c)** $\dfrac{1}{6}$ **d)** $-\dfrac{1}{2}$ **e)** $-\dfrac{5}{6}$

f) 9 **g)** 1 **h)** $\dfrac{1}{27}$ **i)** $\dfrac{25}{81}$

18. a) $\dfrac{19}{16}$ **b)** $\dfrac{5}{6}$ **c)** 4 **d)** $\dfrac{151}{20}$

19. a) i) 8 **ii)** $-\dfrac{1}{8}$ **b) i)** -8 **ii)** $\dfrac{1}{8}$

c) i) -8 **ii)** $\dfrac{1}{8}$ **d) i)** 8 **ii)** $-\dfrac{1}{8}$

e) i) $\dfrac{1}{8}$ **ii)** -8 **f) i)** $-\dfrac{1}{8}$ **ii)** 8

g) i) $-\dfrac{1}{8}$ **ii)** 8 **h) i)** $\dfrac{1}{8}$ **ii)** -8

20. a) 0 **b)** -1 **c)** -2 **d)** 5 **e)** -5 **f)** $\dfrac{1}{5}$

g) -2 **h)** 5 **i)** 1 **j)** -9 **k)** 9 **l)** $\dfrac{1}{2}$

Calculator Power, page 163

1. a) 5.7 cm **b)** 0.3 m **c)** 2 km
d) 49.3 cm **e)** 1.4 m

2. a) 61 000 cm³ to 2 significant digits
b) 56.5 cm, 42.5 cm, 24.5 cm **c)** 58 830.625 cm³
d) 57.5 cm, 43.5 cm, 25.5 cm **e)** 63 781.875 cm³
f) i) 61 000 cm³, 59 000 cm³, 64 000 cm³
ii) 60 000 cm³, 60 000 cm³, 60 000 cm³
g) 1 significant figure

Problem Solving, page 165

1. Answers may vary. **a)** The present time
b) 8 h earlier than the present time

2. a) 5^4 **b)** 2^{18} **c)** 4 **3. a)** 900 **b)** 900
c) 27 000 **4.** 2 cm² **5.** 17 cm **6.** $\dfrac{3}{8}$

Exercises 5-5, page 168

1. a) 1.0×10^3 ✓ **b)** 1.0×10^8 ✓ **c)** 1.0×10^2
d) 7.5×10^2 **e)** 1.1×10^3 **f)** 3.7×10^6
g) 1.0×10^{-4} **h)** 1.0×10^{-7} **i)** 1.0×10^{-6}
j) 8.5×10^{-4} **k)** 9.2×10^{-5} **l)** 8.2×10^{-9}
m) 8.5×10^1 **n)** 3.8×10^{-2} **o)** 9.9×10^3
p) $3.210\ 012 \times 10^6$ **2. a)** 3.0×10^5 km/s
b) 4.843×10^9 **c)** 5.98×10^{24} kg
d) 1.0×10^{-7} s **e)** 4.0×10^{-3} g

3. a) 1.3×10^6°C **b)** 1.0×10^{-5} m
c) 0.000 000 000 000 000 000 000 000 92 g
d) 120 000 000 000 **e)** 4.5×10^9 years
f) 1.13×10^{-8} cm **g)** 150 000 000 km²
h) 360 000 000 km²
i) 5 900 000 000 000 000 000 000 000 kg
j) 8.5×10^9 F

4. a) 3.2×10^5 **b)** 2.47×10^{10} **c)** 4.92×10^8
d) 6.85×10^{12} **e)** 3.87×10^3 **f)** 8.7×10^1
g) 6.72×10^{-3} **h)** 4.37×10^{-5} **i)** 8.41×10^{-3}
j) 4.9×10^{-8} **k)** 1.25×10^2 **l)** 1.85×10^2

5. a) 3 **b)** 1 **c)** -3 **d)** -1 **e)** -3
f) -5 **g)** 3 **h)** 9 **i)** 6 **j)** -7

6. 1.0×10^{26} m, 1.4×10^{22} m, 7.6×10^{20} m,
4.1×10^{16} m, 1.2×10^{13} m, 1.5×10^{11} m,
3.8×10^8 m, 1.3×10^7 m, 8.8×10^3 m,
2.0×10^0 m, 5.0×10^{-3} m, 1.0×10^{-4} m,
1.0×10^{-6} m, 1.0×10^{-10} m, 1.0×10^{-14} m,
1.0×10^{-16} m, 1.0×10^{-20} m

7. Estimates may vary. **a)** 8×10^8 **b)** 5×10^7
c) 1×10^5 **d)** 5×10^1

8. a) 1.1×10^{14} **b)** 3.9×10^6 **c)** 9.9×10^7
d) 5.5×10^4 **e)** 3.6×10^4 **f)** 4.0×10^{-1}

9. Estimates may vary. **a)** 1×10^5 **b)** 1×10^{-4}
c) 1×10^{15} **d)** 4×10^5 **e)** 1×10^{-6}
f) 4×10^1

10. $1\ 000\ 000\ 000 **11. a)** 29.76 t **b)** 10 862.4 t
c) Answers may vary. 760 368 t
12. About 8.3×10^{-4} g **13.** About 1.38×10^{18} t
14. a) 3.1536 m³ **b)** 33 h 20 min
15. a) About 9.5×10^{12} km **b)** 9.5×10^{21} km
16. a) 2.5×10^9 t **b)** About 2×10^8 t **c)** 41 kg
17. 1×10^{-6} mm **18.** 10^{87}
19. a) 1×10^{50} **b)** 1×10^{25} **c)** 1×10^{10}

Mathematics Around Us, page 171

1. a) 500 **b)** 250 **2. a)** 700 **b)** 350
c) 175
3. a) 1688 **b)** 844 **c)** 422

Computer Power, page 172

1. Answers may vary. **a)** 6.9 E + 08
b) 7.2 E + 09 **c)** 4.28 E + 10
2. and 3. Answers may vary.
4. Answers may vary. **a)** 0.052 **b)** 0.0035
c) 0.000096
5. a) 1700000000 **b)** 96300000000
c) 7190000000000 **d)** −620000000000
e) 0.0093 **f)** 0.0000000305
6. Answers may vary. **a)** 1 E + 19 **b)** 10
c) 0.001 **d)** 1 E + 12 **e)** 1 E + 11
f) 1 E + 15
7. Answers may vary. **a)** Add the exponents.
b) Subtract the exponent of the divisor from the
exponent of the dividend.
8. a) 1 E + 26 **b)** 1 E + 10 **c)** 1 E + 13
d) 1 E + 17 **9.** Answers may vary.

Exercises 5-6, page 175

1. a) 9, −9 **b)** 100, −100 **c)** 30, −30
d) 0.4, −0.4 **e)** 120, −120 **f)** 200, −200
g) 0.8, −0.8 **h)** 0.01, −0.01 **i)** 70, −70
j) 0.5, −0.5
2. a) 7 **b)** −0.2 **c)** 40 **d)** 13 **e)** −60
f) 1.2 **g)** −15 **h)** 10^6 **i)** 25 **j)** −4
3. a) 4 m **b)** 100 mm **c)** 2.5 cm **d)** 8 m
e) 100 m **f)** 70 m
4. a) 10 **b)** 7 **c)** 2 **d)** 28 **e)** 40
f) 5 **g)** −31 **h)** 32 **i)** 6
5. a) 10 **b)** 15 **c)** 5 **d)** 7 **e)** 6 **f)** −5
g) 4 **h)** 8 **i)** −32 **j)** −12 **k)** 4 **l)** 10
6. a) −6 **b)** 5 **c)** 20 **d)** 5 **e)** 35
f) −6 **g)** 10 **h)** −9 **i)** 42 **j)** 6
k) 8 **l)** −11
7. a) i) 17 mm **ii)** 68 mm **b) i)** 2.1 cm
ii) 8.4 cm **c) i)** 0.08 m **ii)** 0.32 m **8.** 8 s
9. a) i) 5.02 m **ii)** 15.05 m **b) i)** 8.03 m
ii) 24.08 m **c) i)** 0.90 m **ii)** 2.71 m
d) i) 30.10 cm **ii)** 90.31 cm **e) i)** 0.10 km
ii) 0.30 km **f) i)** 15.05 km **ii)** 45.16 km
10. a) 10 mm **b)** 17 mm **c)** 1.3 m
d) 25 mm **e)** 0.05 km **f)** 10 km
11. a) −56°C **b)** −54°C **c)** −39°C **d)** −28°C

Exercises 5-7, page 179

1. $\sqrt{67}, \sqrt{78}, \sqrt{80}$

2. a) $\sqrt{11}, \sqrt{14}$ **b)** $\sqrt{52}, \sqrt{61}$
c) $\sqrt{140}, \sqrt{130}$ **d)** $\sqrt{118}, \sqrt{110}$
e) $\sqrt{190}, \sqrt{171}$ **f)** $\sqrt{330}, \sqrt{360}$
3. a) 6.2 **b)** 10.9 **c)** 13.1
4. a) 4.2 **b)** 2.8 **c)** 10.5 **d)** 38.4
5. a) 5.4 **b)** 1.7 **c)** 3.7 **d)** 2.5 **e)** 6.6
6. a) 6.6 cm **b)** 1.7 m **c)** 3.1 cm **d)** 6.1 m
7. a) 17 **b)** 38 **c)** 13 **d)** 25 **e)** 91
8. a) 5.89 **b)** 4.62 **c)** 12.27 **d)** 0.79 **e)** 0.22
9. An error symbol is displayed because a negative
number does not have a square root.
10. a) Find the square root of the area and multiply it
by 4 **b)** $P = 4\sqrt{A}$ **c) i)** 20 cm
ii) 32 cm **iii)** About 35 cm **iv)** About 7.8 m
11. a) Divide the diameter by 2, square the result, then
multiply by π. **b)** $A = \dfrac{\pi d^2}{4}$ **c) i)** 79 cm²
ii) 314 cm² **iii)** 794 cm² **iv)** 13 m²
d) Divide the area by π, take the square root of the
answer, then double it. **e)** $d = 2\sqrt{\dfrac{A}{\pi}}$
f) i) 5.3 cm **ii)** 6.5 cm **iii)** 7.1 cm
iv) 2.5 m **12. a)** 59 km **b)** 4 km
13. a) 4.2 s **b)** 6.7 s **c)** 2.1 s **d)** 9.5 s
14. a) i) 8.5 cm **ii)** 2.6 cm **iii)** 12.2 m
iv) 9.2 m **b)** 6.9 cm
15. a) i) 3.1 s **ii)** 1.4 s **b)** 25 cm
16. a) i) 4.4 m/s **ii)** 3.1 m/s **iii)** 1.4 m/s **b)** 20 cm

Review Exercises, page 181

1. a) 17 **b)** 72 **c)** 2.56 **d)** 13 **e)** 1
f) 125 **g)** 32 **h)** $-\dfrac{27}{343}$ **2. a)** −20 **b)** 100
c) 5 **d)** 1 **e)** 43 **f)** 1 **g)** 2 **h)** $\dfrac{17}{5}$
3. a) 6.3 cm² **b)** 8.0 m² **c)** 27.0 cm²
4. a) 857.4 cm³ **b)** 47.0 cm³ **c)** 7.1 m³
5. a) x^9 **b)** x^{24} **c)** x^{18} **d)** x^7 **e)** $15x^6$
f) 2^5 **g)** $27m^6$ **h)** $(-3)^8$ **i)** $25x^2$
j) $5x^6$ **k)** $27x^6$ **l)** $-7y^4$ **6. a)** $6x^3$
b) $-24x^6$ **7. a)** 4096 **b)** 1024 **c)** 6144
8. a) $\dfrac{1}{125}$ **b)** 2 **c)** $-\dfrac{1}{8}$ **d)** $\dfrac{5}{4}$ **e)** $\dfrac{80}{9}$
f) $\dfrac{5}{2}$ **g)** $\dfrac{9}{2}$ **h)** 8 **9. a)** w^{12} **b)** w^3
c) $-5x^8$ **d)** $-8y^6$ **e)** $10y^{-2}$ **f)** $4z^{-4}$

10. a) 0 **b)** -1 **c)** 4 **d)** 1
11. a) 1.0×10^4 **b)** 7.4×10^5 **c)** 1.0×10^{-5}
d) 5.7×10^{-2} **12. a)** 3.577×10^{13}
b) 9.6301×10^8 **c)** 1.6×10^6
13. a) 6 **b)** -0.5 **c)** 120 **d)** 0.09 **e)** 0.6
f) -800 **g)** 0.11 **h)** -0.7
14. a) -30 **b)** 8 **c)** 47
15. a) 8 mm **b)** 0.9 m **c)** 7 cm **d)** 1.5 cm
16. a) 5.29 **b)** 4.17 **c)** 15.81 **d)** 0.66 **17.** 7 cm
18. a) 9 **b)** 4 **c)** -1 **d)** 5 **e)** -4 **f)** 4
19. a) 14 000 m/s **b)** About 70 000 m/s
20. a) 1.6 m **b)** 1.024 m **21.** 10.0 cm

Exercises 6-1, page 185

1. Answers may vary. **a)** Mrs. Adams had $\frac{3}{5}$ of

the profits and Mr. Singh had $\frac{2}{5}$ of the profits.

b) The class had $\frac{7}{12}$ girls and $\frac{5}{12}$ boys.
c) Mrs. Arbor's chain saw needs 25 parts of gasoline to 1 part of oil.
d) The scale of a map is 1 cm to 250 000 cm.
e) Brass is $\frac{3}{5}$ copper and $\frac{2}{5}$ zinc.

2. a) 10:3 **b)** 1:13 **c)** 7:2 **d)** 8:13
e) 1:6 **f)** 1:5 **g)** $\frac{5}{1}$ **h)** $\frac{16}{1}$
3. a) $\frac{5}{8}$ **b)** 7:8 **c)** 6:5 **d)** 8:3
4. Mum's **5. a)** $\frac{1}{5}$ **b)** $\frac{4}{5}$ **6. a)** $\frac{37}{40}$ **b)** 462.5 g
7. a) 2.5:1 **b)** 4:1 **c)** 0.3:1 **d)** 5:1
8. a) 20:24 **b)** 4:24 **c)** 18:24 **d)** 200:24
9. a) 11:9 **b)** 3:55 **c)** 100:3
10. a) 3:8 **b)** 1:8 **11.** 159 cars **12.** 72 cm by 56 cm
13. a) 40:14, 40:17, 40:20, 40:24, 40:28, 52:14, 52:17, 52:20, 52:24, 52:28
b) 40:28, 40:24, 52:28, 40:20, 52:24, 40:17, 52:20, 40:14, 52:17, 52:14 **14.** 2.9×10^{32} kg

Exercises 6-2, page 189

1. a) 11:12 **b)** 2:3 **c)** 3:8 **2. a)** 14.4 g
b) $367.20 **3.** About $11 400
4. $5000, $12 500, $7500
5. $22 400, $11 200, $16 800, $33 600
6. a) 0.18 g **b)** 5.41 g **c)** 0.05 g
7. a) i) 104 **ii)** 97 **b) i)** 9 years **ii)** 9 years

8. a) i) 3.0 **ii)** 1.2 **iii)** 0.9 **b)** 7290 km/h
9. C,264 Hz; D,297 Hz; E,330 Hz; F,352 Hz; G,396 Hz; B,495 Hz; C,528 Hz
10. a) C **b)** B **c)** A **d)** Answers may vary. To be able to know the percent of each nutrient
11. a) $\frac{50}{77}$ **b)** 231 Gm **12.** 40°, 60°, 80°
13. 60°, 90°, 90°, 120° **14. a)** 2:1:3 **b)** 1.5

Exercises 6-3, page 193

1. a) 9 **b)** 6 **c)** 5 **d)** 3 **e)** 33 **f)** 3
g) 128 **h)** 15 **2. a)** 5.5 **b)** $\frac{6}{7}$ **c)** 14.4
d) $\frac{99}{7}$ **e)** $\frac{20}{7}$ **f)** 10.8 **g)** $\frac{21}{5}$ **h)** 26
3. 77 cm **4.** 7.2 m **5.** 138 cm **6. a)** 25
b) 500 **c)** 240 **7.** 5.1 m by 9 m; 45.9 m²
8. Answers may vary. **a)** 330 km **b)** 675 km
c) 120 km **d)** 180 km **e)** 810 km
f) 105 km **9.** 12 cm **10.** Answers may vary.
a) 0.4 cm **b)** 0.2 cm **c)** 0.4 cm

Exercises 6-4, page 196

1. a) i) 30 km **ii)** 75 km **b) i)** 4 L **ii)** 18 L
2. a) i) 40 s **ii)** 3 min 20 s **b) i)** 120 words **ii)** 195 words
3. a) About 26 L **b)** About 1180 km
4. a) i) 1 min 51 s **ii)** About 30 h 52 min
b) i) 32 400 words **ii)** 5 443 200 words
5. 96 **6. a)** 50¢/100 g, 44¢/100 g
b) The 525 g box
7. $539.58 **8.** 194 points **9. a)** 158 d **b)** 360 d
10. a) About 42¢/100 mL, 36¢/100 mL; the 1 L size **b)** The 1 L size
11. $2378.00 **12.** 2 L, $0.57; 1 L, $0.33
13. 22 km/h **14.** 100 km/h **15.** 1.2 min
16. 45.5 h **17.** $\frac{z}{36}$ days

The Mathematical Mind, page 198

1. 1.618 or -0.618 **2.** 1.618 **3.** 1.625

Exercises 6-5, page 203

1. a) 7% **b)** 18.5% **c)** 57% **d)** 0.8%
e) 365% **f)** 36.5% **g)** 540% **h)** 1875%
2. a) 38% **b)** 57% **c)** 81% **d)** 6%
e) 3.5% **f)** 7.2% **g)** 9.1% **h)** 0.7%
i) 0.86% **j)** 0.51% **k)** 0.07% **l)** 360%

m) 306%   **n)** 300.6%   **o)** 3060%

3. a) 0.24   **b)** 0.39   **c)** 0.574   **d)** 0.03
e) 0.058   **f)** 0.115   **g)** 0.016   **h)** 0.009
i) 1.37   **j)** 2.64   **k)** 3.75   **l)** 3.758
m) 0.001   **n)** 0.0203   **o)** 0.0025

4. a) 25%   **b)** 62.5%   **c)** 70%   **d)** 55%
e) About 83%   **f)** 60%   **g)** 160%
h) About 67%   **i)** 130%   **j)** 77.5%
k) About 667%   **l)** 38%   **m)** 4%
n) 17.5% **o)** 5.5% **5.** Estimates may vary.
a) 25% **b)** 33% **c)** 25% **d)** 30%

6. a) 50%   **b)** 75%   **c)** 87.5%   **d)** 1%
e) 0.1%   **f)** About 67%

7. a) $\dfrac{13}{50}$ **b)** $\dfrac{7}{20}$ **c)** $\dfrac{16}{25}$ **d)** $\dfrac{3}{4}$ **e)** $\dfrac{5}{8}$ **f)** $\dfrac{5}{4}$

g) $\dfrac{61}{75}$ **h)** $\dfrac{1}{6}$ **i)** $\dfrac{37}{20}$ **j)** $\dfrac{18}{5}$ **k)** $\dfrac{1}{125}$ **l)** $\dfrac{1}{800}$

8. About 67%   **9.** 250%   **10.** 12%

Problem Solving, page 205

1. 37.5 km/h   **2.** 40 km   **3.** 62.5%
4. 4 min **5.** 360 km **6.** 22 km/h   **7.** 100 km/h

Mathematics Around Us, page 206

1. a) About 98%   **b)** About 89%   **c)** 312 votes
2. a) 346 votes, 315 votes   **b)** 4 votes
3. a) 226 ballots   **b)** 215 votes

Exercises 6-6, page 210

1. a) 10   **b)** 8   **c)** 0.9   **d)** 1.75   **e)** 81.75
f) 6   **g)** 0.665   **h)** 11.7
2. a) 20   **b)** 15   **c)** 25   **d)** 40   **e)** 70
f) 100   **g)** 27   **h)** 80   **i)** 25   **j)** 70
3. a) 20%   **b)** About 11%   **c)** About 167%
d) 90%   **e)** 12.5%   **f)** About 333%
g) 0.1% **h)** 0.05% **4. a)** $48 **b)** $765
c) $36.99 **5.** $193.38 **6.** $99 **7.** About $9383
8. $4 000 000   **9.** 1280 **10.** About 46%
11. $37.44 **12.** $13.31 **13. a)** 7.6% **b)** 20.0%
14. a) 92.5% **b)** 27.75 g **15. a) i)** $2.80
ii) $1.72   **b) i)** $4.71   **ii)** $1.88
16. a) 21.7%   **b)** 6253, answers may vary—the
percent of defective cars is the same every day.
17. a) $197.95 **b)** $168.26 **18.** $61.20
19. a) 7.44% **b)** 850 kg, 70 kg, 0.6 kg, 2 kg, 3 kg,
74.4 kg **20.** 25% **21.** 400% **22. a)** 8.3% **b)** 421 600
people **23.** 14.1% **24.** $112 320

Investigate, page 212

1. d) i) +100%   **ii)** −50%   **iii)** +125%
iv) −43.75%   **v)** −56.25%   **vi)** +31.25%
2. Find the new dimensions, multiply them together,
subtract the original area, express the change in
area as a percent of the original area.

Exercises 6-7, page 215

1. a) $\dfrac{5}{\pi}$ cm   **b)** 3 cm   **c)** π cm   **d)** $\dfrac{1}{\pi^2}$ cm

2. a) 5.0 cm **b)** 9.8 m **c)** 12 mm **d)** 2.5 mm
3. a) 60°   **b)** 240°   **c)** 225°
4. a) 25%   **b)** 33.3%   **c)** 30%   **d)** 40%
e) 65% **f)** 45% **g)** 20% **h)** 37.5% **i)** 97.5%
5. a) 3.60 m²   **b)** 0.40 m²
6. a) 1963 mm²   **b)** 1963 cm²   **c)** 1%
d) 373 cm²   **e)** 19%   **f)** 5%

7. 573 **8.** 150° **9. a) i)** $\dfrac{1}{4}$ **ii)** $\dfrac{1}{8}$ **iii)** $\dfrac{3}{4}$ **iv)** $\dfrac{1}{3}$

b) i) 18.8 cm   **ii)** 9.4 cm   **iii)** 56.5 cm
iv) 25.1 cm   **c)** 135°   **d)** Multiply the
circumference and the sector angle, then divide by
360.

10. a) 1.5   **b)** 2.25   **11.** 4 cm diameter drain,
twice as fast   **12. a)** $\dfrac{3}{2}$ **b)** $\dfrac{3}{1}$ **c)** $\dfrac{2}{1}$

13. a) 30°   **b)** 50°   **c)** 75°   **d)** 127.5°
14. $\dfrac{x+y}{2\pi}$ **15.** 66.7%   **16.** 27 times greater,
assuming the densities are the same.

17. About 6 m

Review Exercises, page 218

1. a) 3:1   **b)** 54 g   **2. a)** $\dfrac{7}{9}$ **b)** 29:34

c) 8:17   **d)** 24:9
3. a) 10.5   **b)** 6.5   **c)** 9   **d)** 63
4. $43 750; $81 250   **5.** $9000; $24 000, $12 000
6. 45.7 m   **7.** 127.5 km   **8.** 30.5 cm
9. a) 4680   **b) i)** 12 min 49 s
ii) 8 days 21 h 40 min **10. a)** 30 L **b)** No
11. 40%   **12.** $140.25   **13.** $199.65/m³
14. a) $3.23   **b)** $1.01   **15.** 182 cm
16. a) 19.0 cm   **b)** 138 cm²

Cumulative Review, Chapters 4-6, page 219

1. a) -13 **b)** 22 **c)** 3 **d)** $4.\overline{8}$ **e)** -14
f) 0.6 **g)** -6 **h)** 3 **i)** 2

2. a) 3 **b)** 3 **c)** -2.6 **d)** 1 **e)** $\dfrac{8}{7}$
f) 1.2 **g)** -3.5 **h)** -1.5

3. a) -2 **b)** -1 **c)** 4 **d)** 7

4. a) i) \$8450 **ii)** \$11 680 **iii)** \$12 725
b) 1080 **5. a)** 8 **b)** 1125 **c)** 27

6. 36 years, 12 years **7.** 8,11

8. a) 24 **b)** 128 **c)** -18 **d)** -8 **e)** $\dfrac{7}{3}$
f) 2 **g)** $\dfrac{1}{9}$ **h)** $\dfrac{9}{4}$ **9. a)** 18 **b)** 32 **c)** 52

d) 1 **e)** 125 **f)** 3 **g)** $\dfrac{75}{7}$ **h)** -58

10. a) x^{10} **b)** x^6 **c)** $-21p^{-7}$ **d)** $-3m^{-14}$
e) $72x^5$ **f)** $16y^6$ **g)** $7a^{10}$ **h)** $9x$ **i)** $6s^8$

11. a) 1.5×10^4 **b)** 2.7×10^6 **c)** 2.1×10^1
d) 1.6×10^{-5} **e)** 3.7×10^{-4} **f)** 1.9×10^{-1}

12. a) 50 **b)** -1.4 **c)** 1500 **d)** 2 **e)** 78 **f)** 13

13. a) 6.48 **b)** 8.00 **c)** -7.42 **14.** \$4701.85

15. a) 1.6 **b)** 75 **c)** 4 **d)** 14

16. \$10 000, \$15 000 **17.** 150 km **18.** 1:750 000

19. a) 75 **b)** 40% **20.** 20% **21.** \$408

22. a) \$22.75 **b)** \$2.00 **23.** 112 cm **24. a)** 60°
b) 19 cm **c)** 170 cm² **25. a)** 17.5 cm **b)** 109 cm²

Chapter 7

Exercises 7-1, page 223

1. a) 14 **b)** 7 **c)** 1 **d)** -1 **e)** -4

2. a) t **b)** x **c)** w **d)** z **e)** No variable

3. a), b), d), e), i), j), k), and **l)** have like terms;
c), f), g), and **h)** have unlike terms.

4. a) $5a, -a$ **b)** $3y^2, y^2$ **c)** $9g, \dfrac{1}{9}g; 9g^2, g^2$
d) $16, -8; d, 0.5d$ **e)** $17q^2, -15q^2$

5. a) $14m$ **b)** $-2k$ **c)** $5x$ **d)** $-3n$
e) $-4a$ **f)** $6x^2$ **g)** $-4y^3$ **h)** $-8c$
i) $-9.4m$ **j)** 0 **k)** $\dfrac{23}{12}x$ **l)** $\dfrac{13}{18}a$

6. a) $-4x - 6y$ **b)** $3a + 4b$ **c)** $4p + 4q$
d) $-7c + 5d$ **e)** $-6m - n$ **f)** $14g - 20h$
g) $11e - 10f$ **h)** $-2x - 19y$

7. a) $8t$ **b)** $a + 2ab$ **c)** $-15m + 5mn$

d) $4s^2 + s^3$ **e)** $-k^3$ **f)** $2c^4 - 3c^2$ **g)** $\dfrac{5}{6}x$

h) $1.2r$ **i)** $\dfrac{7}{20}a^2$ **j)** $-3.0h$ **k)** $-\dfrac{13}{6}c^2$ **l)** $0.4n$

8. a) $4x$ **b)** $-4a$ **c)** $8p$ **d)** $-6n^2$
e) $-5x^3$ **f)** $7y$ **g)** $-0.8c$ **h)** $-6.8x$
i) $6.0b^2$ **j)** $\dfrac{5}{6}a$ **k)** $-\dfrac{1}{2}m$ **l)** 0

9. a) $1.0a$ **b)** $-0.5m$ **c)** $\dfrac{3}{4}x$ **d)** $\dfrac{5}{12}y$
e) $2c^2$ **f)** $13b^2$ **g)** $-16x^3$ **h)** $5x^2y$
i) $3abc$ **j)** $-11mnp$ **k)** $12xyz$ **l)** $-16fgh$

10. a) $-2x - 11y + 3z$ **b)** $3a + b - 8c$
c) $-10e - 4f + 12g$ **d)** $6m - 2p - 5x$
e) $-5d + 3e - 2f$ **f)** $3 - 14x + 3y$
g) $7 + 15a - 15b$ **h)** $-5 + 9x + 6y$

11. a) $7x$ **b)** $-8a$ **c)** $3p^2$ **d)** $-2y^2 - 2y$
e) $5m^2 - 5m$ **f)** $12x^3 - 4x^2$ **g)** $6a^2$
h) $-4x^2 - 2x$ **i)** $4.2c - 3.2c^2$

12. a) $32m^2 - 22m$ **b)** $-65x^2 + 10x$
c) $38c^2 + 25c$ **d)** $-42n + 20n^2$ **e)** $-0.9x^2$
f) $-8.6x^3 + 11.7x^2$ **g)** $-\dfrac{5}{12}c$ **h)** $\dfrac{1}{5}a^2 - \dfrac{5}{6}a$

13. a) $6n^2 + 7n$ **b)** $3x^3 + 3x^2$ **c)** $7.3y^2 - 1.8y$
d) $-a^2 - 3a$ **e)** $\dfrac{3}{4}c^2 + \dfrac{2}{3}c$ **f)** $\dfrac{15}{8}m^3 - \dfrac{3}{4}m^2$
g) $0.7x^2 - 0.3x$ **h)** $-3y + 5y^2$ **i)** $4a^3 + a$

14. a) $8a + 9$ **b)** $10x - 2$ **c)** $-4n + 3$
d) $-7c - 2$ **e)** $4x - 3$ **f)** $4x^2 - 7x$
g) $-5a^2 - a$ **h)** $2m - 3$ First degree:
a), b), c), d), e), h); second degree: f), g)

15. a) $2a^2 - a$ **b)** $5x + 7$ **c)** $5x^2 + 3x$
d) $6m^2 + 1$ **e)** $c - 8$ **f)** $3a^2 - 3a - 3$
g) $2 + 4x$ **h)** $-n^2 - 2n + 4$
i) $\dfrac{7}{10}m + m^2$ **j)** $-\dfrac{1}{4}y^2 + \dfrac{1}{2}y$

16. a) $xy, 2xy; 3x^2y, -5x^2y$ **b)** $3a, -7a; 4ab, -5ab$
c) $5ax, 3ax, 6xa; 4a, -7a$
d) $3a^2b, -3a^2b; -5ab, 6ba$

17. a) $-xy - 5x^2y + 7xy^2$
b) $-xy + 2x^2y - 4x^2y^2 + 3$
c) $ay^2 - 2a^2 + 4a^2y - 7ay$
d) $11w + z - 3wz - 6w^2z$
e) $9ab + 2a^2b - 4a$ **f)** $xy^2 + 5x^2y + 6x - 4y$
g) $-6m^2n - m + 14mn^2$
h) $-8 + 2c^2d + 6cd + 8cd^2$

18. a) $-x + 7y$ **b)** $xy^2 - 8x^2y + 6x^2y^2$
c) $16ab^2 + 4a^2b^2$ **d)** $x^2y - x^2y^2$
e) $-6abc + 2a^2bc + 9abc^2$
f) $9p^2q - pq^2 + 2pq + 6$

g) $-4xyz + 2x^2yz - 3xy^2z + 12xy$

h) $1.1s^2t - 12.0st + 6.0st^2$

19. b) a^2, $3a$, $4a$, 12 **c)** $a^2 + 7a + 12$; second degree

20. b) $2a^3$, $4a^3$; $5a^2$, $8a^2$, $6a^2$; $20a$, $12a$
c) Answers may vary.
d) a^4, $4a^3$, $2a^3$, $8a^2$, $6a^2$, $5a^2$, $20a$, $12a$, 30
e) $a^4 + 6a^3 + 19a^2 + 32a + 30$

21. b) $2a^2b + a^3b + ab^2 + 2ab + b^2 + a^2 + a^3$; fourth degree

Exercises 7-2, page 228

1. a) 2 **b)** 4 **c)** 8 **d)** 8 **e)** $\dfrac{11}{4}$ **f)** 1.75

2. a) -5 **b)** -6 **c)** 0 **d)** 72 **e)** 39 **f)** 15

3. a) 110 **b)** 127 **c)** 96.4

4. a) 138 **b)** -80 **c)** 95.4

5. a) i) $7k^2 + 2k - 3$ **ii)** $7, 2, -3$ **iii)** 6
b) i) $\dfrac{1}{2}k^2 + \dfrac{1}{4}k + \dfrac{1}{3}$ **ii)** $\dfrac{1}{2}, \dfrac{1}{4}, \dfrac{1}{3}$ **iii)** $\dfrac{13}{12}$
c) i) $-8.4k^2 + 2.5k$ **ii)** $-8.4, 2.5$ **iii)** -5.9

6. a) $181°C$ **b)** $220°C$ **7. b) i)** 9 **ii)** 35 **iii)** 54

8. a) 2372 **b)** 1875 **9. a)** 2550 **b)** $10\ 100$

10. a) 1 **b)** 1 **11. a)** 4477 cm^3 **b)** 2596 m^3

12. a) 48 m **b)** 170 m **13.** 192 m/s, 5787 m

14. a) $\$3400$ **b)** $\$5600$ **c)** $\$11\ 000$ **d)** $\$15\ 400$

15. a) i) 5 **ii)** 14 **iii)** 55 **b) ii)** $\$102.38$

The Mathematical Mind, page 230

2. a) $1681 = 41^2$ **b)** Answers may vary, for example, 1601

3. Answers may vary. **a)** 7 **b)** 17 **c)** 82

Computer Power, page 231

1. No **2. a)** 4 **b)** 17 **c)** 41 **d)** 80 **3.** 161

Exercises 7-3, page 235

1. a) $9x + 6$ **b)** $7a + 4$ **c)** $5 - 6m$
d) $6x + 2$ **e)** $3 - 8t$ **f)** $4c - 5$
g) $6n^2 - 8n - 4$ **h)** $-2x^2 + 5x - 4$
i) $7 - 7c - 3c^2$ **j)** $5 - 3n + 3n^2$

2. a) $-2 + 3x$ **b)** $-5a - 4$ **c)** $-\dfrac{1}{2}x + 5$
d) $-4n^2 + 3n - 1$ **e)** $3 + 2t - t^2$
f) $-0.2a^2 - 0.4a + 0.6$

3. a) $-5x + 1$ **b)** $2 + n$ **c)** $10a - 11$
d) $3 + 2t$ **e)** $-6n - 3$ **f)** $2x - 42$
g) $12x - 1$ **h)** $14a^2 - 2a - 10$

i) $x^2 - 4x - 4$ **j)** $k^2 + k - 7$

4. a) $6x - 4$ **b)** $7a + 7$ **c)** $6c - 7$
d) $6x^2 - 6x$ **e)** $m^2 + 3m - 8$
f) $2t^2 + 6t - 4$ **g)** $6 - 4n$ **h)** $6s$
i) $7 - 7x + 7x^2$ **j)** $n^2 + 3$

5. a) $28x + 5$ **b)** $50 - 20x$ **c)** $5n - 6$
d) $-3 - 82t$ **e)** $18n^2 + 30n - 44$
f) $0.3x - 9.2$

6. a) $P = 2.5n - 20\ 000$ **b) i)** $\$5000$ **ii)** $\$30\ 000$
c) i) $12\ 000$ **ii)** $16\ 000$ **iii)** 8000

7. a) $6x^2 + y^2$ **b)** $x^2 + 9xy - 2y^2$
c) $-3x^2 + 10x^2y + 6y^2 - 7$
d) $3x^2 - 6x + 2y^2 - 7y + 14$
e) $5x^2 - 2x + 5$ **f)** $6y^2 + 3y - 5$
g) $9x^2y^2 - 2xy - 6$

8. a) $3x^2y + 2x - y$ **b)** $2a^2 + 2ab$
c) $-2 + 2x^2y - x^2y^2$ **d)** $8z - x^2 + x^2y$
e) $-2ab^2 - 2a^2b$ **f)** p

9. a) $P = -0.1x^2 + 3.0x - 1$
b) i) $\$11.5$ million **ii)** $\$21.5$ million

10. a) i) 40 **ii)** -20 **iii)** 10 **iv)** 100 **b)** 3

11. a) $-7x^2 - 10x + 25$; 17 **b)** $2x^2 - 10x - 5$; 23

12. a) $4a^2b + 5b^2 + a^2$ **b)** $x^2 + 4y^2 + 3x^2y$
c) $mn^2 - 3n^2 + 6m$ **d)** $-a^2 + 2ab^2 + 2b^2$
e) $3x^2y^2 - 3x^2 - 3y^2 + 13$

Exercises 7-4, page 238

1. a) $30n^2$ **b)** $-6a^2$ **c)** $25x^2$ **d)** $-18n^2$
e) $10x^4$ **f)** $6a^2$ **g)** $10x^5$ **h)** $-56y^2$
i) $5x^4$ **j)** $\dfrac{1}{8}n^2$ **k)** $3.0m^3$ **l)** $1.5x^5$

2. a) $144x^2$ **b)** $-170a^3$ **c)** $-200n^4$
d) $140c^5$ **e)** $85x^5$ **f)** $-140n^4$ **g)** $30x^3$
h) $-24n^3$ **i)** $9a^2$ **j)** $4x^4$ **k)** $36x^5$ **l)** $-400m^4$

3. a) x^3y^4 **b)** m^3n^4 **c)** a^3b^4 **d)** c^5d^3
e) p^3q^4 **f)** x^5y^5 **g)** $6x^3y^3$ **h)** $-12x^3y^3$
i) $6a^3b^5$ **j)** $10a^3b^3c^3$ **k)** $-12m^3n^2p^3$ **l)** $10x^3y^3z^2$

4. a) $5x - 15$ **b)** $7a + 7$ **c)** $-6 - 3n$
d) $-4x + 8$ **e)** $-2x + 5$ **f)** $18x - 12$
g) $-30 - 12t$ **h)** $5x^2 - 30x + 15$
i) $6 - 10n + 6n^2$ **j)** $7x^2 - 21x + 63$
k) $0.6x - 1.0$ **l)** $\dfrac{1}{6} - \dfrac{1}{4}a$

5. a) $3x^2 + 2x$ **b)** $5a^2 - a$ **c)** $3n - 7n^2$
d) $-x^2 + 2x$ **e)** $-3c^2 - 5c$ **f)** $3x^3 - x^2$
g) $y^4 - 5y^3$ **h)** $2r^2 - 7r^3$
i) $3n^4 - 5n^3 + n^2$ **j)** $-5x^5 + x^4$
k) $3a^4 - 2a^3 + a^2$ **l)** $-7s + 2s^2 - s^3$

6. a) $10x^2 + 15x$ **b)** $6a^2 - 8a$ **c)** $15c - 6c^2$
d) $-8n^2 + 4n$ **e)** $-14y^3 + 35y$
f) $18k - 6k^2 + 12k^3$ **g)** $6x^3 - 10x^2$

h) $-12a^4 + 8a^3$ **i)** $15s^3 - 10s^2 - 35s$
j) $6p^2 - 9p^3 - 3p^4$ **k)** $-21a^4 + 14a^3 + 28a^2$
l) $-6x^2 + 2.25x^3 + 18x^4$

7. a) $3x^3y - 3x^2y^2$ **b)** $-2a^3b^2 + 2a^2b$
c) $4m^2n - 4mn^2$ **d)** $-3p^2q^2 + 3p^2q$
e) $5a^2b^2 - 5a^3$ **f)** $-4x^3y + 4xy^3$
g) $-2m^3n^2 + 6m^2n^3$ **h)** $14a^3b^2 - 21a^2b^3$
i) $-6p^2q^2r + 12pq^2r^2$ **j)** $1.25m^2n^3 - 2.5m^3n^2$

8. a) $3x^3y + 3x^2y^2 + 3x^2y$
b) $-2a^2b^2 + 2ab - 2a^3b$
c) $-3m^2n + 3m^3n + 3m^2$
d) $-12w^2z + 4w^3z - 40w^2z^2$
e) $2xy^3 - 4x^3y^3 + 6x^2y^3$
f) $18x^2yz^3 - 12x^2y^3z + 6xy^2z^3 - 12x^2y^2z^2$

9. a) 1140   **b)** 1360   **c)** 1563

10. a) $(2x^2 + 3x)$; $(6x + 6)$
b) 125 750 m²; 1506 m

11. a) $8x^2 + 10xy$ **b)** $4m^2 + 5mn$ **12. a)** 2.5 cm
b) 15 cm **13.** 112π cm² **14. a) i)** $15x^3 - 3x^2$
ii) $46x^2 - 8x$ **b)** 4998 cm³, 2198 cm²

15. a) i) $(12x^3 + 24x^2)$
     ii) $(26x^2 + 28x)$
     iii) $12x^2$
b) i) \$959.52   **ii)** \$374.85

Exercises 7-5, page 242

1. a) $x^2 + 8x + 15$ **b)** $a^2 + 6a + 8$
c) $n^2 + 8n + 7$

2. a) $x^2 + 7x + 12$ **b)** $n^2 + 8n + 12$
c) $a^2 - 8a + 15$ **d)** $t^2 - 5t + 4$
e) $x^2 + 3x - 10$ **f)** $n^2 - n - 12$
g) $a^2 - 2a - 48$ **h)** $x^2 + 2x - 63$
i) $x^2 + 7x - 60$ **j)** $s^2 - 14s + 33$
k) $n^2 + n + \dfrac{1}{4}$ **l)** $a^2 - \dfrac{1}{6}a - \dfrac{1}{3}$

3. a) $a^2 - a - 2$ **b)** $n^2 - 5n + 6$
c) $y^2 + y - 20$ **d)** $b^2 - 3b - 18$
e) $a^2 - 16a + 60$ **f)** $n^2 + 22n + 120$
g) $x^2 + 4x - 5$ **h)** $y^2 + 3y - 88$
i) $z^2 - 11z + 30$ **j)** $a^2 - a - 6$
k) $b^2 + 14b + 40$ **l)** $x^2 - 10x + 9$

4. a) $3x^2 - x - 2$ **b)** $2a^2 - 11a + 15$
c) $4n^2 + 13n - 35$ **d)** $6x^2 + 13x - 15$
e) $36x^2 - 9x - 1$ **f)** $10n^2 - 12n + 2$
g) $14c^2 - 3c - 5$ **h)** $18x^2 - 2$
i) $3x^2 + 5x - 2$ **j)** $6a^2 - 13a - 5$
k) $40y^2 - 23y + 3$ **l)** $8x^2 + 2x - 21$

5. a) $5x^2 - 13x - 6$ **b)** $4a^2 + 8a + 3$
c) $16n^2 - 14n + 3$ **d)** $16a^2 + 24a + 9$
e) $12x^2 - 17x + 6$ **f)** $30x^2 - 14x - 4$
g) $12x^2 - 36x + 15$ **h)** $9b^2 - 4$
i) $20a^2 - 31a - 7$ **j)** $8a^2 + 65a + 8$

k) $4a^2 - 12a + 9$ **l)** $9a^2 + 24a + 16$
6. a) $-a^2 + 4a - 3$ **b)** $-x^2 + 2x - 1$
c) $2y^2 + 9y - 5$ **d)** $2z^2 - 2z - 4$
e) $-\dfrac{1}{8}x^2 + \dfrac{3}{4}x + 9$ **f)** $15x^2 - 4x - 4$

7. a) $60 + 5a - 5a^2$ **b)** $-12 + 3n^2$
c) $-3x^2 + 3x + 36$ **d)** $10x^2 - 20x - 80$
e) $12a^2 + 6a - 90$ **f)** $14c^2 + 7c - 105$
g) $50 - 20a + 2a^2$ **h)** $4x^2 - 28x + 40$
i) $-3t^2 + 12t - 12$ **j)** $100x^2 - 55x - 15$
k) $21x^2 - 49x - 42$ **l)** $-4x^2 + 1.6x - 0.16$

8. a) $x^3 + 5x^2 + 3x + 15$
b) $a^3 - 3a^2 + 2a - 6$ **c)** $n^4 + 5n^2 + 6$
d) $x^3 - 5x^2 + 2x - 10$ **e)** $x^4 - 5x^2 + 4$
f) $a^4 - 13a^2 + 36$ **g)** $3x^3 + 2x^2 - 15x - 10$
h) $2n^3 - 4n^2 + n - 2$ **i)** $-3a^4 + 7a^2 - 2$

9. a) $x^2 + 7xy + 10y^2$ **b)** $a^2 - ab - 6b^2$
c) $6m^2 - 5mn + n^2$ **d)** $20x^2 + 7xy - 3y^2$
e) $6r^2 - 17rs - 3s^2$ **f)** $56a^2 + 113ab + 56b^2$
g) $2p^2 - pq - 15q^2$ **h)** $6x^2 - xy - 40y^2$
i) $42a^2 + ab - 56b^2$

10. a) $-x^2 + 2xy - y^2$ **b)** $-a^2 + 3ab - 2b^2$
c) $8q^2 - 10pq + 3p^2$ **d)** $-2y^4 + 7y^2x - 3x^2$
e) $-4p^4 + 17p^2q - 4q^2$ **f)** $18m^2 + 12mn + 2n^2$

11. a) x **b)** $12a$ **c)** $-10n$ **d)** $-6x$ **e)** $-13a$

12. a) $R = -0.5x^2 + 105x - 1000$
b) i) \$3500   **ii)** \$4400

13. i) a) $63x^2 - 108x + 45$ **b)** $32x - 28$
c) 5265 square units; 292 units **ii) a)** $15x^2 + 6x$
b) $16x + 4$ **c)** 1560 square units; 164 units

14. a) $R = -x^2 + 3.5x + 82.5$
b) i) \$85 000   **ii)** \$85 500   **iii)** \$84 000

15. a) $n + 5$ **b)** $x - 4$ **c)** $x - 2$ **d)** $a + 2$
e) $x + 3$ **f)** $t + 5$ **g)** $s - 5$
h) $(x + 5)(x + 4)$ **i)** $(a - 7)(a - 2)$
j) $(n - 5)(n - 5)$

16. a) $x^3 + 7x^2 + 11x + 5$ **b)** $a^3 - a^2 - 10a + 6$
c) $t^3 - t^2 - 17t + 20$
d) $2x^3 - 15x^2 + 26x - 12$
e) $x^3 + 6x^2 + 11x + 6$ **f)** $6x^3 + x^2 - 4x + 1$
g) $3x^3 - 33x^2 + 99x - 60$
h) $6x^4 + 4x^3 - 6x^2 - 4x$

Exercises 7-6, page 247

1. a) $x^2 + 10x + 25$ **b)** $x^2 + 2x + 1$
c) $x^2 - 6x + 9$ **d)** $n^2 - 14n + 49$
e) $c^2 + 8c + 16$ **f)** $x^2 - 2x + 1$
g) $a^2 + 4a + 4$ **h)** $a^2 - 12a + 36$
i) $4 + 4a + a^2$ **j)** $25 - 10x + x^2$
k) $t^2 + 18t + 81$ **l)** $100 - 20m + m^2$

2. a) $x^2 - 4$ **b)** $a^2 - 9$ **c)** $x^2 - 16$

d) $x^2 - 64$ **e)** $y^2 - 1$ **f)** $d^2 - 144$
g) $s^2 - 625$ **h)** $m^2 - 1600$ **i)** $x^2 - 121$
j) $64 - x^2$ **k)** $36 - a^2$ **l)** $81 - y^2$
3. a) $9a^2 - 6a + 1$ **b)** $4a^2 + 12a + 9$
c) $49x^2 - 70x + 25$ **d)** $36a^2 + 48a + 16$
e) $9n^2 - 48n + 64$ **f)** $25 - 90x + 81x^2$
g) $100 - 60c + 9c^2$ **h)** $144x^2 + 120x + 25$
4. a) $9x^2 - 4$ **b)** $16x^2 - 9$ **c)** $9 - 25x^2$
d) $36s^2 - 25$ **e)** $144x^2 - 49$
f) $25y^2 - 169$ **g)** $100a^2 - 121$
h) $16s^2 - 400$
5. a) $x^2 + 14x + 49$ **b)** $a^2 - 4a + 4$
c) $n^2 + 8n + 16$ **d)** $4x^2 - 4x + 1$
e) $25c^2 + 30c + 9$ **f)** $4 - 12m + 9m^2$
g) $16 + 40x + 25x^2$ **h)** $64 - 48x + 9x^2$
i) $25 + 50s + 25s^2$ **j)** $16 - 24a + 9a^2$
k) $9 - 42x + 49x^2$ **l)** $36x^2 - 72x + 36$
6. a) $n^2 + 0.4n + 0.04$ **b)** $x^2 - 2.25$
c) $c^2 - \dfrac{1}{4}$ **d)** $x^2 + \dfrac{1}{2}x + \dfrac{1}{16}$ **e)** $k^2 - \dfrac{4}{9}$
f) $\dfrac{4}{9}a^2 - 1$ **g)** $x^2 - \dfrac{2}{3}x + \dfrac{1}{9}$
h) $4s^2 + \dfrac{4}{5}s + \dfrac{1}{25}$ **i)** $1.44x^2 - 12x + 25$
j) $\dfrac{1}{4}x^2 - \dfrac{1}{9}$ **7. a), b), c), d)** $x^2 - 6x + 9$
8. a) $3x^2 - 12x + 12$ **b)** $4x^2 - 100$
c) $5a^2 - 5$ **d)** $-16x^2 + 48x - 36$
e) $-75 + 30n - 3n^2$ **f)** $18x^2 - 32$
9. a) 961   **b)** 169   **c)** 841   **d)** 10 609
e) 3721   **f)** 8464
10. a) 899   **b)** 896   **c)** 3599   **d)** 3591
e) 9999   **f)** 9975   **g)** 89 996   **h)** 39 900
11. a) 4   **b)** −6   **c)** $\pm 7, \pm 14$ **d)** $\pm 3, \pm 12$
e) $\pm 7, \pm 28$ **f)** $\pm 3y, \pm 30y$
12. a) $x^4 - 5x^2 + 4$ **b)** $x^4 - 1$
c) $a^4 - 34a^2 + 225$ **d)** $a^4 - 625$
e) $-y^4 + 5y^2 - 4$ **f)** $-n^4 + 13n^2 - 36$
13. a) i) $x^2 - 1$ **ii)** $x^3 - 1$ **iii)** $x^4 - 1$
b) $x^5 - 1$ **14. a)** 1 999 999   **c)** 249 999

Investigate, page 248

6. The result is always the square of the number you started with. $(x - 1)^2 + x + x - 1 = x^2$

Exercises 7-7, page 250

1. a) 3 **b)** 4 **c)** $2x$ **d)** $7x$ **e)** y^2 **f)** $4z^2$
2. a) $5(y - 2)$ **b)** $6(2a + 3)$
c) $-3(x^2 - 2x + 4)$ **d)** $2(a^2 - 5a + 1)$
e) $w(4 + 3w - 7w^2)$ **f)** $2y(4y^2 - 2y + 1)$
g) $-2s(3 - s - 2s^2)$ **h)** $-7k^2(1 + 5k - 7k^2)$
i) $6m^2(1 - 6m - 9m^2)$

3. a) $7(2x^2 + 5x - 1)$ **b)** $-5(2 + 5a - 6a^2)$
c) $10(2n^2 - 3n + 4)$ **d)** $5x(1 + 2x + 3x^2)$
e) $3c(3c^2 + 5)$ **f)** $x^2(-x + 1)$
g) $4x(1 - 2x + 3x^2)$ **h)** $-3y^2(2 + y + 4y^2)$
i) $4m(3 + 4m - m^2)$
4. a) $8(2x + 5)$ **b)** $3(5n - 8)$
c) $-2a(a + 3)$ **d)** $a(a^2 - 9a + 3)$
e) $-3(9x^2 + 3x - 1)$ **f)** $x(5x^2 + 3x - 1)$
g) $a(9a^2 + 7a + 18)$ **h)** $-8d(1 + 3d + d^2)$
i) $17k(1 - 5k - 3k^2)$
5. a) xy **b)** $3xy$ **c)** ab **d)** 4   **e)** $-5xy$
f) $6pq$ **g)** $2mn$ **h)** $3x^2y$
6. a) $xy(1 + x)$ **b)** $-3xy(xy - 2)$
c) $ab(1 - ab)$ **d)** $-4(xy + 4)$
e) $5xy(1 + 2xy)$ **f)** $6pq(p - 2q)$
g) $2mn(m - 2n)$ **h)** $3x^2y(1 + 3y)$
i) $-xy(5x^5 + y^5)$
7. a) $b^3(b - 3)$ **b)** $3b^4(1 - 2b)$
c) $-a^2(a^2 - 3a + 2)$ **d)** $21x(1 + 2x + 3x^2)$
e) $-d^4(1 - 5d)$ **f)** $6m(4m^2 + m - 2)$
g) $-3x(4 + 3x + x^2 + 2x^3)$
h) $x^3(2 + 3x - 4x^2 + 5x^3)$ **8.** $S = 2\pi r(h + r)$
9. a) $6a(3 - b^2)$ **b)** $4xy(3x + 4)$
c) $-4abc(2b + 3ac)$ **d)** $5(m^2 + 3mn + 5n^2)$
e) $4xy^2z(x - 4z)$ **f)** $3x(x + 2y^2 - 4xy^2)$
g) $-y(5x - 6 - 3xy)$ **h)** $a^2b^2(9a + 7 + 18b)$
i) $-7a^2b^2(a - 2b + 3)$
j) $-4p^2q^3(3 + 5p - 2q)$
10. a) $3xy(y + 2x - 3)$ **b)** $-2ab(a - 3b + 2)$
c) $5m^2n(n - 2mn + 5)$ **d)** $-7x^2y^2(4 - 2xy + y)$
11. a) $2a^2b(a - 8b^2 + 2ab + 3b - 4ab^2 + 6)$
b) $5x^2y^2(3x^2y - 5xy^2 + 2y - x + 6x^2y^2 - 7)$
12. a) $(a + 6)(a + 7)$ **b)** $(x - 9)(x - 2)$
c) $(1 + y)(-8 - 3y)$ **d)** $(2 - x)(5 + x)$
e) $(x + 3)(2x + 4)$ **f)** $(2a - 1)(-3a + 6)$
13. a) $3(3t - 1)(2t + 3)$ **b)** $a(a + 2)(a - 1)$
c) $5x(x + 7)(x - 2)$ **d)** $-(2n + 3)(n + 4)$
e) $2(r - 3)(r + 4)$ **f)** $x^2(x + 4)(x - 1)$
g) $3a^2(a - 1)(a - 2)$ **h)** $4a(2a - 5)(3a + 4)$
14. a) $(a + 2)(a + b)$ **b)** $(3 - y)(x + y)$
c) $(a + b)(3 + b)$ **d)** $(x - 1)(4 + a)$
e) $(p - q)(2 - p)$ **f)** $(x + y)(y - 4)$
g) $-(m - n)(3 + n)$ **h)** $-(c + d)(5 + d)$

Investigate, page 251

The result is one more than the original number.
$$\sqrt{(x + 2)x + 1} \equiv x + 1$$

Problem Solving, page 253

1. a) $\dfrac{3}{4}, \dfrac{7}{8}$ **b)** $4x + 7y, 5x + 9y$ **c)** 11, 16
d) 29, 35   **2.** 25

3. A-hexagon in circle, B-hexagon in hexagon, C-circle in square, D-square in triangle

4. 20 **5.** $\dfrac{n(n + 1)}{2}$ **6.** $\dfrac{n^2(n + 1)^2}{4}$

Exercises 7-8, page 256

1. a) $(x + 2)(x + 5)$ **b)** $(x + 2)(x + 3)$
c) $(m + 6)(m + 4)$ **d)** $(a + 1)(a + 7)$
e) $(x + 3)^2$ **f)** $(n + 7)^2$ **g)** $(t + 8)(t + 5)$
h) $(x - 6)^2$ **i)** $(x + 4)(x + 5)$

2. a) $(x - 3)(x - 5)$ **b)** $(c - 4)(c - 8)$
c) $(a - 4)^2$ **d)** $(x - 5)(x - 1)$
e) $(x + 1)^2$ **f)** $(n - 2)(n - 7)$
g) $(y - 6)(y - 9)$ **h)** $(s - 9)^2$
i) $(k - 6)(k - 5)$

3. a) $(x - 4)^2$ **b)** $(x + 6)^2$ **c)** $(a + 2)^2$
d) $(p - 1)^2$ **e)** $(x - 3)^2$ **f)** $(t - 5)^2$
g) $(x + 7)^2$ **h)** $(b - 8)^2$ **i)** $(x + 10)^2$

4. a) $(x + 8)(x - 2)$ **b)** $(a + 6)(a - 2)$
c) $(x + 9)(x - 3)$ **d)** $(c + 7)(c - 5)$
e) $(x + 4)(x - 3)$ **f)** $(a + 6)(a - 5)$
g) $(y + 8)(y - 7)$ **h)** $(t - 6)(t + 4)$
i) $(x - 5)(x + 3)$

5. a) $(x - 4)(x - 2)$ **b)** $(x + 3)(x + 6)$
c) $(a - 2)(a - 9)$ **d)** $(m + 4)(m + 7)$
e) $(n - 5)^2$ **f)** $(3 - n)(10 - n)$
g) $(p + 8)^2$ **h)** $(y - 7)(y - 6)$
i) $(x + 8)(x + 7)$

6. a) $(r - 9)(r + 4)$ **b)** $(a - 9)(a + 5)$
c) $(n - 9)(n + 6)$ **d)** $(m - 8)(m + 6)$
e) $(k - 9)(k + 7)$ **f)** $(x - 10)(x + 3)$
g) $(9 - a)^2$ **h)** $(m + 11)^2$ **i)** $(n - 2)^2$

7. a) $(x - 8)(x + 3)$ **b)** $(x + 10)(x - 5)$
c) $(a + 9)(a - 8)$ **d)** $(n - 8)(n + 5)$
e) $(m + 7)(m - 6)$ **f)** $(8 + x)(1 - x)$
g) $(y + 4)(y - 1)$ **h)** $(s - 9)(s + 2)$
i) $(2 - t)(1 + t)$ $2 + 2t - it - t^2$

8. a) $(x + 8)(x - 1)$ **b)** $(a + 7)(a - 2)$
c) $(t - 3)(t + 1)$ **d)** $(n + 7)(n + 6)$
e) $(x - 9)(x - 8)$ **f)** $(c - 6)(c - 5)$
g) $(m + 11)(m - 5)$ **h)** $(a + 1)(a + 9)$
i) $(s + 5)(s - 4)$ **j)** $(c + 12)(c - 3)$
k) $(6 - m)(2 + m)$ **l)** $(5 - y)(3 - y)$

9. a) 240 **b)** $(x - 5)(x + 3)$ **c)** 240

10. a) 2750 **b)** $(x - 9)(x - 4)$ **c)** 2750

11. a) $(x + 9)(x + 7)$ **b)** No factors
c) No factors **d)** $(t + 3)(t + 8)$
e) $(n - 5)(n - 7)$ **f)** No factors
g) $(x + 12)(x - 5)$ **h)** No factors
i) No factors **j)** No factors
k) $(7 + t)(8 - t)$ **l)** No factors

12. a) $2(x + 5)(x + 1)$ **b)** $5(a - 4)(a + 2)$
c) $10(n + 2)(n - 1)$ **d)** $4(a - 5)(a + 1)$
e) $3(x^2 + 5x + 2)$ **f)** $7(a - 2)(a - 3)$
g) $x(x - 3)(x + 1)$ **h)** $a(a^2 - 2a - 9)$
i) $2y(y + 3)(y + 4)$ **j)** $3x(x + 4)(x - 2)$
k) $10n(3 + n)(2 + n)$ **l)** $7s(2 - s)(1 + s)$

13. a) $R = (7 - x)(5 + x)$
b) i) \$36 000 **ii)** \$35 000 **iii)** \$32 000

14. a) $R = (11 - x)(5 + x)$
b) i) \$60 000 **ii)** \$63 000 **iii)** \$64 000
iv) \$60 000 **v)** \$55 000

15. a) $(x + 5y)(x + 3y)$ **b)** $(x - 7y)(x - 2y)$
c) $(x - 5y)(x + y)$ **d)** $(x + 9y)(x - 2y)$
e) $(c - 7d)(c + 3d)$ **f)** $(m + 9n)(m + 5n)$
g) $(3x - y)(2x + y)$ **h)** $(4a + b)(2a - b)$
i) $(7a - b)(4a + b)$ **j)** $(2x + y)(6x + y)$
k) $(5x - 1)^2$ **l)** $(4a - b)(5a - b)$

16. a) $\pm 13, \pm 8, \pm 7$ **b)** $\pm 21, \pm 12, \pm 9$
c) $\pm 17, \pm 7, \pm 3$
d) Answers may vary, for example, 4, 6, -6, -14 ... **e)** Answers may vary, for example, 3, 4, -5, -12, ... **f)** Answers may vary, for example, 1, -3, -8, -35, ...

17. a) $y = (x + 1)(x + 11)$
b) 24, 39, 56, 75, 96, 119, 144, 171, 200, 231
c) 7, -19

18. a) $-10, 3$ **b)** $-17, 9$ **c)** $-1, 12$

Calculator Power, page 258

1. a) 83 200, 85 000, 86 400, 87 400, 88 000
b) 88 000, 88 200, 88 000, 87 400, 86 400
c) Answers may vary. **2.** 210 m by 420 m

3. a) (5,45), (6,32), (7,21), (8,10), (9,5), (10,0), (11,-3), (12,-4), (13,-3), (14,0), (15,5)
b) 12

Exercises 7-9, page 260

1. a) $(x + 5)(x - 5)$ **b)** $(a + 7)(a - 7)$
c) $(x + 6)(x - 6)$ **d)** $(y + 10)(y - 10)$
e) $(x + 1)(x - 1)$ **f)** $(x + 2)(x - 2)$
g) $(m + 8)(m - 8)$ **h)** $(n + 12)(n - 12)$

2. a) $(x + 1)(x - 1)$ **b)** $(x + 4)(x - 4)$
c) $(x + 6)(x - 6)$ **d)** $(x + 2)(x - 2)$

3. a) $(3a + 2)(3a - 2)$ **b)** $(5x + 3)(5x - 3)$
c) $(4s + 1)(4s - 1)$ **d)** $4(3 + 5n)(3 - 5n)$
e) $(10x + 11)(10x - 11)$ **f)** $(12p + 7)(12p - 7)$
g) $\left(\dfrac{1}{2}x + \dfrac{2}{3}\right)\left(\dfrac{1}{2}x - \dfrac{2}{3}\right)$ **h)** $(2.5 + n)(2.5 - n)$

4. a) $(7a + 1)(7a - 1)$ **b)** $4(1 + 3x)(1 - 3x)$
c) $(3 + 8m)(3 - 8m)$ **d)** $(9y + 7)(9y - 7)$

e) $(1.2x + 1)(1.2x - 1)$ **f)** $(40a + 9)(40a - 9)$

g) $(0.8x + 1.1)(0.8x - 1.1)$

h) $\left(\dfrac{1}{3} + \dfrac{1}{4}x\right)\left(\dfrac{1}{3} - \dfrac{1}{4}x\right)$

5. a) $2(x - 3)(x + 3)$ **b)** $5(x - 1)(x + 1)$

c) $3(a + 4)(a - 4)$ **d)** $3(n^2 + 10)$

e) $7(1 - 2y)(1 + 2y)$ **f)** $2(a^2 + 6)$

g) $x(x - 5)(x + 5)$ **h)** $a(a + 7)(a - 7)$

6. a) $(a - b)(a + b)$ **b)** $(x - 2y)(x + 2y)$

c) $(3m + 4n)(3m - 4n)$

d) $(6x - 7y)(6x + 7y)$ **e)** $(ab + c)(ab - c)$

f) $(2ab + 3cd)(2ab - 3cd)$

g) $c^2(2c - 9d)(2c + 9d)$

h) $y^2(5x + 3y)(5x - 3y)$

7. a) $(x^2 + 1)(x - 1)(x + 1)$

b) $(a^2 + 4)(a - 2)(a + 2)$

c) $(4c^2 + 1)(2c + 1)(2c - 1)$

d) $2(1 + x^2)(1 + x)(1 - x)$

Exercises 7-10, page 262

1. a) $4x^3$ **b)** $2y^4$ **c)** $9y^3$ **d)** $-3m^2$

e) $9y^2$ **f)** $\dfrac{3n^2}{5}$ **g)** -5 **h)** $\dfrac{3c^3}{2}$ **i)** $6x^3$

j) $-4y$ **k)** $-\dfrac{9a^2}{4}$ **l)** $\dfrac{3}{2}x$

2. a) $2a + 1$ **b)** $4y - 1$ **c)** $3x^2 - 1$

d) $2a + 5$ **e)** $6x - 1$ **f)** $5 - 2m$

g) $-3 + n$ **h)** $3 - x$ **3. a)** $4x^3y$ **b)** $-6a^2$

c) 7 **d)** $-3b^2$ **e)** $-3x^2y^2$ **f)** $5abc$

4. a) $x - 2$ **b)** $x - 2$ **c)** $6 - 7a$

d) $-4n - 1$ **e)** $-4y^2 + y$ **f)** $-8b^2 - 2b$

g) $m^3 - 6$ **h)** $x^3 + 3x$ **i)** $\dfrac{7}{6} - c$

5. a) $3x^2 - x + 5$ **b)** $1 + 3c - 2c^2$

c) $x^2 - 3x + 2$ **d)** $4 + a - a^2$

e) $3x^2 - 6x + 1$ **f)** $-3a^2 - a + 2$

g) $3 - 2y + y^2$ **h)** $4x^4 - 5x^2 + 1$

i) $3w^4 - 6w^2 + 1$

6. a) $1 - 3x + 9x^3$ **b)** $-4m^3 + 2m - 1$

c) $6a^3 + 3a - 2$ **d)** $2y^4 + 3y^2 - 5$

e) $\dfrac{4n^2 - 6n + 8}{3}$ **f)** $x(-5x^4 + 3x^2 - 1)$

7. a) $1 - 3x^2y^2 + 6xy^3$ **b)** $b(4a^2b^2 - 3ab + 2)$

c) $n(-n^2 + 2mn - 3m^2)$ **d)** $\dfrac{3x^4y^2 - 2x^3y + 1}{x^2}$

e) $3a^2 - 2ab + b^2$ **f)** $yz^2(3 - 2xyz + x^2y^2z^2)$

8. $\dfrac{R}{3}$ **9.** $\dfrac{R}{3}$

Exercises 7-11, page 265

1. $\dfrac{3a^2b}{2}$; $\dfrac{4m^2n^2}{3mn}$; $\dfrac{3}{5}$; $\dfrac{x - 6}{5}$; $\dfrac{3 - 4y}{2y}$; $-\dfrac{4}{3}$; $3x^2 + 1$;

$\dfrac{4 + 3m^2}{2m^3}$ **2. a)** $\dfrac{3x^3}{y^4}$ **b)** $-12m^2n$ **c)** $\dfrac{2xy^2}{3}$

d) $\dfrac{10m}{3}$ **e)** $\dfrac{a^2}{b^2}$ **f)** $\dfrac{-8cd^2}{3}$ **g)** $4xy^2$

h) $\dfrac{-4m^3n^3}{15}$ **i)** $\dfrac{-5x^4y}{6}$

3. a) $\dfrac{2x^4}{y}$ **b)** $\dfrac{5x^3y}{9}$ **c)** $\dfrac{m}{6}$ **d)** $\dfrac{3ab^2}{2}$

e) $-2x^3$ **f)** $\dfrac{5c^2d}{2}$ **g)** $\dfrac{-9y}{8}$ **h)** $\dfrac{3a}{4}$

i) $\dfrac{xy^3}{6}$ **j)** $\dfrac{-4p^3q^2}{5}$ **k)** $\dfrac{-12b^3}{a^3}$ **l)** $\dfrac{4n^6}{35m}$

4. a) $\dfrac{3a + 2}{2}$ **b)** $\dfrac{2x - 2}{5}$ **c)** $\dfrac{2 + 3y}{7}$

d) $\dfrac{4m - 1}{4}$ **e)** $-\dfrac{1 + 4n}{3}$ **f)** $\dfrac{x + 1}{3}$

g) $\dfrac{2y - 7}{5}$ **h)** $\dfrac{5x + 2}{3}$ **i)** $\dfrac{2m + 1}{2}$

5. a) $\dfrac{2}{x}$ **b)** $\dfrac{a - 11}{3a^2}$ **c)** $\dfrac{1 - 2m}{m}$ **d)** $\dfrac{5y + 1}{3y^3}$

e) $\dfrac{3x - 7}{x^4}$ **f)** $\dfrac{2 + n}{2n^2}$ **g)** $\dfrac{6x + 2}{3x^2}$

h) $-\dfrac{y + 1}{y^3}$ **i)** $\dfrac{6a - 3}{5a}$ **6. a)** $\dfrac{-5x}{2}$ **b)** $-4ab^2$

c) $\dfrac{n^3}{4m}$ **d)** $\dfrac{x^2yz^2}{3}$ **e)** $-\dfrac{c}{2}$ **f)** $\dfrac{15}{8z}$

7. a) $\dfrac{x + 5}{2x^2}$ **b)** $\dfrac{-2y + 10}{3y^3}$ **c)** $\dfrac{-2 + m}{2m}$

d) $\dfrac{13 + a}{a^3}$ **e)** $\dfrac{2x - 14}{3x^2}$ **f)** $\dfrac{-2a + 11}{4a^3}$

8. a) $\dfrac{10x - 1}{12}$ **b)** $\dfrac{a - 6}{6}$ **c)** $\dfrac{10 - 17m}{10}$

d) $\dfrac{13y + 5}{12}$ **e)** $\dfrac{n + 17}{14}$ **f)** $\dfrac{3x + 63}{20}$

9. $\dfrac{xy}{x + y}$ **10. a)** $\dfrac{2Dv}{v^2 - w^2}$ **b)** $\dfrac{v^2 - w^2}{v}$

Review Exercises, page 267

1. a) $3n$ **b)** $8x$ **c)** $8y^2$ **d)** $-10y^2$ **e)** $5b^2$

f) $0.9y^3 + 2y$ **2. a)** $-x + 7$; first degree

b) $6y^3 + 13y^2 + 4y$; third degree

c) $3a^4 - a^3 + 2a^2 + 9a$; fourth degree

d) $3a^2 + 5a + 2$; second degree

3. a) 2 **b)** 10 **c)** 44 **d)** 40.25

4. a) $7y + 1$ **b)** $2x - 5$ **c)** $11r - 7$
d) $3y^2 + 3y$ **e)** $5x - 8$ **f)** $-3 + p - 4p^2$
g) $-5q^2 + 8q - 6$ **5. a)** $35a^2$ **b)** $-15b^2$
c) $16y^2$ **d)** $-63x^5$ **e)** $-8y^3$ **f)** $-12x^3y^3$

6. a) $4y - 8$ **b)** $8a - 24$ **c)** $-4x - 8$
d) $15x - 3x^2$ **e)** $2y^2 - 12y$
f) $-15x + 5x^2$ **g)** $35y - 10y^2 + 15y^3$
h) $-18x^3 - 30x^2 + 72x$
i) $-40a - 70a^2 + 20a^3$

7. a) $6y(1 + 3y)$ **b)** $-3a(1 - 4a^3)$
c) $5a^2(1 - 5a)$ **d)** $a(3a^2 + 4a + 7)$
e) $3xy(2x - 1 + 3y)$ **f)** $2ab(4 - 2ab + 3b)$

8. a) $x^2 - 7x + 12$ **b)** $y^2 + 10y + 21$
c) $a^2 + 3a - 10$ **d)** $n^2 + n - 42$
e) $n^2 - 3n - 28$ **f)** $x^2 + 4x - 5$

9. a) $4x^2 - 44x + 120$ **b)** $y^3 + 7y^2 - 18y$
c) $-21y + 18y^2 + 3y^3$

10. a) $x^2 + 6x + 9$ **b)** $y^2 - 10y + 25$
c) $25 - 10q + q^2$ **d)** $36 - 60y + 25y^2$

11. a) $(x - 2)(x - 5)$ **b)** $(x - 3)^2$
c) $(x + 5)(x + 1)$ **d)** $(a - 6)(a + 2)$
e) $(x - 4)(x + 3)$ **f)** $(5 - x)(3 + x)$
g) $(y - 9)(y + 8)$ **h)** $(n + 8)(n - 5)$
i) $(8 - x)(1 + x)$ **j)** $2(x^2 - 6x - 36)$
k) $5(m + 4)(m - 2)$ **l)** $y(y + 3)(y - 1)$

12. a) $a^2 - 16$ **b)** $x^2 - 64$ **c)** $4 - y^2$
d) $\frac{1}{4}n^2 - 1$ **e)** $3x^2 - 108$ **f)** $-45y + 5y^3$

13. a) $(b + 5)(b - 5)$ **b)** $(x + 9)(x - 9)$
c) $(y + 11)(y - 11)$ **d)** $\left(m + \frac{1}{2}\right)\left(m - \frac{1}{2}\right)$
e) $(3x + 4)(3x - 4)$ **f)** $(5 - 2y)(5 + 2y)$
g) $2(x + 4)(x - 4)$ **h)** $4m(4 - m)(4 + m)$

14. a) $(10 + 6x)$ metres   **b)** $(2x^2 + 4x)$ square
metres   **c)** 52 m, 126 m²

15. a) 16°C   **b)** 45°C   **c)** 54°C

16. a) $3x - 4$ **b)** $6 - x$ **c)** $3x + 1$
d) $5 - 3a$ **e)** $x - 4$ **f)** $\frac{5a - 3}{a^2}$

17. a) $3 - c + 2c^2$ **b)** $x^2 + 4x - 1$
c) $\frac{3m - 4m^2 + 5}{2m^3}$ **18. a)** $\frac{-5b^3}{8c}$ **b)** $6x$
c) $\frac{-2}{m^2}$ **d)** $\frac{-7st^3}{4r^4}$ **e)** $\frac{v^2}{60w^2}$ **f)** $\frac{-6c^3}{ab}$

19. a) $\frac{3x + 8}{2}$ **b)** $\frac{-m - 11}{3}$ **c)** $\frac{7a - 2b}{2b}$
d) $\frac{-2u + 11v}{5u}$ **e)** $\frac{2s - 15t}{2t^2}$ **f)** $\frac{5m - 12n}{6}$

Chapter 8

Exercises 8-1, page 272

1. A($-2,5$), B($-4,3$), C($-3,1$), D($-5,-2$),
E($-2,-3$), F($1,-5$),G($3,-3$),H($5,-2$),
I($5,3$), J($3,5$)

3. a) On the y-axis **b)** On a line parallel to the x-axis,
and 4 units below   **c)** On the left of the y-axis
d) To the left of the y-axis, and above the x-axis
e) Along a line through the origin, that is the same
distance from both axes, passing through the
quadrants where x and y are both positive, and x
and y are both negative.

4. d) WHY   **5. c)** Parallelogram

6. OEF, GHI, KLM, RST   **7. a)** $(3,-2)$
b) $(-3,-2)$ **c)** $(-1,4)$ **d)** $(0,3)$

8. a), c) Parallelogram, rhombus, rectangle, square
b) Trapezoid   **d)** Parallelogram, rhombus

9. a) $(9,0)$, $(3,6)$, or $(-3,0)$
b) $(5,-3)$, $(5,9)$, or $(-1,5)$
c) $(-3,-4)$, $(9,6)$, or $(-7,6)$
d) $(2,6)$, $(-2,0)$, or $(2,-6)$ **10.** Square

Exercises 8-2, page 276

1. a) $\{(1,0.50), (2,0.95), (3,1.35), (4,1.70), (5,2.00)\}$
b) $\{(-5,-2), (-4,3), (3,5), (7,2), (5,-1), (2,-3)\}$

2. a) $\{(0,2), (2,6), (4,2), (6,10), (8,12), (10,0),$
$(10,4), (12,8)\}$
b) $\{(-6,-3), (-5,2), (-5,-5), (-3,-2),$
$(-1,1)$ $(0,-5)$, $(3,2)$, $(3,-4)$, $(5,-2)\}$
c) $\{(1,0.5), (2,1), (3,1.5), (4,2), (5,2.5), (6,3)\}$
d) $\{(-5,12), (-4,8), (-3,4), (-2,2), (0,0),$
$(2,2), (3,4), (4,8), (5,12)\}$ **4. a) i)** 15 **ii)** 4
b) $\{(1,1), (2,3), (3,6), (4,10), (5,15), (6,21)\}$

5. a) i) 30, 40   **ii)** 5, 15   **iii)** 15, 20   **iv)** 25
b) i) 6, 10   **ii)** 13   **iii)** 2, 16   **iv)** 2
c) $\{(2,40), (2,30), (6,5), (6,15), (10,15), (10,20),$
$(13,25), (16,30)\}$

6. a) $\{(1,0.15), (2,0.30), (3,0.45), (4,0.60), (5,0.75),$
$(6,0.86), (7,0.97), (8,1.08), (9,1.19), (10,1.30),$
$(11,1.38), (12,1.46), (13,1.54), (14,1.62),$
$(15,1.70)\}$

7. $\{(1,0), (2,0), (3,0), (4,0.32), (5,0.64), (6,0.96),$
$(7,1.28), (8,1.60)\}$

8. b) i) $\{(4,0), (2,5), (0,10)\}$
ii) $\{(0,1), (0,2), (0,3), (0,4), (0,5), (0,6), (0,7),$
$(0,8), (0,9), (0,10), (1,0), (1,1), (1,2),$
$(1,3), (1,4), (1,5), (1,6), (1,7), (2,0), (2,1),$
$(2,2), (2,3), (2,4), (2,5), (3,0), (3,1), (3,2),$
$(4,0)\}$

9. a) $\{(4,0.75), (5,1.50), (6,2.25), (7,3.00), (8,3.75),$
$(9,4.50), (10,5.25), (11,6.00), (12,6.75),$
$(13,7.50), (14,8.25), (15,9.00), (16,9.75)\}$
c) Allowance: y; age: x; $y = 0.75x - 2.25$

Problem Solving, page 279

1. About 9:53   **2.** −25°C   **3.** About 145 m
4. 04:00   **5.** 96 m by 48 m

Exercises 8-3, page 282

1. a) 80 g   **b) i)** About 55 g   **ii)** About 38 g
iii) About 27 g   .**iv)** About 13 g
c) About 5500 years
2. a) Beginning and end of daylight-saving time
b) About 4:30 P.M. on December 21st
c) About 9:50 P.M. on June 21st   **d) i)** About
6:10 P.M.   **ii)** About 8:50 P.M.
iii) About 4:30 P.M.   **e) i)** About January 15
and November 10
ii) About March 15 and October 20
iii) About April 25 and August 20
3. a) {(18,202), (20,200), (30,190), (40,180),
(50,170)}   **c)** 40 years   **d)** 193 beats/min
4. a) i) 13 cm   **ii)** 6 cm   **iii)** 6 cm
b) i) 0.5 s, 2.0 s, 3.0 s, 4.5 s, 5.5 s   **ii)** About
0.75 s, 1.75 s, 3.25 s, 4.25 s, 5.75 s   **c)** 2.5 s
5. b) i) About 55°C   **ii)** About 12.75 min
c) i) About 10°C   **ii)** About 6°C
6. b) About 1954   **c)** About 8 000 000
d) Answers may vary, for example, 27.5 million if
the rate of the last 2 decades is maintained.
7. a) {(0,12), (1,10), (2,8), (3,6), (4,4), (5,2), (6,0)}

Exercises 8-4, page 287

1. a), c) Linear   **2. a), b)**   **3. a)** (0,4), (3,0)
b) (0, −3), (6,0)   **c)** (−2,0)
d) (0,4), (−2,0)   **e)** (0,3)   **f)** (0, −1), (−4,0)
4. a) (0,6), (9,0)   **b)** (0, −4), (3,0)   **c)** (0,7),
(−4,0)   **d)** (0,2), (10,0)   **e)** (0, −6), (3,0)
f) (0,1.5), (3,0)
5. a) About 6.5 h   **b)** About 4.5 h   **c)** About 8.5 h
6. a) About 180 km   **b)** About 2.5 h   **c)** 50 km
d) No

7. a)

x	y
0	2
5	−2
10	−6

b)

x	y
2	0
6	3
10	6

c)

x	y
1	−2
4	0
7	2

d)

x	y
0	0
7	5
−7	−5

e)

x	y
0	−7
7	0
3	−4

f)

x	y
0	3
2	3
4	3

8. b), c) Linear
9. a) {(0,280), (1,180), (2,80), (2.8,0)} **b)** 280 km
c) 2 h 48 min **d) i)** 200 km **ii)** 80 km

10. b) i) About 195°F   **ii)** About 250°F
iii) About 390°F   **c) i)** About 30°C
ii) About 50°C   **iii)** About 95°C
d) i) About −5°C   **ii)** About −20°C
iii) About −25°C   **iv)** About −30°C
11. b) i) About 144 cm **ii)** About 162 cm
iii) About 168 cm **c) i)** About 9 years 4 months
ii) About 10 years **iii)** About 11 years

Investigate, page 289

1. The lines intersect at (1,5).
2. The lines are parallel.   **3.** The lines coincide.
4. a) The graphs intersect at (3,4).
b) The graphs are parallel. **c)** The graphs coincide.
d) The graphs are parallel.
e) The graphs intersect at (−2,5).
f) The graphs coincide. **g)** The graphs coincide.
h) The graphs coincide.
i) The graphs intersect at (−6, −1).
5. Answers may vary. **i)** If the equations, in their
simplest form, have the same y- and x-coefficients,
but different constant terms
ii) If the equations, in their simplest form, are
identical

Problem Solving, page 290

1. a) Odd **b)** Even **c) i)** $-\frac{1}{2}n$ **ii)** $\frac{1}{2}(n+1)$

2. The perimeters are equal. **3. a)** 64 **b)** n^2
4. a) 40 **b)** 60 **5.** 11 units **6.** 20%
7. All orders give the same result.

Mathematics Around Us, page 291

4. The comet is moving faster at (35,0) and (−1,0);
and it is moving slowest at (17, −4.5) and
(17,4.5).

Exercises 8-5, page 294

1. a), d) Linear   **b), c)** Non-linear
2. a) {(0,0), (2,2), (4,8), (6,18), (8,32), (10,50),
(12,72), (14,98), (15,112.5)}
c) About 30 m   **d)** About 12 s
3. a) {(0,335.0), (1,330.1), (2,315.4), (3,290.9),
(4,256.6), (5,212.5), (6,158.6), (7,94.9),
(8,21.4), (9, −61.9)}
c) About 235 m   **d)** About 7 s
4. a) {(100,3.00), (200,1.50), (300,1.00), (400,0.75),
(500,0.60), (600,0.50), (700,0.43), (800,0.38),
(900,0.33), (1000,0.30)}
c) 200 kPa   **d)** 1.2 L

5. a) {(50,51), (75,64), (100,75), (125,85), (150,93), (175,101), (200,109), (225,116), (250,123), (275,129), (300,135)}
  b) i) About 110 km   **ii)** About 140 km
  iii) About 260 km   **c) i)** About 70 km/h
  ii) About 93 km/h   **iii)** About 110 km/h

6. a) {(200,1500), (250,1975), (300,2500), (350,3075), (400,3700), (450,4375), (500,5100), (550,5875), (600,6700)}
  b) i) About 260 km/h   **ii)** About 340 km/h
  iii) About 430 km/h   **c) i)** About 2800 L/h
  ii) About 4700 L/h   **iii)** About 5875 L/h

7. Tables may vary.
  a) {(0,0), (2,1.7), (4,6.9), (6,15.6), (8,27.7), (10,43.3), (12,62.4), (14,84.9), (16,110.9), (18,140.3), (20,173.2)}
  b) The area increases by a factor of 4.

8. a) {(3,8000), (4,16 000), (5,32 000), (6,64 000), (7,128 000), (8,256 000), (9,512 000)}
  b) i) About 23 000   **ii)** About 110 000
  iii) About 300 000   **c) i)** About 2:30 P.M.
  ii) About 5:30 P.M.   **iii)** About 6:30 P.M.

9. a) {(0,0), (4,84), (8,136), (12,156), (16,144), (20,100), (24,24), (25,0)}   **c)** About 12 cm

10. a) {(0,0), (2,252), (4,480), (6,660), (8,768), (10,780), (12,672), (14,420), (15,232.5)}
  c) About 9 cm

11. a) $(2,2)$, $\left(\frac{4}{3},4\right)$, $\left(\frac{5}{4},5\right)$ **c)** $x + y = xy$

12. $x - y = xy$

Computer Power, page 297

3. b) i) 30.4 m   **ii)** 97.9 m   **iii)** 403.1 m
  c) i) 6.5 s   **ii)** 13.0 s   **iii)** 20.9 s

Exercises 8-6, page 300

1. a) $y = 2x$ **b)** $y = -\frac{1}{3}x$ **c)** $y = x + 1$

2. a) $y = x$ **b)** $y = x + 2$ **c)** $y = -x$

3. a) 10   **b)** 18   **c)** $y = x$

4. a) $y = x^2$ **b)** $x + y = 5$ **c)** $y = -\frac{1}{2}x$

5. a) 144   **b)** 400   **c)** $y = x^2$

6. a) 10   **b)** 32   **c)** $y = x + 2$

7. a) i) 12 cm² **ii)** 20 cm² **iii)** 4 cm² **iv)** 30 cm²
  b) $y = 2x$ **8. a)** 13 **b)** 199 **c)** $y = 2x - 1$

9. a) 10   **b)** 31   **c)** 100   **d)** 301
  e) $y = 3x + 1$ **10. a)** $y = x^2 + 1$
b) $y = 2x + 1$ **c)** $y = 3x - 2$

11. a) 10   **b)** 90   **c)** $y = x^2 - x$

Review Exercises, page 303

1. c) A rectangle **2. a)** Along a line parallel to the *y*-axis, and 2 units to its left **b)** Along a line parallel to the *x*-axis, and 3 units above it
  c) Below the *x*-axis and to the right of the *y*-axis

3. a) {(−3,−2), (−2,−1), (−1,0), (0,1), (1,2), (2,3)}
  b) {(5,4), (5,−4), (3,3), (3,−3), (1,1), (1,−1), (0,0)}

4. a) i) 0   **ii)** 5   **iii)** 9   **iv)** 20
  b) i) 4   **ii)** 6   **iii)** 9   **c)** 14

5. b) 0.52 m   **c)** Fourth bounce   **d)** 4   **e)** 3

6. b) About 3 days   **c)** Assume 9 days, about 65%

8. b) 25 **c)** 115 **9. a)** $y = 3x$ **b)** $y = x - 1$

c) $y = -\frac{1}{4}x$ **10. a)** 10 **b)** 21 **c)** 20

d) 41 **e)** $y = 2x + 1$

Chapter 9

Exercises 9-1, page 308

2. PQ, PR, PS, QR, QS

3. a) ∠ADB, ∠BDC, ∠ADC   **b)** ∠PTQ, ∠PTR, ∠PTS, ∠QTR, ∠QTS, ∠RTS

4. a) △MNO, △MPR, △PNQ, △NOQ, △QOR
  b) △ADE, △ADB, △ADC, △ABE, △ABC, △BEC, △CED, △BCD

5. a) Infinite number, 2, 1, 0   **b)** 2, 1, 0

6. Infinite, 1, 0   **7. a)** Infinite number, 1, 0
b) Infinite number, 2, 1, 0

8. a) 6   **b)** infinite   **c)** 8

Exercises 9-2, page 311

1. a) ∠ABC is acute.   **b)** ∠PQR is straight.
  c) ∠XYZ is reflex.   **d)** ∠DEF is right.

2. a) ∠AEC, ∠DEB; ∠AED, ∠CEB
  b) ∠STQ, ∠PTR; ∠STP, ∠QTR

3. a) 97°, 97°   **b)** 80°, 30°   **c)** 50°, 60°

4. 90°   **5. a)** ∠ABC, ∠BCA, ∠CAB acute
  b) ∠ACB, ∠CAB acute; ∠ABC obtuse
  c) ∠ABC right; ∠BAC, ∠BCA acute

6. The lines are perpendicular. **7.** 2, 0 **8.** 286°

9. a) 65° **b)** 55° **c)** 120° **d)** 36° **e)** 70° **f)** 25°

10. a) 0, 1, 2, 3, 4   **b)** 2, 1, 0

11. Answers may vary.

12. a) i), ii) The angles are supplementary.

The Mathematical Mind, page 315

1. Yes   **2.** No   **3.** No   **4.** Yes, yes   **5.** No
6. Both   **7.** Several   **8.** No

Exercises 9-3, page 317

1. a) ∠MLS, ∠NSL; ∠KLS, ∠PSL
b) ∠QLK, ∠LSN; ∠KLS, ∠NSR; ∠QLM,
∠LSP; ∠MLS, ∠PSR
c) ∠KLS, ∠LSN; ∠MLS, ∠PSL
2. a) 75°   **b)** 110°   **c)** 120°
3. a) 120°, 60°, 60°, 60°   **b)** 55°, 115°, 55°
c) 130°, 55°, 75°, 75°
4. No   **5.** No   **6.** 0, 1, 2, 3, infinite
8. 40°, 75°, 65°; 180°

Computer Power, page 319

1. 360°   **2.** Answers may vary. HOME; RT 120;
FD 80; RT 120; FD 80; RT 120; FD 80. 360°
3. The sum of the exterior angles of a triangle is 360°.
4. 180°   **5.** 540°
6. The sum of the interior angles in a triangle is 180°.

Exercises 9-4, page 321

1. △GHJ is right; △DEF is acute; △ABC is right,
△KLM is obtuse.   **2. a)** 80°, acute   **b)** 35°, acute
c) 115°, obtuse   **d)** 90°, right
3. a) 80°   **b)** 20°   **c)** 125°
4. a) △ABC, acute   **b)** △DEF, obtuse
c) △GHJ, right   **d)** △KLM, acute
5. a) The sum of the angles is 180°.   **b)** By folding
6. a) 20°   **b)** 135°   **c)** 100°   **d)** 80°   **e)** 25°   **f)** 70°
7. Reasons may vary. **a)**, **b)** yes; **c)**, **d)**, **e)**, **f)** no
8. Answers may vary. **9. a)** 8   **b) i)** △ABE, △ADE
ii) △ACB, △ECB, △DCE, △DCA
iii) △ABD, △EBD
10. a) Add x and 90°.   **b) i)** 120°   **ii)** 140°   **iii)** 177°
c) Subtract 90° from y.   **d) i)** 20°   **ii)** 70°   **iii)** 85°
e) y = x + 90°
11. a) 125°   **b)** 145°   **c)** 48°   **d)** 36°
12. a) 360°   **b)** 360°   **c)** 360°   **13.** 360°

Problem Solving, page 325

1. Eagles   **2.** About 18 km   **3.** 37.5 cm²   **4.** 1
5. 9 trains   **6.** 10   **7.** 5 min
9. No, the sum of 2 sides of a triangle must be greater
than the third side.
10. Answers may vary. The area is less than 0.08 m².

Exercises 9-5, page 328

1. a) 70°   **b)** 25°   **c)** 75°   **d)** 45°   **e)** 50°
f) 60°   **g)** 150°   **h)** 120°   **i)** 100°
2. a) Yes   **b)** No
3. a) 108°, 144°   **b)** 100°, 40°   **c)** 30°, 90°
d) 27°, 49.5°   **e)** 105°   **f)** 40°, 140°
5. a) Subtract 2x from 180°.
b) i) 40°   **ii)** 130°   **iii)** 94°
c) Subtract y from 180° and divide by 2.
d) i) 50°   **ii)** 35°   **iii)** 81.5°
e) y = 180° − 2x
6. a) Divide x by 2.   **b) i)** 30°   **ii)** 20°   **iii)** 13°
c) Multiply y by 2.   **d) i)** 80°   **ii)** 50°   **iii)** 162°
e) $y = \dfrac{x}{2}$ **7.** 30 m
8. Answers may vary. Move along JM extended
to a point X, such that ∠TXM is 45°. Then,
MX = TM.   **9. a)** 30°, 120° or 75°, 75°
b) 40°, 100° or 70°, 70°   **c)** 80°, 20° or 50°, 50°
d) 45°, 45°   **e)** 35°, 35°   **10. a)** 1   **b)** 3   **c)** 4

Exercises 9-6, page 335

1. a) MR = CL; RX = LP; MX = CP;
∠M = ∠C; ∠R = ∠L; ∠X = ∠P
b) QP = QR; SP = SR; ∠P = ∠R;
∠PQS = ∠RQS; ∠PSQ = ∠RSQ
2. PQ = XW; QR = WZ; RS = ZY, PS = XY,
∠P = ∠X, ∠Q = ∠W, ∠R = ∠Z, ∠S = ∠Y
3. a) △ABC ≅ △DEF SAS   **b)** Not congruent
c) △MNP ≅ △QRS AAS   **d)** Not congruent
e) △MNL ≅ △PNL SSS
f) △RUT ≅ △TSR SSS
4. a) △ABC ≅ △DFE AAS
b) △JKL ≅ △NMO SAS
c) △STU ≅ △AZY SSS (or SAS)
5. a) 4 cm, 5 cm, 6 cm   **b)** 50°, 5 cm, 8 cm
c) 131°, 6 cm, 9 cm   **d)** 4 cm, 2 cm, 3 cm
e) 7 cm, 9 cm, 120°   **f)** 90°, 30°, 5 cm

Exercises 9-7, page 340

1. a) 5   **b)** 13   **c)** 41   **d)** 8   **e)** 9   **f)** 24
2. a) 5.4   **b)** 6.7   **c)** 3.9   **d)** 8.1   **e)** 10.2   **f)** 13.1
3. a) 5.0 cm, 13.0 m   **b)** 6.4 cm, 9.5 cm
c) 5.3 cm, 4.6 cm   **d)** 1.4 units, 1.7 units,
2.0 units   **e)** 2.1 cm   **f)** 28.0 cm
4. 51.4 m   **5.** 8.0 m   **6.** 671 cm
7. No, because the greatest length in the box (the
diagonal) is only 1.14 m long.   **8.** 12.6 m
9. a) 8.5 cm   **b)** 62.5%   **10.** 51 cm, 42 cm
11. a) 12 cm²   **b)** Answers may vary.

Computer Power, page 343

1. a) 47 **b)** 126 **c)** 185 **d)** 47.2
e) 4.79 **f)** 549 **g)** 28.7

2. a) 4.81 cm **b)** 10.83 m **c)** 38.7 cm **d)** 2.38 m

Exercises 9-8, page 349

1. a) i) $\angle$ADC **ii)** $\angle$AOC
b) i) $\angle$AEC, $\angle$AFC **ii)** $\angle$AOC
c) i) $\angle$AIC, $\angle$AHC, $\angle$AGC **ii)** $\angle$AOC

2. a) 60° **b)** 50° **c)** 50° **d)** 90° **e)** 64° **f)** 190°

3. a) 50° **b)** 40° **c)** 30°, 50° **d)** 35°, 25°
e) 45°, 32° **f)** 38°, 90°

4. a) 55°, 110° **b)** 48°, 96° **c)** 67°, 134°
d) 90°, 90° **e)** 65°, 65° **f)** 20°, 40°

5. a) 70°, 80° **b)** 95°, 65° **c)** 155°, 90°
d) 90°, 105° **e)** 115°, 100° **f)** 50°, 70°

6. a) 90°, 90° **b)** 80°, 40° **c)** 60°, 60°
d) 110°, 20° **e)** 60°, 40° **f)** 50°, 15°

7. a) 70°, 110° **b)** 110°, 125°
c) 30°, 75°, 45°, 30°, 75°
d) 65°, 25°, 25°, 65°, 65°
e) 85°, 95°, 75°, 105° **f)** 25°, 130°

8. a) i) y is twice the value of x. **ii)** $y = 2x$
b) i) Subtract x from 90°. **ii)** $y = 90° - x$
c) i) Subtract x from 180°. **ii)** $y = 180° - x$

9. a) 5.4 cm² **b)** 14.3 cm² **c)** 19.6 cm²

10. a) 83.8 cm **b)** 94.2 cm

Mathematics Around Us, page 353

1. As B approaches C, the sum of the angles decreases to 180° just before B coincides with C; as B moves away from C, the sum of the angles increases to a maximum 360° when B and C are on opposite sides of the globe.

3. Great-circle routes because they are shorter.

4. Perth, Australia

5. a) 187° **b)** 266° **c)** 443°

6. a) Yes **b)** No **c)** No **d)** Yes

Review Exercises, page 354

1. a) 116°, 32° **b)** 65°, 52°, 63° **c)** 65°, 130°
d) 75°, 105°, 105° **e)** 70°, 80°, 70° **f)** 30°, 80°
g) 37.5°, 35° **h)** 130°, 100° **i)** 120°, 120°

2. a) $\triangle$ABC $\cong$ $\triangle$EDF SAS
b) $\triangle$ABC $\cong$ $\triangle$HIG SAS

3. a) 10.9, 4.9 **b)** 10.0, 18.0

4. 52 cm **5.** No **6.** 35 cm

7. a) 40°, 50° **b)** 35°, 70° **c)** 130°, 115°

8. a) 55°, 80° **b)** 50°, 40° **c)** 110°, 30°

9. a) 360° **b)** 360° **c)** 360°

10. 4.95 m **11.** 10.4 cm

Cumulative Review, Chapters 7-9, page 356

1. a) $9m - 12n$ **b)** $-6a + 3b$
c) $-3x - 11$ **d)** $4y^2 - 12y - 7$
e) $11x - 13$ **f)** $-3x - 2y + 6$

2. a) i) 33 **ii)** 124 **iii)** 23.25
b) i) -14 **ii)** 35 **iii)** -7.25

3. a) $-15m^2$ **b)** $-\dfrac{1}{8}x^3$ **c)** $48a^5$
d) $8x^3 - 20x^2 + 12x$ **e)** $-14x^3y^7$
f) $-10m^5 + 4m^3 - 8m^2n$

4. a) $x^2 + 7x - 44$ **b)** $2x^2 - 13x + 21$
c) $20 + 51a + 27a^2$ **d)** $9m^2 - 25$
e) $8x^3 + 10x^2 - 3x$ **f)** $-84a^3 + 200a^2 + 64a$

5. a) $3m(2m - 5)$ **b)** $2y(y^2 - 3y + 4)$
c) $(2x + 7)(2x - 7)$ **d)** $(x + 7)(x - 4)$
e) $(m - 6)(m - 3)$ **f)** $(5 - a)(4 + a)$

6. a) $(y + 13)(y + 3)$ **b)** $2(x + 1)(x - 6)$
c) $4a(a - 5)(a + 5)$ **d)** $-3x(x^2 - 5x + 2)$
e) $3\left(m + \dfrac{1}{2}\right)\left(m - \dfrac{1}{2}\right)$ **f)** $y(y - 7)(y - 8)$

7. a) 1160 cm² **b)** 377 cm²

8. a) 9 **b)** 37 **c)** 1 **d)** 21

9. a) $2x - 7$ **b)** $2x^2 - 3x + 5$ **c)** $\dfrac{5x^2}{12y^3}$
d) $-\dfrac{5m^2n}{9}$ **e)** $\dfrac{3x^3y}{2}$ **f)** $-\dfrac{16}{9c}$

10. a) $\dfrac{4x + 1}{3}$ **b)** $\dfrac{6 - m}{5}$ **c)** $\dfrac{8a - 9}{4a}$
d) $\dfrac{121 - 6x}{12}$ **11.** Trapezoid **12. a) i)** 135°
ii) 150° **b) i)** hexagon **ii)** pentagon

13. a) {(1,1), (2,3), (3,6), (4,10), (5,15), (6,21)}
c) Because the sum of the first n natural numbers is never 12.

15. a) 11 **b)** 21 **c)** $y = x + 1$

16. b) i) $6.30 **ii)** $9.90
c) i) 3 min **ii)** 8.5 min

17. a) 50°, 50° **b)** 65°, 75° **c)** 75°, 105°

18. a) $\triangle$ABC $\cong$ $\triangle$FDE, SAS
b) $\triangle$MNP $\cong$ $\triangle$SRQ, SSS;
$\triangle$MNP $\cong$ $\triangle$UTV, ASA

19. a) 11.3 **b)** 14.3, 9.2 **c)** 19.6, 13.9

20. 10.8 m **21. a)** 55°, 110° **b)** 90°, 33°
c) 65°, 115° **22.** No

Chapter 10

Exercises 10-1, page 363

1. a) i) Reflection **ii)** Translation **iii)** Rotation
  b) i) Translation **ii)** Rotation **iii)** Reflection
  c) i) Rotation **ii)** Translation **iii)** Reflection
2. a), f) Reflection or rotation **b)** Reflection
  c) Reflection **d)** Rotation **e)** Rotation
3. a) Rotation **b)** Reflection **c)** Reflection
4. Answers may vary.

Exercises 10-2, page 367

2. b) i) A′(2,4) **ii)** B′(7,8) **iii)** C′(−1,1)
  iv) D′(−2,4)
3. a) A′(1,6), B′(3,7), C′(9,7), D′(8,5), E′(−2,4)
  b) They are the same length.
  c) They are the same length.
  d) They have the same measure.
4. b) A′(5,6), B′(7,9), C′(8,2) **c)** The translation
  does not affect its size or shape, only its position.
5. A′(2,1), B′(6,0), C′(8,−5), D′(4,−4)
6. b) P(−6,6), Q(−4,10), R(−8,7)
7. Lengths and directions of line segments, measures
  of angles, areas of figures
9. c) The line maps onto itself, because the translation
  arrow is parallel to the line.
10. a) A′(−4,3), B′(1,3), C′(1,−2)
  b) A″(1,6), B″(6,6), C″(6,1)
  d) It does give the same result.

Exercises 10-3, page 372

2. a) 3:00 **b)** 12:30 **c)** 9:15 **d)** 4:05
4. a) P′(2,−6), Q′(6,−4), R′(3,−2)
  b) P′(−2,6), Q′(−6,4), R′(−3,2)
5. a) A′(2,−5), B′(6,−5), C′(9,−1), D′(2,−1)
  b) A′(−2,5), B′(−6,5), C′(−9,1), D′(−2,1)
6. x = 1 **7.** y = −2
8. c) i) Isosceles triangle **ii)** Kite
  iii) Isosceles triangle **iv)** Rhombus **v)** Kite
  vi) Quadrilateral
10. a) P′(−2,−4), Q′(4,−2), R′(1,2)
  b) P′(2,4), Q′(−4,2), R′(−1,−2)
11. a) A′(−2,−6), B′(4,−3), C′(3,3), D′(−5,2)
  b) A′(2,6), B′(−4,3), C′(−3,−3), D′(5,−2)
12. Lengths of line segments, measures of angles,
  points on the reflection line, areas of figures

Exercises 10-4, page 378

2. A′(−1,−4), B′(−5,−5), O′(0,0)
3. A′(−1,−3), B′(−4,−7), C′(−6,−4), D′(−3,−1)
4. P′(−5,−3), Q′(7,1), R′(−1,2)

5. K′(−4,−3), L′(−6,1), M′(1,6), N′(3,−4)
6. a) P,P′, and the centre of rotation lie on a straight
  line.
  b) The coordinates of the image have opposite
  values to the coordinates of the original point.
7. c) i) Parallelogram **ii)** Parallelogram
  iii) Square **iv)** Rhombus **v)** Parallelogram
8. a, c
9. Lengths of line segments, measures of angles, areas
  of figures
11. c) The image and the original line coincide because
  the rotation centre lies on the line.

Problem Solving, page 381

1. 12 **2.** 9 **3.** 6 **4.** 9
  1 2 3 2
  5 3 4 7 4
  1 6 8 5
5. a) Yes **c)** The difference of the squares of two
  prime numbers greater than 3 is always a multiple
  of 24.

Exercises 10-5, page 387

1. a), b), d) Enlargements **c), e), f)** Reductions
2. a) $\frac{1}{2}$ **b)** 1.5 **c)** $\frac{2}{3}$ **d)** $\frac{5}{3}$
3. a) 2 **b)** $\frac{7}{5}$ **c)** 9.6 cm², 40.6 cm²
4. a) ii) $\frac{3}{2}$ **iii)** Area A′B′C′D′ = 2.25(Area ABCD)
  b) ii) $\frac{5}{7}$ **iii)** Area △P′Q′R′ = $\frac{1}{2}$(Area △PQR)
  c) ii) $\frac{3}{4}$ **iii)** Area W′X′Y′Z′ = $\frac{1}{2}$(Area WXYZ)
  iv) Corresponding angles are equal.
5. b) 2:1 **c)** 2 **d)** Equal
  e) Area A′B′C′D′E′ = 4(Area ABCDE)
6. a) 10 cm, 24 cm, 26 cm **b)** 25 cm, 60 cm, 65 cm
  c) 2.5 cm, 6 cm, 6.5 cm
  d) 3.75 cm, 9 cm, 9.75 cm
8. a) 100 **b)** 150 **c)** 75 **d)** 125
9. a) About 4.0 km **b)** About 1.6 km
  c) About 1.8 km **10. a)** About 4.4 km
  b) About 5.3 km **c)** About 4.3 km **11. a)** 3 **b)** $\frac{3}{1}$

Exercises 10-6, page 393

1. △ABC ∼ △MNP ∼ △DFE;
  Quad GHKJ ∼ quad CDAB;
  △KLM ∼ △TWS ∼ △TVU

5. a) 10, 9   **b)** 9, 10   **c)** 12, $\frac{40}{3}$ **d)** 9, 7.5
e) $\frac{80}{3}$, 24   **f)** 14.4, 10
6. a) 9 **b)** 10 **c)** 15 **d)** 16 **e)** 10 **f)** 6
7. About 26.5 m   **8.** 38.4 m   **9.** 30 m
10. a) 59 cm by 42 cm   **b)** A4
11. 17 cm by 22 cm   **12.** 28 cm by 35 cm
13. a) 7.2, 7   **b)** 7.04, 3.8   **c)** 16.5, 18
     d) 1.6, 3.2   **14.** 7.1 m

Exercises 10-7, page 398

4. c) Yes   **5. a)** (7.5,0) **b) i)** (4.5,0) **ii)** (0,3.5)
6. 15 units   **7.** 5.0 m by 6.6 m   **8.** 10.7 m

Review Exercises, page 400

1. a), h) Translation   **b), d), e)** Reflection
   c), f), g) Rotation
2. LKJM translation 7 left, 11 up; QPSR rotation of
   270° about O; EFGH reflection in x-axis
3. a) Reflection   **b)** Translation   **c)** Rotation
5. a) A′(3,2), B′(6,−7), C′(9,−1)
   b) P(−3,−1), Q(−5,6), R(−10,3)
6. a) A′(2,−5), B′(−3,−1), C′(1,4)
   b) A′(−2,5), B′(3,1), C′(−1,−4)
7. L′(2,3), M′(−4,3), N′(−4,−5)   **8.** $x = -1$
10. a) 9   **b)** 26.25, 24   **c)** 5   **d)** $\frac{160}{3}$, 18.75
11. 6.1 m **12.** 52 cm by 78 cm **13. a)** 65°, 3, 155°
b) 70°, 40°, 70° **c)** 95°, 85°
15. 360°

Chapter 11

Exercises 11-1, page 405

1. Answers and reasons may vary.   **a)** Circle graph
   b) Pictograph   **c)** Broken-line graph
   d) Continuous-line graph   **e)** Histogram
2. Answers may vary.   **3.** 100%
4. a) 20%   **b)** About 8 min
5. a) Swimming
   b) 1050 kJ   **c)** About 28 min
6. a) January **b)** October **c)** March **d)** 51 cm
7. a) 2.25×10^8 km; 1.5×10^8 km, 1.0×10^8 km,
   5.0×10^7 km
   b) About 4.5 times   **c)** 7.8×10^8 km
   d) The pictograph would need a large number of
   symbols for the farthest planets.

Exercises 11-2, page 410

4. b) i) 175   **ii)** 51%   **c)** Answers may vary.
   1.91-1.95; 1.96-2.00; 2.01-2.05; 2.06-2.10
5. Answers may vary.
   a) 20 to 29,2; 30-39,2; 40-49,4; 50-59,11;
   60-69,33; 70-79,16; 80-89, 7; 90-99,3
   c) 59   **d) i)** 76%   **ii)** 10%
6. b) i) $1500   **ii)** $4500   **iii)** $7200
   iv) $12 000   **9. d) i)** 14 820 000 **ii)** 23 140 000

Mathematics Around Us, page 412

1. a) i) 2.5 cm   **ii)** 1.7 cm

Exercises 11-3, page 415

1. a) 11.2, 11.5, 12   **b)** 3.3, 4, 4
   c) 3.3, 3.4, no mode   **d)** 16, 16, 18
   e) 10.3, 10, 5   **f)** $\frac{1}{2}, \frac{1}{2}, \frac{1}{2}$ **2.** $8.83
3. a) Mean is increased by 2.   **b)** Mean is
   doubled.   **4.** 18 **5.** 70
6. a) Mean: $624.64; median: $530; mode: $670,
   $385, $290   **b)** Answers may vary, the mean.
7. a) A: mean 16; median 16; mode 15, 20;
   B: mean 11.84; median 11; mode 11
   b) Mean 13.92; median 14; mode 11
   c) Answers may vary.
8. Answers may vary. Mean 28; median 35; mode 35
9. Answers may vary.
   a) Mode   **b)** Mean   **c)** Mean   **d)** Mean
   e) Mean   **f)** Mean   **g)** Mean   **h)** Mode
10. Answers may vary.   **a)** 6, 7, 8, 11, 13
   b) 6, 7, 8, 24, 25 **11. a)** No change in the mean;
median and mode may or may not change.
12. 104, this mark cannot be achieved.   **13.** 0
14. 0.051 873 775 2; greater

Computer Power, page 417

1. a) 31.285 714 3, 30   **b)** 517.041 667, 501
2. a) 155.4 cm, 155.35 cm   **b)** 155.4 cm

Exercises 11-4, page 419

Answers may vary.
1. a) No, most colds don't last more than 4 days.
   b) No, fewer people ride bicycles, therefore fewer
   should be hurt.
   c) No, each age group might not contain the same
   number of skiers.
   d) No, skiers who take lessons might attempt more
   difficult slopes.

e) No, the unemployed might not be qualified for the vacancies.

2. The age groups might not contain the same number of people; that is, there may be fewer drivers under 25.   **3.** We need to know how many dentists were surveyed, it might be only 5!

7. a) 0.410, 0.440 **b)** 0.333, 0.200 **c)** 0.500, 0.467
   d) Rooky has a greater batting average in total, but Pops has a greater average if calculated separately.

Mathematics Around Us, page 421

Answers may vary.

Exercises 11-5, page 423

1. a) 70   **b)** 290

2. a) Foreign   **b)** 247   **c)** $864.50

Exercises 11-6, page 425

Answers may vary.

Exercises 11-7, page 429

1. 0.502 **2. a) i)** 0.15 **ii)** 0.15 **iii)** 0.10
b) 100 is not sufficient to answer the questions.
3. Answers may vary.   **4.** 3125
5. Answers may vary.   **d)** The greater the number of tosses, the closer the relative frequency gets to 0.5.
6. 0.53   **7.** Answers may vary.
8. Answers may vary.
9. a) 0.450   **b)** 0.391   **c)** 0.249   **d)** 0.248
   e) Because the total number of times at bat was greater.   **10. a)** Answers may vary.
b) As the length to diameter ratio increases, the cylinder is less likely to land on an end.
11. Answers may vary.

Computer Power, page 431

1. a) a, 29, 0.059 304 703 5; e, 63, 0.128 834 356;
   i, 47, 0.096 114 519 4; n, 39, 0.079 754 601 2;
   o, 31, 0.063 394 683; s, 33, 0.067 484 662 6;
   t, 35, 0.071 574 642 1
b) a, 8, 0.045 977 011 5; e, 22, 0.126 436 782;
   i, 18, 0.103 448 276; n, 14, 0.080 459 770 1;
   o, 13, 0.074 712 643 7; s, 15, 0.086 206 896 6;
   t, 11, 0.063 218 390 8

Exercises 11-8, page 435

1. a) $\frac{1}{2}$ **b)** $\frac{1}{4}$ **c)** $\frac{1}{3}$ **2. a)** $\frac{1}{50}$ **b)** $\frac{3}{25}$ **c)** $\frac{1}{25}$

3. a) $\frac{3}{8}$ **b)** $\frac{1}{4}$ **c)** $\frac{3}{8}$ **d)** $\frac{5}{8}$ **e)** $\frac{3}{4}$ **f)** $\frac{1}{4}$

4. a) i) June 5, 10, 15, 20, 25, 30
   ii) June 2, 9, 16, 23, 30 **iii)** June 30
b) $\frac{1}{5}, \frac{1}{6}, \frac{1}{30}$

5. a) i) Drawing red, drawing white, drawing green
   ii) Yes **b) i)** (H) (H); (H) (T); (T) (H); (T) (T)
   ii) Yes **c) i)** Drawing a, b, ... z **ii)** No
   d) i) Drawing white, drawing blue, drawing red
   ii) No **e) i)** Landing on A, B, ... H
   ii) Yes, if the letters are contained in equal areas.

6. a) $\frac{7}{500}$ **b)** $\frac{7}{370}$ **7.** $\frac{1}{12}$ **8. a)** $\frac{2}{3}$ **b)** $\frac{1}{3}$

9. a) $\frac{1}{4}$ **b)** $\frac{1}{2}$ **c)** 0   **10.** 0

11. a) $\frac{1}{2}$ **b)** $\frac{1}{2}$ **c)** 1   **d)** 0

12. a) $\frac{1}{6}$ **b)** $\frac{1}{2}$ **c)** $\frac{1}{2}$ **d)** $\frac{1}{3}$ **e)** 1   **f)** 0

13. a) 12 or 13   **b)** 50   **c)** 500
14. a) 4   **b)** 17   **c)** 167
15. a) 6 **b)** 8 **c)** 12 or 13 **d)** 4 **16.** 1
17. Bag B   **18. a)** $\frac{1}{3}$ **b)** $\frac{2}{3}$ **c)** $\frac{11}{24}$

19. a) $\frac{1}{6}$ **b)** $\frac{7}{30}$ **c)** $\frac{23}{60}$ **d)** $\frac{1}{2}$

20. a) $\frac{1}{2}$ **b)** $\frac{1}{4}$ **c)** $\frac{1}{26}$ **d)** $\frac{3}{13}$

21. a) 0.29   **b)** 0.36   **22. a) i)** 0.834 43
   ii) 0.467 74   **iii)** 0.366 69   **b)** 0.023 33

Problem Solving, page 439

1. $1.19 **2.** Answers may vary. **3.** $\frac{1}{17}$ **4.** $\frac{613}{648}$
5. a) Yes **b)** Yes **c)** No

The Mathematical Mind, page 440

Reasons may vary. **1. a) i)** Break even
ii) Win **iii)** Lose **iv)** Lose

Exercises 11-9, page 443

1. a) $\frac{1}{8}$ **b)** $\frac{1}{4}$ **2. a)** $\frac{1}{4}$ **b)** $\frac{1}{32}$ **3. b)** $\frac{1}{32}$

4. $\frac{1}{64}$ **5.** $\frac{1}{216}$ **6.** 0.1296 **7.** $\frac{36}{5329}$ **8.** $\frac{1}{1650}$

9. a) i) $\frac{1}{4}$ **ii)** $\frac{1}{5}$ **b) i)** $\frac{4}{9}$ **ii)** $\frac{1}{3}$

c) i) $\dfrac{9}{16}$ ii) $\dfrac{1}{2}$ **10. a)** $\dfrac{1}{8}$ **b)** $\dfrac{1}{20}$

11. a) $\dfrac{1}{16}$ **b)** $\dfrac{1}{4}$ **c)** $\dfrac{1}{169}$ **d)** $\dfrac{1}{2704}$

12. a) $\dfrac{1}{28\ 561}$ **b)** $\dfrac{1}{270\ 725}$ **13. a)** $\dfrac{1}{24}$ **b)** $\dfrac{1}{8}$

14. a) $\dfrac{5}{36}$ **b)** $\dfrac{25}{216}$ **c)** $\dfrac{1\ 953\ 125}{60\ 466\ 176}$

15. a) $\dfrac{1}{16}$ **b)** $\dfrac{15}{16}$ **c)** $\dfrac{1}{4}$ **d)** $\dfrac{3}{4}$

16. a) $\dfrac{35}{36}$ **b)** $\dfrac{1}{6}$ **c)** $\dfrac{1}{18}$ **d)** $\dfrac{7}{9}$ **e)** $\dfrac{11}{36}$ **17.** 5.6%

Exercises 11-10, page 446

Answers may vary.

1. Spin the arrow 10 times and record how often it falls in the correct section. This is one experiment. Repeat it 40 times. Count the number of experiments where the arrow pointed to the correct section 3 or more times. Divide this by 40.

2. **a)** Toss 4 coins and record if you get 3 heads. Repeat this experiment 40 times.
   b) Toss 8 coins and record if you get 5 or more heads. Repeat 40 times.
   c) Toss 3 coins and record if you get all heads. Repeat 40 times.
   d) Toss 2 coins and record if you get both heads. Repeat 40 times.

3. Toss 4 coins and record if you get 2 heads and 2 tails. Repeat 36 times.

4. Toss 8 coins and record if you get at least 3 heads. Repeat 40 times.

5. Toss 8 dice and record if you get at least 2 sixes. Repeat 40 times.

6. Open the book at any page and count how many numbers out of 40 have the last 2 digits even.

7. Toss a coin and a die (each of the 12 combinations represents a month). Do this 5 times and record the results. This represents one experiment. Repeat the experiment at least 15 times. Count the number of times in each experiment that 2 or 3 or 4 or 5 combinations were the same.

Investigate, page 447

Answers may vary.

1. $\dfrac{19}{50}$ **2.** $\dfrac{19}{50}$ **3.** From the table, $\dfrac{1}{5}$

4. From the table, $\dfrac{3}{4}$ **5.** From the table, $\dfrac{8}{33}$

Computer Power, page 448

1. Answers may vary, for example, **a)** 54 H, 46 T
   b) 232 H, 268 T **c)** 504 H, 496 T
2. **a)** 54% **b)** 46.4% **c)** 50.4%
3. The percent gets closer to 50%.
4. Unlikely, but could happen.

Review Exercises, page 449

4. Mean $12 944; median $12 400; mode $12 400
5. 36 **6.** Answers may vary. 1, 16, 23, 24, 25, 25, 25, 25, 25 **7., 8.** Answers may vary.
9. **a)** Yes **b)** 12 **c)** 0.984

10. a) $\dfrac{7}{15}$ **b)** $\dfrac{2}{5}$ **c)** $\dfrac{1}{5}$ **d)** $\dfrac{2}{5}$ **11. a)** $\dfrac{22}{65}$ **b)** $\dfrac{17}{65}$

c) $\dfrac{2}{13}$ **12. a)** $\dfrac{3}{14}$ **b)** $\dfrac{5}{12}$ **c)** $\dfrac{61}{168}$ **d)** $\dfrac{53}{84}$

13. a) $\dfrac{1}{4}$ **b)** $\dfrac{1}{4}$ **c)** $\dfrac{3}{8}$ **14. a)** $\dfrac{9}{38}$ **b)** $\dfrac{21}{190}$

c) $\dfrac{1}{190}$ **d)** 0 **15. a)** $\dfrac{1}{3}$ **b)** $\dfrac{1}{12}$ **c)** $\dfrac{1}{24}$

16. Answers may vary.

Chapter 12

Exercises 12-1, page 454

5. **d)** Answers may vary, for example, ∠AOB is 180° hence half of it (or the sum of half of the angles into which it is divided) is 90°. **6. c)** 131°
7. **b)** 37°, 83°, 8.7 cm **d)** 5.3 cm, 102°
8. **c)** 80°, 100°
9. **b)** The sum of the lengths of any 2 sides of a triangle must be greater than the length of the third side. **10. b)** 8.0 cm
15. **d)** They are parallel, alternate angles equal.
16. Answers may vary, for example, the point where the arcs meet is the same distance from both arms of the angle.

Exercises 12-2, page 458

6. **c)** PQ = 2BC **d)** ∠APQ = ∠ABC **7.** 45°
8. **c) i)** 3.1 cm **ii)** 105° **iii)** 110°
9. **b)** 56°, 41°, 83°
10. **b)** 6.5 cm **c)** 8.7 cm **d)** 7.6 cm
14. Bisector of an angle, perpendicular bisector of a line segment, perpendicular from a point to a line

Investigate, page 459

Any point on the perpendicular bisector of a line segment is equidistant from the ends of the line segment.

Investigate, page 460

The perpendicular bisectors of the sides of any triangle meet at a point.
The angle bisectors of any triangle meet at a point.
The medians of any triangle meet at a point.
The altitudes of any triangle meet at a point.

Exercises 12-3, page 463

1. c) Approximately $(2, \pm 3.5)$ **2.** Answers may vary.
4. a) No, because the points are collinear.
   b) If the points are not collinear
5. Yes, if the points are not collinear
6. Through 4 points if they are the vertices of: a rectangle, a trapezoid with its non-parallel sides equal; a quadrilateral with opposite angles supplementary. Through 5 or more points if they are the vertices of a regular polygon.
7. Infinite number **8.** Infinite number
9. For an isosceles triangle **10. f)** $HG = 2OG$
   g) Yes **11.** Median **12. g)** Yes

Exercises 12-4, page 469

1. a), c) Prisms **b), d)** Pyramids
2. a) 150 cm² **b)** 62 cm² **c)** 143 cm²
3. a) 434 m² **b)** 408 cm² **c)** 756 cm²
4. a) 9280 cm² **b)** 1577 m² **c)** 1876 cm²
5. a) 42.1 m² **b)** 780 cm² **c)** 37 m² **6. b)** 572 cm²
7. a) Number of sides plus 2
   b) Twice the number of sides
   c) Three times the number of sides
8. a), b) Number of sides plus 1
   c) Twice the number of sides
9. a) $260 **b)** $25
   c) $268 ignoring doors and windows

Investigate, page 471

The volume of a pyramid is one-third the volume of a rectangular prism which has the same height and the same base.

Exercises 12-5, page 475

1. a) 3645 cm³ **b)** 252 m³ **c)** 3104 cm³
   d) 5 m³ **e)** 4 cm³ **f)** 3800 cm³
2. a) 2 m³ **b)** 4 m³ **c)** 32 m³
3. 18 m³ **4.** 10 m³ **5.** 4 **6.** 600
7. a) 9 m³ **b)** 5724 cm³ **c)** 7 cm³

8. Answers may vary. **9.** About 5.6 cm
10. 4500 cm³ **11. a)** 431 **b)** 0.053 m³
12. 68.0 cm³ **13. a)** 2 592 100 m³
    b) 1.127 m³ **c)** About 5 711 000 t
14. a) 24 m³ **b)** About 44

Investigate, page 477

The volume of a cone is one-third the volume of a cylinder which has the same height and the same base.

Problem Solving, page 479

1. a) 44 m² **b)** 77 cm² **c)** 66 cm²
2. a) 57 m² **b)** 103 cm² **c)** 82 cm²
3. 9.4 m² **4. a)** 29 cm **b)** 7.5 cm
5. Along the diagonal of the square formed by the black ball and 4 of the squares between it and the colored ball.
6. a) Square **b)** Rectangle **c)** Space quadrilateral
7. Answers may vary, for example, cut a piece of paper which is the height of the tin. Fold it in half so the crease represents half the height. Put the paper in the can and add water to the crease.
8. 1996 mm³

Exercises 12-6, page 482

1. a) 139 506 cm³ **b)** 2788 cm³ **c)** 2494 m³
   d) 2219 cm³ **2. a)** 17 868 cm² **c)** 1063 m²
3. a) 8670 cm³ **b)** 18 246 m³ **4.** 785 cm³
5. 262 cm³ **6.** 19 cm², 25 cm², 460 cm³, 590 cm³
7. 65 cm³ **8.** 6135 m³ **9.** About 16 **10.** $26.46
11. a) 196 cm², 196 cm² **b)** $25.70, $23.54
12. 415.0 m³ **13.** 48.3 cm³
14. 1062 cm³, these are probably outside dimensions, and do not take into account that the can will not be full to the brim.
15. 2 127 000 L **16. a)** About 427 cars **b)** $273.70
17. a) 4.2 m **b)** 3.7 m **c)** 69 m², 77 m²
    d) Because they give maximum volume for minimum surface area.

Investigate, page 484

Answers may vary.

Investigate, page 485

1. The value is approximately π.
4. The surface area of a sphere is equal to π times the square of the diameter.

Exercises 12-7, page 488

1. **a)** 616 cm², 1437 cm³   **b)** 25 m², 11 m³
   c) 17 390 cm², 215 634 cm³
2. **a)** 1963 cm², 8181 cm³ **b)** 531 mm², 1150 mm³
   c) 133 cm², 144 cm³
3. 4189 cm³   **4.** $V = \frac{1}{6}\pi d^3$
5. **a)** 5.10×10^8 km², 1.08×10^{12} km³
   b) 3.80×10^7 km², 2.21×10^{10} km³
   c) 6.05×10^{12} km², 1.40×10^{18} km³
6. **a)** 314 cm² **b)** 524 cm³ **7. a)** 1260 cm²
b) 4190 cm³ **8. a)** $4\pi r^2$, $6\pi r^2$ The cylinder's area is
1.5 times the sphere's area. **b)** $\frac{4}{3}\pi r^3$, $2\pi r^3$
The cylinder's volume is 1.5 times the sphere's volume.
9. 2.8 cm   **10.** 2.9 cm
11. We see twice the area it appears to be.
12. **a)** 1150 cm² **b)** 3650 cm³ **13. a)** 2.5 cm
b) About 19% increase **14. a)** $\frac{C^2}{\pi}$ **b)** $\frac{C^3}{6\pi^2}$

Problem Solving, page 490

1. 4 min **2.** All integers   **3. a)** 45 **b)** $\frac{n(n-1)}{2}$

4. **a)** 4   **b)** 22   **c)** 24   **5.** 42

6. **a)** 100   **b)** n^2 **7.** Answers may vary. $\frac{3}{8}$

8. $28.50   **9.** $n + 1$

Mathematics Around Us, page 491

1. About $\frac{4}{1}$ **2.** About $\frac{2}{1}$ **3.** The bear because it has
the smaller surface area to volume ratio. **4.** Spherical

Review Exercises, page 492

4. **a) i) ii)** Equal distances using compasses
   iii) SSS, FB is common.
   b) Since triangles are congruent, corresponding
   angles are equal and $\angle EBF = \angle FBD$.
7. **a)** 24.75 cm²   **b)** 24.88 cm²   **c)** 3750 mm²
8. $252.80 **9.** $324.29   **10. a)** 262 cm³
b) 5 cm³ **c)** 30 m³ **11.** 16 753 cm³
12. About 1.6 L   **13.** About 0.3 m³   **14.** 202 cm²
15. **a)** 46 cm³   **b)** 2.3 cm
16. **a)** Yes   **b)** Just over 17 cm   **c)** About 30
17. **a)** 669 m²   **b)** 1184 m³

Cumulative Review, Chapters 9-12, page 494

1. **a)** A'(2,6), B'(2,3), C'(7,3)
   b) A'(−1,−6), B'(−1,−3), C'(4,−3)
   c) A'(−4,−1), B'(−1,−1), C'(−1,4)
   d) A'(−2,8), B'(−2,2), C'(8,2)
2. **a)** P'(7,2), Q'(4,−2), R'(9,−4)
   b) D(−9,4), E(−7,0), F(−4,5)
3. The reflection line is $y = x$.
4. **a)** 50 cm²   **b)** 1152 cm²   **5.** About 9.1 m
6. **a)** 384 g   **c) i)** 16%   **ii)** 36%   **iii)** 16%
8. Mean, about 70; median 72; mode 75
9. All increase by 3.
10. **a)** $\frac{15}{16}$ **b)** $\frac{1}{16}$ **11. a) i)** 2,4,6,8,10,12
    ii) 2,3,4,5,6 **iii)** 2,4,6 **b) i)** $\frac{1}{2}$ **ii)** $\frac{5}{12}$ **iii)** $\frac{1}{4}$
12. **a)** $\frac{6}{25}$ **b)** $\frac{4}{25}$ **c)** $\frac{2}{5}$ **d)** 0
13. **a)** $\frac{3}{4}$ **b)** $\frac{1}{4}$ **c)** 0 **d)** 1
14. Answers may vary – both outcomes are not equally
    likely.
17. **a)** 188.2 cm²   **b)** 165 cm²   **c)** 706.9 cm²
18. **a)** 2688 cm³   **b)** 3351 cm³   **c)** 2831 cm³
    d) 3000 cm³
19. 1.6 m³   **20.** About $8017   **21.** 5772 cm³

Index

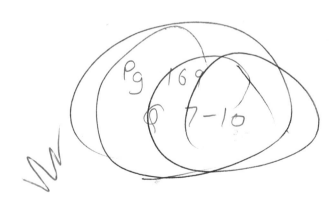

Pg 169

7-10